W9-BLU-576

GREEN
BUILDING
PRODUCTS

The GreenSpec® Guide to
Residential Building Materials

Alex Wilson and Mark Piepkorn · EDITORS

Nadav Malin · CO-EDITOR, GREENSPEC

Angela Battisto · GREENSPEC MANAGER

BUILDING GREEN

Authoritative Information on Environmentally Responsible Building Design and Construction

NEW SOCIETY PUBLISHERS

Green Building Products:
The GreenSpec® Guide to Residential Building Materials

Cataloging in Publication Data: A catalog record for this publication is available from the National Library of Canada.

ISBN: 0-86571-543-2

Cover photo by Randi Baird of a home designed and built by South Mountain Company, Martha's Vineyard, Massachusetts. Used by permission.

Product photos were provided by the manufacturers and are used by permission.

Production notes:

Text design by Joy Wallens-Penford. Cover design by DC Design.

In keeping with the copublishers' missions to build an ecologically sustainable society through their work and actions, this book is printed on acid-free paper that is 100% old growth forest-free (100% post-consumer recycled), processed chlorine-free, and printed with vegetable-based, low-VOC inks.

Printed in Canada.

Inquiries regarding requests to reprint all or part of this book, should be addressed to BuildingGreen, Inc., at the address below.

Copublished by:

BuildingGreen, Inc., 122 Birge Street, Suite 30, Brattleboro, VT 05301, USA   802-257-7300

BuildingGreen's mission is to provide accurate, unbiased, and timely information that will help building professionals improve the environmental performance of buildings and surrounding landscapes. For further information and to learn about our other information resources, please visit our website at: www.BuildingGreen.com.

New Society Publishers, P.O. Box 189, Gabriola Island, BC V0R 1X0, Canada   250-247-9737

New Society Publishers' mission is to publish books that contribute in fundamental ways to building an ecologically sustainable and just society, and to do so with the least possible impact on the environment, in a manner that models this vision. For further information, or to browse our full list of books and purchase securely, visit our website at: www.newsociety.com

Contents

FOREWORD by Sarah Susanka v

INTRODUCTION vi

SITEWORK & LANDSCAPING

Aggregate Surfacing 2
Drip Irrigation System 2
Erosion and Sedimentation Control 2
Fertilizing 3
Geosynthetics 3
Hydro-Mulching 3
Insect Control 5
Landscape Edging 5
Landscape Timbers 5
Native Plants and Seeds 7
Permanent Traffic Control 8
Plastic Lumber 12
Porous Pavement 12
Rubber Aggregate Surfacing 13
Seeding and Soil Supplements 14
Site Furnishings 14
Stormwater Drainage 14
Temporary Traffic Control 15
Tree Grates and Guards 15
Wood-Plastic Composite Lumber 16

OUTDOOR STRUCTURES

Driven Piles 18
Exterior Sun Control Devices 18
Landscape Timbers 18
Plastic Fences and Gates 18
Plastic Lumber 18
Playground Equipment 18
Rainwater Harvesting Systems and Components 19
Shoreline Protection and Mooring Structures 19
Site Furnishings 19
Wood-Plastic Composite Lumber 24

DECKING

Certified Wood Decking 26
Plastic Lumber 27

Preservative-Treated Wood and Treatment Products 31
Wood-Plastic Composite Lumber 31

FOUNDATIONS, FOOTERS & SLABS

Autoclaved Aerated Concrete Masonry Units 34
Coal Fly Ash 34
Concrete Cleaning 34
Concrete Curing 34
Concrete Masonry Units 35
Concrete Pigments 35
Concrete Rehabilitation 35
Dampproofing and Waterproofing 35
Driven Piles 36
Expansion Joint Filler 37
Form Release Agents 37
Forms for Cast-in-Place Concrete 39
Foundation and Load-Bearing Elements 40
Low Density Concrete 41
Masonry Mortar 41
Permanent Forms 41
Rebar Supports 41

STRUCTURAL SYSTEMS & COMPONENTS

Adobe Masonry Units 44
Autoclaved Aerated Concrete Masonry Units 44
Certified Wood Lumber and Timbers 45
Coal Fly Ash 48
Cold-formed Metal Framing 48
Concrete Cleaning 48
Concrete Masonry Units 48
Concrete Pigments 49
Concrete Rehabilitation 49
Engineered Lumber Products 49
Expansion Joint Filler 50
Exterior Wall Assemblies 50
Form Release Agents 50
Heavy Timber Construction 50
Low Density Concrete 50
Masonry Mortar 50

i

Metal Fastenings..51
Metal-Web Wood Joists.....................................51
Permanent Forms...52
Precast Concrete..57
Preservative-Treated Wood and Treatment Products.......57
Reclaimed Lumber and Timbers.....................59
Rough Carpentry Accessories..........................63
Structural Insulated Panels...............................64
Wood Framing Fasteners...................................68
Wood Trusses..69

SHEATHING

Fiberboard and Particleboard Panels..........................72
Sheathing (including Plywood & OSB).........................72

EXTERIOR FINISH & TRIM

Bricks..76
Cast Stone...76
Composition Siding..76
Fiber-Cement Siding...77
Masonry Accessories...78
Rain Screen Products...78
Reclaimed Wood Siding.....................................79
Stone Facing..80
Wood Shingles...81
Wood-Plastic Composite Lumber.....................81

ROOFING

Asphalt Shingles...84
Clay Roofing Tiles...84
Fiber-Cement Roofing Shingles........................85
Fluid-Applied Roofing.......................................85
Green Roof Plants...86
Green Roof Systems..86
Metal Roof Panels...87
Metal Shingles...87
Plastic Shingles...88
Ridge and Soffit Vents......................................89
Roll Roofing Accessories..................................90
Roof Walkway Pads...90
Roofing Underlayment......................................90
Rooftop Planting Media....................................91
Slate Shingles...91
Thermoplastic Membrane Roofing...................93
Wood Shingles...93

DOORS

Door and Window Accessories.........................96
Door Hardware..96
Doors and Windows - General.........................96
Steel Entry Doors...96
Wood and Plastic Doors....................................96

WINDOWS

ABS Plastic Windows.....................................100
Door and Window Accessories.....................100
Doors and Windows - General.....................100
Fiberglass Windows.......................................100
Insulating Glass...102
Metal-Framed Skylights.................................102
Plastic Unit Skylights....................................103
Skylights..105
Vinyl Windows...105
Window Shades and Quilts...........................107
Window Treatment Hardware.......................108
Wood Windows..108

INSULATION

Air Leakage Control.......................................112
Cellulose Insulation.......................................112
Cotton Insulation..117
EPS Foam Insulation......................................118
Fiberglass Insulation......................................123
Foamed-in-Place and Sprayed-On Insulation..............125
Insulation Baffles..126
Non-EPS Foam Board Insulation...................127
Other Insulation..128
Radiant Barriers...128
Rockwool Insulation......................................129
Sealants...130
Structural Insulated Panels...........................130
Vapor Retarders...130
Weatherstripping and Gaskets.....................130

FLOORING & FLOORCOVERINGS

Bamboo Flooring...135
Brick and Stone Flooring...............................137
Carpet Cushion..137
Carpet Tile...138
Ceramic Tile...139
Certified Wood Flooring.................................140

Concrete Pigments 142
Cork Flooring 142
Fiberboard and Particleboard Panels 144
Flooring Adhesives 144
Flooring Underlayment 145
Linoleum Flooring 146
Natural-Fiber Floor Mats 147
Paver Tile 147
Plastic Flooring 148
Reclaimed Wood Flooring 148
Recycled-Glass Tile 154
Resilient Flooring 154
Rubber Flooring 155
Sheet Carpet 156
Slip-Resistant Flooring 157
Suppressed Wood Flooring 157
Terrazzo 158
Tile Setting Materials and Accessories 158

INTERIOR FINISH & TRIM

Acoustical Ceiling Panels 160
Acoustical Wall Finishes 160
Ag-Fiber Particleboard 161
Bamboo and Straw Paneling 161
Certified Millwork 162
Certified Wood Stair Parts 164
Concrete Pigments 164
Cork Wall Covering 164
Countertops 165
Custom Cabinets 166
Fiberboard and Particleboard Panels 167
Fiberboard Millwork 168
Fire-Retardant-Treated Wood and Ag-Fiber 168
Gypsum Board 168
Gypsum Board Accessories 170
Paver Tile 171
Plastic Paneling 171
Prefinished Panels 172
Reclaimed Millwork 173
Reclaimed Wood Stair Parts 177
Recycled-Glass Tile 178
Special Wall Coverings 179
Stone Facing 180
Straw Interior Partition Panels 180
Terrazzo 180

Wall Covering 180
Wall Covering Adhesives 182
Wood Restoration and Cleaning 182

CAULKS & ADHESIVES

Duct Mastic 184
Joint Sealants 184
Sealants 185
Wood and Plastic Adhesives 186

PAINTS & COATINGS

Coatings for Concrete and Masonry 188
Coatings for Steel 189
Decorative Finishes 189
Exterior Paints 189
Exterior Stains 191
Exterior Transparent Finishes 191
Interior Paints 192
Interior Stains 196
Interior Transparent Finishes 197
Mastic Removers 198
Natural and Lime-Based Plaster 198
Paint Strippers 199
Recycled Paints 199
Specialty Sealers 200
Vapor-Retarding Coatings 201

MECHANICAL SYSTEMS/HVAC

Air Conditioning Equipment 204
Air Filters and Air Cleaning Devices 205
Air Outlets and Inlets 205
Boilers and Accessories 205
Duct Mastic 207
Ducts 208
Fans 208
Furnaces 209
Heat Pumps 210
Heat-Recovery and Energy-Recovery Ventilation 212
Humidity Control Equipment 214
HVAC Instrumentation and Controls 214
Masonry Fireplaces 215
Measurement and Control Instrumentation 215
Mechanical Insulation 215
Solar Flat Plate Collectors (Air Heating) ... 216
Space Heaters 216

iii

PLUMBING

Composting Toilet Systems 220
Domestic Water Heat Exchangers 221
Domestic Water Heaters 221
Domestic Water Piping 223
Faucets and Controls 223
Graywater Systems 226
Package Sewage Treatment 226
Rainwater Harvesting Systems and Components.......... 226
Sanitary Waste and Vent Piping 228
Septic and Leach Field Systems 229
Sinks 230
Solar Water Heating Systems and Components 231
Toilets.. 231
Water Supply and Treatment Equipment 233

ELECTRICAL

Electrical Power 236
Hazardous Substances Detection and Alarm........ 236
Inverters and Solar Electric Components 236
Lighting Controls and Building Automation 236
Outlet Boxes 237
Photovoltaic Collectors 237
Solar Energy Industry Information 237
Wind Energy Equipment 237

LIGHTING

Compact Fluorescent Lamps 240
Compact Fluorescent Luminaires 242
Exterior Luminaires 243
Fluorescent Lamps..................................... 244
Interior Luminaires 244
Lamp and Ballast Recycling 244
Lighting Accessories 246
Special Purpose Lighting 246

APPLIANCES

Residential Clothes Washers and Drying Equipment..... 248
Residential Dishwashers 250
Residential Refrigerators 252

FURNITURE & FURNISHINGS

Ag-Fiber Particleboard 256
Bedding 256
Certified Wood Furniture 256

Cork Furniture 258
Fiberboard and Particleboard Panels.......... 258
Fixed Tackboards 258
Natural-Fiber Fabrics 259
Office Furniture 259
Reclaimed Wood Furniture 260
Recycled-Content Furniture........................ 261
Recycling Equipment 262
Storage Shelving 262
Synthetic Fiber Fabrics 262
Tub and Shower Doors 263
Window Shades and Quilts......................... 263

RENEWABLE ENERGY

Inverters and Solar Electric Components 266
Masonry Fireplaces 266
Photovoltaic Collectors 266
Solar Energy Industry Information 268
Solar Flat Plate Collectors (Air Heating) 268
Solar Water Heating Systems and Components 268
Wind Energy Equipment 271

DISTRIBUTORS & RETAILERS

Distributors: Certified Wood....................... 274
Distributors/Retailers: Energy Conservation.............. 275
Distributors/Retailers: Green Building Materials........ 276
Distributors/Retailers: Renewable Energy Equipment ..278
Used Building Materials 280

MISCELLANEOUS

Hazardous Materials Testing and Remediation.......... 286
Hazardous Substances Detection and Alarm.............. 287
Insect Control 288
Lamp and Ballast Recycling 289
Measurement and Control Instrumentation 289
Recycling Equipment 290
Wood Products Certification and Information............. 290

INDEX OF PRODUCTS & MANUFACTURERS 293

ABOUT THE EDITORS 306

ENVIRONMENTAL BENEFITS STATEMENT 306

Foreword

by Sarah Susanka

The book you have in your hands is an important and much-needed tool in building a house that is green—a house that respects the value of our planet's natural resources, that protects its occupants, and that recognizes the impact and legacy it will leave for future generations.

When I first became an architect, back in the 1980s, I was a passive solar "nut," convinced that it was time to loosen our dependence on fossil fuels and embrace the abundant energy available from the sun. Then I moved to Minnesota and discovered that, though this might be an excellent strategy for warmer climates and lower latitudes, in Minneapolis in December there just aren't enough hours of sunlight, even on a really sunny day, to make passive solar strategies work effectively. So I turned into an energy-efficiency nut instead, learning everything I could about how to minimize heat loss in the winter and heat gain in the summer, while still designing homes that were comfortable as well as a delight to live in.

Over the twenty years I practiced residential architecture and energy-efficient design in the Twin Cities, my colleagues and I developed a strategy for building better, not bigger, which came to be known as building Not So Big. My first book, *The Not So Big House*, published in 1998 by Taunton Press, spelled out a recipe for a more sustainably made house—one that was about a third smaller than you thought you needed, with every space used every day. Such a house is filled with the special details of design and construction that make its structure last for centuries rather than decades, and with a character that encourages generations of inhabitants to take care of it, and make it their own, just like the homes of the Arts and Crafts movement did a century ago.

I believe that the very first step in building a green home is to build it just the right size for the way you want to live—you can read more about how to make this happen in the *Not So Big House* series of books, as well as my latest, *Home By Design*.

With a house design that's properly tailored to the activities of your life, and with spaces proportioned to fit our human scale, it is then time to select the products that support your efforts to make a healthy environment for your household, without hurting the planet in the process. For many years, this has presented a quandary. You've known what you WANT to be able to do—to make product selections that align with your values. You've known that you want to do what's best for the Earth and for future generations, and only purchase items that are in keeping with the natural order of things. But until now the problem has been how to find them. Simply having the values is not enough. You need a guide to help find the companies that share your goals and have made the effort to create sustainable products that can fulfill your dream for a truly green home.

This book is that guide. It's written in a way that makes it easy to find the information and product advice you need, and it's a must for anyone—builder, designer, architect or homeowner—who wants to know the unbiased and unembellished truth about what's really "green." The editors at BuildingGreen, including Alex Wilson and Mark Piepkorn, are among the most knowledgeable people in the world on sustainability, energy efficiency, and environmental characteristics of building products. They provide an enormous service to all of us in documenting, in layperson's language, the ins and outs of product selection for a green home.

Green Building Products provides the most comprehensive and useful resource for fulfilling the dreams that so many of us share for a sustainable future for our planetary—as well as our personal—home. Together we CAN make a difference, and this book points the way, giving us the tools to make the decisions that will ensure a better, though not necessarily bigger, future.

Sarah Susanka is an architect and author of the highly acclaimed Not So Big House *series of books, published by Taunton Press.*

Introduction

GREEN HOMES ARE SAFE TO LIVE IN, AFFORDABLE TO operate, and less damaging to the local, regional, and global environments.

Interest in green building has been growing by leaps and bounds in recent years for a number of reasons. Home-owners are alarmed by news about mold and asthma and about the alphabet soup of toxic chemicals that enters our homes through building products, furnishings, and consumer goods. We want the place where we live to be safe. We spend 90% of our time indoors and a significant chunk of that in our homes; these spaces should not make us sick. A green home is a healthy home.

Some people are worried that rising energy prices could make their homes too expensive to live in. In recent years, we have watched wild gyrations in the price of gasoline, natural gas, electricity, and heating oil. Evidence that worldwide oil production may be nearing a peak even as demand continues to grow leads to the concern that significantly higher prices may be just around the corner. (The prices of natural gas and electricity tend to rise and fall with the price of oil.) With more and more people nearing retirement age and facing the prospect of living on a fixed income, many are wisely concerned about the rising costs of operating their homes. This includes energy costs but also the costs of maintaining the home. A green home is affordable to operate—its energy use is low, and it is made with durable, low-maintenance materials.

Finally, more and more homeowners are beginning to recognize that their actions *can* make a difference. There is growing awareness about our impacts on the environment, and an increasing willingness to do something about it. Surveys show that efforts to make their homes more environmentally friendly are high priorities for homeowners and potential homebuyers—even if those measures increase costs.

Doing the right thing by creating a green home makes sense all around. It's good for your family's health, it saves money, and it's good for the environment.

Why Choose Green Building Products?

There are really three stakeholders to benefit from the use of green building products: the people who work with the materials (not only on the job site but also people in the factories where the products are made); the homeowners who live with those materials; and the local, regional, and global environment that is protected through the production and use of these materials.

The direct benefits of green building products to workers and homeowners are the easiest to justify. Manufacturing facilities and construction companies can save money if employees don't have to use special protective gear and if they stay healthier, losing less time to sick leave. And the importance of a safe, healthy home almost goes without saying. Since we spend so much of our time indoors, it's imperative that our indoor environments don't make us sick. Asthma now affects one in eight children, and medical experts are increasingly pointing to homes—and the products we put in them—as the culprits that cause respiratory illnesses. Further, there are a slew of chemicals we introduce to our homes whose health effects we know almost nothing about, such as the plasticizers that make vinyl shower curtains and wallcoverings flexible, brominated flame retardants in foam cushions, and fluoropolymers such as Teflon® used to insulate some wiring and a component in some finishes. Some of these chemicals are now showing up in the blood of humans worldwide and are being linked to behavioral and developmental problems.

Homeowners benefit directly from many products in the operation of their homes: heating, cooling, water use, maintenance, and repairs. Some green building products are more energy-efficient or more water-efficient than conventional products; others are more durable or require less maintenance. These direct benefits will save people money or time over the life of their homes and can easily be justified on those grounds.

Selecting green products solely because they protect the

environment can be more difficult to justify—but is no less important. While most homeowners will be sympathetic to concerns about rainforest destruction, ozone depletion, or toxic chemical releases from manufacturing plants, those impacts are far away, and most of them don't affect us directly. However, growing awareness about global warming is helping people understand the fact that actions in one place can have environmental impacts elsewhere. If, as many scientists believe, global warming is going to become a lot more apparent over the coming years and decades, it may become easier to draw the connection between our purchasing decisions and a wide range of impacts. If that happens, the environment could become a much bigger factor in the way we think, act, and make purchasing decisions.

When it comes to choosing green building products, both direct and indirect benefits are important. The relative priorities of these benefits, though, will vary significantly from person to person.

What Makes a Product Green?

This is a very complicated question. Many different factors come into play in determining the "greenness" of products and materials; very often the distinctions are not black-and-white. Much of the complexity in examining the environmental and health impacts of materials results from the fact that the impacts can occur at different points in the *life cycle* of a product, and those impacts can vary tremendously from product to product.

The science of examining the environmental and health impacts of products is referred to as *life-cycle assessment*, or LCA. This process examines a product from "cradle to grave," considering environmental and health issues involved with all aspects of resource extraction, manufacture, use, and disposal. Instead of "cradle to grave," some prefer to think of this cycle as "cradle to cradle," recognizing the idea of taking a product at the end of its useful life and turning it into the raw material for something else—recycling.

A green product is one whose life-cycle impacts are low. A floor tile made from recycled glass might be considered green because it is made from a waste material—something that would otherwise end up in a landfill. A mineral silicate paint might be green because it is highly durable and won't require frequent recoating or other treatment throughout its life. Metal cabinets might be green because they don't emit VOCs (volatile organic compounds) or other pollutants. A compact fluorescent light bulb might be green because it reduces energy consumption in the home. Sometimes, more than one environmental attribute exists for a product—for example, recycled plastic decking that is made from a waste product, is more durable than standard wooden decking, and doesn't release chemicals that can harm the environment (as can conventional pressure-treated wood).

Product Selection is Only One Part of Green Building

While this book focuses on the selection of products for building and remodeling to make a home more environmentally friendly, it is important to point out that green building is about much more than products. Green building is also about such issues as:

- Energy-efficient design and construction—where windows are located, how much insulation is installed, and how effectively air leakage is controlled;

- House size—not building a larger home than is needed;

- Where the house is built—so that use of automobiles can be minimized and important natural areas can be protected;

- Design and construction detailing to avoid moisture problems—the leading cause of indoor air quality problems in houses.

While the products and materials used in a home are often the most visible aspects of "green," these other issues are at least as important—and often significantly more important. Indeed, it is possible to build a compact, energy-efficient home close to alternative transportation that would be considered green by any measure with very few products and materials that are specifically considered "green." Conversely, a house could be built from 100% green products yet not be very green at all—because it isn't energy-efficient, because it's much bigger than necessary, or because building it damaged an ecologically sensitive area.

Selecting green building products is a very important aspect of green design, but it's not the whole story. Be sure to pay attention to the broader issues. For more information on green building, visit www.BuildingGreen.com.

A challenge in choosing green products is balancing all of these different—and often unrelated—considerations. A product might be made of recycled material but release harmful levels of VOCs; another might be durable but manufactured with chemicals that are significantly hazardous to the environment or to humans. We are often comparing apples to oranges when trying to decide which environmental impacts should carry greater weight. Fortunately, there are some efforts under way to quantify the environmental impacts of building materials using standardized measures.

Building for Environmental and Economic Sustainability (BEES) is a life-cycle assessment software tool that was developed by the National Institute of Standards and Technology (NIST). This tool helps architects, engineers, and environmental building consultants understand environmental and health impacts over a product's life cycle. While relatively few products have been assessed through BEES to date, it offers great promise for life-cycle assessment of building materials as the underlying database grows.

The nonprofit ATHENA™ Sustainable Materials Institute is amassing a comprehensive, public database of life-cycle *inventory* information about generic (as opposed to brand-specific) building materials. These inventories include detailed information on the environmental burdens that result from producing building materials.

Other organizations, including Green Seal, Scientific Certification Systems, the Institute for Market Transformation to Sustainability, and GreenBlue are developing very specific *Environmentally Preferable Product* (EPP) standards for various product categories, such as carpet and textiles. A new effort in California, supported by the California Division of the State Architect, is working on EPP standards for at least 20 different product categories (see www.EPPbuildingproducts.org).

As more rigorous and specific standards for green building products are developed, the selection criteria for product directories—such as this one—will become more quantitative. Until that time, the selection process for a product directory has to be based on the expertise of those creating it. Specifics of how products are selected for this directory are described below.

What is *GreenSpec*?

GreenSpec® is the leading national directory of green building products. Included here are those *GreenSpec* products that are most relevant to home building. Our intent with *GreenSpec* is to highlight the greenest building products; there are products with some green attributes that are not included because there are similar products considered to be greener. While we do our best to be comprehensive, there are doubtless many building products that would qualify for *GreenSpec* but are not yet included. If you have recommendations for products that should be considered, e-mail greenspec@BuildingGreen.com.

Manufacturers do not pay to be included in *GreenSpec*. Decisions about which products to include are based totally on criteria developed by the *GreenSpec* and *Environmental Building News* editorial team. This policy allows us to be nonbiased in selecting products—and in writing the descriptions of those products. Because manufacturers don't pay to be listed in *GreenSpec*, they can't control what is said about the products. In other words, what you read about products in this book is based on the research our staff has done; it is not written by the marketing staff of manufacturing companies.

Product Selection Criteria Used in This Directory

BuildingGreen, Inc. has been researching green building products and publishing information on them since 1992. Through writing hundreds of product reviews in the monthly newsletter *Environmental Building News*, and listing nearly 2,000 products in the comprehensive *GreenSpec*® database of green building products, BuildingGreen has developed very specific criteria for what makes a product green. These criteria include:

PRODUCTS MADE WITH SALVAGED, RECYCLED, OR AGRICULTURAL WASTE CONTENT

The materials used to produce a building product, and where those materials come from, are important green criteria and probably the best known. When many people think of green building products, they think of products made from recycled materials.

• **Salvaged products.** Whenever we can *reuse* a product instead of producing a new one from raw materials—even if those raw materials are from recycled sources—we save resources and energy. Many salvaged materials used in buildings (including bricks, millwork, framing lumber, plumbing fixtures, and period hardware) are mostly sold on a local or regional basis by salvage yards; some are marketed nationally. Certain salvaged products are not recommended, including toilets, faucets, and windows—because the water- and energy-savings of today's high-performance products offer far greater benefit than any there might be in using the old ones. With salvaged wood products, be aware that lead paint may be present. Test painted wood for lead paint (easy-to-use test kits are available) and, if found, avoid the product or have the wood stripped and sealed.

• **Products with post-consumer recycled content.** Recycled content is an important feature of many green products. From an environmental standpoint, *post-consumer* is preferable to *post-industrial* recycled content because post-consumer recycled materials are more likely to be diverted from landfills. For most product categories, there is currently no set standard for the percentage of recycled content required to qualify for inclusion in *GreenSpec*; such standards will increasingly be developed in the future as more products begin using higher percentages of recycled materials.

In some cases, products with recycled content are included with caveats regarding where they should be used. Rubber flooring made from recycled automobile tires is a good example—the caveat is that these products should not be used in most fully enclosed indoor spaces due to potential offgassing of harmful chemicals.

• **Products with post-industrial recycled content.** Post-industrial recycling refers to the use of industrial byproducts—as distinguished from material that has been in consumer use. Examples of post-industrial recycled materials used in building products include iron-ore slag from blast furnace metal refining used in making mineral wool insulation; fly ash from the smoke stacks of coal-burning power plants used in making concrete; and PVC scrap from pipe manufacturing used in making roofing shingles. Usually excluded from this category is the use of scrap within the manufacturing plant where it was generated—material that would

typically have gone back into the manufacturing process anyway. While post-consumer recycled content is a lot better than post-industrial recycled content, the latter can still qualify a product for inclusion in *GreenSpec* in many product categories—especially those where there are no products available with post-consumer recycled content.

Products made from agricultural waste material. A number of products are included in *GreenSpec* because they are derived from agricultural waste products. Most of these are made from straw—the stems left after harvesting cereal grains—though other materials such as rice hulls and sunflower seed hulls are also used in some building products.

PRODUCTS THAT CONSERVE NATURAL RESOURCES

Aside from salvaged or recycled content, there are a number of other ways that products can contribute to the conservation of natural resources. Examples of these include products that use less material than the standard solution for a particular function; products that are especially durable or low-maintenance; wood products that carry third-party certification demonstrating well-managed forestry; and products made from rapidly renewable resources.

• **Products that reduce material use.** Products meeting this criterion may not be distinctly green on their own but are included in *GreenSpec* because of the resource efficiency benefits that they make possible. For example, drywall clips allow the elimination of corner studs in wood house framing; engineered stair stringers reduce lumber waste; pier foundation systems minimize concrete use; and concrete pigments can turn concrete slabs into attractive finished floors, eliminating the need for conventional finish flooring.

• **Products with exceptional durability or low maintenance requirements.** These products are environmentally attractive because they need to be replaced less frequently or their maintenance has very low impact. This criterion is highly variable by product type. Sometimes, durability is a contributing factor to the green designation—but not enough to distinguish the product as green on its own. Included in this category are such products as fiber-cement siding, fiberglass windows, slate shingles, and vitrified clay waste pipe.

• **Certified wood products**. Third-party certification based on standards developed by the Forest Steward-ship Council (FSC) is the best way to ensure that wood products come from well-managed forests. Wood products must go through a chain-of-custody certification process to carry an FSC stamp. Manufactured wood products can meet the FSC certification requirements with less than 100% certified-wood content through *percentage-based claims* (30% certified-wood content is required if only virgin wood fiber is used; certified-wood content as low as 17.5% is allowable if the rest of the fiber content is from recycled sources). With a few special-case exceptions, any nonsalvaged solid-wood product must be FSC-certified to be included in *GreenSpec*. A few manufactured wood products, including engineered lumber and particleboard or medium-density fiberboard (MDF), can be included if they have other environmental attributes—such as the absence of formaldehyde binders.

• **Rapidly renewable products.** Rapidly renewable materials are distinguished from wood by having a shorter harvest rotation—typically 10 years or less. They are biodegradable, often low in VOC emissions, and usually produced from agricultural crops. Because sunlight is generally the primary energy input (via photosynthesis), these products may be less energy-intensive to produce—though transportation and processing energy use should also be considered. Examples include natural linoleum; form-release agents made from plant oils; natural paints; geotextile fabrics from coir and jute; products made with bamboo or cork; and such textiles as organic cotton, wool, and sisal.

PRODUCTS THAT AVOID TOXIC OR OTHER EMISSIONS

Some building products are considered green because they have low manufacturing impacts, are alternatives to conventional products made from chemicals considered problematic, or because they facilitate a reduction in polluting emissions from building maintenance. In this *GreenSpec* criterion, a few product components were singled out for avoidance in most cases: substances that deplete stratospheric ozone; toxic wood preservatives; polyvinyl chloride (PVC); and products containing brominated flame retardants. In a few cases, these substances may be included in a "green" product, but that product has to have other significant environmental benefits (for example, high post-consumer recycled content).

Substitutes for conventional products made with environmentally hazardous components may not, in themselves, be particularly green (i.e., they may be petrochemical-based or relatively high in VOCs), but *relative to the products being replaced* they can be considered green. Most of the products satisfying this criterion are in categories that are dominated by the more harmful products—such as wiring or drainage piping, where PVC products represent most of the industry. We have created several subcategories here for green products:

• **Natural or minimally processed products.** Products that are natural or minimally processed can be green because of low energy use and low risk of chemical releases during manufacture. These can include wood products, agricultural or nonagricultural plant products, and mineral products such as natural stone and slate shingles.

• **Alternatives to conventional preservative-treated wood**. Wood treated with CCA (chromated copper arsenate) contains the toxins arsenic and chromium, and has been eliminated from the market for most uses; but it is still available for some applications. Other wood treatments, such as pentachlorophenol (penta) and creosote, are considered carcinogens—cancer-causing substances.

• **Alternatives to ozone-depleting substances.** Included here are categories in which the majority of products still contain or use HCFCs (hydrochlorofluoro-carbons), such as certain types of foam insulation and most compression-cycle heating and air-conditioning equipment. As ozone-depleting substances are phased out, the relative importance of this criterion drops (for example, polyisocyanurate insulation is no longer made with HCFC-141b as the blowing agent, so the environmental benefit of expanded polystyrene, EPS, over polyiso has disappeared).

• **Alternatives to products made from PVC.** Most PVC products are over 40% chlorine by weight, and hazardous chlorinated hydrocarbons—such as dioxins—can be generated during incineration. Many PVC products also contain plasticizers that may be endocrine disruptors (chemicals that mimic natural hormones and may cause reproductive or developmental problems).

• **Alternatives to other components considered hazardous.** Fluorescent lamps with low mercury levels are considered green through this criterion, as are some products that avoid the use of industry-standard brominated flame retardants.

• **Products that reduce or eliminate pesticide treatments.** Periodic pesticide treatment around buildings can be a significant health and environmental hazard. The use of certain products can obviate the need for pesticide treatments, and such products are therefore considered green. Examples include physical termite barriers, borate-treated building products, and bait systems that eliminate the need for broad-based pesticide applications.

• **Products that reduce pollution or waste from operations.** Alternative wastewater disposal systems reduce groundwater pollution by decomposing organic wastes more effectively. Porous paving products and green (vegetated or "living") roofing systems result in less stormwater runoff and thereby reduce surface water pollution and sewage treatment plant loads. Masonry fireplaces and pellet stoves burn fuel more completely with fewer emissions than conventional fireplaces and wood stoves. Recycling bins and compost systems enable occupants to reduce their solid waste generation.

PRODUCTS THAT REDUCE ENVIRONMENTAL IMPACTS DURING CONSTRUCTION, DEMOLITION, OR RENOVATION

Some building products achieve their environmental benefits by avoiding pollution or other environmental impacts during construction, renovation, or demolition. While this is a fairly small category in terms of the number of products satisfying the criterion, it is nonetheless important. The subcategories here refer to the construction stage where the benefit is typically realized:

• **Products that reduce the impacts of new construction.** Included here are various erosion-control products, foundation products that eliminate the need for excavation, and exterior stains that result in lower VOC emissions into the atmosphere.

• **Products that reduce the impacts of demolition.** Fluorescent lamp and ballast recyclers and low-mercury fluorescent lamps reduce environmental impacts during demolition (as well as renovation).

• **Products that reduce the impacts of renovation.**

Modular carpet tiles minimize environmental impacts during reconfiguration of spaces (renovation).

PRODUCTS THAT SAVE ENERGY OR WATER

The ongoing environmental impacts that result from energy and water used in operating a building often far outweigh the impacts associated with its construction. Many products are included in *GreenSpec* for these benefits. There are several quite distinct subcategories:

• **Building components that reduce heating and cooling loads.** Examples include structural insulated panels (SIPs), insulated concrete forms (ICFs), autoclaved aerated concrete (AAC) blocks, and high-performance windows.

With windows, energy performance requirements for *GreenSpec* listing are based on the National Fenestration Rating Council (NFRC) *unit U-factors*; with U-factors, the lower the number, the better it insulates. The base standard for windows is a unit U-factor of 0.25 or lower for at least one product in a listed product line. If the windows are made from an environmentally attractive material (e.g., high recycled content or superb durability, such as fiberglass), the energy standard is less stringent: a U-factor of 0.30 or lower. If the frame material is nongreen, such as PVC (vinyl), the energy standard is more stringent: a U-factor of 0.20 or lower is required. There are a few exceptions to these standards, such as high-recycled-content windows made for unheated buildings.

• **Equipment that conserves energy.** With energy-consuming equipment such as water heaters, clothes washers, and refrigerators, the criteria for *GreenSpec* listing are based on energy performance ratings that rely on U.S. Department of Energy test standards. In most appliance categories, *GreenSpec* has a higher energy performance threshold than ENERGY STAR®: for example, exceeding those standards by 10% or 20%. With certain product categories, such as compact fluorescent lamps (CFLs), all products qualify from an energy standpoint, but some are eliminated due to performance problems.

• **Renewable energy and fuel cell equipment.** Equipment and products that enable us to use renewable energy instead of fossil fuels and conventionally generated electricity are highly beneficial from an environmental standpoint. Examples include solar water heaters, photovoltaic (PV) systems, and wind turbines. Fuel cells are also included here, even though fuel cells today nearly always use natural gas or another fossil fuel as the hydrogen source—they are considered green because emissions are lower than combustion-based equipment and because the use of fuel cells will help us eventually move beyond fossil fuel dependence.

• **Fixtures and equipment that conserve water.** All toilets and most showerheads today meet federal water efficiency standards—but not all of these products perform satisfactorily. With toilets, *GreenSpec* considers both water use and flush performance based on a standardized test procedure. The emphasis in *GreenSpec* is on toilets that use at least 10% less water than the federally mandated 1.6 gallons per flush (gpf), though some toilets that offer superb flush performance at 1.6 gpf are also included. With faucets, special controls that help conserve water are the usual basis for inclusion. Some other water-saving products, such as rainwater catchment systems, are also found here.

PRODUCTS THAT CONTRIBUTE TO A SAFE, HEALTHY INDOOR ENVIRONMENT

Houses should be healthy to live in, and product selection is a significant determinant of indoor environment quality. Green building products that help to ensure a healthy indoor environment can be separated into several categories:

• **Products that don't release significant pollutants into the building.** Included here are zero- and low-VOC paints, caulks, and adhesives, as well as products with very low emissions, such as manufactured wood products made without formaldehyde binders. Just how low the VOC level needs to be for a given product to qualify for inclusion in *GreenSpec* depends on the product category, but for many products the VOC threshold is 50 grams per liter, which is far below even the most stringent California standards.

• **Products that block the introduction, production, or spread of indoor contaminants.** Certain materials and products are green because they prevent the introduction (or development) of pollutants—especially biological contaminants—into the home. Duct mastic, for example, can block the entry of mold-laden air or insulation fibers into a duct system. "Track-off" systems for entryways help to remove pollutants from the shoes of people entering. Coated duct board—compared with standard rigid fiberglass duct board—prevents fiber shedding and helps control mold growth. And true linoleum naturally controls microbial contamination through the ongoing process of linoleic acid oxidation. (Note that vinyl flooring—which is PVC flooring—is often mistakenly referred to as linoleum. PVC is not considered a green product.)

• **Products that remove indoor pollutants.** Products that qualify for *GreenSpec* based on this criterion include certain ventilation products, filters, radon mitigation equipment, and other equipment that helps to remove pollutants or introduce fresh air. Because ventilation equipment is now fairly standard, only products that are particularly efficient or quiet, or that offer other environmental benefits, are included.

• **Products that warn occupants of health hazards in the building.** Included here are carbon monoxide (CO) detectors, lead paint test kits, and other indoor air quality (IAQ) test kits. Because CO detectors are so common, other features are needed to qualify these products for *GreenSpec*, such as evidence of superb performance.

• **Products that improve light quality.** A growing body of evidence suggests that natural daylight is beneficial to our health and productivity. Products that enable us to bring daylight into a building, such as tubular skylights, are included in *GreenSpec*.

Sitework & Landscaping

Sitework and landscaping are typically the first and last tasks, respectively, on a building site. Steps can be taken at the beginning of sitework that can greatly increase the value—and reduce the cost—of landscaping after construction. Siting of the building itself usually has already occurred, but there is still often an opportunity to influence such issues as solar access and minimizing of site disturbance.

A site survey should precede any sitework to identify sensitive areas and features to be protected, such as wetlands, trees, and other vegetation. It's well worth the effort to save trees if they are healthy and not too close to the structure. Mature trees on a lot can add more than 15% to the value of a house, and appropriately placed trees can reduce a building's conditioning needs by more than 40%.

A tree's root system extends out quite a distance from the trunk—typically at least to the *drip line* of the furthest branches. Even just compacting the soil can harm the roots, so a large area around each protected tree needs to be fenced off. To ensure cooperation of subcontractors in this effort, one strategy is to specifically list in their contract the value of each mature tree and hold them responsible for that value if the tree is damaged.

Invasive plants introduced from other parts of the world can wreak havoc on the ecological balance of a region, so nonnative species should generally be avoided in land-scaping (though noninvasive exotic species—those that don't spread and outcompete native plants—are much less of a concern). Plants that are native to your area are also adapted to your climate, so they tend to need less care and maintenance, and require less watering—saving time and money. Most lawns are planted with nonnative turf grasses, such as Kentucky Bluegrass, which require watering in most U.S. climates. Hardy, native species such as buffalo grass and certain fescues should be used instead, or consider replacing lawn areas with other landscapes that require less water, fertilizer, herbicides, and maintenance.

Handling stormwater runoff can be a major design issue. Conventional solutions include concrete or PVC drainage pipes and, on larger projects, detention ponds; these are expensive and tend to increase the contamination of the water from surface pollutants. Softer solutions include the use of pervious surfaces to allow rainwater infiltration directly into the ground; these are far better environmentally and usually less expensive. Use of swales for rainwater instead of curbs and stormwater drains is also preferred.

Resource-efficient products and building materials for sitework and landscaping include porous paving systems suitable for driveways, walkways, courtyards, and park-ing areas; and landscaping timbers made from recycled plastics, which are more durable in ground contact than preservative-treated wood. Retaining walls and hardscape surfaces can often be made from salvaged materials, such as broken up concrete paving (which some green builders refer to as "urbanite").

Aggregate Surfacing

Salvaged materials, such as brick, can be processed into aggregate surfacing.

Brick Nuggets

Cunningham Brick Co., Inc.
701 N. Main St.
Lexington, NC 27292

Toll-free: 800-672-6181
Phone: 336-248-8541
www.cunninghambrick.com

Brick Nuggets are crushed waste bricks suitable for landscaping uses. They are available in 40-lb. bags and bulk.

Drip Irrigation System

Drip irrigation systems, such as soaker hoses, release measured quantities of water directly to the soil surrounding the intended plants instead of spraying an entire area. Drip irrigation uses water more efficiently and greatly reduces loss through evaporation. Look for products with recycled content.

Fiskars Soaker Hose and Sprinkler Hose

Fiskars, Inc. - Fiskars
  Garden Tools
780 Carolina St.
Sauk City, WI 53583

Toll-free: 800-500-4849
www.fiskars.com

Fiskars Soaker Hose and Sprinkler Hose, formerly Moisture Master, are Green Seal-certified products that contain 65% post-consumer recycled rubber from tires.

Erosion and Sedimentation Control

While polymer-based fabrics dominate the geotextile market, alternatives made from natural fibers are available. These include coir fiber (the strong coconut-husk fiber that is obtained from coconut oil production) and jute, a fiber commonly used to make twine. The primary advantage of natural-fiber geotextiles is their biodegradability once vegetation is established. Unlike polymer-based fabrics, natural-fiber products also absorb moisture and work like a mulch, which benefits seedling establishment.

ANTIWASH/GEOJUTE and GEOCOIR DeKoWe

Belton Industries, Inc.
P.O. Box 127
1205 Hamby Rd.
Belton, SC 29627

Toll-free: 800-845-8753
Phone: 864-338-5711
www.beltonindustries.com

Antiwash®/Geojute® is woven in a 1/2" grid pattern that is suitable for moderate slopes sustaining runoff velocities of up to 8 ft/s. The jute fabric, available in 4'-wide by 225'- or 147'-long rolls, biodegrades in one to two years. Geocoir® DeKoWe®, made from coir, is stronger and more durable than jute geotextiles. This product is available in three different weights: 400, 700, and 900 g/m²; is typically used on steeper slopes; and may last from 4 to 5 years, depending upon the application.

BioFence

Environmental Research Corps
15 Mohawk Ave.
East Freetown, MA 02717

Phone: 508-763-5253
www.biofence.com

BioFence™ is a one-piece silt fence made from 100% biodegradable materials. Beech or maple stakes measuring 42" x 1 1/8" are sewn into 7- to 10-oz., 20-mesh seine weave Hessian Cloth composite stiffened with cornstarch. Aspen wood fiber matting is stitched to the front. This product installs more quickly than conventional silt fence/straw bale combinations and is cost-competitive. Custom fences are available for specific applications.

Erosion Control Blankets

SI Geosolutions
4109 Industry Dr.
Chattanooga, TN 37416

Toll-free: 800-621-0444
www.fixsoil.com

SI Geosolutions offers natural-fiber erosion control and shoreline stabilization products for many applications. Most products are coir-fiber-based, though some contain photodegradable PE netting.

Erosion Control Products

RoLanka International, Inc.
155 Andrew Dr.
Stockbridge, GA 30281

Toll-free: 800-760-3215
Phone: 770-506-8211
www.rolanka.com

RoLanka manufactures a full line of coir-based, soil erosion control blankets and streambank stabilization products.

KoirMat and KoirLog

Nedia Enterprises, Inc.
22187 Vantage Pointe Pl.
Ashburn, VA 20148

Toll-free: 888-725-6999
Phone: 571-223-0200
www.nedia.com

Nedia Enterprises manufactures a full line of primarily coir-based erosion control products. KoirMat™ erosion control matting, made from 100% coir fiber, is suitable for a wide variety of applications. KoirLog™ is a 100% coconut fiber "log" for shoreline and stream channel erosion control applications. KoirLog is available in 6", 8", 12", 16", and 20" diameters and is typically 10' to 20' long.

Fertilizing

The fertilizers included here are organic or produced from wastes diverted from landfills. Due to the shipping energy use (and costs), regional sources are generally preferred.

Cedar Grove Compost

Cedar Grove Composting, Inc.
17825 Cedar Grove Rd. SE
Maple Valley, WA 98038

Toll-free: 877-764-5748
Phone: 206-832-3073
www.cedar-grove.com

Cedar Grove Composting operates the largest single dedicated composting facility in the U.S. in Maple Valley, Washington. The company started by making composted products from a curbside yard-waste collection program in Seattle. The manufacturer has certified the following recycled-content levels (by weight): total recovered material 100% typical.

Premium Compost, Clay Buster, and Lawn Topdressing

Central Maui Landfill / Maui Eko-Systems
P.O. Box 1065
Puunene, HI 96784

Phone: 808-572-8844

Premium Compost, Clay Buster, and Lawn Topdressing are soil amendments that are batch-tested by independent labs and certified by the Hawaii Department of Health. These products are available in 1 1/2 ft³ bags, 1 yd³ bulk bags, and in bulk.

Geosynthetics

Geotextile products increase the durability of subsurface and foundation drainage installations by stopping the migration of fine sediments. Several geosynthetics made from recycled plastic are available, including those listed here. Note: For bioengineering and erosion-control applications, biodegradable, natural-fiber materials are generally preferable.

LowFlow

Polyguard Products, Inc.
3801 S. Business 45
P.O. Box 755
Ennis, TX 75120

Toll-free: 800-541-4994
Phone: 972-875-8421
www.polyguardproducts.com

LowFlow™ is a 100% post-industrial recycled-content plastic geotextile that provides drainage and protection for foundation waterproofing at sites with low transmissivity clay soils. The manufacturer has certified the following recycled-content levels (by weight): total recovered material 100% typical, 100% guaranteed.

Slopetame²

Invisible Structures, Inc.
1600 Jackson St., Ste. 310
Golden, CO 80401

Toll-free: 800-233-1510
Phone: 303-233-8383
www.invisiblestructures.com

Slopetame² is a plastic grid product made from 100% injection-molded recycled HDPE with varying amounts of post-consumer and post-industrial content. Slopetame² is designed to provide immediate erosion control in permanent installations on weak or eroding slopes by resisting undercutting water and soil movement. It has a geotextile backing.

Hydro-Mulching

Hydro-seeding is often the most effective way to sow grass seed over large areas. Cellulose mulch made from recycled newspaper is used as a primary component of hydro-seeding sprays. It prevents erosion, retains soil moisture, and encourages seed germination. There are slight differences among products, but all are similar.

A W I Mulch

All-Weather Insulation Co., LLC
19 W. Industrial Dr.
Springfield, KY 40069

Phone: 859-336-9832

A W I Mulch contains recycled newspaper.

Applegate Mulch

Applegate Insulation Manufacturing
1000 Highview Dr.
Webberville, MI 48892

Toll-free: 800-627-7536
Phone: 517-521-3545
www.applegateinsulation.com

Applegate mulch is made from recycled paper. The manufacturer has certified the following recycled-content levels (by weight): total recovered material 99% typical, 99% guaranteed; post-consumer material 99% typical, 99% guaranteed.

Astro-Mulch

Thermo-Kool of Alaska
P.O. Box 230085
Anchorage, AK 99523

Phone: 907-563-3644

Astro-Mulch contains recycled newspaper. The manufacturer has certified the following recycled-content levels (by weight): total recovered material 99% typical, 85% guaranteed; post-consumer material 99% typical, 85% guaranteed.

Benovert

Benolec, Ltd.
1451 Nobel St.
Sainte-Julie, PQ J3E 1Z4 Canada

Phone: 450-922-2000
www.benolec.com

Benovert hydro-mulch contains recycled newspaper.

Climatizer Hydroseeding Mulch

Climatizer Insulation, Ltd.
120 Claireville Dr.
Etobicoke, ON M9W 5Y3 Canada

Toll-free: 866-871-5495
Phone: 416-798-1235
www.climatizer.com

Climatizer Hydroseeding Mulch contains recycled newspaper.

Fiber Mulch

Thermoguard Co.
125 N. Dyer Rd.
Spokane, WA 99212

Toll-free: 800-541-0579
Phone: 509-535-4600

Thermoguard's hydro-mulch contains recycled newspaper.

Fiber Turf

Erie Energy Products, Inc.
1400 Irwin Dr.
Erie, PA 16505

Toll-free: 800-233-1810
Phone: 814-454-2828
www.erieenergy.com

Fiber Turf is made from recycled newspaper.

Fibrex

Paul's Insulation
P.O. Box 115
Vergas, MN 56587

Toll-free: 800-627-5190
Phone: 218-342-2800

Fibrex hydro-mulch is made from 100% post-consumer recycled newspaper.

Hydro-Spray

National Fiber
50 Depot St.
Belchertown, MA 01007

Toll-free: 800-282-7711
Phone: 413-283-8747
www.natlfiber.com

Hydro-Spray hydro-seeding mulch contains a minimum of 90% recycled, over-issue newsprint.

Hydro-Spray Mulch

Profile Products, LLC
60 Davy Crockett Park Rd.
Limestone, TN 37681

Phone: 423-257-2051
www.profileproducts.com

Hydro-Spray Mulch contains recycled newspaper.

Nu-Wool HydroGreen

Nu-Wool Co., Inc.
2472 Port Sheldon St.
Jenison, MI 49428

Toll-free: 800-748-0128
Phone: 616-669-0100
www.nuwool.com

Nu-Wool® HydroGreen™ hydroseeding mulch is made from 100% recycled paper fibers and contains an organic dye and wetting agent.

Promat - H

Tascon, Inc.
7607 Fairview St.
P.O. Box 41846
Houston, TX 77214

Toll-free: 800-937-1774
www.tasconindustries.com

Promat - H is made from recycled newspaper. The manufacturer has certified the following recycled-content levels (by weight): total recovered material 85% typical, 85% guaranteed; post-consumer material 85% typical, 85% guaranteed.

Thermo-Mulch

Therm-O-Comfort Co. Ltd.
75 S. Edgeware Rd.
St. Thomas, ON N5P 2H7 Canada

Toll-free: 877-684-3766
Phone: 519-631-3400

Thermo-Mulch contains 100% recycled newspaper (80% post-industrial and 20% post-consumer).

Insect Control

see *Miscellaneous: Insect Control*

Landscape Edging

Landscape edging products are good applications for recycled plastics and tire-rubber. The material is impervious, resistant to root penetration, will not rot, and structural requirements are minimal.

Lawn Edging and Tree Rings

Phoenix Recycled Products, Inc.
360 W. Church St.
Batesburg, SC 29006

Phone: 803-532-4425
www.permamulch.com

Phoenix Recycled Products' lawn edging and tree rings are made from recycled-tire rubber and are available in a variety of sizes and colors. The manufacturer has certified the following recycled-content levels (by weight): total recovered material 85% typical, 85% guaranteed; post-consumer material 85% typical, 85% guaranteed.

Lawn Edging, Lattice, and Privacy Fencing

Master Mark Div. of Avon Plastics, Inc.
P.O. Box 662
Albany, MN 56307-0662

Toll-free: 800-535-4838
Phone: 320-845-2111
www.mastermark.com

Master Mark makes a variety of landscape products, such as lawn edging, lattice, and privacy fencing from recycled HDPE plastic. The manufacturer has certified the following recycled-content levels (by weight): post-consumer material 100% typical, 100% guaranteed.

Landscape Timbers

Landscape timbers provide an appropriate use of low-grade, commingled recycled plastics that little else can be produced from. Lighter-weight hollow extrusions, generally made from HDPE, require less energy for shipping. Along with products listed here, many manufacturers of recycled plastic lumber also produce landscape timbers.

Ecoboard Landscape Timbers

American Ecoboard, Inc.
200 Finn Ct.
Farmingdale, NY 11735

Phone: 631-753-5151
www.americanecoboard.com

Ecoboard® landscape timbers are manufactured from recycled HDPE and LDPE with UV-stabilization, flame-retardant, and strength additives. Ecoboard landscape timbers are available in 4x4, 4x6, 5x5, and 6x6 sizes. The manufacturer has certified the following recycled-content levels (by weight): total recovered material 100% typical, 100% guaranteed; post-consumer material 90% typical, 80% guaranteed.

EPS Plastic Landscape Timbers

Engineered Plastic
  Systems
740 B Industrial Dr.
Cary, IL 60013

Phone: 847-462-9001
www.epsplasticlumber
  .com

Photo: David Cook

Environmental Plastic Systems (EPS) plastic landscape
timbers are typically made
from 100% post-consumer
recycled HDPE and are available in 3x4, 4x4, 4x6, and 6x6 dimensions with a smooth or wood-grain finish. Standard colors are dark
brown, black, and charcoal gray; other colors are available for an
additional charge. All EPS plastic products come with a 50-year
limited warranty.

Landscape Timbers

Aloha Plastics Recycling
75 Amala Pl.
Kahului, HI 96732

Phone: 808-877-0822
www.aloha-recycling.com

Aloha Plastics Recycling manufactures a variety of plastic products
primarily from 100% post-consumer HDPE. Aloha Plastics Recycling
landscape timbers contain LDPE as well.

Landscape Timbers

Amazing Recycled Products, Inc.
P.O. Box 312
Denver, CO 80201

Toll-free: 800-241-2174
Phone: 303-699-7693
www.amazingrecycled.com

Amazing Recycled Plastics Landscape Timbers are made from
recycled HDPE plastic and a small amount of waste paper. The
manufacturer has certified the following recycled-content levels
(by weight): total recovered material 100% typical, 100% guaranteed; post-consumer material 80% typical, 75% guaranteed.

Landscape Timbers

American Recycled Plastic, Inc.
1500 Main St.
Palm Bay, FL 32905

Toll-free: 866-674-1525
Phone: 321-674-1525
www.itsrecycled.com

American Recycled Plastic manufactures landscape timbers from
recycled HDPE plastic. The manufacturer has certified the following recycled-content levels (by weight): total recovered material

100% typical, 100% guaranteed; post-consumer material 80%
typical, 80% guaranteed.

Landscape Timbers

Barco Products Co.
11 N. Batavia Ave.
Batavia, IL 60510

Toll-free: 800-757-5460
Phone: 630-879-0084
www.barcoproducts.com

Landscape Timbers are made from 100% recycled plastic (commingled HDPE and LDPE). The product is sized as railroad ties with
premolded holes for rebar stakes and weighs 40 lbs.

Landscape Timbers

The Plastic Lumber Co.
115 W. Bartges St.
Akron, OH 44311

Toll-free: 800-886-8990
Phone: 330-762-8989
www.plasticlumber.com

The Plastic Lumber Company offers approximately 20 different
profiles (up to 6x6) of dimensional plastic lumber available in
12 colors. Commercial and residential decking is also available.
Recycled content is 97% post-consumer.

Landscape Timbers

XPotential Products Inc.
St. Boniface Postal Sta.
P.O. Box 126
Winnipeg, MB R2H 3B4 Canada

Toll-free: 800-863-6619
Phone: 204-224-3933
www.xpotentialproducts.com

XPotential Product's interlocking landscape timbers are made
from 100% recycled materials including the primarily nonmetallic
residue of shredded automobiles (such as carpet, seat cushions,
fabrics, and trace amounts of metal) along with post-consumer
and post-industrial recycled plastics. The timbers measure $2\frac{1}{2}$"
x $3\frac{1}{2}$" x 95" and weigh 36 lbs. each. All the XPotential products
come with a limited lifetime warranty.

Phoenix Recycled-Plastic Landscape Timbers

Phoenix Recycled Plastics
220 Washington St.
Norristown, PA 19401

Phone: 610-277-3900
www.plasticlumberyard.com

Phoenix Recycled Plastics manufactures landscape timbers from
100% recycled plastic. The 8'-long ties are available in 4x4, 6x6,
and 6x8 sizes.

SelecTimber

SelecTech, Inc.
15 Fourth St.
Taunton, MA 02780

Phone: 508-828-4200
www.selectechinc.com

SelecTimber is a 100% recycled polyethylene landscape timber. The structural rib design reduces weight to about half that of solid plastic landscape timbers. The nominal 6x6 product comes in 8' lengths and has molded holes for rebar attachment. The manufacturer has certified the following recycled-content levels (by weight): total recovered material 100% typical, 100% guaranteed; post-consumer material 10% typical, 5% guaranteed.

Native Plants and Seeds

Landscaping with native plants adapted to your local climate and not requiring irrigation, fertilizers, or pesticides will result in lower environmental impact than conventional lawns and landscaping with nonnative plantings. Included here are several of the leading suppliers of native seed and seedlings. While these companies can be good sources, you should start by looking for native plant nurseries in your immediate area, as they're likely to have specific genotypes best adapted to your region.

Native Plant Supplier

Bitterroot Restoration, Inc.
445 Quast Ln.
Corvallis, MT 59828

Phone: 406-961-4991
www.bitterrootrestoration.com

Bitterroot Restoration maintains extensive offerings of native plants appropriate to the western U.S. The company, founded in 1986, provides restoration design and planning services in addition to selling plants. "Plant salvage" is among the services offered—transplanting of plants from land that will be developed. Comprehensive Web site; catalog available.

Native Plant Supplier

The Reveg Edge/Ecoseeds
P.O. Box 361
Redwood City, CA 94064

Phone: 650-325-7333
www.ecoseeds.com

The Reveg Edge, a division of the Redwood City Seed Company, is a unique supplier of native plants in that its plants are custom-grown with seeds supplied by the buyer that were collected from the ecosystem for which the plants are intended. In this way, the established plantings will be appropriate to the intended microclimate. This process allows the company to supply native plants

to any place in the United States. The company, founded in 1971, also offers a wide range of hard-to-find and heirloom vegetable, herb, and medicinal plants under the Ecoseeds™ brand name, in addition to in-depth classes and consulting on establishment of native plants.

Native Seed and Plant Supplier

Ernst Conservation Seeds
9006 Mercer Pike
Meadville, PA 16335

Toll-free: 800-873-3321
Phone: 814-336-2404
www.ernstseed.com

Ernst Conservation Seeds is one of the few native seed and plant suppliers in the Northeast. The company was founded in 1963 and specializes in native wildflowers and grasses, legumes, cover crops, bioengineering materials, wetland restoration and wildlife habitat mixes, and naturalized conservation species.

Native Seed and Plant Supplier

Ion Exchange
1878 Old Mission Dr.
Harpers Ferry, IA 52146

Toll-free: 800-291-2143
www.ionxchange.com

Ion Exchange was founded in 1988 and supplies seedlings and/or seed of more than 250 native grasses and wildflowers. Their selection of grasses, sedges, and rushes is particularly large, with over 40 species—most of which are available in plugs, pots, or seed (by the packet, ounce, or pound). The company has both a printed catalog and an online catalog, which allows searches based on ecosystem, type of plant, and so forth.

Native Seed and Plant Supplier

LaFayette Home Nursery, Inc.
1 Nursery Ln.
LaFayette, IL 61449

Phone: 309-995-3311

One of the oldest suppliers of seed and plants, LaFayette Home Nursery was founded in 1887 and is now run by third- and fourth-generation family members. The company's Prairie Department, which focuses on native plants, was established in 1970.

Native Seed and Plant Supplier

Native American Seed
127 N. 16th St.
Junction, TX 76849

Toll-free: 800-728-4043
www.seedsource.com

Serving Texas and the arid Southwest, Native American Seed has a superb Web site with extensive information, including photos of most of the native plant species they sell. The company, founded in 1974, is committed to supplying seeds that were produced using source seed harvested from sites within the ecoregion being served. In this way, they are able to retain the original genetic integrity of the plants. The parent company is Neiman Environments, Inc., which specializes in large-scale restoration projects of abused, neglected, and/or overgrazed land. The company supplies seed only (from seedlings) from more than 100 species.

Native Seed and Plant Supplier

Prairie Nursery, Inc.
P.O. Box 306
Westfield, WI 53964

Toll-free: 800-476-9453
www.prairienursery.com

Founded in 1972, Prairie Nursery's mission is "to preserve native plants and animals by helping people create attractive, nonpolluting natural landscapes that can support a diversity of wildlife." The company offers over 100 wildflowers and 19 species of grass, sedge, and bulrush in seed form, individual plants, or both, as well as many seed mixes and collections of plants for special purposes. Their 65-page catalog includes more specific information.

Native Seed and Plant Supplier

Prairie Restorations, Inc.
P.O. Box 327
Princeton, MN 55371

Phone: 763-389-4342
www.prairieresto.com

Prairie Restorations supplies native seed and plants for prairie restoration work in the Upper Midwest, offering distribution within a 200-mile radius of their two facilities in Princeton and Hawley, Minnesota—including parts of Wisconsin, Iowa, and the Dakotas. Installation, land management, and consultation services are also available.

Native Seed and Plant Supplier

S&S Seeds, Inc.
P.O. Box 1275
Carpinteria, CA 93014

Phone: 805-684-0436
www.ssseeds.com

Founded in 1975, S&S Seeds is a wholesale producer and supplier of more than 900 plant species including wildflowers, native grasses, and erosion-control seed mixes. The company also offers a line of erosion-control products, including EarthGuard, Flexterra, Bonded Fiber Matrices, Greenfix Erosion Control Blankets, and soil stabilizers.

Native Seed and Plant Supplier

Taylor Creek Restoration Nurseries
17921 Smith Rd.
Brodhead, WI 53520

Phone: 608-897-8641
www.appliedeco.com

Taylor Creek Restoration Nurseries was founded in the late 1970s as the companion company to Applied Ecological Services, an ecological consulting and restoration contracting firm. Taylor Creek Nurseries offers more than 400 species of native plants that are grown on 300 acres and supplied throughout the Midwest. Both seed and plants are available.

Salvaged Native Plants

Willowell Nursery
10008 S.W. 60th St.
Portland, OR 97219

Phone: 503-245-3553

Willowell Nursery maintains a plant rescue program to salvage native plants form lands slated for development in the Portland, Oregon area.

Permanent Traffic Control

Recycled plastics and rubber can effectively be used in the manufacture of roadway markers, speed bumps, parking stops, and traffic signs. Recycled plastic diverts material from the waste stream and has lower embodied energy than portland cement-based concrete products. In addition, the lighter weight of plastic parking bumpers (40–50 lbs. versus 250–300 lbs.) reduces transportation energy consumption and cost of shipping. Plastic parking stops are easily installed with $^5/_8$" rebar stakes, and they never need painting.

Better Than Wood Car Stops

BTW Industries
3939 Hollywood Blvd., Ste. 3B
Hollywood, FL 33021

Phone: 954-962-2100
www.recycledplastic.com

BTW manufactures car stops from recycled HDPE, LDPE, and PP plastics. The manufacturer has certified the following recycled-content levels (by weight): total recovered material 100% typical, 97% guaranteed; post-consumer material 100% typical, 97% guaranteed.

Car Stops

Kay Park Recreation Corp.
1301 Pine St.
Janesville, IA 50647

Toll-free: 800-553-2476
www.kaypark.com

Kay Park Recreation's Car Stops are made from 96% post-consumer recycled, commingled plastic.

Car Stops and Speed Bumps

Aloha Plastics Recycling
75 Amala Pl.
Kahului, HI 96732

Phone: 808-877-0822
www.aloha-recycling.com

Aloha Plastics Recycling manufactures a variety of products, including car stops and speed bumps, from 100% post-consumer HDPE.

Car Stops and Speed Bumps

American Recreational Products
3505 Veterans Memorial Hwy., Ste. Q
Ronkonkoma, NY 11779

Phone: 631-588-4545

American Recreational Products offers wheel stops and speed bumps made from 100% recycled plastic. Products include hardware.

Car Stops and Speed Bumps

Plastic Recycling of Iowa Falls, Inc.
10252 Hwy. 65
Iowa Falls, IA 50126

Toll-free: 800-338-1438
Phone: 641-648-5073
www.hammersplastic.com

Plastic Recycling of Iowa Falls, formerly Hammer's Plastic Recy-

cling, manufactures yellow, blue, and gray car stops and yellow speed bumps from recycled commingled HDPE, LDPE, LLDPE, and other miscellaneous plastics. The manufacturer has certified the following recycled-content levels (by weight): total recovered material 100% typical, 100% guaranteed; post-consumer material 50% typical, 50% guaranteed.

Car Stops and Speed Bumps

Traffic & Parking Control Co., Inc. (Tapco)
800 Wall St.
Elm Grove, WI 53122

Toll-free: 800-236-0112
www.tapconet.com

TAPCO distributes parking control devices from recycled plastic and rubber, such as wheel stops, bollard covers, speed bumps, and speed humps. The manufacturer has certified the following recycled-content levels (by weight): total recovered material 100% typical, 100% guaranteed; post-consumer material 100% typical, 100% guaranteed.

FlexStake Highway Safety Products

Flexstake, Inc.
2150 Andrea Ln. #C
Fort Myers, FL 33912

Toll-free: 800-348-9839
Phone: 941-481-3539
www.flexstake.com

FlexStake Highway Safety Products include various traffic delineators and markers made from over 50% post-consumer recycled plastics. Flexstake products will withstand being "mowed-over" by onrushing traffic.

Impact-Curb

XPotential Products Inc.
St. Boniface Postal Sta.
P.O. Box 126
Winnipeg, MB R2H 3B4 Canada

Toll-free: 800-863-6619
Phone: 204-224-3933
www.xpotentialproducts.com

Impact-Curb™ is a plastic composite parking stop manufactured from recycled materials, including auto shredder residue as well as HDPE and LDPE plastics. Impact-Curb is approximately $5\frac{1}{4}$" x 8" in 6' or 8' lengths and 4" x 6" in 6' or 8' lengths. The manufacturer has certified the following recycled-content levels (by weight): total recovered material 100% typical, 100% guaranteed; post-consumer material 85% typical, 85% guaranteed.

Parking Stops

Bedford Technology, LLC
2424 Armour Rd.
P.O. Box 609
Worthington, MN 56187-0609

Toll-free: 800-721-9037
Phone: 507-372-5558
www.plasticboards.com

Bedford Technology manufactures, among other products, 6' and 8' parking stops made from recycled HDPE plastic. The manufacturer has certified the following recycled-content levels (by weight): total recovered material 99% typical, 99% guaranteed; post-consumer material 65% typical, 50% guaranteed.

Parking Stops and Bollards

Amazing Recycled Products, Inc.
P.O. Box 312
Denver, CO 80201

Toll-free: 800-241-2174
Phone: 303-699-7693
www.amazingrecycled.com

Amazing Recycled Products manufactures parking stops and flat-top bollards (also available customized) with recycled HDPE and waste paper composite material. The parking stops are 4', 6', or 8' long. The manufacturer has certified the following recycled-content levels (by weight): total recovered material 100% typical, 100% guaranteed; post-consumer material 80% typical, 75% guaranteed.

Parking Stops and Speed Bumps

Inteq Corp.
33010 Lakeland Blvd.
Eastlake, OH 44095

Phone: 440-953-0550
www.4-inteqcorp.com

Inteq's Parking Stops and Speed Bumps are made from recycled HDPE plastic. Speed bumps are yellow, and parking stops are yellow, white, gray, black, or blue. The manufacturer has certified the following recycled-content levels (by weight): total recovered material 100% typical, 100% guaranteed; post-consumer material 100% typical, 95% guaranteed.

Parking Stops and Speed Bumps

The Plastic Lumber Co.
115 W. Bartges St.
Akron, OH 44311

Toll-free: 800-886-8990
Phone: 330-762-8989
www.plasticlumber.com

The Plastic Lumber Company's Parking Stops of recycled plastic are 3', 4', or 6' in length and come in yellow, white, gray, blue,

and black. Bright yellow Speed Bumps are 4', 6', or 9' in length. The manufacturer has certified the following recycled-content levels (by weight): post-consumer material 95% typical, 70% guaranteed.

Parking Stops, Speed Bumps, and Bollards

American Recycled Plastic, Inc.
1500 Main St.
Palm Bay, FL 32905

Toll-free: 866-674-1525
Phone: 321-674-1525
www.itsrecycled.com

American Recycled Plastic manufactures parking stops, speed bumps, and bollards from recycled HDPE plastic. The manufacturer has certified the following recycled-content levels (by weight): total recovered material 100% typical, 100% guaranteed; post-consumer material 80% typical, 80% guaranteed.

Parking Stops, Speed Bumps, and Bollards

Litchfield Industries
4 Industrial Dr.
Litchfield, MI 49252

Toll-free: 800-542-5282
Phone: 517-542-2988
www.litchfieldindustries.com

Litchfield Industries manufactures parking stops, speed bumps, and bollards made from 100% post-consumer plastic. Parking stops are 4' long and are available in yellow, blue, white, gray, and black. Speed bumps are 6' long and yellow in color.

Parking Stops, Speed Bumps, and Bollards

Recycled Plastic Man, Inc.
P.O. Box 2248
Englewood, FL 34295

Toll-free: 800-253-7742
Phone: 941-473-1618
www.recycledplasticman.com

Recycled Plastic Man manufactures parking stops, speed bumps, and bollards from post-consumer recycled plastics (primarily HDPE). The manufacturer has certified the following recycled-content levels (by weight): total recovered material 100% guaranteed; post-consumer material 100% guaranteed.

Park-It and Easy Rider

GNR Technologies, Inc.
990 Upton
LaSalle, PQ H8R 2T9 Canada

Toll-free: 800-641-4143
Phone: 514-366-6116
www.gnrtech.com

Park-It and Easy Rider are 100% recycled-rubber parking stops and speed bumps, respectively. These durable products are black with reflective yellow tape markings.

Power-Stop

Tandus Group / C&A Floorcoverings
311 Smith Industrial Blvd.
P.O. Box 1447
Dalton, GA 30722-1447

Toll-free: 800-248-2878
Phone: 706-259-9711
www.tandus.com

Power-Stop is a parking stop made from C&A's ER3 composite material. This very durable composite is made from post-consumer and post-industrial carpeting and carpet-tile waste that includes PVC backing and nylon face fiber.

Restrictor Speed Humps

Recycled Technology, Inc.
19475 S.W. Teton Ave.
Tualatin, OR 97062

Toll-free: 800-455-6287
Phone: 503-691-5845
www.recycledtech.com

Recycled Technology Restrictor Speed Humps for temporary or permanent installations are made from recycled-tire rubber. They are designed to calm traffic, slowing vehicular speeds to 25 mph. The manufacturer has certified the following recycled-content levels (by weight): post-consumer material 94% typical, 93% guaranteed.

SelecStops and SelecBumps

SelecTech, Inc.
15 Fourth St.
Taunton, MA 02780

Phone: 508-828-4200
www.selectechinc.com

SelecStops™ parking stops are made from 100% recycled plastic and are offered in yellow, white, blue, and gray. SelecBumps™ speed bumps are available in black or yellow and are also made from 100% recycled plastic. The manufacturer has certified the following recycled-content levels (by weight): total recovered material 100% typical, 100% guaranteed; post-consumer material 90% typical, 85% guaranteed.

Speed Bumps

Scientific Developments, Inc.
P.O. Box 2522
Eugene, OR 97402

Toll-free: 800-824-6853
www.sdirubber.com

Scientific Developments Speed Bumps are made from recycled-

tire rubber with a UV-stabilized virgin rubber overlay. They are available with very durable, molded-in yellow hypalon stripes. The manufacturer has certified the following recycled-content levels (by weight): total recovered material 95% typical, 95% guaranteed; post-consumer material 95% typical, 75% guaranteed.

Traffic Calming Products

American Rubbertech
112-01 75th Ave.
Forest Hills, NY 11375

Toll-free: 800-228-2309
Phone: 718-520-0401

American Rubbertech produces public safety products from recycled waste tires. The product range consists of delineators, bollards, lane separators, walkways, and universal access ramps. The manufacturer has certified the following recycled-content levels (by weight): total recovered material 100% typical, 100% guaranteed; post-consumer material 100% typical, 100% guaranteed.

Traffic Cones and Safety Delineators

Inteq Corp.
33010 Lakeland Blvd.
Eastlake, OH 44095

Phone: 440-953-0550
www.4-inteqcorp.com

Inteq produces traffic cones and safety delineators with bases of 100% post-consumer rubber or PVC. Tops are made from virgin vinyl to maintain proper safety color. The manufacturer has certified the following recycled-content levels (by weight): total recovered material 80% typical, 80% guaranteed; post-consumer material 80% typical, 80% guaranteed.

Wheel Stops, Speed Bumps, and Bollards

Barco Products Co.
11 N. Batavia Ave.
Batavia, IL 60510

Toll-free: 800-757-5460
Phone: 630-879-0084
www.barcoproducts.com

Barco sells 100% recycled tire rubber speed bumps and 100% recycled plastic speed bumps. The rubber speed bumps come in either interlocking sections (to allow for unlimited lengths) or 6' lengths with safety stripes. Premium color wheel stops (white, blue and yellow) are made of 95% recycled plastic (commingled with HDPE and LDPE). Gray wheel stops contain 85% recycled PVC. Wheel stops are 6' L x 6" W x 4" H with a typical triangular profile. Barco's bollards are made from 96% recycled LDPE and HDPE (50 to 80% post-industrial content).

Plastic Lumber

see *Decking: Plastic Lumber*

Porous Pavement

As the proportion of land covered with impervious surfaces continues to grow, dealing with stormwater in the built environment is increasingly costly, demanding, and important. Natural environments are able to absorb most stormwater loads, maintaining a healthy hydrologic balance. Porous paving seeks to combine the load-carrying capacity we expect of paved areas with the water-infiltration qualities of natural ground cover. Porous pavement can be achieved using specialized formulas of concrete or asphalt (leaving the "fines" out so that the cured pavement remains porous), or by using various types of concrete and plastic unit pavers, including open-grid products that can be filled either with aggregate or with soil and plantings (usually turf). For concrete and asphalt porous pavement, detailed specifications are available that will help your local concrete and asphalt mixing plants satisfy your needs; with these materials, look for a paving contractor familiar with porous pavement, as the installation is quite different. Unit pavers are often used in porous pavement systems. Some unit pavers contain recycled content or are made from salvaged material, such as cobblestone or brick. These pavers are available in a variety of shapes, sizes, and colors, and some are interlocking. To work in porous pavement they need to be installed above a "reservoir" of uniform-sized aggregate (for example, $1^1/_2$" crushed stone), and laid with free-draining, uniform-sized, fine aggregate (such as coarse sand) between the pavers. In addition to infiltrating stormwater, porous paving systems planted with grass also minimize contributions to the urban heat-island effect while providing visually appealing outdoor space.

Concrete Porous Pavers

Capitol Ornamental Concrete Specialties, Inc.
90 Main St.
P.O. Box 3249
South Amboy, NJ 08879

Phone: 732-727-5460
www.capitolconcrete.com

Capitol Ornamental Concrete Specialties offers a number of concrete pavers suitable for porous paving installations, including the Ecologic™ Paver System—an engineered permeable pavement system that uses 4" x 8" and 4" x 4" interlocking concrete pavers installed over an air-entrained soil media.

Draincore²

Invisible Structures, Inc.
1600 Jackson St., Ste. 310
Golden, CO 80401

Toll-free: 800-233-1510
Phone: 303-233-8383
www.invisiblestructures.com

Draincore² is a drainage mat of interconnected plastic rings made from 100% post-industrial recycled HDPE with varying amounts of post-consumer and post-industrial content. This mat is designed to be used in conjunction with geotextiles and appropriate soils for effective subsurface drainage of high use outdoor areas. While the use of natural (biodegradable) products is generally preferred for permanent underground applications, Draincore² has high compressive strength suitable for heavy traffic.

Drainstone and Turfstone

Oldcastle Architectural Products Group
375 Northridge Rd., Ste. 250
Atlanta, GA 30350

Toll-free: 800-899-8455
Phone: 770-804-3363
www.belgardhardscapes.com

Drainstone and Turfstone by Belgard are concrete porous paving products. Drainstone has an octagonal pattern ($3^1/_8$" x 4" x 8") that allows water to infiltrate between adjoining pavers. Turfstone is a larger, precast unit covering $2^2/_3$ ft² each. The 40% open, basketweave pattern supports grass growth in and between the pavers. Both products have a compressive strength greater than 8,000 psi and meet or exceed ASTM tests for water absorption and freeze-thaw stability (C-936 and C-67).

EcoGrid Porous Pavers

Hanover Architectural Products
240 Bender Rd.
Hanover, PA 17331

Toll-free: 800-426-4242
Phone: 717-637-0500
www.hanoverpavers.com

EcoGrid™ Pavers are pervious interlocking concrete paving units which allow moderate vehicle traffic. Each unit is $11^3/_4$" x $11^3/_4$" x 4". EcoGrid Pavers contain a percentage of flyash.

EP Henry ECO Pavers

EP Henry Corporation
201 Park Ave.
P.O. Box 615
Woodbury, NJ 08096

Toll-free: 800-444-3679
www.ephenry.com

EP Henry manufactures the ECO Paver line of cement porous-paving products. ECO I Pavers are solid block pavers that measure $5\frac{1}{2}$" x $8\frac{1}{4}$" x $3\frac{1}{8}$". Monoslabs measure $23\frac{1}{2}$" x $15\frac{5}{8}$" x $4\frac{9}{16}$" and have a grid-like configuration with a multilevel surface. Turf Pavers are formed in a lattice-like pattern and measure $23\frac{5}{8}$" x $15\frac{3}{4}$" x $3\frac{1}{8}$". Each of these pavers may be seeded with grasses.

Salvaged Brick and Cobblestone Pavers

Gavin Historical Bricks
2050 Glendale Rd.
Iowa City, IA 52245

Phone: 319-354-5251
www.historicalbricks.com

Gavin Historical Bricks supplies salvaged paving bricks and cobblestones recovered from buildings and streets from around the country. Shipping is provided nationwide, though the heavy weight reduces the practicality (and environmental attractiveness) of shipping large quantities long distances.

SF-RIMA

Nicolock
640 Muncy Ave.
Lindenhurst, NY 11757

Toll-free: 800-669-9294
Phone: 631-669-0700
www.nicolock.com

SF-RIMA™ paving stones are made from no-slump concrete with a compressive strength of 8,000 psi. These square pavers ($7\frac{3}{4}$" x $7\frac{3}{4}$") can be installed with either wide or narrow spacing, depending upon the orientation of integral spacers. Widely spaced pavers are often seeded with grasses, which may mitigate heat island effects and stormwater runoff. The company also has a manufacturing facility in North Haven, CT.

StoneyCrete

Stoney Creek Materials, LLC
25 Stoney Creek Cove
Austin, TX 78734

Phone: 512-261-0821
www.stoneycreekmaterials.com

StoneyCrete™ is a pervious concrete pavement installed by trained and certified contractors. The mix includes a proprietary additive that improves elasticity and strength: 4,000 psi at 28 days. Where available, fly ash or blast-furnace slag replaces 20% of the Portland cement in the mix.

UNI Eco-Stone

UNI-Group U.S.A.
4362 Northlake Blvd., Ste. 204
Palm Beach Gardens, FL 33410

Toll-free: 800-872-1864
Phone: 561-626-4666
www.uni-groupusa.org

UNI Eco-Stone® is a $3\frac{1}{8}$"-thick interlocking concrete porous paver that measures approximately 9" long by $5\frac{1}{2}$" at its widest point. These pavers can be installed in running bond, basketweave, and herringbone patterns. UNI-Group U.S.A. licenses over two dozen companies around the country to manufacture these pavers.

Rubber Aggregate Surfacing

Granulated rubber made from recycled tires is an appropriate surfacing material for outdoor play areas. Durable and highly resilient when applied to a 6" depth, it creates a softer play environment than pea gravel and, unlike wood chips, will not rot or attract insects. Keep these areas separated from other landscaping materials, so that the nonbiodegradable aggregate can later be removed if uses change.

Granulated Rubber

Rubber Granulators, Inc.
3811 152nd St. NE
Marysville, WA 98271

Phone: 360-658-7754

Rubber Granulators produces granulated rubber made from used tires available in 55-lb. and 2,000-lb. sacks.

Perma-Turf Playground Safety Surface

TIREC Corporation
P.O. Box 604
Mullica Hill, NJ 08062

Toll-free: 800-993-9411
Phone: 856-478-4491
www.perma-turf.com

Perma-Turf® Playground Safety Surface is a fiber-reinforced rubber aggregate made from 100% recycled tires with the steel belting removed. Tirec guarantees its products to be free of steel and backs them with a 50-year guarantee. Perma-Flex® High Performance Arena Footing is a similar product made for equestrian arenas.

RubberStuff

ART (American Rubber Technologies, Inc.)
P.O. Box 6548
Jacksonville, FL 32236-6548

Toll-free: 800-741-5201
www.americanrubber.com

RubberStuff™, made from recycled-tire rubber, is a granulated-rubber safety surface for playground applications. The $1/4$" rubber granules are usually installed at a 6" depth. The manufacturer has certified the following recycled-content levels (by weight): total recovered material 100% typical, 100% guaranteed; post-consumer material 100% typical, 100% guaranteed.

Tire Turf

Continental Turf Systems, Inc.
P.O. Box 389
Continental, OH 45831

Phone: 419-596-4242
www.tireturf.com

Tire Turf is loose, granulated, 100% post-consumer recycled-tire-rubber ground cover for use in playgrounds, horse arenas, and as a landscaping mulch.

Seeding and Soil Supplements

Lawn maintenance is a major source of air pollution and contaminated runoff from fertilizers and pesticides. Close to 40 million gas-powered mowers are used on the lawns of America. While domestic manufacturers have decreased their products' emissions significantly (as required by EPA regulations), an hour of mowing the lawn with a current gas-powered machine still pollutes about as much as driving a late-model car for 13 hours. Compounding the problem, fertilizer runoff from lawns is one of our most significant non-point-source water pollution problems; also, lawn pesticides are commonly applied at rates up to 20 times that of agricultural pesticides. Landscaping that requires less mowing, fertilizing, and pesticide use has significant environmental advantages.

No Mow

Prairie Nursery, Inc.
P.O. Box 306
Westfield, WI 53964

Toll-free: 800-476-9453
www.prairienursery.com

No Mow turfgrass mix consists of six native cool-season fescue varieties for seeding in the northern U.S. and southern Canada. No Mow requires only monthly or annual mowing. These drought-tolerant grasses require minimal irrigation and fertilization, and are appropriate for shady locations. Other prairie wildflowers and grasses for a variety of planting conditions are available.

Site Furnishings

see *Outdoor Structures: Site Furnishings*

Stormwater Drainage

Hydrocarbons, heavy metals, nutrients, and other pollutants collect on pavement and other impervious surfaces. When it rains, these pollutants can enter stormwater flows and pollute nearby surface waters. Large parking lots and "ultra-urban" areas can benefit from proprietary stormwater treatment systems that help remove pollutants (though regular maintenance is critical with such systems). Lower-maintenance "structural practices," such as infiltration trenches, porous pavement, detention ponds, and biofiltration systems, should be used whenever possible. Some stormwater drainage products help reduce downstream flooding by detaining or storing the water; other products are effective at directing rainwater away from foundations, increasing building durability. With storm drainage piping, look for high recycled content.

Rain Run

Presto Products
    Company
670 N. Perkins St.
P.O. Box 2399
Appleton, WI 54912

Toll-free: 800-548-3424
Phone: 920-738-1336
www.prestoproducts.com

Rain Run®, made with recycled plastic, is a splashblock for use at the base of gutter downspouts. The splashblock keeps rainwater away from the foundation and allows it to soak into the ground more effectively.

Rainhandler and Doorbrella

Savetime Corporation
2710 North Ave.
Bridgeport, CT 06604

Toll-free: 800-942-3004
www.rainhandler.com

Rainhandler is an aluminum, multilouvered, self-cleaning device designed to replace gutters. The product breaks up heavy sheets of water into smaller drops that are more easily absorbed into the ground, and spreads the water over a greater area to further facilitate absorption. Doorbrella is an accessory designed to channel water over unprotected doorways to Rainhandlers on each side of the door. Rainhandler is available in brown or white baked-on enamel or unfinished aluminum. Doorbrella is available in brown or aluminum. Both products come with a 25-year limited warranty and a one-year, money-back guarantee.

Temporary Traffic Control

Recycled plastics and rubber can effectively be used in the manufacture of roadway markers and traffic signs. The following listings include such products.

Portable Traffic Delineators

Scientific Developments, Inc.
P.O. Box 2522
Eugene, OR 97402

Toll-free: 800-824-6853
www.sdirubber.com

Scientific Developments' Portable Traffic Delineators have recycled-tire rubber bases and recycled LDPE plastic posts that are orange with reflective bands. The manufacturer has certified the following recycled-content levels (by weight): total recovered material 100% typical, 100% guaranteed; post-consumer material 75% guaranteed.

Street Smart Traffic Control Units

North West Rubber Mats, Ltd.
33850 Industrial Ave.
Abbotsford, BC V2S 7T9 Canada

Toll-free: 800-663-8724
Phone: 604-859-2002
www.northwestrubber.com

Street Smart Traffic Control Units are portable traffic delineators with 100% recycled-tire rubber bases and bright orange nonrecycled posts.

Tree Grates and Guards

Tree grates, guards, and root barriers are good applications for recycled plastic, because of the minimal structural requirements of these products. Tree-ring mats to keep weeds down around trees can be made from recycled-tire rubber.

Arbor Guard and Universal Barriers

DeepRoot Partners, LP
81 Langton St., Ste. 4
San Francisco, CA 94103

Toll-free: 800-458-7668
Phone: 415-437-9700
www.deeproot.com

DeepRoot Partners manufactures Arbor Guard+ tree trunk protectors. Arbor Guard+ protects young trees from rodent and lawn maintenance equipment damage. The product, made of 50% post-consumer recycled polyethylene, is 9" high and expands to protect 4"-diameter trees—or larger if two or more Arbor Guard+ units are connected.

Universal Barriers are designed to protect hard surfaces, such as sidewalks, from uplifting caused by tree roots. The product, made from 50% post-consumer recycled polypropylene (except UB 36-2 and UB 40-2), surrounds the rootball of a young tree and directs the roots downward. DeepRoot Partners also manufactures Linear Barriers for use along a hard surface area instead of around a tree.

CP and DWP Root Barrier Panels

Century Products
1401 N. Kraemer, Ste. B
Anaheim, CA 92806

Toll-free: 800-480-8084
Phone: 714-632-7083
www.centuryrootbarrier.com

CP and DWP Series Root Barrier Panels protect hardscape surfaces from uplifting caused by tree roots. The 50% recycled plastic modular panels are flexible and can be separated into 1' sections. DWP Series panels include deep watering channels that efficiently direct irrigation water to the tree's root zone.

Tree Rings

Phoenix Recycled Products, Inc.
360 W. Church St.
Batesburg, SC 29006

Phone: 803-532-4425
www.permamulch.com

Phoenix Recycled Products fabricates a recycled tire-rubber mat that forms a weed barrier around trees. The manufacturer has certified the following recycled-content levels (by weight): total recovered material 85% typical, 85% guaranteed; post-consumer material 85% typical, 85% guaranteed.

Wood-Plastic Composite Lumber

see *Decking: Wood-Plastic Composite Lumber*

This Space is Available for Your Notes

Outdoor Structures

Outdoor Structures include freestanding built items such as fences, playground equipment, tables, and benches. Also included here are some miscellaneous items that are installed or used out-of-doors, such as exterior sun-shade systems. Green criteria for products in this category include durability, low maintenance, and recycled content. Prefabricated picnic tables, benches, and trash can enclosures made with recycled plastic and wood-plastic composite lumber are available. Products made with durable, rot-resistant, FSC-certified hardwoods such as Ipé can be a good choice.

Driven Piles

see *Foundations, Footers, and Slabs: Driven Piles*

Exterior Sun Control Devices

Products that can be used to selectively block out solar gain, including those that support vegetation along walls, can provide important energy conservation benefits.

greenscreen Trellising System

greenscreen
1743 S. La Cienega Blvd.
Los Angeles, CA 90035

Toll-free: 800-450-3494
Phone: 310-837-0526
www.greenscreen.com

Greenscreen™ is a three-dimensional, welded-wire trellis system that can be installed freestanding or wall-mounted. The basic trellis module is 4' wide, 2" or 3" thick, and 6', 8', 10', or 12' long. Custom-sized panels can be ordered in 2" increments. Greenscreen is available in a wrinkled matte finish of green or black, as well as a glossy finish of green, black, silver, or white. Various accessories, such as planter straps, edge trim, and specialty shapes, are also available. Thoughtful plant selection may be important for success of the system. In addition to the numerous environmental benefits of encouraging the growth of vegetation and that of energy savings from shading, Greenscreens can also play an important role in making the most of growing area in small-space and rooftop applications.

Landscape Timbers

see *Sitework and Landscaping: Landscape Timbers*

Plastic Fences and Gates

Conventional wood fencing—even that made from pressure-treated wood—is prone to degradation and has a short life. This is a good application for recycled plastics because such products are more durable than those made from wood, and the structural requirements are minimal. Recycled-plastic fencing products are significantly greener than virgin-polymer products.

Fencing

Inteq Corp.
33010 Lakeland Blvd.
Eastlake, OH 44095

Phone: 440-953-0550
www.4-inteqcorp.com

Inteq manufactures recycled HDPE plastic fencing (10–100% post-industrial content). The capped hollow posts will accept two, three, or four hollow rails. Inteq's fencing products are available in white, gray, weathered (tan), and black.

Plastic Fences

Aeolian Enterprises, Inc.
P.O. Box 888
Latrobe, PA 15650

Toll-free: 800-269-4672
Phone: 724-539-9460
www.aeo1.com

Aeolian's corral, privacy, and picket fence products are made from recycled HDPE. The percentage of recycled plastic used varies, depending on product color.

Plastic Lumber

see *Decking: Plastic Lumber*

Playground Equipment

Playground equipment included here is made from recycled plastic, high-recycled-content metal, or FSC-certified wood. Forest Stewardship Council (FSC) certification involves third-party evaluation and monitoring of sustainable forestry practices and chain-of-custody certification to ensure that labeled products were derived from FSC-certified forests.

Playfield Equipment

Children's Playstructures, Inc.
12441 Mead Way
Littleton, CO 80125

Phone: 303-791-7626
Toll-free: 800-874-9943
www.childrensplaystructures.com

Children's Playstructures custom-designs, constructs, and installs playground structures for schools and parks made primarily from 100% recycled HDPE plastic lumber produced by U.S. Plastic Lumber Co./Eaglebrook. Children's Playstructures services the Colorado and Wyoming area.

Playground Equipment

Amazing Recycled Products, Inc.
P.O. Box 312
Denver, CO 80201

Toll-free: 800-241-2174
Phone: 303-699-7693
www.amazingrecycled.com

Amazing Recycled Products manufactures a range of children's playground equipment containing from 50–100% post-consumer recycled HDPE. The manufacturer has certified the following recycled-content levels (by weight): total recovered material 75% typical, 50% guaranteed; post-consumer material 75% typical, 50% guaranteed.

Playground Equipment

Landscape Structures Inc.
601 7th St. S
P.O. Box 198
Delano, MN 55328

Phone: 763-972-3391
Toll-free: 888-438-6574
www.playlsi.com

Landscape Structures manufactures playground equipment from various recycled materials. Most notably, wire tunnels and barriers, vertical ladders, roller-slide rollers, rubber floor tiles, and plastic benches, decks, and walls are made from 100% post-consumer recycled materials. Landscape Structures is ISO 14001-certified.

Rainwater Harvesting Systems and Components

see *Plumbing: Rainwater Harvesting Systems and Components*

Shoreline Protection and Mooring Structures

Look for products containing recycled plastic, rubber, and fiberglass.

Easy Dock

American Recreational Products
3505 Veterans Memorial Hwy., Ste. Q
Ronkonkoma, NY 11779

Phone: 631-588-4545

EasyDock is a one-piece floating dock made from 100% recycled plastic. Interconnecting docks are available in several sizes.

ForeverDock

Phoenix Recycled Plastics
220 Washington St.
Norristown, PA 19401

Phone: 610-277-3900
www.plasticlumberyard.com

ForeverDock® Floating Dock Kits are constructed with Phoenix recycled plastic lumber made from 100% recycled HDPE. Docks can be shipped complete or in kit form and are available in 8 standard colors as well as custom colors.

Site Furnishings

Most of the products here are green because of recycled content. Recycled plastic site furnishings are most commonly made from either HDPE or commingled plastics. Recycled commingled plastics may have slightly inconsistent properties, but this is a lower-grade waste material that is generally more of a disposal problem. Other products in this category are made from salvaged materials or FSC-certified wood. Forest Stewardship Council (FSC) certification involves third-party evaluation and monitoring of sustainable forestry practices and chain-of-custody certification to ensure that labeled products were derived from FSC-certified forests.

2nd Site Systems

Victor Stanley, Inc.
P.O. Drawer 330
Dunkirk, MD 20754

Toll-free: 800-368-2573
Phone: 301-855-8300
www.victorstanley.com

2nd Site Systems utilizes a patented slat design of 100% recycled plastic lumber reinforced with recycled steel bar. Products include park benches, picnic tables, and trash receptacles.

Benches and Picnic Tables

RecycleTech Products
12 N. Charlotte St.
Mulliken, MI 48861

Toll-free: 877-609-2243
www.recycletechproducts.com

RecycleTech Products manufactures park benches and picnic tables from recycled HDPE. The manufacturer has certified the following recycled-content levels (by weight): total recovered material 95% typical, 95% guaranteed; post-consumer material 80% typical, 60% guaranteed.

Benches and Recycling and Waste Receptacles

Recycled Plastics Marketing, Inc.
16541 Redmond Way
PMB #354-C
Redmond, WA 98052-4482

Toll-free: 800-867-3201
Phone: 425-867-3200
www.rrpm.com

Recycled Plastics Marketing manufactures outdoor benches from a minimum of 80% post-consumer recycled HDPE and recycling and waste receptacles from 100% post-consumer recycled HDPE and polypropylene.

Benches and Table Sets

Doty & Sons Concrete Products, Inc.
1275 E. State St.
Sycamore, IL 60178

Toll-free: 800-233-3907
www.dotyconcrete.com

Doty & Sons Concrete Products uses recycled HDPE plastic in its precast concrete site amenities, including benches and table sets. The manufacturer has certified the following recycled-content levels (by weight): total recovered material 17% typical; post-consumer material 17% typical, 17% guaranteed.

Benches, Picnic Tables, and Landscape Ties

American Recreational Products
3505 Veterans Memorial Hwy., Ste. Q
Ronkonkoma, NY 11779

Phone: 631-588-4545

American Recreational Products offers benches, picnic tables, and landscape ties made from 100% recycled commingled plastics. Products are typically made from 50% post-consumer plastic and 50% post-industrial plastic.

Benches, Picnic Tables, and Planters

Cascades Re-Plast, Inc.
2001 McGill College Ave.,
  Ste. 230
Montreal, PQ H3A 1G1
  Canada

Toll-free: 888-703-6515
Phone: 514-284-9850
www.cascadesreplast.com

Cascades Re-Plast manufactures an assortment of recycled-plastic outdoor furniture and accessories in brown, beige, green, gray, and black.

Benches, Picnic Tables, and Recycling Receptacles

EagleOne Golf Products
1201 W. Katella Ave.
Orange, CA 92867

Toll-free: 800-448-4409
Phone: 714-997-1400
www.eagleonegolf.com

EagleOne Golf Products offers site amenities, including benches, picnic tables, and recycling receptacles, made from recycled HDPE plastic. The manufacturer has certified the following recycled-content levels (by weight): total recovered material 90% typical, 80% guaranteed; post-consumer material 90% typical, 80% guaranteed.

Benches, Picnic Tables, and Trash Receptacles

Aloha Plastics Recycling
75 Amala Pl.
Kahului, HI 96732

Phone: 808-877-0822
www.aloha-recycling.com

Aloha Plastics Recycling manufactures a variety of products, including benches, picnic tables, and trash receptacles, from 100% post-consumer HDPE.

Benches, Picnic Tables, Waste Receptacles, and Planters

Inteq Corp.
33010 Lakeland Blvd.
Eastlake, OH 44095

Phone: 440-953-0550
www.4-inteqcorp.com

Inteq's benches and picnic tables are made from recycled HDPE plastic. Tables are either standard 6' or 8' length or hexagonal. Benches come in a variety of styles and can be custom designed. Inteq's waste receptacles and planters contain recycled HDPE plastic and are available in many styles including custom production. All are offered in a variety of colors. Recycled content is up to 90% (minimum 20% post-consumer).

Benches, Picnic Tables, Waste Receptacles, and Planters

Kay Park Recreation Corp.
1301 Pine St.
Janesville, IA 50647

Toll-free: 800-553-2476
www.kaypark.com

Kay Park Recreation manufactures picnic tables, benches, waste receptacles, and planters containing 96% post-consumer recycled commingled plastics.

Benches, Tables, Chairs, Waste Receptacles, and Planters

The Plastic Lumber Co.
115 W. Bartges St.
Akron, OH 44311

Toll-free: 800-886-8990
Phone: 330-762-8989
www.plasticlumber.com

The Plastic Lumber Company offers site furnishings made from recycled plastic. Commercial-grade benches, picnic tables, and waste receptacles/recycling centers are available in a variety of color combinations and are made with 97% post-consumer recycled content.

Better Than Wood - Benches and Picnic Tables

BTW Industries
3939 Hollywood Blvd., Ste. 3B
Hollywood, FL 33021

Phone: 954-962-2100
www.recycledplastic.com

BTW has been manufacturing outdoor furniture from recycled HDPE, LDPE, and PP plastic since 1990. These products contain UV inhibitors and are available in gray and redwood. The manufacturer has certified the following recycled-content levels (by weight): total recovered material 100% typical, 97% guaranteed; post-consumer material 100% typical, 97% guaranteed.

Certified Ipe Outdoor Furniture

Modern Outdoor
12328 Gladstone Ave., Ste. 3
Lake View Terrace, CA 91342

Phone: 818-838-7060
www.modernoutdoor.com

Modern Outdoor offers domestically produced, high-style outdoor furniture made from Brazilian Ipe hardwood. Due to difficulties in sourcing FSC-certified Ipe, the manufacturer may use wood certified under the less-stringent ITTO (International Tropical Timber Organization) or IBAMA (Brazilian Institute of Environment and Renewable Resources) programs. Specify FSC-certified (Forest Stewardship Council) wood. The furniture uses electro-polished stainless steel frames. Stainless steel contains little or no recycled content and is not recyclable, but it is very long-lasting.

Certified Outdoor Furniture

Forest World Group
219 W. Manhattan Ave.
Santa Fe, NM 87501

Toll-free: 800-468-6139
Phone: 505-983-1200
www.naturallydurable.com

Forest World Group, formerly Sylvania Certified, sells outdoor furniture constructed of FSC-certified lesser-known tropical wood species, such as roble, curupau, and ipé.

Certified Teak Outdoor Furniture

Smith and Hawken
P.O. Box 8690
Pueblo, CO 81008-9998

Toll-free: 800-776-3336
www.smithandhawkentrade.com

Smith and Hawken sells a wide selection of FSC-certified teak outdoor furniture.

Certified Teak Outdoor Furniture

TTD, Inc.
8232 Williston Rd.
Williston, VT 05495

Toll-free: 866-490-2448
Phone: 802-878-1489
www.triptrap.com

TTD, Inc. is the North American distributor for Trip Trap Denmark teak furniture. Three of the company's lines of park and garden furniture—Drachmann, Vitas Bering, and Selandia, a line of folding chairs and tables—have products available for an upcharge in FSC-certified teak. Trip Trap Denmark is ISO 14001-certified.

Conservancy Series - Benches, Picnic Tables, and Recycling Receptacles

Florida Playground and Steel Co.
4701 S. 50th St.
Tampa, FL 33619

Toll-free: 800-444-2655
Phone: 813-247-2812
www.fla-playground.com

Conservancy Series benches, picnic tables, and recycling receptacles are made from recycled plastic/wood composite materials and steel.

Earthcare Series

Litchfield Industries
4 Industrial Dr.
Litchfield, MI 49252

Toll-free: 800-542-5282
Phone: 517-542-2988
www.litchfieldindustries.com

The Earthcare Series of site furnishings is made from 100% post-consumer recycled plastic. The Series includes picnic tables, benches, and trash receptacles.

Eco Outdoor Series

Ecologic, Inc.
921 Sherwood Dr.
Lake Bluff, IL 60044

Toll-free: 800-899-8004
Phone: 847-234-5855
www.ecoloft.com

Ecologic is a large producer of furniture based on recycled HDPE plastic. They have an extensive range of outdoor furniture suitable for residential and public spaces, ranging from individual Adirondack chairs and ottomans to tables, benches, trash receptacles (designed to take standard Rubbermaid inserts), and fan trellises. Some of these products contain recycled steel to add stiffness. The entire line is manufactured with 97.5% recycled content. UV protection is integral to the plastic in each component.

Fountains and Bird Feeders

Torrens Sculpture Designs
P.O. Box 1819
Gig Harbor, WA 98335

Toll-free: 800-786-7736
www.tomtorrens.com

Torrens Sculpture Designs custom-builds fountains and bird feeders from reclaimed oxygen tanks. Additional metals used include reclaimed steel, copper, and aluminum

Perennial Park Outdoor Furniture

Engineered Plastic
Systems
740 B Industrial Dr.
Cary, IL 60013

Phone: 847-462-9001
www.epsplasticlumber.
com

Photo: David Cook

Environmental Plastic Systems manufactures Perennial Park outdoor furniture and accessories from 100% recycled HDPE (typically 100% post-consumer content). Products include benches and picnic tables, planter benches, and serving tables. A selection of kid-sized and handicapped-accessible tables, as well as custom orders, are also available. Colors currently include white, gray, redwood, forest green, black, cedar, primary red, and tan. All EPS plastic products come with a 50-year limited warranty.

Phoenix Recycled Plastic Site Furnishings

Phoenix Recycled Plastics
220 Washington St.
Norristown, PA 19401

Phone: 610-277-3900
www.plasticlumberyard.com

Phoenix Recycled Plastics manufactures a wide range of outdoor site furnishings from 100% recycled plastic. Products include picnic tables and benches, chairs (Adirondack and others), "gliders" and porch swings, as well as hexagonal, rectangular, and wheelchair-accessible tables.

Picnic Tables and Benches

Plastic Recycling of Iowa Falls, Inc.
10252 Hwy. 65
Iowa Falls, IA 50126

Toll-free: 800-338-1438
Phone: 641-648-5073
www.hammersplastic.com

Plastic Recycling of Iowa Falls, formerly Hammer's Plastic Recycling, manufactures several park benches and picnic tables, including ADA-compliant products, of commingled recycled HDPE, LDPE, LLDPE, and other miscellaneous plastics. The manufacturer has certified the following recycled-content levels (by weight): total recovered material 100% typical, 100% guaranteed; post-consumer material 50% typical, 50% guaranteed.

Picnic Tables, Benches, Planters, and Waste Receptacles

Barco Products Co.
11 N. Batavia Ave.
Batavia, IL 60510

Toll-free: 800-757-5460
Phone: 630-879-0084
www.barcoproducts.com

Barco Products sells 8 different picnic tables and 13 park benches with 100% recycled plastic content (commingled HDPE and LDPE), averaging 40% post-consumer. Two of the picnic table designs are ADA wheelchair accessible. The company also offers planters and waste receptacles made from 100% recycled HDPE (90 to 100% post-consumer content).

Pilot Rock Site Furnishings

R. J. Thomas Manufacturing Co., Inc.
P.O. Box 946
Cherokee, IA 51012-0946

Toll-free: 800-762-5002
Phone: 712-225-5115
www.pilotrock.com

Pilot Rock Site Furnishings are made from recycled HDPE and LDPE plastic. The Pilot Rock line includes benches, picnic tables, waste receptacles, and car stops. The manufacturer has certified the following recycled-content levels (by weight): total recovered material 100% typical, 100% guaranteed; post-consumer material 75% typical, 60% guaranteed.

Planters

SelecTech, Inc.
15 Fourth St.
Taunton, MA 02780

Phone: 508-828-4200
www.selectechinc.com

SelecTech's planters are made from 100% recycled LDPE. The planters are available in terra-cotta in a variety of sizes and come with a 50-year limited warranty. The manufacturer has certified the following recycled-content levels (by weight): total recovered material 100% typical, 100% guaranteed; post-consumer material 0% typical, 0% guaranteed.

Poly-Wood

Poly-Wood Inc.
1001 W. Brooklyn St.
Syracuse, IN 46567

Toll-free: 877-457-3284
Phone: 574-457-3284
www.polywoodinc.com

Poly-Wood manufactures outdoor residential furniture from 98% recycled HDPE plastic.

Polywood Site Furnishings

Polywood, Inc.
125 National Rd.
Edison, NJ 08817

Toll-free: 800-915-0043
Phone: 732-248-8810
www.polywood.com

Polywood manufactures park and site furnishings from Polywood plastic lumber utilizing a patented blend of recycled plastics. Polywood's site furniture includes benches, picnic tables (some with wheelchair access), waste receptacles and bike racks. The manufacturer has certified the following recycled-content levels (by weight): total recovered material 100% typical, 100% guaranteed; post-consumer material 100% typical, 100% guaranteed.

Re-Bench

Falcon Products, Inc.
9387 Dielman Industrial Dr.
St. Louis, MO 63132

Toll-free: 800-873-3252
Phone: 314-991-9200
www.falconproducts.com

The Re-Bench is a park bench with recycled plastic slats fastened to recycled cast iron supports. The Re-Bench is available in three colors: cedar, weathered redwood, and white. Seat height is 18", depth is 17" and overall height is $34^{5}/_{8}$".

Recycle Design Site Furnishings

U.S. Plastic Lumber, Ltd.
2600 W. Roosevelt Rd.
Chicago, IL 60608

Toll-free: 800-653-2784
Phone: 312-491-2500
www.usplasticlumber.com

The award-winning Recycle Design site furnishings are made with 100% post-consumer recycled HDPE Durawood PE plastic lumber and steel or aluminum structural components. The Recycle Design line includes benches, picnic tables, and waste receptacles.

Recycled Plastic Site Amenities

DuMor, Inc.
P.O. Box 142
Mifflintown, PA 17059

Toll-free: 800-598-4018
Phone: 717-436-2106
www.dumor.com

DuMor offers a wide array of site amenities made from recycled HDPE plastic lumber. Products include benches, picnic tables, planters, and waste receptacles. The manufacturer has certified the following recycled-content levels (by weight): total recovered material 95% typical, 95% guaranteed; post-consumer material 95% typical, 95% guaranteed.

Site Furnishings

American Recycled Plastic, Inc.
1500 Main St.
Palm Bay, FL 32905

Toll-free: 866-674-1525
Phone: 321-674-1525
www.itsrecycled.com

American Recycled Products manufactures a large variety of site furnishings, including benches, outdoor tables, waste receptacles, waste receptacle skirting, mailboxes, planters, and custom wildlife structures from recycled HDPE. The manufacturer has certified the following recycled-content levels (by weight): total recovered material 100% typical, 100% guaranteed; post-consumer material 80% typical, 80% guaranteed.

Site Furnishings

BJM Industries, Inc.
R.R. 1, Box 257A
Kittanning, PA 16201

Phone: 724-548-2440
www.bjmindustries.com

BJM Industries manufactures site furnishings, such as picnic tables, park and garden benches, and planters, from Millennium Lumber—a combination of post-consumer recycled HDPE and post-industrial recycled cellulose (from diaper factory trimmings).

Ski and Snowboard Furniture

Reeski, Inc.
P.O. Box 781
Aspen, CO 81612

Toll-free: 800-826-5447
Phone: 970-704-0866
www.reeski.com

Reeski manufactures chairs, benches, coat racks, and more from used skis and snowboards. Reeski offers many durable and creative designs; custom orders are welcome. Furniture often includes 100% recycled plastic lumber. Uncertified redwood is used for some items. The manufacturer has certified the following recycled-content levels (by weight): post-consumer material 99% typical, 99% guaranteed.

Wood-Plastic Composite Lumber

see *Decking: Wood-Plastic Composite Lumber*

This Space is Available for Your Notes

Decking

Until 2004, most preservative-treated wood was pressure-treated with CCA (chromated copper arsenate). Concerns about arsenic and chromium leaching from decks and fences led to the removal of CCA-treated lumber from the market. Disposal of the existing billions of board feet of CCA-treated wood already in use will be an ongoing problem as it reaches the end of its useful life. Degradation of CCA-treated wood leaves residual toxins; burning it results in airborne toxins or, if burned in controlled incinerators, highly toxic ash.

Direct substitutes for CCA-treated wood include less toxic products such as ACQ (ammoniacal copper quaternary) and CBA (copper boron azole). ACQ is corrosive to standard steel over time—so stainless steel screws and nails and double-coated, hot-dipped galvanized hangers and hardware are typically recommended. CBA is less corrosive to steel. Aluminum hardware shouldn't be used with either. Both ACQ and CBA rely on copper as the active ingredient, and copper is highly toxic to many aquatic organisms; for this reason neither should be used on boardwalks, docks, or decks overhanging ponds, marshes, or other aquatic locations. Neither ACQ nor CBA are approved for saltwater applications. For wood that isn't exposed to weather, borate-based preservatives (without copper) are effective against insects while being much less toxic than other chemicals.

There are also problems associated with using naturally rot-resistant wood species, such as redwood and cedar. Clear-heart redwood is generally cut from old-growth forests. Redwood trees take a long time to mature, and there are very few remaining stands of privately owned redwood. Small but increasing amounts of redwood and cedar are available from certified, well-managed forests. The quick-growing second-growth redwood and cedar, with wide growth rings, is less resistant to rot and insects than old-growth wood. Sustainably harvested, long-lasting exotic hardwoods such as Ipé, imported from Brazil and Bolivia, are increasingly available; look for third-party FSC certification. Forest Stewardship Council (FSC) certification involves third-party evaluation and monitoring of sustainable forestry practices—and chain-of-custody verification that wood products were derived from certified forests.

In some settings, a patio made from local stone makes an attractive alternative to a wood deck.

For exposed applications, recycled plastic lumber is an excellent alternative that will handily outlast most wooden decking materials: 50-year warranties aren't uncommon. Products combining recycled plastic with wood fiber offer a more wood-like feel and less thermal expansion in the sun. Prefabricated picnic tables, benches, and garbage can enclosures made with these materials are available.

Certified Wood Decking

Products listed here are produced from FSC-certified wood. Forest Stewardship Council (FSC) certification involves third-party evaluation and monitoring of sustainable forestry practices.

Certified Decking

Cascadia Forest Goods, LLC
38083 Wheeler Rd.
Dexter, OR 97431

Phone: 541-485-4477
www.cascadiaforestgoods.com

Cascadia Forest Goods (CFG) is a supplier of FSC-certified and recycled forest products, including cedar decking. CFG also distributes FSC-certified flooring and decking from Central and South America, including ipé and pucte.

Certified Decking

Collins Companies
1618 S.W. First Ave., Ste. 500
Portland, OR 97201

Toll-free: 800-329-1219
Phone: 503-417-7755
www.collinswood.com

The CollinsWood® line includes FSC-certified particleboard, FSC-certified TruWood® engineered (hardboard) siding, and FSC-certified hardwood and softwood lumber and millwork. In 1993, Collins Pine Company became the first privately owned timber management company to receive FSC certification in the U.S. CollinsWood has been a leader in the forest and wood products certification movement since its inception.

Certified Decking

Forest World Group
219 W. Manhattan Ave.
Santa Fe, NM 87501

Toll-free: 800-468-6139
Phone: 505-983-1200
www.naturallydurable.com

Forest World Group, formerly Sylvania Certified, sells decking lumber of FSC-certified ipé and lesser-known naturally durable tropical species as alternatives for pressure-treated wood decking.

Certified Decking

Harwood Products
1 Main St.
Branscomb, CA 95417

Toll-free: 800-441-4140 (CA only)
Phone: 707-984-6181
www.harwoodp.com

Harwood Products offers certified redwood decking and timbers, Douglas fir lumber and timbers, and white fir lumber.

Certified Decking

Randall Custom Lumber, Ltd.
3530 S.E. Arcadia Rd.
Shelton, WA 98584

Phone: 360-426-8518
www.rclumber.com

Randall Custom Lumber manufactures FSC-certified decking, flooring, hard and softwood lumber, and stair parts. Some of their certified species are ash, red cedar, red alder, Douglas fir, madrone, and maple.

Certified Iron Woods Decking

Cecco Trading, Inc.
600 E. Vienna Ave.
Milwaukee, WI 53212-1637

Phone: 414-445-8989
www.ironwoods.com

Iron Woods® is a brand of ipé decking from the Brazilian forest that is offered FSC-certified with an upcharge. Iron Woods' natural durability rating of 25+ years is the highest of woods tested by the U.S. Forest Products Lab. The product is available in all standard decking, porch flooring, and dimensional lumber sizes from 2x2 to 4x12 and up to 20' long in standard even lengths. Iron Woods decking is Class A fire-rated and comes with a 25-year fully transferable limited warranty.

Certified Tropical Hardwood Decking

Sustainable Forest Systems LP
990 Carib Ln.
Vero Beach, FL 32963

Phone: 772-473-0328

Sustainable Forest Systems has operated tropical hardwood timberlands and associated processing since 1994. They offer a wide range of FSC-certified tropical hardwood products.

FSC Pau Lope

Greenheart Durawoods, Inc.
6901 Chestnut Ave.
Merchantville, NJ 08109

Toll-free: 800-783-7220
Phone: 856-663-2700
www.paulope.com

FSC Pau Lope® is an extremely hard and durable, insect- and fire-resistant, FSC-certified tropical hardwood decking material. Pau Lope can be left to weather to a silvery gray or oiled periodically to maintain its color. Greenheart Durawoods offers both certified and noncertified decking, so FSC-certified product must be specified.

Plastic Lumber

In 2000, the EPA estimated that 24.7 million tons of the U.S. solid waste stream was plastics. Just 1.2 tons of it was recycled; the rest went to landfills, where it occupies about 25% of the overall landfill space. Plastic lumber makes good use of recycled plastic and is an effective replacement for pressure-treated lumber, protecting timber resources and preventing the use of chemical lumber treatments. Plastic lumber won't rot, absorb water, splinter, or crack; it's also resilient to shock, making it an extremely durable component in exterior and marine applications. It can accept most types of fasteners and is workable with standard saws and carbide blades. Plastic lumber usually isn't a suitable replacement for load-bearing structural components, however; the physical characteristics of plastic polymers, while durable, don't provide the rigidity necessary for primary structural support. Some companies have addressed this weakness by reinforcing their products with fiberglass or steel. In addition, plastic lumber experiences greater rates of thermal expansion and contraction, which can give rise to problems in certain applications.

Aztec Recycled Plastic Lumber

Amazing Recycled Products, Inc.
P.O. Box 312
Denver, CO 80201

Toll-free: 800-241-2174
Phone: 303-699-7693
www.amazingrecycled.com

Aztec Recycled Plastic Lumber is a molded HDPE product that includes a small percentage of waste-paper content. The waste paper imparts some slip-resistant qualities to the matte-finished product. Aztec is available in standard dimensions and lengths of 6', 8', 10', and 12'. The manufacturer has certified the following recycled-content levels (by weight): total recovered material 100% typical, 100% guaranteed; post-consumer material 80% typical, 75% guaranteed.

Better Than Wood

BTW Industries
3939 Hollywood Blvd., Ste. 3B
Hollywood, FL 33021

Phone: 954-962-2100
www.recycledplastic.com

Since 1990 BTW has manufactured dimensional lumber from recycled HDPE, LDPE, and PP plastics in gray and redwood colors. The manufacturer has certified the following recycled-content levels (by weight): total recovered material 100% typical, 97% guaranteed; post-consumer material 100% typical, 97% guaranteed.

Carefree Xteriors HDPE

U.S. Plastic Lumber, Ltd.
2600 W. Roosevelt Rd.
Chicago, IL 60608

Toll-free: 800-653-2784
Phone: 312-491-2500
www.usplasticlumber.com

Carefree Xteriors HDPE, formerly the Carefree Decking System, consists of decking, rail caps, spindles, and bull-nose stair treads made from 100% post-consumer HDPE. Decking lumber and stair treads are also available in a knurled, nonskid finish.

DuraBord Plastic Lumber

Recycled Plastics Marketing, Inc.
16541 Redmond Way
PMB #354-C
Redmond, WA 98052-4482

Toll-free: 800-867-3201
Phone: 425-867-3200
www.rrpm.com

Recycled Plastics Marketing manufactures DuraBord™ plastic lumber from 100% recycled HDPE (minimum 80% post-consumer content). DuraBord is available in a variety of colors including cedar, gray, sand, weathered wood, and white, and comes with a 50-year limited warranty.

Ecoboard Plastic Lumber

American Ecoboard, Inc.
200 Finn Ct.
Farmingdale, NY 11735

Phone: 631-753-5151
www.americanecoboard.com

Ecoboard® lumber is manufactured in a wide array of dimensions and colors. These products contain recycled HDPE and LDPE, as well as UV-stabilization, flame-retardant, and strength additives. The manufacturer has certified the following recycled-content levels (by weight): total recovered material 100% typical, 100% guaranteed; post-consumer material 90% typical, 80% guaranteed.

EPS Plastic Lumber

Engineered Plastic Systems
740 B Industrial Dr.
Cary, IL 60013

Phone: 847-462-9001
www.epsplasticlumber.com

Environmental Plastic Systems (EPS) plastic lumber is typically made from 100% post-consumer recycled HDPE and is available in a variety of sizes with a smooth or wood-grain finish. Available colors include white, gray, redwood, forest green, black, cedar, primary red, and tan. All EPS plastic products come with a 50-year limited warranty.

Impact-Post

XPotential Products Inc.
St. Boniface Postal Sta.
P.O. Box 126
Winnipeg, MB R2H 3B4
Canada

Toll-free: 800-863-6619
Phone: 204-224-3933
www.xpotentialproducts.
com

Impact-Post™ is a plastic-composite product manufactured with recycled materials including auto shredder residue as well as HDPE and LDPE plastics. Impact-Post comes in two sizes (6" x 6" x 8' and 4" x 4" x 8'). The manufacturer has certified the following recycled-content levels (by weight): total recovered material 100% typical, 100% guaranteed; post-consumer material 85% typical, 85% guaranteed.

Leisure Deck

The Plastic Lumber Co.
115 W. Bartges St.
Akron, OH 44311

Toll-free: 800-886-8990
Phone: 330-762-8989
www.plasticlumber.com

Leisure Deck™ is available in 1x6 and $^5/_4$x6 boards in plank, tongue & groove, or groove & groove, in seven colors. Several railing, post, and trim options are available, as is a line of outdoor furniture. Leisure Deck boards and accessories are made from 100% recycled HDPE, 97% post-consumer.

Marine Lumber

Plastic Pilings, Inc.
1485 S. Willow Ave.
Rialto, CA 92376

Phone: 909-874-4080
www.plasticpilings.com

Plastic Pilings manufactures various structural plastic lumber products including members from 3" x 6" to 12" x 20" and up to 50' in length. This recycled plastic product has a reinforced tubular-steel or fiberglass core. The manufacturer has certified the following recycled-content levels (by weight): total recovered material 50% typical; post-consumer material 50% typical.

Millennium Lumber

BJM Industries, Inc.
R.R. 1 Box 257A
Kittanning, PA 16201

Phone: 724-548-2440
www.bjmindustries.com

Millennium Lumber is manufactured from a combination of post-consumer recycled HDPE and post-industrial recycled cellulose (from diaper factory trimmings). Millennium Lumber is available in standard lengths from 8' to 16' and up to 30' by special order in a variety of colors and profiles.

Perma-Deck

Cascades Re-Plast, Inc.
2001 McGill College
    Ave., Ste. 230
Montreal, PQ H3A 1G1
Canada

Toll-free: 888-703-6515
Phone: 514-284-9850
www.cascadesreplast.
com

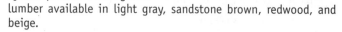

Perma-deck® is 100% recycled plastic decking and lumber available in light gray, sandstone brown, redwood, and beige.

Perma-Deck Plastic Lumber

Environmental Building Products, Inc.
P.O. Box 261310
Highlands Ranch, CO 80163

Phone: 303-470-7555
www.environmentalbuildingproducts.com

Environmental Building Products markets and distributes plastic lumber throughout the Rocky Mountain region and western United States. Perma-Deck is a wood-grained plastic lumber made from recycled HDPE, PP, and PS plastic, and it comes in sandstone brown, beige, redwood, and light gray. The product has a 50-year limited warranty against splitting, warping, peeling, rot, and insect infestation. The manufacturer has certified the following recycled-content levels (by weight): total recovered material 100% typical, 90% guaranteed; post-consumer material 50% typical, 30% guaranteed.

Plastic Lumber

Aeolian Enterprises, Inc.
P.O. Box 888
Latrobe, PA 15650

Toll-free: 800-269-4672
Phone: 724-539-9460
www.aeo1.com

Aeolian Enterprises manufactures hollow and solid-profile plastic lumber made from recycled HDPE (recycled content varies with color). Solid-profile products are planed to achieve a uniform flat surface and texture during fabrication. Aeolian offers various dimensions including nominal 1x4, 1x6, and $^5/_4$x6.

Plastic Lumber

American Recycled Plastic, Inc.
1500 Main St.
Palm Bay, FL 32905

Toll-free: 866-674-1525
Phone: 321-674-1525
www.itsrecycled.com

American Recycled Plastic manufactures lumber from recycled HDPE plastic. The manufacturer has certified the following recycled-content levels (by weight): total recovered material 100% typical, 100% guaranteed; post-consumer material 80% typical, 80% guaranteed.

Plastic Lumber

Bedford Technology, LLC
2424 Armour Rd.
P.O. Box 609
Worthington, MN 56187

Toll-free: 800-721-9037
Phone: 507-372-5558
www.plasticboards.com

Bedford Technology offers recycled HDPE plastic lumber in a variety of dimensions, including $^5/_4$ decking, two-by lumber, and large timbers up to 12x12. Bedford's standard product colors are black, brown, gray, and cedar with other colors available. The manufacturer has certified the following recycled-content levels (by weight): total recovered material 99% typical, 99% guaranteed; post-consumer material 65% typical, 50% guaranteed.

Plastic Lumber

Environmental Recycling, Inc.
8000 Hall St.
St. Louis, MO 63147

Phone: 314-382-7766

Environmental Recycling offers a full line of 100% recycled HDPE plastic lumber in common dimensions and gray, redwood, and black colors. They specialize in flooring systems for commercial trucks.

Plastic Lumber

Inteq Corp.
33010 Lakeland Blvd.
Eastlake, OH 44095

Phone: 440-953-0550
www.4-inteqcorp.com

Inteq manufactures a variety of recycled HDPE plastic lumber. Nonstructural landscape timbers are available in multiple colors up to 12' in length in standard sizes of 4x4, 4x6, and 6x6. Decking and railing material is also made from recycled HDPE plastic and is available in multiple colors. Additionally, Inteq offers structural and nonstructural recycled plastic lumber in standard dimensions. Nonstructural is 100% HDPE, and structural contains 15% recycled fiberglass. Inteq asks customers to consult with them before utilizing the structural lumber. The manufacturer has certified the following recycled-content levels (by weight): total recovered material 100% typical, 100% guaranteed; post-consumer material 100% typical, 100% guaranteed.

Plastic Lumber

Re-Source Building Products
1685 Holmes Rd.
Elgin, IL 60123

Toll-free: 800-231-9721
Phone: 847-931-4771
www.plastival.com

Re-Source Building Products manufactures plastic lumber from 98% recycled HDPE in 30 different profiles including deck and railing components.

Plastic Lumber

Recycled Plastic Man, Inc.
P.O. Box 2248
Englewood, FL 34295

Toll-free: 800-253-7742
Phone: 941-473-1618
www.recycledplasticman.com

Recycled Plastic Man manufactures extruded plastic lumber of commingled HDPE for marine and residential use in a variety of profiles and colors. The manufacturer has certified the following recycled-content levels (by weight): total recovered material 100% guaranteed; post-consumer material 100% guaranteed.

Plastic Lumber

The Plastic Lumber Company, Inc.
115 W. Bartges St.
Akron, OH 44311

Toll-free: 800-886-8990
Phone: 330-762-8989
www.plasticlumber.com

The Plastic Lumber Company offers approximately 20 different profiles of dimensional plastic lumber available in 12 different colors. Sizes range from $1/2$" x $2^1/2$" to 6x6. Commercial and residential decking is also available. Recycled content is 97% post-consumer.

Polywood Plastic Lumber

Polywood, Inc.
125 National Rd.
Edison, NJ 08817

Toll-free: 800-915-0043
Phone: 732-248-8810
www.polywood.com

Polywood manufactures structural-grade plastic lumber for industrial projects, Polytie™ engineered composite crossties, dimensional lumber, and park and site furnishings. Polywood products are manufactured utilizing a patented blend of recycled plastics and are available in black, white, and a choice of wood-tone colors. The manufacturer has certified the following recycled-

content levels (by weight): total recovered material 100% typical, 100% guaranteed; post-consumer material 100% typical, 100% guaranteed.

Recycled Plastic Lumber

Aloha Plastics Recycling
75 Amala Pl.
Kahului, HI 96732

Phone: 808-877-0822
www.aloha-recycling.com

Aloha Plastics Recycling manufactures a variety of plastic products including plastic lumber from 100% post-consumer HDPE. Aloha Plastic Lumber is available in brown, green, black, and gray in a variety of dimensions and profiles.

Recycled Plastic Lumber

Plastic Recycling of Iowa Falls, Inc.
10252 Hwy. 65
Iowa Falls, IA 50126

Toll-free: 800-338-1438
Phone: 641-648-5073
www.hammersplastic.com

Plastic Recycling of Iowa Falls, formerly Hammer's Plastic Recycling, manufactures a full line of recycled plastic lumber (in lengths up to 12') and assembled products (picnic tables, park benches, etc.) in a variety of colors of commingled recycled HDPE, LDPE, LLDPE, and miscellaneous plastics. The manufacturer has certified the following recycled-content levels (by weight): total recovered material 100% typical, 100% guaranteed; post-consumer material 50% typical, 50% guaranteed.

Rumber Lumber

Rumber Materials Inc.
621 W. Division St.
Muenster, TX 76252

Toll-free: 877-786-2371
Phone: 940-759-4181
www.rumber.com

Rumber® Lumber, made from recycled HDPE plastic and recycled-tire rubber, is available in 2x2, 2x4, 2x6, 2x8, 2x12, and 4x4 dimensions in standard lengths of 6' to 24'. The manufacturer has certified the following recycled-content levels (by weight): total recovered material 100% typical, 100% guaranteed; post-consumer material 50% typical, 50% guaranteed.

SeaTimber

Seaward International, Inc.
3470 Martinsburg Pike
P.O. Box 98
Clearbrook, VA 22624

Toll-free: 800-828-5360
Phone: 540-667-5191
www.seaward.com

SeaTimber® recycled plastic lumber with fiberglass reinforcement was developed as an alternative to preservative-treated lumber for marine applications. SeaTimber contains UV inhibitors, is impervious to marine borers, and has been U.S. government-approved for structural marine applications.

The Forever Deck

Phoenix Recycled Plastics
220 Washington St.
Norristown, PA 19401

Phone: 610-277-3900
www.plasticlumberyard.com

The Forever Deck® is constructed with Phoenix recycled plastic lumber made from 100% recycled HDPE. Phoenix also offers fiberglass-reinforced lumber graded for structural applications. The manufacturer has certified the following recycled-content levels (by weight): total recovered material 100% typical, 100% guaranteed; post-consumer material 30% typical.

Preservative-Treated Wood and Treatment Products

see *Structural Systems & Components: Preservative-Treated Wood and Treatment Products*

Wood-Plastic Composite Lumber

Wood-plastic composite lumber incorporates some of the characteristics of wood with those of plastic lumber. Recycled plastic resin (usually polyethylene) is combined with wood fiber—which may be post-industrial recycled content or virgin fiber—to create a product that has various advantages over both solid wood and solid plastic. Like plastic lumber, it will not rot, crack, or splinter, while the wood fiber adds considerable strength. Wood-plastic composite materials generally have a more natural coloring and appearance than 100%-plastic materials. The wood fibers, however, may absorb water and fade in color over time. Some wood-plastic composite lumber is graded for structural use, primarily as deck substructure and marine use. This is not true of all wood-plastic composites, so check with the manufacturer for specific product indications.

Carefree Xteriors Composite

U.S. Plastic Lumber, Ltd.
2600 W. Roosevelt Rd.
Chicago, IL 60608

Toll-free: 800-653-2784
Phone: 312-491-2500
www.usplasticlumber.com

Carefree Xteriors® Composite decking is made from a patented mix of oak sawdust from post-industrial sources and recycled HDPE. Carefree Xteriors Composite planking is available in ⁵/₄x6 dimensions and matching railing products. The planking contains approximately 35% recycled plastic and 65% wood fiber. Carefree Xteriors Composite was previously known as SmartDeck®.

ChoiceDek

AERT, Inc.
(Advanced Environmental Recycling Technologies, Inc.)
P.O. Box 1237
Springdale, AR 72765

Toll-free: 800-951-5117
Phone: 479-756-7400
www.choicedek.com

AERT manufactures ChoiceDek™, a decking product composed of 48% recycled plastic and 52% recycled wood fibers. ChoiceDek is a brown color when installed and weathers to silver-gray in 4 to 6 months. The underside of a ChoiceDek board has large corrugations to improve the strength-to-weight ratio. The manufacturer has certified the following recycled-content levels (by weight): total recovered material 100% typical, 95% guaranteed; post-consumer material 10-20% typical, 0% guaranteed.

Nexwood

Nexwood Industries, Ltd.
1327 Clark Blvd.
Brampton, ON L6T 5R5 Canada

Toll-free: 888-763-9966
Phone: 905-799-9686
www.nexwood.com

Nexwood™ is a 98%-recycled HDPE and cellulose fiber composite decking product. Unlike similar products, this three-celled, hollow-core material is rigid. For residential decks Nexwood is suitable for installation on 24" centers with the 2x6 profile. For commercial decks, boardwalks, and docks, 16" on-center support is recommended. Nexwood is currently available in 2x6 and ⁵/₄ tongue and groove, as well as fence and rail components in 4X4, 2X4, 2X2, and fascia board. End caps are also available in all profiles except 2X4. In the future, Nexwood ⁵/₄ radius edge board will be available.

Rhino Deck

Master Mark Div. of Avon Plastics, Inc.
P.O. Box 662
Albany, MN 56307-0662

Toll-free: 800-535-4838
Phone: 320-845-2111
www.mastermark.com

Rhino Deck® composite deck building components include lumber, posts, spindles, a rail system, and planks in 8' and 20' lengths. Decking products are made from recycled HDPE plastic. The manufacturer has certified the following recycled-content levels (by weight): total recovered material 50% typical, 50% guaranteed; post-consumer material 50% typical, 50% guaranteed.

Trex

Trex Company, Inc.
160 Exeter Dr.
Winchester, VA 22603

Toll-free: 800-289-8739
Phone: 540-542-6300
www.trex.com

Trex® was the first wood-plastic composite product brought to market. Available in a number of common dimensions and 5 colors, Trex is a wood-polymer lumber made from waste wood fibers and recycled HDPE and LDPE plastic. The manufacturer has certified the following recycled-content levels (by weight): total recovered material 97% typical, 94% guaranteed; post-consumer material 68% typical, 65% guaranteed.

WeatherBest Decking

Louisiana Pacific Corp. - WeatherBest Premium Decking
Nashville, TN 28078

Toll-free: 800-343-3651
Phone: 615-986-5600
www.lpcorp.com

WeatherBest™ Basic and WeatherBest Select are smooth-faced composite decking products that weather to varying shades of grey or ivory. WeatherBest Premium has a reversible, random wood-grained pattern over rough-sawn boards and is available in five colors with minimal fading. All three lines are made with 100% recycled wood and HDPE, and have a limited 10-year warranty. Available sizes include standard 8', 12', 16', and 20' lengths in a nominal ⁵/₄x6 solid plank for 16" on-center installations. Fascia, post sleeves, post caps, balusters, and side rails are available in all colors.

Foundations, Footers & Slabs

Conventional foundations, footers, and slabs use a lot of concrete, which is energy-intensive and polluting to produce—up to a ton of CO_2 is released in producing a ton of cement. Admixture components such as calcium chloride (an accelerator), gypsum (a retarder), and sulfonated melamine formaldehyde (SMF, a plasticizer) also affect the environmental impact of the concrete. Depending on the chemical, the impact may be on-site or at the plant. Also, concrete foundations and slabs do not provide much by way of thermal insulation, though they can provide thermal storage. Foundations, footers, and slabs should always be detailed to reduce thermal bridging as much as possible.

Forming can account for a significant portion of the total cost of poured concrete. Essentially things get built twice: once in forms and again in concrete. Plywood has been the mainstay of concrete-forming companies for many years, though some companies have invested in reusable, durable forms—a more resource-efficient solution that is still relatively labor-intensive. Reusable forms also require form-release agents, most of which are petrochemical-based and offgas large amounts of volatile organic compounds (VOCs). Vegetable-based form-release oils are also available.

For large buildings and some sites with poor soil conditions, foundations are engineered to specific structural requirements, and fairly extensive use of concrete may well be necessary. Replacing up to 25% of the cement in a concrete mixture with fly ash from coal-burning power plants will reduce the environmental impact of producing the material, and this substitution can actually strengthen the concrete. Fine-ground blast-furnace slag from metal foundries can have similar properties to those of fly ash.

For homes and smaller buildings, alternative foundation systems are available that can reduce concrete use and increase energy efficiency. Many such products consist of stay-in-place insulating concrete forms (ICFs) made of polystyrene foam or a cementitious matrix of recycled foam or recycled wood fibers. Expanded polystyrene (EPS) foam should be preferred until extruded polysterene (XPS) foam insulation becomes available without ozone-depleting HCFCs. Some EPS foam products have an integral borate treatment, which helps keep damaging insects out of the foam. The brominated flame retardants used in most EPS foam have health and environmental risks that are generating significant concern.

Precast concrete foundation walls are available in some areas. They use less concrete than site-cast foundations and are designed to accommodate interior insulation.

The depth of a foundation wall (and thus the amount of material required) can be reduced by raising the frost line, generally by placing foam insulation horizontally (usually extending about 4') around the foundation. These "frost-protected shallow foundations" can save money and materials where crawl-space or slab-on-grade foundations are used in cold climates. "Rubble trench" foundations are another option—one that was favored by Frank Lloyd Wright. Pier foundations, which can reduce excavation requirements and concrete use significantly, may also be an appropriate choice.

Non-asphalt-based dampproofing reduces the risk of introducing chemicals into local aquifers and VOCs into the building, and they can be longer lasting. In some parts of the country, rigid mineral wool panels are available that help insulate foundation walls while also providing effective drainage. Mineral wool typically includes iron-ore slag—a post-industrial waste product. And recycled aggregate or crushed glass can be used in the concrete or as backfill for foundation drains.

Foundations can also be designed with termite shields or be backfilled with special termite-proof sand, so that toxic soil treatments are not required. Pesticides commonly used around foundations introduce hazardous chemicals to the environment and must be periodically reapplied.

Autoclaved Aerated Concrete Masonry Units

see *Structural Systems & Components: Autoclaved Aerated Concrete Masonry Units*

Coal Fly Ash

Coal fly ash is a waste product of coal-fired power plants and can be used as a substitute for up to 60% of the portland cement in a concrete mixture, depending on the application. It makes the concrete stronger and gives it improved workability compared with a conventional mix. The environmental advantages include reducing the use of high-embodied-energy portland cement and reusing an otherwise-landfilled waste product. Other industrial and agricultural waste products, including ground blast-furnace slag and rice-hull ash, can also be used to replace some of the portland cement in concrete. With any such substitutions, be sure that the mixtures are properly engineered for the application. Fly ash is generally supplied in bulk to ready-mix plants, which do the custom-mixing.

MRT Blended Hydraulic Cement

Mineral Resource Technologies, LLC
2700 Research Forest Dr., Ste. 150
The Woodlands, TX 77381-4226

Toll-free: 800-615-1100
Phone: 281-362-1060

MRT Blended Hydraulic Cement, an alternative to portland cement, is made from Class C fly ash and other ingredients. It is available in bulk for ready-mix plants or in bags for mixing on-site. The manufacturer has certified the following recycled-content levels (by weight): total recovered material 83% typical, 80% guaranteed; post-consumer material 83% typical, 80% guaranteed.

Concrete Cleaning

With concrete cleaning agents, look for biodegradable, biobased materials.

Nu Look Concrete & Masonry Cleaner

Envirosafe Manufacturing
Corporation
7634-B Progress Cir.
W. Melbourne, FL 32904

Toll-free: 800-800-5737
www.envirosafemfg.com

Envirosafe Nu Look Concrete & Masonry Cleaner #40-44 is a fluid-applied cleaner that removes dirt, oil, and stains from concrete. Nu Look is biodegradable, noncarcinogenic, and water-soluble with a pH of less than 1.0. Nu Look Gel is slightly more viscous for vertical surfaces.

Concrete Curing

Concrete curing compounds are admixtures that aid in concrete setting and curing or give the finished concrete certain properties. Look for biobased and low-VOC products.

Cure and Seal

Natural Soy, LLC
2 Liberty St.
Watkins, IA 52354

Toll-free: 888-655-0039
Phone: 319-227-7418

Natural Soy's Cure and Seal, made from soy oil and other natural ingredients, is designed to retain the hydration water in freshly worked concrete. It also repels water and assists in the prevention of surface scaling of concrete induced by freeze-thaw cycles and the impact of deicing salts. Cure and Seal will not prevent the penetration of motor or other heavier oils. It is available in 5-, 55-, and 250-gallon containers and should be applied at a rate of 1 gal/200 ft^2.

SealTight Green Line

W. R. Meadows, Inc.
300 Industrial Dr.
P.O. Box 338
Hampshire, IL 60140-0338

Toll-free: 800-342-5976
Phone: 847-683-4500
www.wrmeadows.com

W. R. Meadows' Green Line includes over 60 water-emulsion, low-solvent (or, in some cases, solvent-free) concrete products. The product line includes:

Sealtight 1100-Clear—an all-resin curing compound used in both interior and exterior applications.

Sealtight 1200-White—a resin-based curing compound that also protects concrete from solar radiant heat.

Sealtight Vocomp®-20 and Vocomp-25—acrylic curing and sealing compounds. They become clear after application and resist yellowing from UV light.

Concrete Masonry Units

see *Structural Systems & Components: Concrete Masonry Units*

Concrete Pigments

see *Flooring & Floorcoverings: Concrete Pigments*

Concrete Rehabilitation

Look for concrete-repair mortars with high fly-ash content.

Emaco T415 and Emaco T430

Degussa Building Systems / MBT Protection and Repair
889 Valley Park Dr.
Shakopee, MN 55379

Toll-free: 800-433-9517
Phone: 612-496-6000
www.degussabuildingsystems.com

Emaco T415 and Emaco T430 are concrete-repair mortars with high levels of fly ash content, an industrial waste product from coal-fired power plants. These products produced by Degussa Building Systems, formerly known as ChemRex.

Dampproofing and Waterproofing

Conventional dampproofing products are asphalt-based coatings that typically have high VOC content and may contaminate groundwater. Most of the listed products have lower VOC emissions.

Aquafin-IC Crystalline Waterproofing

Aquafin, Inc.
P.O. Box 1440
Columbia, MD 21044

Toll-free: 888-482-6339
Phone: 410-964-1410
www.aquafin.net

Aquafin-IC is a penetrating, inorganic, cementitious material used to permanently waterproof and protect new or existing structurally sound concrete and concrete masonry by reacting with moisture and free lime in the concrete. Aquafin-IC resists strong hydrostatic pressure and can be used in both interior and exterior below-grade applications. It is "breathable," nontoxic, releases no VOCs, and is suitable for potable water storage applications. Aquafin-IC may take up to a month to reach full waterproofing potential.

Bentonite Waterproofing Systems

CETCO - Building Materials Group
1500 W. Shure Dr.
Arlington Heights, IL 60004

Toll-free: 800-527-9948
Phone: 847-392-5800
www.cetco.com

CETCO produces several waterproofing membranes using sodium bentonite, a natural clay with extremely low permeability and self-sealing properties. These membranes may be used beneath concrete slabs, against backfilled foundation walls, and for property line construction, such as lagging and metal sheet piling retention walls. Also, CETCO provides bentonite-based concrete joint waterstops that activate and swell to form a positive seal. CETCO claims that the products typically contain no VOCs and require no solvent-based primers or adhesives. Bentonite waterproofing can be installed on "green" concrete as soon as the forms are removed in a wide range of weather conditions, including freezing temperatures.

Delta-MS

Quad Lock Building Products
Cosella Dörken Products Inc.
4655 Delta Way
Beamville, ON L0R 1B4
  Canada

Toll-free: 888-433-5824
Phone: 905-563-3255
www.deltams.com

Delta-MS is an air-gap membrane constructed from 6 mm-thick HDPE, with a pattern of dimples approximately $5/8$" in diameter molded into the surface. When installed, the membrane is held off the wall approximately $5/16$" to allow any moisture in the concrete to migrate to the outer surface, condense on the inside surface of the membrane, and flow into the foundation drain. Because HDPE is impervious, soil moisture is unable to penetrate but will also flow to the foundation drain. Using Delta-MS avoids the need for asphalt-based spray-on dampproofings, which are prone to suffer cracking as the concrete cures and sometimes cracks. Delta-MS can be installed rapidly (in approximately 2 hours for an average basement).

DynoSeal Waterproofing Sealer

American Formulating & Manufacturing (AFM)
3251 Third Ave.
San Diego, CA 92103

Toll-free: 800-239-0321
Phone: 619-239-0321
www.afmsafecoat.com

DynoSeal is an asphaltic emulsion waterproof sealer, with a VOC content of less than 100 g/l, for use on foundations and other wet applications. The product containers have over 90% post-consumer recycled-plastic content. The Dyno line of AFM coatings also includes driveway sealers and UV-stabilized rooftop coatings.

Rub-R-Wall Foundation Waterproofing

Rubber Polymer Corp.
1135 W. Portage Trl. Ext.
Akron, OH 44313-8283

Toll-free: 800-860-7721
Phone: 330-945-7721
www.rpcinfo.com

Rub-R-Wall® foundation waterproofing is made from synthetic rubber. This product is spray-applied under high pressure (3,000 psi) and temperature (140–160°F) by factory-certified professionals. The resulting rubber coating requires protection from backfilling with either $1/4$" EPS foam or a woven geotextile. Rub-R-Wall has a lifetime limited warranty for residential applications and a 10-year warranty for commercial applications.

Xypex Concentrate

Xypex Chemical Corporation
13731 Mayfield Pl.
Richmond, BC V6V 2G9 Canada

Toll-free: 800-961-4477
Phone: 604-273-5265
www.xypex.com

Xypex Concentrate is a nontoxic powder consisting of portland cement, very fine treated silica sand, and various active proprietary chemicals. Mixed with water to form a slurry, it penetrates the pores of concrete and masonry structures, plugging them with a non-soluble crystalline formation that becomes an integral part of the structure. This product is approved for use on potable water structures and contains no VOCs. Xypex Concentrate is available in powder form in 20-lb. pails, 60-lb. pails, and 50-lb. bags. Other formulations for the protection and waterproofing of concrete are available. Xypex products also protect reinforcing steel.

Driven Piles

Marine borers are a constant threat to submerged wooden pilings, even when chemically treated. Ironically, this problem has worsened as marine environments have been cleaned up. Treated-wood pilings may introduce hazardous chemicals to marine ecosystems, and their periodic replacement is expensive. Recycled-content plastic pilings are impervious to marine borers and are an appropriate solution for building durable docks and piers. These pilings are usually extruded around steel or fiberglass reinforcing rods and treated with UV inhibitors and antioxidants. While more expensive than wooden pilings, if maintenance and durability are considered, recycled-plastic pilings often have lower life-cycle costs.

Carefree Xteriors Structural Pilings

U.S. Plastic Lumber, Ltd.
2600 W. Roosevelt Rd.
Chicago, IL 60608

Toll-free: 800-653-2784
Phone: 312-491-2500
www.usplasticlumber.com

The makers of Carefree Xteriors® Structural plastic lumber, formerly Trimax™, also produce 100% recycled material fiberglass-reinforced, recycled-plastic marine pilings. The 10"-diameter pilings contain post-consumer plastic resins and fiberglass. They come in gray and are available by special order in light gray, green, tan, redwood, and white.

Dock and Piling Cap

Recycled Plastic Man, Inc.
P.O. Box 2248
Englewood, FL 34295

Toll-free: 800-253-7742
Phone: 941-473-1618
www.recycledplasticman.com

Recycled Plastic Man manufactures plastic pilings and caps made from recycled plastic. The manufacturer has certified the following recycled-content levels (by weight): total recovered material 100% guaranteed; post-consumer material 100% guaranteed.

Ecoboard Marine Pilings

American Ecoboard, Inc.
200 Finn Ct.
Farmingdale, NY 11735

Phone: 631-753-5151
www.americanecoboard.com

Ecoboard® marine pilings are manufactured from recycled HDPE and LDPE with UV-stabilization, flame-retardant, and strength additives. According to the manufacturer, Ecoboard pilings have been tested as a friction pile where load-bearing capability needed to exceed 15 tons of vertical loading with a minimum of "creep" or failure. The pilings tested to a 60-ton load, at which time the test was stopped. The manufacturer has certified the following recycled-content levels (by weight): total recovered material 98% typical, 90% guaranteed; post-consumer material 90% typical, 70% guaranteed.

Expansion Joint Filler

Filling the expansion joints in concrete construction is a good use of panels made from recycled newspaper or waste agricultural materials, because the strength requirements are minimal. For radon control, less permeable joint sealants may be preferable.

Homex 300

Homasote Company
932 Lower Ferry Rd.
P.O. Box 7240
West Trenton, NJ 08628

Toll-free: 800-257-9491
Phone: 609-883-3300
www.homasote.com

Homex® 300 can be used both as an expansion joint filler and a clean, curvable light-duty forming material for concrete slabs. This 100% post-consumer waste paper material, with weather- and termite-resistant additives, is available in up to 10' lengths, various widths, and $1/2$", $3/4$", and 1" thicknesses.

Form Release Agents

Concrete form-release agents are applied to concrete forms to allow easier stripping of forms. Conventional form-release oils can be a major source of VOCs, soil contamination, and human health risks. Increasingly, biodegradable, nonpetroleum alternatives are available. These products contain just a tiny fraction of the federally permitted VOC limit for concrete form-release agents—currently 450 g/l. Many of these products produce a smoother finished surface with fewer "bug holes." Most of the products included here are made from agricultural crops; a few are water-based and must be protected from freezing temperatures during storage.

Asphalt Release

Franmar Chemical, Inc.
P.O. Box 97
Normal, IL 61761

Toll-free: 800-538-5069
Phone: 309-452-7526
www.franmar.com

Franmar makes soy-based asphalt and concrete form-release agents.

Bio-Form

Leahy-Wolf Company
1951 N. 25th Ave.
Franklin Park, IL 60131

Toll-free: 888-873-5327
Phone: 847-455-5710
www.leahywolf.com

Bio-Form® is a biodegradable, zero-VOC concrete form-release agent made primarily from rapeseed oil (in food-grade form known as Canola oil). It can be used below freezing point and covers 2,000 ft²/gal on pretreated high-density overlay forms. Bio-Form is available in 5- and 55-gallon containers and 275-gallon tanks. Though more expensive than conventional products, it has been reported to perform better.

Crete-Lease 20-VOC

Cresset Chemical Company
One Cresset Center, Box 367
Weston, OH 43569

Toll-free: 800-367-2020
Phone: 419-669-2041
www.cresset.com

Crete-Lease 20-VOC is a water-based form-release agent. Available in 5- and 55-gallon containers and 275-gallon totes.

Duogard II

W. R. Meadows, Inc.
300 Industrial Dr.
P.O. Box 338
Hampshire, IL 60140-0338

Toll-free: 800-342-5976
Phone: 847-683-4500
www.wrmeadows.com

Duogard II is a water-emulsion concrete form-release agent with a VOC content of 55 g/l. It is available in 5- and 55-gallon containers.

Enviroform and Aquastrip

Conspec®
4226 Kansas Ave.
Kansas City, KS 66106

Toll-free: 800-348-7351
Phone: 913-279-4800
www.conspecmkt.com

Enviroform is a 100% biodegradable, plant-oil-based, zero-VOC form-release agent. Aquastrip is a water-based, solvent-containing, VOC-compliant release agent.

FORMSHIELD WB

Tamms Industries
3835 State Rte. 72
Kirkland, IL 60146

Toll-free: 800-862-2667
Phone: 815-522-3394
www.tamms.com

Formshield WB (formerly Aquaform) is a water-based form-release agent available in 5- and 55-gallon containers.

Greenplus Form Release Agent ES

Greenland Corporation
7016-30 St. SE
Calgary, AB T2C 1N9 Canada

Toll-free: 800-598-7636
Phone: 403-720-7049
www.greenpluslubes.com

Greenland Corporation manufactures the Greenplus line of rapidly biodegradable, vegetable oil-based lubricants suitable for a wide variety of lubricating applications. Customized products are also available, as well as technical support for the proper product choice, and ongoing support. Included in the line is Greenplus Form Release Agent ES for use with metal, wood, plastic, and fiberglass forms. Greenplus Form Release Agent does not react with portland cement or its common admixtures.

Soy Form Release and Natural Form Oil

Natural Soy, LLC
2 Liberty St.
Watkins, IA 52354

Toll-free: 888-655-0039
Phone: 319-227-7418

Natural Soy produces Soy Form Oil form-release agent containing soy oil, surfactant, and water. It prevents the adhesion of concrete to forms and molds and can be used to clean forms for reuse. It is sprayable, cleans up with water, and has no VOCs or other hazards. It is available in 5-, 55-, and 250-gallon containers. 1 gallon covers approximately 300 ft². Natural Form Oil is a nonwater-based version for use in freezing conditions.

SOYsolv Concrete Form Release Agent

SOYsolv®
6154 N. CR 33
Tiffin, OH 44883

Toll-free: 800-231-4274
Phone: 419-992-4570
www.soysolv.com

Water-based, nonflammable, nontoxic SOYsolv Concrete Form Release is made from soybean oil and cleans up with soap and water.

Forms for Cast-in-Place Concrete

Products included here are less resource-intensive than conventional concrete-forming products, permit the construction of foundations using less concrete, or are made from recycled-content materials or plywood certified according to the standards of the Forest Stewardship Council (FSC). Concrete construction tubes made from recycled paper, in conjunction with recycled-plastic or fabric footing forms, offer a quick, resource-efficient means of pouring structural piers. While most commonly used for decks, outdoor stairs, and the like, pier foundations are also used for entire buildings and can be particularly appropriate on ecologically fragile sites. Concrete pier foundations greatly reduce concrete use compared with full-height frost walls, though proper detailing to control air leakage and heat loss is difficult and extremely important. Cement production takes about 6 million Btu per ton of cement produced; most of that energy is used in coal-fired cement kilns, resulting in high carbon dioxide, nitrous oxide, and sulfur emissions. Judicious use of concrete is an important green-building consideration.

Bigfoot System Footing Forms

F&S Manufacturing, Inc.
6750 Hwy. #3
Martin's Point, NS B0J 2E0
    Canada

Toll-free: 800-934-0393
Phone: 902-627-1600
www.bigfootsystems.com

The Bigfoot System® is a one-piece, lightweight, recycled, high-density polyethylene (HDPE) form for site-forming pier footings. The funnel-shaped form replaces site-built solid-wood footings. The construction tube and the footing pour as one unit. Bigfoot Systems will accept all 6", 8", 10", 12", 14", 16", and 18" cardboard construction tubes. Tubes are attached to the Bigfoot Systems using four screws.

Caraustar Concrete Column Forms

Caraustar ICPG Corp.
Evergreen Industrial Park
100 Forest La.
Beardstown, IL 62618

Phone: 217-323-5225
www.caraustar.com

Caraustar (formerly Smurfit) Concrete Column Forms are recycled-paper concrete forms with a polyethylene-impregnated virgin kraft interior layer (to aid release) and a waxed exterior. The recycled-paper content is estimated to be 90% from mixed, post-industrial, and post-consumer sources, according to the company. Smurfit Concrete Column Forms are available from 6" to 48" in diameter (2" increments up to 24").

Fastfoot, Fastbag, and Fast-Tube Fabric Forms

Fab-Form Industries Ltd.
Unit #212, 6333 148th St.
Surrey, BC V3S 3C3
    Canada

Toll-free: 888-303-3278
Phone: 604-596-3278
www.fab-form.com

Fastfoot® is a fabric concrete footing form system for linear foundations. Specially designed steel "yokes" hold pairs of 2x4s, which hold the fabric in a trough formation. After the 2x4s are leveled, the trough is filled with concrete. The 2x4s can be nailed to the partially cured concrete as bracing for the foundation forms or removed for reuse. Fastfoot is well suited to rocky or uneven ground. Fastfoot Lite is a simplified version, which uses the same fabric with 2x4s and stakes. Fastbag®, for pier footings, is a nonwoven polypropylene "pillowcase" with a hole in the top that is nailed to the ground and filled with concrete. As the plastic fabric forms are not removed, there may be some indoor air quality benefits from the capillary break between footings and soil. The company also now offers Fast-Tube™ for forming concrete columns.

GreenCore Plyform

ROMEX World Trade Company, LLC - sales agent for ROM
P.O. Box 1110
Alexandria, LA 71309

Toll-free: 800-299-5174
Phone: 318-445-1973
www.martco.com

GreenCore Plyform® FSC-certified concrete forming panels are available in BB grade and $^{19}/_{32}$" and $^{23}/_{32}$" thicknesses. These panels are edge-sealed and oiled with NOX-CRETE Concrete Forming Oil, a petroleum-based product made by Chemtrec in Omaha, Nebraska. The mill also produces industrial plywood. GreenCore Plyform is certified using partial-content rules for certification (some fiber used in the mill comes from land not owned by the company), but 100% FSC-certified product can be provided. Roy O. Martin Lumber Management, LLC (ROM) is the first company to receive FSC-certification in the state of Louisiana, and they offer the first FSC-certified OSB and FSC-certified utility poles.

Recycled Paper Formworks/Brick Ledger Void Forms

SureVoid Products, Inc.
1895 W. Dartmouth
Englewood, CO 80110

Toll-free: 800-458-5444
Phone: 303-762-0324
www.surevoid.com

SureVoid® produces a range of corrugated paper construction products, referred to commonly as "void forms" or "carton forms." These forms create a space between concrete structures and expansive soils (soils high in clay content that expand when wet) to isolate the concrete from the swelling ground. They can also provide a temporary support platform until the grade beam or structural slab has set and can support itself across drilled piers, pads, or intermittent footings. As the corrugated paper eventually absorbs ground moisture and loses strength, it creates a space for wet soil to expand into without causing damage. An alternative use for these products is to displace concrete volume as a means of reducing weight and cost.

SONOTUBES

Sonoco Products Co.
N. Second St.
Hartsville, SC 29550

Toll-free: 888-875-8754
Phone: 843-383-7000
www.sonoco.com

Sonotube® fiber forms are cylindrical recycled paperboard forms available from 6" to 60" in diameter. These are the most widely used concrete column forms; in fact, the brand name is often used generically.

The Footing Tube

The Footing Tube
28 Amberwood Ln.
Fredericton, NB E3C 1L7 Canada

Toll-free: 888-929-2011
Phone: 506-452-8919
www.foottube.com

The Footing Tube™ is a tapered, one-piece, 100% recycled polyethylene footing and pier form primarily for decks and additions. The 62"-high form, which can hold a volume of 4.8 ft³ of concrete, has a diameter of 24" at the base of the footing and 8" at the top of the pier. According to the company, the taper and smooth plastic of the sides of a properly installed tube increases resistance to frost uplift in comparison to typical cylindrical formwork. The Footing Tube works in frost-prone areas to 5' depths. Currently distributed only in Canada, but the company will ship to the U.S.

Foundation and Load-Bearing Elements

Conventional foundation excavation can disturb plantings and soil, and cause sediment runoff and erosion. In fragile environments, such as boardwalks and decking in wetlands, and in erosion-prone areas, consider foundation-anchor systems that don't require excavation.

Diamond Pier

Pin Foundations, Inc.
8607 58th Ave. NW
Gig Harbor, WA 98332

Phone: 253-858-8809
www.pinfoundations.com

Diamond Pier™ DP-100 and DP-50 permit installation of pier foundations with neither excavation nor site-poured concrete. These products are structural foundation systems for decks, outbuildings, and boardwalks. Held in place with four steel pins driven through the piers and deep into the ground at angles, they are particularly appropriate for fragile ecosystems, poor soils, or difficult access sites. Pin Foundations has also developed the L.I.F.T.™ system for continuous perimeter foundations that does not require excavation (see listing this section). The company's Butterfly™ and Speed Pile™ systems are no longer offered.

Instant Foundation System

A. B. Chance, Division of Hubbell Power Systems, Inc.
210 N. Allen
Centralia, MO 65240

Phone: 573-682-8414
www.abchance.com

A. B. Chance manufactures the Instant Foundation®, a unique screw-anchor foundation system for supporting walkways in ecologically sensitive areas. The steel piers are screwed into the ground or wetland using portable rotary augering equipment, eliminating the need for any excavation or concrete. A. B. Chance also manufactures galvanized-steel hardware to complete the installations.

L.I.F.T. Foundation Systems

Pin Foundations, Inc.
8607 58th Ave. NW
Gig Harbor, WA 98332

Phone: 253-858-8809
www.pinfoundations.
    com

The L.I.F.T.™ systems allow installation of foundations without excavation. Structural foundations for homes are fixed in the ground with a combination of a surface concrete perimeter beam and driven steel pins reaching deep into dense soil. The L.I.F.T. systems are particularly appropriate for the preservation of natural groundwater flows and where problematic soils drive up the cost of conventional foundations. The company also offers single, stand-alone versions of the technology for pier foundations that are used for support of boardwalks and decks and are well suited to the protection of fragile ecosystems (see listing this section).

Low Density Concrete

Slag is a byproduct of steel production. It's typically landfilled but can be used as a replacement for stone aggregate in concrete, which can improve the concrete's strength-to-weight ratio and its thermal properties.

True Lite Slag Concrete Aggregate

Lafarge North America (Chicago and Hamilton Slag)
139 Windermere Rd.
Hamilton, ON L8H 3Y2 Canada

Phone: 219-378-1193
www.lafargenorthamerica.com

True Lite lightweight expanded blast furnace slag aggregate from Lafarge is the recovered nonmetallic mineral components from iron blast furnaces. It can reduce concrete's weight with little or no reduction in strength, and improve its sound attenuation and thermal properties. The slag is inert and is otherwise typically landfilled. A finer grind of this slag has properties similar to fly ash.

Masonry Mortar

see *Structural Systems & Components: Masonry Mortar*

Permanent Forms

see *Structural Systems & Components: Permanent Forms*

Rebar Supports

Rebar supports for concrete formwork hold rebar in place during pours. They have minimal structural requirements, making them good candidates for manufacturing with recycled waste plastic. Look for products with high recycled content.

Rebar Supports

Eclipse Plastic, Inc.
12504 Roosevelt Rd.
Snohomish, WA 98290

Toll-free: 800-278-4276
Phone: 360-863-9213

Eclipse Plastic manufactures and sells directly a variety of rebar support devices made from 100% recycled engineering-grade plastic.

This Space is Available for Your Notes

This Space is Available for Your Notes

Structural Systems & Components

The structure of a building should be designed for durability and soundness—unless it's a temporary structure, in which case it should accommodate disassembly and reuse of the materials. Some structural materials may compromise the building's energy efficiency by creating thermal bridges from interior to exterior that allow heat to bypass the insulation; these should be addressed during building design.

For houses and small commercial buildings, wood is by far the most common framing material. Even with wood from certified, well-managed forests, measures should be taken to minimize the use of wood framing and maximize the amount of insulation in the building envelope. "Advanced framing" measures include framing at 24" on-center instead of 16", using single top plates (and lining up roof framing over the wall studs), using two- or three-stud corners, and insulating headers above openings.

Larger framing members, such as 2x10s and 2x12s, are made from mature trees that often come from scarce old-growth forests; engineered lumber products, such as trusses and I-joists, should be preferred. Finger-jointed lumber, which uses short pieces of wood that might otherwise become waste, makes straighter boards that are less prone to warp.

There are alternatives to wood. Light-gauge steel framing is used as a piece-for-piece substitute for wood framing. While it does contain some recycled content, the sheet steel used for light-gauge framing generally contains less recycled material than heavier types of steel. Steel is also quite energy-intensive to produce (high in embodied energy). Most important, however, is that steel conducts heat 400 times more readily than wood: steel framing can easily compromise a building's thermal performance unless insulation is specially designed to block thermal bridging.

Masonry construction is common in many areas. Hollow-core concrete masonry units (CMUs) are hard to insulate effectively. A special type of masonry block called autoclaved aerated concrete (AAC) insulates much better than standard concrete block. Other types of block should generally be insulated on the exterior, or between the concrete block and the exterior skin.

Concrete wall systems that are more typically used for foundations—including insulated concrete forms (ICFs)—can also be used to form above-grade walls. Making concrete is energy-intensive and polluting: the production of a ton of cement releases up to a ton of carbon dioxide. Admixture components also affect the environmental impact of concrete. Though concrete walls can provide thermal storage, they don't provide much thermal insulation; concrete walls for conditioned spaces should always be insulated.

Structural insulated panels (SIPs—sometimes called stress-skin or foam-core panels), usually made with foam insulation sandwiched between oriented-strand board (OSB) skins, are a viable alternative for houses and other small buildings. They insulate well, are usually quite airtight, and go up quickly. Some panels are available with mineral-wool insulation or compressed straw as the core instead of plastic foam.

Foam-core panels are often used to enclose post-and-beam or timber-frame structures. These heavy timber structures use a great deal of wood, but they're likely to be very durable—the finish materials and exterior skins can be replaced multiple times in the life of a solid timber frame. If the wood is local or from well-managed forests, this construction system may represent a good choice. Some timber framers use salvaged timbers from buildings that are being demolished.

Other alternative structural systems include adobe, rammed earth, straw-bale construction, and cob construction (a hand-formed mixture of sand, clay and straw). Log homes use a great deal of wood and don't insulate very well. Like their mainstream cousins, some proponents of alternative materials or methods claim mass-enhanced "effective R-values," which are relevant only under certain conditions.

Adobe Masonry Units

Adobe is a natural building material common to the U.S. Southwest. It can be very durable if protected from erosion; many Native American adobe structures built hundreds of years ago are still standing. Made from soil that has suitable sand and clay content and then air-dried in the sun, adobe bricks typically have extremely low greenhouse gas emissions and embodied energy. Most commercially available adobe bricks are stabilized with cement or asphalt additives, but adobe bricks are very commonly made on-site without stabilizers. Walls made of adobe bricks are most often protected from the weather with a parge coat of stucco or plaster, or large overhangs.

Adobe Block

Adobe Factory
P.O. Box 519
Alcalde, NM 87511

Phone: 505-852-4131

Adobe Factory is northern New Mexico's main adobe manufacturer and supplier.

Adobe Block

Clay Mine Adobe, Inc.
6401 W. Old Ajo Hwy.
Tucson, AZ 85735

Phone: 520-578-2222
www.claymineadobe.com

Clay Mine Adobe, founded in 1996, manufactures adobe block with a custom portland cement stabilizer, wheat straw (optional), and washed coarse aggregate admixture. Clay Mine adobe block requires no sealing and retains the authentic look of unstabilized adobe. It is available in a variety of standard as well as custom sizes and natural custom colors including a burnt adobe look. Clay plaster, cement-stabilized and unstabilized in a variety of earth tones, is also available in 95-pound bags.

Adobe Block

Mule Creek Adobe
547 Hwy. 78
P.O. Box 33
Mule Creek, NM 88051

Phone: 505-535-2973
www.mulecreekadobe.com

Mule Creek Adobe is a family-owned business that manufactures stabilized adobe with about 4% asphalt emulsion using traditional ladder forms and a student work force. As the drying process is dictated by the seasons (May to mid-September) and production is limited, the company recommends reserving block several months in advance. Block is available in 6 sizes. "Holey" or voided block is also available for running electrical wiring and plumbing.

Adobe Block

New Mexico Earth Adobes
P.O. Box 10506
Albuquerque, NM 87184

Phone: 505-898-1271

New Mexico Earth Adobes is an adobe block supplier serving the central and northern New Mexico, and southern Colorado regions. Blocks are 4" x 10" x 14" and weigh approximately 30 lbs. each.

Adobe Block

Old Pueblo Adobe Company
9353 N. Casa Grande Hwy.
Tucson, AZ 85743

Toll-free: 800-327-4705
Phone: 520-744-9268
www.oldpuebloadobe.com

Old Pueblo Adobe Company manufactures adobe and Southwestern building supplies as well as offering a variety of antique Mexican Ranchero furnishings, accessories, and building products for sale in their Tucson showroom.

Adobe Block

Rio Abajo Adobe
7 Industrial Park Ln.
Belen, NM 87002

Phone: 505-864-6191

Rio Abajo Adobe manufactures adobe brick and offers consulting services for small to large adobe block manufacturing startups or people building adobe homes.

Autoclaved Aerated Concrete Masonry Units

Commercial production of autoclaved aerated concrete (AAC) began in 1930 in Europe, where it has been widely used for decades. Concrete masonry units (CMUs) made from AAC are lighter than conventional CMUs, they generally have no cores, and they provide higher insulation levels (R-values of up to 1.25 per inch, an order of magnitude higher than standard concrete). The insulating value of AAC allows it to function simultaneously as structure and insulation system. It has about 20% of the density—though only about 10% of the compressive strength—of regular concrete. Manufacturers may increase the product's strength by including reinforcing steel rods or mesh. Structural applications of unreinforced AAC are limited to low-rise buildings; in high-rise buildings it may be used in partition and curtain walls. AAC has very good sound-absorbing characteristics and can be worked with conventional carpenter's tools, making site modifications relatively easy. It's also nontoxic, fire-resistant, and insect-resistant, but because it's a porous material, AAC must be protected from moisture with claddings or coatings. It can be produced using coal fly ash as a substitute for some of the sand in conventional AAC.

Autoclaved Aerated Concrete

ACCOA Aerated Concrete Corporation of America
3351 W. Orange Blossom Trl.
Apopka, FL 32712

Toll-free: 888-901-2226
Phone: 407-884-0051
www.accoaac.com

ACCO AAC blocks, lintels, and panels are made by Aerated Concrete Corporation of America.

Autoclaved Aerated Concrete

Babb International Inc.
2400 Hebel Blvd.
P.O. Box 834
Adel, GA 31620

Toll-free: 800-994-3235
Phone: 229-896-1209
www.babb.com

In June 2001, autoclaved aerated concrete (AAC) manufacturer Babb International acquired Matrix (a licensee of the Hebel AAC process) to become the largest manufacturer of AAC products in the U.S. Many block and panel sizes of AAC are available, including blocks larger than standard CMU-size, larger "jumbo" units, panels, and a variety of specially manufactured shapes and pre-assembled wall sections—with integral reinforcement. AAC products are made from a mixture of poured concrete, fly ash, and sand. Babb products can be used for interior and exterior applications. In exterior wall applications, they must not be exposed but can be painted with a textured paint, coated with a stucco finish specially made for AAC, or clad with standard siding.

Autoclaved Aerated Concrete

E-Crete
2151 E. Broadway Rd. #115
Tempe, AZ 85282

Toll-free: 888-432-7383 x11
Phone: 480-596-3819 x11
www.e-crete.com

E-Crete has been producing autoclaved aerated concrete (AAC) blocks in a plant near Phoenix, Arizona since December 2000. The company uses sterile mine tailings from an adjacent closed copper mine to substitute for the silica content, which represents 25% of the dry weight content. E-Crete reports a steady-state insulating value of approximately R-1.2 per inch for their most common block (density of 31 lbs/ft³). Factoring in the benefits

of the thermal mass boosts this R-value by a factor of 2 or more in their southwestern climate (with lots of sunshine and large temperature swings). E-Crete plans to expand to reinforced panel production and block operations in other locations as market conditions permit.

Autoclaved Aerated Concrete

Texas Contec, Inc.
1535 Brady Blvd., Ste. 2
San Antonio, TX 78237-4355

Toll-free: 877-926-6832
Phone: 210-402-3223
www.texascontec.com

Contec AAC, formed in 1995, manufactures AAC at its plant in Monterrey, Mexico. Texas Contec is their U.S. distributor and offers a full line of AAC products, accessories, and technical services.

Certified Wood Lumber and Timbers

Certified wood products are verified by a third party as originating from well-managed forests. GreenSpec recognizes the Forest Stewardship Council (FSC) standards as currently the most rigorous and also the only certification system that provides for chain-of-custody certification to ensure that products used were derived from certified forests. Some companies listed here sell both certified and noncertified wood products, or products that have been certified according to different, less stringent environmental standards. To make certain that you get environmentally responsible wood products, be sure to specify your interest in FSC-certified wood.

Certified Hardwood and Softwood Lumber

Lashway Lumber, Inc.
P.O. Box 768
Williamsburg, MA 01096

Phone: 413-268-7685

Lashway Lumber mills FSC-certified North American hardwood and softwood lumber.

Certified Hardwood and Softwood Lumber and Timbers

Cascadia Forest Goods, LLC
38083 Wheeler Rd.
Dexter, OR 97431

Phone: 541-485-4477
www.cascadiaforestgoods.com

Cascadia Forest Goods (CFG) is a supplier of FSC-certified and recycled forest products, including timbers, beams, and siding. CFG's woods come from the Pacific Northwest and British Columbia, such as: Douglas fir, incense and western red cedar, Sitka and Englemann spruce, ponderosa and sugar pine, and regional hardwoods (madrone, white and black oak, broadleaf maple, alder, and chinkapin).

Certified Hardwood Lumber

Allard Lumber Company
354 Old Ferry Rd.
Brattleboro, VT 05301

Phone: 802-254-4939
www.allardlumber.com

Allard Lumber is a manufacturer and wholesaler of FSC-certified northern hardwood lumber, including white hard maple, red oak, and cherry.

Certified Hardwood Lumber

Dwight Lewis Lumber / Lewis Lumber Products
30 S. Main St.
P.O. Box 356
Picture Rocks, PA 17762

Toll-free: 800-233-8450
Phone: 570-584-4460
lewislp.com

Dwight Lewis Lumber sells FSC-certified moldings, flooring, paneling, and hardwoods, subject to availability. Certified species are cherry, hard and soft maple, and red oak.

Certified Hardwood Lumber

Maine Woods Company, LLC
Fish Lake Rd.
P.O. Box 111
Portage, ME 04768

Phone: 207-435-4393
www.mainewoods.net

Maine Woods Company, LLC, owned in part by Seven Islands Land Company, operates a state-of-the-art sawmill in northern Maine producing primarily hard maple and yellow birch lumber and flooring. Smaller quantities of American beech, red maple, and white ash are also produced. A portion of the mill output is FSC-certified.

Certified Hardwood Lumber and Timbers

ROMEX World Trade Company, LLC - sales agent for ROM
P.O. Box 1110
Alexandria, LA 71309

Toll-free: 800-299-5174
Phone: 318-445-1973
www.martco.com

Roy O. Martin Lumber Management, LLC has received certification of its 585,000 acres of forestland and four mills according to standards of the Forest Stewardship Council (FSC). This is the first FSC certification of any forest management operation in Louisiana. Roy O. Martin produces FSC-certified lumber in red oak, white oak, ash, hackberry, pecan, sap gum (sweet gum), cypress, and several other species at the company's hardwood lumber mill in LeMoyen. While the majority of the mill's output is red oak, ROM has become one of the largest suppliers of southern ash and cypress. Lumber accounts for 75% of production, with the rest in timbers, railroad ties, and pallet cants.

Certified Iron Woods Lumber

Cecco Trading, Inc.
600 E. Vienna Ave.
Milwaukee, WI 53212-1637

Phone: 414-445-8989
www.ironwoods.com

Iron Woods® is a brand of ipé decking and lumber from the Brazilian forest that is offered FSC-certified with an upcharge. Iron Woods' natural durability rating of 25+ years is the highest of woods tested by the U.S. Forest Products Lab. The product is available in all standard decking, porch flooring, and dimensional lumber sizes from 2x2 to 4x12 and up to 20' long in standard even lengths. Iron Woods lumber is Class A fire-rated and comes with a 25-year fully transferable limited warranty.

Certified Lumber

McDowell Lumber Company, Inc.
Rte. 46 S
P.O. Box 148
Crosby, PA 16724

Phone: 814-887-2717
www.mcdowelllumber.com

McDowell Lumber deals in FSC-certified lumber, flooring, wainscoting, and veneer in over 15 species including red oak, cherry, hard and soft maple, ash, and a variety of other hardwoods harvested in Pennsylvania.

Certified Lumber

Menominee Tribal Enterprises
Hwy. 47 N
P.O. Box 10
Neopit, WI 54150

Phone: 715-756-2311
www.menominee.edu/mte/index.html

Menominee Tribal Enterprises (MTE) offers a full line of certified wood products harvested from the 220,000-acre Menominee Forest. MTE is continuing its development of value-added products from the 16 wood species harvested. Menominee forest lands were the first certified to FSC standards in North America.

Certified Lumber and Timbers

Harwood Products
1 Main St.
Branscomb, CA 95417

Toll-free: 800-441-4140 (CA only)
Phone: 707-984-6181
www.harwoodp.com

Harwood Products offers certified redwood decking and timbers, Douglas fir lumber and timbers, and white fir lumber.

Certified Millwork

Midwest Hardwood
Corporation
9540 83rd Ave. N
Maple Grove, MN 55369

Phone: 763-425-8700
www.midwesthardwood.
com

Midwest Hardwood Corporation's Sawmill Division offers some varieties of FSC-certified northern hardwood lumber. The wood is harvested from forests in Wisconsin, Michigan, and Minnesota.

Certified Redwood Lumber

Big Creek Lumber Company
3564 Hwy. 1
Davenport, CA 95017

Phone: 831-457-5023
www.big-creek.com

Big Creek Lumber Company was among the first certified producer of redwood lumber. Big Creek harvests timber on its 6,800 acres of FSC-certified second- and third-growth forestland in the Santa Cruz Mountains of coastal California. Wholesale and retail quantities available.

Certified Spruce-Pine-Fir (SFP) Lumber

Materiaux Blanchet, Inc.
5055 W. Hamel Blvd., Ste. 225
Quebec City, PQ G2E 2G6 Canada

Phone: 418-871-2626
www.mbi-quebec.com

Materiaux Blanchet, Inc. produces a full range of graded, kiln-dried, FSC-certified spruce-pine-fir dimensional lumber from Seven Islands Land Company timber.

Certified Tropical Hardwood

Sustainable Forest Systems LP
990 Carib Ln.
Vero Beach, FL 32963

Phone: 772-473-0328

Sustainable Forest Systems has operated tropical hardwood timberlands and associated processing since 1994. They offer a wide range of FSC-certified tropical hardwood products.

Certified Wood Products

Randall Custom Lumber, Ltd.
3530 S.E. Arcadia Rd.
Shelton, WA 98584

Phone: 360-426-8518
www.rclumber.com

Randall Custom Lumber manufactures FSC-certified decking, flooring, hard and softwood lumber, and stair parts. Some of their certified species are ash, red cedar, red alder, Douglas fir, madrone, and maple.

CollinsWood Certified Wood Products

Collins Companies
1618 S.W. First Ave., Ste. 500
Portland, OR 97201

Toll-free: 800-329-1219
Phone: 503-417-7755
www.collinswood.com

The CollinsWood® line includes FSC-certified particleboard, FSC-certified TruWood® engineered (hardboard) siding, and FSC-certified hardwood and softwood lumber and millwork. In 1993, Collins Pine Company became the first privately owned timber management company to receive FSC certification in the U.S. CollinsWood has been a leader in the forest and wood products certification movement since its inception.

Horse- and Biodiesel-Harvested Hardwood and Softwood Lumber

JH Lumber & Wood Products
1701 Chase Rd.
Berlin, VT 05602

Phone: 802-229-4148

JH Lumber & Wood Products mills kiln-dried North American hardwood and softwood lumber. Logging is done with horses and biodiesel-powered equipment and soon will occur on over 1,400 acres of forest land.

Coal Fly Ash

see *Foundations, Footers, and Slabs: Coal Fly Ash*

Cold-formed Metal Framing

Commonly used for interior partitioning of commercial buildings, light-gauge steel framing is increasingly being used in residential construction. Compared to solid wood, steel studs are lightweight, dimensionally stable, resistant to insect damage, and of consistent quality. Cold-rolled steel framing typically contains 20–25% recycled material (10–15% post-consumer content), though some manufacturers have in excess of 90% recycled content. Steel studs are also recyclable at the end of the building's useful life. Despite the advantages of light-gauge steel, its use can cripple a building's energy performance when improperly used in exterior wall applications because of thermal bridging through the highly conductive steel. Foam insulation is often recommended on the inside or outside surface of a wall to address this problem.

Residential Steel Framing Systems

Tri-Steel Homes
5400 S. Stemmons Fwy.
Denton, TX 76210

Toll-free: 800-874-7833
Phone: 940-497-7070
www.tri-steel.com

Tri-Steel Homes fabricates steel framing for residential construction. Over 66% of the steel content in the studs is recycled scrap material, such as from automobiles.

Tri-Chord Steel Systems

Tri-Chord Steel Systems, Inc.
4411 S. 40th St., Ste. 1
Phoenix, AZ 85040

Phone: 602-426-8700
www.tri-chordsteelsystems.com

The Tri-Chord STUD and Truss Systems were designed to minimize thermal bridging. In profile, the studs and trusses have triangular sections at each edge and discrete webs spanning the wall cavity, instead of a solid heat-conducting steel web. Contains 66–68% post-consumer recycled content.

Concrete Cleaning

see *Foundations, Footers, and Slabs: Concrete Cleaning*

Concrete Masonry Units

CMU (concrete masonry unit) construction is increasing in popularity. Like many conventional products, CMUs can be used in "green" ways—for example, using a decorative type of block without additional finish materials. Energy performance is a concern with most CMU systems; included here are specially designed products with EPS (expanded polystyrene) insulation inserts. CMUs may also contain post-industrial recycled material, such as fly ash or ground blast-furnace slag.

IMSI Block

SouthWest Management
887 W. Center St.
Orem, UT 84057

Phone: 801-724-9870
www.floridaaffordablehousing.com

IMSI® Block is a uniquely molded concrete block available in 8" and 12" sizes designed to minimize thermal bridging and to receive molded EPS insulation inserts. IMSI Block is reinforced with rebar and grout in some of the interior cells as determined by structural engineering. All electrical and plumbing are run within the block so no furring or sheetrock is required for a finished wall. IMSI, Ltd. holds the patent on the IMSI Wall System. SouthWest Management and associates are the license holders for the production, sales, marketing, and distribution of the IMSI Wall System.

Omni Block

Omni Block, Inc.
15125 N. Hayden Rd.
#123
Scottsdale, AZ 85260

Phone: 480-661-9009
www.omniblock.com

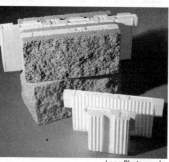
Lenz Photography

Omni Block is a uniquely molded concrete block (not foam) available in 8" and 12" sizes designed to minimize thermal bridging and to receive molded EPS insulation inserts. Omni Block is reinforced with rebar and grout in some of the interior cells as determined per structural engineering. All electrical and plumbing are run within the block so no furring or sheetrock is required for a finished wall.

Concrete Pigments

see *Flooring & Floorcoverings: Concrete Pigments*

Concrete Rehabilitation

see *Foundations, Footers, and Slabs: Concrete Rehabilitation*

Engineered Lumber Products

While not free from ecological concerns, engineered lumber products provide a significant environmental advantage over solid wood by utilizing fast-growing, small-diameter trees efficiently. The selection offered here is limited to products that do not include formaldehyde binders; or, if they do, offer other green features such as FSC-certified content. (Certification to Forest Stewardship Council—FSC—standards involves third-party evaluation and monitoring of sustainable forestry practices.) Phenol-formaldehyde binders, while not emitting as much formaldehyde as urea-formaldehyde binders, still may pose an indoor air quality concern.

Certified Engineered Wood

Standard Structures, Inc.
P.O. Box K
Santa Rosa, CA 95402

Toll-free: 800-862-4936
Phone: 707-836-8100
www.standardstructures.com

Standard Structures was the first manufacturer of certified engineered wood products. FSC-certified glulam beams, wood I-joists, and open-web trusses are available. The company uses conventional phenol resorcinol formaldehyde binders. With some products, special orders may be required for certified-wood fabrication.

Insul-Beam

Premier Building Systems - Division of Premier Industries, Inc.
4609 70th Ave. E
Fife, WA 98424

Toll-free: 800-275-7086
Phone: 253-926-2020
www.pbspanel.com

Insul-Beam is an insulated header with laminated veneer lumber facings and a core of EPS foam insulation. EPS may contain up to 15% recycled content. Insul-Beam can be used in place of site-fabricated headers and will improve building envelope energy performance. This product is available for 2x4, 2x6, and 2x8 framing in lengths up to 24'. Engineering data is available.

New TJI Joists

Trus Joist-Weyerhaeuser
200 E. Mallard Dr.
Boise, ID 83706

Toll-free: 800-338-0515
Phone: 208-364-1200
www.trusjoist.com

Trus Joist is a wooden I-joist with Timberstrand® LSL flanges, instead of LVL. Timberstrand is formaldehyde-free and is a more efficient conversion of log to lumber than LVL.

SWII Headers

Superior Wood Systems
1301 Garfield Ave.
P.O. Box 1208
Superior, WI 54880

Toll-free: 800-375-9992
Phone: 715-392-1822
www.swi-joist.com

SWII headers are engineered, insulated headers that deliver superior thermal performance when compared to solid-wood, site-fabricated headers. SWII headers consist of solid 2"-thick wood top and bottom chords and dual OSB web members that encase an EPS foam core. The SWII-62 Insulated Header insulates to R-18.

TimberStrand LSL Studs, Headers, and Rim Boards

Trus Joist-Weyerhaeuser
200 E. Mallard Dr.
Boise, ID 83706

Toll-free: 800-338-0515
Phone: 208-364-1200
www.trusjoist.com

Laminated Strand Lumber (LSL) is manufactured from fast-growing aspen and poplar trees that are debarked and shredded into strands. The strands are coated with a formaldehyde-free MDI (methyl diisocyanate) binder and pressed into huge billets that are milled into dimensional lumber. LSL lumber is very consistent and stable; it does not warp and twist like solid wood. Additional research will be needed to determine whether intensive utilization of aspen stands on 20-year rotations could be detrimental to long-term forest ecosystem health. However, the conversion rate from log to lumber is about twice that for conventionally sawn lumber. TimberStrand® LSL Studs, Headers, and Rim Boards are available in 2x4 and 2x6 studs and 2x10 Rim Boards up to 22' long. They are formaldehyde-free, dimensionally stable, and straighter than conventional lumber.

Expansion Joint Filler

see *Foundations, Footers, and Slabs: Expansion Joint Filler*

Exterior Wall Assemblies

Look for superior energy performance and use of FSC-certified wood and other green materials. (Certification to Forest Stewardship Council—FSC—standards involves third-party evaluation and monitoring of sustainable forestry practices.)

3-D Panel Construction System

3-D Panel Construction Systems
2610 Sidney Lanier Dr.
Ft. Myers, FL 33906

Phone: 912-264-3772
www.3-dpanelworks.com

The ICS 3-D Panel Construction System has a core of EPS foam insulation encased in reinforcing wire mesh that is field-coated with concrete.

Form Release Agents

see *Foundations, Footers, and Slabs: Form Release Agents*

Heavy Timber Construction

Log and heavy timber construction has significant appeal in North America for its rustic qualities. Though the embodied energy of wood is relatively low, heavy timber construction—such as in log houses—is rarely environmentally preferable compared with more conventional building systems. Conventional framing is more wood-efficient, and in most cases, results in a more energy-efficient building envelope. Products listed here have environmental features that separate them from conventional timber and log products.

EcoLog Homes

Haliburton Forest: EcoLog Concepts
Box 202, Kennisis Lake Rd.
R.R. 1
Haliburton, ON K0M 1S0 Canada

Phone: 705-754-4663
www.haliburtonforest.com

EcoLog Homes are built of certified hemlock logs from the 50,000-acre Haliburton Forest and Wildlife Reserve. The company's annual capacity is limited by the sustainable yield of the forest to 20 building kits per year.

Low Density Concrete

see *Foundations, Footers, and Slabs: Low Density Concrete*

Masonry Mortar

Look for masonry mortar products with high fly-ash content or little or no portland cement.

MRT E-Z Joint

MRT / Atlanta Distribution Center
319 McDonough Blvd.
Atlanta, GA 30315

Phone: 404-635-0050
www.mrtus.com

MRT E-Z Joint™ is a masonry cement that relies entirely on Type C fly ash for its hydraulic properties. MRT E-Z Joint cements consists of about 80% fly ash combined with various additives. Actual fly ash levels range from 75–85% for Type M cement to 50% for Type N. Some of these additives are standard in cement products, while others are more specialized and proprietary. The product is available in three formulations and performs very much like standard masonry cement but requires less water. It is available in a range

 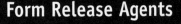

of colors by custom order. MRT E-Z Joint is currently only produced in the Atlanta area, but the company has plans for facilities in other areas as well. The company was previously known as Mineral Recycling Technologies, Inc.

St. Astier Natural Hydraulic Lime Mortar

TransMineral USA, Inc.
201 Purrington Rd.
Petaluma, CA 94952

Phone: 707-769-0661
www.limes.us

St. Astier Natural Hydraulic Lime, or NHL, is a 100% natural product that has been in production since 1851. St. Astier NHL Mortar is widely used in the restoration of old buildings. This natural hydraulic lime mortar imported from France allows stone to "breathe" naturally.

Metal Fastenings

Look for high recycled content in steel fasteners.

Maze Nails

Maze Nails
100 Church St.
Peru, IL 61354

Toll-free: 800-435-5949
www.mazenails.com

Maze Nails are made from domestic remelted steel in all standard and most specialty nail styles and sizes. Maze's Stormguard line of nails is galvanized with a double hot-dipped zinc coating for extra durability.

Metal-Web Wood Joists

Metal-web wood joists are lightweight, high-strength framing members that can provide long, clear spans and don't require drilling for mechanical and electrical systems. Metal-web wood joists are also very resource-efficient.

Open-Web Trusses

Trus Joist-Weyerhaeuser
200 E. Mallard Dr.
Boise, ID 83706

Toll-free: 800-338-0515
Phone: 208-364-1200
www.trusjoist.com

Trus Joist-Weyerhaeuser's open-web trusses are manufactured with solid-wood top and bottom chords and steel-tube web members. All trusses are custom-engineered and manufactured for specific applications.

Posi-Strut

MiTek Industries
14515 N. Outer 40 Dr., Ste. 300
Chesterfield, MO 63017

Toll-free: 800-325-8075
Phone: 314-434-1200
www.mitekinc.com

Posi-Struts offer a high-strength 20-gauge steel alternative to wood webs for floor joists and roof rafters; their open-web configuration eliminates the need for cutting and drilling, and they feature standard 2' o.c. spacing to cut down on cost and labor over conventional webs.

SpaceJoist

Jager Building Systems
#220, 6223 - 2nd St. SE
Calgary, AB T2H 1J5 Canada

Phone: 403-259-0727
www.jager.ca

The Jager SpaceJoist™ is a truss for wood-framed construction with solid-wood top and bottom flanges and open-metal web members. SpaceJoists can have trimmable, I-joist-type ends.

TrimJoist

TrimJoist
5146 Hwy. 182 E
P.O. Box 2286
Columbus, MS 39704

Toll-free: 800-844-8281
Phone: 662-327-7950
www.trimjoist.com

TrimJoist's open-web trusses are manufactured with solid-wood top and bottom chords and solid-wood web members joined with metal plate connectors. TrimJoists have trimmable, I-joist-type ends.

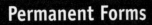

Permanent Forms

Insulating concrete forms (ICFs) provide a labor-efficient means of building insulated poured-concrete walls, floors, and roof decks. ICFs are permanent forms with integral insulation—they aren't disassembled after the concrete has cured. Most of these products are made from expanded polystyrene (EPS) foam produced with a non-ozone-depleting blowing agent. Other permanent forms are made from a composite of wood waste and cement or of EPS beads and cement. The environmental advantages of ICF walls include higher R-values and reduced concrete content compared with conventionally formed concrete walls. Be aware that the R-values claimed by ICF manufacturers are not arrived at in a consistent manner and may be misleading. For comparison purposes, "steady-state" R-values should be used when that information is available. Mass-enhanced or "effective" R-values are only relevant in certain climates or under certain conditions, but they're often listed in product literature. Some EPS foams used in ICFs contain borates to protect against possible damage from wood-boring insects. The brominated flame retardants used in most EPS foam have health and environmental risks that are generating significant concern.

Amazon Grid-Wall ICFs

Amazon Forms One, Inc.
19068 Marbach Ln.
San Antonio, TX 78266

Toll-free: 866-651-3322
Phone: 210-651-3322
www.amazongridwall.com

Amazon Grid-Wall™ is an insulated concrete form system made from polystyrene (85% by volume, 100% of which is post-consumer recycled) and cement. The standard form measures 4' long x 10" thick x 16" tall with 6" diameter voids running horizontally and vertically 16" o.c. Grid-Wall forms are dry stacked but must be spot glued with a polystyrene-compatible adhesive to keep the forms from shifting during the concrete pour. Grid-Wall does not require drywall on the interior; stucco can be applied to the exterior using only one coat and no wire lath. Grid-Wall forms are termite- and fire-resistant and can be molded with power tools or a rasp.

Arxx High Performance Wall System

Arxx Building Products
800 Division St.
Cobourg, ON K9A 5V2 Canada

Toll-free: 800-293-3210
Phone: 905-373-0004
www.arxxbuild.com

The standard ICF of the Arxx High Performance Wall System, formerly known as Blue Maxx™, is comprised of two $2^5/_8$"-thick EPS panels separated by 99% post-industrial recycled polypropylene plastic webbing on 8" centers. The webbing serves as strapping for attachment of interior and exterior finishes and as support for steel reinforcing rods within the wall. Each standard interlocking Arxx block is 4' long, $16^3/_4$" high, and $11^1/_2$" thick with a steady-state R-value of 22.1. Other thicknesses and configurations are available, as are a number of accessories that facilitate construction.

Baleblock System

Celestial Construction, Inc.
1599 Luisa St.
Santa Fe, NM 87505

Phone: 505-820-2818
www.baleblock.com

The Baleblock™ system uses straw bales with two predrilled 4" holes to form an insulating straw-bale wall with a "post-and-beam" reinforced-concrete structure.

Cempo Form

Cempo Forms, Inc.
P.O. Box 9300
Pahrump, NV 89060

Phone: 775-727-6565
www.cempo.com

Cempo Form is a 100% recycled EPS and cement-composite permanent form system. The standard forms are available in 8", 10", and 12" thicknesses in a 32" x 48" block (about 150 lbs.—most often chosen by owner-builders) and a 32" x 96" block (300 lbs.—more commonly used by contractors). Cempo Form can be easily worked with hand tools, and can be cut and shaped for a variety of details. The company is in the process of testing for R-value.

Durisol Wallforms

Durisol Building Systems Inc.
67 Frid St.
Hamilton, ON L8P 4M3
Canada

Phone: 905-521-0999
www.durisol.com

Durisol Wallforms are the original stay-in-place concrete forms introduced in 1945. They are made from a composite of mineralized wood chips and portland cement. Each wallform provides approximately 3 ft² of wall. Mineral wool insulation inserts are available in several sizes to provide steady-state R-values up to R-21. The structural design permits use in multistory buildings. The Durisol material can also be specified in custom shapes for use as precast noise-absorption panels, retaining walls, floor forms, and roof panels. The manufacturer has certified the following recycled-content levels (by weight): total recovered material 40% typical, 35% guaranteed; post-consumer material 0% typical, 0% guaranteed.

ECO-Block ICFs

ECO-Block, LLC
11220 Grader St.,
   Ste. 700
Dallas, TX 75238

Toll-free: 800-503-0901
Phone: 214-503-1644
www.eco-block.com

Eco-Block® EPS ICFs have embedded HDPE webs that serve as recessed furring strips on the exterior of the units and as attachment points for snap-on 100% recycled polypropylene connectors on the interior. Connectors of 4", 6", or 8" can be used singly or spliced together, allowing for concrete thicknesses from 4" to 24" (in varying increments). Eco-Blocks have an R-value of 22 based upon 5" of EPS in the wall profile. The Eco-Block system includes flaring brick ledge panels and is also amenable to tilt-up construction with insulation on one side only. ICF blocks are shipped compactly and assembled on-site.

Faswall Wallforms

K-X Faswall Corp.
P.O. Box 180
Windsor, SC 29865

Toll-free: 800-491-7891
Phone: 803-642-9346
www.faswall.com

Faswall® is a fiber-cement block ICF. These ICFs are made of cement with optional fly ash content and K-X Aggregate (waste wood chips treated with mineral solutions to improve durability and cementitious bonding). A standard wallform block measures 16" x 8" x 11$\frac{1}{2}$" with a 6"-deep core and weighs 22 lbs. Split-double, large-core, and corner wallforms are also available.

Greenblock

Greenblock Worldwide Corp.
P.O. Box 749
Woodland Park, CO 80866

Toll-free: 800-216-1820
Phone: 719-687-0645
www.greenblock.com

Greenblock™ is an insulating concrete form made from EPS and held together by plastic webs for structural integrity and minimal thermal bridging. Greenblocks have 2" of foam on the interior side of the block and 2$\frac{1}{2}$" on the exterior side. Greenblock forms have been used in Europe for over 30 years.

ICF Block System

ICF Industries, Inc.
570 S. Dayton - Lakeview Rd.
New Carlisle, OH 45344

Toll-free: 877-423-4800
Phone: 937-845-8347
www.iceblock.net

The ICF Block™ System utilizes 16" x 48" x 9$\frac{1}{4}$"-wide (or 11"-wide) EPS foam blocks with 6" (or 8") concrete cores. Steel studs are embedded on 12" centers within the blocks to facilitate attachment of interior and exterior finishes. Thermal bridging is minimized because the studs are not exposed on the exterior of the EPS block. ICF Industries was formerly I.C.E. Block Building Systems, and the product was known as I.C.E. Block™.

Insulated Concrete Forms

Pacemaker Plastics Co., Inc.
126 New Pace Rd.
P.O. Box 279
Newcomerstown, OH 43832-0279

Toll-free: 800-446-2188
Phone: 740-498-4181
www.pacemakerplastics.com

Pacemaker Plastics Company manufactures a UL- and code-listed expanded polystyrene foam ICF system that results in wall thicknesses of 4" to 12".

Insul-Deck ICFs for Floors, Roofs, and Walls

Insul-Deck®
7000 Houston Rd.,
   Bldg. 100, Ste. 3
Florence, KY 41042

Toll-free: 800-475-6720
Phone: 859-525-6720
www.insul-deck.org

Insul-Deck® is an interlocking ICF for joisted concrete floors, roofs, tilt-walls, and pre-cast walls. Molded from EPS with integral steel functioning as support beams and receptors for drywall attachment, Insul-Deck can span up to 30' or more, allowing for clear-span basements. Integral channels (approximately 4$\frac{3}{4}$" in diameter) for utility lines enable ducting within the insulated space and improved energy performance. Panels are available in any length, with variable thicknesses for R-values from 16 to 34. According to the manufacturer, the finished Insul-Deck system is 30–40% lighter than comparable poured-in-place slab floor systems and provides the same load capacity.

IntegraSpec ICF

Phil-Insul Corp.
735 Arlington Park Pl.,
    Unit 11U
Kingston, ON K7M 8M8
Canada

Toll-free: 800-382-9102
Phone: 613-634-1319
www.integraspec.com

IntegraSpec® ICF consists of two $2^1/_2$"-thick interlocking expanded polystyrene form panels (48" long x $12^1/_4$" high) held together with ABS plastic spacers of 4", 6", or 8" to create insulated concrete walls with corresponding concrete core thicknesses. The spacers can be combined to increase core thickness and also function as furring strips/studs. The completely reversible panels are shipped flat. IntegraSpec ICF has an R-value of 22+ per ASHRAE Fundamentals (1997) and is manufactured in both Canada and the U.S.

Keeva ICFs

Keeva International, Inc.
4615 E. Sierra Morena St.
Mesa, AZ 85215

Phone: 480-855-6641
www.keeva.com

Keeva International insulated concrete forms are molded from expanded polystyrene. The standard interlocking form weighs 3 lbs. and measures 8" x 12" x 48" with six 5" x 5" vertical cavities allowing for vertical concrete columns 8", 16", or 24" on center. These are combined with the company's Lintel form, which contains horizontal channels, to form a post-and-beam-like concrete assembly. Little bracing is necessary. The company reports an R-value of 20.4 and claims to require 35–65% less concrete than other ICF systems. Finish materials are attached to metal furring strips installed on the surface of the forms.

Lite-Form and Fold-Form

Lite-Form International
1950 W. 29th St.
So. Sioux City, NE 68776

Toll-free: 800-551-3313
www.liteform.com

Owens Corning's Lite-Form ICFs are comprised of two rigid-foam planks measuring 8' x 8" x 2" held together by plastic spacer ties that can be sized to offer concrete thicknesses from 4" to 24" (in 2" increments). Lite-Form is available in EPS or XPS foam. Only the EPS is being specified here. Owens Corning's Fold-Form is an interlocking, foldable ICF. The forms are made from two 1' x 4' x 2" sheets of rigid EPS foam insulation held together with plastic spacer ties. Fold-Form folds flat for more compact shipping and storage. Form widths are available to create concrete thicknesses of 4" to 16" (also in 2" increments). Both Lite-Form and Fold-Form

have calculated R-values of 26 for finished walls. In-Wall bracing is available for all walls over 4' in height.

Pentstar Concrete Form Masonry Units

Pentstar, Corp.
7308 Aspen Ln. N, Ste. 114
Minneapolis, MN 55428

Toll-free: 877-645-9704
Phone: 763-315-9342
www.pentstar.com

Pentstar® Concrete Form Masonry Units, a hybrid of unit masonry and ICF construction, are comprised of two masonry faces tied together by post-industrial recycled reinforced nylon connectors. Between the two masonry faces (starting on the outside) is a 1" dead-air space weep cavity and 2" of rigid foam (EPS or Celotex) that creates a $5^1/_2$" cavity for the concrete pour. The units are designed to be laid up with mortar, creating a hollow form that works like an ICF. With the insulation to the outside of the concrete pour and inner masonry, thermal mass effects are a significant part of the wall's thermal performance. An additional benefit is that the forms can also serve as the finish on both exterior and interior surfaces.

Perform Wall Panels

Perform Wall, LLC
5776 N. Mesa
El Paso, TX 79912

Toll-free: 888-727-8725
Phone: 915-587-8885
www.performwall.com

Perform Wall Panels are made from 85% (by volume) post-consumer EPS and 15% Portland cement molded into 8.5"-, 10"-, 12"-, and 14"-thick blocks. Flat stock is available in 2" or 4" thicknesses. Because of the insulating beads, the insulating value is considerably higher than that for concrete alone. Perform Wall claims R-11 for a finished 10" standard block wall.

PolySteel Forms

American PolySteel, LLC
5150 Edith Blvd. NE, Ste. F
Albuquerque, NM 87107

Toll-free: 800-977-3676
Phone: 505-345-8153
www.polysteel.com

American PolySteel manufactures a variety of ICF products utilizing expanded polystyrene foam form pieces and steel connectors/attachment studs rather than the much more common plastic ties. In 2002 the company reconfigured its forms so that the steel connectors are now recessed $1/_2$" below the surface of the form, thereby improving thermal performance. PolySteel manufactures both a "waffle-grid" and "flat-wall" form, as well as an insulated concrete deck form. The company also incorporates AFM Corporation's Perform Guard® borate treatment in their forms to protect against insect damage.

Premier ICFs

Insulfoam (Division of Premier Industries, Inc.)
1019 Pacific Ave., Ste. 1501
Tacoma, WA 98402

Toll-free: 800-248-5995
Phone: 253-572-5111
www.insulfoam.com

Insulfoam manufactures interlocking insulated concrete forms from expanded polystyrene (EPS) containing up to 15% post-consumer recycled content. The forms are borate-treated for insect resistance. No assembly of individual forms is required. The company claims an average R-value of 27 (minimum R-20, but with 30% of the wall a solid $9^1/_2$" of EPS at R-45, Insulfoam calculates an average of approximately R-27). The company manufactures ICFs at their plants in Alaska, California, Washington, and Nebraska and accepts EPS scrap from its larger customers. The manufacturer has certified the following recycled-content levels (by weight): total recovered material 15% typical, 10% guaranteed; post-consumer material 15% typical, 10% guaranteed.

QUAD-LOCK ICFs

QUAD-LOCK Building Systems Ltd.
7398 - 132nd St.
Surrey, BC V3W 4M7 Canada

Toll-free: 888-711-LOCK
Phone: 604-590-3111
www.quadlock.com

The QUAD-LOCK® Solid Concrete Wall System is an interlocking expanded polystyrene (EPS) ICF system. EPS panels are 12" high, 48" long, and can be either $2^1/_4$" or $4^1/_4$" thick. The panels are joined with HDPE plastic connectors to create walls of nominal 4", 6", 8", 10", or 12" thickness (thicker walls can be accomplished by tying together any variation of connectors). The company claims an R-value of 21.7 for the $2^1/_4$" panels.

R-Control ICF System

Advance Foam Plastics, Inc. - California Division
748 N. McKeever Ave.
Azusa, CA 91702

Phone: 626-334-5358
www.afprcontrol.com

Advance Foam Plastics is a licensed manufacturer of AFM Corporation's R-Control® ICF System. The R-Control system consists of 1' x 8' R-Control PerformGuard® insect-resistant EPS foam panels joined by plastic form ties on 12" centers. Ties vary in length to create 4", 6", 8", and 10" walls with a nominal R-value of 20.

R-Control ICF System

Advance Foam Plastics, Inc. - Colorado Division
5250 N. Sherman St.
Denver, CO 80216

Toll-free: 800-525-8697
Phone: 303-297-3844
www.afprcontrol.com

Advance Foam Plastics is a licensed manufacturer of AFM Corporation's R-Control® ICF System. The R-Control system consists of 1' x 8' R-Control PerformGuard® insect-resistant EPS foam panels joined by plastic form ties on 12" centers. Ties vary in length to create 4", 6", 8", and 10" walls with a nominal R-value of 20.

R-Control ICF System

Advance Foam Plastics, Inc. - Nevada Division
920 Kleppe Ln.
Sparks, NV 89431

Toll-free: 800-444-9290
Phone: 775-355-7655
www.afprcontrol.com

Advance Foam Plastics is a licensed manufacturer of AFM Corporation's R-Control® ICF System. The R-Control system consists of 1' x 8' R-Control PerformGuard® insect-resistant EPS foam panels joined by plastic form ties on 12" centers. Ties vary in length to create 4", 6", 8", and 10" walls with a nominal R-value of 20.

R-Control ICF System

Advance Foam Plastics, Inc. - Utah Division
111 W. Fireclay Ave.
Murray, UT 84107

Toll-free: 877-775-8847
Phone: 801-265-3465
www.afprcontrol.com

Advance Foam Plastics is a licensed manufacturer of AFM Corporation's R-Control® ICF System. The R-Control system consists of 1' x 8' R-Control PerformGuard® insect-resistant EPS foam panels joined by plastic form ties on 12" centers. Ties vary in length to create 4", 6", 8", and 10" walls with a nominal R-value of 20.

R-Control ICF System

Big Sky Insulations, Inc.
P.O. Box 838
Belgrade, MT 59714

Toll-free: 800-766-3626
Phone: 406-388-4146
www.bsiinc.com

Big Sky Insulations is a licensed manufacturer of AFM Corporation's R-Control® ICF System. The R-Control system consists of 1' x 8' R-Control PerformGuard® insect-resistant EPS foam panels joined by plastic form ties on 12" centers. Ties vary in length to create 4", 6", 8", and 10" walls with a nominal R-value of 20.

R-Control ICF System

Stanark Foam / R-CONTROL
10101 Hwy. 70 E
N. Little Rock, AR 72117

Toll-free: 800-632-4586
Phone: 501-945-1114
www.stanark.com

Stanark Foam is a licensed manufacturer of AFM Corporation's R-Control® ICF System. The R-Control system consists of 1' x 8' R-Control PerformGuard® insect-resistant EPS foam panels joined by plastic form ties on 12" centers. Ties vary in length to create 4", 6", 8", and 10" walls with a nominal R-value of 20.

Reddi-Deck Floor and Roof-Deck ICFs

Reddi Form, Inc.
10 Park Pl., Ste. 5-B
Butler, NJ 07405

Toll-free: 800-334-4303
www.reddiform.com

Reddi-Deck™ is a stay-in-place, self-supporting insulating concrete forming system for joisted concrete floor and roof decks. The Reddi-Deck panels are produced by a continuous molding production line integrating the insulating capabilities of EPS with the structural strength of metal inserts. According to the manufacturer, the systems are half the weight of comparable hollow-core, precast systems, which in turn reduces the load on walls and foundations.

Reward Wall Systems

Reward Wall Systems, Inc.
9931 S. 136th St., #100
Omaha, NE 68138-3936

Toll-free: 800-468-6344
Phone: 402-592-7077
www.rewardwalls.com

Reward Wall Systems manufactures two complete and diverse lines of insulating concrete forms—the iForm™ flat wall form and the eForm™ waffle grid form. Both forms are used in residential and commercial structures including large-scale high-rise projects. Reward's iForm is made from two 2.4"-thick premolded 48" x 16" slabs of EPS held together with plastic ties that are embedded in the EPS. The ties provide strength while the concrete is poured and serve as a nailing surface for interior and exterior finishes such as drywall and siding. The forms remain in place and become part of the wall providing a steady-state R-value of 22. Reward's eForm, with an interior waffle-grid configuration, is available with pre-formed 90° and 45° corners. According to the manufacturer, eForm can save up to 30% on concrete costs over flat wall forms.

SAFE Block

DuraBuild
2303 R.R. 6205 S, Ste. 135-373
Lakeway, TX 78734

Phone: 512-844-4414

SAFE Block™, formerly TechBLOC™, offers an ICF system providing 2½" of EPS insulation for both inner and outer surfaces. SAFE Block comes in 48" x 16" panels attached by plastic connectors to give concrete thicknesses of 4", 6", 8", 10", or 12". The inserted connectors can also serve as fastening points for interior drywall and exterior finishes.

SmartBlock

American ConForm
  Industries, Inc.
7231 Garden Grove Blvd.,
  Ste. L
Garden Grove, CA 92841

Toll-free: 800-266-3676
Phone: 714-662-1100
www.smartblock.com

SmartBlocks, made from EPS, are available to form a solid concrete wall in 4", 6", 8", 10", and 12" nominal sizes or as a screen concrete wall measuring 40" x 10" x 10" with a 6½" wide (standard size) post-and-beam concrete-core structure. SmartBlock walls possess superior acoustic insulation and use plastic connectors with 25% recycled content. American ConForm claims R-22 to R-24 insulation values.

Standard ICFs

Standard ICFs
7 Prebles Way
Gray, ME 04039

Toll-free: 888-584-3766
Phone: 207-657-2222
www.standardicf.com

Standard ICF Corporation®, formerly Therm-O-Wall, manufactures the 895 ICFs™ System. The system consists primarily of two forms; a standard form made from two 2⅜"-thick EPS panels separated by recycled-HDPE plastic brackets; and a corner form of the same materials. Standard panels are 48" L x 16" H x 11¼" W, providing for a concrete thickness of 6½". The imbedded brackets are placed 12" on center and also function as furring strips for finish material attachment. The company claims an R-value of 26.

Tech Block

Tech Block International, LLC
1315 E. Gibson Ln., B-2
Phoenix, AZ 85034

Phone: 602-254-5414
www.techblock.com

Tech Blocks are patented exterior wall blocks composed of a mixture of polystyrene beads and cement paste. Bonded to the blocks is ³/₄" OSB, which becomes the inside surface of the wall and acts as an attachment surface for drywall. Underneath the drywall, the OSB acts as backing for hanging cabinetry, drape hardware, base, casing, etc. The exterior of the blocks is ready for stucco without the need for wire mesh. The Tech Block Wall System resists fire, sound, water, and termites. Each Tech Block weighs about 85 lbs. and measures 48" x 16" x 11" thick, with a steady-state R-value of 35+, according to the manufacturer. Tech Block International, LLC, is an ENERGY STAR® Partner with plants in Arizona, California, and Georgia, and has plans for plants in Texas and New Mexico.

TF System Vertical ICFs

Wisconsin Thermo-Form, Inc.
185 E. Walnut
Sturgeon Bay, WI 54235

Toll-free: 800-360-4634
Phone: 920-746-9100
www.tfsystem.com

Wisconsin Thermo-Form, an ENERGY STAR® Homes Ally, manufactures the TF System™ of unique, vertically oriented insulated concrete forms. This system utilizes a standard 2¹/₂" x 12" x 8' expanded polystyrene plank (or custom planks variable in height up to 12') and preformed corner planks. The planks are joined by 26-gauge galvanized steel I-Beam studs, which enable planks to slide up to allow access to the inside of the forms until a top cap is installed. Wall thicknesses of 4", 6", 8", 10", and 12" are possible, with the company claiming an R-value of 25. Forms are shipped flat. Bracing requirements are minimal, and compressive strength allows for the installation of floor systems before pouring.

Thermal Foams TF ICF

Thermal Foams, Inc.
2101 Kenmore Ave.
Buffalo, NY 14207

Phone: 716-874-6474
www.thermalfoams.com

Thermal Foams Inc. is an authorized manufacturer/distributor of the TF Insulated Concrete Building System. The TF ICF system is a vertical plank system that consists of Thermal Foams EPS foam panels joined together with metal I-beams that vary in height and are available in widths to create 4", 6", 8", 10", and 12" walls with a nominal R-value of 22.

Precast Concrete

Precast structural concrete products speed construction and often lead to lower environmental damage on the construction site (compared to pouring concrete on-site). Waste from overage is also eliminated through precasting at a plant. Through aeration, the weight of precast concrete components can often be reduced by up to a third, significantly reducing structural loading requirements and material use in high-rise buildings. Aerated concrete also insulates better, which can be a factor in some applications. Substitution of fly ash or other post-industrial waste materials can further improve environmental performance.

Superior Walls

Superior Walls of America, Ltd.
937 East Earl Rd.
New Holland, PA 17557

Toll-free: 800-452-9255
www.superiorwalls.com

Superior Walls™ is a custom precast foundation wall system with integrated footer, concrete "studs," and bond beam that is insulated at the factory with extruded polystyrene (currently made with ozone-depleting HCFC-141b). Superior Wall Panels are lifted by crane into place and locked together. The R-5 line has 1" of rigid insulation to achieve an R-value of 5, which may be increased with additional insulation to R-24. The Xi line has 2¹/₂" of rigid insulation for R-12.5, which may be increased with additional insulation to R-31.5.

Preservative-Treated Wood and Treatment Products

The durability of preservative-treated wood is the most important advantage to its use. Extending the service life of wood products reduces the demands on forests for replacement timber. As of January 2004, sales of lumber treated with the preservative CCA (chromated copper arsenate) were banned for consumer applications. Disposal by incineration is the most significant environmental concern associated with the billions of board feet already in use that were treated with this preservative: toxins such as arsenic may become airborne, and those that don't get into the air end up in the ash, where they're highly leachable. Less toxic applications such as ACQ (ammoniacal copper quaternary) and CBA (copper boron azole) are available. For wood that isn't exposed to weather, borate-based preservatives are effective against insects while being much less toxic than other chemicals. Wood treated with the copper-based ACQ and CBA should be avoided near aquatic ecosystems, since copper is highly toxic to many aquatic organisms. Note that ACQ-treated wood is more corrosive to steel fasteners than CCA-treated wood; follow manufacturers' recommendations for fastener selection.

ACQ Preserve Treated Wood

Chemical Specialties, Inc.
200 E. Woodlawn Rd., Ste. 250
Charlotte, NC 28217

Toll-free: 800-421-8661
Phone: 704-522-0825
www.treatedwood.com

Preserve® pressure-treated wood is protected against rot, decay, and termite damage with ACQ® (alkaline copper and quarternary ammonium compounds). ACQ Preserve, like conventional CCA-treated wood, can be used for a variety of applications in above-ground or ground-contact applications where protection from fungal decay and termites is required. Preserve Plus®, offering superior water resistance, is also available. Preserve is the oldest of several recently introduced alternatives to CCA-treated wood, which do not use arsenic or chromium. Because of the toxicity of copper to aquatic organisms and because ACQ may leach out of the wood, recycled-plastic lumber and wood-plastic composite lumber products are preferable near aquatic ecosystems. Preserve wood scraps and cut-offs should be disposed of in landfills in accordance with local, state, and federal regulations.

Advance Guard

Osmose Wood Preserving, Inc.
P.O. Box O
Griffin, GA 30224

Toll-free: 800-241-0240
www.osmose.com

Osmose introduced Advance Guard™ lumber and plywood pressure-treated with Tim-Bor® sodium-borate in 2000. The product was developed to deal with the growing problem of termites—especially Formosan termites in the southern U.S. and Hawaii. Advance Guard can be used for framing houses, though it costs significantly more than untreated lumber. The product is being co-marketed with LP's SmartGuard line of zinc borate-treated OSB sheathing and siding products and a special formulation of Cocoon cellulose insulation. Advance Guard treated lumber is offered with a 20-year limited warranty.

LifeTime

Valhalla Wood Preservatives, Ltd.
PO Box 328
Salt Spring Is., BC V8K2R7 Canada

Phone: 250-538-5516
www.valhalco.com

Valhalla claims LifeTime wood treatment as a nontoxic family recipe that outperforms pressure-treated wood. LifeTime, which can also be used as a wood stain, is packaged as a powder for mixing with water to create an acidic solution that can be applied by roller, brush, or sprayer. Some prominent green building experts have reported good success with LifeTime, though comprehensive test results have not been made available.

NatureWood

Osmose Wood Preserving, Inc.
P.O. Box O
Griffin, GA 30224

Toll-free: 800-241-0240
www.osmose.com

Osmose uses copper oxide and quaternary compounds dissolved in an alkaline carrier to produce NatureWood®, an alternative to CCA-treated wood products that is made without chromium or arsenic. NatureWood is approved by the American Wood Preservers' Association for use in above-ground and ground-contact applications. The company offers a limited-lifetime, nontransferable warranty for farm and residential use. Due to the leachability of copper into water, use of NatureWood should be avoided in wetlands and around surface waters.

Tim-Bor and Bora-Care

Nisus Corporation
100 Nisus Dr.
Rockford, TN 37853

Toll-free: 800-264-0870
Phone: 865-577-6119
www.nisuscorp.com

Bora-Care® is a boron-based wood treatment that protects against termites, carpenter ants, wood-destroying beetles, and decay fungi. Bora-Care contains glycol for deeper penetration of the boron into the wood. Bora-Care has low toxicity to people but is highly toxic to beetle larvae.

Tim-Bor®, formerly offered by U.S. Borax, is a similar wood preservative except that it does not contain glycol. Borate products are not effective in damp or wet areas. Despite research efforts, no effective means has been found to keep borate preservatives from leaching out of wet wood. Overall, Tim-Bor is a very safe product appropriate for use throughout buildings and where toxic CCA-treated wood is commonly used in regions of the country prone to termite infestations. Nisus is currently pursuing research on a product designed to prevent the leaching of borates from Bora-Care and Tim-Bor.

Wolmanized Natural Select Wood

Arch Treatment Technologies, Inc.
1955 Lake Park Dr., Ste. 250
Smyrna, GA 30080

Phone: 770-801-6600
www.wolmanizedwood.com

Arch Treatment Technologies manufactures copper azole; a non-arsenic, nonchromium replacement for CCA. Pressure-treated wood produced with copper azole is being marketed under the name Natural Select™ and manufactured by independent licensed manufacturers around the country. Natural Select wood, which is browner in color than CCA-treated woods, is approved for above-ground and soil-contact applications and comes with a limited lifetime warranty in most residential and agricultural applications.

Reclaimed Lumber and Timbers

As the demands on forest resources have increased, nonforest sources of wood have grown in importance. Reclaimed wood is usually salvaged from buildings slated for demolition, abandoned railroad trestles, and "sinker logs" that sank decades ago during river-based log drives. It can also be obtained from trees that have been recently harvested from urban or suburban areas (such as disease-killed trees). Reclaimed wood is often available in species, coloration, and wood quality that is no longer available today in newly harvested timber. In some cases, reclaimed wood suppliers have only limited quantities with matching coloration or weathering patterns; ample lead time and accurate materials estimates can help ensure the availability of the desired wood. Lowering the uniformity standards for finished wood can also increase the potential for use of reclaimed wood. Environmentally desirable because it isn't tied to recent timber harvesting, use of reclaimed wood can also reduce the quantity of material going into landfills. As with other resources, the supply of reclaimed wood is limited. Efficient and appropriate use of reclaimed wood is important for its long-term availability.

Barnwood and Hand-Hewn Beams

Conklin's Authentic Antique Barnwood
R.R. 1, Box 70
Susquehanna, PA 18847

Phone: 570-465-3832
www.conklinsbarnwood.com

Conklin's Authentic Antique Barnwood sells hand-hewn beams and barn boards in both "as is" and remilled condition.

Reclaimed Hand-Hewn Beams

Chestnut Specialists, Inc.
400 Harwinton Ave.
Plymouth, CT 06782

Phone: 860-283-4209
www.chestnutspec.com

Chestnut Specialists, Inc. dismantles buildings and offers the reclaimed timbers for sale. Products include rough timber and original planks, hand-hewn barn beams, and weathered barn siding, either remilled or in their original milled or hand-hewn condition.

Reclaimed Hand-Hewn Beams

Safe Solutions, LLC
166 Malden Tpke.
Saugerties, NY 12477

Phone: 845-246-3622
www.safesolutionsllc.com

Safe Solutions sells antique hand-hewn beams from disassembled barns. Species include oak, chestnut, walnut, maple, and other hardwoods.

Reclaimed Lumber

Pinocchio's
18651 Hare Creek Ter.
Fort Bragg, CA 95437

Phone: 707-964-6272
www.mcn.org/b/rmoore/

Pinocchio's offers raw and remilled lumber from Douglas fir and redwood in both standard-dimension and custom sizes.

Reclaimed Lumber

TerraMai
1104 Firenze
P.O. Box 696
McCloud, CA 96057

Toll-free: 800-220-9062
Phone: 530-964-2740
www.terramai.com

TerraMai (formerly Jefferson Recycled Woodworks) stocks reclaimed Douglas fir, redwood, ponderosa pine, sugar pine, oak, and red cedar among its 700,000-board-foot inventory. All of TerraMai's varied products are reclaimed. Milling and grading services are available.

Reclaimed Lumber and Timbers

Antique Woods & Colonial Restorations, Inc.
121 Quarry Rd.
Gouverneur, NY 13642

Toll-free: 888-261-4284
www.vintagewoods.com

Antique Woods & Colonial Restorations, Inc. (formerly Vintage Barns, Woods & Restorations) sells reclaimed and remilled wood products including flooring, siding, and whole barn frames.

Reclaimed Lumber and Timbers

Big Timberworks, Inc.
P.O. Box 368
Gallatin Gateway, MT 59730

Phone: 406-763-4639
www.bigtimberworks.com

Big Timberworks offers custom-milled, reclaimed lumber and timbers in a variety of species. The company specializes in shipping timber frame houses all over the country for supervised construction but also sells custom-cut, reclaimed wood from their sawmill in Montana.

Reclaimed Lumber and Timbers

Black's Farmwood
P.O. Box 2836
San Rafael, CA 94912

Toll-free: 877-321-WOOD
Phone: 415-499-8300
www.blacksfarmwood.com

Black's Farmwood sells reclaimed wood products from deconstructed buildings and river bottoms. Products are available in a variety of species and include salvaged timbers and beams, remilled flooring, and barn siding. The company has a showroom in Lucas Valley and uses two mills, one in Kentucky and another in New York.

Reclaimed Lumber and Timbers

Caldwell Building Wreckers
195 Bayshore Blvd.
San Francisco, CA 94124

Phone: 415-550-6777
www.caldwell-bldg-salvage.com

Caldwell Building Wreckers salvages a wide variety of building products including lumber, beams, and timbers. The company also offers custom remilling.

Reclaimed Lumber and Timbers

Centre Mills Antique Floors
P.O. Box 16
Aspers, PA 17304

Phone: 717-334-0249
www.centremillsantiquefloors.com

Centre Mills Antique Floors salvages and remills a variety of hand-hewn wood products made from such species such as chestnut, oak, white pine, and hemlock. Centre Mills also has 7 acres of architectural artifacts containing bricks, mantles, wavy glass, old doors, and used slates.

Reclaimed Lumber and Timbers

Craftmark Reclaimed Wood, Inc.
P.O. Box 237
McMinnville, OR 97128

Phone: 503-472-6929
www.craftmarkinc.com

Craftmark Reclaimed Wood offers reclaimed timber and beam packages in a variety of species, including Douglas fir, heart pine, and white oak, typically salvaged from deconstructed warehouse buildings that are 70–100 years old.

Reclaimed Lumber and Timbers

Crossroads Recycled Lumber
57839 Road 225
P.O. Box 928
North Fork, CA 93643

Toll-free: 888-842-3201
Phone: 559-877-3645
www.crossroadslumber.com

Crossroads Recycled Lumber sells raw and remilled salvaged Douglas fir, sugar pine, ponderosa pine, cedar, and redwood lumber, timbers, and beams.

Reclaimed Lumber and Timbers

D. Litchfield & Co. Ltd.
3046 Westwood St.
Port Coquitlam, BC V3C 3L7 Canada

Toll-free: 877-303-2222
Phone: 604-464-7525
www.dlitchfield.com

Litchfield carries a large, steady supply of all types of reclaimed lumber and beams salvaged through their deconstruction operations.

Reclaimed Lumber and Timbers

Endura Wood Products, Ltd.
1303 S.E. 6th Ave.
Portland, OR 97214

Phone: 503-233-7090
www.endurawood.com

Endura Wood Products currently has access to over 3.5 million board feet of Douglas fir that is being reclaimed from the old Portland Dry Dock #2. Also available is a limited supply of Douglas fir with a distinct red hue that has been reclaimed from maraschino cherry vats.

Reclaimed Lumber and Timbers

J. Hoffman Lumber Co.
1330 E. State St.
Sycamore, IL 60178

Phone: 630-513-6680

J. Hoffman Lumber Co. is the Midwest's only sawmill/millwork company specializing in reclaimed antique heart pine, Douglas fir, and white pine.

Reclaimed Lumber and Timbers

Legacy Antique Woods
114 Sibley Rd.
Honeoye Falls, NY 14472

Phone: 585-624-1011
www.legacyantiquewoods.com

Legacy Antique Woods salvages timbers, boards, and decking from barns and industrial buildings. Material can be purchased "as is" or resawn into boardstock or molder blanks. Primary species offered are chestnut, oak, Douglas fir, heart pine, and white pine with other species typically available as well.

Reclaimed Lumber and Timbers

Longleaf Lumber
70–80 Webster Ave.
Somerville, MA 02143

Phone: 617-625-3659
www.longleaflumber.com

Longleaf Lumber, founded in 1997, dismantles old buildings and remills antique timbers into millwork and flooring at the company's sawmill in the Boston area. Longleaf specializes in heart pine, but other salvaged woods such as chestnut, red and white oak, eastern white pine, and maple are often available from buildings dismantled in various locations around the New England region. Longleaf also sells unmilled reclaimed timbers and reclaimed barn siding. In addition to the sawmill, the company operates a retail store at their Webster Avenue location.

Reclaimed Lumber and Timbers

Maxwell Pacific
P.O. Box 4127
Malibu, CA 90264

Phone: 310-457-4533

Maxwell Pacific, primarily a wholesaler of reclaimed wood products, also offers reclaimed flooring, lumber, and timbers for sale to contractors.

Reclaimed Lumber and Timbers

Michael Evenson Natural Resources
P.O. Box 157
Petrolia, CA 95558

Phone: 707-629-3679
www.oldgrowthtimbers.com

Natural Resources dismantles buildings and remills salvaged lumber for resale. Available species include redwood, Douglas fir, and western red cedar.

Reclaimed Lumber and Timbers

Mountain Lumber
P.O. Box 289
Ruckersville, VA 22968

Toll-free: 800-445-2671
www.mountainlumber.com

Mountain Lumber reclaims timbers from buildings slated for demolition and ships them to their mill in Virginia for remilling into wide-plank flooring, beams, and architectural millwork. They specialize in heart pine, oak, and American chestnut.

Reclaimed Lumber and Timbers

R. W. Rhine Inc.
1124 112th St. E
Tacoma, WA 98445

Toll-free: 800-963-8270
Phone: 253-531-7223

R. W. Rhine stocks a wide variety of salvaged lumber and beams supplied by its extensive deconstruction operations.

Reclaimed Lumber and Timbers

Re-Tech Wood Products
1324 Russell Rd.
P.O. Box 215
Forks, WA 98331

Phone: 360-374-4141
www.retechwoodproducts.com

Re-Tech reclaims and remills timber for a wide variety of custom millwork and complete custom timber frame packages for houses. They also make specialty cuts in timber to order.

Reclaimed Lumber and Timbers

Resource Woodworks, Inc.
627 E. 60th St.
Tacoma, WA 98404

Phone: 253-474-3757
www.rw-timber.com

Resource Woodworks specializes in Douglas fir and redwood timbers salvaged from demolition projects and remilled to custom specifications.

Reclaimed Lumber and Timbers

Vintage Material Supply Co.
4705 E. 5th St.
Austin, TX 78702

Phone: 512-386-6404
www.vintagematerialsupply.com

Vintage Material Supply Co. offers "as is" and remilled salvaged post-and-beam frames, hand-hewn beams, large timbers, and dimensional lumber recovered from such sources as demolished buildings, ranch recovery, urban logging, and river bottoms. Species include old-growth longleaf pine, cypress, white oak, fir, mesquite, and walnut. The company also offers consulting services in vintage wood reclamation.

Reclaimed Lumber and Timbers

Vintage Timberworks
47100 Rainbow Canyon Rd.
Temecula, CA 92592

Phone: 909-695-1003
www.vintagetimber.com

Vintage Timberworks offers a wide range of reclaimed wood products salvaged from buildings in the U.S., Canada, and Australia that are typically at least 70 years old. Reclaimed timber and beams are available in a variety of species and are offered "as is," remilled, and/or refinished (distressed, hand-hewed, sandblasted, etc.). The company also can arrange for building demolition and material reclamation.

Reclaimed Lumber and Timbers

What Its Worth, Inc.
P.O. Box 162135
Austin, TX 78716

Phone: 512-328-8837
www.wiwpine.com

What Its Worth can provide reclaimed longleaf yellow pine and Douglas fir to custom specs. Their milled product is 100% heartwood, and the wood's harvesting usually predates 1925.

Reclaimed Lumber Trestlewood Division

Heartwood Industries
3658 State Road 1414
Hartford, KY 42347

Toll-free: 800-318-9439
Phone: 270-298-0084
www.whiskeywood.com

Heartwood is an international distributor of dimension lumber and timbers salvaged from warehouses and whiskey distilleries. They specialize in flooring but also offer custom millwork and moldings in longleaf yellow pine, oak, chestnut, and cypress.

Reclaimed Timbers

Duluth Timber Co.
P.O. Box 16717
Duluth, MN 55816-0717

Phone: 218-727-2145
www.duluthtimber.com

Duluth Timber reclaims and remills mainly Douglas fir and longleaf yellow pine, but also redwood and cypress. Demolition and salvage of warehouses and sheep-shearing sheds in Australia has yielded a supply of Australian hardwoods such as jarrah and Mountain ash. Duluth has mills in Minnesota, California, and Washington.

Reclaimed Timbers and Millwork

Pioneer Millworks
1180 Commercial Dr.
Farmington, NY 14425

Toll-free: 800-951-9663
Phone: 585-924-9970
www.pioneermillworks.com

Pioneer Millworks salvages timbers and remills Douglas fir, longleaf yellow pine, oak, redwood, chestnut, and white pine. They offer a number of molding profiles in addition to timbers, cabinetry, stair parts, flooring, and doors.

Reclaimed Wood Products

Vintage Log and Lumber, Inc.
Glen Ray Rd.
P.O. Box 2F
Alderson, WV 24910

Toll-free: 877-653-5647
Phone: 304-445-2300
www.vintagelog.com

Vintage Log and Lumber salvages the materials in log cabins and timber-frame barns in Kentucky, Ohio, Pennsylvania, and West Virginia. The company's inventory includes salvaged redwood, chestnut, oak, pine, and poplar boards, beams, flooring, and split rails. They also sell complete hand-hewn log cabins and timber-frame barns.

Reclaimed Wood Timbers

Havillah Shake Company
521 N. Siwash Creek Rd.
Tonasket, WA 98855

Phone: 509-486-1467

Havillah Shake Company is a small rural business that manufactures wood flooring, paneling, and furniture primarily from reclaimed wood sources. They also offer large timbers cut to order from recycled and reclaimed sources.

Reclaimed-Wood Timbers

A Reclaimed Lumber Co.
9 Old Post Rd.
Madison, CT 06443

Phone: 203-214-9705
www.woodwood.com

A Reclaimed Lumber Co. salvages wood from old water and wine tanks, mill buildings, bridge timbers, river-recovery log operations, and other sources to be custom-remilled into a variety of wood products including timbers. A wide variety of species are available, as are antique hand-hewn timbers. Wood is sourced from all over the country, and much of their product is processed at their Connecticut mill, but the company makes an effort to provide locally available wood that they will process locally.

Timeless Timber

Timeless Timber, Inc.
2200 E. Lake Shore Dr.
Ashland, WI 54806

Phone: 715-685-9663
www.timelesstimber.com

Timeless Timber, Inc., formerly The Superior Water-Logged Lumber Company, harvests logs that sank during the log drives of the 1800s. Domestic species include red and white oak, maple, birch, white pine, basswood, elm, and cypress. The company was certified in June of 2000 by Scientific Certification Systems as a producer of timber from 100% salvaged wood.

Trestlewood Timbers

Trestlewood
694 N. 1890 W, Ste. 44A
P.O. Box 1728
Provo, UT 84601

Toll-free: 877-375-2779
Phone: 801-375-2779
www.trestlewood.com

Trestlewood deals exclusively in reclaimed wood. Their wood comes from the Lucin Cutoff railroad trestle, which crosses the Great Salt Lake, and other salvage projects. Trestlewood products include flooring, millwork, timbers, decking, and siding. Available species include Douglas fir, redwood, southern yellow pine, longleaf yellow pine, oak, and other hardwoods.

Wood Materials from Urban Trees

CitiLog™
6 Bywood Ln.
Ewing, NJ 08628

Phone: 609-538-8680
www.citilogs.com

CitiLog, also known as D. Stubby Warmbold, is SmartWood-certified for the harvesting of trees in urban areas of New Jersey and Pennsylvania. Wood is sent by rail to Amish craftsmen in central Pennsylvania who take extra care to turn the lesser graded wood into higher quality products such as flooring, lumber, custom architectural millwork, furniture, and kitchen cabinets. Where appropriate, wood is now harvested using horses.

Rough Carpentry Accessories

Especially when structural requirements are minimal, look for recycled-content products.

EZ-Shim

EZ-Shim
P.O. Box 4820
Santa Barbara, CA 93140

Toll-free: 800-772-0024
Phone: 805-682-2155
www.ezshim.com

EZ-Shim™ is a load-bearing, injection-molded shim made from recycled ABS plastic with prescored grooves for breaking off excess shim stock after installation. EZ-Shim measures $1^1/_8$" x 8" x $^5/_{16}$" at its thick end. There are 10 shims per sheet. The manufacturer has certified the following recycled-content levels (by weight): total recovered material 100% typical, 100% guaranteed.

Structural Insulated Panels

Most structural insulated panels (SIPs) consist of oriented strand board (OSB) sandwiching an insulating foam core. SIPs are gaining market share in the residential and light commercial building market because they're quick to assemble and provide superb energy performance. The insulating core of SIPs is most commonly made from expanded polystyrene (EPS), though in some cases polyurethane foam, or even compressed straw or mineral wool, is used. SIPs are manufactured in a range of thicknesses providing different R-values. Of the foam core materials, EPS used to have an environmental advantage over polyurethane because the latter was blown with ozone-depleting HCFCs, but that is no longer the case. The polyurethane (or polyisocyanurate) used in SIPS is now blown with ozone-safe hydrocarbons. In response to problems with insects burrowing in SIP foam cores, look for products that incorporate borate compounds; without the borate treatment, it's sometimes necessary to use insecticides or special termite trap systems on an ongoing basis in and around SIP buildings. SIP buildings can be quickly assembled, particularly when panels are factory-cut, including door and window openings.

Acsys Panel System

Acsys Inc.
9297 N. Government Way, Ste. G
Hayden, ID 83835

Toll-free: 866-362-2797
www.acsys.net

The Acsys Building System is a structural insulated panel-type product employing an engineered 16- to 20-gauge corrugated galvanized steel endoskeletal core (rather than the more common exoskeleton of OSB). The steel is embedded in molded EPS, which offers R-values ranging from 25 to 50 (panel thicknesses of 6", 8", 10", and 12"). The EPS typically contains 7–10% recycled content from packaging waste, according to the manufacturer. Available in 2' and 4' widths up to 18' long, it may be used with steel framing or as a fully load-bearing system. The panels interconnect with ship-lap joints (secured by galvanized screws) and may be lifted into place by two people. 18-gauge galvanized steel top- and bottom-mounting tracks, as well as corner locater plates, are provided. Panels are typically finished on the exterior with acrylic stucco and on the interior with drywall.

Agriboard

Agriboard Industries, L.C.
P.O. Box 151
Electra, TX 76360

Toll-free: 866-495-3595
Phone: 940-495-3590
www.agriboard.com

After being purchased by one of the original investors in the company, Agriboard™ Industries is back in business manufac-

turing an engineered insulated panel construction system; its straw core is bound only with high heat and pressure. 4" cores are laminated single- or double-ply between two sheets of OSB using a polyurethane adhesive, though Agriboard has plans to switch to a soy-based adhesive, as well as straw-based outer panels. According to the company, the structural wall panels offer excellent thermal and acoustical insulation, have up to a 2-hour fire transmission rating, and are lower in cost and two to three times stronger than conventional wood-frame construction in compressive load, racking, and bending. Agriboard also offers a new ceramic and fiberglass composite, water- and UV-resistant, factory-applied exterior coating.

Enercept Super Insulated Building System

Enercept, Inc.
3100 Ninth Ave. SE
Watertown, SD 57201

Toll-free: 800-658-3303
Phone: 605-882-2222
www.enercept.com

Enercept SIPs consist of a core of expanded polystyrene laminated between two sheets of oriented strand board (OSB).

EPS and Polyurethane SIPs

Winter Panel Corporation
74 Glen Orne Dr.
Brattleboro, VT 05301

Phone: 802-254-3435
www.winterpanel.com

Winter Panel produces structural insulated panels with EPS or polyisocyanurate (polyurethane) foam cores. EPS has always been blown with non-ozone-depleting, non-global-warming pentane. As of late 2003, Winter Panel's polyiso foam is also blown using pentane. The 4¹/₂"- or 6¹/₂"-thick panels are available in Structurewall™ (a direct substitute for 2x4 or 2x6 framing using OSB as the outer skins), Curtainwall panels (nonstructural with gypsum wallboard on interior side, OSB on outside), and Woodclad™ (Structurewall panels with 1x8 v-groove pine cladding on interior finish side). The EPS-core panels are less expensive, while the polyurethane panels have a higher R-value. Panels with custom skins, cores, and thicknesses are also available.

Industry Representation

Structural Insulated Panel Association
P.O. Box 1699
Gig Harbor, WA 98335

Phone: 253-858-7472
www.sips.org

The Structural Insulated Panel Association (SIPA) represents the industry in promoting the advantages of SIPs to designers, contractors, and homeowners.

Insulspan SIPs

Insulspan
9012 E. U.S. Hwy. 223
P.O. Box 38
Blissfield, MI 49228

Toll-free: 800-726-3510
Phone: 517-486-4844
www.insulspan.com

Insulspan's SIPs are produced with EPS foam cores laminated between OSB sheathing.

R-Control Panels

Advance Foam Plastics, Inc. - California Division
748 N. McKeever Ave.
Azusa, CA 91702

Phone: 626-334-5358
www.afprcontrol.com

Advance Foam Plastics is a licensed manufacturer of AFM Corporation's R-Control® Structural Insulated Panels made from R-Control Perform Guard® EPS cores and OSB skins. Panel dimensions range from 4' x 8' to 8' x 24' in thicknesses of $4^1/_2$" to $12^1/_4$". AFM has gone through full structural and fire testing of its system, including relevant building code listings.

R-Control Panels

Advance Foam Plastics, Inc. - Colorado Division
5250 N. Sherman St.
Denver, CO 80216

Toll-free: 800-525-8697
Phone: 303-297-3844
www.afprcontrol.com

Advance Foam Plastics is a licensed manufacturer of AFM Corporation's R-Control® Structural Insulated Panels made from R-Control Perform Guard® EPS cores and OSB skins. Panel dimensions range from 4' x 8' to 8' x 24' in thicknesses of $4^1/_2$" to $12^1/_4$". AFM has gone through full structural and fire testing of its system, including relevant building code listings.

R-Control Panels

Advance Foam Plastics, Inc. - Nevada Division
920 Kleppe Ln.
Sparks, NV 89431

Toll-free: 800-444-9290
Phone: 775-355-7655
www.afprcontrol.com

Advance Foam Plastics is a licensed manufacturer of AFM Corporation's R-Control® Structural Insulated Panels made from R-Control

Perform Guard® EPS cores and OSB skins. Panel dimensions range from 4' x 8' to 8' x 24' in thicknesses of $4^1/_2$" to $12^1/_4$". AFM has gone through full structural and fire testing of its system, including relevant building code listings.

R-Control Panels

Advance Foam Plastics, Inc. - Utah Division
111 W. Fireclay Ave.
Murray, UT 84107

Toll-free: 877-775-8847
Phone: 801-265-3465
www.afprcontrol.com

Advance Foam Plastics is a licensed manufacturer of AFM Corporation's R-Control® Structural Insulated Panels made from R-Control Perform Guard® EPS cores and OSB skins. Panel dimensions range from 4' x 8' to 8' x 24' in thicknesses of $4^1/_2$" to $12^1/_4$". AFM has gone through full structural and fire testing of its system, including relevant building code listings.

R-Control Panels

AFM Corporation
211 River Ridge Cir. #102
Burnsville, MN 55337

Toll-free: 800-255-0176
Phone: 952-474-0809
www.r-control.com

R-Control® SIPs are made from R-Control Perform Guard® EPS cores and OSB skins. The panel dimensions range from 4' x 8' to 8' x 24' in thicknesses of $4^1/_2$" to $12^1/_4$". AFM has gone through full structural and fire testing of its system, including relevant building code listings. AFM also licenses several dozen manufacturers throughout the U.S. to produce these and several other EPS products.

R-Control Panels

Allied Foam Products, Inc.
2731 White Sulphur Rd.
Gainesville, GA 30501

Toll-free: 800-533-2613
Phone: 770-536-7900
www.alliedfoamprod.com

Allied Foam Products is a licensed manufacturer of AFM Corporation's R-Control® Structural Insulated Panels made from R-Control Perform Guard® EPS cores and OSB skins. Panel dimensions range from 4' x 8' to 8' x 24' in thicknesses of $4^1/_2$" to $12^1/_4$". AFM has gone through full structural and fire testing of its system, including relevant building code listings.

R-Control Panels

Big Sky Insulations, Inc.
P.O. Box 838
Belgrade, MT 59714

Toll-free: 800-766-3626
Phone: 406-388-4146
www.bsiinc.com

Big Sky Insulation is a licensed manufacturer of AFM Corporation's R-Control® Structural Insulated Panels made from R-Control Perform Guard® EPS cores and OSB skins. Panel dimensions range from 4' x 8' to 8' x 24' in thicknesses of $4^1/_2$" to $12^1/_4$". AFM has gone through full structural and fire testing of its system, including relevant building code listings.

R-Control Panels

Branch River Foam Plastics, Inc.
15 Thurber Blvd.
Smithfield, RI 02917

Toll-free: 800-336-3626
Phone: 401-232-0270
www.branchriver.com

Branch River Foam Plastics is a licensed manufacturer of AFM Corporation's R-Control® Structural Insulated Panels made from R-Control Perform Guard® EPS cores and OSB skins. Panel dimensions range from 4' x 8' to 8' x 24' in thicknesses of $4^1/_2$" to $12^1/_4$". AFM has gone through full structural and fire testing of its system, including relevant building code listings.

R-Control Panels

Contour Products, Inc. - Newton Division
1418 Cow Palace Rd.
Newton, KS 67114

Toll-free: 800-835-2161
Phone: 316-283-1100
www.contourfoam.com

Contour Products is a licensed manufacturer of AFM Corporation's R-Control® Structural Insulated Panels made from R-Control Perform Guard® EPS cores and OSB skins. Panel dimensions range from 4' x 8' to 8' x 24' in thicknesses of $4^1/_2$" to $12^1/_4$". AFM has gone through full structural and fire testing of its system, including relevant building code listings. For sales information, contact the company's Kansas City Division.

R-Control Panels

Heartland EPS, Inc. - Headquarters
90 Trowbridge Dr.
P.O. Box 669
Fond du Lac, WI 54936

Toll-free: 800-236-5377
Phone: 920-924-4050
www.heartlandeps.com

Heartland EPS is a licensed manufacturer of AFM Corporation's R-Control® Structural Insulated Panels made from R-Control Perform Guard® EPS cores and OSB skins. Panel dimensions range from 4' x 8' to 8' x 24' in thicknesses of $4^1/_2$" to $12^1/_4$". AFM has gone through full structural and fire testing of its system, including relevant building code listings.

R-Control Panels

Pacific Allied Products, Ltd.
91-110 Kaomi Loop
Kapolei, HI 96707

Toll-free: 888-824-3626
Phone: 808-682-2038
www.pacificalliedproducts.com

Pacific Allied Products is a licensed manufacturer of AFM Corporation's R-Control® Structural Insulated Panels made from R-Control Perform Guard® EPS cores and OSB skins. Panel dimensions range from 4' x 8' to 8' x 24' in thicknesses of $4^1/_2$" to $12^1/_4$". AFM has gone through full structural and fire testing of its system, including relevant building code listings.

R-Control Panels

Poly-Foam, Inc.
116 Pine St. S
Lester Prairie, MN 55354

Phone: 320-395-2551
www.polyfoaminc.com

Poly-Foam is a licensed manufacturer of AFM Corporation's R-Control® Structural Insulated Panels made from R-Control Perform Guard® EPS cores and OSB skins. Panel dimensions range from 4' x 8' to 8' x 24' in thicknesses of $4^1/_2$" to $12^1/_4$". AFM has gone through full structural and fire testing of its system, including relevant building code listings.

R-Control Panels

Stanark Foam / R-CONTROL
10101 Hwy. 70 E
N. Little Rock, AR 72117

Toll-free: 800-632-4586
Phone: 501-945-1114
www.stanark.com

Stanark Foam is a licensed manufacturer of AFM Corporation's R-Control® Structural Insulated Panels made from R-Control Perform

Guard® EPS cores and OSB skins. Panel dimensions range from 4' x 8' to 8' x 24' in thicknesses of $4^1/_2$" to $12^1/_4$". AFM has gone through full structural and fire testing of its system, including relevant building code listings.

R-Control Panels

Therma Foam, Inc.
P.O. Box 161128
Fort Worth, TX 76161

Toll-free: 800-333-3626
Phone: 817-624-7204
www.thermafoam.com

Therma Foam is a licensed manufacturer of AFM Corporation's R-Control® Structural Insulated Panels made from R-Control Perform Guard® EPS cores and OSB skins. Panel dimensions range from 4' x 8' to 8' x 24' in thicknesses of $4^1/_2$" to $12^1/_4$". AFM has gone through full structural and fire testing of its system, including relevant building code listings.

R-Control SIP Panels

Insulated Building Systems, Inc.
326 McGhee Rd.
Winchester, VA 22603

Phone: 540-662-0882
www.rcontrolibs.com

Insulated Building Systems is a licensed manufacturer of AFM Corporation's R-Control® Structural Insulated Panels made from R-Control Perform Guard® EPS cores and OSB skins. Panel dimensions range from 4' x 8' to 8' x 24' in thicknesses of $4^1/_2$" to $12^1/_4$". AFM has gone through full structural and fire testing of its system, including relevant building code listings.

R-Control SIP Panels

Team Industries, Inc.
4580 Airwest Dr. SE
P.O. Box 888691
Grand Rapids, MI 49588

Toll-free: 800-356-5548
Phone: 616-698-2001
www.teamindustries.com

Team Industries is a licensed manufacturer of AFM Corporation's R-Control® Structural Insulated Panels made from R-Control Perform Guard® EPS cores and OSB skins. Panel dimensions range from 4' x 8' to 8' x 24' in thicknesses of $4^1/_2$" to $12^1/_4$". AFM has gone through full structural and fire testing of its system, including relevant building code listings.

Structural Insulated Panels

Extreme Panels/Insulspan™
475 E. Fourth St. N
P.O. Box 435
Cottonwood, MN 56229

Toll-free: 800-977-2635
Phone: 507-423-5530
www.extremepanel.com

Extreme Panels/Insulspan manufactures structural insulated panels for residential, commercial, and agricultural applications. Insulspan panels are made with oriented strand board manufactured to APA standards for maximum strength and durability, and are available with expanded polystyrene cores.

Structural Insulated Panels

FischerSIPs, Inc.
1843 Northwestern Pkwy.
Louisville, KY 40203

Toll-free: 800-792-7477
Phone: 502-778-5577
www.fischersips.com

A FischerSIP™ is made by laminating an expanded polystyrene foam core between two sheets of $^7/_{16}$" oriented strand board (OSB). Panels can be manufactured in sizes ranging from 4' x 8' to 8' x 24'.

Structural Insulated Panels

Foam Laminates of Vermont
P.O. Box 102
Hinesburg, VT 05461

Toll-free: 800-545-6290
Phone: 802-453-4438
www.foamlaminates.com

Foam Laminates of Vermont started manufacturing structural insulated panels in 1982 in conjunction with their sister company, Vermont Frames. Exterior skins are generally plywood or OSB. Insulating cores are either expanded polystyrene (EPS) or polyisocyanurate. Only products with an EPS core are being specified here.

Structural Insulated Panels

General Panel Corporation
109 Perma R Rd.
Johnson City, TN 37604

Toll-free: 800-251-7532
www.sipsproducts.com

General Panel Corporation, formerly Perma R and previously listed as Apache Products Company, produces an EPS-core SIP system.

Structural Insulated Panels

Pacemaker Plastics Co., Inc.
126 New Pace Rd.
P.O. Box 279
Newcomerstown, OH 43832-0279

Toll-free: 800-446-2188
Phone: 740-498-4181
www.pacemakerplastics.com

Pacemaker Plastics Co. is a manufacturer of Structural Insulated Panels with full fire and structural testing, and related UL and building code listings. The panels are made with EPS cores and OSB skins. Dimensions range from 4' x 8' to 8' x 28' in thicknesses of $4^9/_{16}$" (R-16) to $12^9/_{16}$" (R-45).

Structural Insulated Panels

PORTERCorp
4240 N. 136th Ave.
Holland, MI 49424

Toll-free: 800-354-7721
Phone: 616-399-1963
www.portersips.com

Photo: Gary Burmeister

PORTERCorp (formerly W. H. Porter) SIPs are made with an EPS foam core and come in any size that can be cut from a 4' x 24' or 8' x 24' sheet of oriented strand board. Panels with custom angles and/or cut-outs are also available. Panels are available in thicknesses of $4^1/_2$", $6^1/_2$", $8^1/_4$", $10^1/_4$", and $12^1/_4$" and provide R-values ranging from 15.8 to 45.7.

Structural Insulated Panels

Premier Building Systems - Division of Premier Industries, Inc.
4609 70th Ave. E
Fife, WA 98424

Toll-free: 800-275-7086
Phone: 253-926-2020
www.pbspanel.com

Premier Building Systems manufactures SIPs with borate-treated EPS foam insulation and OSB skins. Other substrates are available upon request. EPS may contain up to 15% recycled content. Panels are available in sizes of 4' x 8' up to 8' x 24' and range in thickness from 4" to 12" (with R-values of 15, 23, 30, 37, and 45). The company has SIP manufacturing plants in Fife, Washington, and Phoenix, Arizona.

Structural Insulated Panels

Shelter Enterprises, Inc.
8 Saratoga St.
P.O. Box 618
Cohoes, NY 12047

Toll-free: 800-836-0719
Phone: 518-237-4100
www.shelter-ent.com

Shelter custom-builds stress skin panels and interior wall panels in sizes up to 8' x 40'. Shelter produces their own EPS foam for the core. 98% of the EPS waste is recycled into other products. Other core materials are available upon request.

Thermal Foam SIPs

Thermal Foams, Inc.
2101 Kenmore Ave.
Buffalo, NY 14207

Phone: 716-874-6474
www.thermalfoams.com

Thermal Foams Inc. is a manufacturer of structural insulated panels made from Thermal Foams EPS cores and OSB Skins. Panel sizes range from 4' x 8' to 8' x 24' in thicknesses of $4^1/_2$" to $12^1/_4$". Thermal Foams has gone through full structural and fire testing of its systems with an approved model code testing facility.

Thermapan Structural Insulated Panels

Thermapan Structural Insulated Panels Inc.
1380 Commerce Pkwy.
P.O. Box 429
Fort Erie, ON L2A 5M4 Canada

Toll-free: 877-443-9255
www.thermapan.com

Thermapan SIP, formerly known as The Wall™, is an EPS-core structural insulated panel system.

Wood Framing Fasteners

Let-in metal wall bracing, which provides racking resistance, can eliminate or reduce the need for wall sheathing in light-frame construction. Follow structural requirements carefully, and obtain design review by a structural engineer if uncertain. Also check with a building official before substituting let-in bracing for structural sheathing.

S365, S366, S367 Wall Bracing

USP Structural Connectors
703 Rogers Dr.
Montgomery, MN 56069

Toll-free: 800-328-5934
Phone: 507-364-7333
www.uspconnectors.com

S365, S366, and S367 Wall Bracing requires a shallow ($1/2$"-deep) kerf cut.

TWB and RCWB Wall Bracing

Simpson Strong-Tie Connectors
4120 Dublin Blvd., Ste. 400
Dublin, CA 94568

Toll-free: 800-999-5099
Phone: 925-560-9000
www.strongtie.com

Simpson TWB and RCWB Wall Bracing are let-in metal bracing products available in both T and L cross-sections requiring $15/16$" and $9/16$" deep kerf cuts, respectively. They are designed to fulfill the same code bracing requirements as 1x4 let-in bracing. TWB and RCWB are available in lengths of 9'9", 11'4", and 14'2".

Wood Trusses

Roof and floor trusses are inherently more wood-efficient than dimension-lumber rafters and joists. To qualify for GreenSpec, however, truss products must include other environmental features, such as use of FSC-certified wood in their fabrication. (Certification to Forest Stewardship Council—FSC—standards involves third-party evaluation and monitoring of sustainable forestry practices.)

Hayward Truss

Hayward Corporation
P.O. Box 16009
Monterey, CA 93942

Phone: 831-643-1900

Hayward Corporation, formerly Hayward Lumber, produces trusses through their Hayward Building Systems division using FSC-certified lumber, now manufactured in a solar-powered facility soon to be LEED®-certified.

This Space is Available for Your Notes

Sheathing

Sheathing generally serves as a secondary weather barrier behind the exterior finish. It can also be the primary substrate for attaching the finish layer, and often provides diagonal bracing for the structure.

The most common sheathing materials for residential and light commercial construction are plywood and oriented-strand board (OSB). Plywood requires trees of a diameter large enough for veneers to be peeled off as the cylindrical core is turned on a lathe. OSB can be manufactured from fast-growing trees of relatively low commercial value, and uses a higher percentage of the tree. OSB sheathing and wood *I-joist* framing, used together, can reduce wood requirements dramatically while providing superior structural integrity. Most OSB and plywood uses phenol-formaldehyde (PF) adhesive that offgasses less formaldehyde than the urea-formaldehyde (UF) commonly used in interior particleboard and paneling. Some OSB uses primarily a polyurethane-type (MDI) resin for its adhesive; it emits no formaldehyde but is more toxic in its uncured state, placing factory workers at risk.

Recycled-content sheathing is available in various types. A sandwich material with aluminum foil facings over recycled paperboard is available that meets most wind load requirements and costs less than OSB. Exterior gypsum sheathing, typically made with recycled paper facings, is often used on commercial buildings and is particularly good under stucco for houses. Some exterior gypsum sheathing products use fiberglass facings or integral fibers that do not support mold growth.

Fiberboard and Particleboard Panels

see *Interior Finish & Trim: Fiberboard and Particleboard Panels*

Sheathing (including Plywood & OSB)

Sheathing comprises a significant portion of the materials used with many building types. Careful consideration of product selection and use can reduce the environmental impacts of a project. Wall sheathing is often used only as an additional layer of weather protection, although it may also be required for racking resistance. When let-in diagonal bracing is used to provide racking resistance, wood-panel sheathing can sometimes be eliminated or replaced with more resource-efficient or insulative products. Wood products can carry the FSC label under a percentage-based standard if they contain at least 30% FSC-certified wood fiber content—even less if the rest is recovered material. (Certification to Forest Stewardship Council—FSC—standards involves third-party evaluation and monitoring of sustainable forestry practices.) Urea-formaldehyde (UF) and phenol-formaldehyde (PF) binders are used in plywood, while OSB can be made with those binders or the non-formaldehyde-emitting methyl diisocyanate (MDI), a polyurethane binder. UF binders, used exclusively in interior-grade products, can offgas significant concentrations of formaldehyde gas—an indoor air quality concern and a probable human carcinogen. Paradoxically, exterior-rated products using PF binders are less of an offgassing concern. MDI binders do not offgas any formaldehyde. All plywood included here is FSC-certified. Oriented-strand board (OSB) can be an efficient use of forest resources because it can be produced from small-diameter or low-grade tree species; OSB products listed here are included because of the presence of nonformaldehyde binders, the incorporation of nontoxic (to humans) borate insect treatments, or FSC certification. Our listings also include sheathing products that have various environmental advantages over conventional OSB and plywood.

4-Way Floor Deck, N.C.F.R., and Firestall Roof Deck

Homasote Company
932 Lower Ferry Rd.
P.O. Box 7240
West Trenton, NJ 08628

Toll-free: 800-257-9491
Phone: 609-883-3300
www.homasote.com

4-Way® Floor Deck, N.C.F.R.®, and Firestall® Roof Deck are structural high-density fiberboard panels made from 100% recycled newspaper, paraffin binders, and additives for pest and fire resistance. Homasote has been manufacturing products from recycled paper since the early 1900s. 4-Way Floor Deck is a tongue-and-groove multi-ply subfloor that is structural, sound deadening, and moderately insulative (R-2.5/in.), available in $1^{11}/_{32}$" & $1^3/_4$" thicknesses. 4-Way can be installed on 16" and 24" centers. N.C.F.R. is a Class A fire-rated panel for interior and exterior use. Firestall Roof Deck has a 1-hr UL P535 fire rating that includes 28 assemblies; it is manufactured with 1 to 4 plies of Homasote® and a face ply of N.C.F.R. in tongue-and-groove panels from 1" to $1^3/_8$" and $1^7/_8$" thick.

AdvanTech OSB

J. M. Huber Wood
  Products
One Resource Sq.
10925 David Taylor Dr.,
  Ste. 300
Charlotte, NC 28262

Toll-free: 800-933-9220
Phone: 704-547-0671
www.huberwood.com

AdvanTech™ OSB from Huber is an OSB made primarily with formaldehyde-free MDI resin (a small quantity of phenolic resin is added to improve certain properties). Due to its greater moisture resistance than conventional OSB, AdvanTech carries a 50-year warranty. This product has been certified by GREENGUARD for low emissions.

BarrierPanel, TechShield Radiant Barrier, and BarrierFloor OSB

LP
414 Union St., Ste. 2000
Nashville, TN 37219

Toll-free: 888-820-0325
Phone: 877-744-5600
www.lpcorp.com

Part of the SmartGuard™ family, a venture between LP Corp. and Osmose, these products are treated with zinc borate for resistance to termites, carpenter ants, and fungal decay. LP's BarrierPanel™ is an OSB sheathing product suitable for wall, roof, and (double-layer) subfloor applications in residential and light commercial buildings. TechShield™ Radiant Barrier is an OSB roof sheathing with a radiant-foil overlay to minimize radiant heat gain. LP's BarrierFloor™ T&G OSB subflooring is edge-coated to reduce swelling. All carry a 20-year transferable warranty.

Certified Pine Plywood

ROMEX World Trade Company, LLC - sales agent for ROM
P.O. Box 1110
Alexandria, LA 71309

Toll-free: 800-299-5174
Phone: 318-445-1973
www.martco.com

Roy O. Martin Lumber Management, LLC (ROM) has received SmartWood certification for its 585,000 acres of forestland and four mills according to standards of the Forest Stewardship Council (FSC). This is the first FSC certification of any forest management operation in Louisiana. ROM's FSC-certified pine plywood, formerly under the name of SmartCore®, is produced by Martco Plywood in Chopin, Louisiana. Sanded plywood is available in AA, AB, AC, BC, and A-Flat grades in 4' x 8' panels standard thicknesses of $1/4$", $11/32$", $15/32$", $19/32$" and $23/32$". As with the company's OSB plant, some fiber used in the Chopin mill comes from non-company-owned land, but the company can provide 100% FSC-certified product. ROM's pine plywood is also now available sided with a foil radiant barrier, or printed with the company's new "GRID" panel marking system.

Energy Brace and Thermo Ply

Ludlow Coated Products
700 Centreville Rd.
Constantine, MI 49042

Toll-free: 800-345-8881
Phone: 269-435-2425
www.ludlowcp.com

EnergyBrace® and Thermo Ply® are thin, lightweight structural sheathing panels manufactured from 100% recycled cardboard and aluminum-foil facings. The plies are pressure-laminated with a special water-resistant, nontoxic adhesive. Thermo Ply is available in three grades: nonstructural, structural, and super strength. Although Thermo Ply structural is less than $1/8$" thick, when properly secured with 3" fastener spacing on the perimeter and 6" spacing on intermediate studs, the racking strength meets building codes even in seismically active areas. Thermo Ply super strength is applicable with studs on 24" centers. All grades are available in the following sizes: 4' x 8', 4' x 9', $4^3/4$" x 8', and $4^3/4$" x 9'.

EnerMax Radiant Barrier Sheathing

EMCO Building Products Corporation
9510 St-Patrick St.
LaSalle, PQ H8R 1R9 Canada

Toll-free: 800-567-2726
www.emcobp.com

EnerMax™ is a $1/2$"-thick, lightweight structural sheathing radiant barrier panel made from reclaimed sawdust and wood shavings with a nontoxic binder. The company claims that the product's vapor-resistant aluminum-foil skin can boost the wall R-value by 4.7 (this will depend on the application, however). EnerMax comes in 4' x 8'1" and $4^1/2$" x 12' sizes with preprinted nailmarks at 8" intervals. The company also produces High Performance sheathing, which includes an asphalt coating on all six sides.

Fiberboard - Regular and High Density

Huebert Brothers Products, LLC
1545 E. Morgan St.
Boonville, MO 65233-0167

Toll-free: 800-748-7147
www.huebertfiberboard.com

Huebert Fiberboard is made from waste wood chips and cellulose fiber with a carbon-based black emulsion surface coating. This insulating roof sheathing product for mopped roofs contains 40–60% recycled materials, of which 20% is post-consumer. The company claims R-values of roughly 2.78/in. for the $1/2$"-, 1"-, and 2"-thick panels.

Polar-Ply Radiant-Barrier

Superior Radiant
  Insulation
P.O. Box 247
San Dimas, CA 91773

Toll-free: 888-774-4422
Phone: 909-305-1450
www.superiorrb.com

Superior Radiant Insulation manufactures several radiant barrier and insulation products. Among them is Polar-Ply™ aluminum foil-faced OSB or plywood sheathing.

Tuff-Strand Certified OSB

ROMEX World Trade Company, LLC - sales agent for ROM
P.O. Box 1110
Alexandria, LA 71309

Toll-free: 800-299-5174
Phone: 318-445-1973
www.martco.com

Roy O. Martin Lumber Management, LLC (ROM) has gained FSC-certification of its 585,000 acres of forestland and four mills. In addition to this being the first FSC certification of any forest management operation in Louisiana, ROM has made available the first-ever FSC-certified oriented strand board (OSB). Tuff-Strand® is a fairly conventional OSB produced by the Martco Partnership plant in LeMoyen, Louisiana. The 4' x 8' panels are available in three standard thicknesses: $7/16$", $15/32$", and $19/32$". The mill is fed by up to 70% company-owned timber, and while OSB is typically certified using FSC's partial-content rules, the company can provide 100% FSC-certified product. Tuff-Strand's binder is 100% phenol formaldehyde. FSC-certified Tuff-Strand is also now available sided with a foil radiant barrier, or printed with the company's new "GRID" panel marking system.

This Space is Available for Your Notes

Exterior Finish & Trim

The exterior finish is a building's first defense against the weather, and its most visible aspect.

Building systems that rely on the exterior finish as the sole weather barrier are susceptible to failure—especially in climates with wind-driven rain or without good drying conditions. The driving forces of wind and other air-pressure factors will force moisture through even the smallest openings. Because of this, siding or curtain wall systems designed around the *rain-screen* principle are much more effective and durable. This strategy uses a vented exterior finish and a tightly sealed secondary barrier that work together to equalize the pressure on both sides of the exterior finish, taking away the forces that would otherwise drive moisture inwards.

Recycled-wood-fiber composite siding and trim are more stable than materials made from natural wood, hold paint better, and generally cost less. Some hardboard products have had durability problems when improperly installed or when installed without adequate drying provisions in wet climates.

Fiber-cement siding is very durable, looks like wood when it's painted, and provides a fire-resistant surface. The wood fibers provide strength, elasticity, and good paint-holding ability.

Locally produced brick and stone are long-lasting, low-maintenance finishes that reduce transportation costs and environmental impacts. Molded cementitious stone replaces the environmental impacts of quarrying and dressing natural stone with the impacts of producing cement.

Bricks

Clay bricks are the most common form of earthen building product in the U.S. Bricks are typically fired in large kilns at very high temperatures, which results in significant embodied energy. High-temperature firing enables waste materials—even toxic materials like oil-contaminated soil—to be safely incorporated into certain products. Traditionally used as a load-bearing material, clay bricks are now more commonly used as exterior cladding. Different colors of brick are created with different clays, additives, and firing techniques. Bricks can easily be salvaged from building demolition, providing significant resource savings compared with new brick—though salvaged brick may need to be tested for structural properties and moisture resistance.

Cunningham Bricks

Cunningham Brick Co., Inc.
701 N. Main St.
Lexington, NC 27292

Toll-free: 800-672-6181
Phone: 336-248-8541
www.cunninghambrick.com

Cunningham Brick manufactures bricks that incorporate 1.3% manganese dioxide by weight, a toxic metal waste from battery production. Vitrified manganese imparts a darker color to the bricks and is considered safe after firing. The product may not be widely available.

Salvaged Building Brick

Gavin Historical Bricks
2050 Glendale Rd.
Iowa City, IA 52245

Phone: 319-354-5251
www.historicalbricks.com

Gavin Historical Bricks supplies salvaged brick and cobblestone recovered from buildings and streets from around the country. Bricks are used in new construction to provide an antique look, as well as for historic restoration projects. Custom brick matching is available. Shipping is provided nationwide, though the heavy weight reduces the practicality (and environmental attractiveness) of shipping large quantities long distances.

Cast Stone

With simulated-stone products, look for recycled content such as fly ash.

LodeStone Fly-Ash Based Veneer Block

LodeStone Companies
2708 Glenwood
Denton, TX 76209

Phone: 940-483-1761
www.lodestoneproducts.com

Custom Cast Stone, formerly Texas Cast Stone, manufactures LodeStone™, a standardized architectural cast stone product. Class C coal fly ash replaces between 65 and 80% of the portland cement used in typical cast stone. LodeStone veneer blocks are 3" thick at the mortar joints with either a smooth or a chiseled face, in nominal sizes ranging from 8" x 12" to 16" x 32". A handful of trim profiles and end pieces are also available. LodeStone Companies promotes and markets the LodeStone product line.

Composition Siding

Composition siding products are environmentally attractive because they utilize low-grade or waste wood fiber (such as newsprint or sawdust), or strands of fast-growing wood mixed with binding agents and finishes. Although composition siding is resource-efficient relative to solid wood, some products in the past have demonstrated poor durability. Quality composition siding products, if durable, can be affordable green products.

FSC-Certified TruWood Siding

Collins Products, LLC
P.O. Box 16
Klamath Falls, OR 97601

Toll-free: 800-547-1793
Phone: 541-885-3289
www.collinswood.com

Collins Products, a subsidiary of Collins Companies, has introduced an FSC-certified version of its engineered (hardboard) TruWood® siding. It is made from FSC-certified wood chips (using FSC's partial-content rules, with an actual certified fiber content of 32%), phenol formaldehyde binder (5–6% by weight), paraffin wax, acrylic sealants, and finishes. The product is also certified by Scientific Certification Systems to contain a minimum of 50% recycled or recovered wood fiber (minimum 4% post-consumer recycled, 20% post-industrial recycled, and the remainder "recovered"). According to Collins, when compared with cedar siding, TruWood is less expensive, holds paint longer, has no knots or raised grain, and requires less paint to cover. TruWood siding comes with a limited 30-year warranty in a wide variety of both lap and panel products with various textures and finishes. Distributed by Weyerhaeuser in the western U.S.

LP SmartSide Siding and Exterior Trim Products

LP SmartSide
10115 Kincey Ave., Ste. 150
Huntersville, NC 28078

Toll-free: 800-648-6893
www.lpcorp.com

LP's SmartSide™ siding and exterior trim includes formaldehyde-free OSB-based (lap and panel), soffit, and fascia trim products treated during manufacture with zinc borate. Products are delivered with a paint-based overlay to enhance weather resistance. A 30-year transferable warranty with 7-year 100% repair/replacement and a 30-year termite resistance guarantee is offered. Introduced in 1997, SmartSide Siding was joined in 2000 by other LP Smart-Guard® termite-resistant building products.

Fiber-Cement Siding

Fiber-cement building materials earn green points for durability. Fiber-cement, the new generation of what was once an asbestos-containing material, is today made from portland cement, sand, clay, and wood fiber. Environmental concerns include the embodied energy of portland cement and the source of the wood fiber-some products use wood from such distant locations as New Zealand and Russia. Although the current generation of fiber-cement products isn't yet proven over the long haul, that material is quite stable, and products carry up to 50-year warranties. Most fiber-cement siding is available factory primed. It takes paint very well, and proper painting is important for long-term durability.

Cemplank and Cempanel

Cemplank, Inc.
Excelsior Industrial Park
P.O. Box 99
Blandon, PA 19510

Toll-free: 877-236-7526
Phone: 610-926-5533
www.cemplank.com

Cemplank lap siding and Cempanel vertical siding have cedar textures. Cemplank is $^5/_{16}$" thick and 12' long and is available in widths from 6" ($4^3/_4$" exposure) to 12" ($10^3/_4$" exposure). Cemplank is a division of James Hardie Building Products, with manufacturing locations in Pennsylvania and South Carolina.

Fiber-Cement Siding

CertainTeed Corporation
750 E. Swedesford Rd.
P.O. Box 860
Valley Forge, PA 19482

Toll-free: 800-233-8990

Phone: 610-341-7739
www.certainteed.com

CertainTeed WeatherBoards™ Fiber-Cement siding is available in lap, panel, and soffit products with smooth, cedar, or stucco (panel only) textures. Lap siding is available in widths from $6^1/_4$" to 12". Panel siding comes in 4' x 8', 9', or 10' sheets. The DuraPress™ manufacturing system enhances the freeze-thaw resistance of the siding by compressing the siding at more than 500 psi, prior to an autoclaving process. CertainTeed delivers the siding with FiberTect sealant, which penetrates the siding surface to provide moisture protection while acting as the base coat for painting.

GAF Siding

GAF Materials Corp.
1361 Alps Rd.
Wayne, NJ 07470

Toll-free: 800-223-1948
Phone: 877-423-7663
www.gaf.com

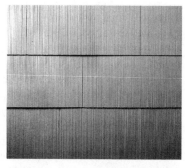

GAF manufactures several lines of fiber-cement siding products with different textures and dimensions.

Hardiplank, Hardipanel, and Hardie Shingleside

James Hardie Building
   Products, Inc.
26300 La Alameda,
   Ste. 250
Mission Viejo, CA 92691

Toll-free: 888-542-7343
Phone: 949-348-1800
www.jameshardie.com

Hardiplank® lap siding is 12' long and is available in widths ranging from $6^1/_4$" (5" exposure) to 12" ($10^3/_4$" exposure). Textures include Smooth, Select Cedarmill, Colonial Smooth, Colonial Roughsawn, Beaded Smooth, and Beaded Cedarmill. Straight-Edge Shingle Plank® emulates the look of shingles in an embossed lap-siding product; it comes in 12' lengths and is $8^1/_4$" wide with a 7" exposure. Hardipanel® vertical siding is available in 4' x 8', 4' x 9', and 4' x 10' sheets in Smooth, Stucco, or Sierra textures with vertical grooves at 8" spacings. Hardiplank and Hardipanel carry 50-year limited warranties. Available accessories include Hardisoffit and Harditrim. Hardie® Shingleside® offers the look of cedar shingles in a fiber-cement siding. Shingleside is available in a variety of styles and profiles and comes with a 30-year limited warranty.

MaxiPlank and MaxiPanel

MaxiTile, Inc.
849 E. Sandhill Ave.
Carson, CA 90746

Toll-free: 800-338-8453
Phone: 310-217-0316
www.maxitile.com

MaxiPlank and MaxiPanel siding products are available in several surface textures and patterns. MaxiPlank is produced in 12' lengths and widths from $6^{1}/_{4}$" to 12". MaxiPanel measures 4' x 8', 4' x 9', and 4' x 10'.

Nichiha Fiber-Cement Rainscreen Siding

Nichiha USA, Inc.
5855 Oakbrook Pkwy.
Norcross, GA 30093

Toll-free: 866-424-4421
Phone: 770-805-9466
www.nichiha.com

Nichiha Corporation, one of Japan's largest building materials manufacturers, is now offering its products in the U.S. market. Nichiha's lines of panelized fiber-cement siding install with special clips that hold the panels away from the sheathing to provide a rainscreen to control water intrusion and increase the durability of the entire wall system. The panels are ship-lapped on four sides and have the appearance of bricks, shakes, or stone. (A lap siding is also available.) Most panels come in 6', 8', or 10' sections, in heights ranging from approximately 8" to 18" and thicknesses ranging from $1/_{2}$" to 1". Depending on the product, the manufacturer offers a 30-year or 50-year transferable warranty.

Masonry Accessories

All masonry accessories should be chosen and installed with the durability and functioning of the complete wall system in mind. Most products included here are designed to improve the durability and performance of masonry wall systems. Forces affecting the conditions in masonry walls include bulk water penetration, wicking of moisture, and solar-driven moisture movement.

CavClear Masonry Mat

Archovations, Inc.
P.O. Box 241
Hudson, WI 54016

Toll-free: 888-436-2620
Phone: 715-381-5773
www.cavclear.com

CavClear® Masonry Mat is an airspace maintenance and drainage material designed to be installed full-height behind brick or stone. The matting prevents obstruction of the cavity drainage airspace and also prevents formation of energy-conducting mortar bridges. A properly functioning drainage system free of all mortar obstructions is the prerequisite for a masonry design to achieve maximum thermal efficiencies and reduced maintenance and repair costs. CavClear is a nonwoven plastic mesh made from 100% recycled plastic (25% minimum post-consumer content) and is available in thicknesses of $1/_{2}$", $3/_{4}$", 1", $1^{1}/_{4}$" and $1^{3}/_{4}$". It is also available bonded to EPS insulation.

CavClear Weep Vents

Archovations, Inc.
P.O. Box 241
Hudson, WI 54016

Toll-free: 888-436-2620
Phone: 715-381-5773
www.cavclear.com

CavClear® Weep Vents are 100% recycled-plastic, nonwoven mesh vents with a flame-retardant binder designed for use in the vertical joints between brick masonry units in masonry cavity wall construction. When installed as intended, CavClear Weep Vents help provide moisture drainage and airflow. The vents come in light gray and manilla colors, with other colors subject to availability, and are part of a complete line of products that aid in keeping cavity airspaces clear.

Mortar Net

Mortar Net USA, Ltd.
541 S. Lake St.
Gary, IN 46403

Toll-free: 800-664-6638
www.mortarnet.com

Mortar Net is a 90%-open, fibrous-mesh wall drainage system used to maintain airflow and allow moisture migration from behind masonry veneer facades. 2"-thick Mortar Net for Brick, Mortar Net Block, and Mortar Net Weep Vents are made from 50% recycled 200-dernier polyester; at least 17% is post-consumer and up to 33% is post-industrial polyester. Mortar Net is designed to keep mortar droppings from blocking weep holes.

Rain Screen Products

In wall assemblies with wood, fiber-cement, or similar sidings, durability and coating longevity can be significantly increased if an air space behind the siding allows it to dry uniformly after rain events. This is called a "rain screen." Such detailing can also help prevent mold growth.

Home Slicker

Benjamin Obdyke Inc.
199 Precision Dr.
Horsham, PA 19044

Toll-free: 800-523-5261
Phone: 215-672-7200
www.benjaminobdyke.com

Home Slicker® is a ventilating and self-draining rainscreen for use under siding, which provides a thermal break and moisture protection for sidewalls. Home Slicker's 3-dimensional, 0.264"-thick nylon matrix provides a continuous space for drying, drainage, and pressure equalization. For use under sidings such as wood, fiber-cement, EIFS, brick, and vinyl, Home Slicker comes with a 50-year limited warranty.

Reclaimed Wood Siding

Reclaimed-wood siding, though not commonly available, is environmentally attractive. It is milled from large timbers recovered from old buildings and other structures—generally not from wood that previously served as siding. Due to slower growth and straighter grain, quality, stability, and durability, reclaimed siding is often superior to new siding. However, the finite supply of reclaimed wood resources suggests that the material may be more suited to higher-visibility uses, such as furniture, interior trim, and flooring.

Reclaimed-Wood Siding

A Reclaimed Lumber Co.
9 Old Post Rd.
Madison, CT 06443

Phone: 203-214-9705
www.woodwood.com

A Reclaimed Lumber Co. salvages wood from old water and wine tanks, mill buildings, bridge timbers, river-recovery log operations, and other sources and custom mills it into a variety of wood products including siding. Typical species include redwood, tidewater red cypress, and Western red cedar, with other species available as well. Wood is sourced from all over the country, and much of their product is processed at their Connecticut mill, but the company tries to provide wood that is local to the customer and will make arrangements to process it locally.

Reclaimed-Wood Siding

Antique Woods & Colonial Restorations, Inc.
121 Quarry Rd.
Gouverneur, NY 13642

Toll-free: 888-261-4284
www.vintagewoods.com

Antique Woods & Colonial Restorations, Inc. (formerly Vintage

Barns, Woods & Restorations) sells reclaimed and remilled wood products including flooring, siding, and whole barn frames.

Reclaimed-Wood Siding

Big Timberworks, Inc.
P.O. Box 368
Gallatin Gateway, MT 59730

Phone: 406-763-4639
www.bigtimberworks.com

Big Timberworks offers reclaimed and remilled wood in a variety of species for residential and commercial applications such as siding, flooring, and stair parts.

Reclaimed-Wood Siding

Black's Farmwood
P.O. Box 2836
San Rafael, CA 94912

Toll-free: 877-321-WOOD
Phone: 415-499-8300
www.blacksfarmwood.com

Black's Farmwood sells reclaimed wood products from deconstructed buildings and river bottoms. Products are available in a variety of species and include salvaged timbers and beams, remilled flooring, and barn siding. The company has a showroom in Lucas Valley and uses two mills, one in Kentucky and another in New York.

Reclaimed-Wood Siding

Centre Mills Antique Floors
P.O. Box 16
Aspers, PA 17304

Phone: 717-334-0249
www.centremillsantiquefloors.com

Centre Mills Antique Floors salvages and remills a variety of hand-hewn wood products made from such species as chestnut, oak, white pine, and hemlock. Centre Mills also has 7 acres of architectural artifacts containing bricks, mantles, wavy glass, old doors, and used slates.

Reclaimed-Wood Siding

Chestnut Specialists, Inc.
400 Harwinton Ave.
Plymouth, CT 06782

Phone: 860-283-4209
www.chestnutspec.com

Chestnut Specialists dismantles buildings and remills reclaimed timbers for resale in a variety of products, including siding.

Reclaimed-Wood Siding

Duluth Timber Co.
P.O. Box 16717
Duluth, MN 55816-0717

Phone: 218-727-2145
www.duluthtimber.com

Duluth Timber reclaims and remills mainly Douglas fir and longleaf yellow pine, but also redwood and cypress. Demolition and salvage of warehouses and sheep-shearing sheds in Australia has yielded a supply of Australian hardwoods such as jarrah and Mountain ash. Duluth has mills in Minnesota, California, and Washington.

Reclaimed-Wood Siding

J. Hoffman Lumber Co.
1330 E. State St.
Sycamore, IL 60178

Phone: 630-513-6680

J. Hoffman Lumber Co. is the Midwest's only sawmill/millwork company specializing in reclaimed antique heart pine, Douglas fir, and white pine. Reclaimed lumber is remilled into flooring, siding, and other millwork.

Reclaimed-Wood Siding

Legacy Antique Woods
114 Sibley Rd.
Honeoye Falls, NY 14472

Phone: 585-624-1011
www.legacyantiquewoods.com

Legacy Antique Woods salvages timbers, boards, and decking from barns and industrial buildings. Material can be purchased "as is" or resawn into boardstock or molder blanks. Primary species offered are chestnut, oak, Douglas fir, heart pine, and white pine with other species typically available as well.

Reclaimed-Wood Siding

Longleaf Lumber
70-80 Webster Ave.
Somerville, MA 02143

Phone: 617-625-3659
www.longleaflumber.com

Longleaf Lumber, founded in 1997, dismantles old buildings and remills antique timbers into millwork and flooring at the company's sawmill in the Boston area. Longleaf specializes in heart pine, but other salvaged woods such as chestnut, red and white oak, eastern white pine, and maple are often available from dismantled buildings around New England. Longleaf also sells unmilled reclaimed timbers and reclaimed barn siding. In addition to the sawmill, the company operates a retail store at their Webster Avenue location.

Reclaimed-Wood Siding

Safe Solutions, LLC
166 Malden Tpke.
Saugerties, NY 12477

Phone: 845-661-7989
www.safesolutionsllc.com

Safe Solutions remills tongue-and-groove barnwood hardwood flooring and siding out of antique reclaimed wood from disassembled barns. A technique called skip planing is used to mill the boards, leaving the original milling marks for aesthetic purposes. Siding is available in oak, chestnut, walnut, maple, and other hardwoods.

Reclaimed-Wood Siding

Trestlewood
694 N. 1890 W, Ste. 44A
P.O. Box 1728
Provo, UT 84601

Toll-free: 877-375-2779
Phone: 801-375-2779
www.trestlewood.com

Trestlewood deals exclusively in reclaimed wood. Their wood comes from the Lucin Cutoff railroad trestle, which crosses the Great Salt Lake, and other salvage projects. Trestlewood products include flooring, millwork, timbers, decking, and siding. Available species include Douglas fir, redwood, southern yellow pine, longleaf yellow pine, oak, and other hardwoods.

River-Reclaimed Wood Siding

Goodwin Heart Pine Company
106 S.W. 109th Pl.
Micanopy, FL 32667

Toll-free: 800-336-3118
Phone: 352-466-0339
www.heartpine.com

Goodwin manufactures wood siding made from antique heart pine and heart cypress logs—200 years old or older—that have been recovered from Southern river bottoms. Siding is kiln-dried, graded, and precision-milled.

Stone Facing

With simulated-stone products, look for recycled content such as fly ash.

CDS Cast Stone Panels

CDS Manufacturing, Inc.
441 S. Virginia St.
Quincy, FL 32351

Toll-free: 888-847-3188
Phone: 850-875-4651
www.cdsmanufacturing.net

CDS Manufacturing produces a variety of cast stone products from a blend of natural minerals and post-consumer and/or post-industrial materials. CDS "Green" Stone™, which is lighter in weight than natural stone, requires no special substructure, clips, or hangers to install and can be fabricated into wall panels, crown or base molding, and a variety of other decorative elements. Recycled materials can include glass, drywall, fiberglass, cellulose, and reclaimed water. Recycled content ranges from 20 to 70% and can be customized to fit design specifications. Realistic stone replications are available in travertine, coral, and limestone textures, as well as custom textures and colors. The manufacturer has certified the following recycled-content levels (by weight): total recovered material 20% typical, 20% guaranteed; post-consumer material 20% typical, 20% guaranteed.

Wood Shingles

see *Roofing: Wood Shingles*

Wood-Plastic Composite Lumber

see *Decking: Wood-Plastic Composite Lumber*

This Space is Available for Your Notes

Roofing

Roofs provide one of the most fundamental functions of a building: shelter from the elements. They must endure drastic temperature swings, long-term exposure to ultraviolet (UV) light, high winds, rain, hail and, depending on the climate, snow. In conflict with these performance and durability requirements, much of the roofing industry is driven by highly competitive economics and thin profit margins. Since shingles are rarely recycled, the 15- or 20-year typical life span of asphalt composite roofing products makes them highly resource-intensive. The National Roofing Contractors Association estimates that 75% of the dollars spent on roofing in the U.S. are for replacing or repairing existing roofs.

Durability is critical in roofing because a failure can mean serious damage not just to the roof itself but also to the building and its contents. Such damage multiplies the economic and environmental cost of less reliable roofing materials. Most roofing failures take place at joints and penetrations, so it's not just the material itself that must be durable but the entire system, including flashings and edge treatments. Proper installation is vital.

Roofing can also have a significant impact on cooling loads—within the building and even in the surrounding community. Use of lighter colored, low-solar absorptance roofing surfaces is one of the key measures advocated in the "Cooling Our Communities" program of the U.S. EPA. Reflective roofing can significantly assist appropriate insulation in dramatically reducing summertime solar gain into the building and thereby lowering the cooling load. Roofs with high solar reflectance also help to minimize the "urban heat island" effect, which raises the ambient temperature in urbanized areas.

Low-slope roofs, common on commercial buildings, are typically single-ply membranes or built-up asphalt with polyisocyanurate insulation underneath. When these roofs are replaced, the insulation usually has to be replaced as well, taking up landfill space and creating new resource demands for the replacement materials. Systems that separate the insulation from the membrane,

and that use a polystyrene insulation which can get wet and dry out without deteriorating, are often preferable because the insulation can be reused. In "protected membrane" applications, the rigid insulation (usually extruded polystyrene, XPS) is actually installed on top of the roofing membrane, with concrete pavers on top of the insulation.

Most intriguing environmentally are green roofs (living roofs) in which soil and plantings are used over the waterproof membrane and specialized green roof components. These living layers help replace the ecological functions that are lost when a building footprint covers open land. By using drought-tolerant, low-growing sedums, the planting media requirements with a green roof are fairly minimal.

Asphalt shingles with fiberglass or organic-fiber mats are still the most common choice for sloped roofing applications. Due to the durability concerns described above, only the heaviest-duty asphalt shingles (with a minimum 30-year warranty) should be considered. Alternatives are available in steel, plastic, rubber, and fiber-cement that use recycled-content materials and come in shake or shingle styles. Clay and concrete tiles are also an option, especially where hail isn't a serious threat. Weight is an issue with some of these products. Sheet steel is also increasingly popular on sloped roofs. Steel roofing should have a thick, galvanized or galvalume coating or be factory-coated with a highly durable finish, such as polyvinylidene fluoride (Kynar 500™), for maximum life.

The movement to integrate solar electricity generation into buildings—called Building-Integrated Photovoltaics (BIPV)—has reached the roofing industry with the introduction of photovoltaic (PV) shingles and larger integrated roofing panels. These are still quite pricey, and an electrician may have to work with the roofers during installation. Once installed, however, they produce electricity that can help power the building, with excess sold to the utility company in most states.

Asphalt Shingles

It's estimated that 75% of the total annual roofing dollars spent in the U.S. are spent on reroofing—and this reroofing generates tremendous quantities of waste. Asphalt shingles represent a large portion of the waste generated from steep-slope reroofing; avoiding asphalt roofing products is recommended because of poor durability and difficulty of recycling. Products included here incorporate recycled content.

Ondura

Tallant Industries, Inc.
4900 Ondura Dr.
Fredericksburg, VA 22407

Toll-free: 800-777-7663
Phone: 540-898-7000
www.ondura.com

Ondura corrugated asphalt roofing is composed of 50% asphalt and 50% cellulose fiber (by weight). The cellulose fiber is 100% post-consumer recycled mixed-paper waste. Ondura claims that their product is safe for rainwater collection systems. Ondura sheets measure 48" x 79" (4.5 sheets per square). Ondura tiles measure 48" x 19¾" (24 tiles per square). The manufacturer has certified the following recycled-content levels (by weight): total recovered material 50% typical, 50% guaranteed; post-consumer material 50% typical, 50% guaranteed.

Clay Roofing Tiles

Clay tiles are durable and made from abundant raw materials. As typically installed, roof tiles are also effective at preventing heat gain through the roof. In some climates and with some products, hail may be a concern.

Clay Roofing Tiles

Gladding, McBean & Co.
P.O. Box 97
Lincoln, CA 95648

Toll-free: 800-776-1133
Phone: 916-645-3341
www.gladdingmcbean.com

Gladding, McBean manufactures clay roofing tiles in a large variety of shapes, sizes, and fire-flashed blends, all of which are suitable for freeze/thaw climates.

Clay Roofing Tiles

Ludowici Roof Tile, Inc.
4757 Tile Plant Rd.
New Lexington, OH 43764

Toll-free: 800-945-8453
Phone: 740-342-1995
www.ludowici.com

Ludowici Clay Roof Tiles are available in 47 standard profiles and 43 standard colors in matte, gloss, weathered, sanded, and combed finishes. The company also offers an expanding lineup of larger, more affordable clay roofing tiles that reduce installation time and create less of a load for the roof deck. Recommended in freeze/thaw climates, all Ludowici standard grade tiles and fittings are covered by a 75-year limited warranty.

Clay Roofing Tiles

MCA Clay Tile
1985 Sampson Ave.
Corona, CA 92879

Toll-free: 800-736-6221
www.mca-tile.com

Among the tiles manufactured by MCA Clay Tile are a one-piece, S-shaped mission style tile in natural or glazed colors, the Corona Tapered Mission Tile available in standard and custom colors and blends, and an interlocking flat tile (MF 108 Flat) in Natural Red and glazed colors. MCA also manufactures Turret Tile®, which allows for a true turret- or fan-shaped installation. MCA's Oriental Style is an interlocking tile in the Japanese tradition. It is available in various glazed colors with many accessories and ornaments available. All MCA tiles have a limited 50-year warranty.

Claylite and ClayMax

US Tile Company
909 Railroad St.
Corona, CA 92882

Toll-free: 800-252-9548
www.ustile.com

Claylite® and ClayMax® are over 40% lighter than standard roofing tile. Claylite is configured in the traditional "S" tile shape, while ClayMax is in the form of a twin "S." US Tile® (UST) also manufactures tiles of standard weight. All UST tiles are a true tapered mission style to provide a tight fit; they are offered in over 20 colors and have a transferable lifetime limited warranty ($50 transfer fee).

Salvaged Clay and Concrete Tile Roofing

Custom Tile Roofing, Inc.
2875 West Hampden Ave.
Englewood, CO 80110

Phone: 303-761-3831
www.customtileroofing.com

Custom Tile Roofing maintains an inventory of close to 400,000 pieces of reclaimed roofing tiles.

Fiber-Cement Roofing Shingles

Fiber-cement building materials earn green points for their durability. The new generation of fiber-cement doesn't contain asbestos; it's made from portland cement, sand, clay, and wood fiber. Environmental concerns with fiber-cement include the embodied energy of portland cement and the source of the wood fiber—some fiber-cement products use wood from such distant locations as New Zealand and Russia. Although newer fiber-cement products are not yet proven over the long haul, the material is quite stable and typically carries a 50-year warranty. Of particular concern with roof shingle products in cold climates are the effects of freeze-thaw cycling; some products have coatings or polymer constituents to minimize water absorption.

FireFree Plus PMFC

Re-Con Building Products, Inc.
4850 S.W. Scholls Ferry Rd., Ste. 203
Portland, OR 97225

Toll-free: 877-276-7663
Phone: 503-226-7706
www.re-con.com

FireFree™ PMFC™ roofing is a polymer-modified fiber-cement product available in Rustic Shake™ or Quarry Slate™ styles. Both products have high recycled content. Rustic Shake is available in three colors; Quarry Slate is available in six colors. These products are Class A fire-rated and backed by a 50-year warranty.

Fluid-Applied Roofing

Look for green features such as low-VOC emissions, recycled content, and reflective surfaces to reduce heat gain.

Astec Coatings

Insulating Coatings Corp. (ICC)
103 Main St.
Binghamton, NY 13905

Toll-free: 800-223-8494
Phone: 607-723-1727
www.icc-astec.com

Astec Coatings are water-based ceramic, elastomeric building coatings with superior energy performance. White Astec coatings reflect solar radiation, as does the ceramic radiant barrier within the coating. ICC products are applied with a paint roller or spray equipment.

Metacrylics

Metacrylics
142 N. 27th St.
San Jose, CA 95116

Toll-free: 800-660-6950
Phone: 408-280-7733
www.metacrylics.com

Metacrylics is an elastomeric acrylic and stitchbond polyester roofing system. The water-based, UV-resistant acrylic coating can be applied to a large number of materials, including tar and gravel and corrugated metal, walking decks, exterior walls, and below-grade waterproofing. Available in 65 colors, white is the heat-reflective option for which Metacrylics qualifies as an ENERGY STAR® Certified Roofs product. According to the manufacturer, Metacrylics had the highest Cool Roof Rating combination of any product (Solar Reflectance: 87 and Thermal Emittance: 90). Metacrylics is not for use with potable water collection systems. The company offers a 10-year limited warranty that can be reinstated indefinitely with reapplication of the topcoat.

Sealoflex Waterproofing System

Sealoflex, Inc.
2516 Oscar Johnson Dr.
Charleston, SC 29405

Toll-free: 800-770-6466
Phone: 843-554-6466
www.sealoflex.com

The Sealoflex Waterproofing System consists of a highly flexible emulsion saturant, a nonwoven polyester fabric, and a UV-resistant finish coat. Sealoflex coatings are VOC-compliant.

Green Roof Plants

These listings are sources for appropriate plants for green (living) roofs.

Green Roof Plants

Green Roof Plants - Emory Knoll Farms
3410 Ady Rd.
Street, MD 21154

Phone: 410-452-5880
www.greenroofplants.com

Green Roof Plants (Emory Knoll Farms) is the only company in North America known to specialize solely in plants for extensive (low-profile) green roofs. In operation for six generations, the company has shifted production solely to green roof applications. The company's greenhouse is powered by a 3 kW PV system, and solar power also powers water pumping. The company has an organic growing focus and makes maximum use of reclaimed, recycled, recyclable, and natural materials. Most nutrients are provided by the farm's 25 llamas. The company propagates hundreds of species of sedum for green roof projects throughout North America.

Green Roof Plants

Intrinsic Perennial Gardens, Inc.
10702 Seaman Rd.
Hebron, IL 60034

Toll-free: 800-648-2788
Phone: 815-648-2788
www.intrinsicperennial
gardens.com

Intrinsic Perennial Gardens offers over 100 varieties of sedum, as well as other hardy perennials appropriate for green roof applications, and primarily serves the Midwest.

Photo: Brent Horvath

Green Roof Systems

Green roof systems for low-slope roofs protect the roof membrane, reduce stormwater flows, and help green our built environment through rooftop plantings. Green roofs, which are more common in Europe, can detain over 50% of rainwater from a typical storm: stormwater detention reduces the loads placed on storm sewers, making it a particularly attractive system in urban areas that have combined sewer overflow (CSO) events during heavy rains. Multilayered green roof systems are thicker than conventional roofs, and additional structural support is typically required. A green roof includes drainage, geotextile, soil, and vegetation layers; sedums or a thick sod of native grasses interspersed with

wildflowers can be a wonderful architectural element which helps to reduce building heat gain and the urban heat island effect. Plantings also absorb CO_2.

AMERGREEN Roof Garden System

American Wick Drain Corporation
1209 Airport Rd.
Monroe, NC 28110

Toll-free: 800-242-9425
Phone: 704-238-9200
www.americanwick.com

The Amergreen™ Roof Garden System consists of a needle-punched, nonwoven polypropylene geotextile filter fabric with an optional copper hydroxide root-barrier coating, a polystyrene "drain core" with water-storing cones that also provides airflow, and another polypropylene geotextile separation layer. Their 50RS system has a $7/16$"-deep drain core, while the 100RS has a 1" core. Amerigreen also manufactures products appropriate for reducing hydrostatic pressure on earth-sheltered homes.

Eco-Roof Systems

Building Logics, Inc.
1033 Downshire Chase
Virginia Beach, VA 23452

Phone: 757-340-4201
www.buildinglogics.com

Using the Famogreen name, Building Logics, Inc. supplies green roof systems with the German FAMOS APAO modified bitumen membrane and vegetation mats. Specialized versions of the membrane are available with a copper-impregnated spun-polyester root barrier and/or a lightweight hydrogel to retain water. Technical support for the design and specification of soil mixes and plants is available.

Roofmeadow

Roofscapes, Inc.
7114 McCallum St.
Philadelphia, PA 19119

Phone: 215-247-8784
www.roofmeadow.com

Roofscapes is a design and consulting firm that specializes in lightweight green roofs. Services offered include design and consulting, installation, construction inspection, and service and maintenance. Roofscapes is affiliated with Optigrun International AG, a German company with over 30 years of green roof experience.

Metal Roof Panels

Metal roofing, properly installed, is highly durable and readily recyclable at the end of its useful life. Using dissimilar metals for roofing, flashing, and fastening isn't recommended because they're susceptible to galvanic corrosion in the presence of water. Metal is also a preferred material for roofs used in rainwater catchment systems. In northern climates, snow readily slides off metal roofs, avoiding the damage caused by ice dams. In recent years, manufacturers have introduced low-slope metal roofing systems to complement more conventional steep-slope products.

Met-Tile

Met-Tile
P.O. Box 4268
Ontario, CA 91761

Phone: 909-947-0311
www.met-tile.com

Met-Tile metal roofing is corrugated and detailed to give the appearance of clay roofing tiles. It is made from recycled steel with a "galvalume" (zinc-alloy) coating for durability and an additional water-based coating in a choice of 10 colors. It comes in lengths from 2' to 25'. Met-tile roofs are custom-designed to order.

Metal Shingles

Metals are readily recyclable, and certain metal roofing products also have high recycled content. These products can be a part of a long-lasting roof when installed with appropriate fasteners and proper flashing. The use of dissimilar metals for roofing, flashing, and fastening isn't recommended because they're susceptible to galvanic corrosion in the presence of water. Metal is also a preferred material for roofs used in rainwater catchment systems. In northern climates, snow readily slides off metal roofs, avoiding the damage caused by ice dams.

MetalWorks Steel Shingles

Tamko Roofing Products, Inc.
220 W. 4th St.
P.O. Box 1404
Joplin, MO 64801

Toll-free: 800-641-4691
Phone: 417-624-6644
www.metalworksroof.com

MetalWorks (formerly AstonWood) Steel Shingles are made from as much as 50% recycled material. The shingles consist of G90 galvanized steel with a Kynar 500® or Hylar

5000® coating. These wood and slate shingle look-alike products are 12" x 40" and interconnect on all four sides. Shingles are available in a variety of colors. Because of their light weight, these steel shingles can be installed over two existing layers of asphalt shingles. MetalWorks shingles carry a lifetime warranty.

Progress Aluminum Roofing

Inteq Corp.
33010 Lakeland Blvd.
Eastlake, OH 44095

Phone: 440-953-0550
www.4-inteqcorp.com

Inteq produces Progress Roofing made from recycled aluminum. The 12" x 24" interlocking roofing panels are formed to look like cedar shakes. The product is available in 10 colors with a Kynar® coating. The manufacturer has certified the following recycled-content levels (by weight): total recovered material 97% typical, 97% guaranteed; post-consumer material 80% typical, 80% guaranteed.

Recycled Metal Shingles

Zappone Manufacturing
2928 N. Pittsburg St.
Spokane, WA 99207

Toll-free: 800-285-2677
Phone: 509-483-6408
www.zappone.com

Zappone shingles are made from either recycled copper or aluminum. Both products contain a concealed nailing flange and a four-way interlocking mechanism. Shingles measure $9\frac{1}{8}$" x 15" with a 8" x $14\frac{1}{2}$" exposure. Aluminum shingles have a Kynar 500 finish in a choice of 6 colors. Recycled aluminum fasteners and accessories are also available. The manufacturer has certified the following recycled-content levels for copper shingles (by weight): total recovered material 85% typical, 85% guaranteed; post-consumer material 75% typical, 75% guaranteed. The manufacturer has certified the following recycled-content levels for aluminum shingles (by weight): total recovered material 100% typical, 100% guaranteed; post-consumer material 100% typical, 100% guaranteed.

Rustic Shingle

Classic Products, Inc.
8510 Industry Park Dr.
P.O. Box 701
Piqua, OH 45356

Toll-free: 800-543-8938
Phone: 937-773-9840
www.classicroof.com

Rustic Shingle is made from an alloy with recycled-aluminum content (mostly beverage cans). The shingles are formed to resemble wood shakes and finished with a baked-on Kynar coating. The Rustic Shingle System consists of 12" x 24" interconnecting panels and matching preformed accessories. The shingles are available in 11 colors. The manufacturer has certified the following recycled-content levels (by weight): post-consumer material 98% typical.

Plastic Shingles

Plastic roofing products, like plastic lumber, provide a use for plastics in the solid-waste stream. Products included here appear very durable, but as with plastic lumber, the long-term effects of UV light, and expansion and contraction of the material, are still unknown. Some of these products carry 50-year warranties—significantly longer than those of asphalt shingles. Another environmental benefit of some of these products is their end-of-life recyclability. Most of the plastic shingles included here appear similar to natural slate.

AmeriSlate

American Roof Manufacturing, LLC
1160 Chess
Foster City, CA 94404

Phone: 650-570-7663

AmeriSlate™ is a unique roofing material manufactured from post-consumer tires that are cut to shape with the treads buffed off. The finishing process involves a coating of crushed stone or roofing granules adhered with a proprietary fire-retardant epoxy. AmeriSlate is available in a range of colors as well as uncoated black and is unconditionally warranted (except for tornadoes) for 75 years. AmeriSlate is an incarnation of FlexShake™, the manufacturing rights to which American Roof Manufacturing purchased in 2003.

Authentic Roof 2000

Crowe Building Products Ltd.
116 Burris St.
Hamilton, ON L8M 2J5 Canada

Phone: 905-529-6818
www.authentic-roof.com

Authentic Roof™ was the first slate-look recycled polymer and rubber roofing material. This product's weight is only 25% that of slate, and the shingles can be installed quickly. Authentic 2000 is produced using Baljen TPO (thermoplastic olefin) and is available in a choice of 6 colors and 3 slate patterns: full, mitered-edge, and beavertail. Authentic shingles carry a Class A, B, or C fire rating and a 50-year warranty.

Eco-shake

Re-New Wood, Inc.
104 N. Eighth St.
P.O. Box 1093
Wagoner, OK 74467

Toll-free: 800-420-7576
Phone: 918-485-5803
www.ecoshake.com

Eco-shake® is a roofing shingle made from post-industrial recycled PVC (recycled content varies due to market availability) and 100% reclaimed wood fibers. The product has the look of a wood shake and is available in three standard colors: umber, teak, and charcoal. Custom colors are also available.

Enviroshake

Wellington Polymer
Technology Inc.
650 Riverview Dr., #1
P.O. Box 1462
Chatham, ON N7M 5W8
Canada

Toll-free: 866-423-3302
Phone: 519-380-9265
www.enviroshake.com

Enviroshake™ Simulated Cedar Shakes are manufactured from approximately 95% recycled material by weight. About half of the recycled content is post-industrial recycled plastics and half is agricultural flax- and hemp-fiber waste, with a small percentage of post-consumer recycled-tire rubber. The remaining portion is comprised of proprietary binders. Enviroshake starts out dark brown and ages to a silver-gray that resembles weathered cedar shakes. The 20"-long shakes come in bundles of mixed widths of 12", 8", 6", and 4" and carry a 50-year limited warranty. Custom molded ridge caps are also available.

Euroslate

GEM, Inc.
9330 48 St. SE
Calgary, AB T2C 2R2 Canada

Phone: 403-215-3333
www.euroslate.ca

Euroslate is an interlocking roofing system with the look of slate tiles. The product is made with 60-70% recycled tire crumb rubber, plus another 15% of a recycled component that the manufacturer will not divulge. The materials are heat-formed with a binder, also proprietary. The system is lightweight (under 4 lbs/ft^2) and recyclable, and the manufacturer is in the process of obtaining Class A fire-resistance certification at this writing. Available colors include silver, brown, red, green, gold, sand, slate, and black. Colors are integral, so those other than black may reduce the overall recycled content of the product. A licensed installer is required. The manufacturer indicates that installation time is significantly reduced over more common options.

Majestic Slate Tiles

EcoStar
104 Terrace Dr.
Mundelein, IL 60060

Toll-free: 800-211-7170
www.premiumroofs.com

Majestic Slate Tiles are 100% post-industrial recycled and re-cyclable, lightweight shingles made from industrial rubber and plastics. The coloration of Majestic Slate varies slightly, imitating differences in color of natural slate. Preformed ridge slates are also available. EcoStar is a division of Carlisle Syntec, Inc.

Progress Plastic Roofing Shingles

Inteq Corp.
33010 Lakeland Blvd.
Eastlake, OH 44095

Phone: 440-953-0550
www.4-inteqcorp.com

Inteq Corp. manufactures Progress Roofing in simulated slate, wood shake, and terra cotta tile profiles from recycled HDPE. All three styles have uniform color throughout and come with a 50-year warranty. Slate and wood shake styles have a UL Class A fire rating; Terra Cotta style are rated Class C. Recycled content is 60% post-industrial, with up to 15% post-consumer content available.

Welsh Simulated Slate Shingles

Welsh Mountain Slate Inc.
249 Bridge St.
Campbellford, ON K0L 1L0 Canada

Toll-free: 800-865-8784
Phone: 705-653-2525
www.welshmountainslate.com

Welsh Mountain Slate manufactures simulated slate roofing shingles from 100% recycled tire rubber and re-engineered polymers. The standard shingles measure 18" long x 12" wide x $\frac{1}{4}$" thick (tapered) and are marked for 6" or 7" exposure. Preformed hip and ridge cap tiles are also available. Welsh Mountain Slate shingles are Class C fire-rated and come in green and three shades of gray. The company will ship factory-direct anywhere in Canada and the U.S., and offers a 50-year warranty.

Ridge and Soffit Vents

Adequate ventilation of attic spaces helps keep buildings with pitched roofs cooler in the summer and reduces the risks of ice dams in the winter. Some evidence indicates that certain roofing materials experience less thermal stress and last longer on properly ventilated roofs, though this contention is hotly debated. Ridge vents in conjunction with soffit vents create an effective ventilation flow, with air entering at the soffits and exiting at the ridge. The ventilation performance of ridge and soffit vents is superior to either gable-end vents or rooftop ventilators. Insulated roofs require an air channel between the insulation and the roof sheathing. Ventilating underlayment products installed beneath roof shingles and tiles allows the roofing to dry uniformly between rain events—increasing life and minimizing mold growth.

Cedar Breather

Benjamin Obdyke Inc.
199 Precision Dr.
Horsham, PA 19044

Toll-free: 800-523-5261
Phone: 215-672-7200
www.benjaminobdyke.com

Cedar Breather® is a fire-resistant underlayment for use with wood shingles or shakes, providing continuous airflow between the solid roof deck and shingles. Cedar Breather's 0.27"-thick, 3-dimensional nylon matrix allows the entire underside of the shingle to dry, eliminating excess moisture, preventing thermal cupping and warping, and reducing potential rotting. Cedar Breather eliminates the need for furring strips and comes with a 50-year warranty.

Cobra Ridge Vents

GAF Materials Corp.
1361 Alps Rd.
Wayne, NJ 07470

Toll-free: 800-223-1948
Phone: 877-423-7663
www.gaf.com

GAF's Cobra ridge vents are made from recycled fibers formed into an airy, fibrous mat that, when capped with asphalt shingles, provides a low-profile ridge vent.

Roll Roofing Accessories

Look for recycled content.

Rolath

Bedford Technology, LLC
2424 Armour Rd.
P.O. Box 609
Worthington, MN 56187

Toll-free: 800-721-9037
Phone: 507-372-5558
www.plasticboards.com

Rolath is a $1\frac{1}{4}$"-wide strapping product made from recycled plastic. Most of the product's content is waste from Bedford Technology's other manufacturing operations. Rolath is most often used to secure roofing felt but is also effective at securing polyethylene film and building wraps. The manufacturer has certified the following recycled-content levels (by weight): total recovered material 99% typical, 95% guaranteed; post-consumer material 0% typical, 0% guaranteed.

Roof Walkway Pads

Roof walk boards made from recycled-tire rubber or other post-consumer waste products make good use of waste material in a durable, reusable product. They're typically applied over membrane roofs to prevent damage while maintaining roofing or roof-mounted mechanical equipment. They are very effective for walkways on green roofs. Residential uses also include poolsides and concrete decks. These heavy duty mats come in a variety of sizes and thicknesses.

Roof Walkway Pads and Paving Risers

North West Rubber Mats, Ltd.
33850 Industrial Ave.
Abbotsford, BC V2S 7T9 Canada

Toll-free: 800-663-8724
Phone: 604-859-2002
www.northwestrubber.com

North West Rubber's Roof Walkway Pads are made from recycled-tire rubber for use in protecting low-slope membrane roofs. The pads are $\frac{3}{8}$", $\frac{1}{2}$", or $\frac{3}{4}$" thick. Paving Risers, made from 100% recycled-tire-derived styrene butadiene rubber, come in squares (6" x 6" and $\frac{3}{8}$" or $\frac{5}{8}$" thick) or circles (4" in diameter and 1" thick) that are used to support cement roof pavers above the roof membrane surface.

Roof-Guard Pads

Humane Manufacturing LLC
805 Moore St.
Baraboo, WI 53913-2796

Toll-free: 800-369-6263
Phone: 608-356-8336
www.humanemfg.com

Roof-Guard Pads are made from recycled-tire rubber, are interlocking, and come in sizes ranging from 2' x 3' to 4' x 6'. They are available with either a raised button or impressed pattern. The manufacturer has certified the following recycled-content levels (by weight): total recovered material 93% typical, 93% guaranteed; post-consumer material 93% typical, 93% guaranteed.

UltraGard PVC WBP-100 Heavy Duty Walkway Pad

Johns Manville Corporation
P.O. Box 5108
Denver, CO 80217

Toll-free: 800-654-3103
Phone: 303-978-2000
www.jm.com

UltraGard PVC WBP-100 Heavy Duty Walkway Pad is a recycled thermoplastic-content pad for high-traffic areas of low-slope roofs. This product is available in 3'- and 4'-wide rolls.

Roofing Underlayment

Roofing underlayment provides additional moisture and ice protection; it installs between the roof sheathing and the finish roofing material. Look for recycled content.

Recycled-Rubber Roofing Underlayment

CETCO
1500 W. Shure Dr.
Arlington Heights, IL 60004

Toll-free: 800-527-9948
Phone: 847-818-7918
www.strongsealroofing.com

StrongSeal™ Recycled Rubberized Products manufactures roofing underlayments from recycled tire rubber with 40% recycled content. Duck's Back (25 mils thick) is the company's nail-down version, and StrongSeal Plus (40 mils) is a peel-and-stick version. These products do not contain asphalt and, according to the manufacturer, can be exposed to the elements for a period of 12 months. StrongSeal is backed by an industry leading material warranty.

Rooftop Planting Media

These are sources for appropriate planting media for green (living) roofs.

Rooftop Planting Media

Midwest Trading - Horticultural Supplies, Inc.
P.O. Box 1005
St. Charles, IL 60174

Phone: 847-742-1840
www.midwest-trading.com

Midwest Trading is a regional supplier of mulch mixes and planting media, including media optimized for green roofs. Green roof planting media should have high absorptivity (high total pore space) and low organic content—properties appropriate for green roofs. A partner company, Midwest Groundcovers, has a number of sedums available for green roof applications.

Rooftop Planting Media

White Premium
    Organics, Inc.
2560 Foxfield Rd.,
    Ste. 200
St. Charles, IL 60174

Toll-free: 866-586-1563
Phone: 630-377-9966
www.garveyintl.com

White Premium Organics produces growing mixes specially formulated for rooftop applications. The mixes consist of approximately 80% inorganic matter such as expanded slate or calcined clay with sand, and 20% organic matter such as composted bark, rice hulls, or mushroom compost. These materials have the significant bulk density needed for rooftop applications, resist decomposing, provide excellent aeration, and won't clog filtration systems, according to the company. Media is available for extensive (2"-4" soil depth), semi-intensive (4"-6" soil depth), and intensive (6" soil depth and deeper) roof garden systems. White Premium Organics serves most of the Midwest area of the U.S.

Slate Shingles

Natural slate roofing is an excellent product from an environmental standpoint. Besides being a minimally processed material, slate also has superb durability: properly installed slate roofs last 70 to 100 or more years with only minor maintenance. Additionally, slates can easily be salvaged and reused on new building projects. However, they are heavy—proximity to slate quarries and adequately strong roof structures must be considered.

Salvaged Slate and Clay Tile Roofing

Alluvium Construction
200 Lake Shore Dr.
Marlton, NJ 08053

Phone: 856-767-2700
www.historicroofs.com

Alluvium Construction specializes in reclaimed slate and tile roofing in all quantities, types, and colors. Domestic or imported new slate may also be ordered. If purchasing new slate, domestic slate from nearby quarries is recommended.

Salvaged Slate and Clay Tile Roofing

Durable Slate Co.
1050 N. Fourth St.
Columbus, OH 43201

Toll-free: 800-666-7445
Phone: 614-299-5522
www.durableslate.com

Durable Slate Co. stocks well over 600,000 pieces of salvaged slate and 400,000 pieces of salvaged clay tiles. Durable Slate is able to match colors and styles of slate and tile that are no longer produced.

Salvaged Slate and Clay Tile Roofing

Emack Slate Company, Inc.
9 Office Park Cir., Ste. 120
Birmingham, AL 35223

Phone: 205-879-3424
www.emackslate.com

Emack Slate maintains an inventory of salvaged slate and clay tiles. Domestic or imported new slate may also be ordered. If purchasing new slate, domestic slate from nearby quarries is recommended.

Salvaged Slate and Clay Tile Roofing

Reclaimed Roofs, Inc.
7454 Lancaster Pike #328
Hockessin, DE 19707

Phone: 302-369-9187
www.reclaimedroofs.com

Reclaimed Roofs provides salvaged roofing slates and tiles. Its owner sits on the Board of Directors for the National Slate Association.

Salvaged Slate and Clay Tile Roofing

Renaissance Roofing, Inc.
P.O. Box 5024
Rockford, IL 61125

Toll-free: 800-699-5695
Phone: 815-547-1725
www.claytileroof.com

Renaissance Roofing, Inc. is a supplier of salvaged clay tile and slate roofing materials.

Salvaged Slate and Clay Tile Roofing

The Roof Tile and Slate Company
1209 Carroll St.
Carrollton, TX 75006

Toll-free: 800-446-0220
Phone: 972-446-0005
www.claytile.com

The Roof Tile and Slate Company maintains a large inventory of salvaged slate and tile. New domestic slate and tile are also available.

Salvaged Slate and Clay Tile Roofing

TileSearch, Inc.
216 James St.
P.O. Box 1694
Roanoke, TX 76262

Phone: 817-491-2444
www.tilesearch.net

TileSearch is a national search service for new and salvaged slate and clay tile roofing. TileSearch also supplies slate for floor tiling.

Salvaged Slate Roofing

Echeguren Slate
1495 Illinois St.
San Francisco, CA 94107

Phone: 415-206-9343
www.echeguren.com

Echeguren Slate offers salvaged roofing slate in sizes from 8" x 12" to 12" x 24", $3/16$" to $3/4$" thick. Domestic or imported new slate for roofing and flooring may also be ordered. If purchasing new slate, domestic slate from nearby quarries is recommended.

Slate Roofing Shingles

Hilltop Slate Inc.
Rte. 22-A
Middle Granville, NY 12849

Phone: 518-642-2270
www.hilltopslate.com

Hilltop Slate, in business since 1948, is a producer of slate roofing shingles with six quarries in New York and Vermont. Hilltop Slate is part of the Slate Products division of the Alfred McAlpine Group and a sister company to Penrhyn, the largest producer of slate products in the world.

Slate Roofing Shingles

Vermont Structural
   Slate Co., Inc.
3 Prospect St.
P.O. Box 98
Fair Haven, VT 05743

Toll-free: 800-343-1900
Phone: 802-265-4933
www.vermontstructural
   slate.com

Vermont Structural Slate has been a producer of slate products since 1859. The company offers roofing shingles in several colors from their Vermont quarries as well as slate from around the world.

Slate Roofing Shingles

Virginia Slate Company
100 E. Main St.
Richmond, VA 23219

Toll-free: 888-827-5283
Phone: 804-282-7929
www.virginiaslate.com

The Virginia Slate Company has been producing slate roofing shingles from its Buckingham County quarry since 1860. Slate can be purchased directly from their own quarry. Virginia Slate also offers slate from other producers in a variety of color choices. Their premium roofing slate carries a 100-year limited warranty.

Thermoplastic Membrane Roofing

Single-ply roofing membranes, typically used on large commercial buildings, are occasionally used on homes and light-commercial buildings for low-slope roof areas and beneath upper-floor walk-out decks. They can be ballasted, mechanically fastened, or fully adhered. Thermoplastic membranes can be heat-welded at seams, minimizing use of solvent-based adhesives. PVC has long been the most common thermoplastic membrane material. For roof membranes, PVC requires plasticizers for flexibility; these chemicals, which may dissipate over time and cause brittleness, are a major cause of membrane failure. PVC is targeted by some environmental groups for its chlorine content and the risk of dioxin production in the event of an unintentional fire or during improperly controlled incineration. Phthalate plasticizers, commonly used with PVC, also may mimic natural hormones in humans and other animals, causing health problems. Concerns about the environmental and health impacts and performance characteristics of PVC have led to the development of thermoplastic olefin (TPO) membranes. Polyolefins are a class of polymers that includes polyethylene and polypropylene. These materials obtain their flexibility through the copolymers rather than plasticizers; however, without the addition of fire retardants, some do not pass necessary fire tests for unballasted applications.

Stevens EP

Stevens Roofing Systems
9 Sullivan Rd.
Holyoke, MA 01040

Toll-free: 800-621-7663
Phone: 413-533-8100
www.stevensroofing.com

Stevens Roofing Systems is one of the world's largest TPO producers. The Stevens EP family of nonhalogenated TPO membranes uses hydrated mineral salts as a fire retardant. Stevens EP membranes are available in nominal 45-, 60-, and 80-mil thickness, and in standard 76.5"-wide rolls. No solvents or adhesives are required, and no known toxins are released if the product is incinerated.

The material is available in many colors and can be installed using several attachment methods. White Stevens EP is highly reflective, reducing energy loads and avoiding contributions to the urban heat island effect. It also meets the EPA ENERGY STAR® Roof Products guidelines.

UltraPly TPO

Firestone Building Products Company
525 Congressional Blvd.
Carmel, IN 46032

Toll-free: 800-428-4442
Phone: 317-575-7000
www.firestonebpco.com

Firestone's UltraPly TPO is a heat-weldable, solar-reflective roofing material that meets fire codes without chlorine or other halogenated fire-retardants. This prevents the release of hydrochloric acid (HCl), dioxins, or related compounds in the event of fire.

Wood Shingles

Wood shingles and shakes are traditionally and most commonly made from old-growth western red cedar. Although the embodied energy of this product is quite low, the harvesting of western red cedar is, in most cases, unsustainable. If a wood shingle roof is desired and fire-related concerns aren't prohibitive, using certified eastern white cedar shingles, commonly used as wall siding, is an option.

Certified PR Shingles

Industries Maibec, Inc.
660 Lenoir St.
Sainte-Foy, PQ G1X 3W3 Canada

Toll-free: 800-363-1930
Phone: 418-659-3323
www.maibec.com

PR® Shingles are made from eastern white cedar from the Seven Islands Land Company that is chain-of-custody certified by SCS. Shingles are available in three options: unfinished (natural); kiln-dried and factory-stained in gray, beige, or a limited choice of colors; and factory-treated with an oil finish. While most commonly used on walls, they may be appropriate in some roofing applications if installed more thickly.

This Space is Available for Your Notes

Doors

Exterior doors are usually solid wood or foam wrapped in metal or some other weather-resistant material. Most foam insulation in doors (polyisocyanurate) used to contain ozone-depleting HCFCs, but that is no longer the case.

Most insulated doors are relatively similar in energy efficiency since the market is so competitive; they're distinguished largely by the quality of their weather-stripping and threshold. Insulating values of R-5 to R-7 are common.

Interior doors are usually wood, molded hardboard, or hollow core. Since Lauan plywood comes from nonsustainably harvested rainforest wood, it should be avoided. Molded hardboard is often made with some recycled content and pressed into shape; some hardboard is made with urea-formaldehyde and should be avoided. While solid wood is beautiful and a natural, minimally processed product, clear stock is becoming harder to get and may come from old-growth forests.

An increasing number of manufacturers are offering doors using wood from certified sources. Certification to Forest Stewardship Council—FSC—standards involves third-party evaluation and monitoring of sustainable forestry practices.

Door and Window Accessories

Look for recycled content, FSC-certified wood, or use of salvaged materials. (Certification to Forest Stewardship Council—FSC—standards involves third-party evaluation and monitoring of sustainable forestry practices.)

Decorative Metalwork

Resource Revival, Inc.
2267 N. Interstate Ave.
Portland, OR 97227

Toll-free: 800-866-8823
Phone: 503-282-1449
www.resourcerevival.com

Resource Revival uses the metal parts of discarded bicycles, including frames, and constructs unique and intriguing door and window grates. The manufacturer has certified the following recycled-content levels (by weight): total recovered material 50% typical, 50% guaranteed; post-consumer material 50% typical, 50% guaranteed.

Door Hardware

Innovative products can reduce air leakage, improving energy performance.

Door-Tite Strike Plate

Door-Tite, Inc.
3219 Creston Ct.
Dublin, OH 43017

Toll-free: 877-366-7848
www.door-tite.com

Door-Tite™ Strike Plate is a simple but very effective one-piece strike plate that automatically adjusts to such conditions as ill-fitting doors and seasonal shrinkage/swelling of doors and door frames to provide an energy-saving tight fit. Door-Tite installs like a standard strike plate and has six step-like protrusions which fit into the latch cavity. As the door closes, the latch moves down the steps until it settles on a step that gives a tight fit.

Doors and Windows - General

see *Windows: Doors and Windows - General*

Steel Entry Doors

Even though steel conducts heat more readily than wood, steel entry doors that include foam insulation and are installed in wooden frames with quality weatherstripping generally provide better energy performance than wood entry doors. In choosing an insulated entry door, consider the R-value of the insulation, weatherstripping, and glazing materials.

Contours Steel Doors

Jeld-Wen, Inc.
3303 Lakeport Blvd.
P.O. Box 1329
Klamath Falls, OR 97601

Toll-free: 800-535-3936
Phone: 541-882-3451
www.jeld-wen.com

The Contours steel entry door has an EPS foam core and is available with low-e coated insulating glass. By contrast, most insulation used in entry doors is polyurethane, which is made with ozone-depleting HCFCs. The Contours line replaces Jeld-Wen's Energy Saver line.

Wood and Plastic Doors

Products listed here include doors made from FSC-certified wood, reclaimed wood, and/or a composite of materials. (Certification to Forest Stewardship Council—FSC—standards involves third-party evaluation and monitoring of sustainable forestry practices.) As with other wood products, specifying certified-wood doors promotes long-term forest management for the benefit of forest ecosystems, timber resources, and local economies. Reclaimed wood doors, like other reclaimed wood products, don't carry the environmental burdens of recent timber harvesting. Previously harvested woods remilled into wood doors can provide rich colors and beauty generally not available from today's faster-growing timber. From an energy performance perspective, wood entry doors are usually not the best option. Composite entry doors, like steel doors, are available with foam insulation; these doors far outperform traditional solid-wood doors in terms of energy conservation. Composite doors may also be made from recovered and/or recycled materials.

Alterna by Doorcraft

Jeld-Wen, Inc.
3303 Lakeport Blvd.
P.O. Box 1329
Klamath Falls, OR 97601

Toll-free: 800-535-3936
Phone: 541-882-3451
www.jeld-wen.com

Alterna by Doorcraft entry doors from Jeld-Wen are the first doors with an EPS foam core instead of the more common polyurethane foam insulation. These non-ozone-depleting doors are faced with a phenol-bonded wood-fiber composite mounted on laminated veneer lumber (LVL) frame members. Paint is required to protect the composite exterior.

Certified Stave Core Doors

Marshfield DoorSystems™
1401 E. 4th St.
P.O. Box 7780
Marshfield, WI 54449-7780

Toll-free: 800-869-3667
Phone: 715-384-2141
www.marshfielddoors.com

Marshfield DoorSystems' Environmental-Class Architectural Wood Doors are FSC-certified stave core doors available for nonrated as well as 20-minute rated applications with either neutral- or positive- pressure fire labels. The composite products in this door do not contain any added urea-formaldehyde. Doors are available with a wide range of veneer options, Styled™ faces, medium-density overlay (MDO), or plastic laminate. Also available is the Enviroclad™ UV factory finish, which uses water-based stains and ultraviolet-cured topcoats, and releases no VOCs. Glue used in the stave core contains 1-5% formaldehyde, but, according to the manufacturer, the doors are encapsulated and will not release any formaldehyde.

Certified Wood Doors

A. E. Sampson & Son, Inc.
171 Camden Rd.
Warren, ME 04864

Toll-free: 800-769-6196
Phone: 207-273-4000
www.aesampsonandson.com

A. E. Sampson & Son manufactures chain-of-custody FSC-certified wooden doors. Hardwoods, including maple and birch, are sourced from the Seven Islands Land Company forests in northern and western Maine. Doors are custom-made with mortise and tenon joinery, stile, and rail.

Certified Wood Doors

Algoma Hardwoods, Inc.
1001 Perry St.
Algoma, WI 54201

Toll-free: 800-678-8910
Phone: 920-487-5221
www.algomahardwoods.com

Algoma Hardwoods manufactures and supplies FSC-certified interior wood doors for residential and commercial custom orders. Lead time for orders of 20 to 30 doors is 10 weeks. The primary species is red oak, with some birch and cherry available as well.

Certified Wood Doors

Eggers Industries
1 Eggers Dr.
P.O. Box 88
Two Rivers, WI 54241

Phone: 920-793-1351
www.eggersindustries.com

Eggers Industries manufactures architectural wood doors in flush as well as stile-and-rail styles that are Smartwood-certified according to the standards of the Forest Stewardship Council. The doors are certified by partial-content rules to contain over 70% certified wood. Current certified offerings include nonrated and 20-minute doors, negative or positive pressure. Some products, such as the wood composite doors, contain urea formaldehyde resins; check with the manufacturer.

Certified Wood Doors

VT Industries, Inc.
1000 Industrial Park
Box 490
Holstein, IA 51025

Toll-free: 800-827-1615
Phone: 712-368-4381
www.vtindustries.com

VT Industries offers a line of architectural wood doors certified by Smartwood according to the standards of the Forest Stewardship Council.

Interior and Exterior Doors

The Bead & Batten Door
1054 Rammell Mt. Rd.
Tetonia, ID 83452

Phone: 208-456-2711
www.alternativetimberstructures.com

The Bead & Batten Door specializes in custom-building of doors in unusual sizes and thicknesses from reclaimed and new woods.

Recycled-Content Wood Doors

Executive Door Company
3939 W. Clarendon
Phoenix, AZ 85019

Phone: 602-272-8076
www.executivedoor.com

Executive Door Company manufactures Environmental residential and commercial interior and exterior doors from medium-density fiberboard (MDF). The doors are certified by Scientific Certification Systems (SCS) to be constructed of 100% recovered and recycled wood fibers with at least 30% post-industrial recycled waste content. Executive Door offers a lifetime warranty against splitting, cracking, or warping.

This Space is Available for Your Notes

Windows

Windows are one of the most high-tech products in residential construction. Since the early 1980s, the energy performance of typical windows has increased by over 50%, the result of both improvements in glazing and in frame construction. The National Fenestration Rating Council (NFRC) publishes the energy performance of certified window products; in some states, manufacturers are required to label their windows with the NFRC's rating. These ratings are like the EPA mileage rating for cars—they may not provide actual energy consumption in a particular application, but are useful for comparison.

The emergence of energy-efficient windows is a key part of a breakthrough in the overall design of houses and light-commercial buildings. Glazed surfaces no longer have to lose a lot of heat or feel cold in winter, so heating systems can be much smaller and less expensive. For example, heating elements are no longer required beneath windows to compensate for the drafts and cold surfaces that windows used to generate. In a well-designed, highly energy-efficient house, central heating may no longer be necessary at all—though air distribution systems are still important to ensure good indoor air quality.

Low-e glass coatings, which increase the R-value of standard double-glazing from 2 to about 3, are gaining in market share each year. The premium of 10–20% for low-e easily pays for itself in a few years in most applications. The added benefit is a warmer window surface that's more comfortable to be near both in cold weather and in very hot weather. Double low-e and HeatMirror™ coatings on suspended films are available in premium windows, and can increase the center-of-glass insulating value up to R-9.

By careful selection of low-e coatings, windows can be "tuned" to optimize the performance of a structure—balancing heat loss, solar gain, and visible light transmission through the glass. In hot climates, coatings that transmit less solar gain should generally be preferred. In cold climates, where solar gain can be beneficial in winter, glazing that transmits more solar energy is preferable on the south side of a building. On the east and west, less solar gain is preferable even in cold climates, because solar gain is greatest on these orientations during the summer, when air conditioning is likely to be used.

Use of an inert, low-conductivity gas in the space between layers of glazing is another way to improve thermal performance. Most low-e windows have argon gas fill; some super-energy-efficient windows have krypton or a mix of argon and krypton between the glazing layers.

Although standard for many years, aluminum windows are disappearing from most cold-climate markets. If aluminum frames are used, they should be constructed with a *thermal break* between the inner and outer surfaces to improve energy performance. Aluminum windows are rapidly being replaced by vinyl frames.

Vinyl frames are much better than aluminum in terms of thermal performance, but there are some environmental concerns associated with the production and eventual disposal of PVC (polyvinyl chloride). Vinyl windows vary greatly in quality; many have weather-sealing problems over the life of the window due to the expansion and contraction of the plastic. They're better suited to sliders and double hung windows than casements, because those styles are prone to warping and sagging. There are also concerns about the PVC resin itself and various compounds that are added to it to provide UV stability, flexibility, and flame resistance.

Wood windows are still the standard for energy efficiency. Vinyl or aluminum cladding adds value in its low maintenance qualities. Wood window manufacturers are facing increasing difficulty in finding affordable, knot-free material from which to manufacture their product; some are using finger-jointed material with an interior coating and exterior cladding.

Other energy-efficient frame materials include fiberglass, with or without foam insulation in the hollow channels, and composites such as a combination of recycled vinyl and wood fibers.

With any window materials, durability of the edge seals and spacers that separate the layers of glass is extremely important, as failure of this seal will cause condensation inside the window (fogging), and the loss of any low-conductivity gas fill.

ABS Plastic Windows

Like vinyl, ABS is very low-maintenance. Because there's no chlorine in ABS, there's no risk of dioxin generation during an accidental fire or incineration at the end of the product's life.

High-Performance Non-PVC Thermoplastic Windows

Thermal Line Windows, Inc.
3601 30th Ave. NW
P.O. Box 579
Mandan, ND 58554

Toll-free: 800-662-1832
Phone: 701-663-1832
www.tlwindows.com

A regional company (12-state Midwestern region) founded in 1984, Thermaline produces both vinyl (PVC) windows and windows made from an engineered ABS plastic called Compozit™. This is a thermoplastic material engineered by GE Plastics division under the name Cycolac/Geloy. Performance is similar to PVC, and the material contains no chlorine. The highest-performance Compozit windows are triple-glazed with two low-e coatings and krypton gas-fill; they have NFRC-listed unit U-factors as low as 0.20 for residential-sized windows and 0.19 for commercial.

Door and Window Accessories

see *Doors: Door and Window Accessories*

Doors and Windows - General

These listings are for industry representation and ratings organizations for doors and windows.

Industry Representation

National Fenestration Rating Council
8484 Georgia Ave., Ste. 320
Silver Spring, MD 20910

Phone: 301-589-1776
www.nfrc.org

The National Fenestration Rating Council (NFRC) administers a voluntary, uniform rating and labeling system for the energy performance of windows, doors, and skylights.

The Efficient Windows Collaborative

Alliance to Save Energy
1200 18th St. NW, Ste. 900
Washington, DC 20036

Phone: 202-530-2231
www.efficientwindows.org

The Efficient Windows Collaborative is actively involved in promoting energy-efficient windows. A nonprofit coalition comprised of industry, government, and other interested groups, their website provides free resources and information.

Fiberglass Windows

Fiberglass has some distinct advantages over wood, vinyl, and metal for window frame and sash construction. As high-quality wood resources become scarce, fiberglass (a composite of polyester resin and glass fibers) is likely to become more common because of its energy performance and durability. Pultruded fiberglass frame members have a hollow profile that's usually insulated with fiberglass or polyurethane foam. Because the conduction through window frames is a significant source of heat loss, insulated fiberglass frames are an attractive option. The coefficient of thermal expansion of fiberglass is low, very similar to that of glass; limited differential expansion and contraction between the sash and glazing materials puts less stress on the glazing's edge seals. Durability of fiberglass as an exterior material is also good. Most fiberglass windows have factory-applied, baked-on coatings and can be repainted. To be included in GreenSpec, fiberglass window lines must include products with NFRC unit U-factors of 0.30 or lower.

High-Performance Fiberglass Windows

Accurate Dorwin Company
1535 Seel Ave.
Winnipeg, MB R3T 1C6 Canada

Toll-free: 888-982-4640
Phone: 204-982-8370
www.accuratedorwin.com

Accurate Dorwin's pultruded fiberglass windows are double- or triple-glazed with one or two low-e coatings, extruded silicone spacers, and argon-filled cavities. U-factors for Accurate Dorwin windows range as low as 0.15 (corresponding to an R-value of 6.7).

High-Performance Fiberglass Windows

Comfort Line
5500 Enterprise Blvd.
Toledo, OH 43612

Toll-free: 800-522-4999
Phone: 419-729-8520
www.comfortlineinc.com

Comfort Line manufactures fiberglass pultruded frame windows with hollow-core, sealed-frame members. Comfort Line's most advanced glazing option is a triple-glazed, krypton-filled panel with two low-e coatings and warm edge spacers.

High-Performance Fiberglass Windows

Duxton Windows & Doors
10 Higgins Ave.
Winnipeg, MB R3B 0A2 Canada

Phone: 204-339-6456
www.duxtonwindows.com

Duxton Windows & Doors manufactures advanced, high-performance windows and doors with pultruded-fiberglass frames. Glazing options include multiple low-e coatings on glass, suspended Heat Mirror films, and a 90:10 mixture of krypton and argon gas-fill. The highest-performance windows easily meet GreenSpec criteria for fiberglass windows, though NFRC unit U-factor testing has not been completed. The company lists center-of-glass R-values as high as 7.6.

High-Performance Fiberglass Windows

Fibertec Window & Door Mfg. Ltd.
157 Rivermede Rd., Unit 2
Concord, ON L4K 3M4 Canada

Toll-free: 888-232-4956
Phone: 905-660-7102
www.fibertec.com

Fibertec™ fiberglass windows have foam-insulated frames and can include Heat Mirror™ or low-e coatings, argon gas-fill, and warm-edge spacers. Fibertec's Santoprene™ weather stripping is applied in three locations for more effective sealing against air infiltration.

High-Performance Fiberglass Windows

Inline Fiberglass Ltd.
30 Constellation Ct.
Toronto, ON M9W 1K1
Canada

Phone: 416-679-1171
www.inlinefiberglass.com

Inline Fiberglass, a world leader in pultrusion technology, manufactures fiberglass windows and doors. A number of units meet or exceed the 0.30 U-value threshold for GreenSpec with some quadruple-glazed, krypton-filled units rating as low as 0.18. The company also licenses their pultrusion technology to other manufacturers.

High-Performance Fiberglass Windows

Integrity Windows and Doors - Marvin Marketing Office
2020 Silver Bell Rd., Ste. 15
Eagan, MN 55122-1042

Toll-free: 800-328-0268
Phone: 651-452-3039
www.integritywindows.com

Integrity™ windows from Marvin feature exterior frame and sash components made from Ultrex™, a pultruded composite of fiberglass and polyester resin. Solid wood jambs are bonded to the interior of the Ultrex frame, giving the windows a natural-wood appearance. Integrity's glazing options are limited to low-e2 with argon insulating glass, but a few products meet the *GreenSpec* 0.30 U-factor threshold.

High-Performance Fiberglass Windows

Milgard Manufacturing, Inc.
965 54th Ave. E
Tacoma, WA 98424

Toll-free: 800-562-8444
Phone: 253-922-6030
www.milgard.com

Milgard is the largest window manufacturer in the West and produces vinyl, thermally broken aluminum, pultruded fiberglass windows, and fiberglass-clad wood windows. All Milgard windows are custom-manufactured, and the company offers a wide range of glazing options, including several that meet the *GreenSpec* energy performance criteria.

High-Performance Fiberglass Windows

Thermotech Windows, Ltd.
42 Antares Dr.
Ottawa, ON K2E 7Y4 Canada

Phone: 613-225-1101
www.thermotechwindows.com

Thermotech's most energy-efficient windows include silicone foam Super Spacers™, triple panes, and low-e glazing (LOF or AFG), resulting in some of the highest-performance windows in North America (many glazing options produce window unit U-factors below 0.20). Thermotech promotes the use of different glazings on different orientations to optimize energy performance. The company offers up to 4 different IG (insulating glass) options on a whole house or project order. Other features include: 15% post-industrial recycled-content fiberglass frames, near-zero-solvent waterborne paint, offcut-sourced polystyrene insulation, and river-bottom-recovered pine jamb extensions.

Insulating Glass

Specifying glazing is common in commercial building applications and with some residential window products. The high-performance glazings listed here help control heating and cooling loads. Careful selection of glazing for specific applications (orientation, building type, etc.) is critical for optimum energy performance and building comfort.

Comfort E2, Comfort Ti, and Solar Glass

AFG Industries, Inc.
1400 Lincoln St.
Kingsport, TN 37660

Toll-free: 800-251-0441
Phone: 423-229-7200
www.afgglass.com

AFG Industries is a leading manufacturer of float glass and solar glass products. AFG manufactures Comfort E2 and Comfort Ti for the residential market and several specialized solar glass products for PV, passive, and active solar applications.

Heat Mirror Glass

Alpen Glass
5400 Spine Rd.
Boulder, CO 80301

Toll-free: 800-882-4466
Phone: 303-530-1150
www.alpeninc.com

Alpen Glass manufactures insulating glass with Heat Mirror™-coated films suspended between two panes of glass filled with argon or krypton gas. Alpen offers high-performance glazings with 99.5% reduction in UV transmission.

Lo E2

Cardinal IG
775 Prairie Center Dr., Ste. 200
Eden Prairie, MN 55344

Toll-free: 800-843-1484
Phone: 952-929-3134
www.cardinalcorp.com

Lo E2 is a soft-coat, low-e glazing with an emissivity of 0.04. When combined with clear glass in a double-pane unit, thermal heat flow is significantly reduced, as is solar heat gain. In applications where passive solar heating is desired, a glazing with a higher solar heat gain coefficient is preferable.

Pilkington Energy Advantage

Pilkington NA
811 Madison Ave.
P.O. Box 0799
Toledo, OH 43695-0799

Toll-free: 800-221-0444
Phone: 419-247-3731
www.pilkington.com

Pilkington® Energy Advantage is a hard-coat (pyrolytic), low-e glass with an emissivity of 0.15. In a double-pane unit, a SHGC of 0.7 is achieved. This is an excellent glazing for use in passive solar buildings on southern orientations where solar gain needs to be high.

Superglass Quad with Heat Mirror

Southwall Technologies
1029 Corporation Way
Palo Alto, CA 94303

Toll-free: 800-365-8794
Phone: 650-962-9111
www.southwall.com

Southwall developed and manufactures solar radiation control films, including Heat Mirror® with a range of performance properties. These films are fabricated into insulated-glass units (IGUs) and laminated glass by approximately 30 manufacturers in North America. Southwall's highest-performing Superglass® incorporates two Heat Mirror suspended films and three gas-filled cavities between dual panes of glass. Center-of-glass R-values above R-10 can be achieved with dual Heat Mirror films and low-conductivity gas-fill.

Metal-Framed Skylights

There have been a number of innovations in the area of metal-framed skylights. Active skylighting systems rely on reflectors and sun-tracking mechanisms to increase daylight entry; these systems boost daylighting primarily during early-morning and late-afternoon hours when the sun is low and little direct sun-

light typically enters a conventional skylight. Another technology, prismatic skylights, refracts sunlight to boost daylighting performance.

SunOptics Skylights

SunOptics Skylights
6201 27th St.
Sacramento, CA 95822

Toll-free: 800-289-4700
Phone: 916-395-4700
www.sunoptics.com

SunOptics manufactures prismatic skylights in which tiny prisms are embedded in the skylight glazing to refract visible light into the skylight, while reflecting infrared and UV light to keep it out. SunOptics skylights transmit more visible light than conventional white-acrylic skylights. Available single-, double-, triple-, and quad-glazed, they are designed with thermal breaks in the frames to reduce heat loss and prevent condensation. SunOptics also makes photo-cell-controlled louvers.

Plastic Unit Skylights

Tubular skylights, or light pipes, allow daylight to be transferred from the roof to occupied space below, even when there's a considerable distance involved (such as through an unheated attic). The system is composed of three parts: an acrylic rooftop dome and flashing, a reflective light pipe, and an interior diffuser. With most of these products, the reflective tube can bend around obstructions, or connect nonaligned roof and ceiling penetrations. Some products include other features such as compact-fluorescent lights or ventilation fans.

Brighten Up and SolaMaster Tubular Skylights

Solatube International, Inc.
2210 Oak Ridge Way
Vista, CA 92083

Toll-free: 800-966-7652
www.solatube.com

Solatube is the world's leading manufacturer of tubular skylights. For residential and smaller commercial applications, the Brighten Up® series is available in 10" and 14" units and features Solatube's patented Spectralight® Infinity tubing material and Light Intercepting Transfer Device (LITD®). The SolaMaster® Series, featuring a 21" unit, is suitable for commercial buildings and larger residential areas and accommodates a wide variety of ceilings. Installing one 21" SolaMaster can displace approximately two traditional light fixtures, each using three FO32T8 fluorescent lamps, according to the manufacturer. Seamless one-piece flashing is available in both the Brighten Up and SolaMaster series. All Solatube skylights are offered with optional light kits, and the 10" Brighten Up unit is available with an optional ventilation fan. A motorized "Daylight Dimmer" butterfly baffle, which is controlled by a wall-mounted switch, is also available for all sizes, adjusting the skylight's output from 100% to approximately 2%.

HUVCO Skylights

HUVCO, Proactive Energy Solutions
3416 Prices Distillery Rd.
Ijamsville, MD 21754

Toll-free: 800-832-6116
Phone: 301-432-7184
www.huvco.com

High Performance Tubular Skylights (HPTS) from HUVCO come in two diameter sizes: 8" and 12", with recommended maximum pipe lengths of 12' and 20'. The "typical light outputs" under ideal conditions are 100W and 250W, respectively. HUVCO also custom produces the High Performance Daylighting System (HPDS) for commercial applications, utilizing a columniation lens, reflective light well, and diffuser, and ranging in size from 1' x 1' up to 4' x 8'.

ODL Tubular Skylight

ODL, Inc.
215 E. Roosevelt Ave.
Zeeland, MI 49464

Toll-free: 800-288-1800
Phone: 616-772-9111
www.odl.com

ODL manufactures tubular skylights in 10" and 14" diameters. The light tube is coated with a highly reflective silver film and comes with a standard prismatic light diffuser at the ceiling to improve light spread. The product is designed for either contractor or DIY installations. ODL offers the option of an electric light kit, which may reduce light output by approximately 2–3% (when the pipe is straight), according to the manufacturer.

Solar Bright Tubular Skylights

Solar Bright Corporation
836 Deville Dr.
Largo, FL 33771

Toll-free: 800-780-1759
Phone: 727-584-8875
www.solarbright.com

Solar Bright Tubular Skylights are 10"-diameter, factory-preassembled units lined with mirrored 3M Silverlux aluminum coating. Each tube illuminates an area of 11' x 11'. Solar Bright offers a lifetime warranty.

Sun Tunnel Tubular Skylights

Velux
1418 Evans Pond Rd.
Greenwood, SC 29649

Toll-free: 800-888-3589
www.veluxusa.com

The Sun Tunnel has a flexible tube (most other tubular skylights offer only elbows to make slight bends). Double diffusion panes produce even light distribution and reduce the likelihood of condensation. The company indicates that thorough testing shows there is no appreciable heat gain or loss with the Sun Tunnel. It is available in 14" and 22" diameters and carries a 7-year warranty. These tubular skylights were formerly manufactured by Sun Tunnel Skylights, Inc.

Sun-Dome Tubular Skylights

Daylighting Technologies, Inc.
8352 Garden Rd.
West Palm Beach, FL 33404

Toll-free: 800-596-8414
Phone: 561-840-0095
www.sun-dome.com

Daylighting Technologies produces 10", 13", and 21" tubular skylights with aluminum flashing and high-impact Lexan polycarbonate domes for both residential and commercial applications. The domes are large-missile impact-tested and Dade County hurricane-approved. The adjustable tubes provide up to 97% reflectivity, according to the company. Daylighting Technologies also provides lighting retrofit systems with fluorescent bulbs, electronic dimmable ballasts, and light sensors to provide constant light levels in all applications.

SunPipe Tubular Skylights

Sun Pipe Co., Inc.
P.O. Box 5760
Elgin, IL 60121-5760

Toll-free: 800-844-4786
Phone: 847-888-9222
www.sunpipe.com

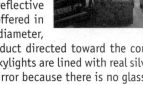

Sun Pipe introduced tubular skylights to the U.S. in 1991. The lined, reflective aluminum pipe is offered in 9", 13", and 21" diameter, with the larger product directed toward the commercial market. SunPipe® Tubular Skylights are lined with real silver, which is more reflective than a mirror because there is no glass on top of it, according to the manufacturer. The company's light control damper, the "Eclipse," is scheduled for release in late 2004.

SunScope Tubular Skylights

Sky-Tech Industries, Inc.
#140, 27019 TWP Rd. 514
Spruce Grove, AB T7Y 1G6 Canada

Toll-free: 800-449-0644
Phone: 780-438-6770
www.sunscope.com

SunScope tubular skylights are available with a diameter of 8½", 13", or 21" and in lengths up to 20'. An optional SunScoop is available that boosts light capture on sunny days—this feature is especially useful in northern climates, where the sun remains lower in the sky.

Sun-Tek Tube

Sun-Tek Manufacturing
10303 General Dr.
Orlando, FL 32824

Toll-free: 800-334-5854
Phone: 407-859-2117
www.sun-tek.com

The Sun-Tek Tube® is a tubular skylight available in 10"-, 14"-, and 21"-diameter sizes. The company also manufactures a curb-mount tube and a multi-tubed skylight, the Spyder, that can illuminate multiple locations with only a single opening in the roof.

Tru-Lite Tubular Skylights

Tru-Lite Skylights, Inc.
13695 E. Davies Pl.
Centennial, CO 80112

Toll-free: 800-873-3309
Phone: 303-783-5700
www.tru-lite.com

Tru-Lite Tubular Skylights® are available in 12" and 16" diameters to illuminate up to 500 ft². No structural modifications or roof curbing are needed. The tube can be raised above the roof plane to improve low-angle daylight collection.

Tubular Skylight

Tubular Skylight, Inc.
753 Cattleman Rd.
Sarasota, FL 34232-2852

Toll-free: 800-315-8823
Phone: 941-378-8823
www.tubular-skylight.com

Tubular Skylights are available in four sizes: 5½", 8", 13", and 21" diameter.

Skylights

Daylighting serves several green purposes. Studies show that natural daylighting can improve the general well-being of building occupants as well as provide such measurable benefits as increased workplace productivity and enhanced school performance. The energy benefit from daylighting generally comes from both savings in electric lighting and cooling-load avoidance. Not all daylighting systems save energy—careful energy modeling can help determine energy benefits in particular applications. As with window and glazing products, the energy performance of skylights and roof windows varies greatly among different products and should be carefully considered.

Roof Windows and Skylights

Roto Frank of America
Research Park
P.O. Box 599
Chester, CT 06412-0599

Toll-free: 800-243-0893
Phone: 860-526-4996
www.roto-roofwindows.com

Roto skylights have double-glazed, low-e, argon-filled glazing.

Roof Windows And Skylights

Velux
1418 Evans Pond Rd.
Greenwood, SC 29649

Toll-free: 800-888-3589
www.veluxusa.com

Velux roof windows and skylights are solid-wood framed and come standard with low-e2 coatings and argon gas-fill. Velux products are EPA ENERGY STAR®-approved.

Roof Windows and Skylights with Heat Mirror

Thermo-Vu Sunlite® Industries, Inc.
895 Waverly Ave.
Holtsville, NY 11742

Toll-free: 800-883-5483
Phone: 631-475-1500
www.thermo-vu.com

Thermo-Vu Sunlite manufactures a number of roof windows and skylights with Heat Mirror™ from Southwall Technologies as a glazing option. According to the company, the U-value of low-e insulated glass units without multiple air spaces is degraded by convection currents that occur in sloped installations but not in vertically installed windows. Heat Mirror™ 66 suffers only a 6% sloped U-value performance loss, as opposed to 10–31% in other products. Heat Mirror reduces noise by as much as 56%, compared with regular double-pane glass, and blocks over 99.5% of damaging UV rays. The units are available with several film

options offering varying degrees of infrared wave reflection for best match to climate zone.

Vinyl Windows

A number of environmental problems are associated with vinyl (PVC)—relating to disposal through incineration and to various additives that are compounded into the vinyl products (stabilizers, plasticizers, flame retardants). Because vinyl is a fairly durable, low-maintenance, and inexpensive material for window fabrication, some are included in this directory. To be approved for inclusion, however, vinyl windows must contain recycled content, or the NFRC-based unit U-factor must be extremely low (0.20 or lower). Achieving this level of energy performance requires a combination of leading-edge technologies. Some of the highest-performance windows on the market are vinyl replacement windows—in part because these products are marketed directly to homeowners, who are generally more open to energy-saving features than the building professionals who typically specify windows for new construction.

High-Performance Vinyl Replacement Windows

Accent Windows, Inc.
12300 Pecos St.
Westminster, CO 80234

Toll-free: 888-284-3948
Phone: 303-420-2002
www.accentwindows.com

Accent Windows is a Colorado manufacturer of vinyl replacement windows. The company uses low-e glass coatings (LoElite™) or suspended Heat Mirror™ films, along with argon or argon/krypton gas-fills to achieve some of the highest energy performance of any replacement windows. Unit U-factors are as low as 0.15. The company estimates that 50–60% of sales are of super-high-performance products (unit U-factor less than 0.30). All Accent windows are custom-manufactured, so the dimensions will be optimized to the window opening. The company serves the mountain region from Billings, Montana to Albuquerque, New Mexico.

High-Performance Vinyl Replacement Windows

Gilkey Window Company, Inc.
3625 Hauck Rd.
Cincinnati, OH 45241

Toll-free: 800-878-7771
Phone: 513-769-4527
www.gilkey.com

Gilkey Window is a regional manufacturer of custom vinyl replacement windows serving Ohio, Kentucky, and the Upper Midwest. The company offers a wide range of glazing options and actively promotes super-high-performance windows and the strategy of using glazings specifically "tuned" to the orientation. Among the glazing options is a "quad" option with both a low-e coating on two glass panes and a suspended Heat Mirror® coating, with krypton gas-fill and warm-edge glass spacers. The NFRC Certified Products Directory lists products with unit U-factors as low as 0.14 (R-7.1). Company sales reps carry Btu meters to explain and demonstrate energy savings potential to prospective customers, and a 20% energy savings guarantee is provided with certain windows.

High-Performance Vinyl Replacement Windows

Gorell Enterprises, Inc.
1380 Wayne Ave.
Indiana, PA 15701

Toll-free: 800-9-GORELL
Phone: 724-465-1800
www.gorell.com

Gorell was founded as a manufacturer of vinyl windows in 1994. The company offers a number of energy-conserving glazing options for replacement and new-construction applications, including several that meet the GreenSpec criteria for vinyl windows. All Gorell windows feature heavy-duty construction with four-point fusion welding and the PPG Intercept spacer system. Gorell's highest-performing glass is Thermal Master III, a triple-glazed unit with two low-e coatings and krypton gas-fill. The highest-performance Gorell products in the NFRC Certified Products Directory have unit U-factors as low as 0.17.

High-Performance Vinyl Replacement Windows

Kensington Windows, Inc.
One Kiski Valley Industrial Park
R.R. 1
Vandergrift, PA 15690

Toll-free: 800-444-4972
Phone: 724-845-8133
www.kensingtonwindows.com

Kensington is a manufacturer of fairly high-end vinyl replacement windows sold primarily through dealers east of the Rocky Mountains. The company emphasizes energy efficiency and offers dozens of products that exceed the GreenSpec criteria for super

energy performance. The highest-performance windows have two panes with low-e coatings, plus a suspended Heat Mirror film (for a total of three low-e coatings), krypton gas-fill, and foam-filled vinyl frames.

High-Performance Vinyl Replacement Windows

SCHÜCO Homecraft, LP
240 Pane Rd.
Newington, CT 06111

Toll-free: 877-472-4826
www.schuco-usa.com

Schuco Homecraft is the U.S. division of a large European manufacturer that has been producing windows for 40 years. The company offers triple-glazed windows with two low-e coatings and krypton gas-fill. They also use a unique thermoplastic edge spacer, which the company claims outperforms conventional metal spacers both in terms of energy performance and durability.

High-Performance Vinyl Replacement Windows

Stanek Vinyl Windows Corp.
4570 Willow Pkwy.
Cuyahoga Heights, OH 44125

Toll-free: 800-962-5512
Phone: 216-341-7700
www.stanekwindows.com

Stanek Windows is predominantly a regional manufacturer of vinyl replacement windows serving the Cleveland, Ohio area, though the company now sells product in some other areas of the East and Midwest. Included in its offerings are a number of remarkably high-energy-performance windows, including System 9 and System 13—the latter are $1^1/_8$"-thick quad-glazed windows with two Heat Mirror® suspended films, a low-e coating on one of the panes of glass, and krypton gas-fill. NFRC-based unit U-factors as low as 0.17 are listed in the NFRC Certified Products Directory, while the company's Web site shows center-of-glass R-values of 12.5! Styles offered include casement, double-hung, bays, bows, sliders, and patio doors. All products are custom-fabricated using reinforced vinyl extrusions.

High-Performance Vinyl Replacement Windows

Thermal Industries, Inc.
301 Brushton Ave.
Pittsburgh, PA 15221-2168

Toll-free: 800-245-1540
www.ThermalIndustries.com

Thermal Industries, a subsidiary of the Atrium Company, is a Pittsburgh-based manufacturer of custom vinyl replacement windows serving many regions of the eastern U.S. The company's highest-performance glass package, Super Peak Performance™ Glass, has three layers of glass, two low-e coatings, krypton gas-fill, and low-conductivity warm-edge spacers between the panes of glass. The NFRC Certified Products Directory lists unit U-factors as low as 0.18.

Renewal by Andersen Windows

Andersen Windows
9900 Jamaica Ave. S
Cottage Grove, MN 55016

Toll-free: 866-773-6392
Phone: 651-264-4000
www.andersenwindows.com

Andersen's Renewal by Andersen® line of windows features frames and sashes made from Fibrex® material, a post-industrial wood and waste-PVC composite with a coextruded virgin PVC exterior coating. Low-e2 from Cardinal IG is standard in all products. Andersen has been recognized by the EPA and DOE, through their ENERGY STAR® programs, for offering and promoting the use of high-performance windows. In 1998 Andersen Windows became the first ENERGY STAR Windows Partner. The highest-performance Renewal by Andersen® windows in the NFRC Certified Products Directory have unit U-factors of 0.29 and qualify for GreenSpec because of their recycled content.

Window Shades and Quilts

Certain designs of window shades and blinds can significantly reduce heat loss or heat gain through windows; these may be appropriate retrofits for older, leaky windows, when window replacement can't be justified. In new construction or when replacement can be justified, installing high-performance windows is usually a better option than investing in energy-conserving blinds or shades.

Earthshade Natural Fiber Window Treatments

Earthshade
P.O. Box 1003
Great Barrington, MA
   01230

Phone: 413-528-5443
www.earthshade.com

Made from mostly wildcrafted grasses and reeds grown without the use of fertilizers or pesticides, Earthshade custom window treatments are handwoven in Mexico and assembled in Texas. The grasses and reeds are handharvested, sundried, and if treated at all, bathed in hydrogen peroxide to meet import regulations. Glues are water-based, and the only finishes are a water-based stain on one pattern (others are baked to achieve their color) and an optional water-based flame retardant for commercial spaces. Nylon cords are used to operate the shades though the company is currently testing hemp as a replacement. Earthshade natural window treatments are available in 10 operating styles and come with the

industry standard lifetime limited warranty making them suitable for both contract and residential applications.

Shades & Blinds

Hunter Douglas Window Covering
1 Duette Way
Broomfield, CO 80020

Toll-free: 800-438-3883
www.hunterdouglas.com

The Duette® Honeycomb shades from Hunter Douglas offer significantly better energy performance than standard shades because of the unique accordion-fold design. When lowered, the fabric opens up providing pockets of trapped air. The opaque Duette shades include a reflective layer to boost energy performance.

Warm Windows

Cozy Curtains
4295 Duncan Dr.
Missoula, MT 59802

Toll-free: 800-342-9955
www.cozycurtains.com

Warm Windows® is a custom-made insulating Roman-shade system which folds above the window when not in use. The shades are made up of 4 layers: High Density Dacron Holofil II®, a polyethylene moisture vapor barrier, metalized Mylar®, and the customer's choice of fabric. The company reports an R-value of 7.69 for installations over single-pane and 8.69 over double-pane windows. Shades attach to a board over the window frame with Velcro® and are pulled up and down with a cord. Magnetic strips around the frame and concealed within the shade provide a magnetically tight seal. Cozy Curtains also offers individual components for sale for do-it-yourselfers.

Window Coverings

Sailshade/Cloth Construction
P.O. Box 3935
Westport, MA 02790

Phone: 508-677-3160
www.sailshade.com

Sailshade window coverings are estimated to provide R-8 insulating values in combination with a double-glazed window when in use. When not in use, they fold compactly in a "self-created valance" to maximize solar gain.

Window Quilt

Northern Cross Industries
113 Technology Dr.
P.O. Box 975
Brattleboro, VT 05301

Toll-free: 800-257-4501
Phone: 802-257-4501

Window Quilt is an insulating blind for windows. Blinds roll up at the top of the window, and the edges fit into a track, making the blind fairly airtight. The product makes the most sense for older windows; with new construction or when windows are being replaced, investing in super-high-performance windows generally makes more sense.

Window Treatment Hardware

Look for products with recycled content or specialized features that save energy or achieve other environmental benefits.

Drapery Rods

Antique Drapery Rod Co., Inc.
140 Glass St.
Dallas, TX 75207

Phone: 214-653-1733
www.antiquedraperyrod.com

Antique Drapery Rod Co. manufactures drapery rods from 100% recycled steel produced at an energy-efficient mini-mill. Other steel products contain minimum 65% post-consumer recycled content. Aluminum products are made from 100% post-consumer content. The company uses recycled wood for their drapery rods, brackets, and rings, as well as offering rods and rings made from bamboo. Wood stains are water-based and low-VOC. The bamboo "tortoise shell" finish is produced using only fire, earth, and water. Antique Drapery Rod minimizes packaging material and uses shipping materials with high recycled content.

Window Treatment Hardware

S&L Designs
P.O. Box 222325
Dallas, TX 75222

Toll-free: 800-788-0358
Phone: 214-742-6417
www.s-ldesigns.com

S&L Designs manufactures decorative window treatment hardware, including rods, finials, and tiebacks. Most products are handcrafted from recycled-content metals; items made from aluminum have 100% recycled content. The company donates part of its profits to environmental causes.

Wood Windows

As with all products made from wood, the source of that wood should be an important consideration. Currently, only a very few manufacturers use FSC-certified wood as a standard frame material, though more use it in certain components or as a special-order option. (Certification to Forest Stewardship Council—FSC—standards involves third-party evaluation and monitoring of sustainable forestry practices.) Energy performance is the primary green consideration of wood windows, and new developments in window technology enable today's products to far outperform those of a few decades ago. Among the improvements are multiple glazing layers, low-conductivity gas fills, better seals on insulated glazing units, heat-reflective (low-emissivity) coatings, advanced weather-stripping, and new frame systems. Low-emissivity coatings which allow short-wavelength solar radiation (sunlight) to pass through but reflect long-wavelength radiation (heat) back into the conditioned space are now standard options from all major window manufacturers. Low-e coatings are usually applied to the outside of the interior pane of a double-glazed panel. Further improvement in energy performance is achieved with triple-glazing and multiple low-e coatings; sometimes an additional glazing layer is provided as a suspended polyester film. To qualify for GreenSpec, wood windows must achieve an NFRC-certified unit U-factor of 0.25 or lower—a manufacturer must both offer these super-high-performance windows and actively market them. The U-factor threshold is higher (less stringent) for fiberglass, certified-wood, or recycled-content frame materials—and more stringent (lower U-factors) for vinyl because of environmental concerns with PVC.

Certified Wood Windows

J. S. Benson Woodworking &
   Design, LLC
118 Birge St.
Brattleboro, VT 05301

Toll-free: 800-339-3515
Phone: 802-254-3515
www.jsbensonwoodworking.com

J. S. Benson Woodworking & Design is a manufacturer of high-end, custom, true-divided-lite windows both for the renovation and new construction market. Available in FSC-certified mahogany. The company offers dual-sealed insulated units using clear annealed glass. Energy features include low-e coatings, argon-fill, and warm-edge insulated glass spacers.

Designer Series SmartSash

Pella Corporation
102 Main St.
Pella, IA 50219

Toll-free: 800-847-3552
Phone: 641-621-1000
www.pella.com

Pella's SmartSash® wood windows and doors are made from ponderosa pine, eastern white pine, sugar pine, and some white fir. They are available with an interior removable panel of glass and with an exterior panel of either single-pane or double-pane argon-filled, low-emissivity SmartSash glazing. The exterior is clad with recycled aluminum finished with a baked-on EnduraClad™ coating. A number of Pella windows have unit U-factors at or below 0.25.

Heat Smart

Loewen Windows
77 Hwy. #52 W
Box 2260
Steinbach, MB R0A 2A0
Canada

Toll-free: 800-563-9367
Phone: 204-326-6446
www.loewen.com

Loewen Window's Heat Smart glazing is available in three versions: double-glazed with low-e coatings and argon gas-fill; triple-glazed with one low-e coating and one argon-filled cavity; and triple-glazed with two low-e coatings and two argon-filled cavities. Loewen uses desiccant-filled aluminum spacers. All products are NFRC-rated. Loewen Windows is a founding member of the DOE Efficient Window Collaborative and is an ENERGY STAR® window partner. Loewen windows incorporate some FSC-certified wood.

High-Performance Wood Windows

Jeld-Wen Windows & Doors, Willmar Collection
485 Watt St.
Winnipeg, MB R2K 2R9 Canada

Toll-free: 888-945-5627
Phone: 204-668-8230
www.willmar.ca

Willmar Windows, part of the Jeld-Wen family, manufactures wood windows with 8 glazing options. Included in Willmar's selection are a number of dual-pane and triple-pane glazing options available with Solar Gain and Solar Shield low-e coatings featuring warm-edge Intercept spacers, and with low-conductivity gas-fill. In addition to solid wood, Willmar Windows are available in metal-clad and copper-clad models. The company also makes 100% vinyl windows.

High-Performance Wood Windows

Marvin Windows and
Doors
Hwy. 11 W
P.O. Box 100
Warroad, MN 56763

Toll-free: 888-537-8268
Phone: 218-386-1430
www.marvin.com

Marvin offers a High-R glazing option with its wood windows that includes triple glazing with two low-e coatings and argon or krypton gas-fill. U-factors as low as 0.18 for Marvin wood windows are found in the NFRC Certified Products Directory, with many products having U-factors below 0.25.

High-Performance Wood Windows

Paramount Windows, Inc.
105 Panet Rd.
Winnipeg, MB R2J 0S1 Canada

Toll-free: 800-519-0508
Phone: 204-233-4966
www.paramountwindows.com

Paramount Windows, founded in 1948, has been promoting highly energy-efficient windows for decades. The company introduced insulated-glass windows in 1957 and triple-glazed windows (Canada's first) in 1962. The company primarily produces wood and aluminum-clad wood windows but also offers vinyl windows—mostly for the replacement market. Several glazing options are available: EnerPlus 4 is triple-glazed with one low-e coating, argon gas-fill in one of the interpane spaces, and two energy-saving spacers. EnerPlus 6 is triple-glazed with two low-e coatings, and argon gas-fill in both interpane spaces. The lowest NFRC U-factor ratings are 0.22. The company's wood supplier recently gained FSC certification, so FSC-certified wood windows can be special-ordered for larger jobs.

High-Performance Wood Windows

Weather Shield Manufacturing, Inc.
1 Weathershield Plz.
P.O. Box 309
Medford, WI 54451

Toll-free: 800-477-6808
Phone: 715-748-2100
www.weathershield.com

Weather Shield offers a wide range of wood window products and glazing options. The highest performing glazing options are Value R6 and Value R10. Value R6 is a triple-glazed, argon-filled panel with two low-e surfaces. Value R10 is similar to Value R6 but contains a krypton/argon gas mix. Among the lowest unit U-factors found in the NFRC Certified Products Directory are 0.16 for commercial-sized fixed windows and 0.17 for residential-sized.

This Space is Available for Your Notes

Insulation

Insulation is one of the most important components of any environmentally responsible house or light commercial building because it reduces energy consumption and the pollution that usually results. In this sense, any insulation material is a "green" product. Good design and appropriate levels of insulation can minimize, or even eliminate, the need for central heating and cooling in many buildings.

Insulation is a key part of the building envelope and an important element in the entire building as an integrated system. Choosing an insulation material should include considering how it works with the rest of the wall, roof, and floor system—and what additional functions, such as air-sealing, the material might serve.

Different types of insulation also have varying impacts in terms of their raw materials and manufacture. These life-cycle impacts should be considered along with factors such as R-value, air-sealing ability, and cost.

The *quality of installation* also makes a big difference in how well insulation performs. If insulation is not installed property, it will not achieve the energy savings its rated R-value would suggest; a California study concluded that a 4% void in fiberglass batts resulted in a 50% decrease in insulation effectiveness.

The type of structural framing also affects the performance of insulation. Steel studs conduct heat much more readily than wood studs, so they create *thermal bridging* that can bypass insulation installed in the cavities. Steel-framed exterior walls should have insulative sheathing installed over the framing members to reduce this problem—in fact, the U.S. Department of Energy recommends that insulative sheathing should be used with steel framing in all U.S. climates.

Fiberglass insulation is the standard in the industry today. High-density fiberglass makes the same wall cavity 15–20% more effective in reducing heat loss. Most fiberglass manufacturers now incorporate at least 30% recycled material; some products are third-party certified for their recycled-glass content. The potential for health problems due to fiber shedding is controversial; loose fill is a greater risk than batts in this regard. While concern has been expressed that airborne fibers might be carcinogenic, those concerns have been allayed to some extent in recent years. Most fiberglass batts are manufactured with phenol formaldehyde as a binder, though some products use alternative binders or no binder at all.

Cellulose insulation is primarily made out of recycled newspaper, though some uses pre-consumer waste. When it is damp-sprayed into open cavities, or blown into closed cavities at relatively high density, it forms a good infiltration barrier that adds to the airtightness of the house—and it's less contractor-dependent for quality control in filling voids than fiberglass batts.

Rigid foam insulation applied to framing yields added infiltration resistance, reduced frame conduction losses, and higher overall wall R-value. Extruded polystyrene (XPS) and polyisocyanurate (polyiso) rigid foam insulation used to be made with ozone-depleting CFC blowing agents, but when ozone depletion was identified as a major environmental problem, the CFCs were replaced with HCFCs through international agreement. HCFCs were eliminated from polyiso insulation as of January, 2003, but they are not scheduled to be totally eliminated from XPS until 2020. Polyiso is now produced with hydrocarbon blowing agents. Expanded polystyrene (EPS) rigid foam has long been made with non-ozone-depleting pentane rather than HCFCs.

Air Leakage Control

These are products designed to limit air infiltration through openings in the building envelope.

Fireplace DraftStopper

Battic Door Attic Stair
Covers
P.O. Box 15
Mansfield, MA 02048-0015

Phone: 508-320-9082
www.batticdoor.com

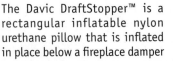

The Davic DraftStopper™ is a rectangular inflatable nylon urethane pillow that is inflated in place below a fireplace damper to stop drafts that occur even when the damper is shut. After installation, the filling tube hangs down into the fireplace with an orange warning label to prevent fires from being lit when the unit is installed. Significant energy savings can be achieved. Until the fall of 2003, the DraftStopper was made with PVC—some PVC units may still be for sale.

R-U Seal

Contractor Products
   International, Ltd.
P.O. Box 83
Quechee, VT 05059

Toll-free: 800-782-1932
Phone: 802-295-8904
www.ruseal.com

R-U Seal® combines moisture and air barriers with insulation into a single product for sealing around windows and doors as part of the initial installation. It consists of a polyethylene envelope over a fiberglass blanket (which is installed in the rough opening) with a crosslinked polyethylene gasket (which is attached to sheathing). R-U Seal is available for 2x4 and 2x6 framed construction; other sizes can be special ordered. A modified version, Retro-Seal, is available for replacement windows.

The Battic Door Attic Stair Cover

Battic Door Attic Stair Covers
P.O. Box 15
Mansfield, MA 02048-0015

Phone: 508-320-9082
www.batticdoor.com

The Battic Door is a simple and inexpensive product for weatherstripping attic hatches that have folding stairways. Essentially a heavy-duty cardboard box that embeds itself into foam weatherstripping installed on the top of the stairway frame, the unit allows easy access to the attic, while providing an airtight seal when dropped into place. Available in two sizes to fit 22" to $22^1/_2$" x 54" as well as 25" to $25^1/_2$" x 54" rough openings. A reflective insulation kit (R-7) and an encapsulated-fiberglass slip-on insulation kit (R-50) are also available.

The Energy Guardian

Energy Sentry Solutions
P.O. Box 400
Paoli, PA 19301

Phone: 610-993-9585
www.energysentrysolutions.com

Made from high-density EPS, The Energy Guardian™ is an insulating and air-sealing cover for attic hatches and pull-down ladders. These patent-pending units consist of a frame and a snug-fitting lid, which is simply put aside and then put in place again when entering and exiting the attic. The ladder-cover version fits any opening less than 35" x 63" and allows $7^1/_2$" clearance for a folded ladder. A second frame can be added for $16^1/_2$" total clearance. The attic hatch cover is designed to fit any opening measuring less than 28" x 32". For areas with little clearance, a 2" frame is available for 7" of total clearance; a 10" frame allows 15" of clearance. The manufacturer claims an R-value of 30 and offers a lifetime warranty. Significant energy savings can be achieved.

Cellulose Insulation

Cellulose insulation has several environmental advantages. Most contains 75–80% post-consumer recycled newspaper and nontoxic borate and/or ammonium sulfate fire retardants. The energy performance is comparable to high-density fiberglass batts at roughly R-3.7 per inch—but cellulose insulation generally packs more tightly so is more effective at controlling air leakage. Cellulose insulation can be "loose-filled" into attic spaces, sometimes in a "stabilized" form to resist settling. For wall applications, cellulose can either be installed as a wet-spray (damp-spray) product with a water-activated adhesive in open wall cavities before drywalling, or be installed in closed cavities using a "dense-pack" process with a density of 3 lbs. per cubic foot or greater.

All-Weather Insulation

All-Weather Insulation Co., LLC
19 W. Industrial Dr.
Springfield, KY 40069

Phone: 859-336-9832

All-Weather Cellulose Insulation contains recycled newspaper.

Applegate Loosefill and Applegate Stabilized Cellulose Insulation

Applegate Insulation
  Manufacturing
1000 Highview Dr.
Webberville, MI 48892

Toll-free: 800-627-7536
Phone: 517-521-3545
www.applegateinsulation.
com

Applegate insulation is made from recycled paper. The manufacturer has certified the following recycled-content levels (by weight): total recovered material 85% typical, 80% guaranteed; post-consumer material 85% typical, 80% guaranteed.

Attic Insulation and Wall Cavity Spray

ThermoCon Manufacturing / Applegate Inc.
2500 Jackson St.
Monroe, LA 71202

Toll-free: 800-854-1907
Phone: 318-323-1337
www.thermocon.com

Attic Insulation and Wall Cavity Spray are cellulose insulations made from recycled newspaper.

AZ Energy Saver

Paul's Insulation
P.O. Box 115
Vergas, MN 56587

Toll-free: 800-627-5190
Phone: 218-342-2800

AZ Energy Saver is cellulose insulation made from 100% post-consumer recycled newspaper.

Benotherm

Benolec, Ltd.
1451 Nobel St.
Sainte-Julie, PQ J3E 1Z4 Canada

Phone: 450-922-2000
www.benolec.com

Benotherm cellulose insulation contains recycled newspaper.

Bonded, Insul Therm, and Tasco

Bonded Insulation Co., Inc.
78 N. Pawling St.
Hagaman, NY 12086

Toll-free: 800-836-3290
Phone: 518-842-1470

Bonded, Insul Therm, and Tasco cellulose insulations contain recycled newspaper.

Cell-Pak Advantage

Cell-Pak, Inc.
204 McIntire Ln.
Decatur, AL 35603

Toll-free: 800-325-5320
Phone: 256-260-2151
www.cellpak.com

Cell-Pak Advantage cellulose insulation, formerly Celluguard Light Wallboard, contains 85% recycled newspaper.

Cellulose Insulation

Advanced Fiber Technology, Inc.
100 Crossroads Blvd.
Bucyrus, OH 44820

Phone: 419-562-1337
www.advancedfiber.com

Advanced Fiber Technology manufactures cellulose insulation from recycled wastepaper. The company would not disclose which fire retardant is used in this insulation. Advanced Fiber Technology is also a manufacturer of cellulose insulation processing equipment.

Cellulose Insulation

Arctic Insulation, Inc.
1216 N. 11th Ave.
Greeley, CO 80631

Phone: 970-351-0587

Arctic Insulation's cellulose insulation contains recycled newspaper.

Cellulose Insulation

Can-Cell Industries, Inc.
14715 114th Ave.
Edmonton, AB T5M 2Y8
Canada

Toll-free: 800-661-5031
www.can-cell.com

Can-Cell Industries manufactures Weathershield loose-fill cellulose, WallBAR stabilized cavity-fill cellulose, K-13 spray-applied thermal and acoustical insulation, and Sonaspray "fc" acoustical spray insulation from recycled newspaper. Typical post-consumer recycled content is 85%. Can-Cell Industries now manufactures K-13 and Sonaspray "fc" for the entire Canadian market.

Cellulose Insulation

Clayville Insulation
P.O. Box 713
Burley, ID 83318

Toll-free: 800-584-9022
Phone: 208-678-9791
www.safelink.net/clayinsu

Clayville insulation is made from recycled newspaper.

Cellulose Insulation

Redi-Therm Insulation, Inc.
3061 S. 3600 W
Salt Lake City, UT 84119

Phone: 801-972-6551

Redi-Therm cellulose insulation is made from recycled paper.

Clean and Xcell

Central Fiber Corp.
4814 Fiber Ln.
Wellsville, KS 66092

Toll-free: 800-654-6117
Phone: 785-883-4600
www.centralfiber.com

Clean and Xcell cellulose insulation is made from recycled newspaper.

Climatizer Plus and Enviro-Batt

Climatizer Insulation, Ltd.
120 Claireville Dr.
Etobicoke, ON M9W 5Y3 Canada

Toll-free: 866-871-5495
Phone: 416-798-1235
www.climatizer.com

Climatizer Plus thermal and acoustical cellulose insulation contains recycled newspaper. It may be hand-poured or pneumatically placed with a blowing machine and delivery hose. Enviro-Batt™ contains less than 2% formaldehyde-free, no-VOC adhesive activated by a very small amount of water during pneumatic installation; moisture-loading is only 20% of that experienced with typical wet-cellulose applications. Both products contain at least 85% post-consumer recycled paper fibers.

Cocoon Loose-Fill and Cocoon2 Stabilized Insulation

U.S. GreenFiber, LLC
809 W. Hill St., Ste. A
Charlotte, NC 28208

Toll-free: 800-228-0024
Phone: 704-379-0644
www.us-gf.com

Cocoon® Loose-fill Insulation consists of 85% recycled paper fiber (at least 80% post-consumer paper content) that has been treated with borates to meet and exceed fire resistance requirements. Cocoon Insulation is blown into attics and is also used in retrofit sidewall applications. Cocoon2® products consist of 85% recycled paper fiber (at least 80% post-consumer paper content) and have an added adhesive for use in walls, attics, floors, ceilings, and other enclosed spaces.

Comfort-Zone

Mason City Recycling
1410 S. Monroe
P.O. Box 1534
Mason City, IA 50402

Toll-free: 800-373-1200
Phone: 641-423-1200
www.netconx.net/~mcrc

Comfort-Zone cellulose insulation is manufactured from recycled newspaper. The manufacturer has certified the following recycled-content levels (by weight): total recovered material 80% typical, 80% guaranteed; post-consumer material 80% guaranteed.

Dry Pac Wall System

Par/PAC™
53 Cove Side Rd.
P.O. Box 242
South Bristol, ME 04568

Toll-free: 877-937-3257
www.parpac.com

Par/PAC's Dry Pac Wall System™ is a patented cellulose insulation in which a non-elastic, polyester-reinforced vapor retarder (Par/PAC poly) is stapled to wooden wall studs prior to drywalling and Good News-Reused™ cellulose insulation is dry-blown into the cavity at a high density. The poly layer allows inspection of the insulation to prevent voids. Cellulose insulation contains recycled newspaper.

Energy Control

Energy Control, Inc.
804 W. Mill St.
P.O. Box 327
Ossian, IN 46777

Toll-free: 800-451-6429
Phone: 260-622-7614

Manufactured under the brand names Energy Control II and Forest Wool, Energy Control cellulose insulation contains over 80% recycled newspaper.

Enviro-Pro, Sound Wall, and Spray-On

Tascon, Inc.
7607 Fairview St.
P.O. Box 41846
Houston, TX 77214

Toll-free: 800-937-1774
www.tasconindustries.com

Enviro-Pro, Sound Wall, and Spray-On are made from recycled newspaper. The manufacturer has certified the following recycled-content levels (by weight): total recovered material 80% typical, 80% guaranteed; post-consumer material 80% typical, 80% guaranteed.

Fiber-lite, Pk Class 1, Wal-Mat, SATAC, and In-Cide PC

P. K. Insulation Manufacturing Co.
2417 Davis Blvd.
Joplin, MO 64804

Toll-free: 800-641-4296
Phone: 417-781-6380
www.pkinsulation.com

P. K. Insulation's cellulose insulation products contain recycled newsprint and paper and a formulated boric acid fire retardant. The manufacturer has certified the following recycled-content levels (by weight): total recovered material 82% typical, 80% guaranteed; post-consumer material 5% typical, 3% guaranteed.

Fibre-Wool Cellulose

Tri-State Insulation Co.
P.O. Box 106
Miller, SD 57362-0106

Toll-free: 800-658-3531
Phone: 605-853-2442

Tri-State's Fibre-Wool cellulose insulation contains 100% recycled newspaper (minimum 80% post-consumer).

Good News - Reused

Mountain Fiber Insulation
1880 Anvil Rd.
P.O. Box 337
Hyrum, UT 84319

Toll-free: 800-669-4951
Phone: 435-245-6081

Good News - Reused cellulose insulation is made from recycled newspaper. The manufacturer has certified the following recycled-content levels (by weight): total recovered material 80% typical, 80% guaranteed; post-consumer material 80% typical, 80% guaranteed.

Good News - Reused, House Blanket, Weather Blanket, and Comfort Control

Modern Insulation
1206 S. Monroe St.
Spencer, WI 54479

Phone: 715-659-2446

Modern Insulations' cellulose insulation products contain 80% post-consumer recycled newspaper.

Igloo Cellulose Insulation

Igloo Cellulose, Inc.
195 Brunswick
Pointe Claire, PQ H9R 4Z1 Canada

Toll-free: 800-363-7876
www.cellulose.com

Contains 85% recycled newspaper and special natural additives.

Isolite, Thermalite, and Isopro

Thermoguard Co.
125 N. Dyer Rd.
Spokane, WA 99212

Toll-free: 800-541-0579
Phone: 509-535-4600

Thermoguard offers a loose-fill cellulose insulation and two different spray-on adhesive insulations, one with a mesh backing. Both are designed for wet-spray installation. Thermoguard is UL-approved. Thermoguard insulation contains recycled newspaper.

K-13 and SonaSpray "fc" Insulation

International Cellulose Corporation
12315 Robin Blvd.
P.O. Box 450006
Houston, TX 77045-0006

Toll-free: 800-444-1252
Phone: 713-433-6701
www.spray-on.com

K-13 is designed for surface-spray applications. It gives a rough finish and can be applied up to 5" thick. SonaSpray® "fc" gives a finished ceiling and can be applied 1" thick. Fire resistance is obtained by adding Borax. Both products, made from recycled ONP, OCC, and other papers, are available in standard colors or custom tints. K-13 has an insulation R-value of 3.8 per inch. SonaSpray "fc" has an NRC (noise reduction) of 0.65 at $1/2$" and 0.90 at 1". The manufacturer has certified the following recycled-content levels (by weight): total recovered material 80% typical, 80% guaranteed.

Mono-Therm

Thermo-Kool of Alaska
P.O. Box 230085
Anchorage, AK 99523

Phone: 907-563-3644

Mono-Therm insulation contains recycled newspaper. The manufacturer has certified the following recycled-content levels (by weight): total recovered material 86% typical, 85% guaranteed; post-consumer material 86% typical, 85% guaranteed.

Nu-Wool Engineered Cellulose Insulation

Nu-Wool Co., Inc.
2472 Port Sheldon St.
Jenison, MI 49428

Toll-free: 800-748-0128
Phone: 616-669-0100
www.nuwool.com

Nu-Wool cellulose insulation is made from recycled newspaper. The manufacturer has certified the following recycled-content levels (by weight): total recovered material 85% typical, 85% guaranteed; post-consumer material 85% typical, 85% guaranteed.

Regal Wall Net and Insulweb

Regal Industries, Inc.
9564 E. County Rd. 600 S
Crothersville, IN 47229

Toll-free: 800-848-9687
Phone: 812-793-2214
www.regalind.com

Regal Industries offers two products that are stapled or glued to the interior face of stud framing to contain blown-in cellulose insulation prior to the installation of drywall. Regal Wall Insulweb is a clothlike product, while Regal Wall Net is a more expensive plastic netting. Glue is available either latex-based by the gallon for warm weather, or solvent-based for cold weather in a 5-gal. container. The solvent-based adhesive has higher VOC emissions.

Therm Shield

Erie Energy Products, Inc.
1400 Irwin Dr.
Erie, PA 16505

Toll-free: 800-233-1810
Phone: 814-454-2828
www.erieenergy.com

Therm Shield cellulose insulation contains recycled newspaper.

Thermo-Cel and Cel-Pak

National Fiber
50 Depot St.
Belchertown, MA 01007

Toll-free: 800-282-7711
Phone: 413-283-8747
www.natlfiber.com

Photo: Bill Hulstrunk

Thermo-Cel, Cel-Pak, and NuWool WallSeal cellulose insulation contain recycled newspaper. Delivery is available to the 9 northeastern states. The manufacturer has certified the following recycled-content levels (by weight): total recovered material 83% typical, 82% guaranteed; post-consumer material 83% typical, 82% guaranteed.

Thermolok and Thermospray

Hamilton Manufacturing, Inc.
901 Russet St.
Twin Falls, ID 83303

Toll-free: 800-777-9689
Phone: 208-733-9689
www.hmi-mfg.com

Thermolok and Thermospray cellulose insulation contain 100% boron and recycled newspaper.

Toc-Light

Therm-O-Comfort Co. Ltd.
75 S. Edgeware Rd.
St. Thomas, ON N5P 2H7 Canada

Toll-free: 877-684-3766
Phone: 519-631-3400

Therm-O-Comfort cellulose insulation is a fiberized product made of 100% recycled newspaper (80% post-industrial and 20% post-consumer) and boric acid/ammonium sulfate fire retardant. It is available in both loose fill and stabilized forms.

Walkote Mix II, Loose Fill, and Craftkote

Western Fibers, Inc.
P.O. Box 745
Hollis, OK 73550

Phone: 580-688-9223

Walkote Mix II, Loose Fill, and Craftkote cellulose insulation products contain recycled newspaper and cardboard.

Weather Blanket, House Blanket, Comfort Control, and Good News - Reused

Champion Insulation, Inc.
P.O. Box 320
Lomira, WI 53048

Phone: 920-269-4311
www.championinsulation.com

Champion Insulation's cellulose insulation products are manufactured using over 85% post-consumer recycled newsprint. The manufacturer has certified the following recycled-content levels (by weight): total recovered material 85% typical, 85% guaranteed; post-consumer material 85% typical, 85% guaranteed.

Weathershield

Thermo-Cell Industries, Ltd.
2015 Lanthier
Orleans, ON K4A 3V2 Canada

Toll-free: 800-267-1433
www.thermocell.com

Weathershield cellulose insulation contains 95% recycled newspaper (by weight) from a mix of post-consumer and post-industrial sources.

Cotton Insulation

Cotton insulation is made from post-industrial recycled cotton textiles, such as denim. Nontoxic flame retardants similar to those used in clothing are added. Unlike fiberglass and mineral wool, there are no mineral microfibers that can cause respiratory problems.

Inno-Therm Fiber Insulation

InnoTherm
1633 Shea Rd.
P.O. Box 226
Newton, NC 28658

Toll-free: 877-466-0612
Phone: 828-466-1147
www.innotherm.com

Inno-Therm is made of recycled cotton and denim or from custom-tailored thermal fibers. It contains no melamine or phenolic resins, can be installed without safety precautions, and is recyclable. Available in $15^1/_2$"- and $23^1/_2$"-wide rolls; R11 and R13 are $3^1/_2$" thick, and R19 is $5^1/_2$" thick. This insulation meets or exceeds standards for thermal resistance, flame and smoke spread ratings, water vapor sorption, odor emission, and fungi resistance.

UltraTouch Natural Fiber Insulation

Bonded Logic, Inc.
411 E. Ray Rd.
Chandler, AZ 85225

Phone: 480-812-9114
www.bondedlogic.com

Bonded Logic makes UltraTouch from post-industrial recycled denim and other cotton-fiber textile trimmings. This insulation contains no mineral fibers and carries no warning labels for installers or occupants. It is completely recyclable at the end of its useful life and has been ASTM tested for thermal resistance, surface-burning characteristics, water-vapor absorption, mold/fungi resistance, and odor emission. Available in batts that are either 16" or 24" wide, UltraTouch comes in $3^1/_2$" (R-13) or $5^1/_2$" (R-19) thicknesses. The manufacturer has certified the following recycled-content levels (by weight): total recovered material 75% typical, 75% guaranteed; post-consumer material 0% typical, 0% guaranteed.

EPS Foam Insulation

Expanded polystyrene (EPS) insulation has long been the rigid foam board of choice for those seeking to minimize the greenhouse gas and ozone-depletion effects of their rigid-insulation choices. Pentane gas is used to expand EPS; it doesn't deplete stratospheric ozone or contribute to global warming, though it does contribute to ground-level smog. Modern EPS plants can be built to recover 95% of pentane used in production (required in California), reducing this impact. Since polyiso manufacturers completed the switch to hydrocarbon blowing agents in 2003, this environmental advantage of EPS over polyiso has disappeared. EPS will remain environmentally preferable to most extruded polystyrene (XPS) until closer to 2010, when XPS manufacturers are scheduled to eliminate use of HCFCs. A downside of EPS insulation is that most is made with the brominated flame retardant HCBD (hexachlorobutadiene) at a concentration of 0.5 to 2.0% by weight.

CavClear EPS Insulation System

Archovations, Inc.
P.O. Box 241
Hudson, WI 54016

Toll-free: 888-436-2620
Phone: 715-381-5773
www.cavclear.com

The CavClear® EPS Insulation System is an insulation and airspace maintenance and drainage system designed to be installed full-height behind brick or stone. The system consists of the CavClear Masonry Mat bonded to EPS insulation. Masonry Mat prevents obstruction of the cavity drainage airspace and also prevents energy-conducting mortar bridges from forming. A properly functioning drainage system free of all mortar obstructions is the prerequisite for a masonry design to achieve maximum thermal efficiencies and reduced maintenance and repair costs. Masonry Mat is a nonwoven plastic mesh made from 100% recycled plastic (25% minimum post-consumer content).

Cellofoam and Fan-Fold

Cellofoam North America, Inc.
1917 Rockdale Industrial Blvd.
P.O. Box 406
Conyers, GA 30012

Toll-free: 800-241-3634
Phone: 770-929-3688
www.cellofoam.com

Cellofoam manufactures EPS insulation products for siding underlayment, foundation perimeter, and other rigid insulation applications.

EPS Foam

Alamo Foam, Inc.
P.O. Box 47107
San Antonio, TX 78265

Phone: 210-646-8288

Alamo Foam manufactures EPS foam for roofing and other insulation applications.

EPS Foam

Drew Foam, Inc.
144 Industrial Dr.
Monticello, AR 71655

Toll-free: 800-643-1206
Phone: 870-367-6245
www.drewfoam.com

Drew Foam manufactures EPS foam insulation for underlayment, perimeter, and roofing applications.

EPS Foam

Insulfoam (Division of Premier Industries, Inc.)
1019 Pacific Ave., Ste. 1501
Tacoma, WA 98402

Toll-free: 800-248-5995
Phone: 253-572-5111
www.insulfoam.com

Insulfoam manufactures a large variety of expanded polystyrene insulation products including the polyethylene-skinned R-TECH family of perimeter foundation, wall, and roof insulation (in standard sheathing and fanfold configurations); standard roof insulation and the custom-cut Insultaper Tapered Roof Drainage System; Insul-Lam and Insul-Vent, nailable deck panels for use on steel and wood roof systems; as well as their Garage Door Insulation Kit. Insulfoam insulation products are made from up to 15% post-consumer recycled EPS with the company accepting EPS scrap from its larger customers. The manufacturer has certified the following recycled-content levels (by weight): total recovered material 15% typical, 10% guaranteed; post-consumer material 15% typical, 10% guaranteed.

EPS Foam

Perma "R" Products
2064 Sunset Dr.
P.O. Box 279
Grenada, MS 38902

Toll-free: 800-647-6130
Phone: 662-226-8075
www.leclairindustries.com

Perma "R" Products manufactures EPS foam insulation for foundation perimeter and other building insulation applications.

EPS Foam

Plymouth Foam Incorporated
1800 Sunset Dr.
Plymouth, WI 53073

Toll-free: 800-669-1176
Phone: 920-893-0535
www.plymouthfoam.com

Plymouth Foam manufactures fanfold and rigid siding underlayment insulation, roofing insulations, and sill plate gaskets made from EPS foam. In addition to their Plymouth, Wisconsin plant, Plymouth Foam also operates manufacturing plants in Becker, Minnesota and Newcomerstown, Ohio.

EPS Foam

Shelter Enterprises, Inc.
8 Saratoga St.
P.O. Box 618
Cohoes, NY 12047

Toll-free: 800-836-0719
Phone: 518-237-4100
www.shelter-ent.com

Shelter Enterprises manufactures EPS foam insulation for underlayment, roofing, perimeter, EIFS, concrete core-fill, SIP, and sill-sealing applications.

EPS Foam

Tri State Foam Products, Inc.
P.O. Box 2337
Martinsville, VA 24113

Toll-free: 800-277-0967
Phone: 276-638-3592
www.tri-state-foam.com

Tri State Foam Products manufactures EPS foam insulation for roofing, perimeter, precast concrete void-fill, and EIFS applications.

EPS Foam Insulation Components

BASF Corporation
3000 Continental Dr. N
Mount Olive, NJ 07828

Toll-free: 800-447-7180
Phone: 973-426-3919
www.plasticsportal.net

BASF produces components for manufacturing low-pentane foam insulation.

Perform and Perform Guard EPS

Advance Foam Plastics, Inc. - California Division
748 N. McKeever Ave.
Azusa, CA 91702

Phone: 626-334-5358
www.afprcontrol.com

Advance Foam Plastics is a licensed manufacturer of AFM Corporation's Perform® EPS Insulation, a non-ozone-depleting foam insulation manufactured in various sizes for many insulation applications. Perform Guard® is Perform EPS formulated with a boron insect repellent. Contour Taper Tile® roof insulation is Perform EPS shaped to achieve appropriate pitches for low-slope roofs.

Perform and Perform Guard EPS

Advance Foam Plastics, Inc. - Colorado Division
5250 N. Sherman St.
Denver, CO 80216

Toll-free: 800-525-8697
Phone: 303-297-3844
www.afprcontrol.com

Advance Foam Plastics is a licensed manufacturer of AFM Corporation's Perform® EPS Insulation, a non-ozone-depleting foam insulation manufactured in various sizes for many insulation applications. Perform Guard® is Perform EPS formulated with a boron insect repellent. Contour Taper Tile® roof insulation is Perform EPS shaped to achieve appropriate pitches for low-slope roofs.

Perform and Perform Guard EPS

Advance Foam Plastics, Inc. - Nevada Division
920 Kleppe Ln.
Sparks, NV 89431

Toll-free: 800-444-9290
Phone: 775-355-7655
www.afprcontrol.com

Advance Foam Plastics is a licensed manufacturer of AFM Corporation's Perform® EPS Insulation, a non-ozone-depleting foam insulation manufactured in various sizes for many insulation applications. Perform Guard® is Perform EPS formulated with a boron insect repellent. Contour Taper Tile® roof insulation is Perform EPS shaped to achieve appropriate pitches for low-slope roofs.

Perform and Perform Guard EPS

Advance Foam Plastics, Inc. - Utah Division
111 W. Fireclay Ave.
Murray, UT 84107

Toll-free: 877-775-8847
Phone: 801-265-3465
www.afprcontrol.com

Advance Foam Plastics is a licensed manufacturer of AFM Corporation's Perform® EPS Insulation, a non-ozone-depleting foam insulation manufactured in various sizes for many insulation applications. Perform Guard® is Perform EPS formulated with a boron insect repellent. Contour Taper Tile® roof insulation is Perform EPS shaped to achieve appropriate pitches for low-slope roofs.

Perform and Perform Guard EPS

AFM Corporation
211 River Ridge Cir. #102
Burnsville, MN 55337

Toll-free: 800-255-0176
Phone: 952-474-0809
www.r-control.com

Perform EPS Insulation is a non-ozone-depleting foam insulation manufactured in various sizes for many insulation applications. Contour Taper Tile® roof insulation is Perform EPS cut to achieve appropriate pitches for low-slope roofs.
Perform Guard® is termite-resistant EPS formulated with a borate additive. AFM also makes use of Perform Guard to manufacture structural insulated panels (SIPs) and insulated concrete forms (ICFs). AFM licenses several dozen manufacturers throughout the U.S. to produce these products as well.

Perform and Perform Guard EPS

Allied Foam Products, Inc.
2731 White Sulphur Rd.
Gainesville, GA 30501

Toll-free: 800-533-2613
Phone: 770-536-7900
www.alliedfoamprod.com

Allied Foam Products is a licensed manufacturer of AFM Corporation's Perform® EPS Insulation, a non-ozone-depleting foam insulation manufactured in various sizes for many insulation applications. Perform Guard® is Perform EPS formulated with a boron insect repellent. Contour Taper Tile® roof insulation is Perform EPS shaped to achieve appropriate pitches for low-slope roofs.

Perform and Perform Guard EPS

Big Sky Insulations, Inc.
P.O. Box 838
Belgrade, MT 59714

Toll-free: 800-766-3626
Phone: 406-388-4146
www.bsiinc.com

Big Sky Insulation is a licensed manufacturer of AFM Corporation's Perform® EPS Insulation, a non-ozone-depleting foam insulation manufactured in various sizes for many insulation applications. Perform Guard® is Perform EPS formulated with a boron insect repellent. Contour Taper Tile® roof insulation is Perform EPS shaped to achieve appropriate pitches for low-slope roofs.

Perform and Perform Guard EPS

Branch River Foam Plastics, Inc.
15 Thurber Blvd.
Smithfield, RI 02917

Toll-free: 800-336-3626
Phone: 401-232-0270
www.branchriver.com

Branch River Foam Plastics is a licensed manufacturer of AFM Corporation's Perform® EPS Insulation, a non-ozone-depleting foam insulation manufactured in various sizes for many insulation applications. Perform Guard® is Perform EPS formulated with a boron insect repellent. Contour Taper Tile® roof insulation is Perform EPS shaped to achieve appropriate pitches for low-slope roofs.

Perform and Perform Guard EPS

Contour Products, Inc. - Kansas City Division
4001 Kaw Dr.
Kansas City, KS 66102

Toll-free: 800-638-3626
Phone: 913-321-4114
www.contourfoam.com

Contour Products is a licensed manufacturer of AFM Corporation's Perform® EPS Insulation, a non-ozone-depleting foam insulation manufactured in various sizes for many insulation applications. Perform Guard® is Perform EPS formulated with a boron insect repellent. Contour Taper Tile® roof insulation is Perform EPS shaped to achieve appropriate pitches for low-slope roofs.

Perform and Perform Guard EPS

Contour Products, Inc. - Newton Division
1418 Cow Palace Rd.
Newton, KS 67114

Toll-free: 800-835-2161
Phone: 316-283-1100
www.contourfoam.com

Contour Products is a licensed manufacturer of AFM Corporation's Perform® EPS Insulation, a non-ozone-depleting foam insulation manufactured in various sizes for many insulation applications. Perform Guard® is Perform EPS formulated with a boron insect repellent. Contour Taper Tile® roof insulation is Perform EPS shaped to achieve appropriate pitches for low-slope roofs. For sales information, contact the company's Kansas City Division.

Perform and Perform Guard EPS

Flexible Packaging Company
Bayamon Gardens Sta.
P.O. Box 4321
Bayamon Gardens (San Juan), PR 00958

Phone: 787-780-0466

Flexible Packaging Company is a licensed manufacturer of AFM Corporation's Perform® EPS Insulation, a non-ozone-depleting foam insulation manufactured in various sizes for many insulation applications. Perform Guard® is Perform EPS formulated with a boron insect repellent. Contour Taper Tile® roof insulation is Perform EPS shaped to achieve appropriate pitches for low-slope roofs.

Perform and Perform Guard EPS

Heartland EPS, Inc. - Headquarters
90 Trowbridge Dr.
P.O. Box 669
Fond du Lac, WI 54936

Toll-free: 800-236-5377
Phone: 920-924-4050
www.heartlandeps.com

Heartland EPS is a licensed manufacturer of AFM Corporation's Perform® EPS Insulation, a non-ozone-depleting foam insulation manufactured in various sizes for many insulation applications. Perform Guard® is Perform EPS formulated with a boron insect repellent. Contour Taper Tile® roof insulation is Perform EPS shaped to achieve appropriate pitches for low-slope roofs.

Perform and Perform Guard EPS

Heartland EPS, Inc. - Illinois Division
3751 Sunset Ave.
Waukegan, IL 60087

Toll-free: 800-800-0359
Phone: 847-263-0200
www.heartlandeps.com

Heartland EPS, formerly Wisconsin EPS, is a licensed manufacturer of AFM Corporation's Perform® EPS Insulation, a non-ozone-depleting foam insulation manufactured in various sizes for many insulation applications. Perform Guard® is Perform EPS formulated with a boron insect repellent. Contour Taper Tile® roof insulation is Perform EPS shaped to achieve appropriate pitches for low-slope roofs.

Perform and Perform Guard EPS

Heartland EPS, Inc. - Iowa Division
809 E. 15th St.
Washington, IA 52353

Toll-free: 888-633-6033
Phone: 319-653-6216
www.heartlandeps.com

Heartland EPS is a licensed manufacturer of AFM Corporation's Perform® EPS Insulation, a non-ozone-depleting foam insulation manufactured in various sizes for many insulation applications. Perform Guard® is Perform EPS formulated with a boron insect repellent. Contour Taper Tile® roof insulation is Perform EPS shaped to achieve appropriate pitches for low-slope roofs.

Perform and Perform Guard EPS

Insulated Building Systems, Inc.
326 McGhee Rd.
Winchester, VA 22603

Phone: 540-662-0882
www.rcontrolibs.com

Insulated Building Systems is a licensed manufacturer of AFM Corporation's Perform® EPS Insulation, a non-ozone-depleting foam insulation manufactured in various sizes for many insulation applications. Perform Guard® is Perform EPS formulated with a boron insect repellent. Contour Taper Tile® roof insulation is Perform EPS shaped to achieve appropriate pitches for low-slope roofs.

Perform and Perform Guard EPS

Pacific Allied Products, Ltd.
91-110 Kaomi Loop
Kapolei, HI 96707

Toll-free: 888-824-3626
Phone: 808-682-2038
www.pacificalliedproducts.com

Pacific Allied Products is a licensed manufacturer of AFM Corporation's Perform® EPS Insulation, a non-ozone-depleting foam insulation manufactured in various sizes for many insulation applications. Perform Guard® is Perform EPS formulated with a borate insect repellent. Contour Taper Tile® roof insulation is Perform EPS shaped to achieve appropriate pitches for low-slope roofs.

Perform and Perform Guard EPS

Poly-Foam, Inc.
116 Pine St. S
Lester Prairie, MN 55354

Phone: 320-395-2551
www.polyfoaminc.com

Poly-Foam is a licensed manufacturer of AFM Corporation's Perform® EPS Insulation, a non-ozone-depleting foam insulation manufactured in various sizes for many insulation applications. Perform Guard® is Perform EPS formulated with a boron insect repellent. Contour Taper Tile® roof insulation is Perform EPS shaped to achieve appropriate pitches for low-slope roofs.

Perform and Perform Guard EPS

Stanark Foam / R-CONTROL
10101 Hwy. 70 E
N. Little Rock, AR 72117

Toll-free: 800-632-4586
Phone: 501-945-1114
www.stanark.com

Stanark Foam is a licensed manufacturer of AFM Corporation's Perform® EPS Insulation, a non-ozone-depleting foam insulation manufactured in various sizes for many insulation applications. Perform Guard® is Perform EPS formulated with a boron insect repellent. Contour Taper Tile® roof insulation is Perform EPS shaped to achieve appropriate pitches for low-slope roofs.

Perform and Perform Guard EPS

Team Industries, Inc.
4580 Airwest Dr. SE
P.O. Box 888691
Grand Rapids, MI 49588

Toll-free: 800-356-5548
Phone: 616-698-2001
www.teamindustries.com

Team Industries is a licensed manufacturer of AFM Corporation's Perform® EPS Insulation, a non-ozone-depleting foam insulation manufactured in various sizes for many insulation applications. Perform Guard® is Perform EPS formulated with a boron insect repellent. Contour Taper Tile® roof insulation is Perform EPS shaped to achieve appropriate pitches for low-slope roofs.

Perform and Perform Guard EPS

Therma Foam, Inc.
P.O. Box 161128
Fort Worth, TX 76161

Toll-free: 800-333-3626
Phone: 817-624-7204
www.thermafoam.com

Therma Foam is a licensed manufacturer of AFM Corporation's Perform® EPS Insulation, a non-ozone-depleting foam insulation manufactured in various sizes for many insulation applications. Perform Guard® is Perform EPS formulated with a boron insect repellent. Contour Taper Tile® roof insulation is Perform EPS shaped to achieve appropriate pitches for low-slope roofs.

Perform and Perform Guard EPS

Thermal Foams/Syracuse, Inc.
6173 S. Bay Rd.
P.O. Box 1981
Cicero, NY 13039

Toll-free: 800-873-6267
Phone: 315-699-8734
www.thermalfoams.com

Thermal Foams is a licensed manufacturer of AFM Corporation's Perform® EPS Insulation, a non-ozone-depleting foam insulation manufactured in various sizes for many insulation applications. Perform Guard® is Perform EPS formulated with a boron insect repellent. Contour Taper Tile® roof insulation is Perform EPS shaped to achieve appropriate pitches for low-slope roofs.

PlastiSpan Insulation

Plasti-Fab Ltd.
270, 3015 Fifth Ave. NE
Calgary, AB T2A 6T8 Canada

Toll-free: 888-446-5377
Phone: 403-248-9306
www.plastifab.com

Plasti-Fab manufactures PlastiSpan® EPS Insulation, a non-ozone-depleting foam product available in various sizes for many insulation applications. PlastiSpan can be shaped to achieve appropriate pitches for low-slope roofs.

Polar 10 and Polar Guard Rigid EPS

Polar Industries
32 Grammar Ave.
Prospect, CT 06712

Toll-free: 800-237-3763
Phone: 203-758-6651
www.polarcentral.com

Polar 10 is a 2-lb. density, $2^{1}/_{3}$"-thick EPS board that is manufactured to be comparable to XPS. The boards are processed from 40–60% industrial scrap through a process called pulfusion, which gives the EPS a durable, hydrophobic skin. The $2^{1}/_{3}$" thickness achieves an R-value of 10 and thus enables this EPS product to meet Northeast energy codes. The 2-lb. density gives the EPS greater compressive and tensile strength. Polar Industries also manufactures other EPS products including Polar Guard, a standard 1-lb. density EPS board (also manufactured with the pulfusion process). Polar Guard is available in $^{3}/_{4}$", 1", and 2" thicknesses.

RayLite, BackerBoard, and StyroStud

DiversiFoam Products
9091 County Rd. 50
P.O. Box 44
Rockford, MN 55373

Toll-free: 800-669-0100
Phone: 763-477-5854
www.diversifoam.com

DiversiFoam manufactures various EPS foam insulation products.

Thermal Foams EPS

Thermal Foams, Inc.
2101 Kenmore Ave.
Buffalo, NY 14207

Phone: 716-874-6474
www.thermalfoams.com

Thermal Foams manufactures EPS insulation in various sizes for many insulation applications. Flat and tapered roof insulation are shaped to achieve appropriate pitches for low-slope roofs. Thermal Foams' roof insulation can have up to 15% recycled content.

Fiberglass Insulation

Most fiberglass insulation is made primarily from silica spun into glass fibers and contains a phenol-formaldehyde (PF) binder, though formaldehyde-free products have been introduced. Most of the PF is removed in a baking process, but offgassing from fiberglass can be a moderate indoor air quality (IAQ) concern. Airborne fiberglass fibers have been implicated as a suspected carcinogenic hazard, though concerns have been downgraded since 2000. Most fiberglass insulation today has at least 30% recycled-glass content, including both post-industrial glass cullet and post-consumer bottle glass. Recycled content varies from plant to plant, with some plants using as much as 40% post-consumer recycled beverage glass as the raw material.

CertainTeed Building Insulation

CertainTeed Corporation
750 E. Swedesford Rd.
P.O. Box 860
Valley Forge, PA 19482

Toll-free: 800-233-8990
Phone: 610-341-7739
www.certainteed.com

CertainTeed Building Insulation is manufactured with recycled glass cullet. One of CertainTeed's plants manufactures insulation products with 35% post-consumer recycled-glass content. These products carry the GREENGUARD certification for low emissions. The manufacturer has certified the following recycled-content levels (by weight): total recovered material 20% typical; post-consumer material 10% typical.

Climate Pro Blowing Wool

Johns Manville Corporation
P.O. Box 5108
Denver, CO 80217

Toll-free: 800-654-3103
Phone: 303-978-2000
www.jm.com

Climate Pro® Blowing Wool is a formaldehyde-free loose-fill fiberglass insulation containing 20% post-consumer and 5% post-industrial recycled glass. Climate-Pro can achieve an R-value of R-70 over $1/2$" ceiling drywall without exceeding ceiling weight limits.

ComfortTherm

Johns Manville Corporation
P.O. Box 5108
Denver, CO 80217

Toll-free: 800-654-3103
Phone: 303-978-2000
www.jm.com

ComfortTherm® is a poly-encapsulated fiberglass insulation designed for metal- and wood-framing as well as for directly above suspended ceilings. Available in batts or rolls, R-values range from 11 to 38. ComfortTherm is formaldehyde-free and contains 20% post-consumer and 5% post-industrial recycled glass.

Fiberglass Insulation

Ottawa Fibre, Inc.
1365 Johnston Rd.
Ottawa, ON K1V 8Z1
Canada

Phone: 613-247-7116
www.ofigroup.com

Ottawa Fibre fiberglass insulation is made from 80% recycled glass (typical), of which 100% is usually post-consumer content. Ottawa Fibre's Golden Glow residential insulation is available in four configurations; unfaced, kraft-faced, foil-faced, and FSK-faced. R-values range from R-6 to R-38, depending on density and thickness. The company also offers a wide range of fiberglass insulation products including commercial and industrial insulation and ceiling tiles.

Formaldehyde-Free Insulation Batts

Johns Manville Corporation
P.O. Box 5108
Denver, CO 80217

Toll-free: 800-654-3103
Phone: 303-978-2000
www.jm.com

Johns Manville Corporation eliminated the use of formaldehyde in their insulation products in 2002. Their thermal- and sound-insulating fiberglass batts use an acrylic binder, and come in rolls either unfaced or with foil, FSK, or Kraft facing.

Industry Representation

North American Insulation Manufacturers Association
44 Canal Center Plz., Ste. 310
Alexandria, VA 22314

Phone: 703-684-0084
www.naima.org

The North American Insulation Manufacturers Association (NAIMA) is the trade association of North American manufacturers of fiberglass, rock wool, and slag wool insulation products. Insulation often incorporates recycled glass and iron slag. The association has certified the following recycled-content levels (by weight): total recovered material 70% typical; post-consumer material 40% typical.

InsulSafe 4

CertainTeed Corporation
750 E. Swedesford Rd.
P.O. Box 860
Valley Forge, PA 19482

Toll-free: 800-233-8990
Phone: 610-341-7739
www.certainteed.com

InsulSafe® 4 is a formaldehyde-free, loose-fill, fiberglass insulation suitable for open-blow attic applications.
InsulSafe 4 contains recycled glass cullet. This product carries the GREENGUARD certification for low emissions. The manufacturer has certified the following recycled-content levels (by weight): total recovered material 20% typical; post-consumer material 10% typical.

Miraflex

Owens Corning
1 Owens Corning Pkwy.
Toledo, OH 43659

Toll-free: 800-438-7465
Phone: 419-248-8000
www.owenscorning.com

Miraflex® is a formaldehyde-free fiberglass insulation. The batts are held together by the twisted nature of the Miraflex fibers, avoiding chemical binders altogether. Twisting the fibers makes them less friable than regular fiberglass, reducing the amount of loose airborne fibers. For attics, polyethylene-wrapped batts are 8³/₄" with an R-value of 25. Wall batts, available only by special order, are 3¹/₂", faced in poly-kraft with polyethylene wraps, and provide an R-value of 13. Packaged Miraflex can be compressed into much smaller rolls than conventional fiberglass insulation, yielding reductions in embodied energy. This product carries the GREENGUARD certification for low emissions.

Monoglass Spray-On Insulation

Monoglass, Inc.
430 North Tower
650 W. 41st Ave.
Vancouver, BC V5Z 2M9 Canada

Toll-free: 888-777-2966
Phone: 604-261-7712
www.monoglass.com

Monoglass® Spray-On Insulation is a combination of elongated, recycled-cullet glass fibers and water-based, nontoxic adhesives that can be spray-applied to virtually any surface or configuration. Without additional support, Monoglass can be applied overhead to a maximum of 5" (R-20) and applied vertically to 7" (R-28). Monoglass is white in color, noncombustible, and can be applied over fireproofing. Monoglass contains no formaldehyde and does not support fungal growth or encourage infestation by pests. The manufacturer has certified the following recycled-content levels (by weight): total recovered material 37% typical, 37% guaranteed; post-consumer material 25% typical, 25% guaranteed.

OPTIMA

CertainTeed Corporation
750 E. Swedesford Rd.
P.O. Box 860
Valley Forge, PA 19482

Toll-free: 800-233-8990
Phone: 610-341-7739
www.certainteed.com

Optima® is an insulation system composed of a non-woven fabric facing behind which Optima is blown.
Optima fiberglass is blown dry, without additives or moisture, and can be used in closed-cavity, retrofit applications. Some of the glass fibers are from recycled glass cullet. This product carries

the GREENGUARD certification for low emissions. The manufacturer has certified the following recycled-content levels (by weight): total recovered material 20% typical; post-consumer material 10% typical.

PINK Fiberglas Building Insulation

Owens Corning
1 Owens Corning Pkwy.
Toledo, OH 43659

Toll-free: 800-438-7465
Phone: 419-248-8000
www.owenscorning.com

Owens Corning Pink fiber glass insulation products are certified by Scientific Certification Systems to contain at least 30% recycled glass (4% post-consumer and 26% post-industrial). A wide range of insulation products are manufactured by Owens Corning. This product carries the GREENGUARD certification for low emissions.

Foamed-in-Place and Sprayed-On Insulation

Foamed-in-place insulation has the advantage of filling wall and ceiling cavities completely, providing high R-values (3.6 to 6.5 per inch) and blocking air leakage very effectively. Installation requires special equipment, however, and must be done by licensed contractors. Most foamed-in-place insulation products are fairly high-density (2 lbs. per cubic foot) closed-cell polyure- thanes—and some of these still use the ozone-depleting HCFC- 141b blowing agent. Open-cell, low-density polyurethane foams have been produced with water or carbon dioxide as the blowing agent for some time. Compared with closed-cell polyurethane, open-cell products also use significantly less material, making them attractive from a resource standpoint.

Air Krete Foam Insulation

Air Krete, Inc.
2710 E. Brutus St.
P.O. Box 380
Weedsport, NY 13166

Phone: 315-834-6609
www.airkrete.com

Air Krete is a cementitious foam in- sulation product that is ultra-light, inorganic, nonflammable, nontoxic, ozone-safe, pest-resistant, and moisture-resistant. Mixed with an expanding agent, it is blown with pressurized air. It contains no fluorocarbons and can be used in high temperature areas. It is foamed in place in new or existing wall cavities by licensed Air Krete contractors. Air Krete has an R-value of 3.9/in. at 75°F. If

not installed properly, a higher-density (lower R-value) foam may be produced. The foam density can be varied to withstand high- vibration environments (along busy roadways) where the highly friable foam would otherwise deteriorate in the wall cavity.

BioBase 501

Bio-Based Systems
10A Wolfer Industrial Pk.
Spring Valley, IL 61362

Phone: 800-803-5189
www.biobased.net

BioBase 501 soybean-oil-based polyurethane spray foam insula- tion functions much like petroleum-based polyurethane foam. The polyol component of the two-part urethane consists of about 40% soy-derived oil. The open-cell foam is installed at a density of 0.5 lbs/ft^3 using CO_2 as the blowing agent. It expands to 100 times its original liquid size. The product has an R-value of 3.7/in. (R-13 at $3^1/_2$") and is applied with customized equipment by certified installers. BioBase 501 was named "Outstanding Green Product of the Year" by the National Association of Homebuilders (NAHB) Green Builders Conference in Baltimore.

Fiberiffic 2000

Ark-Seal
2185 S. Jason St.
Denver, CO 80223

Toll-free: 800-237-7841
Phone: 303-934-7772
www.fiberiffic.com

Ark-Seal manufactures the Fiberiffic® 2000 spray equipment and supplies the latex binder to spray-on loose-fill insulation (cel- lulose is the greenest option) with a latex foam binder similar in composition to interior latex paint. This product contains no HCFCs. It can be troweled to a smooth surface or used in blown-in applications. R-values range from 4/in. with fiberglass to 3.6/in. with cellulose, to 3.5/in. with rockwool and cotton. It can be painted, waterproofed, or coated with stucco.

HealthySeal Spray-in-Place Foam Insulation

HealthySeal
P.O. Box 1868
Hardeeville, SC 29927

Phone: 800-769-3626
www.healthyseal.com

HealthySeal™ 500 is a water-blown, 0.5-lb., two-part, open-cell, expanding polyurethane foam insulation system made with a soy- based polyol from Urethane Soy Systems Co., which comprises about 25% of the end product. Its thermal performance is R-3.8/ in., with the added benefit of air sealing in the cavities.

Icynene Insulation System

Icynene, Inc.
6747 Campobello Rd.
Mississauga, ON L5N 2L7
Canada

Toll-free: 800-758-7325
Phone: 905-363-4040
www.icynene.com

The Icynene Insulation System was the first HCFC-free, low-density, open-cell polyurethane insulation to be introduced and is the most widely recognized brand. The foam is typically sprayed into open wall, ceiling, and floor cavities in a thin layer. It expands about 100 times its original volume and then is trimmed flush with the framing members before drywall is installed. Icynene's R-value is about R-3.6/in. A slightly different formulation of Icynene can be poured into closed wall cavities in retrofit applications. Like all polyurethane foams, Icynene is hazardous during installation.

RTC Polyurethane Insulation

Resin Technology Division of Henry Co.
2270 Castle Harbor Pl.
Ontario, CA 91761

Toll-free: 800-729-0795
Phone: 909-947-7224
www.resintechnology.com

Resin Technology formulates several water-blown, open-cell polyurethane foam insulation products with installed densities of 0.5 to 0.8 lbs/ft³, depending on specific requirements. The company reports an R-value of close to 3.1/in. As with all polyurethane foams, this insulation requires appropriate, professional precautions during installation.

Sealection 500

Demilec USA, Inc.
2925 Galleria Dr.
Arlington, TX 76011

Toll-free: 877-336-4532
Phone: 817-640-4900
www.sealection500.com

Sealection™ 500 is a low-density polyurethane foam that is 100% water-blown and contains no HCFCs or hydrocarbon blowing agents. The product insulates to R-3.8/in. This product has passed the established offgassing tests and is approved by the Environmental Choice Program (a private ecolabeling program in Canada). Like all polyurethane foams, Sealection is hazardous during installation.

SUPERGREEN FOAM

Foam-Tech, Division of Building Envelope Solutions, Inc.
P.O. Box 87, Rte. 5
N. Thetford, VT 05054

Phone: 802-333-4333
www.foam-tech.com

SuperGreen Foam™ is a closed-cell, high-density polyurethane foam containing no HCFCs. The blowing agent is HFC-134a. Super-Green insulates to between R-6 and R-7/in. Like all polyurethane foams, SuperGreen is hazardous during installation. Foam-Tech is a foamed-in-place building insulation contractor that holds a patent license to produce SuperGreen using components manufactured by Preferred Foam Products.

Insulation Baffles

Proper ventilation in attics and roofs is generally essential to maintaining insulation performance-reducing heat gain and (in cold climates) preventing ice dams. Insulation performance suffers when moisture, trapped under the roof sheathing, condenses on the insulation below. The highly conductive nature of water renders wet insulation much less effective—and wet insulation can also result in rotting wood framing members and mold growth. Insulation baffles play an important role in maintaining proper ventilation of vaulted (cathedral) ceilings. Insulation baffles, made from corrugated cardboard, foam, or plastic, ensure that a properly sized cavity is maintained between the top of the insulation and the roof decking. Avoid extruded polystyrene (XPS) baffles that are produced with HCFC blowing agents, and look for products with recycled content.

Attic Vents Chutes

Plymouth Foam Incorporated
1800 Sunset Dr.
Plymouth, WI 53073

Toll-free: 800-669-1176
Phone: 920-893-0535
www.plymouthfoam.com

Attic Vents Chutes are insulation baffles made from EPS foam for 16" and 24" on-center rafter bays. They are not known to contain recycled polystyrene. Plymouth Foam operates manufacturing plants in Plymouth, Wisconsin; Becker, Minnesota; and Newcomerstown, Ohio.

DUROVENT and proVent

ADO Products
21800 129th Ave. N
P.O. Box 236
Rogers, MN 55374

Toll-free: 866-240-4933
Phone: 763-428-7802
www.adoproducts.com

Durovent is made from EPS foam with up to 40% recycled content; proVent is made from polystyrene plastic and has up to 80% recycled content. Both these products are 48" long and available for 16" and 24" rafter spacings. Durovent is for new construction, while proVent is designed for remodeling applications. The thinner profile of proVent allows this product to be shipped more compactly, and its greater durability results in less breakage and other damage than occurs with EPS foam.

Insul-Tray

Insulation Solutions, Inc.
2711 N. Main St.
East Peoria, IL 61611

Toll-free: 866-698-6562
Phone: 309-698-0062
www.insulationsolutions.com

Insul-Tray insulation baffles are made from 100% recycled-content corrugated cardboard with or without a radiant-barrier foil facing for 16" and 24" on-center rafter bays and wall cavities. The radiant barrier reduces heat gain and heat loss through the roof as long as the baffles have an air space next to them.

Perma-Vent

Cellofoam North America, Inc.
1917 Rockdale Industrial Blvd.
P.O. Box 406
Conyers, GA 30012

Toll-free: 800-241-3634
Phone: 770-929-3688
www.cellofoam.com

Perma-Vent is an EPS foam insulation baffle for 16" and 24" on-center rafter bays. This product is not known to contain recycled polystyrene.

PermaVent Attic Baffle

Perma "R" Products
2064 Sunset Dr.
P.O. Box 279
Grenada, MS 38902

Toll-free: 800-647-6130
Phone: 662-226-8075
www.leclairindustries.com

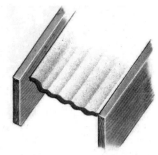

PermaVent Attic Baffles are insulation baffles for 16" and 24" on-center rafter bays. The product measures $3/8$" x 22" x 48" for 24" o.c. rafters; break along center perforations for 16" o.c. installations.

StyroVent

DiversiFoam Products
9091 County Rd. 50
P.O. Box 44
Rockford, MN 55373

Toll-free: 800-669-0100
Phone: 763-477-5854
www.diversifoam.com

StyroVent Attic Ventilation Chute, made from RayLite brand EPS, comes in two sizes: StyroVent Mini is for 16" on-center construction and measures 15" W x $2^{1}/_{4}$" D x 48" L; StyroVent Maxi, for 24" on-center construction, measures $23^{1}/_{4}$" W x $2^{1}/_{2}$" D x 48" L.

Non-EPS Foam Board Insulation

Foam insulation products are all petroleum-derived, but most have superior air-sealing, moisture resistance, and insulating properties compared to fiberglass and other fiber-insulation materials. Many foams require a blowing agent to create the foaming action. CFCs (chlorofluorocarbons) have been eliminated for this purpose because of their high ozone-depleting potential (ODP). CFCs were originally replaced by HCFCs (hydrochlorofluorocarbons), which have much lower ODPs. Polyisocyanurate (polyiso) is a common insulation for low-slope roofing and residential/light commercial walls; since 2003, all U.S. polyiso is produced using non-ozone-depleting hydrocarbon blowing agents. Extruded polystyrene (XPS), commonly used for foundation insulation because of its impermeability to water and high R-value, is still blown with HCFC-142b—although European manufacturers have converted to non-ozone-depleting blowing agents. Only a few specialized XPS insulation materials in the U.S. are currently produced without HCFCs.

ACFoam

Atlas Roofing Corp.
2000 RiverEdge Pkwy.,
   Ste. 800
Atlanta, GA 30328

Phone: 770-952-1442
www.atlasroofing.com

ACFoam® was the first North American polyisocyanurate foam insulation to be blown with hydrocarbons rather than HCFCs; it has zero ODP and zero GWP. ACFoam with ACUltra™ is sold under various brand names for both commercial and residential roofing and wall sheathing applications. This product also contains recovered materials and meets ASTM C-1289, UL, and FM standards. ACFoam-II (a roof insulation) contains between 16% and 43% recovered materials by weight, depending on thickness.

Styrofoam High Performance Underlayment

Dow Chemical Co., Styrofoam Brand Products
200 Larkin Ctr.
Midland, MI 48674

Toll-free: 800-441-4369
Phone: 989-636-1000
www.styrofoam.com

Styrofoam® High Performance Underlayment from Dow is the first U.S.-manufactured extruded polystyrene (XPS) foam board with zero ODP. This product, blown with HFC-152a, is designed for residential wall-sheathing applications. It comes in 4' x 50' fanfold sections, several different facings, and in thicknesses of $^{1}/_{4}$" (R-1) and $^{3}/_{8}$" (R-1.5).

Other Insulation

With innovative or nonconventional insulation materials, look for recovered-material content, less-processed formulations, and other green features.

Wool Insulation

Good Shepherd Wool
   Insulation
R.R. #3
Rocky Mountain House,
   AB T4T 2A3 Canada

Phone: 403-845-6705
www.goodshepherd
   wool.com

Good Shepherd Wool Insulation is sold in batts for frame houses and wool rope for

log homes. The only additive is a boron-based fire retardant and vermin and insect repellent.

Radiant Barriers

Radiant barriers reflect radiant heat in attics and ceilings—and in some cases, walls. These products can be foil-faced kraft paper, foil-faced polyethylene film, or foil facings on rigid insulation or wood-fiber sheathing. Radiant barrier products usually don't include significant recycled content because of the lower reflectivity of recycled aluminum; the high embodied energy of virgin aluminum is made up for many times over through improved building energy performance.

Astro-Foil

Innovative Energy
10653 W. 181 Ave.
Lowell, IN 46356

Toll-free: 800-745-3645
Phone: 219-696-3639
www.insul.net

Astro-Foil has two layers of polyethylene film with air bubbles sandwiched between layers of reflective aluminum foil. The company claims the following insulation performance, based on ASTM C-236 Hot Box testing procedures, depending on the direction of heatflow: down, R-15; up, R-5.4; and horizontal, R-7.3.

F-2, FSKF, and Type 4, 5, & 6

Superior Radiant Insulation
P.O. Box 247
San Dimas, CA 91773

Toll-free: 888-774-4422
Phone: 909-305-1450
www.superiorrb.com

Superior Radiant Insulation manufactures several radiant barrier and insulation products. F-2 is 100-lb. kraft paper-faced with foil on both sides. Similarly, FSKF has two foil facings on 30-lb. kraft with a nylon or fiberglass mesh scrim layer. Type 4, 5, and 6 are multilayer radiant barriers with chipboard stapling flanges for use in 2x4 and 2x6 framing. Superior Radiant Insulation also manufactures an aluminum foil-faced OSB or plywood sheathing.

K Shield Reflective Barrier

Key Solutions Marketing
P.O. Box 5090
Scottsdale, AZ 85261

Toll-free: 800-776-9765
Phone: 480-948-5150

The K Shield Reflective Barrier is made from aluminum-foil facings with a core of either 100# kraft paper or plastic film. Available in 500 and 1,000 ft² rolls, 25$^{1}/_{2}$" and 51" wide.

Low-E Insulation

Environmentally Safe Products, Inc.
313 W. Golden Ln.
New Oxford, PA 17350

Toll-free: 800-289-5693
www.low-e.com

Low-E Insulation has a core of microcell polyethylene foam insulation, which has 40% recycled content, and facings of polished aluminum foil. The product is reported to reflect 97% of the radiant energy that strikes its surfaces. Based on the direction of heat flow, the company claims the following insulation performance (ASTM C-236) for the $1/4$" version: down, R-10.74; up, R-7.55; and horizontal, R-7.75.

Reflectix

Reflectix, Inc.
1 School St.
P.O. Box 108
Markleville, IN 46056

Toll-free: 800-879-3645
Phone: 765-533-4332
www.reflectixinc.com

Reflectix combines an aluminum-foil facing with bubble-wrap packaging to form a $5/16$"-thick insulating radiant barrier. Reflectix comes in various roll widths and lengths.

TempShield Material

Sealed Air Corp. - Air Cellular Insulation
301 Mayhill Ave.
Saddle Brook, NJ 07663

Toll-free: 800-648-9093
Phone: 201-712-7000
www.sealedair.com

TempShield™ reflective-foil, air-cellular insulation consists of one or two layers of Barrier Bubble® air-cellular material laminated between layers of aluminum foil. The company claims up to 97% radiant-heat reflection for this insulation, which has 20% recycled-plastic content. TempShield insulation is a Class A/Class 1 fire-retardant product and comes in standard rolls of 4' x 125'.

The Insulator

Bonded Logic, Inc.
411 E. Ray Rd.
Chandler, AZ 85225

Phone: 480-812-9114
www.bondedlogic.com

The Insulator™ Thermal-Acoustic Insulation is a $3/8$"-thick thermal

and acoustic insulation made from post-industrial denim and cotton fiber and faced on either one or both sides with an aluminum barrier (also available in a two- or three-ply version). The product is formaldehyde-free and comes in 4' x 6' or 4' x 75' rolls (in $3/8$" thickness only). The Insulator is thermally bonded using a synthetic fiber binder and is treated with a boric acid antimicrobial agent. It is Class A fire-rated, and no protective clothing or gear is necessary for installation. The $3/8$" pad has a noise reduction coefficient of 0.45 and an R-value of 1.47.

Rockwool Insulation

Mineral wool insulation is made from either molten slag—a waste product of steel production—or natural rock, such as basalt and diabase. Some products contain a mix of these two. Mineral wool can be blown in as loose-fill, used in batts, spray-applied with a binding adhesive, or formed into rigid board stock. Typical R-values are 2.8 to 3.7 per inch. Mineral wool has a higher density than fiberglass, so it has better sound-blocking properties. It's also more fire-resistant than fiberglass. Rigid boardstock mineral wool insulation is a superb foundation insulation and drainage material, because it is extremely hydrophobic.

ThermaFiber Insulation Products

ThermaFiber LLC
3711 W. Mill St.
Wabash, IN 46992

Toll-free: 888-834-2371
Phone: 260-563-2111
www.thermafiber.com

Thermafiber Firespan, Safing Insulation, Curtain Wall Insulation, FS15, FS25, Sound Attenuation Firewall Blankets (SAFB's), are mineral-fiber insulation products manufactured with high proportions of slag, a post-industrial recycled material. The products come in a wide variety of densities, facings, thicknesses, and R-values as rigid or loose-fill material. These products have been evaluated by an independent testing facility for low pollutant emissions. ThermaTech Attic Blowing Wool, Side Wall Spray, and Foundation Wall Spray, according to the manufacturer, contain no formaldehyde or chemical additives, are noncombustible and odor-free, will not absorb moisture or support mildew or fungus, and will not rot or decay.

Thermal-Pruf, Dendamix, and Sound-Pruf

American Sprayed Fibers, Inc.
1550 E. 91st Dr.
Merrillville, IN 46410

Toll-free: 800-824-2997
Phone: 219-769-0180
www.asfiusa.com

Thermal-Pruf™ is a blend of cellulose and premium rock wool insulation that can be spray-applied onto steel, aluminum, concrete, brick, block, or wood. In addition to achieving an R-value of 3.9/in., Thermal-Pruf also provides fireproofing and acoustical insulation. It can be applied to exterior as well as interior locations and be left textured, rolled to a smooth finish, or overcoated with approved weather-coating systems. American Sprayed Fibers also offers two additional spray-on systems that provide thermal insulation: Dendamix™, made specifically for fireproofing, and Sound-Pruf™ for soundproofing. The manufacturer has certified the following recycled-content levels (by weight): total recovered material 100% guaranteed; post-consumer material 100% guaranteed.

Sealants

see *Caulks & Adhesives: Sealants*

Structural Insulated Panels

see *Structural Systems & Components: Structural Insulated Panels*

Vapor Retarders

With polyethylene-film vapor retarders, look for products with high recycled content.

Construction Film

Gempak
9611 James Ave. S
Bloomington, MN 55431

Toll-free: 800-328-4556
Phone: 952-881-8673

Gempak, formerly Strout Plastics, manufactures construction film that generally contains 100% recycled LDPE. With some production runs, contamination of recycled materials necessitates the addition of virgin resins to produce a quality product.

MemBrain Smart Vapor Retarder

CertainTeed Corporation
750 E. Swedesford Rd.
P.O. Box 860
Valley Forge, PA 19482

Toll-free: 800-233-8990
Phone: 610-341-7739
www.certainteed.com

MemBrain™ Smart Vapor Retarder is made from a transparent polyamide-based (Nylon-6) material, which changes permeability according to relative humidity and can increase the drying potential of closed building envelope systems. The 2-mil-thick, high-tensile-strength sheeting is as strong as a 6-mil sheet of polyethylene. Its moisture permeability varies from less than 1 perm at low relative humidity to more than 20 perms at high (95%) relative humidity. MemBrain is intended for use in heating and mixed climates, and is not suitable for cooling climates with high outdoor humidity or in buildings with high constant indoor relative humidity. Interior finish materials and cavity-fill insulation must also be highly permeable.

Weatherstripping and Gaskets

Quality weatherstripping and gaskets are very important in achieving airtight, low-energy buildings. Specialized gaskets can also be used as a moisture-control strategy, as in the "Airtight Drywall Approach" for light-frame construction.

Weatherstripping and Gaskets

M-D Building Products
4041 N. Santa Fe Ave.
Oklahoma City, OK 73118

Toll-free: 800-654-8454
Phone: 405-528-4411
www.mdteam.com

M-D manufactures a wide range of weatherstripping and weatherization products.

Weatherstripping and Gaskets

Resource Conservation Technology, Inc.
2633 N. Calvert St.
Baltimore, MD 21218

Phone: 410-366-1146
www.conservationtechnology.com

Resource Conservation Technology specializes in building gaskets, weatherstripping, and air barriers. The company provides high quality products and service.

Weatherstripping and Joint Sealants

illbruck Sealant Systems, inc.
14617 Carriage Ln.
Burnsville, MN 55306

Toll-free: 800-438-0684
Phone: 612-521-3555
www.illbruck.com/en

illbruck Sealant Systems, inc. offers weatherstripping products that can be used alone or together as part of a system. The company's i2112™ platform focuses on window and door installation. Products include: illbruck Vapor Permeable Tape, illbruck Window Flashing Tape, Perennator 2112™ Window & Perimeter Silicone, and illbruck Insulation Tape. illbruck's willseal 600 is a precompressed, self-expanding polyurethane foam joint sealant for joint sizes from 1/8" to 1 1/2" (in rolls) and from 1 3/4" and wider (in sticks). illbruck products are manufactured in Europe.

This Space is Available for Your Notes

This Space is Available for Your Notes

Flooring & Floorcoverings

Flooring and floorcoverings are subject to physical abuse from feet and heavy objects; and since they're the lowest spot in a room, they tend to collect dirt, moisture, and other contaminants. A good flooring material should be very durable—to reduce the frequency of replacement—and it should be easy to clean. At the same time, softer surfaces may be preferred for reasons of comfort, noise absorption, and style, setting up a potential conflict in choices. Raw material and manufacturing impacts must also be considered with many types of carpeting and other floorcoverings.

Carpet systems, including carpet pads and adhesives, have been identified by the EPA as a potential source of indoor air pollution. Testing and monitoring are ongoing; the Green Label and more stringent Green Label Plus programs of the Carpet and Rug Institute help prevent the most severe instances of toxic offgassing from new carpet. High-end commercial carpets tend to be more chemically stable than inexpensive residential-quality carpets; some manufacturers are willing to provide detailed air-quality testing data on their products. Carpets may also contribute to air quality problems by trapping pollutants and moisture, and damp carpeting can provide a medium for growth of mold, mildew, and dust mites. Flexible-foam carpet padding frequently contains brominated flame retardants (BFRs); these compounds, chemically similar to PCBs, are raising health concerns because they are being found in human blood and breast milk worldwide, and there is evidence of health effects. BFRs from carpet padding can be released into the living space, especially as the carpet padding ages. In residences, hard flooring surfaces with area rugs, which can be thoroughly cleaned, are often preferable to wall-to-wall carpeting.

Modular carpet tiles can be replaced selectively, reducing the cost and environmental impact of recarpeting an entire room when one area becomes worn or damaged. Some carpet tiles also contain a high percentage of recycled content, and others can be resurfaced and reused. Carpet tiles with random patterns allow easy replacement of individual tiles. Although carpet recycling is technologically difficult due to the contaminants and multiple components of used carpet, some companies now have extensive recycling programs. When installing new carpeting, it may be possible to have the old carpeting hauled away for recycling at a price no higher than the cost of disposal.

A wide variety of high quality carpet is made from recycled soda bottles (PET) and offers the feel and performance of conventional carpet in residential or other low-traffic settings. Natural-fiber carpet with jute backing is a good alternative to synthetic fibers, particularly if the carpeting is made domestically. Imported wool carpet is typically treated with pesticides before it can enter the country.

The underlayment used between a subfloor and floorcovering is often made from Lauan, a tropical hardwood that comes from unsustainable logging operations in Southeast Asia. Other underlayment products are available and should be chosen in consultation with your floorcovering supplier. For example, a recycled-content, formaldehyde-free, gypsum-based underlayment is available and is recommended by major tile manufacturers as a substrate. Under carpet, a recycled-newsprint-and-paraffin product is a good alternative.

Vinyl flooring, whose primary component is polyvinyl chloride (PVC), may be a source of VOC offgassing, both from the flooring itself and from the adhesive. There's also concern about toxic byproducts, such as dioxin, which may be produced if the material is incinerated at the end of its useful life. Natural linoleum, made primarily from cork and linseed oil, is a possible substitute, though it's currently manufactured only in Europe. VOCs are also released from linoleum—but these are from minimally processed linseed oil and are not generally considered as harmful as those from petrochemical sources. Nevertheless, some chemically sensitive people may find them problematic. Adhesives used for linoleum must also be screened carefully for toxic offgassing.

Ceramic and porcelain tile have a high embodied energy, but their durability makes them environmentally sound in the long run. Some high-quality ceramic tile incorporates recycled glass from automobile windshields. Regionally produced stone flooring is a good natural finish when sealed with low-toxic sealers.

Terrazzo is a long-lasting, nontoxic floorcovering option

that uses crushed stone, and sometimes post-consumer recycled glass, in a cementitious matrix. The embodied energy of portland cement is a consideration. Epoxy-based "synthetic terrazzo" may also utilize recycled glass; while the 100%-solids product is considered safe for installers and is benign when cured, bispehonal-A (BPA) is used in the manufacture of epoxy. BPA is a bioaccumulating chemical considered by some experts to be an endocrine disrupter even at minute quantities. Like brominated flame retardants, BPA has been showing up in nature in increasing amounts.

Hardwood flooring from certified well-managed forests may be an excellent environmental choice. Other hard-woods come from forestry operations that may or may not be environmentally responsible. Tropical hardwoods, in particular, should be avoided unless FSC-certified due to the sensitivity of those ecosystems. Certification to Forest Stewardship Council—FSC—standards involves third-party evaluation and monitoring of sustainable forestry practices. Reclaimed and recycled wood flooring milled from the large timbers of old structures, trestle bridges, or "sinker logs" is another option.

Fast-growing bamboo is manufactured into hardwood-type strip flooring by a number of Southeast Asian companies, offering an intriguing alternative to standard hardwood.

Bamboo Flooring

Bamboo has long been an important building material in the Far East, and this durable and dimensionally stable material is finding increasing use as flooring in North America. Over 1,000 species of bamboo—which is a grass, not a tree—exist worldwide. Most bamboo for flooring comes from the Hunan province of China; this species grows to a harvestable size for flooring manufacture, with stems four to six inches in diameter, in three to five years. It's not a food source for pandas, which generally inhabit higher-elevation forests. Despite the long-distance transport of the product to the United States, the durability, hardness, and short regeneration time of bamboo provide justification for using it for flooring instead of wood. Bamboo flooring products are all very similar in fabrication and dimensions; they're glued together in either three horizontal layers of flat grain, or multiple layers of vertical grain, spanning the width of the flooring strip. With either approach, the lamination is typically done with urea-formaldehyde binders, which is the primary negative aspect. In addition to the natural blonde color, this product is often available in dark amber, the result of a pressure-steaming carbonization process. Whether or not socially responsible worker conditions exist in bamboo flooring factories has been impossible to verify.

Bamboo Flooring

California Bamboo Flooring Co.
134 Paul Dr., Ste. 102
San Rafael, CA 94903

Toll-free: 888-548-7548
www.californiabamboo.com

The California Bamboo Flooring Co. product, available in natural and amber colors, is finished with three layers of UV-cured ceramic topcoat. These flat-grain flooring strips measure $5/8$" x $3^5/8$" x 6' and are available in both 1-ply vertical-grained or 3-ply horizontal-grained, all-bamboo configurations.

Bamboo Flooring

International Black Jewel
160 Bullock Dr.
Markham, ON L3P 1W2 Canada

Phone: 905-477-8899
www.amatibambu.com

International Black Jewel, formerly Amati Bambu, flat-grain flooring includes a vertically laminated central ply in the $3/4$" x 4" x 36" strips. It is available in natural color or stained with a water-based stain, with or without a polyurethane coating.

Bamboo Flooring

Jackson Industries LLC
P.O. Box 142588
Gainesville, FL 32614-2588

Phone: 352-372-6600
www.jacksonllc.com

Jackson Bamboo Flooring is available horizontally laminated in standard dimensions of $3/8$" x 3" x $36^1/4$" in natural and carbonized colors (carbonized is available in three shades by special order, as is a vertically laminated version). The flooring is treated with a boric acid insecticide and finished with an aluminum oxide anti-scratch finish in a semi-gloss sheen (matte and gloss are available by special order). Trim molding, T-molding, quarter round, stair nose, threshold, and horizontal and vertical reducers are also available. The manufacturer of Jackson Bamboo Flooring is ISO 9002-certified. Products are currently sold through Lowe's Home Improvement Warehouses in the Southeast USA and come with a 15-year limited warranty.

Bamboo Flooring

MOSO International NA, Ltd.
2220 40th Ave. E
Seattle, WA 98112

Toll-free: 800-617-2324
www.moso.com

MOSO bamboo flooring is available as strip or plank, flat- or vertical-pressed, and pre- or unfinished in natural or caramel hues. Prefinished flooring is coated with five coats of UV-cured polyurethane acrylic—the second coat applied has aluminum oxide added for improved wear resistance. Strip flooring measures 3.62" wide and is available in 3' or 6' lengths. Plank flooring is available in 6' lengths in widths slightly less than 6". An engineered version of the plank flooring is available single-face in 7' lengths and in widths of 7.48". Laminations are bonded with urea-formaldehyde; however, the manufacturer claims that the product exceeds stringent European standards for formaldehyde emissions. All MOSO products are manufactured in P.R. China.

Bamboo Flooring

Wellmade USA, Inc.
P.O. Box 2704
Wilsonville, OR 97070

Phone: 503-784-1050
www.bamboofloorings.com

Wellmade's bamboo flooring panels are available $3/8$", $1/2$", $5/8$", and $3/4$" thick by $3^5/8$" or $3^4/5$" wide, and 36", $37^4/5$", or 72" in length. Planks are T&G on all sides, available in natural or carbonized colors, and come prefinished with three coats of UV-cured acrylic or an aluminum oxide lacquer. Also available are wide and narrow molding, stair nosing, stair tread, and base molding in natural or carbonized colors.

Bamboo Hardwoods Flooring

Bamboo Hardwoods, Inc.
510 S. Industrial Way
Seattle, WA 98108

Toll-free: 800-783-0557
Phone: 206-264-2414
www.bamboohardwoods.com

Bamboo Hardwoods, a U.S. company with a factory in Vietnam, sells both unfinished and prefinished flooring. The unfinished product is vertically laminated, and the prefinished product includes a rubber-tree-wood inner core. These flooring products are manufactured with a melamine adhesive and a boric acid insecticide. The rubberwood used is harvested from over-mature trees on rubber plantations that are out of production. Bamboo Hardwoods also reports that their engineered floor now uses a much harder bamboo (measuring 2048 on the Janka Ball Hardness Test)—the hardest bamboo ever discovered, according to the company.

BamPlank Bamboo Flooring

Bamboo Depot
635 Indiana Rd.
Benicia, CA 94510

Toll-free: 888-273-6888
Phone: 707-751-3898
www.bamboobridge.com

BamPlank™ tongue-and-groove flooring measures $5/8$" x $3^1/8$" x 36" and is available in natural and carbonized finishes and in vertical or horizontal 3-ply laminations. The binder used between the laminations is primarily a casein-based (milk protein) product, with a trace amount of urea-formaldehyde.

Bamtex Bamboo Flooring

Mintec Corporation
100 E. Pennsylvania Ave., Ste. 210
Towson, MD 21286

Toll-free: 888-964-6832
Phone: 410-296-6688
www.bamtex.com

Bamtex Bamboo Flooring is available in natural or carbonated colors in finished or unfinished $3^5/8$" x 36" or 72" strips. Bamtex also offers various sizes of paneling and large boards.

GreenWood Bamboo Flooring

GreenWood Products Company
260 Calle Pintoresco
San Clemente, CA 92673

Phone: 949 369-2733
www.greenwoodflooring.com

GreenWood Products Company offers horizontally and vertically laminated bamboo flooring in natural or carbonized colors with a 7-coat aluminum oxide urethane finish. Both styles are $5/8$" thick

and measure $3^5/8$" x 72". The horizontal style is also offered in a 6"-wide version. Formaldehyde emissions are a very low 0.0127 ppm.

Hanlite Bamboo Flooring

Hanlite Enterprises Corp.
8344 Charlotte Way
Denver, CO 80221

Phone: 303-428-8889
www.hanlitebamboo.com

Hanlite bamboo flooring is available in vertically and horizontally laminated planks measuring 72" x $4^1/8$" x $5/8$". The flooring comes in light and dark natural colors, as well as light and dark carbonized colors. Horizontally and vertically laminated stair treads, stair nosing, stair panels, base board, base shoe, reducers, T-moldings, and vent registers are also available. Hanlite bamboo flooring is produced using DYNO adhesives (made in Sweden) with ultra-low formaldehyde emissions of 0.0127 ppm, and a German-made UV-cured base coat and Miraphen anti-scratch finish coat. Hanlite also offers 4' x 8' bamboo plywood, as well as 8' veneer sheets in 17" and 24" widths.

Jarwin Bamboo Flooring

E.Z. Oriental, Inc.
1455 Monterey Pass, Ste. 105
Monterey Park, CA 91754

Toll-free: 888-395-8887
Phone: 323-526-1188
www.bamboofloor.net

E.Z. Oriental Inc. manufactures bamboo flooring which consists of three layers of bamboo laminated vertically or horizontally. It comes with a scratch-resistant matte finish in natural or carbonized colors.

Plyboo Bamboo Flooring

Smith & Fong Company
375 Oyster Point Blvd. #3
S. San Francisco, CA 94080

Toll-free: 866-835-9859
www.plyboo.com

Plyboo® Bamboo Flooring comes either flat or vertical grained in a natural or amber color. Unfinished or prefinished with polyurethane, all flooring measures $5/8$" x $3^3/4$" x 38" or 75" and comes 18 ft² per box. Plyboo is laminated with a low- or no-VOC adhesive. The company also offers a comprehensive range of trim moldings in stairnosing, threshold, reducer, and baseshoe profiles, and baseboard prefinished in amber or natural color.

Silkroad Bamboo Flooring

K&M Bamboo Products, Inc.
300 Esna Park Dr., Unit 26
Markham, ON L3R 1H3 Canada

Phone: 905-947-1688
www.silkroadflooring.com

K&M Bamboo Products Inc. offers Silkroad™ horizontally or vertically laminated bamboo flooring in natural or carbonized colors, $3^5/_8$" wide x $^5/_8$" or $^1/_2$" thick, and 36" or 72" long. Also offered are a carbonized composite lamination ($3^5/_8$" wide x $^1/_2$" thick x 36" long) and an amber horizontally-laminated plank ($3^5/_8$" wide x $^5/_8$" thick x 36" long). Accessories include bull-nosing, baseboards, reducers, T-moldings, quarter-rounds, and stair treads. Finish options are 100% UV-cured urethane and aluminum oxide. Silkroad bamboo has a total VOC emission of .017 mg/m²/hr and is the first—and currently the only—flooring product to be certified by the Canadian government's Environmental Choice Program (EcoLogo). K&M also offers bamboo plywood and veneer, as well as cork and FSC-certified maple flooring.

Sun Brand Bamboo Flooring

Bamboo Flooring Intl. Corp. (BFI)
20950 Currier Rd.
Walnut, CA 91789

Toll-free: 800-827-9261
Phone: 909-594-4189
www.bamboo-flooring.com

Sun Brand flat-grain bamboo flooring measures $^5/_8$" x $3^5/_8$" x 24" or 36" and is prefinished with a UV-cured acrylic urethane. The plies are laminated using a urea-formaldehyde adhesive.

Teragren Bamboo Flooring, Flooring Accessories & Stair Parts

Teragren LLC
121715 Miller Rd. NE, Ste. 301
Bainbridge Island, WA 98110

Toll-free: 800-929-6333
Phone: 206-842-9477
www.teragren.com

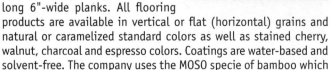

Teragren LLC (formerly TimberGrass LLC) manufactures bamboo flooring in tongue-and-groove, unfinished or prefinished $3^5/_8$"-wide solid strips in multiple lengths, or 6-foot-long 6"-wide planks. All flooring products are available in vertical or flat (horizontal) grains and natural or caramelized standard colors as well as stained cherry, walnut, charcoal and espresso colors. Coatings are water-based and solvent-free. The company uses the MOSO specie of bamboo which

is harvested at maturity at 6 years. Teragren also manufactures coordinating stair parts, flooring accessories and vents, panels & veneer. All products have 0.0155 ppm of formaldehyde.

Tomorrow's Timber Bamboo Flooring

Plyboo America, Inc.
745 Chestnut Ridge Rd.
Kirkville, NY 13082

Toll-free: 800-210-1719
Phone: 315-687-3240
www.plyboo-america.com

Tomorrow's Timber Bamboo Flooring comes in natural or amber color, with a flat or vertical grain, and either unfinished or finished with a UV-cured polyurethane in matte or satin. The product is $^5/_8$" x $3^5/_8$" x 36"; other lengths and widths are available.

Brick and Stone Flooring

Brick and stone, particularly if locally produced or salvaged, can provide an extremely long-lasting, low-maintenance, visually interesting floor with low environmental costs. These materials create an unyielding surface that may be hard on joints and feet, however; and uneven floors may collect dirt and debris in low spots and prove difficult or even dangerous for some to traverse.

Salvaged-Brick Flooring

Gavin Historical Bricks
2050 Glendale Rd.
Iowa City, IA 52245

Phone: 319-354-5251
www.historicalbricks.com

Gavin Historical Bricks supplies salvaged brick and cobblestone recovered from buildings and streets from around the country. The company handcuts their antique brick into $^1/_2$" floor tile for a variety of applications. Shipping is provided nationwide.

Carpet Cushion

Carpet cushions may be made from a variety of recycled, natural, and/or synthetic materials. Natural materials include jute fibers and animal hair; synthetic materials include nylon and polypropylene waste from carpet manufacturing, recycled-tire rubber, and rebond polyurethane (reprocessed from virgin prime flexible polyurethane products). As with carpet itself, care should be taken not to expose the cushion to moisture—including long-term moisture from concrete slabs—to minimize the potential for microbial growth. Flexible-foam carpet padding frequently contains brominated flame retardants (BFRs) which have been identified as a growing health and environmental concern (see discussion under Flooring and Floorcoverings introduction above). Carpet cushion is used primarily in residential applications.

Carpet Padding

Earth Weave Carpet Mills, Inc.
P.O. Box 6120
Dalton, GA 30722

Phone: 706-278-8200
www.earthweave.com

Earth Weave Carpet Mills offers a natural rubber rug gripper padding and a 100% natural wool padding (made from 80% post-industrial waste).

Diamond Bond Cushion

Reliance Carpet Cushion Division
15902 S. Main St.
Gardena, CA 90248

Toll-free: 800-522-5252
Phone: 323-321-2300

Diamond Bond Carpet Cushion products are made from recycled textile waste fibers. Rather than using a chemical bonding agent, as do most other manufacturers, Reliance uses heat as a bonding agent in the Diamond Bond Cushion products. The manufacturer has certified the following recycled-content levels (by weight): total recovered material 100% typical, 100% guaranteed; post-consumer material 0% typical, 0% guaranteed.

EcoSoft Carpet Cushion

DuPont Commercial Flooring
175 TownPark Dr. NW, Ste. 400
Kennesaw, GA 30144

Toll-free: 800-438-7668
Phone: 770-420-7791
www.flooring.dupont.com

EcoSoft carpet cushion is 100% recycled fibers with half the recycled content coming from reclaimed commercial carpet.

Endurance II

Shaw Contract Group
616 E. Walnut Ave.
P.O. Drawer 2128
Dalton, GA 30722

Toll-free: 800-441-7429
Phone: 706-275-1700
www.shawcontract.com

Endurance II™ is made from 100% post-industrial recycled fiber from carpet manufacturing, needle-punched to a synthetic interliner. It is available in 20- to 40-oz. weights.

PL and DublBac Series Carpet Cushion

Leggett & Platt, Inc. - Fairmont Division
2245 W. Pershing Rd.
Chicago, IL 60609

Toll-free: 800-621-6907
Phone: 773-376-1300

PL and DublBac Series carpet cushion is made from bonded 100% recycled polyurethane foam from post-industrial and post-consumer sources.

Rug-Hold 100% Natural

Rug-Hold - Division of
    Leggett and Platt, Inc.
4530 Patten Dr. E
Atlanta, GA 30336

Toll-free: 800-451-4653
Phone: 404-691-9500
www.rughold.com

Rug-Hold® 100% Natural rug underlayment is made of jute fiber coated with natural rubber. All Rug-Hold products use natural rubber.

Synthetic Fiber Carpet Cushion

Reliance Carpet Cushion Division
15902 S. Main St.
Gardena, CA 90248

Toll-free: 800-522-5252
Phone: 323-321-2300

Inter-Loc, Embassy, Marathon, Ambassador, and the Environmental Performance Collection of products, including Natural Wonder, Performa Bond, Berber Tradition, Broadloom Delight, and Berber Select synthetic fiber carpet cushions, are manufactured with 100% post-consumer carpet fiber content.

UnderFleece

Appleseed Wool Corp.
55 Bell St.
Plymouth, OH 44865

Toll-free: 800-881-9665
Phone: 419-687-9665

UnderFleece™ carpet cushion is made from 100% wool felt needled to a woven jute scrim and contains no glues, dyes, mothproofing, or other chemical treatments.

Carpet Tile

Carpet tile is an environmentally preferable alternative to carpeting because damaged or stained carpet tiles can be replaced individually without having to replace carpeting on an entire floor. Though primarily used in commercial buildings, carpet tile is beginning to appear for residential applications as well.

Interface FLOR with Ingeo PLA Fiber

Interface Flooring Systems, Inc.
Orchard Hill Rd.
P.O. Box 1503
LaGrange, GA 30241

Toll-free: 800-336-0225
Phone: 706-882-1891
www.interfaceflooring.com

The Spring Planting line in Interface's FLOR collection of residential carpet tile products is the first floorcovering to use Ingeo® PLA (polylactic acid) fibers. Cargill Dow's Ingeo is a form of polyester derived from corn. The face fiber in this line is made entirely of Ingeo, while the other nine lines in this collection use more conventional fibers. The FLOR collection uses PVC backings.

Ceramic Tile

Tile is an inherently low-toxic, waterproof, durable finish material for flooring, walls, and other applications. While tile is somewhat energy-intensive to manufacture, the materials involved are readily available and mined with fairly low impact. Some products are made from post-consumer or post-industrial wastes.

Debris Series Ceramic Tile

Fireclay Tile
495 W. Julian St.
San Jose, CA 95110

Phone: 408-275-1182
www.fireclaytile.com

Fireclay Tile manufactures the Debris Series of handmade tile using post-industrial and post-consumer recycled material. The Debris Series' terra cotta clay body contains 47.5% recycled broken window panes and clear glass bottles. These tiles are finished with lead-free transparent glazes.

Eco-Cycle and Eco-Cycle Stone

Crossville Porcelain Stone
P.O. Box 1168
Crossville, TN 38557

Phone: 931-484-2110
www.crossville-ceramics.com

Crossville Porcelain Stone offers a line of ceramic tile called GeoStone EcoCycle made from 50–100% unfired raw materials generated during the manufacturing process of standard-color porcelain tiles, including a small percentage of dust from the air and water filtration systems. The tiles measure 12" x 12" with matching 4" x 12" bullnose trim. Available in five colors, GeoStone EcoCycle is recommended for interior floors and walls as well as exterior walls.

Eco-Tile

Quarry Tile Company
6328 E. Utah Ave.
Spokane, WA 99212

Phone: 509-536-2812
www.quarrytile.com

Eco-Tile™ is a commercial-grade, glazed ceramic tile made with approximately 70% recycled solid waste as defined by the EPA's CPG program. This waste content is made up of post-consumer recycled glass (about 25%), post-industrial grinding paste from the computer industry, and post-industrial mining waste from the sand and gravel industry (post-industrial content about 45%). The company also utilizes reprocessed glaze waste from their other manufacturing operations. Glaze from overspray, body scrap, and process waste is recycled in a closed-loop, zero-discharge, water reclamation system. Eco-Tile may contain up to 10% by weight of this material. All the recycled content in Eco-Tile comes from within a 10- to 350-mile radius of the plant and replaces virgin materials from as far away as 2,300 miles. Currently produced in over 50 colors and 5 sizes, Eco-Tile must be special-ordered (minimum 300 ft²).

Certified Wood Flooring

The availability of domestic hardwood from third-party FSC-certified forests makes flooring a great application for certified wood. (Certification to Forest Stewardship Council—FSC—standards involves third-party evaluation and monitoring of sustainable forestry practices.)

Certified Cherry Flooring

Green River Lumber
29 Locust Hill Rd.
P.O. Box 329
Great Barrington, MA 01230

Phone: 413-528-9000
www.greenriverlumber.com

Green River Certified Cherry Flooring is a solid hardwood flooring milled from well-managed, FSC-certified forests in Pennsylvania. The cherry hardwood flooring is $^{25}/_{32}$" thick and comes in $2^1/_4$", 3", 4", and 5" widths (actual face width).

Certified Hardwood Flooring

Maine Woods Company, LLC
Fish Lake Rd.
P.O. Box 111
Portage, ME 04768

Phone: 207-435-4393
www.mainewoods.net

Maine Woods Company, LLC, owned in part by Seven Islands Land Company, operates a state-of-the-art sawmill in northern Maine producing primarily hard maple and yellow birch lumber and flooring. Smaller quantities of American beech, red maple, and white ash are also produced. A portion of the mill output is FSC-certified.

Certified Parquet Flooring

Parquet By Dian
16601 S. Main St.
Gardena, CA 90248

Phone: 310-527-3779
www.parquet.com

Parquet By Dian (PBD) received its chain-of-custody SmartWood Certification in September 2001. This square-edged flooring results in a much longer life than traditional tongue-and-groove (T&G) flooring, which can be sanded down only as far as the tongue. In addition, the manufacturer claims they can produce 2 ft² of parquet from 1 board foot of lumber, whereas manufacturers of T&G can only produce 1 ft² of $^3/_4$" strip flooring. The $^7/_{16}$"-thick pieces of FSC-certified wood are preassembled into "tile" sections held together by adhesive sheets of plastic and then installed with polyurethane adhesive. Sealing the perimeter and apply-

ing a surface finish results in an installation that is essentially waterproof, according to the manufacturer. PBD flooring can be installed immediately (no acclimation time is required), and the product is available in a large variety of patterns and a number of wood species.

Certified Wood Flooring

A. E. Sampson & Son, Inc.
171 Camden Rd.
Warren, ME 04864

Toll-free: 800-769-6196
Phone: 207-273-4000
www.aesampsonandson.com

A. E. Sampson & Son offers FSC-certified wood flooring in birch or maple, in several grades.

Certified Wood Flooring

Cascadia Forest Goods, LLC
38083 Wheeler Rd.
Dexter, OR 97431

Phone: 541-485-4477
www.cascadiaforestgoods.com

Cascadia Forest Goods (CFG) is a supplier of FSC-certified and recycled forest products, including flooring. Some of the available species include madrone, white oak, clear vertical grain (CVG) Douglas fir, birch, big-leaf maple, and myrtlewood. Exotic species of Central and South America are also available, including Santa Maria, catalox, chechen negro, jobillo, machiche, ramon blanco, sauche, and others. CFG supplies both solid and engineered wood flooring.

Certified Wood Flooring

Dwight Lewis Lumber / Lewis Lumber Products
30 S. Main St.
P.O. Box 356
Picture Rocks, PA 17762

Toll-free: 800-233-8450
Phone: 570-584-4460
lewislp.com

Dwight Lewis Lumber sells FSC-certified moldings, flooring, paneling, and hardwoods, subject to availability. Certified species are cherry, hard and soft maple, and red oak.

Certified Wood Flooring

Endura Wood Products, Ltd.
1303 S.E. 6th Ave.
Portland, OR 97214

Phone: 503-233-7090
www.endurawood.com

Endura offers FSC-certified flooring ranging from exotic hardwoods such as jatoba to Oregon white oak. Contact the company for a list of currently available species. The company also offers reclaimed wood flooring.

Certified Wood Flooring

Kane Hardwood, A Collins Company
P.O. Box 807
Kane, PA 16735

Phone: 814-837-6941
www.CollinsWood.com

One side of Kane Hardwood's tongue-and-groove VersaWood™ can be used for paneling, the other for flooring. VersaWood is available FSC-certified in red oak, cherry, and red maple. It comes in $2^3/_4$" and $5^3/_4$" widths and in prime, rustic, and natural grades.

Certified Wood Flooring

McDowell Lumber Company, Inc.
Rte. 46 S
P.O. Box 148
Crosby, PA 16724

Phone: 814-887-2717
www.mcdowelllumber.com

McDowell Lumber deals in FSC-certified lumber, flooring, wainscoting, and veneer in over 15 species including red oak, cherry, hard and soft maple, ash, and a variety of other hardwoods harvested in Pennsylvania.

Certified Wood Flooring

Plaza Hardwood, Inc.
219 W. Manhattan Ave.
Santa Fe, NM 87501

Toll-free: 800-662-6306
Phone: 505-992-3260
www.plzfloor.com

Plaza Hardwood offers FSC-certified maple, birch, cherry, ash, red oak, and white oak flooring.

Certified Wood Flooring

Randall Custom Lumber, Ltd.
3530 S.E. Arcadia Rd.
Shelton, WA 98584

Phone: 360-426-8518
www.rclumber.com

Randall Custom Lumber manufactures FSC-certified decking, flooring, hard and softwood lumber, and stair parts. Some of their certified species are ash, red cedar, red alder, Douglas fir, madrone, and maple.

Certified Wood Flooring

Tembec, Inc., Huntsville Division
80 Old North Rd.
P.O. Box 5616
Huntsville, ON P1H 2J4 Canada

Toll-free: 800-461-5386
Phone: 705-789-2371
www.muskokaflooring.com

Tembec's Muskoka wood flooring is produced (on a special-order basis) from FSC-certified maple harvested from lands that the company manages.

Certified Wood Flooring

Whitethorn Construction
545 Shelter Cove Rd.
P.O. Box 400
Whitethorn, CA 95589

Phone: 707-986-7412
www.whitethornconstruction.com

Whitethorn specializes in FSC-certified tan oak flooring, available in varied earth-tones in widths ranging from $2^1/_4$" to $4^1/_4$".

Certified Wood Flooring

Windfall Lumber and Milling
210 Thurston St.
Olympia, WA 98501

Phone: 360-352-2250
www.windfalllumber.com

Windfall is a distributor of FSC-certified hardwoods, flooring, and structural lumber. Windfall also manufactures specialty wood products such as flooring and moldings.

WFI SingleStrip - The American Quartered Collection

Wood Flooring International (WFI)
1810 Underwood Blvd.
Delran, NJ 08075

Phone: 856-764-2501
www.wflooring.com

The American Quartered collection of WFI's SingleStrip flooring is a long-length engineered wood floor with the look of solid wood plank flooring. At least 75% of the wood used to manufacture the line is FSC-certified. The core/back components (which comprise 75% of the flooring by volume) are 100% FSC-certified. The $1/8$" solid wood wear layer (which makes up 25% of the total volume and is recycled from veneer manufacturing) can be resanded up to three times. This $9/16$"-thick, 3"- or 5"-wide square-edge flooring comes in random lengths between 1' and 7' long in 6" increments. The collection is finished with a 9-coat, UV-cured acrylic urethane with aluminum oxide base coats and anti-scratch top coats in satin gloss. Available species are red and white oak, as well as North American cherry, maple, and walnut.

Concrete Pigments

Coloring pigments in concrete add architectural interest using very little additional material—thus turning concrete into a finished floor. In this way, the need for additional products can sometimes be avoided, eliminating the environmental impacts associated with those materials.

Davis Colors

Davis Colors
3700 E. Olympic Blvd.
Los Angeles, CA 90023

Toll-free: 800-356-4848
Phone: 323-269-7311
www.daviscolors.com

Davis Colors produces color additives for portland cement-based concrete paving and finished floor surfaces, concrete products, and structures. Made from recycled or reclaimed steel and iron, Davis Colors are added to the concrete mix with the company's Chameleon™ computer-operated automatic dosing system or with Mix-Ready® bags that dissolve when tossed directly into an operating ready-mix truck. With integral color, the high embodied energy of concrete is offset by the dual structural and finish floor role of the colored concrete.

EnvironOxide Pigments

Hoover Color Corporation
2170 Julia Simpkins Rd.
P.O. Box 218
Hiwassee, VA 24347

Phone: 540-980-7233
www.hoovercolor.com

Hoover Color Corp., in partnership with Iron Oxide Recovery, Inc. (IOR), produces a range of earth-tone pigments made with Environ-Oxide™, a natural iron oxide product recovered from abandoned coal mine drainage. Settling ponds and constructed wetlands are used in a patented process to contain the mine runoff. The process yields a premium quality pigment that is nontoxic, nonbleeding, and weather-resistant while cleaning water that would otherwise pollute the receiving stream. The product can be used as a colorant in a wide range of building products, including concrete, cement block, paint, wood stain, and brick. For general information, contact IOR at 412-571-2204; for sales, contact Hoover Color at 540-980-7233. Iron oxide pigments made from EnvironOxide must be specifically requested.

Cork Flooring

Cork is a natural flooring material that's been used for more than a century. Obtained from the outer bark of the cork oak (Quercus suber), it can be harvested sustainably without killing the tree. The cork regenerates in about 10 years. Grown in Portugal, Algeria, Spain, Morocco, France, Italy, and Tunisia, all cork flooring products available in the U.S. are imported. There's almost no material waste from the manufacturing process, but agglomerating the cork requires binders to hold the ground granules together. Urea-formaldehyde binders should be avoided in favor of urea-melamine, phenol-formaldehyde, polyurethane, or all-natural protein binders. Cork flooring is typically available in a variety of shades in tile form, and in some cases is sandwiched with other flooring materials. It's durable, sound-absorbing, and naturally moisture-, rot-, and mold-resistant. Cork is typically finished with a polyurethane or wax coating, which is periodically reapplied. While cork is naturally fire-resistant, wax finishes reduce this quality. Cork-PVC laminate tiles or cork tiles with a PVC wear layer are not considered green.

Cork Floating Floor and Parquet Tile

Natural Cork, Inc.
1710 North Leg Ct.
Augusta, GA 30909

Toll-free: 800-404-2675
Phone: 706-733-6120
www.naturalcork.com

Natural Cork Floating Floor™ is a tongue-and-groove cork plank product measuring $1/2$" x $11^{13}/_{16}$" x $35^{11}/_{16}$" and is available prefinished with an acrylic coating. The Floating Floor is constructed with a cork surface layer, exterior grade fiberboard core featuring CLIC installation, and cork underlayment. Parquet Tile measures $3/_{16}$" x 12" x 12" and is prefinished with an acrylic coating. Parquet Tile can also be purchased unfinished in $3/_{16}$" x 12" x 24".

Dodge Cork Tile

Dodge-Regupol, Inc.
P.O. Box 989
Lancaster, PA 17608

Toll-free: 866-883-7780
Phone: 717-295-3400
www.regupol.com

Dodge™ Cork Tile is available in three different shades. The 12" x 12" tiles are $3/_{16}$" or $5/_{16}$" thick and finished with wax, matte polyurethane, polyurethane satin ($3/_{16}$" only), or glossy polyurethane.

Expanko Cork Tiles

Expanko Cork Co.
3135 Lower Valley
Parksburg, PA 19365

Toll-free: 800-345-6202
Phone: 610-436-8300
www.expanko.com

Expanko cork tiles are 12" or 24" square and come in $3/_{16}$" and $5/_{16}$" thicknesses. They are available in 12 different face patterns either unfinished or finished with a polyurethane or wax coating.

Globus Cork Flooring

Globus Cork
741 E. 136th St.
Bronx, NY 10454

Phone: 718-742-7264
www.corkfloor.com

Globus Cork Flooring is available in a wide range of sizes and shapes (including triangles, hexagons, and baseboard tiles) and comes in more than 40 colors. All pigments, finishes, and adhesives are water-based and solvent-free. The cork granules are agglomerated with a polyurethane binder. The tiles come with a latex-based adhesive on their underside and are installed using a second adhesive on the subfloor. Finished with three coats of water-based varnish, the company suggests that a commercial-grade finish coat be applied in the field by the installer.

Nova Cork

Nova Distinctive Floors
1710 E. Sepulveda Blvd.
Carson, CA 90745

Toll-free: 866-576-2458
www.novafloorings.com

Nova Cork™ Floating Floor cork flooring, available in 28 designer patterns, is FSC and SCS certified. The $7/_{16}$" x 12" x 36" planks snap together with a glueless "Klick" system. They consist of 3 layers—a high-density cork wear layer with a water-based polyurethane finish; a high-density tongue-and-groove fiberboard layer made with recycled fibers; and a low-density cork base layer. This product has a 20-year residential warranty; 10-year commercial. Nova Distinctive Floors is the exclusive North American distributor/importer of Nova Cork, which is manufactured in Switzerland.

ProntoKorQ

KorQinc
155 E. 56th St.
New York, NY 10022

Phone: 212-758-2593
www.korqinc.com

ProntoKorQ is a tongue-and-groove floating cork flooring product that comes in $3/8$" x 12" x 36" planks. Cork floor tiles measure $3/_{16}$" x 12" x 12". Both products are available in several patterns and unfinished or prefinished with a water-based varnish. KorQ also offers baseboard and molding products made from agglomerated cork.

WE Cork Flooring

WE Cork
16 Kingston Rd., Unit 6
Exeter, NH 03833

Toll-free: 800-666-2675
Phone: 603-778-8558
www.wecork.com

WE Cork Classic Collection cork flooring comes in tiles and planks measuring 12" x 12" x $^3/_{16}$" and 4" x 36" x $^3/_{16}$", respectively. The flooring is available in light, medium, dark, or leopard shades and either unfinished, waxed, or in varnished matte. The company also manufactures a line of floating floors, which do not require gluing, and two lines of sound-control underlayment for flooring, WECU Soundless™ and WECU Soundless +™.

Wicanders Natural Cork

Amorim Flooring North America, Inc.
7513 Connelley Dr., Ste. M - Front
Hanover, MD 21076

Toll-free: 800-828-2675
Phone: 410-553-6062
www.wicanders.com

Wicanders Series 100 is a PVC-free floating natural cork flooring system. The tiles are made with a phenolic resin binder and measure 900 x 295 x 10.5 mm; they are available in 5 collections with a total of 108 designs. Series 200 is a glue-down version, available in 600 x 300 mm and 600 x 600 mm tiles, 6 mm thick, in more than 100 designs.

Fiberboard and Particleboard Panels

see *Interior Finish & Trim: Fiberboard and Particleboard Panels*

Flooring Adhesives

Flooring adhesives can be a major source of indoor air quality problems, often more so than the flooring products they adhere. Water-based adhesives have lower VOC emissions than solvent-based products. While some products are sold as multipurpose, others are specific to a particular application or product (linoleum, for example, requires special adhesives due to its linseed oil content). If a flooring manufacturer recommends a specific low- or zero-VOC, water-based product for use with its material, then use it; otherwise consider a product known to minimize indoor air pollution and check with the flooring product manufacturer to find out whether that product can be used with their flooring material. Some California districts restrict the manufac-

ture, sale, and installation of flooring adhesives that exceed a VOC content of 150 grams per liter. Most of the products listed here are zero-VOC.

#965 Flooring and Tread Adhesive

Johnsonite
16910 Munn Rd.
Chagrin Falls, OH 44023

Toll-free: 800-899-8916
Phone: 440-543-8916
www.johnsonite.com

Johnsonite's #965 is a high-strength, solvent-free, water-based, acrylic latex adhesive. It was formulated for rubber sheet flooring as well as rubber and vinyl stair treads and nosings on porous and nonporous surfaces.

380 Natural All-Purpose Floor Adhesive

Sinan Co.
P.O. Box 857
Davis, CA 95617

Phone: 530-753-3104
www.dcn.davis.ca.us/go/sinan

Sinan 380 Natural All-Purpose Floor Adhesive is a water-based product made with organic binders for use with cork, wood, linoleum, and carpeting. Sinan products are made from all-natural, primarily plant-based materials, all of which are listed on the packaging.

BioShield Cork Adhesive #16

Eco Design/BioShield Paint Company
1330 Rufina Cir.
Santa Fe, NM 87507

Toll-free: 800-621-2591
Phone: 505-438-3448
www.bioshieldpaint.com

BioShield Cork Adhesive #16 is a water-based, solvent-free adhesive specially designed for cork flooring.

Envirotec Floor Covering Adhesives

W. F. Taylor Company
11545 Pacific Ave.
Fontana, CA 92337

Toll-free: 800-397-4583
Phone: 909-360-6677
www.wftaylor.com

Envirotec is W. F. Taylor Company's line of nontoxic, solvent-free, low-VOC adhesive products. These products include multipurpose flooring adhesives, carpet adhesives, and cove base adhesives.

Henry GreenLine Flooring Adhesives

The W. W. Henry Company
400 Ardex Park Dr.
Aliquippa, PA 15001

Toll-free: 800-232-4832
Phone: 724-203-5000
www.wwhenry.com

Henry® GreenLine™ Flooring Adhesives are latex-based, hypoallergenic, zero-VOC flooring adhesives with almost no discernible odor. Four versions include GL33 for vinyl composition tile (VCT), GL62 for most commercial carpets in heavy traffic areas (for all backings except vinyl), GL83 for residential and commercial linoleum sheet flooring, and GL23 for commercial carpets and residential and commercial felt-back sheet flooring. While still wet, clean-up is with soap and water; dried adhesive is cleaned with mineral spirits. Greenline comes with Henry's Best 10-year warranty.

Safe-Set Adhesives

Chicago Adhesive Products Co.
1165 Arbor Dr.
Romeoville, IL 60446

Toll-free: 800-621-0220
www.chapco-adhesive.com

Safe-Set products are solvent-free, zero-VOC, nonflammable, non-toxic floor covering adhesives and carpet seaming tapes.

Flooring Underlayment

Underlayment products for flooring serve several functions and can be made from a variety of materials. Environmentally preferable materials for flooring underlayment include natural cork, strawboard, and recycled-paper-based fiberboard. Using underlayment products beneath wood, tile, resilient flooring, or carpet and carpet cushion provides a level surface and helps insulate floors from sound transmission and, to a limited extent, heat loss. Cork rolls and sheets provide particularly high added resilience to the floor system, with significantly less thickness than fiberboard products or a gypsum-cement poured-in-place slab. Use of a sound-deadening underlayment below a hard-surface floor can reduce the need to further control sound transmission with carpeting or rugs.

Acousti-Cork

Amorim Industrial Solutions
26112 110th St.
P.O. Box 25
Trevor, WI 53179

Toll-free: 800-255-2675
Phone: 262-862-2311
www.amorimsolutions.com

Acousti-Cork sheets and rolls are made with a polyurethane-based binder. They may be used under a variety of flooring types, although an additional board underlayment is advised for use with vinyl sheet and vinyl composition tile.

Photo: Larry Lyons

Cork Underlayment

Natural Cork, Inc.
1710 North Leg Ct.
Augusta, GA 30909

Toll-free: 800-404-2675
Phone: 706-733-6120
www.naturalcork.com

Natural Cork sound control underlayment comes in $5/64$", $1/8$", or $1/4$" thicknesses in 4' x 50' rolls or $1/4$" and $1/2$" thicknesses in 2' x 3' sheets.

Fiberock Aqua-Tough Underlayment

USG Corporation
125 S. Franklin St.
Chicago, IL 60606

Toll-free: 800-874-4968
Phone: 312-606-4000
www.usg.com

Fiberock® Underlayment with Aqua-Tough™ technology is a gypsum and cellulose blend flooring underlayment suitable for a wide range of floor coverings. USG manufactures this product in an Ohio plant using a chemical process to recover synthetic gypsum from the flue-gas desulfurization (FGD) of coal-fired power plants. Because Fiberock Aqua-Tough is engineered with a uniform, highly indentation-resistant surface and no adhesives, solvents, or resins, its use avoids some of the problems often associated with wood-based underlayments. Though not for areas with prolonged exposure to standing water, the Aqua-Tough technology provides water resistance throughout the product. Fiberock Aqua-Tough Underlayment has been certified by Scientific Certification Systems (SCS) to contain 95% recycled material, 85% of which is post-industrial recycled gypsum and 10% recycled paper fiber.

Homasote 440 SoundBarrier and ComfortBase

Homasote Company
932 Lower Ferry Rd.
P.O. Box 7240
West Trenton, NJ 08628

Toll-free: 800-257-9491
Phone: 609-883-3300
www.homasote.com

Homasote 440 Sound Barrier® panels are high-density fiberboard made from 100% recycled wastepaper and a formaldehyde-free paraffin binder. They are designed to provide sound control as a flooring underlayment and in wall assemblies, and are part of a UL-listed 1-hr floor assembly and wall assembly (UL Design Number V448). 440 SoundBarrier is available in $^3/_8$", $^1/_2$", $^5/_8$", and $^3/_4$" thicknesses and a variety of sizes from 4' x 4' up to 4' x 10'. Comfort Base™ is similar to SoundBarrier but is specifically designed for use as a "floating" underlayment over a concrete slab. A grooved grid pattern on the bottom side provides ventilation to remove trapped moisture from the slab. This product helps insulate basement and slab-on-grade floors with an R-value of 1.2. Homasote recycles more than 250 tons of newsprint per day and has been manufacturing building panels from waste papers since 1909.

Nova Underlayment

Nova Distinctive Floors
1710 E. Sepulveda Blvd.
Carson, CA 90745

Toll-free: 866-576-2458
www.novafloorings.com

Nova Cork rolled cork underlayment can be used under a wide variety of floorcoverings, and has a 20-year residential warranty; 10-year commercial. It's available as 6 mm-thick 4' x 50" rolls (200 ft^2 per roll), 6 mm-thick 2' x 3' sheets (300 ft^2 per carton), and 12 mm-thick 2' x 3' sheets (150 ft^2 per carton). NovaCork is manufactured in Switzerland.

WoodStalk Underlayment

Dow BioProducts
11 WoodStalk Way
P.O. Box 328
Elie, MB R0H 0H0 Canada

Toll-free: 800-441-4DOW
www.dow-bioproducts.com

Dow BioProducts, a wholly-owned subsidiary of Dow Chemical Canada, produces WoodStalk Underlayment (formerly produced by Isobord under the name IsoUnderlay) from straw fiber and formaldehyde-free resins. It can be used in place of lauan plywood as a leveling system under carpet, laminate flooring, vinyl sheet flooring, and hardwood flooring.

Linoleum Flooring

Natural linoleum is a durable, low-maintenance flooring made from linseed oil, pine rosin, sawdust, cork dust, limestone, natural pigments, and a jute backing. Linoleum does not contain significant petroleum-based products or chlorinated chemicals, as does vinyl (PVC) flooring—which is often mistakenly referred to as "linoleum." From a raw materials standpoint, linoleum is an outstanding product: all of its ingredients are minimally processed and commonly available. Linoleum does raise some red flags when it comes to indoor air quality—the ongoing oxidation of linoleic acid in the flooring leads to offgassing of volatile organic compounds (VOCs). Some argue that linoleum's VOCs, as compared to petroleum-derived VOCs, are a lesser health threat. As with all offgassing products, the VOC emissions taper off over time. Adhesives for linoleum installation differ from vinyl flooring adhesives; and a smooth, dry surface is essential for proper installation. Linoleum can also be used for desktop and conference table surfaces. The material provides a pleasantly resilient writing surface.

DLW Linoleum

Armstrong World Industries, Inc.
2500 Columbia Ave.
Lancaster, PA 17604

Toll-free: 877-276-7876
Phone: 717-397-0611
www.armstrong.com

DLW linoleum is made in Germany and comes in a wide variety of colors and styles in both sheet and tile. Tile is available by special order only. Marmorette is available in 2, 2.5 and 3.2 mm thicknesses. Colorette and Uni Walton are available in 2.5 and 3.2 mm thicknesses, and Linorette is 2.5 mm thick. Linodur is a heavy-duty 4 mm product. In 1998, Armstrong World Industries, the largest manufacturer of vinyl flooring (and out of the linoleum industry since the 1970s) purchased DLW, reentering this product field.

Linosom Linoleum

Tarkett Commercial
4103 Parkway Dr.
P.O. Box 354
Florence, AL 35631

Toll-free: 800-366-2689
Phone: 256-766-0234
www.domco.com

Linosom™ linoleum is available in five lines: Veneto, Toscano, Etrusco, Trentino, and Narnidur. Elafono is an underlayment. Linosom comes in a wide variety of colors, including unique earth-toned patterns. It is available only in sheet form in 2, 2.5, 3.2, and 4 mm thicknesses.

Manufactured in Italy, Linosom is available in the U.S. through Tarkett Commercial, formerly Azrock, a division of Domco Tarkett, Inc. Also available from Tarkett Commercial is Linosport, a 4 mm linoleum flooring for indoor recreational facilities.

Marmoleum and Artoleum

Forbo Linoleum, Inc.
P.O. Box 667
Hazleton, PA 18201

Toll-free: 800-842-7839
Phone: 570-459-0771
www.forbolinoleumNA.com

Forbo, the largest producer of linoleum in the world, operates a sophisticated production facility that helps it meet criteria for the Netherlands Environmental Quality Mark and the Nordic Swan Label. The product also received the Sequoia Award from the U.S. Association of Woodworking and Furnishing Suppliers (AWFS) in recognition of the company's commitment to environmental innovation. A large range of colors and styles is available, including custom-designed borders. Marmoleum® and Artoleum® are available in sheet form. Marmoleum Dual is also available as a 20" x 20" or 13" x 13" tile mounted on a polyester backing to improve dimensional stability.

Nova Linoleum

Nova Distinctive Floors
1710 E. Sepulveda Blvd.
Carson, CA 90745

Toll-free: 866-576-2458
www.novafloorings.com

Nova Linoleum™ planks, available in 11 colors, measure $^{7}/_{16}$" x 12" x 36". They consist of 3 layers: a $^{5}/_{64}$" linoleum wear layer; a high-density fiberboard core; and a $^{5}/_{64}$" cork composition layer. This floating floor system snaps together with a glueless "Klick" system. Nova Linoleum is manufactured in Switzerland and includes a 20-year residential warranty; 10-year commercial.

Prontolino

KorQinc
155 E. 56th St.
New York, NY 10022

Phone: 212-758-2593
www.korqinc.com

Prontolino is a linoleum-cork hybrid flooring product. It comes in $^{3}/_{8}$" x 12" x 36" tongue-and-groove planks of natural linoleum laminated onto a thick cork backing. The linoleum surface is available in 9 colors.

Natural-Fiber Floor Mats

These mats are made from durable natural fibers in a variety of styles and weaves. Common natural fibers for matting include sisal (often used in wall coverings), jute (used to make rope and burlap bags), and coir (from coconut husks). Natural-fiber mats generally don't have backings or chemical treatments. They're durable but may shed broken fibers, requiring periodic sweeping or vacuuming of the surrounding floor area.

Plain Herringbone-Weave Cocoa Matting

Allied Mat & Matting, Inc.
52-08 Grand Ave.
Maspeth, NY 11378

Toll-free: 800-452-5588
Phone: 718-381-9824
www.alliedmat.com

Plain Herringbone-Weave Cocoa Matting is made from coir fiber and is approximately $^{3}/_{8}$" thick. It is available in rolls that are 36", 45", 54", or 72" wide.

Paver Tile

Tile is an inherently low-toxic, durable finish material for flooring, walls, and other applications. While tile is fairly energy-intensive to manufacture, the materials involved are readily available and mined with relatively low impact. Some products are made from post-consumer or post-industrial wastes.

Debris Series Paver Tile

Fireclay Tile
495 W. Julian St.
San Jose, CA 95110

Phone: 408-275-1182
www.fireclaytile.com

Fireclay Tile manufactures the Debris Series of handmade tile using post-industrial and post-consumer recycled material. The Debris Series' terra cotta body is made from 25% recycled granite dust, 19% broken window panes, and 8.5% recycled brown and green glass bottles. The tiles can be unglazed or glazed. The glazes do not contain lead.

Plastic Flooring

The plastic flooring products listed here use up to 100% post-consumer and/or post-industrial recycled plastic to create inexpensive, often interlocking, floor tiles that are particularly appropriate in wet areas. Though not always durable enough for heavy traffic areas, plastic flooring is suitable for outdoor showers and certain other utilitarian spaces where easy maintenance and some resilience are required. Textures and open-weave construction also lend slip-resistance to some products.

Turtle Tiles

Turtle Plastics
7400 Industrial Pkwy.
Lorain, OH 44053

Phone: 440-282-8008
www.turtleplastics.com

Turtle Tiles are open-weave floor tiles made from recycled PVC plastic. The interlocking tiles are $^3/_4$" thick" x 12" x 12" and come in 20 solid colors. The manufacturer has certified the following recycled-content levels (by weight): total recovered material 100% guaranteed; post-consumer material 50% guaranteed.

Reclaimed Wood Flooring

Reclaimed Wood Flooring is made from timbers salvaged from old buildings, bridges, or other timber structures. It may also be manufactured from logs salvaged from river bottoms, or from trees being removed in urban and suburban areas. White pine, longleaf yellow pine, cypress, oak, walnut, and chestnut may be available from Eastern and Midwestern suppliers. Western suppliers commonly stock Douglas fir. Plan your needs with plenty of lead time, as availability and pricing fluctuate widely.

Durapalm Palm Flooring

Smith & Fong Company
375 Oyster Point Blvd. #3
S. San Francisco, CA 94080

Toll-free: 866-835-9859
www.plyboo.com

Photo: John Wells

Smith & Fong's Durapalm® flooring is made from plantation-grown coconut palm trees that no longer produce coconuts. The $^3/_4$" x 3" x 3' to 6' tongue-and-groove planks range from dark to medium-red mahogany in color, contain no formaldehyde or VOCs, and are available unfinished or prefinished with an 8-coat ceramic/urethane UV-cured finish. Smith & Fong reports that they use only the darker, harder palm for a durable surface (1600 PSI Janka Ball Test, ASTM D1037). Reducer, baseshoe, and stairnosing and threshold molding are available.

Flooring from Urban Trees

CitiLog™
6 Bywood Ln.
Ewing, NJ 08628

Phone: 609-538-8680
www.citilogs.com

CitiLog, also known as D. Stubby Warmbold, is SmartWood-certified for the harvesting of trees in urban areas of New Jersey and Pennsylvania. Wood is sent by rail to Amish craftsmen in central Pennsylvania who take extra care to turn the lesser graded wood into higher quality products such as flooring, lumber, custom architectural millwork, furniture, and kitchen cabinets. Where appropriate, wood is now harvested using horses.

Flooring from Urban Trees

Urban Hardwoods
5021 Colorado Ave. S
Seattle, WA 98134

Phone: 206-766-8199
www.urbanhardwoods.com

Urban Hardwoods salvages urban trees from within a 50-mile radius of the company and mills them into furniture, flooring, and other millwork. Urban Hardwoods continually designs products to make use of manufacturing "fall-down." The remainder of the waste material is given away or sold as firewood, or is used for heating their facility. The company utilizes plant-based solvents, when needed, to clean tools and machinery, and ships 99% of their products blanket-wrapped (all blankets are reused). They will also accept products back at the end of their useful life and refurbish them or reuse the material to manufacture new products. The company is seeking certification from SmartWood under the "Rediscovered Wood" category.

MultiLayer and Solid-Plank Antique Wood Flooring

Natural Wood Flooring, Inc.
174 Emily Dr., Ste. B
Winterville, NC 28590

Toll-free: 800-726 7463
Phone: 252-353-1077

Natural Wood Flooring, Inc., formerly The Joinery Co., sells antique heart pine flooring in engineered MultiLayer® and in solid plank. Environmentally friendly adhesives and finishes are used throughout.

Reclaimed Flooring

Vintage Timberworks
47100 Rainbow Canyon Rd.
Temecula, CA 92592

Phone: 909-695-1003
www.vintagetimber.com

Vintage Timberworks offers a wide range of reclaimed wood products salvaged in the U.S., Canada, and Australia from buildings that are typically over 70 years old. Reclaimed flooring is available remilled or "as is," requiring denailing and T&G clean-up. Douglas fir and oak flooring can be milled in a wide variety of widths and lengths. Most other species are limited in width and length to available stock.

Reclaimed Heart Pine Flooring

Albany Woodworks, Inc.
P.O. Box 729
Albany, LA 70711-0729

Toll-free: 1-800-551-1282
Phone: 225-567-1155
www.albanywoodworks.com

Albany Woodworks' reclaimed antique heart pine is available in tongue-and-groove, center-matched random lengths.

Reclaimed Heart Pine Flooring

Heart Pine Lumber and Millworks
3645 Five Chop Rd.
P.O. Box 1844
Orangeburg, SC 29116

Phone: 803-534-8478

Heart Pine Lumber and Millworks, formerly Wood Floors, Inc., offers reclaimed heart pine lumber remilled into three grades of tongue-and-groove flooring. The top grade is 90–100% red heart pine, the second grade contains 50% heart pine and is yellowish in color, and the third grade is a light yellow streaked with green-blue and red. All flooring is available in either uniform or random widths.

Reclaimed Heart Pine Flooring

J. L. Powell & Co., Inc.
723 Pine Log Rd.
Whiteville, NC 28472

Toll-free: 800-227-2007
Phone: 910-642-8989
www.plankfloors.com

J. L. Powell offers reclaimed and remilled antique heart pine flooring.

Reclaimed Heart Pine Flooring

Mayse Woodworking Co.
319 Richardson Rd.
Lansdale, PA 19446

Toll-free: 888-566-4532
Phone: 215-822-8307

Mayse produces Classic American Heart Pine™ in three flooring styles: American Country Heart Pine™, Signature Heart Pine™, and Federal Heart Pine™. The flooring is remanufactured from recycled heart pine beams into $^{7}/_{8}$" tongue-and-groove flooring in widths ranging from 2" to 12", in knotty, clear, and vertical-grain.

Reclaimed Tropical Hardwood Flooring

TerraMai
1104 Firenze
P.O. Box 696
McCloud, CA 96057

Toll-free: 800-220-9062
Phone: 530-964-2740
www.terramai.com

TerraMai (formerly AsiaRain Jungle Hardwoods) produces flooring from reclaimed tropical hardwoods such as old railroad ties. Flooring is available in either the "Jungle Mix" or "Species" collections. "Jungle Mix" colors vary from tans and golds to pinks, reds, and dark earth tones. By varying percentages of different species in this mix, three distinct hues can be obtained (gold, rose, or dark earth tones). "Species" is sorted by color to create the illusion of a single-species floor. All flooring is available in "Character" (with evidence of previous use) and "Select" (clear) grades.

Reclaimed Wood Flooring

Aged Woods / Yesteryear Floorworks Company
2331 E. Market St.
York, PA 17402

Toll-free: 800-233-9307
Phone: 717-840-0330
www.agedwoods.com

Aged Woods® / Yesteryear Floorworks Company™ offers reclaimed wood flooring lines in oak, cherry, chestnut, white pine, longleaf heart pine, yellow pine, walnut, hemlock, hickory, poplar, and maple. Most of the flooring is ³/₄" tongue-and-groove and of random widths and lengths within given ranges. Matching stair parts are available in conjunction with flooring orders.

Reclaimed Wood Flooring

Antique Speciality Flooring
100 W. Main St.
Plantsville, CT 06479

Toll-free: 888-SAVE WOOD
Phone: 860-621-6787

Antique Speciality Flooring offers reclaimed, random-width wood flooring in tongue-and-groove planks of chestnut, oak, heart pine, white pine, and hemlock.

Reclaimed Wood Flooring

Antique Woods & Colonial Restorations, Inc.
121 Quarry Rd.
Gouverneur, NY 13642

Toll-free: 888-261-4284
www.vintagewoods.com

Antique Woods & Colonial Restorations, Inc. (formerly Vintage Barns, Woods & Restorations) sells reclaimed and remilled wood products including flooring, siding, and whole barn frames.

Reclaimed Wood Flooring

Architectural Timber and Millwork
P.O. Box 719
Hadley, MA 01035

Toll-free: 800-430-5473
Phone: 413-586-3045
www.atimber.com

Architectural Timber and Millwork salvages wood from existing structures slated for demolition and remills it into wide-plank and contemporary-plank flooring. Their flooring is available in a variety of species, including a running inventory of heart pine.

Reclaimed Wood Flooring

Big Timberworks, Inc.
P.O. Box 368
Gallatin Gateway, MT 59730

Phone: 406-763-4639
www.bigtimberworks.com

Big Timberworks offers reclaimed and remilled wood for residential and commercial applications in a variety of species.

Reclaimed Wood Flooring

Black's Farmwood
P.O. Box 2836
San Rafael, CA 94912

Toll-free: 877-321-WOOD
Phone: 415-499-8300
www.blacksfarmwood.com

Black's Farmwood sells reclaimed wood products from deconstructed buildings and river bottoms. Products are available in a variety of species and include salvaged timbers and beams, remilled flooring, and barn siding. The company has a showroom in Lucas Valley and uses two mills, one in Kentucky and another in New York.

Reclaimed Wood Flooring

Carlisle Restoration Lumber
1676 Rte. 9
Stoddard, NH 03464

Toll-free: 800-595-9663
Phone: 603-446-3937
www.wideplankflooring.com

Carlisle Restoration specializes in large-dimension antique flooring, available in heart pine, chestnut, and oak.

Reclaimed Wood Flooring

Centre Mills Antique Floors
P.O. Box 16
Aspers, PA 17304

Phone: 717-334-0249
www.centremillsantiquefloors.com

Centre Mills Antique Floors salvages, remills, and sells several species and types of flooring, including antique chestnut, to wholesale customers ordering a minimum of 1,000 ft².

Reclaimed Wood Flooring

Chestnut Specialists, Inc.
400 Harwinton Ave.
Plymouth, CT 06782

Phone: 860-283-4209
www.chestnutspec.com

Chestnut Specialists reclaims timbers from old buildings and remills them into T&G, planed, and square-edge flooring. Various species of kiln-dried flooring are available.

Reclaimed Wood Flooring

Conklin's Authentic Antique Barnwood
R.R. 1, Box 70
Susquehanna, PA 18847

Phone: 570-465-3832
www.conklinsbarnwood.com

Conklin's Authentic Antique Barnwood salvages flooring and re-sells it either "as is" or remilled. Antique flooring is available in chestnut, oak, pine, hemlock, and random heart.

Reclaimed Wood Flooring

Craftmark Reclaimed Wood, Inc.
P.O. Box 237
McMinnville, OR 97128

Phone: 503-472-6929
www.craftmarkinc.com

Craftmark Reclaimed Wood specializes in wide-plank flooring of multiple species remilled from wood typically salvaged from de-constructed warehouse buildings that are 70–100 years old.

Reclaimed Wood Flooring

Crossroads Recycled Lumber
57839 Road 225
P.O. Box 928
North Fork, CA 93643

Toll-free: 888-842-3201
Phone: 559-877-3645
www.crossroadslumber.com

Crossroads reclaimed wood flooring is available in 3" to 12" widths primarily in pine and Douglas fir.

Reclaimed Wood Flooring

Duluth Timber Co.
P.O. Box 16717
Duluth, MN 55816-0717

Phone: 218-727-2145
www.duluthtimber.com

Duluth Timber reclaims and remills mainly Douglas fir and longleaf yellow pine, but also redwood and cypress. Demolition and salvage of warehouses and sheep-shearing sheds in Australia has yielded a supply of Australian hardwoods such as jarrah and Mountain ash. Duluth has mills in Minnesota, California, and Washington.

Reclaimed Wood Flooring

Early New England Restorations
32 Taugwonk Spur
Stonington, CT 06378

Phone: 860-599-4393

Early New England Restorations, formerly Horse Drawn Pine, remills pine plank flooring.

Reclaimed Wood Flooring

Green Mountain Woodworks
P.O. Box 1433
Phoenix, OR 97535

Toll-free: 866-888-7478
Phone: 541-535-5880
www.greenmountainwoodworks.com

Green Mountain Woodworks offers a full line of unique hardwood flooring, emphasizing environmentally responsible, antique re-claimed, and Northwest woods. Green Mountain Woodworks clearly defines the "EcoStatus" of each wood, including FSC-certified, those from ecosystem restoration projects, reclaimed/recycled woods, and woods rescued from low value or waste streams (fire wood and pulp/chip).

Reclaimed Wood Flooring

Havillah Shake Company
521 N. Siwash Creek Rd.
Tonasket, WA 98855

Phone: 509-486-1467

Havillah Shake Company is a small rural business that manufactures wood flooring, paneling, and furniture primarily from reclaimed wood sources.

Reclaimed Wood Flooring

Heartwood Industries
3658 State Road 1414
Hartford, KY 42347

Toll-free: 800-318-9439
Phone: 270-298-0084
www.whiskeywood.com

Heartwood offers salvaged and remilled flooring in longleaf pine, oak, chestnut, cypress, red cedar, and Douglas fir.

Reclaimed Wood Flooring

J. Hoffman Lumber Co.
1330 E. State St.
Sycamore, IL 60178

Phone: 630-513-6680

J. Hoffman Lumber Co. is the Midwest's only sawmill/millwork company specializing in reclaimed antique heart pine, Douglas fir, and white pine. Reclaimed lumber is remilled into flooring, siding, and other millwork.

Reclaimed Wood Flooring

Legacy Antique Woods
114 Sibley Rd.
Honeoye Falls, NY 14472

Phone: 585-624-1011
www.legacyantique
woods.com

Legacy Antique Woods salvages timbers, boards, and decking from barns and industrial buildings. Material can be purchased "as is" or resawn into boardstock or molder blanks. Primary species offered are chestnut, oak, Douglas fir, heart pine, and white pine with other species typically available.

Reclaimed Wood Flooring

Longleaf Lumber
70-80 Webster Ave.
Somerville, MA 02143

Phone: 617-625-3659
www.longleaflumber.com

Longleaf Lumber, founded in 1997, dismantles old buildings and remills antique timbers into millwork and flooring at the company's sawmill in the Boston area. Longleaf specializes in heart pine, but other salvaged woods such as chestnut, red and white oak, eastern white pine, and maple are often available from dismantled buildings around New England. Longleaf also sells unmilled reclaimed timbers and reclaimed barn siding. In addition to the sawmill, the company operates a retail store at their Webster Avenue location.

Reclaimed Wood Flooring

Maxwell Pacific
P.O. Box 4127
Malibu, CA 90264

Phone: 310-457-4533

Maxwell Pacific is primarily a wholesaler of reclaimed wood products but also offers reclaimed flooring, lumber, and timbers for sale to contractors.

Reclaimed Wood Flooring

Mountain Lumber
P.O. Box 289
Ruckersville, VA 22968

Toll-free: 800-445-2671
www.mountainlumber.com

Mountain Lumber has a large stock of reclaimed tongue-and-groove, solid plank flooring. Most varieties are end-matched. Species include heart pine, oak, and American chestnut.

Reclaimed Wood Flooring

Pioneer Millworks
1180 Commercial Dr.
Farmington, NY 14425

Toll-free: 800-951-9663
Phone: 585-924-9970
www.pioneermillworks.com

Pioneer Millworks remills salvaged wood into flooring and millwork. The primary species is longleaf yellow pine. Other species that are often available include redwood, bald cypress, chestnut, and white oak.

Reclaimed Wood Flooring

Re-Tech Wood Products
1324 Russell Rd.
P.O. Box 215
Forks, WA 98331

Phone: 360-374-4141
www.retechwoodproducts.com

Re-Tech salvages solid and glue-laminated fir beams and cuts them for several different lines of flooring. They also salvage fir and cedar for high-end flooring from "buckskins," which are blowdown trees (felled by windstorms) from past years.

Reclaimed Wood Flooring

Resource Woodworks, Inc.
627 E. 60th St.
Tacoma, WA 98404

Phone: 253-474-3757
www.rwtimber.com

Resource Woodworks specializes in milling flooring from reclaimed Douglas fir and other available species.

Reclaimed Wood Flooring

Safe Solutions, LLC
166 Malden Tpke.
Saugerties, NY 12477

Phone: 845-661-7989
www.safesolutionsllc.com

Safe Solutions remills tongue-and-groove barnwood hardwood flooring and siding out of antique reclaimed wood from disassembled barns. The company uses a technique called skip planing to mill the boards while leaving some of the original milling marks for aesthetic purposes. Flooring is available in oak, chestnut, walnut, maple, and other hardwoods.

Reclaimed Wood Flooring

Sylvan Brandt
651 E. Main St.
Lititz, PA 17543

Phone: 717-626-4520
www.sylvanbrandt.com

Sylvan Brandt reclaimed wood flooring is made from resawn beams and barn siding. Tongue-and-groove planks of oak, heart pine, white pine, and hemlock are available.

Reclaimed Wood Flooring

TerraMai
1104 Firenze
P.O. Box 696
McCloud, CA 96057

Toll-free: 800-220-9062
Phone: 530-964-2740
www.terramai.com

TerraMai (formerly Jefferson Recycled Woodworks) produces several grades of flooring from reclaimed lumber, ranging from clear tongue-and-groove to rough-cut plank. Douglas fir, ponderosa pine, and southern yellow pine are among their most popular species.

Reclaimed Wood Flooring

The Woods Company, Inc.
985 Superior Ave.
Chambersburg, PA 17201-7864

Phone: 717-263-6524
www.thewoodscompany.com

The Woods Co. specializes in wide-plank flooring and custom interior millwork made from wood reclaimed from demolished buildings.

Reclaimed Wood Flooring

Trestlewood
694 N. 1890 W, Ste. 44A
P.O. Box 1728
Provo, UT 84601

Toll-free: 877-375-2779
Phone: 801-375-2779
www.trestlewood.com

Trestlewood deals exclusively in reclaimed wood. Their wood comes from the Lucin Cutoff railroad trestle, which crosses the Great Salt Lake, and other salvage projects. Trestlewood products include flooring, millwork, timbers, decking, and siding. Available species include Douglas fir, redwood, southern yellow pine, longleaf yellow pine, oak, and other hardwoods.

Reclaimed Wood Flooring

Vintage Lumber Co.
P.O. Box 485
Woodsboro, MD 21798

Toll-free: 800-499-7859
www.vintagelumber.com

Since 1973, Vintage Lumber has been reusing historic old wood obtained from dismantled derelict barns to produce reclaimed antique solid wood flooring. "The Vintage Collection" uses old beams and boards, ranging in age from 50-200 years, which are milled into Vintage and Vintage/Distressed plank flooring. Vintage Lumber mills the lower grades of native Appalachian hardwoods into rustic/character flooring in "The American Country Collection." Both collections are milled in random widths and end-matched in 2'-10' lengths.

Reclaimed Wood Flooring

Vintage Material Supply Co.
4705 E. 5th St.
Austin, TX 78702

Phone: 512-386-6404
www.vintagematerialsupply.com

Vintage Material Supply Co. offers salvaged wood flooring available "as is" with edges cleaned, as well as new flooring milled from wood recovered from such sources as demolished buildings, ranch recovery, urban logging, and river bottoms. Primary species include old-growth longleaf pine, Tidewater cypress, mesquite, and walnut.

Reclaimed Wood Flooring

What Its Worth, Inc.
P.O. Box 162135
Austin, TX 78716

Phone: 512-328-8837
www.wiwpine.com

What Its Worth offers reclaimed pure heart longleaf yellow pine remilled into tongue-and-groove or square-edge flooring. Widths start at $2\frac{1}{2}$"; What Its Worth will provide flooring up to 12" wide upon request. Their milled product is 100% heartwood, and the wood's harvesting usually predates 1925.

Reclaimed-Wood Flooring

A Reclaimed Lumber Co.
9 Old Post Rd.
Madison, CT 06443

Phone: 203-214-9705
www.woodwood.com

A Reclaimed Lumber Co. salvages wood from old water and wine tanks, mill buildings, bridge timbers, river-recovery log operations, and other sources and custom mills it into a variety of wood products including plank flooring. Typical flooring species are long leaf yellow pine, Douglas fir, red and white oak, and chestnut. Wood is sourced from all over the country, and much of their product is processed at their Connecticut mill, but the company makes an effort to provide customers with locally available wood that they will process locally.

Reclaimed-Wood Flooring

Endura Wood Products, Ltd.
1303 S.E. 6th Ave.
Portland, OR 97214

Phone: 503-233-7090
www.endurawood.com

Endura Wood Products currently has access to over 3.5 million board feet of Douglas fir that is being reclaimed from the old Portland Dry Dock #2. This reclaimed wood can be milled into both character grade and clear flooring. Also offered is a limited supply of Douglas fir reclaimed from maraschino cherry vats that can be milled into $2\frac{1}{4}$" wide red-hued flooring.

River-Reclaimed Wood Flooring

Goodwin Heart Pine Company
106 S.W. 109th Pl.
Micanopy, FL 32667

Toll-free: 800-336-3118
Phone: 352-466-0339
www.heartpine.com

Goodwin manufactures antique wood flooring made from antique heart pine and heart cypress logs—200 years old or older—recovered from Southern river bottoms. Flooring is kiln-dried, graded, and precision-milled. Reclaimed timbers from old buildings are also available.

Recycled-Glass Tile

see *Interior Finish & Trim: Recycled-Glass Tile*

Resilient Flooring

Standard products in resilient flooring today include vinyl sheet flooring, vinyl tile, and vinyl composition tile (VCT), which replaced vinyl-asbestos tile after asbestos lost favor. All of these standard products are made with polyvinyl chloride (PVC), which may result in environmental problems during manufacture or disposal (particularly incineration). Some environmental groups are calling for a phaseout of PVC. Included here are products that don't fit into specific resilient-flooring categories.

Stratica

Amtico International Inc.
6480 Roswell Rd.
Atlanta, GA 30328

Toll-free: 800-404-0102
Phone: 404-267-1900
www.stratica.com

Stratica is a chlorine-free, low-VOC, durable alternative to vinyl or VCT flooring. It is flexible yet free of plasticizers, which are used in sheet vinyl flooring. Stratica manufacture meets ISO 14001 standards for environmental management. Stratica is lightweight, flexible, and extremely durable. It is made with a base layer of mineral-filled copolymer and a DuPont Surlyn® wear layer and is sold primarily in 13" x 13" tiles. Stratica is available in a wide range of solid colors and patterns including marble, granite, stone, various woods, and terrazzo.

Rubber Flooring

Each year in the United States more than 200 million tires are discarded; most enter landfills. Today's recycled-rubber industry is expanding quickly to make use of this wasted resource. Recycled-tire rubber provides a highly durable, resilient, slip-resistant, anti-fatigue surface suitable for a variety of flooring requirements. Rubber granules from ground tires may be vulcanized (reformed under high heat using a sulfur additive), or agglomerated with a synthetic binding matrix, such as polyurethane. Products may have color integrated as flecks, the binding matrix may be colored, or color may be added as a wear layer. The rubber and its binders or additives, however, may be significant sources of indoor air pollutants, including VOCs and heavy metals. Thus, we do not widely recommend rubber flooring for most indoor spaces, particularly residential buildings. Indoor/outdoor spaces, such as entrances and skating rinks, or commercial/industrial areas with high ventilation rates, are potentially excellent applications for these recycled-content products.

CushionWalk Pavers

Dinoflex Manufacturing, Ltd.
P.O. Box 3309
Salmon Arm, BC V1E 4S1 Canada

Toll-free: 877-713-1899
Phone: 252-832-7780
www.dinoflex.com

Cushion Walk Pavers are made from 91% recycled-tire rubber and are designed primarily for covering patios, rooftop decks, and walkways. Paving tiles are available in terra-cotta red, forest green, stone beige, teak brown, and midnight black.

Mondo Commercial Flooring

Mondo America Inc.
2655 Francis Hughes
Laval, PQ H7L 3S8 Canada

Toll-free: 800-361-3747 (U.S.)
Phone: 450-967-5800
www.mondousa.com

Mondo produces commercial flooring made from natural and synthetic rubber, mineral fillers, and color pigments. Unlike products such as VCT and sheet vinyl, these durable, easy-to-clean floorcoverings require no maintenance coatings. The products contain no PVC, solvents, halogens, plasticizers, or heavy metals and are available in tiles or rolls. Made in a variety of styles and colors suitable for a wide range of applications, Mondo Commercial Flooring is nonporous, heat weldable, and fungus-resistant (ASTM G-21-90). The products are also compliant with California Indoor Air Quality Requirement section 01350.

PlayGuard

CSSI
175 Fountain Ave.
Lancaster, PA 17601

Toll-free: 800-851-4746
Phone: 717-481-2935
www.carlsurf.com

PlayGuard, a resilient shock-absorbing tile system made from ground-up used tire treads, has a firm surface that is suitable for wheelchairs and mobility aids. PlayGuard 24" x 24" rubber pavers come in a variety of colors for indoor and outdoor use in playgrounds and recreation rooms. They may also be used as ballast on low-slope roof systems. PlayGuard also offers standard and ADA-compliant perimeter access ramps, molded 45° and 90° corners, and half tiles to complete the system. The manufacturer has certified the following recycled-content levels (by weight): total recovered material 50% typical, 50% guaranteed; post-consumer material 50% typical, 50% guaranteed.

Softpave

CSSI
175 Fountain Ave.
Lancaster, PA 17601

Toll-free: 800-851-4746
Phone: 717-481-2935
www.carlsurf.com

Softpave ™ is made from recycled-tire rubber with a polyurethane binder. The 1"-thick, 24" x 24" pavers have a disc tread pattern on the bottom and a smooth, tile, or brick pattern on the top surface. They come in black, charcoal, red-flecked, green-flecked, or rust. Step tiles, stair nosings, and edge pieces are also available. The manufacturer has certified the following recycled-content levels (by weight): total recovered material 50% typical, 50% guaranteed; post-consumer material 50% typical, 50% guaranteed.

SuperFlexx Paver Tiles

U.S. Rubber Recycling, Inc.
2225 Via Cerro, Unit B
Riverside, CA 92509

Toll-free: 888-473-8453
Phone: 909-342-0177
www.usrubber.com

SuperFlexx Paver Tiles are made from high-density, urethane-bonded primary crumb rubber buffings. The ³/₄" x 24" x 24" tiles, available in red, green, or black, are suitable for in-door/outdoor usage, especially in wet areas.

Sheet Carpet

Carpeting is almost ubiquitous in our homes, schools, and office buildings. Almost two billion square yards of carpeting are sold each year, nearly all of it made from petrochemicals. Carpet is a good absorber of sound and impact, yielding a surface associated with comfort. Its absorbent nature, however, also makes it a good medium for holding moisture and harboring dirt, mold, and dust mites. This, along with potential offgassing from the carpet and its adhesive, has led to indoor air quality concerns.

Bio-Floor Collection

Earth Weave Carpet Mills, Inc.
P.O. Box 6120
Dalton, GA 30722

Phone: 706-278-8200
www.earthweave.com

Earth Weave Carpet Mills produces wall-to-wall carpeting and area rugs from 100% biodegradable, all natural materials such as wool, hemp, jute, and natural rubber. Their Bio-Floor line of wool carpeting is nonwoven and uses a 100% biodegradable adhesive to bond the wool to a hemp-cotton primary backing and then a secondary backing of jute fibers. No chemical treatments are used, and color variation is achieved through the selection of naturally pigmented wool.

Commercial and Residential Carpet

Mohawk Industries, Inc.
160 S. Industrial Blvd.
Calhoun, GA 30703

Phone: 800-622-6227
www.mohawkind.com

In partnership with Honeywell, Mohawk Commercial offers ten carpets that feature ColorStrand™ Infinity™ Forever Renewable nylon, all with a recycled content of 25%. These floor coverings can be continually renewed in a closed-loop process that preserves all of the original quality. Residential polyester Mohawk carpets have 100% recycled-content face fiber from recovery of soda-bottle PET.

Metafloor

Lees Carpets, Division of Burlington Industries
3330 W. Friendly Ave.
Greensboro, NC 27420

Toll-free: 800-523-5647
www.leescarpets.com

Metafloor, a carpet and hard-surface-flooring hybrid, uses at least 50% less nylon than typical carpet and, as a result, is less likely to trap dirt. It comes as a 12'-wide broadloom product currently available in a single collection of patterns called "Collective Voice." The company claims that Metafloor is highly durable and very inexpensive to maintain—with only water and mild detergent needed to remove most common stains. The secondary backing has 50% recycled content in the form of nylon scraps from other processes in the facility. A lifetime warranty covers edge unravel, delamination, and tuft bind integrity. Metafloor became the first floorcovering product ever to win "Best of Show" at NeoCon.

Natural Design Collection and Natural Textures Collection

Design Materials, Inc.
241 S. 55th St.
Kansas City, KS 66106

Toll-free: 800-654-6451
Phone: 913-342-9796
www.dmikc.com

These carpet collections from Design Materials are made from natural fibers. Products in the Natural Design Collection are made from sisal, coir, and reed, while those in the Natural Textures Collection are made from sisal, wool, and jute. They come in 13'2"-wide broadloom rolls in a variety of colors, patterns, and weaves.

Natural Fiber Floor Coverings

Sisal Rugs Direct
P.O. Box 313
Excelsior, MN 55331

Toll-free: 800-287-3144
Phone: 952-448-9602
www.sisalrugs.com

Sisal Rugs Direct markets broadloom and area rugs of sisal, sisal/wool blend, seagrass, and mountain grass imported from Brazil, China, and Africa with natural latex-rubber backings.

Nature's Carpet

Colin Campbell & Sons, Ltd.
1428 W. 7th Ave.
Vancouver, BC V6H 1C1 Canada

Toll-free: 800-667-5001
Phone: 604-734-2758
www.naturescarpet.com

Nature's Carpet, made from 100% New Zealand raw wool, is completely free of chemical residues from all stages of the process—from the washing and spinning of the wool through manufacture of the finished carpet. The line currently consists of six loop-pile carpets in natural wool hues, two loop-pile ribbed products, and one cut-pile carpet with vegetable-dyed colors. The backing is made from jute and strengthened with unbleached cotton. Nature's Carpet uses no moth treatment, uses natural latex rather than synthetic, and has negligible VOC ratings. The carpet has been used extensively for people with chemical sensitivities.

Visio

Lees Carpets, Division of Burlington Industries
3330 W. Friendly Ave.
Greensboro, NC 27420

Toll-free: 800-523-5647
www.leescarpets.com

The Visio Collection uses high-recycled-content Antron Legacy EPP nylon 6,6 fiber from Dupont and Lees' Unibond RE backing, resulting in 20% post-consumer and 19% post-industrial recycled content (the recycled content of both constituents is certified by Scientific Certification Systems). This collection was designed by Ken Wilson and Colleen Waguespack of Envision Design. Lees' patented Duracolor yarn-dyeing process uses heat to integrate the dye into the fiber and provide stain resistance. Several other collections from Lees have similar construction but use Antron Legacy EPP fiber without recycled content. These include the Modern Collection, the Geologic Collection, and Colorburst broadloom for schools.

Wool and Cotton Carpet

Carousel Carpet Mills
3315 Superior Ln.
Bowie , MD 20715

Phone: 301-262-2650
www.carouselcarpets.com

Carousel produces carpets made from wool, linen, and cotton fibers, with a poly backing. They also make custom carpets and rugs.

Slip-Resistant Flooring

Slip-resistant flooring is necessary for many public or industrial entryways, work areas, and high-traffic areas, particularly where exposure to water is expected. Residential applications can include poolsides and concrete decks. The products listed here are all made from recycled tires, using both the rubber and the nylon tire cord elements bonded to a backing to create a thick, heavy-duty, slip-resistant surface. The synthetic materials are also highly resistant to water damage and organic deterioration. Be aware, however, that these products may be significant sources of VOCs and are thus best used in well-ventilated areas or for other high-traffic, indoor/outdoor applications.

Nova Walkway Pads

EcoStar
104 Terrace Dr.
Mundelein, IL 60060

Toll-free: 800-211-7170
www.premiumroofs.com

EcoStar produces Nova Walkway Pads from Starloy, a proprietary polymer made from 100% recycled post-industrial rubber and plastic. Nova is nonabsorbent, impact-resistant, nonslip, and interlocks for easy installation in areas such as roofs. EcoStar is a division of Carlisle SynTec, Inc.

Suppressed Wood Flooring

Suppressed wood comes from trees growing in the understory of mature forests—usually where forestry practices have prevented fires, so natural thinning and succession hasn't occurred. It is now generally recognized that overly dense forests increase fire hazard and leave trees vulnerable to insect infestation and disease. These small, slow-growing trees were once regarded as waste, suitable only for fuel and firewood. Attributes of these trees include close grain, fine texture, and small tight knots. This can provide a raw material for joinery, flooring, and panels.

Flooring & Floorcoverings

Alpine Grade Douglas Fir Flooring

Green Mountain Woodworks
P.O. Box 1433
Phoenix, OR 97535

Toll-free: 866-888-7478
Phone: 541-535-5880
www.greenmountainwoodworks.com

Green Mountain Woodworks produces this Douglas fir flooring from trees thinned out of overly dense forests in southwest Oregon. Green Mountain Woodworks is associated with the Healthy Forests Healthy Communities Partnership, which works with communities in National Forests to develop locally owned small businesses that make products from the wood recovered during forest restoration. (Timber from National Forests is not eligible for FSC certification.)

Terrazzo

Some terrazzo products include recycled content. Be aware that different binders are used in terrazzo products, not all of which are environmentally attractive.

QuartzStone

Quartzitec
15 Turner Ct.
Sussex, NB E4E 2S1
Canada

Toll-free: 877-255-9600
Phone: 506-433-9600
www.quartzitec.com

QuartzStone tiles are manufactured from quartz fragments bound with white portland cement rather than the more common polyester resin. The tiles measure 11.8" x 11.8" and 15.7" x 15.7" and are available in 3 series with 40 colors. Unit pavers are also available in 8 colors. Both products can be color-customized.

Recycled-Glass "Terrazzo" Tile

Wausau Tile, Inc.
9001 Business Hwy. 51
P.O. Box 1520
Wausau, WI 54402

Toll-free: 800-388-8728
Phone: 715-359-3121
www.wausautile.com

Wausau Tile, one of the largest terrazzo manufacturers in the world, produces a line of terrazzo-like tile from recycled glass (approximately 60% recycled glass by weight) using technology developed by the Civil Engineering Dept. of Columbia University.

According to the company, the patented chemical additives result in a much stronger and more water-resistant product than traditional terrazzo.

Tile Setting Materials and Accessories

Tile adhesives, like many other adhesives, can have high VOC levels. VOCs contribute to poor indoor air quality (IAQ), and they're a major component of smog. Tile adhesives included here have low VOC levels.

D-5 Premium and D-40 Duraflex Thin-Set Mortar

Bostik Findley
211 Boston St.
Middleton, MA 01949

Toll-free: 800-366-7837
www.bostik.com

D-5 Premium Thin-Set Mortar (formerly D-505+) and D-40™ Duraflex™ are zero-VOC, thin-set tile mortars.

Safecoat 3 in 1 Adhesive

American Formulating & Manufacturing (AFM)
3251 Third Ave.
San Diego, CA 92103

Toll-free: 800-239-0321
Phone: 619-239-0321
www.afmsafecoat.com

Safecoat 3 in 1 Adhesive is designed for hard composition—ceramic, vinyl, parquet, formica, and slate—floor and counter tiles. It is a water-based alternative to solvent-based adhesives and has significantly lower VOC content of 44 g/l (82 g/l less water).

158

Copyright © BuildingGreen, Inc.

Interior Finish & Trim

Particleboard and medium-density fiberboard (MDF) are almost always made with a urea formaldehyde (UF) binder. This is one of the largest in-home sources of formaldehyde gas—a known human carcinogen. These products can offgas for 5 years or more into the living space. UF-based particleboard and MDF are typically used for cabinet boxes, substrates for countertops, shelving, and stair treads. If possible, these materials should be avoided. Any UF-based materials used in a building should be sealed with a low-toxic, low-permeability coating.

A few formaldehyde-free particleboard and MDF products are available, including some made with straw instead of wood fiber. These are made with a urethane-type (MDI) resin. Be aware that MDI is highly toxic before it cures, so its use increases the health risk to factory workers if a manufacturer doesn't have good safety standards. Once cured, MDI-based wood panel products are very stable, without measurable offgassing.

Conventional drywall is quite attractive from an environmental standpoint. It is typically made from 100% recycled paper backing and natural gypsum, which is plentiful and can be low-impact to extract. More and more drywall today contains post-industrial waste in the form of synthetic gypsum created by sulfur removal systems in the smokestacks of coal-burning power plants. This material is sometimes referred to as flue-gas desulfurization gypsum.

The joint compound used to finish drywall contains synthetic additives that may affect some chemically sensitive people; specialty alternatives are available. Dry-mix, setting-type joint compounds, which are sold in powder form and mixed on site, contain fewer additives.

Cabinets made from nontoxic materials and finishes or solid wood are available. People with chemical sensitivities often find enameled-metal cabinets to be the least problematic.

Clear wood trim materials are increasingly difficult to find (or more expensive), and they place a high demand on virgin timber. On the other hand, this is an application where high-quality wood can be fully seen and celebrated. Finger-jointed trim for painted applications, and veneer-covered, finger-jointed trim for stain applications, are good substitutes.

Whenever possible, woods used in interior finish and trim should be from certified well-managed forests; third-party certification to standards developed by the Forest Stewardship Council (FSC) provides a way that users can verify environmental claims. Currently there are two U.S.-based organizations that certify forest operations (and wood products): Scientific Certifications Systems, and the Rainforest Alliance (SmartWood).

Tropical hardwoods should be avoided unless they come from FSC-certified sustainable sources, as their harvest can cause irreparable damage to tropical rainforests. Only a few of the many species of tropical woods have much commercial value—often large areas of forest are damaged in pursuit of a few trees. The roads left behind by loggers provide access for slash-and-burn farmers and other settlers, so penetration by logging operations is frequently the beginning of a chain of activities that totally destroy the forest. Fortunately, well-managed tropical forests are increasingly becoming certified.

Acoustical Ceiling Panels

Acoustical ceiling materials vary depending on the specific performance criteria desired (e.g., durability, light reflectance, sound absorption, washability, design flexibility, fire resistance). Most common in commercial suspended ceilings are wet-pressed mineral-fiber tiles and panels, typically made from a mixture of waste paper, mineral fiber (which may include slag, a waste product from steel-making), cornstarch, and various other mineral-based components. A number of these products have high recycled content; some, however, may contain low levels of formaldehyde. Fiberglass ceiling panels are also available with recycled content, though the percentage is typically lower than with mineral-fiber products. Most fiberglass ceiling panel products use a phenol-formaldehyde binder. Though far more common in Europe, wood-fiber-based ceiling panel products are also available in the U.S.—these are free of mineral fibers and formaldehyde but are typically more expensive, and they contain no recycled content. Metal ceiling products may or may not include a backing of fiberglass. Products for use in food service facilities, hospitals, or other areas with high sanitary standards have a PVC covering or scrubbable paint finish. Incineration of PVC (polyvinyl chloride) may release dioxins and furans. Residential acoustical ceiling panels are not available in as many materials or styles as commercial products.

InStar Straw-Panel Acoustical Ceiling System

Affordable Building Systems LLC
2750 State Hwy. 160
Whitewright, TX 75491

Toll-free: 866-364-1198
Phone: 903-364-1198
www.affordablebuildingsystems.com

The InStar™ Acoustical Ceiling System is comprised of 2"-thick compressed-straw panels—bound together by the natural lignin in the straw when the straw is processed with high heat and immense pressure. The core is covered with hydro-Kraft paper using PVA glue. The system is supported by a pre-engineered, recycled-steel structural support system with a powder-coat paint finish. A variety of configurations are offered for different acoustical needs. The standard system provides an NRC of 0.65, an STC of 34, and an OITC of 29. A number of environmentally attractive finish material options are available for the panels.

Mineral Fiber and Glass Based Drop-in Ceiling Tile

Armstrong World Industries, Inc.
2500 Columbia Ave.
Lancaster, PA 17604

Toll-free: 877-276-7876
Phone: 717-397-0611
www.armstrong.com

Armstrong Ceiling Systems offer a complete line of acoustical ceiling products that include both post-consumer and post-industrial waste, as well as abundant natural materials, including recycled newspaper, mineral wool, perlite, and cornstarch. Armstrong Ceilings offers products that contain up to 82% recycled content. Through its ceiling recycling program, old ceiling tiles are recycled and made into new ones.

X-Technology, Acoustone, and Auratone Panels and Tiles

USG Corporation
125 S. Franklin St.
Chicago, IL 60606

Toll-free: 800-874-4968
Phone: 312-606-4000
www.usg.com

USG Interiors manufactures a wide range of recycled-content mineral-fiber ceiling panels and tiles made from slag, waste paper, synthetic gypsum, and corn starch. The X-Technology line has the highest total recycled content at 85%, followed by Acoustone at 68%. Some Auratone products have recycled content of up to 62%.

Acoustical Wall Finishes

These wall finishes provide acoustic dampening and may be panelized or trowel-applied products. Look for recycled content and non-urea formaldehyde binders.

BASWAphon Acoustic Insulation

Artisan Sound Control, LLC
1164 Lloyd Rd.
Wickliffe, OH 44092

Phone: 440-585-3580
www.artisansound.com

The BASWAphon seamless finish system has acoustic dampening properties and the appearance of plaster or painted drywall. The

system, which may be applied to walls or ceilings—including curves, vaults, and domes—is comprised of 5 components: a 32 mm-thick mineral wool supporting panel (74% post-consumer recycled glass and phenol-formaldehyde binder), a factory-applied precoating, and a trowel-applied gap filler containing glass-foam spheres (75% post-consumer recycled glass and vinyl acetate-copolymer binders), and trowel-applied base and top coats (95% recycled marble dust with a vinyl-acetate copolymer binders and acrylic-copolymer binder, respectively). The supporting panels are glued to the substrate with USG Durabond® adhesive. BASWAphon comes in 40 mm and 68 mm thicknesses and can be colored with integral pigments. The materials for the system are manufactured in Sweden.

Ag-Fiber Particleboard

Straw is a byproduct that remains after the harvesting of grains such as wheat, oats, rice, and rye. If too much straw is tilled into the soil, it can rob the soil of nitrogen while it is being decomposed by soil bacteria; and environmental or safety regulations increasingly prohibit the burning of straw in the field. These concerns make the use of straw as a building material attractive. One application is in the form of particleboard—the finely chopped fibers are pressed into panels along with a formaldehyde-free MDI (methyl diisocyanate) binder, which imparts greater strength and moisture-resistance to the material than conventional urea-formaldehyde (UF) binders. Straw particleboard is 20% lighter than wood particleboard and provides good machinability.

PrimeBoard

PrimeBoard, Inc.
2441 N. 15th St.
Wahpeton, ND 58075

Phone: 701-642-3286
www.primeboard.com

PrimeBoard® was the first M3-rated particleboard made from wheat straw and a formaldehyde-free binder. Now made from a blend of agricultural-residue fibers, panels are available in a range of thicknesses, sizes, and grades. PrimeBoard also offers custom-cut panels as well as panels pressed with all-paper-based laminates in a wide range of colors.

PUREKOR Composite Panels

Panel Source International
18 Rayborn Cres., Ste. 101
St. Albert, AB T8N 5C1 Canada

Toll-free: 877-464-7246
Phone: 780-458-1007
www.panelsource.net

Panel Source International offers a composite particleboard product made from wheat-straw fiber and a formaldehyde-free Resin. The PUREKOR product is available from 4x8 to 5x12 sizes in thicknesses ranging from $\frac{1}{4}$" to $1\frac{1}{2}$". Standard density is 45 lbs., and grades produced include mill grade, M1, M2, and premium.

WoodStalk

Dow BioProducts
11 WoodStalk Way
P.O. Box 328
Elie, MB R0H 0H0 Canada

Toll-free: 800-441-4DOW
www.dow-bioproducts.com

Dow BioProducts, a wholly-owned subsidiary of Dow Chemical Canada, produces WoodStalk™ fiberboard panels (formerly produced by Isobord Enterprises under the name Isobord) from straw particles and a formaldehyde-free pMDI binder. WoodStalk panels are produced in 4' x 8', 4' x 9', 4' x 10', 4' x 12', and 5' x 8' sheets in thicknesses ranging from $\frac{1}{4}$" to $1\frac{1}{8}$" and meet the ANSI-M3 composite panel board standard.

Bamboo and Straw Paneling

Paneling for interior spaces is typically produced from either solid hardwoods or urea-formaldehyde-bonded fiberboard. Frame and panel construction and fine moldings are resource-intensive uses of solid wood, and UF binders may result in formaldehyde offgassing and indoor air quality (IAQ) problems. The following alternatives to hardwood paneling are made from fast-growing straw or bamboo. Some are free of UF binders.

Bamboo Paneling and Veneer

MOSO International NA, Ltd.
2220 40th Ave. E
Seattle, WA 98112

Toll-free: 800-617-2324
www.moso.com

MOSO bamboo flooring, veneer, and paneling is manufactured in China. Veneer and paneling are available in thicknesses from $1/42$" to 1". Sheet sizes are to specification up to dimensions of 5' x 8'. Laminations are bonded with urea-formaldehyde; however, the manufacturer claims that the product exceeds stringent European standards for formaldehyde emissions.

Bamtex Bamboo Paneling

Mintec Corporation
100 E. Pennsylvania Ave., Ste. 210
Towson, MD 21286

Toll-free: 888-964-6832
Phone: 410-296-6688
www.bamtex.com

Bamtex Bamboo Flooring is available in natural or carbonated colors in finished or unfinished $3^5/8$" x 36" or 72" strips. Bamtex also offers various sizes of paneling and large boards.

New England Classic Raised Panel System

New England Classic
3 Adams St.
South Portland, ME 04106

Toll-free: 888-460-6324
Phone: 207-799-5936
www.newenglandclassic.com

New England Classic produces a range of wainscoting and wall paneling systems, available in six styles from traditional to modern, made from formaldehyde-free wheat straw (WoodStalk™) panels. Stiles, rails, chair rail (cap), and shoe are produced from MDF, with a "low-emission" or no-added-formaldehyde option. Classic Traditional and Classic American are available preprimed for painting, or with oak, maple, and cherry ready-to-finish or factory finished wood veneers. Classic Modern is available with cherry or maple ready-to-finish or factory-finished wood veneer. Classic Traditional, Classic American, and Classic Modern are also available with mahogany, anigre, and walnut veneer by special order. Classic Beadboard is available preprimed or in oak, maple, or cherry.

Plyboo Bamboo Paneling, Plywood, and Veneer

Smith & Fong Company
375 Oyster Point Blvd. #3
S. San Francisco, CA 94080

Toll-free: 866-835-9859
www.plyboo.com

Photo courtesy of Cheng Design

Plyboo® tambour, fabric-backed, flexible paneling is available in a $3/16$" x 48" x 96" size with either a sanded or "raw" surface. Sanded comes prefinished or unfinished in an amber or natural color. The "raw" paneling, which retains the outside skin of the bamboo and has a more rustic appeal, comes unfinished in a natural green/yellow or amber color.

Plyboo bamboo plywood is available in a variety of dimensions and sizes. $1/4$" and $1/2$" solid bamboo plywood comes in a 16" x 72" size; $3/4$" plywood is available in both 30" x 72" and 48" x 96" sizes; and $1/8$" plywood is 48" x 96" with plywood backing. All these sizes are available in either vertical or flat grain in an amber or natural color.

Plyboo bamboo veneer has a vertical pattern in natural or amber color in a 0.6 mm x 12" x 98". There is also a $1/8$" bamboo veneer in a 48" x 96" size with a plywood backing. Veneers are provided with either paper or fleece backing.

Teragren Bamboo Panels and Veneer

Teragren LLC
121715 Miller Rd. NE, Ste. 301
Bainbridge Island, WA 98110

Toll-free: 800-929-6333
Phone: 206-842-9477
www.teragren.com

Teragren manufactures bamboo panels and veneer for cabinetry, furniture, interior paneling, counter tops, and other interior applications as a direct replacement for wood products. Stock panels are available in 1' x 6' x $5/8$" or $3/4$"; and 4' x 8' x $3/4$", $1/4$", or $1/8$". Paper-backed and unbacked veneers are available in sheets and strips; contact for sizes. Note that while the adhesive used to manufacture the panels and veneer exceeds E1 standards, it is not food grade; if the surface is to be used for food preparation, a food grade sealer is recommended.

Certified Millwork

Certified wood products are third-party verified as originating from well-managed forests based on Forest Stewardship Council (FSC) standards. Some companies listed here may sell both certified and noncertified products or carry other types of certification that don't qualify for GreenSpec. To ensure the use of environmen-

tally responsible wood products, be sure to specify your interest in FSC-certified wood when contacting these companies.

Certified Millwork

Anderson-Tully
1725 N. Washington St.
P.O. Box 38
Vicksburg, MS 39180

Phone: 601-636-3876
www.andersontully.com

Anderson-Tully Company (ATCO) received its FSC certification from SmartWood after years of uncertified but well-managed forestry practices. Anderson-Tully has long been offering an extensive number of species (with cottonwood and hackberry leading the list) due to its practice of finding markets for lesser-used tree species rather than eliminating them.

Certified Millwork

Cascadia Forest Goods, LLC
38083 Wheeler Rd.
Dexter, OR 97431

Phone: 541-485-4477
www.cascadiaforestgoods.com

Cascadia Forest Goods (CFG) is a supplier of FSC-certified and recycled forest products, including flooring, paneling, and trim. CFG's woods are primarily those from the Pacific Northwest and British Columbia, such as: Douglas fir, incense and western red cedar, Sitka and Englemann spruce, ponderosa and sugar pine, and regional hardwoods (madrone, white and black oak, broadleaf maple, alder, and chinkapin).

Certified Millwork

Collins Companies
1618 S.W. First Ave., Ste. 500
Portland, OR 97201

Toll-free: 800-329-1219
Phone: 503-417-7755
www.collinswood.com

The CollinsWood® line includes FSC-certified particleboard, FSC-certified TruWood® engineered (hardboard) siding, and FSC-certified hardwood and softwood lumber and millwork. In 1993, Collins Pine Company became the first privately owned timber management company to receive FSC certification in the U.S. CollinsWood has been a leader in the forest and wood products certification movement since its inception.

Certified Millwork

Dwight Lewis Lumber / Lewis Lumber Products
30 S. Main St.
P.O. Box 356
Picture Rocks, PA 17762

Toll-free: 800-233-8450
Phone: 570-584-4460
lewislp.com

Dwight Lewis Lumber sells FSC-certified moldings, flooring, paneling, and hardwoods, subject to availability. Certified species are cherry, hard and soft maple, and red oak.

Certified Millwork

Les Produits Forestiers Becesco
2900, 95ième Rue
St-Georges, QC G6A 1E3 Canada

Phone: 418-227-3671

Les Produits Forestiers Becesco is a certified hardwood lumber supplier milling oak, beech, birch, hard maple, and soft maple.

Certified Millwork

Menominee Tribal Enterprises
Hwy. 47 N
P.O. Box 10
Neopit, WI 54150

Phone: 715-756-2311
www.menominee.edu/mte/index.html

Menominee Tribal Enterprises (MTE) offers a full line of certified wood products harvested from the 220,000-acre Menominee Forest. MTE is continuing its development of value-added products from the 16 wood species harvested. Menominee forest lands were the first certified to FSC standards in North America.

Certified Millwork

Mt. Baker Plywood
2929 Roeder Ave.
P.O. Box 997
Bellingham, WA 98225

Phone: 360-733-3960
www.mountbakerproducts.com

Mt. Baker Plywood manufactures FSC-certified paneling and panel products.

Certified Millwork

Windfall Lumber and Milling
210 Thurston St.
Olympia, WA 98501

Phone: 360-352-2250
www.windfalllumber.com

Windfall Lumber and Milling is a distributor of FSC-certified hardwoods, flooring, and structural lumber. Windfall also manufactures specialty wood products such as flooring and moldings.

Certified Wainscot

McDowell Lumber Company, Inc.
Rte. 46 S
P.O. Box 148
Crosby, PA 16724

Phone: 814-887-2717
www.mcdowelllumber.com

McDowell Lumber deals in FSC-certified lumber, flooring, wainscoting, and veneer in over 15 species including red oak, cherry, hard and soft maple, ash, and a variety of other hardwoods harvested in Pennsylvania.

Certified Wood Moldings

Colonial Craft
501 Main St.
Luck, WI 54853

Toll-free: 800-289-6653
Phone: 715-472-2223
www.colonialcraft.com

Colonial Craft offers FSC-certified hardwood moldings. All other Colonial Craft products, including architectural moldings, can be produced from certified wood upon request.

FSC-Certified Wood Paneling

Wood Ceilings
25310 Jeans Rd.
Veneta, OR 97487

Toll-free: 866-935-9663
Phone: 541-935-9663
www.woodceilings.com

Wood Ceilings—formerly Pacific Wood Systems—crafts architectural suspended ceiling panel systems and wall paneling of FSC-certified woods including black cherry, western hemlock, red oak, maple, mahogany, and teak (when available).

Certified Wood Stair Parts

FSC-certified wood products are third-party verified as originating from well-managed forests based on Forest Stewardship Council (FSC) standards. Some companies listed here may sell both certified and noncertified products or products certified according to other, less stringent environmental standards. To ensure the use of environmentally responsible wood products, be sure to specify your interest in FSC-certified wood when contacting these companies.

Certified Stair Parts

B. W. Creative Wood Industries Ltd.
23282 River Rd.
Maple Ridge, BC V2W 1B6 Canada

Phone: 604-467-5147
www.bwcreativewood.com

B. W. Creative Wood specializes in stair parts fabricated of FSC-certified white fir. They also offer FSC-certified post caps and ball tops for porches and decks.

Certified Stair Parts

Randall Custom Lumber, Ltd.
3530 S.E. Arcadia Rd.
Shelton, WA 98584

Phone: 360-426-8518
www.rclumber.com

Randall Custom Lumber manufactures FSC-certified decking, flooring, hard and softwood lumber, and stair parts. Some of their certified species are ash, red cedar, red alder, Douglas fir, madrone, and maple.

Concrete Pigments

see *Flooring & Floorcoverings: Concrete Pigments*

Cork Wall Covering

Long used as a wall covering, cork is available in sheets or tiles of various thicknesses. It's tackable, self-healing, durable, sound-absorbing, and naturally resistant to moisture, rot, mold, and fire.

Cork Wall Covering

KorQinc
155 E. 56th St.
New York, NY 10022

Phone: 212-758-2593
www.korqinc.com

KorQ wall covering is made from a thin layer of cork laminated onto a cotton backing. It is available in rolls and may also be used for other fabric-like applications. KorQ wall tiles measuring $^3/_6$" x 12" x 12" or $^3/_{16}$" x 12" x 24" are also available.

Natural Cork Wall Tile

Natural Cork, Inc.
1710 North Leg Ct.
Augusta, GA 30909

Toll-free: 800-404-2675
Phone: 706-733-6120
www.naturalcork.com

Natural Cork Wall Tile is $^1/_8$" thick, 12" high x 24" wide, features a peel-and-stick application and comes prefinished with a wax coating in 6 patterns.

Countertops

Countertops have particular performance demands because of their high use and exposure to water, especially at the seams of sink cutouts and backsplashes. A variety of suitable countertop products with environmental advantages are available. In addition to the products listed here, ceramic tile or natural linoleum surfaces offer green countertop options.

Certified Butcher Block Countertops

Endura Wood Products, Ltd.
1303 S.E. 6th Ave.
Portland, OR 97214

Phone: 503-233-7090
www.endurawood.com

Endura Wood Products manufactures and installs a number of butcher block products including tables, countertops, end-grain chopping blocks, and rolling kitchen carts from FSC-certified domestic and exotic hardwoods. Species offered include hard rock maple, Oregon white oak, Pacific madrone, cherry, myrtlewood, and machiche.

IceStone Countertops

IceStone, Inc.
Brooklyn Navy Yard
65 Flushing Ave., Bldg. 12
Brooklyn, NY 11025

Phone: 718-624-4900
www.icestone.biz

IceStone™ is a terrazzo-like countertop material made from a minimum of 75% recycled glass, 17–18% type-3 white portland cement, and small quantities of proprietary ingredients. Although IceStone would not divulge the process they use to avoid the alkali-silica reaction (ASR) that typically affects concrete with glass aggregate, they claim it does not involve the use of epoxy, which is sometimes used for this purpose. IceStone is produced in standard $1^1/_4$"-thick , 4' x 8' slabs. A 2"-thick product is also available. The slabs are shipped to local stone-finishing companies for cutting, routing, sandblasting, and polishing. IceStone is available in 18 standard colors, based largely on the color of the recycled glass used in the product. The cement matrix can also be pigmented, providing a wide range of color options.

Recycled-Paper Countertops

All Paper Recycling, Inc.
502 Fourth Ave. NW, Ste. 7
New Prague, MN 56071

Phone: 952-758-6577
www.shetkastone.com

All Paper Recycling manufactures tables and countertops using a patented process and 100% recycled paper. The material, called Shetkastone, can be recycled over and over again through the same process. This process uses no binders or adhesives, just pre-consumer and post-consumer waste paper, including items such as wax paper and phone books. The material has a Class A fire rating without the addition of chemicals and a 400-pound screw test. The company will provide samples and additional information for a $35 fee.

Syndecrete

Syndesis
2908 Colorado Ave.
Santa Monica, CA 90404

Phone: 310-829-9932
www.syndesisinc.com

Syndecrete® is a cement-based, precast lightweight composite containing fly ash and post-industrial recycled polypropylene fiber waste from carpet manufacturing.
To date, Syndecrete has developed 11 standard colors and a library of over 500 custom colors and mix designs. Syndecrete has half the weight and twice the compressive strength of standard concrete. The product is more resistant to chipping and cracking than conventional concrete, tile, or stone and has a workability more akin to wood than cement-based materials. Applications of this high-end product include: countertops, table tops, tiles, fireplace surrounds, landscape elements, sinks, bathtubs, and showers. The manufacturer has certified the following recycled-content levels (by weight): total recovered material 80% typical, 15% guaranteed; post-consumer material 40% typical, 15% guaranteed.

Vetrazzo

Counter Production
710 Bancroft Way
Berkeley, CA 94710

Toll-free: 866-809-4898
Phone: 510-843-6916
www.counterproduction.
com

Photo: Fernando Aguila

Vetrazzo countertops have mixed colors of recycled-glass chips embedded in a masonry binder for a terrazzo-like look. Vetrazzo is available in a wide variety of colors and in thicknesses up to 1$\frac{1}{2}$". The manufacturer has certified the following recycled-content levels (by weight): total recovered material 90% typical, 80% guaranteed; post-consumer material 90% typical, 80% guaranteed.

Custom Cabinets

Environmental features to look for with custom cabinets include FSC-certified wood, recovered-fiber wood products, ag-fiber panels, low-formaldehyde wood products, and low-VOC finishes. (Certification to Forest Stewardship Council—FSC—standards involves third-party evaluation and monitoring of sustainable forestry practices.)

Green Leaf Series

Cabinet King, Inc.
15375 Brookpark Rd.
Brookpark, OH 44142

Toll-free: 877-422-2463
Phone: 216-898-1230
www.cabinetking.com

Photo: Schuman Architectural Photography

Cabinet King's Green Leaf series uses PrimeBoard® ag-fiber particleboard (made from agricultural residue fibers and a formaldehyde-free binder) for sides, tops, bottoms, backs, shelving, and drawer bottoms, and FSC-certified wood for frames and drawers (sides and backs). Finishes are either Safecoat® Acrylacq or PrimeBoard's all-paper-based melamine. Forbo Marmoleum® will also soon be available as a countertop option. Adhesives are water-based. Cabinet King is also a dealer for cabinets made by other companies, as well as a line of green building products including PrimeBoard, Marmoleum, Safecoat finishes, Titebond® solvent-free construction adhesive, and Bonded Logic recycled cotton insulation.

Greenline

Forefront Designs
1075 Shelley St.
Springfield, OR 97477

Toll-free: 888-245-0075
Phone: 541-747-4884
www.forefrontdesigns.com

Greenline builds cabinets, casework, and countertops using wheatboard structural cores, FSC-certified veneers, high pressure plastic laminates, and various ISO 14001-certified materials. Casework is formaldehyde- and solvent-free and is suitable for laboratories, hospitals, schools, assisted living centers, and other commercial projects. Environmental interior design and consultation are available.

Neil Kelly Naturals Collection

Neil Kelly Cabinets
804 N. Alberta
Portland, OR 97217

Phone: 503-335-9207
www.neilkellycabinets.
com

The Neil Kelly "Naturals Collection" is an award-winning cabinet line that features formaldehyde-free wheatboard case material, low-VOC finishes, and optional FSC-certified lumber doors/drawers. Unlimited customization and virtually any desired upgrade are available.

Fiberboard and Particleboard Panels

Medium-density fiberboard (MDF) is usually manufactured from sawmill waste and a urea-formaldehyde (UF) binder. Formaldehyde, a known human carcinogen, offgasses from UF binders and can be especially problematic for chemically sensitive individuals. Most of the following MDF products are formaldehyde-free, contain FSC-certified wood content, or are made from recovered waste fiber. (Certification to Forest Stewardship Council—FSC—standards involves third-party evaluation and monitoring of sustainable forestry practices.) Particleboard is made from larger wood fiber particles than MDF, and has a lower density; and it doesn't mill as cleanly. The particleboard products listed here are low- or zero-formaldehyde products or are made from FSC-certified wood fiber or ag-fiber (such as straw).

Certified Particleboard

Collins Products, LLC
P.O. Box 16
Klamath Falls, OR 97601

Toll-free: 800-547-1793
Phone: 541-885-3289
www.collinswood.com

The CollinsWood® line includes FSC-certified particleboard, FSC-certified TruWood® engineered (hardboard) siding, and FSC-certified hardwood and softwood lumber and millwork. In 1993, Collins Pine Company became the first privately owned timber management company to receive FSC certification in the U.S. CollinsWood has been a leader in the forest and wood products certification movement since its inception.

Medex and Medite II

SierraPine Ltd.
3010 Lava Ridge Ct. #220
Roseville, CA 95661

Toll-free: 800-676-3339
Phone: 916-772-3422
www.sierrapine.com

SierraPine's Medex MDF, for use in high-moisture applications, and Medite II MDF, for interior use, are manufactured with a polyurea resin matrix adhesive rather than conventional formaldehyde-based resins. (Medite FR, a Class 1, fire-retardant MDF panel, is now manufactured with formaldehyde.) SierraPine has earned certification from Scientific Certification Systems (SCS) for using up to 100% recovered and recycled wood fiber for MDF.

Resincore-I Particleboard

Rodman Industries
P.O. Box 88
Oconomowoc, WI 53066

Phone: 262-569-5820
www.rodmanindustries.com

Resincore-I particleboard is manufactured with phenol-formaldehyde binders, which result in lower formaldehyde offgassing and impart greater moisture resistance to the product than particleboard produced with urea-formaldehyde binders.

Versaroc Cement-Bonded Particleboard

U.S. Architectural Products
55 Industrial Cir.
Lincoln, RI 28730

Toll-free: 800-243-6677
www.architecturalproducts.com

Versaroc® from U.S. Architectural Products is a structural cement-bonded particle board made with mineralized wood particles and portland cement. It can be worked with typical carpentry tools; fasteners should be treated for corrosion resistance. The formaldehyde-free, termite-resistant, noncombustible product is available in stock nominal ("uncalibrated") thicknesses of 10 mm ($^3/_8$"), 12 mm ($^1/_2$"), and 19 mm ($^3/_4$"); several other thicknesses may be special-ordered. "Calibrated" stock is sanded to more precise thicknesses for applications requiring tighter tolerances. These boards are available square-edged in 48" widths; or tongue-and-groove in 46$^1/_2$" widths for thickness of 16 mm ($^5/_8$") or more. Stocked length is 96"; shorter or longer boards (up to 120") are available by special order, as are widths less than 48" square or 46$^1/_2$" tongue-and-groove. All orders can be factory-sealed on all surfaces with an acrylic paint sealer.

Weyerhaeuser Particleboard and MDF

Weyerhaeuser
P.O. Box 9777
Federal Way, WA 98063-9777

Toll-free: 800-525-5440
Phone: 253-924-2345
www.weyerhaeuser.com

Weyerhaeuser's full line of U.S.-made composite panel products (formerly manufactured by Willamette) has been certified by Scientific Certification Systems (SCS) to contain recycled and recovered wood fiber. Duraflake Particleboard, Eugene MDF, Simsboro Particleboard, Malvern MDF, and Bennettsville MDF have been certified by SCS to contain 100% recycled and recovered wood. The manufacturer reports the bulk of this recycled content to be post-industrial, with Duraflake Particleboard and Eugene MDF containing a minimum of 5% and 25% post-consumer content, respectively.

Fiberboard Millwork

Pressures on timber supply are especially acute for high-visibility, solid-wood products like window sash and molding, which have traditionally been produced from old-growth trees. Medium-density fiberboard (MDF) molding made from post-industrial wood wastes is an excellent substitute for paint-grade moldings. The consistent quality and economical price of MDF moldings is broadening its market share. Some MDF is available with nonformaldehyde binder.

Certified Veneer-Faced Trim

S. J. Morse Company
Rte. 50
P.O. Box 600
Capon Bridge, WV 26711

Phone: 304-856-3423
www.sjmorse.com

The S. J. Morse Company now offers custom-made, veneer-faced trim in six FSC-certified species—three domestics: oak, cherry, and maple; and three relatively unknown Brazilian species: Amapa, Taurari Vermelho, and Cupiuba. The trim is available in any specified width and can be provided with a clear finish (a water-based option is available) or be left unfinished for custom staining and finishing. FSC-certified, recycled-content, or ag-fiber cores are offered, including formaldehyde-free options. Other custom veneer products are also available FSC-certified: window seats, wide window and door jambs, column wraps, ceiling panels, and kitchen cabinet door faces.

Medite MDF Molding

SierraPine Ltd.
3010 Lava Ridge Ct. #220
Roseville, CA 95661

Toll-free: 800-676-3339
Phone: 916-772-3422
www.sierrapine.com

SierraPine's Medite Division produces MDF moldings that are made with a formaldehyde-free MDI binder and are factory-primed with a water-based paint. SierraPine moldings are manufactured in knot-free, blemish-free, 16' lengths. SierraPine has earned certification from Scientific Certification Systems (SCS) for using up to 100% recovered and recycled wood fiber for MDF.

Fire-Retardant-Treated Wood and Ag-Fiber

Some of these fire-resistant products are available with formaldehyde-free binders.

Pyroblock Fire-Retardant Particleboard, MDF, and Plywood

Panel Source International
18 Rayborn Cres., Ste. 101
St. Albert, AB T8N 5C1 Canada

Toll-free: 877-464-7246
Phone: 780-458-1007
www.panelsource.net

Pyroblock® PB Plus ag-fiber Particleboard Pyroblock MDF Plus and Plywood Plus Fire-Retardant Panels are urea formaldehyde-free. Unlike conventional fire-retardant panels, in which a fire-retardant chemical is incorporated throughout the product, Pyroblock Panels rely on an intumescent coating. This coating expands and chars when subjected to heat and thereby insulates and protects the substrate from fire. According to the company, the product is inert when cured. Pyroblock meets applicable flame spread standards (ASTM E-84(01) in the U.S., and CAN/ULC 102-M in Canada). Available sizes are 4' or 5' wide by 8', 9', or 10' long by $1/8$" to $1^1/4$" thick. Product is also available as an FSC-certified product

Gypsum Board

Gypsum board, or drywall, is typically made with 100% recycled, unbleached paper facings that are bonded without adhesives onto a gypsum core. Though mined virgin gypsum is still widely used in gypsum board production, recycled and synthetic gypsum comprise an increasing portion of product manufacturing. Recycled gypsum board is derived from in-plant scrap and some clean construction waste; advances in recycling technology allow separation of the paper from the core so that each may be recycled separately. Synthetic, or flue-gas, gypsum is a waste product obtained from stack scrubbers that remove sulfur from coal-fired power plant emissions. (In these scrubbers, calcium carbonate is converted to calcium sulfate, or gypsum.) Synthetic gypsum may replace up to 100% of the natural gypsum in drywall. Each of the companies listed here has at least one U.S. plant operating or planned that uses 100% synthetic gypsum. Reducing waste is an important consideration in green building projects; 54"-wide gypsum board may allow more efficient wall coverage in rooms with 9' ceilings. Be aware that paper facings may provide a medium for mold growth in conditions of high humidity and low air circulation; some drywall is made with integral cellulose or fiberglass fibers instead of paper facing to eliminate mold risk.

Fiberock Gypsum Fiber Panels

USG Corporation
125 S. Franklin St.
Chicago, IL 60606

Toll-free: 800-874-4968
Phone: 312-606-4000
www.usg.com

Fiberock™ Abuse-Resistant Gypsum Fiber Panels incorporate perlite and recycled newsprint into the synthetic gypsum core. Unlike standard drywall, there are no paper facings. The resulting fiber-reinforced panels are stronger, stiffer, and denser than regular drywall, provide better screw/nail retention and increased thermal mass. This product has a total recycled content exceeding 95% by weight.

Gold Bond Gypsum Wallboard

National Gypsum Company
2001 Rexford Rd.
Charlotte, NC 28211

Toll-free: 800-628-4662
Phone: 704-365-7300
www.national-gypsum.com

National Gypsum manufactures Gold Bond® gypsum wallboard with synthetic gypsum in some plants.

G-P Gypsum Board

G-P Gypsum Corporation
55 Park Pl.
Atlanta, GA 30303

Phone: 404-652-4000
www.gp.com/gypsum

G-P Gypsum operates 18 manufacturing plants for gypsum board. The Wheatfield, Indiana and Tacoma, Washington plants use synthetic gypsum, while the remaining plants use varying amounts of recycled gypboard. The manufacturer has certified the following recycled-content levels (by weight): total recovered material 8% typical, 6% guaranteed; post-consumer material 0% typical, 0% guaranteed.

Sheetrock Brand Gypsum Panels

USG Corporation
125 S. Franklin St.
Chicago, IL 60606

Toll-free: 800-874-4968
Phone: 312-606-4000
www.usg.com

Sheetrock® Brand Gypsum Panels are USG's standard drywall product. USG uses flue gas desulfurization (FGD) gypsum, an industrial waste product derived from pollution-control equipment at coal-fired power plants, in its standard drywall product. The company used over 3 million tons of this material in 2001—more than any other wallboard manufacturer. However, this FGD gypsum content varies day-to-day and plant-to-plant due to availability. The recycled content of their boards nationwide for 2001 was over 36% by weight, according to the company. In addition, all USG wallboard uses 100% recycled (post-consumer) paper. Seven of their plants use 90%-plus FGD gypsum in the board they produce. Seven additional plants use a blend of FGD and mined gypsum.

Temple-Inland Gypsum

Temple-Inland Forest Products
303 S. Temple Dr.
P.O. Drawer N
Diboll, TX 75941

Toll-free: 800-231-6060
Phone: 936-829-5511
www.templeinland.com

Temple-Inland produces over 60% of its wallboard using synthetic gypsum derived from flue-gas desulphurization. All wallboard coming from their Tennessee and Arkansas plants has an SCS-certified recycled content of 99% with the exception of sheathing and moisture-resistant wallboard, which is certified to contain 95% recycled content. Wallboard can be specified from these plants and comes with endtapes designating production source. The manufacturer has certified the following recycled-content levels (by weight): total recovered material 99% typical, 95% guaranteed; post-consumer material 6% typical, 4% guaranteed.

Gypsum Board Accessories

This section includes environmentally attractive accessories for gypsum board construction, such as low-VOC joint compounds and drywall clips or "stops." Using drywall clips at corners and partition-wall intersections allows a reduction in steel or wood studs, saving resources and reducing costs. Used at corners, drywall clips allow slight movement of drywall panels to accommodate expansion and contraction of framing members, minimizing cracking and call-backs. In addition, drywall clips and stops do not take up space that insulation could occupy in wall cavities where interior partitions meet exterior walls.

ButtHanger and EZ-Backer

Flat-Fast, Inc.
1122 Siddonsburg Rd.
Mechanicsburg, PA 17055

Toll-free: 888-292-1002
Phone: 717-766-6084
www.butthanger.com

The ButtHanger, a simple device made from wood strapping and metal cross pieces, eliminates the single most problematic aspect of interior finish work—the drywall butt joint. By enabling the laying out and hanging of board finish ends to space rather than to framing, the Butthanger bends the butt ends inward about $1/8$". This changes a labor-intensive and difficult 3'-wide mud joint into a quick and easy 1'-wide one while both reducing cut-off waste and joint compound used for butt joints. EZ-Backer is an all-steel commercial version of the ButtHanger.

DC1 Drywall Clip

USP Structural Connectors
703 Rogers Dr.
Montgomery, MN 56069

Toll-free: 800-328-5934
Phone: 507-364-7333
www.uspconnectors.com

The DC1 Drywall Clip is a galvanized steel clip that is installed with nails.

Murco M100 Joint Compound

Murco Wall Products
2032 N. Commerce
Fort Worth, TX 76106

Toll-free: 800-446-7124
Phone: 817-626-1987
www.murcowall.com

Murco Wall Products manufactures a powdered all-purpose joint cement and texture compound formulated with inert fillers and natural binders only. It does not contain any preservatives or slow-releasing compounds and is zero-VOC. M100 mixes easily with tap water.

No-Nail and Stud Claw

Stud Claw USA
5370 Chestnut Ridge Rd.
Orchard Park, NY 14127

Phone: 716-662-7877

No-Nail™ is a sheet metal drywall clip that creates floating corners. It friction-fits to one sheet of drywall and grips the adjoining sheet with its own spurs. This clip can accommodate non-right-angle applications such as cathedral ceilings. The Stud Claw is a metal wire clip that grips two-by wood framing with spurs and also facilitates floating corners. Two sizes are available: GC-15 ($1^1/_2$") for single top plates and studs, and GC-30 (3") for double plates.

Prest-on Corner Clips

Prest-on Company
312 Lookout Pt.
Hot Springs, AR 71913

Toll-free: 800-323-1813
Phone: 501-767-3855
www.prest-on.com

Prest-on's steel Corner Clips are "pressed" onto the drywall and nailed or screwed to the structural member. This product is not designed for floating corners.

QuikSand Sanding Blocks

Earthstone International
555 Republic Dr., Ste. 440
Plano, TX 75074

Toll-free: 888-994-6327
www.goearthstone.com

Earthstone® QuikSand®, made with limestone and 96% post-consumer recycled glass, is a hand-held, self-sharpening, pumice-like block for smoothing and feathering drywall joint compound or spackling, or removing adhesives and other imperfections from unfinished or finished drywall surfaces. The blocks may be used wet or dry. Used dry, they produce less airborne dust than sandpaper or screens. The porous material won't clog or rip, according to the manufacturer. Versions of this product are also available for rough wood, painted surfaces, and rusted metal.

Simpson Drywall Stop (DS)

Simpson Strong-Tie
Connectors
4120 Dublin Blvd., Ste. 400
Dublin, CA 94568

Toll-free: 800-999-5099
Phone: 925-560-9000
www.strongtie.com

The Simpson Drywall Stop (DS)
is a galvanized steel product that installs with nails.

The Nailer

The Millennium Group, Inc.
P.O. Box 1848
Estes Park, CO 80517

Toll-free: 800-280-2304
Phone: 970-663-1200
www.thenailer.com

The Nailer® is a 100% recycled-content, high-density polyethylene (HDPE) plastic drywall stop or backer. The Nailer installs with flat-head nails or staples and the standard component "Tec" screw for steel studs. Drywall may be screwed or glued to The Nailer or may simply be floated behind the adjacent drywall sheet. The Nailer allows for full-size friction fit insulation in wall cavities and can reduce cracking due to truss uplift.

Paver Tile

see *Flooring & Floorcoverings: Paver Tile*

Plastic Paneling

Recycled plastic paneling is an appropriate use for some of the various post-consumer plastic materials entering the waste stream—in particular, high-density polyethylene (HDPE) from milk and detergent bottles. Plastic materials are resistant to water and microbial growth, making them appropriate for wet locations such as bathrooms and industrial or agricultural facilities.

Eco Panels

Recycled Plastics, Inc.
609 County Rd. 82 NW
Garfield, MN 56332

Phone: 320-834-2293
www.gipo-rpi.com

Eco Panels are extruded sheets made from 100% recycled HDPE. Depending upon specific color patterns, Eco Panels contain 0–50%

post-industrial recycled HDPE, with the balance being post-consumer recycled. Eco Panels are available in 10 custom colors as well as black and white, and measure 4' x 8' in thicknesses from $1/8$" to $3/4$". They can be cut, sanded, routed, milled, drilled and otherwise handled with conventional wood and metal working tools and machines. In addition, the material can be shaped by thermoforming and welding.

EPS Plastic Plywood

Engineered Plastic Systems
740 B Industrial Dr.
Cary, IL 60013

Phone: 847-462-9001
www.epsplasticlumber.com

Environmental Plastic Systems (EPS) manufactures plastic "plywood" from 100% recycled HDPE (typical post-consumer content 100%). The product is available in white only and in thicknesses of $3/8$", $1/2$", $3/4$", 1", and $1 1/8$". All EPS plastic products are covered by a 50-year limited warranty.

Origins

Yemm & Hart Ltd.
1417 Madison 308
Marquand, MO 63655

Phone: 573-783-5434
www.yemmhart.com

Yemm & Hart manufactures several types of recycled HDPE-plastic panels. The Origins line of panels, made from milk jugs and detergent bottles, is available in 21 patterns and 30 solid colors. Origins comes in 4' x 8' and 5' x 10' sheets in thicknesses from $1/8$" to 2", as well as toilet and shower partitions and sign stock. The manufacturer has certified the following recycled-content levels (by weight): total recovered material 100% typical, 100% guaranteed; post-consumer material 100% typical, 100% guaranteed.

Phoenix Recycled Plastic Panels

Phoenix Recycled Plastics
220 Washington St.
Norristown, PA 19401

Phone: 610-277-3900
www.plasticlumberyard.com

Phoenix Recycled Plastics manufactures plastic sheeting from 100% recycled plastic. The black or white panels come in 4' x 8' sheets in $1/8$", $1/4$", $3/8$", and $1/2$" thicknesses and 4' x 10' sheets in a $1/2$" thickness.

Plastic Panels

Coon Manufacturing, Inc.
708 N.E. 115th St.
P.O. Box 108
Spickard, MO 64679

Toll-free: 800-843-1532
Phone: 660-485-6299
www.coonmfginc.com

Coon Manufacturing markets their recycled plastic products for agricultural construction applications. Their plastic sheet goods are rugged, smooth or corrugated, recycled high-density polyethylene panels available in various sizes. Coon complements their white panels with plastic molding products and stainless steel hardware.

Plastic Panels

Iowa Plastics, Inc.
322 N. Main Ave.
Sioux Center, IA 51250

Phone: 712-722-0692

Iowa Plastics manufactures 4' x 8' panels in thicknesses from $1/16$" to $1/2$". Panels come in white and black and are made from 98% post-consumer recycled HDPE. Custom sizes are also available. The manufacturer has certified the following recycled-content levels (by weight): post-consumer material 98% typical, 98% guaranteed.

Sandhill Plastics Sheeting

Sandhill Plastics
119 W. 19th St.
Kearney, NE 68848

Phone: 308-236-5025

Sandhill Plastics manufactures plastic sheeting of 100% post-consumer HDPE used primarily for agricultural applications. Standard sheets measure 4' x 8' in thicknesses ranging from $1/16$" to $5/8$".

Prefinished Panels

The following products are an eclectic assortment of unusual prefinished panels that offer an alternative to traditional prefinished paneling. These are made with recycled content, nontoxic binders, agricultural-waste fiber such as straw, and/or FSC-certified wood. Certification to Forest Stewardship Council (FSC) standards involves third-party evaluation and monitoring of sustainable forestry practices.

DesignWall, NovaCork, and Burlap Panels

Homasote Company
932 Lower Ferry Rd.
P.O. Box 7240
West Trenton, NJ 08628

Toll-free: 800-257-9491
Phone: 609-883-3300
www.homasote.com

DesignWall®, NovaCork®, and Burlap Panels all consist of a Homasote 100% recycled newspaper fiber and paraffin binder substrate with various decorative coverings. DesignWall is a substrate of Class A fire-rated N.C.F.R. board wrapped in Class A fire-rated Guilford of Maine fabric covering. NovaCork is available as a Class A board and is covered with cork veneer. Burlap Panels are standard 440 Homasote covered with burlap. All three products are available in 4' x 8' and 4' x 10' panels.

Environ Biocomposite, Dakota Burl, and Biofiber Wheat

Phenix Biocomposites, LLC
P.O. Box 609
Mankato, MN 56002

Toll-free: 800-324-8187
Phone: 507-388-3434
www.phenixbiocomposites.com

Environ® is a biocomposite panel containing recycled newsprint, soy flour, pigment, and a water-based catalyst that converts the soy flour into a resin. This tough material looks like granite and works like hardwood. It is not appropriate for moisture-prone applications. Dakota Burl™ composite panels are made primarily from post-process, sunflower-seed hulls. Biofiber™ panels are made from finely chopped post-harvest wheat straw combined with a high-performance urethane resin. All the panels come in standard 4' x 8' sheets in $1/2$", $3/4$", and 1" thicknesses.

Meadoboard Straw Panels

Meadowood Industries, Inc.
33242 Red Bridge Rd.
Albany, OR 97321

Phone: 541-259-1303
www.meadowoodindustries.com

Meadoboard™ is a formaldehyde-free rye grass straw panel available in 4' x 8' sheets from $1/8$" to 1" thick. This coarse-textured interior finish material can be custom-molded into various shapes. Meadowood is not an M3-rated structural panel product. Rye grass straw is an agricultural waste product from grass seed production.

Tricel Honeycomb

Tricel Corp.
2100 Swanson Ct.
Gurnee, IL 60031

Toll-free: 800-352-3300
Phone: 847-336-1321
www.tricelcorp.com

Tricel Honeycomb recycled-content paper core panels have either plywood, foil, or paper board exteriors bonded with phenolic resins.

Unicor

National Shelter Products, Inc.
22526 S.E. 64th Pl., Ste. 230
Issaquah, WA 98027

Toll-free: 800-552-7775
Phone: 425-557-7968

Unicor™ wallboard is made from recycled corrugated containers and bottle carrier stock from the beverage industry bonded with PVA (white glue) adhesive. Unicor is mainly used as a sheathing panel in RV, manufactured housing, and residential construction applications. It is not rated for use as a shear panel.

Reclaimed Millwork

As the demands on forest resources have increased, nonforest sources of wood have grown in importance. Reclaimed wood is usually salvaged from buildings slated for demolition, abandoned railroad trestles, and "sinker logs" that sank decades ago during river-based log drives. It can also be from trees that have been recently harvested from urban or suburban areas (such as disease-killed trees). Reclaimed wood is often available in species, coloration, and wood quality not available in newly harvested timber. In some cases, reclaimed wood suppliers have only limited quantities with matching coloration or weathering patterns; ample lead time and accurate materials estimates can help ensure the availability of the desired wood. Lowering the uniformity standards for finished wood can also increase the potential for use of reclaimed wood. Environmentally desirable because it isn't tied to recent timber harvesting, reclaimed wood is a reuse of materials which can reduce the quantity of material going into landfills. As with other resources, the supply of reclaimed wood is limited. Efficient and appropriate use of reclaimed wood is important for its long-term availability. Be aware that reclaimed wood may contain lead paint; testing is recommended if lead paint residue is suspected.

Classic American Heart Pine Millwork

Mayse Woodworking Co.
319 Richardson Rd.
Lansdale, PA 19446

Toll-free: 888-566-4532
Phone: 215-822-8307

Mayse Woodworking offers reclaimed heart pine millwork including trim, moldings, stair treads, and risers.

Millwork from Urban Trees

CitiLog™
6 Bywood Ln.
Ewing, NJ 08628

Phone: 609-538-8680
www.citilogs.com

CitiLog, also known as D. Stubby Warmbold, is SmartWood-certified for the harvesting of trees in urban areas of New Jersey and Pennsylvania. Wood is sent by rail to Amish craftsmen in central Pennsylvania who take extra care to turn the lesser graded wood into higher quality products such as flooring, lumber, custom architectural millwork, furniture, and kitchen cabinets. Where appropriate, wood is now harvested using horses.

Millwork from Urban Trees

Urban Hardwoods
5021 Colorado Ave. S
Seattle, WA 98134

Phone: 206-766-8199
www.urbanhardwoods.com

Urban Hardwoods salvages urban trees from within a 50-mile radius of the company and mills them into furniture, flooring, and other millwork. Urban Hardwoods continually designs products to make use of manufacturing "fall-down." The remainder of the waste material is given away or sold as firewood, or is used for heating their facility. The company utilizes plant-based solvents, when needed, to clean tools and machinery, and ships 99% of their products blanket-wrapped (all blankets are reused). They will also accept products back at the end of their useful life and refurbish them or reuse the material to manufacture new products. The company is seeking certification from SmartWood under the "Rediscovered Wood" category.

Reclaimed and Urban-Harvested Millwork

Jackel Enterprises
347 Locust St.
Watsonville, CA 95076

Toll-free: 800-711-9663
Phone: 831-768-3880
www.jackelenterprises.com

Jackel Enterprises processes urban and suburban forestry—the low-impact removal of city-owned and back-yard trees, ranch maintenance, and the like. Species include redwood, Douglas fir, Monterey cypress, black acacia, and California black walnut. Jackel also processes forest floor salvage from private parties, primarily old growth redwood, as well as milling recycled hardwoods and softwoods, including Douglas fir, redwood, western red cedar, heart pine, bald cypress, walnut, oak, and hickory. For the next year the mill that supplies their fine-grain, vertical Douglas fir is milling SmartWood-certified lumber purchased from the Hoopa Indians.

Reclaimed Millwork

Aged Woods / Yesteryear Floorworks Company
2331 E. Market St.
York, PA 17402

Toll-free: 800-233-9307
Phone: 717-840-0330
www.agedwoods.com

Aged Woods® / Yesteryear Floorworks Company™ is a full-service mill that uses reclaimed, kiln-dried wood to produce stair parts, moldings, cabinetry, and paneling. They salvage their materials from barns that are typically between 75 and 200 years old. Available species include American chestnut, longleaf heart pine, maple, cherry, walnut, hemlock, hickory, poplar, pine, and oak.

Reclaimed Millwork

Albany Woodworks, Inc.
P.O. Box 729
Albany, LA 70711-0729

Toll-free: 1-800-551-1282
Phone: 225-567-1155
www.albanywoodworks.com

Albany Woodworks mills various architectural woodwork products of reclaimed woods including heart pine and heart cypress.

Reclaimed Millwork

Architectural Timber and Millwork
P.O. Box 719
Hadley, MA 01035

Toll-free: 800-430-5473
Phone: 413-586-3045
www.atimber.com

Architectural Timber and Millwork specializes in custom architectural millwork fabricated from reclaimed wood. They source their materials from different parts of the country, providing a widely varied species inventory.

Reclaimed Millwork

Big Timberworks, Inc.
P.O. Box 368
Gallatin Gateway, MT 59730

Phone: 406-763-4639
www.bigtimberworks.com

Big Timberworks sells siding, paneling, moldings, stair parts, flooring, cabinets, and beams manufactured from reclaimed and remilled lumber.

Reclaimed Millwork

Centre Mills Antique Floors
P.O. Box 16
Aspers, PA 17304

Phone: 717-334-0249
www.centremillsantiquefloors.com

Centre Mills Antique Floors salvages and remills a variety of hand-hewn wood products made from such species as chestnut, oak, white pine, and hemlock. Centre Mills also has 7 acres of architectural artifacts, including bricks, mantles, wavy glass, old doors, and used slates.

Reclaimed Millwork

Craftmark Reclaimed Wood, Inc.
P.O. Box 237
McMinnville, OR 97128

Phone: 503-472-6929
www.craftmarkinc.com

Craftmark Reclaimed Wood specializes in custom molding and stair treads utilizing reclaimed wood typically from deconstructed warehouse buildings that are 70–100 years old. Species include Douglas fir, heart pine, and white oak.

Reclaimed Millwork

Duluth Timber Co.
P.O. Box 16717
Duluth, MN 55816-0717

Phone: 218-727-2145
www.duluthtimber.com

Duluth Timber reclaims and remills mainly Douglas fir and longleaf yellow pine, but also redwood and cypress. Demolition and salvage of warehouses and sheep-shearing sheds in Australia has yielded a supply of Australian hardwoods such as jarrah and Mountain ash. Duluth has mills in Minnesota, California, and Washington.

Reclaimed Millwork

J. Hoffman Lumber Co.
1330 E. State St.
Sycamore, IL 60178

Phone: 630-513-6680

J. Hoffman Lumber Co. is the Midwest's only sawmill/millwork company specializing in reclaimed antique heart pine, Douglas fir, and white pine. Reclaimed lumber is remilled into flooring, siding, and other millwork.

Reclaimed Millwork

J. L. Powell & Co., Inc.
723 Pine Log Rd.
Whiteville, NC 28472

Toll-free: 800-227-2007
Phone: 910-642-8989
www.plankfloors.com

J. L. Powell & Co. specializes in custom architectural millwork, including stair parts, produced from reclaimed antique heart pine.

Reclaimed Millwork

Legacy Antique Woods
114 Sibley Rd.
Honeoye Falls, NY 14472

Phone: 585-624-1011
www.legacyantiquewoods.com

Legacy Antique Woods salvages timbers, boards, and decking from barns and industrial buildings. Material can be purchased "as is" or resawn into boardstock or molder blanks. Primary species offered are chestnut, oak, Douglas fir, heart pine, and white pine with other species typically available as well.

Reclaimed Millwork

Longleaf Lumber
70–80 Webster Ave.
Somerville, MA 02143

Phone: 617-625-3659
www.longleaflumber.com

Longleaf Lumber, founded in 1997, dismantles old buildings and remills antique timbers into millwork and flooring at the company's sawmill in the Boston area. Longleaf specializes in heart pine, but other salvaged woods such as chestnut, red and white oak, eastern white pine, and maple are often available from dismantled buildings around New England. Longleaf also sells unmilled reclaimed timbers and reclaimed barn siding. In addition to the sawmill, the company operates a retail store at their Webster Avenue location.

Reclaimed Millwork

Mountain Lumber
P.O. Box 289
Ruckersville, VA 22968

Toll-free: 800-445-2671
www.mountainlumber.com

Mountain Lumber provides an extensive list of mill services for their reclaimed antique woods, including heart pine, oak, and American chestnut. Millwork includes stair parts, moldings, countertops, and rough lumber for cabinetry and paneling.

Reclaimed Millwork

Pioneer Millworks
1180 Commercial Dr.
Farmington, NY 14425

Toll-free: 800-951-9663
Phone: 585-924-9970
www.pioneermillworks.com

Pioneer Millworks salvages timbers and remills Douglas fir, longleaf yellow pine, oak, redwood, chestnut, and white pine. They offer a number of molding profiles in addition to timbers, cabinetry, stair parts, flooring, and doors.

Reclaimed Millwork

Re-Tech Wood Products
1324 Russell Rd.
P.O. Box 215
Forks, WA 98331

Phone: 360-374-4141
www.retechwoodproducts.com

Re-Tech reclaims and remills timber for a wide variety of custom millwork and complete custom timber-frame packages for houses. They also make specialty cuts in timber to order.

Reclaimed Millwork

TerraMai
1104 Firenze
P.O. Box 696
McCloud, CA 96057

Toll-free: 800-220-9062
Phone: 530-964-2740
www.terramai.com

TerraMai (formerly Jefferson Recycled Woodworks) mills various architectural woodwork products of reclaimed woods.

Reclaimed Millwork

The G. R. Plume Co.
1373 W. Smith Rd., Ste. A-1
Ferndale, WA 98248

Phone: 360-384-2800

The G. R. Plume Co. produces custom architectural millwork and timbers fabricated from reclaimed Douglas fir.

Reclaimed Millwork

Trestlewood
694 N. 1890 W, Ste. 44A
P.O. Box 1728
Provo, UT 84601

Toll-free: 877-375-2779
Phone: 801-375-2779
www.trestlewood.com

Trestlewood deals exclusively in reclaimed wood. Their wood comes from the Lucin Cutoff railroad trestle, which crosses the Great Salt Lake, and other salvage projects. Trestlewood products include flooring, millwork, timbers, decking, and siding. Available species include Douglas fir, redwood, southern yellow pine, longleaf yellow pine, oak, and other hardwoods.

Reclaimed Millwork

Vintage Log and Lumber, Inc.
Glen Ray Rd.
P.O. Box 2F
Alderson, WV 24910

Toll-free: 877-653-5647
Phone: 304-445-2300
www.vintagelog.com

Vintage Log and Lumber salvages the materials in log cabins and timber-frame barns in Kentucky, Ohio, Pennsylvania, and West Virginia. The company's inventory includes salvaged redwood, chestnut, oak, pine, and poplar boards, beams, flooring, and split rails. They also sell complete hand-hewn log cabins and timber-frame barns.

Reclaimed Millwork

Vintage Material Supply Co.
4705 E. 5th St.
Austin, TX 78702

Phone: 512-386-6404
www.vintagematerialsupply.com

Vintage Material Supply Co. mills architectural woodwork products from reclaimed woods recovered from such sources as demolished buildings, ranch recovery, urban logging, and river bottoms. Reclaimed species include old-growth longleaf pine, sinker pine and cypress, and native Texas timbers. Products offered include post-and-beam frames, exposed trusses, entry doors, interior doors, windows, staircases, staircase parts, paneling, fireplace mantels, and custom furniture. The company also offers consulting services in vintage wood reclamation.

Reclaimed Millwork

Vintage Timberworks
47100 Rainbow Canyon Rd.
Temecula, CA 92592

Phone: 909-695-1003
www.vintagetimber.com

Vintage Timberworks offers millwork remilled from wood salvaged in the U.S., Canada, and Australia from buildings that are typically at least 70 years old. Typical species include Douglas fir, cedar, and redwood. The company also arranges for building demolition and material reclamation in the U.S. and Canada.

Reclaimed Millwork

What Its Worth, Inc.
P.O. Box 162135
Austin, TX 78716

Phone: 512-328-8837
www.wiwpine.com

What Its Worth specializes in vertical-grain longleaf heart pine flooring and millstock, along with posts and beams in both heart pine and Douglas fir. Their milled product is 100% heartwood, and the wood's harvesting usually predates 1925.

Reclaimed Paneling

Carlisle Restoration Lumber
1676 Rte. 9
Stoddard, NH 03464

Toll-free: 800-595-9663
Phone: 603-446-3937
www.wideplankflooring.com

Carlisle Restoration produces paneling from reclaimed antique pine, chestnut, and oak.

Reclaimed Paneling

Crossroads Recycled Lumber
57839 Road 225
P.O. Box 928
North Fork, CA 93643

Toll-free: 888-842-3201
Phone: 559-877-3645
www.crossroadslumber.com

Crossroads reclaimed wood paneling is available in 3" to 12" widths primarily in hemlock, pine, and Douglas fir.

Reclaimed Paneling and Trim

Resource Woodworks, Inc.
627 E. 60th St.
Tacoma, WA 98404

Phone: 253-474-3757
www.rwtimber.com

Resource Woodworks fills custom orders of reclaimed, remilled Douglas fir, cedar, and redwood paneling and trim.

Reclaimed-Wood Millwork

A Reclaimed Lumber Co.
9 Old Post Rd.
Madison, CT 06443

Phone: 203-214-9705
www.woodwood.com

A Reclaimed Lumber Co. salvages wood from old water and wine tanks, mill buildings, bridge timbers, river-recovery log operations, and other sources. This wood is custom-remilled into a variety of wood products, including plank flooring, siding, molding, paneling, wainscoting, and other millwork. Available species include black cherry and walnut, beech, chestnut, gray elm, rock maple, red and white oak, Eastern hemlock spruce, Douglas fir, and red, white, and yellow pine. Wood is sourced from all over the country, and much of their product is processed at their Connecticut mill, but the company makes an effort to provide locally available wood that they will process locally.

River-Reclaimed Wood Millwork

Goodwin Heart Pine Company
106 S.W. 109th Pl.
Micanopy, FL 32667

Toll-free: 800-336-3118
Phone: 352-466-0339
www.heartpine.com

Goodwin offers custom millwork made from antique heart pine and antique heart cypress reclaimed from Southern river bottoms. Decorative wood moldings are architecturally drawn and are designed to classic proportions. Stair treads, balusters, newels, and rails are also available.

Reclaimed Wood Stair Parts

Reclaimed wood stair parts are environmentally attractive because new trees don't have to be cut and material is diverted from the waste stream. Often the quality of reclaimed wood is superior to newly milled wood because the reclaimed material is from old-growth trees that are no longer available for harvest. Be aware that reclaimed wood may contain lead paint; testing is recommended if lead paint residue is suspected.

Reclaimed-Wood Stair Parts

A Reclaimed Lumber Co.
9 Old Post Rd.
Madison, CT 06443

Phone: 203-214-9705
www.woodwood.com

A Reclaimed Lumber Co. salvages wood from old water and wine tanks, mill buildings, bridge timbers, river-recovery log operations, and other sources and custom remills it into a variety of wood products including stair parts. Typical species include long leaf yellow pine, Douglas fir, oak, and chestnut. Wood is sourced from all over the country, and much of their product is processed at their Connecticut mill, but the company makes an effort to provide locally available wood that they will process locally.

Reclaimed-Wood Stair Parts

Aged Woods / Yesteryear Floorworks Company
2331 E. Market St.
York, PA 17402

Toll-free: 800-233-9307
Phone: 717-840-0330
www.agedwoods.com

Aged Woods® / Yesteryear Floorworks Company™ is a full-service mill that uses reclaimed, kiln-dried wood to produce stair parts, moldings, cabinetry, and paneling. They salvage their materials from barns usually from 75 to 200 years old. Available species include American chestnut, cherry, maple, walnut, hickory, hemlock, poplar, pine, and oak.

Reclaimed-Wood Stair Parts

Big Timberworks, Inc.
P.O. Box 368
Gallatin Gateway, MT 59730

Phone: 406-763-4639
www.bigtimberworks.com

Big Timberworks produces a variety of custom millwork products through their Wood Supply Division. Products include stair parts, railings, door and window parts, custom furniture, and trims.

Reclaimed-Wood Stair Parts

Endura Wood Products, Ltd.
1303 S.E. 6th Ave.
Portland, OR 97214

Phone: 503-233-7090
www.endurawood.com

Endura Wood Products currently has access to over 3.5 million board feet of Douglas fir that is being reclaimed from the old Portland Dry Dock #2. Also available is a limited supply of Douglas fir with a distinct red hue that has been reclaimed from maraschino cherry vats (to fabricate stair treads, this material would have to be edge-glued).

Reclaimed-Wood Stair Parts

J. L. Powell & Co., Inc.
723 Pine Log Rd.
Whiteville, NC 28472

Toll-free: 800-227-2007
Phone: 910-642-8989
www.plankfloors.com

J. L. Powell & Co. specializes in custom architectural millwork, including stair parts, produced from reclaimed antique heart pine.

Reclaimed-Wood Stair Parts

Mayse Woodworking Co.
319 Richardson Rd.
Lansdale, PA 19446

Toll-free: 888-566-4532
Phone: 215-822-8307

Mayse Woodworking offers reclaimed heart pine millwork including trim, moldings, stair treads, and risers in three styles: American Country, Signature, and Federal.

Reclaimed-Wood Stair Parts

Mountain Lumber
P.O. Box 289
Ruckersville, VA 22968

Toll-free: 800-445-2671
www.mountainlumber.com

Mountain Lumber provides an extensive list of mill services for their reclaimed antique woods, including heart pine, oak, and American chestnut. Millwork includes stair parts, moldings, countertops, and rough lumber for cabinetry and paneling.

Reclaimed-Wood Stair Parts

Pioneer Millworks
1180 Commercial Dr.
Farmington, NY 14425

Toll-free: 800-951-9663
Phone: 585-924-9970
www.pioneermillworks.com

Pioneer Millworks salvages timbers and remills Douglas fir, longleaf yellow pine, oak, redwood, chestnut, and white pine. They offer a number of molding profiles in addition to timbers, cabinetry, stair parts, flooring, and doors.

Reclaimed-Wood Stair Parts

Vintage Material Supply Co.
4705 E. 5th St.
Austin, TX 78702

Phone: 512-386-6404
www.vintagematerialsupply.com

Vintage Material Supply Co. mills staircase parts and fabricates complete staircases, including freestanding spirals, from reclaimed wood recovered from such sources as demolished buildings, ranch recovery, urban logging, and river bottoms. Species include primarily old-growth longleaf pine, cypress, mesquite, and walnut.

Reclaimed-Wood Stair Parts

What Its Worth, Inc.
P.O. Box 162135
Austin, TX 78716

Phone: 512-328-8837
www.wiwpine.com

What Its Worth can provide reclaimed longleaf yellow pine and Douglas fir to custom specs. Their milled product is 100% heartwood, and the wood's harvesting usually predates 1925.

River-Reclaimed Wood Stair Parts

Goodwin Heart Pine Company
106 S.W. 109th Pl.
Micanopy, FL 32667

Toll-free: 800-336-3118
Phone: 352-466-0339
www.heartpine.com

Goodwin offers a full line of stair parts made from antique heart pine and antique heart cypress reclaimed from Southern river bottoms. Stair treads can be solid or laminated, and a full range of standard balusters, newels, and rails is available.

Recycled-Glass Tile

A number of attractive specialty tiles are produced from recycled glass.

Architectural Accents

Aurora Glass
2345 W. Broadway
Eugene, OR 97402

Toll-free: 888-291- 9311
Phone: 541-681-3260
www.auroraglass.org

Aurora Glass Architectural Accents include glass tiles, rosette blocks, sconces, and drawer pulls made from 100% recycled glass. Aurora Glass is a program of St. Vincent de Paul of Lane County, Inc. The glass foundry's profits support homeless and low-income people through emergency services, housing, jobs, training, and other charitable endeavors. The manufacturer has certified the following recycled-content levels (by weight): total recovered material 100% typical, 100% guaranteed; post-consumer material 86% typical, 86% guaranteed.

Blazestone

Bedrock Industries
1401 W. Garfield
Seattle, WA 98119

Toll-free: 877-283-7625
Phone: 206-283-7625
www.bedrockindustries.com

Blazestone® tiles are made from 100% recycled glass, most of which is post-consumer content. They come in 2" x 2", 2" x 4", 4" x 4", 5" x 5", 5" x 10", and 4" hex sizes, as well as mosaic pieces. Color varies with the recycled glass materials used. Bedrock also makes architectural accents and non-architectural accessories from recycled glass. Three of the 28 colors offered are made exclusively from 100% post-industrial waste. For the others, the manufacturer has certified the following recycled-content levels (by weight): total recovered material 100% typical, 100% guaranteed; post-consumer material 50% typical, 50% guaranteed.

Oceanside Glass Tiles

Oceanside Glasstile Co.
2293 Cosmos Ct.
Carlsbad, CA 92009

Toll-free: 877-648-8222
Phone: 760-929-4000
www.glasstile.com

Oceanside produces four styles of tile all handcast from 85% post-consumer recycled glass. They are semi-transparent, have an iridescent surface, and are available in a range of colors. Tessera is available in 29 colors and 3 sizes. Casa California includes larger-format tiles with a full line of decoratives. Minerali is a specialty tile with wide color variation and a textured surface. Haiku features opal glass with Asian motifs.

Recycled-Glass Tiles

Sandhill Industries
6898 S. Supply Rd., Ste. 100
Boise, ID 83716

Phone: 208-345-6508
www.sandhillind.com

Sandhill Industries manufactures wall and floor tile from 100% post-industrial plate glass. The company's manufacturing process can produce both glossy and matte finishes, and results in no wastewater or air emissions. Tiles come in a standard variety of square, bar, and triangle sizes, as well as rail pieces and film-mounted mosaic patterns. A wide assortment of colors, shapes, and textures can be produced by special order. The manufacturer has certified the following recycled-content levels (by weight): total recovered material 100% typical, 100% guaranteed; post-consumer material 0% typical, 0% guaranteed.

Terra Classic and Terra Traffic

Terra Green Ceramics
1650 Progress Dr.
Richmond, IN 47374

Phone: 765-935-4760
www.terragreenceramics.com

Terra Green Ceramic Tiles are made with 58% recycled aviation glass. Terra Classic and Terra Traffic (slip-resistant) are each available in 17 colors, several sizes, and with a wide range of accessories.

Special Wall Coverings

Listings here include unusual wall covering products; look for recycled content or natural materials. Because large amounts of adhesive may be needed for some special wall coverings, low-VOC products are a high priority.

No-Flame Sisal Wallcovering

Design Materials, Inc.
241 S. 55th St.
Kansas City, KS 66106

Toll-free: 800-654-6451
Phone: 913-342-9796
www.dmikc.com

No-Flame Sisal Wallcovering is manufactured in Merida, Mexico. A natural fiber obtained from the Agave plant (Agave sisalana), sisal can be woven into durable, resilient, sound-absorbing, and tackable fabrics and textiles of various thicknesses. Its hydroscopic property helps modify a room's humidity without conducting static electricity. It can be directly applied to concrete masonry walls and other surfaces with a trowel-on adhesive. The sisal fiber for this product is treated with borax for fire retardance, dyed, spun into yarn, and woven into sheets with a boucle weave construction. The end-product is available in 12 colors. Design Materials also offers a zero-VOC adhesive.

Plaster in a Roll and Faster Plaster Underliner

Flexi-Wall Systems
208 Carolina Dr.
P.O. Box 89
Liberty, SC 29657-0089

Toll-free: 800-843-5394
Phone: 864-843-3104
www.flexiwall.com

Plaster in a Roll™ is a 35-mil-thick jute fabric wall covering impregnated with gypsum plaster and a factory-applied clear coating. It comes in 48"-wide rolls and can be applied to any rigid wall or ceiling surface. It is available in two textures: Classics, available in 16 colors; and Images, available in 10 colors. Flexi-Wall Adhesive #500, used to adhere the product to the surface, also crystallizes the gypsum. Faster Plaster™ Underliner is a similar 50-mil wall liner designed to be adhered to concrete or masonry as a substrate for painting, plastering, or application of a finish wall covering.

Stone Facing

see *Exterior Finish: Stone Facing*

Straw Interior Partition Panels

Straw, a byproduct of agricultural production, is gaining acceptance as a building material. Although its use in straw-bale houses is perhaps more widely recognized, compressed-straw panels and particleboard are becoming a more significant presence. The straw panels listed here are formed under high temperature between heavyweight kraft paper similar to that used in drywall. The 2"- to 4"-thick panels listed here are nonstructural, appropriate for interior partition walls and ceilings. They offer excellent sound control and have been used for decades in parts of Europe and Australia.

Easiboard/Easiwall Panels

Pierce Enterprises, Inc.
7208 S. Tucson Way, Ste. 120
Centennial, CO 80112

Toll-free: 866-447-8729
Phone: 303-792-0719

Easiwall panels, made from straw with fiberglass mesh and recycled-content kraft paper facings, provide a quick panelized system for interior partitioning of spaces. The panels are predrilled for electrical and communications wiring and are quickly installed with metal clips—no framing needed. Until their U.S. factory is completed, product is being supplied from manufacturing facilities abroad.

Prestowall

Affordable Building Systems LLC
2750 State Hwy. 160
Whitewright, TX 75491

Toll-free: 866-364-1198
Phone: 903-364-1198
www.affordablebuildingsystems.com

The Prestowall™ system is designed to replace standard stud and drywall construction for interior walls. These $2\frac{1}{4}$"-thick straw panels, measuring 4' wide, are bound together with only high heat and pressure using straw that originated from within a 20-mile radius of the manufacturing plant. The panels are tapered at the vertical edges to 2" with slots to receive biscuit connector disks for fastening panels together with screws. Joints can be taped and finished just like drywall. Two preformed $\frac{3}{4}$" channels per panel are available for wiring. Prestowall comes with a recycled paperboard finish and is resistant to mold, termites, and fire—with a Class A fire rating possible for commercial use and a Class B rating for residential use. Straw panels bound in this way are exceptionally strong and do not offgas pollutants.

Terrazzo

see *Flooring & Floorcoverings: Terrazzo*

Wall Covering

Textile and vinyl wall coverings are commonly used in commercial buildings for sound control and durability. Paper and vinyl "wallpaper" is widely used in homes. Avoiding vinyl (PVC) products is environmentally desirable for several reasons: interior finishes containing PVC can be a significant source of VOCs (tests have shown that VOC levels do drop off dramatically within weeks after installation); during disposal at the end of the wall covering's useful life, toxins (including dioxin) may be released if the material is incinerated improperly; combustion of PVC during accidental building fires can produce both dioxin and hydrochloric acid, which is extremely hazardous for firefighters and escaping building occupants; phthalate plasticizers in many vinyl products, including wall coverings, are also increasingly being identified as health concerns, particularly due to their ability to mimic natural hormones; finally, most vinyl wall coverings have very low moisture permeability, and there is potential for mold growth if moisture is trapped behind these wall coverings. The following synthetic and natural-fiber products are alternatives to PVC-based wall coverings. Using low-VOC adhesives is another important step in establishing good indoor air quality.

DuraWeave

Roos International Ltd. Inc.
1020 N.W. 6th St., Ste. H
Deerfield Beach, FL 33442

Toll-free: 800-888-2776
Phone: 954-429-3883
www.roosintl.com

DuraWeave™ Wallcovering, formerly distributed by Southeastern Sales Co., is a woven glass textile wall covering. Designed to be painted, DuraWeave is available in a large variety of textures and patterns and is washable (when painted), nontoxic, nonflammable, and repairable. DuraWeave allows walls to breathe and is particularly resistant to mold and mildew in high-moisture areas. It can be applied to nearly all wall surfaces, providing additional reinforcement and bridging minor imperfections and cracks.

EnVision

Tapeter Decorative Wall Solutions, LLC
1020 N.W. 6th St., Ste. H
Deerfield Beach, FL 33442

Toll-free: 877-867-4430
Phone: 954-429-8516

The EnVision™ lines of Type I and Type II commercial wallcovering are made from a nonwoven polyester-cellulose blend. These textured, breathable wallcoverings have a protective scrubbable finish and are designed expressly as an alternative to vinyl wallcovering. EnVision is produced with water based inks, and is Class A fire rated. Type I is available in 3 designs and 8 coordinating colors; Type II in 6 designs and 8 coordinating colors. Both types are available in a 54"-wide contract size.

Innvironments Collection

Innovations in Wallcoverings, Inc.
150 Varick St.
New York, NY 10013

Toll-free: 800-227-8053
Phone: 212-807-6300
www.innovationsusa.com

The Innvironments® Collection is comprised of breathable, Class A fire-rated wall coverings manufactured from materials such as sisal, cellulose, honeysuckle vines, and cork using water soluble inks that contain no heavy metals. The Allegory® Series, which has a Type II wall covering rating, is made from 50% wood fiber and 50% spun-woven polyester. Because Allegory is permeable, it avoids IAQ problems associated with nonpermeable wall coverings associated with PVC-based products.

Moment

Roos International Ltd. Inc.
1020 N.W. 6th St., Ste. H
Deerfield Beach, FL 33442

Toll-free: 800-888-2776
Phone: 954-429-3883
www.roosintl.com

Moment, formerly distributed by Tapeter Decorative Wall Solutions, is a sturdy (Type I) nonwoven, breathable wall covering designed expressly as an alternative to vinyl wall covering. A protective finish resists grease and stains while providing a scrubbable surface. Moment contains 38% cellulose fiber, 37% polyester, and 25% acrylic polymers; is entirely free of PVC and chlorine; and may be fully recycled. Moment is available in a range of 40 colors and carries a Class A fire rating.

Rauhsaser

Better Wall System
P.O. Box 567
Kenora, ON P9N 3X5 Canada

Toll-free: 800-461-2130
Phone: 807-548-2130

Rauhsaser (Rough Fiber), a thick wallpaper designed to be painted, is made from recycled paper with a wood chip texture. Five patterns are available. This product was previously sold in the U.S. under the name CoverAge.

Texturglas

Roos International Ltd. Inc.
1020 N.W. 6th St., Ste. H
Deerfield Beach, FL 33442

Toll-free: 800-888-2776
Phone: 954-429-3883
www.roosintl.com

Texturglas is a woven glass textile wall covering that is durable, flame-retardant, washable (when painted), and repairable. Texturglas allows walls to breath and is suitable for high-moisture areas. This products can be applied to nearly all wall surfaces providing additional reinforcement and bridging minor imperfections and cracks. Available in a large variety of patterns and textures, Texturglas can be painted approximately 8 times without losing its texture and provides an estimated service life of over 30 years.

The South Seas Collection

Newcastle Fabrics Corp.
80 Wythe Ave.
Brooklyn, NY 11211

Toll-free: 800-404-5560
Phone: 718-782-5560
www.newcastlefabrics.com

The South Seas Collection is a series of wall coverings made from hand-woven natural fibers in a wide variety of patterns.

Wall Covering Adhesives

Look for low-VOC adhesives. A large quantity of adhesive is required for wall coverings, especially when highly porous materials such as sisal are installed. Testing a small area of the covering with the chosen adhesive is recommended to determine whether offgassing or unpleasant odors will be a problem; this is especially important if any building occupants suffer from chemical sensitivity.

389 Natural Wallpaper Adhesive

Sinan Co.
P.O. Box 857
Davis, CA 95617

Phone: 530-753-3104
www.dcn.davis.ca.us/go/sinan

Sinan 389 Natural Wallpaper Adhesive is sold in powder form to be mixed with water. It is suitable for up to medium-weight paper-based wall coverings. Sinan products are made from all-natural, primarily plant-based materials, all of which are listed on the packaging.

Wood Restoration and Cleaning

Products included here are for cleaning, refinishing, preserving, and treating wood. Look for low-VOC fluids and chemicals, and products with high recycled content. Epoxy wood-consolidation products may be low-VOC, but the manufacture of epoxy utilizes bisphenol-A (BPA), a bioaccumulating chemical that many scientists believe is endocrine-disrupting even at very minute levels. (Endocrine-disrupting chemicals mimic natural hormones and may cause reproductive or developmental problems.)

PowerSand Sanding Blocks

Earthstone International
555 Republic Dr., Ste. 440
Plano, TX 75074

Toll-free: 888-994-6327
www.goearthstone.com

Earthstone® PowerSand®, made with limestone and 90% post-consumer recycled glass, are self-sharpening, pumice-like blocks or discs that attach to palm-sized power sanders or electric drills (with mount adapters). QuikSand® is a hand-held version of the product. In addition to smoothing wood, they can be used to remove finishes from most substrates without the need for stripping chemicals. The PowerSand blocks produce less airborne dust than sandpaper, and the porous material won't clog or rip. One block is the approximate equivalent of 25 sheets of sandpaper, so fewer change-outs are required.

This Space is Available for Your Notes

Caulks & Adhesives

Caulks and adhesives are applied wet, and then dry or cure in place. During that process a carrier evaporates, leaving the active agents in place. For most products this carrier was traditionally a volatile organic solvent that turned into an airborne volatile organic compound (VOC) as it evaporated. Air quality regulations and health concerns have driven a shift toward waterborne products. Evaporating water isn't a health concern, though other components of the coating or adhesive still generally release some VOCs.

Caulks and adhesives have their greatest effect on indoor air quality during and immediately after installation. The health hazard is particularly acute for installers. Most conventional products offgas VOCs, formaldehyde, and other chemicals that are added to enhance the performance or extend shelf-life of the product. Little scientific data is available on the health effects of many of these chemicals—and even less on the effects of exposure to a *combination* of such chemicals that may occur in buildings. Quality substitutions, which are lower in toxicity or nontoxic, are available for all of these products.

Even so-called zero-VOC materials may still release small amounts of organic compounds. People with chemical sensitivities should always test these products before applying them on their projects, or having them applied by workers. Aside from solvents with well-known health effects (such as benzene, toluene, or xylene), the scientific community offers little guidance on the distinction between acceptable and problematic VOCs.

In most categories, the GreenSpec criteria for "low-VOC" products is 50 grams per liter, which is well below even the most stringent VOC regulations in California.

Glue-down carpets and resilient flooring should be applied only with low-VOC adhesives. Alternative carpet fastening methods should also be considered—these include:

- tackless strips, commonly used in residential settings;

- a hook-and-loop (Velcro®-type) tape system that allows sections of carpet to be lifted and re-attached as needed;

- peel-and-stick adhesive systems, such as those used on modular carpet tiles—the acrylic adhesives used on tiles are generally considered safer.

Duct Mastic

see *Mechanical Systems/HVAC: Duct Mastic*

Joint Sealants

Environmental considerations for caulking materials include durability and VOC content.

#930 Epoxy Caulking Compound

Johnsonite
16910 Munn Rd.
Chagrin Falls, OH 44023

Toll-free: 800-899-8916
Phone: 440-543-8916
www.johnsonite.com

Johnsonite's #930 is a two-part, nonflammable epoxy compound for repairing cracks, holes, depressions, and worn and broken edges on wood, concrete, or metal steps. It provides a uniform bonding support for treads and nosings. The compound is available in a dual-cartridge applicator.

Liquid Nails Brand Super Caulk and Painter's Caulk

Maaco Adhesives
925 Euclid Ave.
Cleveland, OH 44115

Toll-free: 800-634-0015
Phone: 216-344-7304
www.liquidnails.com

Liquid Nails® Brand Super Caulk (LC130) is a water-based acrylic latex sealant that has a VOC content of 49 g/l (white) and 50 g/l (clear). Liquid Nails Brand Painter's Caulk (LC135) is a water-based acrylic latex sealant that has a VOC content of 70 g/l.

OSI Sealants

OSI Sealants, Inc.
7405 Products Dr.
Mentor, OH 44060

Toll-free: 800-321-3578
Phone: 440-255-8900
www.osisealants.com

The following Polyseamseal products are water-based with VOC levels from 2 g/l to 32 g/l: Acrylic Caulk with Silicone; Outdoor Window, Door & Siding Sealant; Painters Latex Caulk; All-Purpose Adhesive Caulk and Tub & Tile Adhesive Caulk (both in clear).

The following Pro Series products are water-based and low-VOC: H2U Acrylic Urethane Sealant (<5 g/l VOC), PC-158 Painter's Choice Latex Caulk (24 g/l), SA-167 Siliconized Acrylic Latex Caulk (colors 41 g/l, clear <5 g/l), CS-150 Latex Concrete Crack Sealant (40 g/l), SC-175 Acoustical Sound Sealant (25 g/l), SW-325 Shear & Drywall Adhesive (<3 g/l), QB-350 Latex Multi Purpose Construction Adhesive (22 g/l), SF-550 High Performance Latex Deck & Subfloor Adhesive (<2 g/l), and SF-555 Fiberglass Construction Adhesive (<2 g/l).

The following PL products are water-based and low-VOC: Tub & Shower Surround Adhesive (<3 g/l VOC), Latex FRP Adhesive (<3 g/l), Ceramic Tile Adhesive (15 g/l), Cove Base Adhesive (20 g/l), and Water Based Contact Cement (10 g/l).

Pecora Sealants

Pecora Corporation
165 Wambold Rd.
Harleysville, PA 19438

Toll-free: 800-523-6688
Phone: 215-723-6051
www.pecora.com

AC-20® + Silicone is a one-part, water-based acrylic/silicone sealant with a VOC content of 31 g/l. It is available in 11 standard colors. Pecora 864, 890, and 895 are all one-part silicone sealants with VOC contents of 12 g/l. Urexpan® NR-200 (two-part) and Urexpan NR-201 (one-part) are both polyurethane traffic-grade sealants. Both parts of NR-200 are zero-VOC, while NR-201 has a VOC content of 45 g/l. Pro-Sil 1, at less than 15 g/l VOCs, is a one-part hybrid polymer sealant used for sealing perimeters, expansion joints, EIFS, etc.

Phenoseal and Sealant

Phenoseal
P.O. Box 428
Franklin, MA 02038

Toll-free: 800-343-4963
Phone: 508-528-2200
www.phenoseal.com

Phenoseal is a vinyl acetate homopolymer-based adhesive caulk. (Note that vinyl acetate does not contain chlorine, so is very different from PVC.) This product is often tolerated by the environmentally sensitive. Uncured Phenoseal can be cleaned up with water. Sealant is a water-based acrylic latex window and door sealant.

Quick Shield VOC-Free Sealant

Geocel Corporation
P.O. Box 398
Elkhart, IN 46515

Toll-free: 800-348-7615
Phone: 574-264-0645
www.geocelusa.com

Quick Shield is a white, one-part, quick-setting, interior/exterior flexible sealant that contains no VOCs. It is resistant to water within 5 minutes and is paintable within 10 minutes. Quick Shield bonds to wood, aluminum, brick, and concrete without a primer. It cleans up with water, is mold- and mildew-resistant, and is rated to last 50 years.

Sealants

Resource Conservation Technology, Inc.
2633 N. Calvert St.
Baltimore, MD 21218

Phone: 410-366-1146
www.conservationtechnology.com

Resource Conservation Technology specializes in building gaskets, weather stripping, and air barriers. The company provides high quality products and service.

Tremflex 834 and Tremco Spectrem 1

Tremco, Inc.
3735 Green Rd.
Beachwood, OH 44122

Toll-free: 800-852-8173
Phone: 216-292-5000
www.tremcosealants.com

Tremflex 834 is a water-based, siliconized acrylic latex sealant with a VOC content of 13.7 g/l. It is mildew-resistant and can be used in bathrooms and kitchens, as well as for general interior and exterior caulking, as a back bedding glazing compound, and as an acoustical sealant. It is paintable and comes in white only.

Tremco Spectrem 1 is a one-part, zero-VOC, moisture-curing silicone joint sealant suitable for high-movement building joint applications such as aluminum curtain walls, precast concrete panels, metal panels, and window perimeters.

Sealants

The challenge of sealing building envelopes against air infiltration is made easier with foam sealants. Look for products with blowing agents that are non-ozone-depleting and have low global-warming potential. Be aware that a label "no CFCs" is not the same as "ozone-safe"; HCFC propellants/blowing agents, while not as bad as CFCs, still deplete ozone. Foam sealants are commonly available in high-expanding and low-expanding formulations; low-expanding foam is the material of choice for sealing window and door rough openings—it performs significantly better than fiberglass and will be less likely than high-expanding foams to swell the openings (which can make opening and closing difficult). Foam sealants are useful in many applications, especially in building renovation. Some products are available only in disposable cans; the use of bulk tanks and reusable dispensing guns can reduce the environmental costs of using these sealants by minimizing waste.

CF 128

Hilti, Inc.
P.O. Box 21148
Tulsa, OK 74121

Toll-free: 800-879-8000
Phone: 918-252-6000
www.us.hilti.com

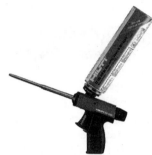

CF 128 is a single-component, polyurethane-based foam sealant propelled by HFC-134a, propane, and isobutane blowing agents. This minimally expanding product is dispensed from a can with a reusable gun (CF-DS1). CF 116 is a similar product dispensed with a disposable nozzle.

PurFil IG

Todol Products
25 Washington Ave.
P.O. Box 398
Natick, MA 01760

Toll-free: 800-252-3818
Phone: 508-651-3818
www.todol.com

PurFil IG uses HFC-134a as its propellant and a mix of propane and isobutane as the blowing agent. It is available in disposable cans with application guns.

Touch'n Foam

Convenience Products
866 Horan Dr.
Fenton, MO 63026-2416

Toll-free: 800-325-6180
Phone: 636-349-5333
www.convenienceproducts.com

Touch'n Foam is an HCFC-free foam sealant that uses a mixture of propane and isobutane as the blowing agent. It is available in triple-expanding or low-expanding formulations in disposable cans.

Universal Foam Sealant

illbruck Sealant Systems, inc.
14617 Carriage Ln.
Burnsville, MN 55306

Toll-free: 800-438-0684
Phone: 612-521-3555
www.illbruck.com/en

illbruck's Universal Foam Sealant is an HCFC-free, one-component, moisture-cure polyurethane foam for filling, bonding, and sealing. Manufactured in the Netherlands, the product is hydrocarbon-blown and is dispensed from a gun-grade or tube-grade aerosol can. Universal Foam Sealant has a light green color; other colors are available upon request.

Wood and Plastic Adhesives

Adhesives are a significant potential source of indoor air quality concerns, so these products should be selected with care. Water-based adhesives have lower VOC emissions than solvent-based products. While some are sold as multipurpose, others are specific to particular applications. If a manufacturer recommends a low- or zero-VOC, water-based product for use with its material, then use that product; otherwise consider one known to minimize indoor air pollution. For inclusion in GreenSpec, the VOC limit is 50 grams per liter.

Speed Grip

Geocel Corporation
P.O. Box 398
Elkhart, IN 46515

Toll-free: 800-348-7615
Phone: 574-264-0645
www.geocelusa.com

Speed Grip construction adhesive—with a 100% VOC-free, chemically reactive formula—is suitable for use on a variety of porous and nonporous surfaces including plastic, wood, concrete, brick, plasterboard, carpet, and metal. This adhesive is intended for applications such as panel installation, sheathing, windows, and other building components. Speed Grip cleans up with water.

Titebond Solvent Free Construction Adhesive

Franklin International
2020 Bruck St.
Columbus, OH 43207

Toll-free: 800-877-4583
Phone: 614-443-0241
www.titebond.com

Titebond® is a solvent-free, nonflammable construction adhesive that contains 6.6 g/l VOCs. Its performance is equivalent to conventional adhesives. Titebond complies with the requirements of the APA, AFG-01 test for subfloors. It costs about 10% more than conventional solvent-based adhesives. The company also produces specialized solvent-free adhesives for such applications as subflooring, drywall, cove-base, and acoustical ceiling tile.

This Space is Available for Your Notes

Paints & Coatings

Paints and coatings are applied as a fluid, and they dry or cure in place. During that process a carrier evaporates, leaving the active agents in place. For most products this carrier was traditionally a volatile organic solvent that turned into an airborne volatile organic compound (VOC) as it evaporated. Air quality regulations and health concerns have driven a shift toward waterborne products. Evaporating water isn't a health concern, though other components of the coating or adhesive still generally release some VOCs.

Paints and coatings have their greatest effect on indoor air quality during and immediately after installation. The health hazard is particularly acute for installers. Most conventional products offgas VOCs, formaldehyde, and other chemicals that are added to enhance the performance or extend shelf-life of the product. Little scientific data is available on the health effects of many of these chemicals—and even less on the effects of exposure to a *combination* of such chemicals that may occur in buildings. Quality substitutions, which are lower in toxicity or nontoxic, are available for all of these products.

Even so-called zero-VOC materials may still release small amounts of organic compounds. People with chemical sensitivities should always test these products before applying them on their projects, or having them applied by workers. Alternatives to conventional paints made from plant-based solvents may also release significant amounts of VOCs, but many people find these compounds less objectionable than those derived from petrochemicals. Aside from solvents with well-known health effects (such as benzene, toluene, or xylene), the scientific community offers little guidance on the distinction between acceptable and problematic VOCs.

In most categories, the *GreenSpec* criteria for "low-VOC" products is 50 grams per liter, which is well below even the most stringent VOC regulations in California.

While wet-applied products emit the most VOCs immediately after curing, some continue to *offgas* such compounds for a long time. In addition, VOCs emitted during curing can become attached to other surfaces in the space, especially fabrics, and then be re-emitted over time. To reduce this problem, painting should be done with soft surfaces covered and direct ventilation provided until the coating is dry.

For wood-floor finishes, waterborne polyurethane is suggested. It contains no crosslinking agent—a type of chemical that adds hardness but is toxic. Waterborne finishes have been tested for durability, and they wear comparably to solvent-based ones. Installers often prefer waterborne finishing products because they dry quickly, allowing several coats to be applied in one day.

Coatings for Concrete and Masonry

Federal VOC-content limits include 350 grams per liter for concrete-curing compounds and 700 grams per liter for concrete curing and sealing compounds. A range of products, particularly waterborne ones, are available that fall well below these limits. For inclusion in GreenSpec, the VOC limit is 50 grams per liter.

9400 Impregnant

Palmer Industries, Inc.
10611 Old Annapolis Rd.
Frederick, MD 21701-3347

Toll-free: 800-545-7383
Phone: 301-898-7848
www.palmerindustriesinc.com

A water-repellent, UV-protective coating for masonry, concrete, and other cementitious materials, formulated without solvents for minimal toxicity.

Ashford Formula

Curecrete Distribution, Inc.
1203 W. Spring Creek Pl.
Springville, UT 84663

Toll-free: 800-998-5664
Phone: 801-489-5663
www.ashfordformula.com

Ashford Formula is a permanent, penetrating concrete hardener, densifier, dustproofer, and sealer for new or existing concrete. As it progressively seals, the concrete becomes watertight but remains breathable and will develop a shine through use or by scrubbing. The product also locks in salts to eliminate the formation of concrete dust. Ashford Formula is water-based, nontoxic, nonflammable, and releases no VOCs. It is effective on concrete, stucco, terrazzo, concrete block, and similar materials.

Penetrating Waterstop

American Formulating & Manufacturing (AFM)
3251 Third Ave.
San Diego, CA 92103

Toll-free: 800-239-0321
Phone: 619-239-0321
www.afmsafecoat.com

Safecoat® Penetrating WaterStop is a zero-VOC sealer that increases water-repellency and helps control the migration of free salts identified as efflorescence on brick walls, concrete foundations, stucco, stone, and most unglazed tile. It is nonflammable and free of formaldehyde and hazardous ingredients.

Radcon Formula #7

Parker International Ltd. / USA
110 Revere Dr.
Greensboro, NC 27407

Phone: 336-854-9236
www.parker-intl-ltd.com

Radcon® Formula #7 is a water-based, zero-VOC, biochemically modified silicate solution that is spray-applied over cured concrete during a three-day process (may be steam-applied in one day). Radcon penetrates and reacts with calcium and water to form a subsurface, nonsoluble, calcium-silicate-hydrate gel waterproofing complex in pores, capillaries, and cracks up to $1/8$" wide. The product also remains active in the presence of water to seal new hairline cracks. In humid environments, Radcon enables concrete to outgas moisture, eliminating the problems of premature delamination of membranes, and it can also serve to replace membranes altogether, according to the company. Not suitable for negative hydrostatic pressure situations, such as the inside face of continually wet basements or retaining walls. Radcon is specifically designed for high-thermal-stress situations and is biodegradable, nonflammable, and safe for potable water applications.

Trojan Masonry Sealer

Envirosafe Manufacturing
    Corporation
7634-B Progress Cir.
W. Melbourne, FL 32904

Toll-free: 800-800-5737
www.envirosafemfg.com

Trojan Masonry Sealer, a penetrating sealer for permanently waterproofing masonry, is a water-dispersed thermoplastic polyester polymer that dries to form a monolithic barrier filling voids and coating the interior particles of concrete to block moisture transmission. Trojan Masonry Sealer releases no VOCs, is nontoxic, nonflammable, noncaustic, and is suitable for use indoors or out on concrete, cement, brick, stucco, plaster, mortar, terrazzo, and most natural stones.

Weather-Bos Sealers

Weather-Bos International
316 California Ave., Ste. 1082
Reno, NV 89509

Toll-free: 800-664-3978
www.weatherbos.com

Weather-Bos sealers are made from natural, nontoxic vegetable oils and resins as well as other natural ingredients. These sealers are low-odor, water-reducible, nonflammable, and free of harmful fungicides. The small amount of pigment in some formulas provides UV protection. Masonry Boss™ waterproofs and protects brick, adobe, concrete, tile, and stone.

Paints, rust inhibitors, and other coatings for steel have traditionally been lead-based and/or very high in VOCs. A few environmentally preferable products exist.

234 Natural Metal Primer

Sinan Co.
P.O. Box 857
Davis, CA 95617

Phone: 530-753-3104
www.dcn.davis.ca.us/go/sinan

Sinan 234 Natural Metal Primer is formulated for priming clean steel and metal materials for interior and exterior applications. Sinan products are made from all-natural, primarily plant-based materials, all of which are listed on the packaging.

Direct to Metal Coating

Fuhr International LLC
P.O. Box 86
Winigan, MO 63566

Toll-free: 800-558-7437
Phone: 660-857-4300
www.fuhrinternational.com

Direct to Metal (DTM) is a low-VOC (32 g/l) acrylic coating for metal surfaces to provide protection against oxidation and corrosion. DTM may be used as both primer and finish, is suitable for interior and limited exterior use, and is available in clear, white, black, primer red, and custom colors.

MetalCoat Acrylic Metal Primer

American Formulating & Manufacturing (AFM)
3251 Third Ave.
San Diego, CA 92103

Toll-free: 800-239-0321
Phone: 619-239-0321
www.afmsafecoat.com

MetalCoat Acrylic Metal Primer is a thermoplastic emulsion primer fortified with rust-inhibiting pigments. It is designed for use on iron, steel, aluminum, and galvanized metal but is not recommended for copper. The product contains no hazardous chemicals and has a low-VOC content of 44 g/l (88 less water).

Decorative Finishes

Decorative finishes are typically high-grade, multicolored and/or textured coatings for interior and exterior applications. Textures and colors are achieved by proprietary mixtures of pigments, oils,

and inorganic fillers. The products listed here are waterborne and have relatively low-VOC content. They offer a durable and environmentally preferable alternative to common vinyl wall coverings, which offgas plasticizers and pose heightened health risks during a fire or end-of-life incineration. For inclusion in GreenSpec, the VOC limit is 50 grams per liter.

Silacote Textured Coating

Silacote USA LLC
110 Revere Dr.
Greensboro, NC 27407

Toll-free: 800-766-3157
Phone: 336-854-9236
www.silacote.com

Silacote's Liquid Rock texture paint is made from natural inorganic compounds such as quartz, chalk, other minerals, and mineral colorants with a potassium silicate binder. It contains no heavy metals, and is zero-VOC (including the colorants). It can be trowelled or tooled for a durable textured finish over interior or exterior inorganic substrates such as concrete, lime plaster, marble, natural stone, brick, and new gypsum wallboard. This water-based product chemically bonds (petrifies) with the substrate, forming a microcrystalline structure that reflects light and heat. It comes in white only; Silacote's Mineral Silicate Paints can be used to achieve a chemically bonded color coat if required.

Exterior Paints

Paints for exterior surfaces may be listed here for a number of reasons, including minimal offgassing and superior durability. Included are mineral silicate paints that chemically react with mineral surfaces (stucco, plaster, concrete, etc.) in a process called petrification to form a highly durable finish. Mineral silicate paints can also be used indoors. For inclusion in GreenSpec, the VOC limit is 50 grams per liter.

Best Duracryl Exterior Paint

Best Paint, Inc.
5205 Ballard Ave. NW
Seattle, WA 98107

Phone: 206-783-9938
www.bestpaintco.com

Best Paint's Duracryl Exterior Paint is a 100% acrylic resin formula, which contains a low-toxic zinc compound for mold and mildew protection. Best Paint's water-based formula contains less than 50 g/l VOC (less water) and is manufactured for interior and exterior applications with a semi-gloss or eggshell finish. Duracryl Exterior Primer is also available. Suitable for wood, stucco, masonry, primed metal, and other typical surfaces.

Eco-House Mineral Silicate Paint

Eco-House, Inc.
P.O. Box 220, Stn. A
Fredericton, NB E3B 4Y9 Canada

Phone: 506-366-3529
www.eco-house.com

Eco-House, Inc. was the first manufacturer to produce mineral silicate paints in North America. The binder is potassium silicate dissolved in water (also known as "waterglass"), which petrifies when it chemically reacts with lime. Used on plaster, concrete, and other mineral surfaces, this product is not suitable for wood, metal, or any flexible surface. According to Eco-House, silicate paints are solvent-free, completely odorless after 1-2 days, made from widely available materials (water, quartz sand, potash, lime, and silicate minerals), naturally antimicrobial (not requiring fungicides), non-combustible at any temperature, and extremely durable.

Ecological Interior/Exterior Paint

Innovative Formulations Corporation
1810 S. Sixth Ave.
Tucson, AZ 85713

Toll-free: 800-346-7265
Phone: 520-628-1553

Ecological Paint are professional-quality, odor-free, interior/exterior, zero-VOC, hypo-allergenic, water-based acrylic urethanes, which contain no known hazardous, toxic, or carcinogenic materials. Available with or without a mold inhibitor in semi-gloss, high-gloss, eggshell, satin, and flat.

EverKote 300

Edison Coatings, Inc.
3 Northwest Dr.
Plainville, CT 06062

Toll-free: 800-697-8055
Phone: 860-747-2220
www.edisoncoatings.com

EverKote 300 is a waterborne, inorganic mineral-silicate coating made with a potassium silicate binder, sometimes known as "waterglass," that forms a chemical bond (petrifies) with suitable substrates. It is appropriate for application on calcareous stone (such as limestone or marble), masonry, concrete, cement plaster, ceramics, as well as on iron and other metals. EverKote 300 is extremely durable, nonflammable, UV-resistant, breathable, and naturally antimicrobial. It is available in two grades: low-viscosity, semi-transparent Penetral; and medium-viscosity, opaque Patinar. EverKote 300 comes in a flat (matte) finish in 900 standard colors; custom color matching is also available.

Keim Mineral Silicate Paint

Cohalan Company, Inc.
3 Port Lewes
Lewes, DE 19958

Phone: 302-644-1007
www.keimmineralsystems.com

Keim Mineral Systems invented mineral silicate paints in Bavaria (Germany) in 1878, and Keim paints are widely used around the world today. The binder is potassium silicate dissolved in water (also known as "waterglass"). This is combined with inorganic fillers and natural earth oxide to produce an inorganic "liquid stone" finish through a process of petrification. Durability in excess of 100 years has been reported, according to Keim. Used on plaster, concrete, and other mineral surfaces; not suitable for wood, metal, or any flexible surface. Available in both exterior and interior products, with 270 standard colors and thousands of custom colors available. Keim mineral silicate paints are solvent-free, odorless, nontoxic, vapor-permeable, naturally resistant to fungi and algae, noncombustible, light-reflective, colorfast, resistant to acid rain, and extremely durable. Keim Mineral Systems carries ISO 14001 certification.

Rodda Low-VOC Exterior Paint

Rodda Paint
6107 N. Marine Dr.
Portland, OR 97203

Toll-free: 800-452-2315
Phone: 503-737-6033
www.roddapaint.com

Rodda Paint's Horizon line includes the first exterior paint that meets Green Seal's GS-11 standard for coatings. The 100% acrylic exterior products are low-VOC and certified to meet Green Seal's requirements regarding VOC levels and toxic ingredients. The Horizon line includes 42 different products in various finishes for interior, exterior, and priming applications. Rodda is a founding member of the Oregon Natural Step Network, a statewide group of businesses working towards environmental sustainability.

Safecoat Exterior Satin Enamel

American Formulating & Manufacturing (AFM)
3251 Third Ave.
San Diego, CA 92103

Toll-free: 800-239-0321
Phone: 619-239-0321
www.afmsafecoat.com

Safecoat Exterior Satin Enamel contains no ammonia, formaldehyde, ethylene glycol, mildewcides, or fungicides. This premium exterior paint has a VOC content of 17 g/l (42 g/l less water), virtually no odor during application and none when dry, and a satin sheen. It is suitable for use on wood, stucco, aluminum, vinyl, and fully-cured concrete.

Silacote Mineral Silicate Paint

Silacote USA LLC
110 Revere Dr.
Greensboro, NC 27407

Toll-free: 800-766-3157
Phone: 336-854-9236
www.silacote.com

Silacote Mineral Silicate Paint is made from natural inorganic compounds such as quartz, other minerals, and mineral colorants with a potassium silicate binder. It is suitable for coating inorganic substrates such as concrete, lime plaster, marble, natural stone, brick, and new gypsum wallboard. For interior and exterior applications, Silacote is breathable, nontoxic, noncombustible, zero-VOC (including colorants), and will not support mold growth. This water-based product chemically bonds (petrifies) with the substrate, producing a coating with a life expectancy of 25-30+ years, according to the manufacturer. Silacote forms a microcrystalline structure that reflects light and heat. Fully tintable, with a large number of colors available; colors not affected by UV or acid rain.

Exterior Stains

VOC emissions are the primary concern with exterior stains and paints. Look for low-VOC products. For inclusion in GreenSpec, *the VOC limit is 50 grams per liter.*

BioShield Exterior Stains

Eco Design/BioShield Paint
 Company
1330 Rufina Cir.
Santa Fe, NM 87507

Toll-free: 800-621-2591
Phone: 505-438-3448
www.bioshieldpaint.com

The BioShield product line, available online and through the BioShield Paint Catalog, includes paints, waxes, finishes, and thinners derived from low-toxic, non-petroleum-based ingredients.

NatureStain

NatureStain Co.
2153 E. Cedar St., Ste. 6
Tempe, AZ 85281

Phone: 480-303-8379
www.naturestain.com

NatureStain™, a semi-transparent stain for fiber-cement siding, is a blend of acrylic emulsion and a soybean oil derivative. The product penetrates fiber-cement siding and, according to the manufacturer, is not compromised by movement and moisture changes—as acrylic latex paint products can be. NatureStain is low-VOC (less than 25 g/l), nontoxic, biodegradable, and cleans up with soap and water. The manufacturer offers a 10-year limited warranty for product applied by hand on installed siding and a 15-year limited warranty for product machine-applied or hand-applied to siding while lying flat.

ZVOC Exterior Waterbased Stain

Fuhr International LLC
P.O. Box 86
Winigan, MO 63566

Toll-free: 800-558-7437
Phone: 660-857-4300
www.fuhrinternational.com

ZVOC® Exterior Waterbased Stain is a zero-VOC acrylic wood stain for both interior and exterior use that is suitable for a wide variety of applications, including kitchen cabinets, decks, and windows and doors.

Exterior Transparent Finishes

The products included here have low VOC levels, are derived from natural oils, or are biodegradable.

9400W Impregnant

Palmer Industries, Inc.
10611 Old Annapolis Rd.
Frederick, MD 21701-3347

Toll-free: 800-545-7383
Phone: 301-898-7848
www.palmerindustriesinc.com

9400W Impregnant is a water-repellent, UV-protective coating for wood, formulated without solvents for minimal toxicity.

BioShield Exterior Transparent Finishes

Eco Design/BioShield Paint Company
1330 Rufina Cir.
Santa Fe, NM 87507

Toll-free: 800-621-2591
Phone: 505-438-3448
www.bioshieldpaint.com

The BioShield product line, available online and through the BioShield Paint Catalog, includes paints, waxes, finishes, and thinners derived from low-toxic, non-petroleum-based ingredients.

Broda Pro-Tek-Tor

Broda Coatings Ltd.
1434 Rupert St.
N. Vancouver, BC V7J 1E9
Canada

Toll-free: 888-311-5339
Phone: 604-980-3325
www.cbrproducts.com

Broda Pro-Tek-Tor Natural Oil Wood Finish is an oil-based, waterborne, non-film-forming, penetrating wood finish. This product needs only soap and water cleanup, and is available in clear, transparent, semi-transparent, and semi-solid formulations. Mold and mildew resistance is provided by liquid microbiocides with low acute oral toxicity.

GCP 1000

Genesis Coatings, Inc.
2780 La Mirada Dr., Ste. B
Vista, CA 92083

Toll-free: 800-533-4273
Phone: 760-599-6011
www.genesiscoatings.com

GCP 1000 coating is an odorless, water-based, zero-VOC, two-part aliphatic polyurethane designed to be a high-performance general maintenance coating that is resistant to scuff marks and other unwanted markings. Genesis Coatings has also developed nontoxic, biodegradable graffiti removers: Graffiti Gold Remover, Graffiti Eaze Away, and Graffiti Terminator.

Weather-Bos Finishes

Weather-Bos International
316 California Ave., Ste. 1082
Reno, NV 89509

Toll-free: 800-664-3978
www.weatherbos.com

Weather-Bos transparent finishes are made from natural, nontoxic vegetable oils and resins as well as other natural ingredients. These finishes are low-odor, water-reducible, nonflammable, and free of harmful fungicides. The small amount of pigment in some formulas provides UV protection. The Boss™ is the company's original all-purpose wood finish; Deck Boss™ protects and weatherproofs wood decks; and Log Boss™ is for use on log homes.

Zar Exterior Polyurethane

United Gilsonite Laboratories (UGL)
P.O. Box 70
Scranton, PA 18501

Toll-free: 800-272-3235
Phone: 570-344-1202
www.ugl.com

Zar Exterior Water-Based Polyurethane is an amber-colored protective finish for exterior wood surfaces as well as fiberglass and metal entry doors. The product contains ultraviolet-radiation inhibitors to provide additional protection from UV rays.

Interior Paints

A primary consideration for most interior paints is their potential impact on occupant health. To this end, very-low-VOC or zero-VOC paints are generally preferred, though some chemically sensitive people find that even these can be difficult to tolerate. Note that liquid carriers (including water and exempt VOCs) are usually excluded when stating VOC levels, which are expressed as grams of VOC per liter of VOC-plus-paint-solids. Most zero-VOC paints still use colorant systems that contain VOCs, so custom-coloring will increase emissions. Some paints are made from minimally processed plants and minerals; while these products may contain relatively high levels of VOCs, they may not be as troublesome as the compounds released from petrochemical-based paints. Some paints included here have other environmental features. For inclusion in GreenSpec, the VOC limit is 50 grams per liter.

Air-Care Odorless Paints

Coronado Paint Company
308 Old County Rd.
Edgewater, FL 32132-0308

Toll-free: 800-883-4193
Phone: 386-428-6461
www.coronadopaint.com

The Air-Care line consists of Odorless Acrylic Primer, Odorless Acrylic Flat, Odorless Acrylic Eggshell, and Low Odor Acrylic Semi-Gloss. All these formulations are zero-VOC, though colorants add some VOCs.

American Pride Vegetable-Oil-Modified Latex Paint

Southern Diversified Products, LLC
2714 Hardy St.
Hattiesburg, MS 39401

Phone: 601-264-0442
www.americanpridepaint.com

Southern Diversified Products is manufacturing a vegetable-oil-modified line of interior latex paints called "American Pride" that is partially based on a castor oil acrylated monomer developed by polymer science researchers at the University of Southern Mississippi. American Pride has a VOC content of around 3 g/l and virtually no smell, allowing interior painting without evacuating a building or providing additional ventilation. The paint is the second to be certified under the paint standard by the independent nonprofit Green Seal and, according to the organization, performs well compared to other high-end interior latex paints, while being priced competitively with them. American Pride's flat white has a scrub rating of 880 strokes (ASTM D2486-89), while its eggshell white withstood 2,600 strokes. The paints are currently for sale at individual dealers throughout Mississippi and by special order in other parts of the country.

Best Paints

Best Paint, Inc.
5205 Ballard Ave. NW
Seattle, WA 98107

Phone: 206-783-9938
www.bestpaintco.com

Best Paint products are zero-VOC, with no biocide. They are available in flat, satin, eggshell, and semi-gloss in a wide range of colors for indoor use.

BioShield Interior Paint

Eco Design/BioShield Paint Company
1330 Rufina Cir.
Santa Fe, NM 87507

Toll-free: 800-621-2591
Phone: 505-438-3448
www.bioshieldpaint.com

The BioShield product line, available online and through the BioShield Paint Catalog, includes paints, waxes, finishes, and thinners derived from low-toxic, non-petroleum-based ingredients. The wall paint and milk paint have very low VOC contents.

Devoe Paint: Wonder Pure

The Glidden Company
925 Euclid Ave.
Cleveland, OH 44115

Toll-free: 800-834-6077
Phone: 216-344-8000
www.iciduluxpaints.com

The Wonder-Pure line of Devoe Paint, manufactured by Glidden, is zero-VOC. The line includes Primer (DR3160), Interior Flat (DR3101), Eggshell (DR3201), and Semi-Gloss (DR3301). They are available only through independent Glidden dealers.

EarthTech Paints and Finishes

EarthTech
29638 Gigi Rd.
Evergreen, CO 80439

Phone: 303-674-7873

EarthTech's commercial, light-industrial, and architectural paints are all zero-VOC and available in 5 bases: white, neutral, medium, accent, and deep.

EnviroKote Interior Low Odor Paint

Frazee Paint
6625 Miramar Rd.
San Diego, CA 92121

Toll-free: 800-477-9991
Phone: 858-276-9500
www.frazeepaint.com

EnviroKote paint is a very-low-VOC acrylic latex available in flat, eggshell, and semi-gloss formulations. White and medium-tint base paints are available.

Enviro-Safe Paint

Chem-Safe Products Company
110 W. Elizabeth St.
Austin, TX 78704

Phone: 512-326-4474
www.ecowise.com

Enviro-Safe zero-VOC paints are available in flat, satin, and semi-gloss for interior use, and satin for exterior use. The product line uses a grapefruit-derived low-toxic preservative, so shelf life is guaranteed for only one year.

Eurolux Waterborne Acrylics

Fine Paints of Europe
P.O. Box 419
Woodstock, VT 05091

Toll-free: 800-332-1556
Phone: 802-457-2468
www.finepaintsofeurope.com

Eurolux waterborne acrylic paints are made in Holland. They have less than 30 g/l VOCs and are very durable, high-quality coatings at a premium price.

Gold Label Premium Enviro Paints

Spectra-tone Paint Company
1595 E. San Bernardino
San Bernardino, CA 92408-2946

Toll-free: 800-272-4687
Phone: 909-478-3485
www.spectra-tone.com

Gold Label Premium Enviro Paints for interior use are VOC-free and come in flat (#410), low-lustre enamel (#8800), and semi-gloss (#9900). The product line is made with a terpolymer resin that may not be as durable as acrylic latex resins.

Harmony Coating System

The Sherwin-Williams Company
   Stores Group
101 Prospect Ave. NW
Cleveland, OH 44115

Toll-free: 800-321-8194
Phone: 216-566-2000
www.sherwinwilliams.com

Harmony Interior Latex Flat, Eg-Shel, Semi-Gloss, and Primer provide a durable, low-odor, anti-microbial, interior paint system formulated without silica. These products can be used, without typical odor complaints, in occupied areas because of the very low odor during application and drying. The Harmony line contains zero-VOCs and replaces the company's low-VOC HealthSpec line.

Healthy Milk Paint

Antique Drapery Rod Co., Inc.
140 Glass St.
Dallas, TX 75207

Phone: 214-653-1733
www.antiquedraperyrod.com

Healthy Milk Paint™ comes in a ready-to-use liquid form that contains 85–98% food-grade ingredients, depending on the color, and no VOCs. Food-grade fungicides are used to prevent mold. A variety of colors are offered, and custom-mixing is available. The company also offers Healthy Milk Stucco, Tea Stain, and Milk Paint Aromatherapies. Healthy Milk Paint is manufactured by Walker Paint Co., a division of Antique Drapery Rod Co.

Kelly-Moore Enviro-Cote

Kelly-Moore Paint Co.
987 Commercial St.
San Carlos, CA 94070

Toll-free: 800-874-4436 ext. 157 (corporate offices)
Phone: 916-921-0165
www.kellymoore.com

Kelly-Moore Enviro-Cote acrylic satin enamel paint is zero-VOC, their Acry-prime has a maximum VOC content of 15 g/l, semi-gloss enamel has a maximum VOC content of 6 g/l, and flat finish paints have VOC contents of less than 13 g/l.

Kurfees Fresh Air

Progress Paint Manufacturing Co., Inc.
201 E. Market St.
P.O. Box 33188
Louisville, KY 40202

Toll-free: 800-626-6407
Phone: 502-587-8685
www.progresspaint.com

Kurfees Fresh Air interior paint has a calculated maximum VOC content of 24 g/l and is available in flat, eggshell, and satin finishes or as primer.

LifeMaster 2000

ICI Paints
925 Euclid Ave.
Cleveland, OH 44115

Toll-free: 800-984-5444
Phone: 216-344-8000
www.iciduluxpaints.com

LifeMaster 2000 interior latex paints have zero-VOC content and are available in Flat (LM9100), Eggshell (LM9300), and Semi-gloss (LM9200) finishes.

Milk Paint

Old Fashioned Milk
   Paint Co.
436 Main St.
P.O. Box 222
Groton, MA 01450

Phone: 978-448-6336
www.milkpaint.com

Milk Paint is a powdered paint made from casein (milk protein) mixed with lime, clay, and earth pigments. Water is added to make a pint, quart, or gallon size. It is available in 16 historical colors, which can be blended or tinted. Milk Paint is marketed primarily as a paint for wood furniture; however, different additives and clear sealers can be used to enhance durability and adhesion to nonporous surfaces. Although Milk Paint contains a natural mildewcide, the use of a clear sealer over the paint in damp areas such as bathrooms is recommended.

Murco LE-1000 and GF-1000

Murco Wall Products
2032 N. Commerce
Fort Worth, TX 76106

Toll-free: 800-446-7124
Phone: 817-626-1987
www.murcowall.com

Murco paints are water-based, low-VOC, latex products for interior use, popular with chemically sensitive individuals. Available in flat (GF-1000) and high-gloss (LE-1000).

Natural Paints

Sinan Co.
P.O. Box 857
Davis, CA 95617

Phone: 530-753-3104
www.dcn.davis.ca.us/go/sinan

Sinan natural interior paint products include primers, a professional wall paint (satin only), and a milk paint in powder form. Manufactured only in white, they can be tinted using a concentrate available in 8 earth-tone colors. Sinan products are made from all-natural, primarily plant-based materials, all of which are listed on the packaging.

No-VOC Paints

Republic Paints
1128 N. Highland Ave.
Hollywood, CA 90038

Toll-free: 888-957-3060
Phone: 323-957-3060
www.republicpaints.com

Republic Odorless interior paint has a calculated zero-VOC content and is available in flat, eggshell, and satin finishes or as primer in a range of colors.

Pristine Eco-Spec

Benjamin Moore & Co.
51 Chestnut Ridge Rd.
Montvale, NJ 07645

Toll-free: 800-344-0400
Phone: 201-573-9600
www.benjaminmoore.com

Pristine® Eco-Spec® is a zero-VOC 100% acrylic latex interior paint available in primer/sealer, flat, eggshell, and semi-gloss. The product line is for the professional contractor market.

Pure Performance

PPG Architectural Finishes
One PPG Pl.
Pittsburgh, PA 15272

Toll-free: 800-441-9695
Phone: 412-434-3131
www.ppgaf.com

PPG Architectural Finishes sells a zero-VOC interior latex paint line, Pure Performance, under its Pittsburgh Paints brand. The paint comes in a full range of sheens and can be tinted to any Pittsburgh Paints color (tints contribute a minimal amount of VOCs—2 g/l maximum). Pure Performance, which is replacing the company's second-to-the-top Wallhide line, is the first paint certified under the Green Seal standard and meets the special "Class A" rating reserved for zero-VOC paints. PPG claims that the Pure Performance line, made with vinyl acetate ethylene resin, is the first to offer zero-VOC with no compromise on durability and at a price similar to that of conventional paints.

Radiance Paints

Degussa Building Systems / Radiance
889 Valley Park Dr.
Shakopee, MN 55379

Toll-free: 800-766-6776
Phone: 612-496-6000
www.degussabuildingsystems.com

Radiance™ paint products contain tiny metallic particles that impart low-e characteristics to painted surfaces. Radiance Interior Wall Finish is used for vertical applications, while Radiance Low-E Attic and Decking Radiant Barrier is for the underside of roof decks. Energy savings from the paint in most situations will be fairly low, except when the walls or ceiling are very poorly insulated. Radiance paints are produced by Degussa Building Systems, formerly known as ChemRex.

Rodda Zero-VOC Interior Paint

Rodda Paint
6107 N. Marine Dr.
Portland, OR 97203

Toll-free: 800-452-2315
Phone: 503-737-6033
www.roddapaint.com

Rodda Paint's Horizon line includes 42 different products in various finishes for interior, exterior, and priming applications. The interior products are nominally zero-VOC, with less than one gram of VOCs per liter. The Horizon line also includes the first exterior paint that meets Green Seal's GS-11 standard for coatings. Rodda is a founding member of the Oregon Natural Step Network, a statewide group of businesses working towards environmental sustainability.

Safecoat Enamels

American Formulating & Manufacturing (AFM)
3251 Third Ave.
San Diego, CA 92103

Toll-free: 800-239-0321
Phone: 619-239-0321
www.afmsafecoat.com

Safecoat Enamels do not contain extenders, heavy-metal drying agents, formaldehyde, acetone, or heavy-duty preservatives. The result is a higher quality resin content and, therefore, higher-quality paint film than most commercial paints provide, with none of the usual chemical additives. Additionally, Safecoat finishes help seal in VOCs of building materials or previously applied finishes. Safecoat Enamels are available in a variety of finishes and can be tinted to virtually any color. Safecoat paints have long been used by people with chemical sensitivities.

Safecoat Zero-VOC Flat, Eggshell, and Semi-gloss

American Formulating & Manufacturing (AFM)
3251 Third Ave.
San Diego, CA 92103

Toll-free: 800-239-0321
Phone: 619-239-0321
www.afmsafecoat.com

Safecoat Zero-VOC Flat, Zero-VOC Eggshell, and Zero-VOC Semi-gloss are premium quality zero-VOC paints with little odor when wet and none when dry. Safecoat paints are tinted using zero-VOC colorants. None of these paints contains formaldehyde, ammonia, crystalline silica, or ethylene glycol.

The Real Milk Paint Co.

The Real Milk Paint Co.
11 West Pumping Station Rd.
Quakertown, PA 18951

Toll-free: 800-339-9748
Phone: 215-538-3886
www.realmilkpaint.com

The Real Milk Paint Company's Real Milk Paint is derived from purified milk protein, lime, natural fillers, and nontoxic lead-free pigments. Real Milk Paint comes ready to be mixed with water for a desired consistency from thin wash to thick paint. Once mixed with water, the paint will remain usable from 2 to 4 weeks. Real Milk Paint is virtually odorless during application and drying, and contains no VOCs.

Wonder-Pure No-VOC/Odor

Devoe Paint
925 Euclid Ave.
Cleveland, OH 44115-1487

Toll-free: 866-391-1955
www.devoepaint.com

Wonder-Pure™ No-VOC/Odor interior paint has a calculated zero-VOC content and is available in flat, eggshell, and semi-gloss. Tinted colors may contain small quantities of VOCs. Wonder-Pure is also available in a primer/sealer.

ZVOC White Primer and Topcoat

Fuhr International LLC
P.O. Box 86
Winigan, MO 63566

Toll-free: 800-558-7437
Phone: 660-857-4300
www.fuhrinternational.com

ZVOC White Primer and Topcoat are zero-VOC, water-based acrylic wood coatings suitable for interior and exterior use. The Primer is acceptable as a "primed only" finish for use on wood products that will receive a finish coat of some type to be determined at a later date. The Topcoat is compatible with a wide variety of primers. Typical application of each product is one to two coats.

Interior Stains

The products included here have low VOC levels, are derived from natural oils, or are biodegradable.

BioShield Interior Stains

Eco Design/BioShield Paint Company
1330 Rufina Cir.
Santa Fe, NM 87507

Toll-free: 800-621-2591
Phone: 505-438-3448
www.bioshieldpaint.com

The BioShield product line, available online and through the BioShield Paint Catalog, includes paints, waxes, finishes, and thinners derived from low-toxic, non-petroleum-based ingredients.

Sinan 160 Series Natural Stain

Sinan Co.
P.O. Box 857
Davis, CA 95617

Phone: 530-753-3104
www.dcn.davis.ca.us/go/sinan

Sinan products are made from all-natural, primarily plant-based materials, all of which are listed on the packaging. Sinan 160 Series Natural Stain is available in 12 earth-tone colors and can be thinned using purified water.

Interior Transparent Finishes

In recent years, polyurethane and other clear interior finishes have dramatically decreased the amount of volatile organic compounds (VOCs) that they offgas. Waterborne polyurethanes are becoming common alternatives to conventional solvent-based products. The products included here have low VOC levels, are derived from natural materials, or have exceptional durability. For inclusion in GreenSpec, the VOC limit is 50 grams per liter.

Aqua ZAR

United Gilsonite Laboratories (UGL)
P.O. Box 70
Scranton, PA 18501

Toll-free: 800-272-3235
Phone: 570-344-1202
www.ugl.com

Aqua ZAR® Water-Based Polyurethane is a low-odor, nonyellowing, clear interior wood finish available in gloss and satin. According to the manufacturer, Aqua Zar's fast-drying, low-odor formula resists most household chemicals and abrasions.

BioShield Interior Transparent Finishes

Eco Design/BioShield Paint
   Company
1330 Rufina Cir.
Santa Fe, NM 87507

Toll-free: 800-621-2591
Phone: 505-438-3448
www.bioshieldpaint.com

The BioShield product line, available online and through the BioShield Paint Catalog, includes paints, waxes, finishes, and thinners derived from low-toxic, non-petroleum-based ingredients.

Land Ark Wood Finishes

Land Ark Wood Finishes
213 Townes Rd.
N. Augusta, SC 29860

Phone: 803-279-4116

Land Ark wood finishes are formulated for use on timber frames as well as both exterior and interior finish applications. These finishes—including tung oil, linseed oil, beeswax, D-limonene (cold-pressed from orange peels), and resin (from pine trees)—have no chemical additives, petroleum products, or heavy-metal driers and are completely biodegradable.

OSMO Hardwax Oil

Environmental Home Center
1724 Fourth Ave. S
Seattle, WA 98134

Toll-free: 800-281-9785
Phone: 206-682-7332
www.environmentalhomecenter.com

OSMO Hardwax Oil, formerly known as OS Hardwax Oil, is a penetrating floor finish made from natural vegetable oils and waxes, and contains no biocides or preservatives. Because OSMO is very high in solids, it can be applied in only two coats and is very durable. The finish may also be spot-repaired.

Pure Tung Oil

The Real Milk Paint Co.
11 West Pumping Station Rd.
Quakertown, PA 18951

Toll-free: 800-339-9748
Phone: 215-538-3886
www.realmilkpaint.com

The Real Milk Paint Company's 100% Pure Tung Oil contains no petroleum distillates or other additives and has a light, nutty odor. Tung oil, which comes from the seed of the tung tree, is a suitable treatment for wood and stone, forming a tough, flexible, water- and alkali-resistant coating. Pure Tung Oil produces a nontoxic finish that is suitable for food preparation surfaces. Other applications include children's toys and furniture, wooden instruments, and wood paneling and molding. A light coating on metal surfaces acts as an effective rust inhibitor.

Sutherland Welles Low-Toxic Wood Finishes

Sutherland Welles, Ltd.
P.O. Box 1387
Morrisville, VT 05661

Toll-free: 800-322-1245
Phone: 802-888-3222
www.sutherlandwelles.com

Sutherland Welles Low-Toxic Wood Finishes are polymerized tung oils with natural Di-Citrusol™ solvent and reduced chemical driers. The products are botanicals, free of petroleum distillates, and are available in various lustres and as a sealer. Performance and coverage of the low-toxic products are comparable to those features of conventional lines, according to the company. Millie's All Purpose Penetrating Wood Oil is formulated with polymerized tung oil, Di-Citrusol™ and beeswax; no chemical driers are added.

Tried & True Wood Finishes

Tried & True Wood
    Finishes
14 Prospect St.
Trumansburg, NY 14886

Phone: 607-387-9280
www.triedandtruewood
    finish.com

Photo: Ortiz Studios

Tried & True™ Wood Finishes are made from polymerized linseed oil through a proprietary heat treatment process. Original Wood Finish includes beeswax. Varnish Oil includes varnish resin (hardened tree sap). All are nontoxic with zero VOCs and no heavy-metal driers. The ingredients are derived from renewable agricultural resources. By contrast, conventional "boiled" linseed oil finishes typically include toxic, heavy-metal drying agents. Tried & True finishes are appropriate for a wide range of applications from interior millwork to fine furniture. Application labor costs are similar to those for conventional products. The Danish Oil Finish may also be used as a rammed-earth floor finish, while the Varnish Oil may be used as a concrete countertop sealant as well as a sealer for terra cotta and thrown-tile products.

ZVOC High Solids Clear Coat, Wax Seal & Finish, and Sanding Sealer

Fuhr International LLC
P.O. Box 86
Winigan, MO 63566

Toll-free: 800-558-7437
Phone: 660-857-4300
www.fuhrinternational.com

High Solids Clear Coat, Wax Seal & Finish, and Sanding Sealer are part of Fuhr International's ZVOC® line of zero-VOC coatings. High Solids Clear Coat and Wax Seal & Finish are water-based acrylic products for use on interior and exterior wood substrates. Both finishes were designed for the kitchen cabinet industry and exceed KCMA finish-coat testing requirements with proper application, but they are also suitable for a variety of other applications. Sanding Sealer is a water-based acrylic sanding sealer designed as a companion product for Fuhr's line of ZVOC finishes.

Mastic Removers

Look for low-VOC, nontoxic, biodegradable products.

BEANedoo Mastic Remover

Franmar Chemical, Inc.
P.O. Box 97
Normal, IL 61761

Toll-free: 800-538-5069
Phone: 309-452-7526
www.franmar.com

FranMar's BEANedoo® Mastic Remover is made from soybeans to remove ceramic tile mastic, asbestos mastic, and carpet mastic. BEANedoo Mastic Remover has no odor, is nontoxic, noncaustic, 100% biodegradable, and rinses with water.

Natural and Lime-Based Plaster

Lime plasters have lower embodied energy than portland-cement-based plasters, and they don't include petroleum-based ingredients, as acrylic plasters do. Integral natural pigments obviate the need for painting. Also included are wall coatings made from ingredients such as clay, sand, and cellulose.

American Clay Natural Earth Plaster

American Clay Enterprises, LLC
2601 Karsten Court, SE
Albuquerque, NM 87102

Toll-free: 866-404-1634
Phone: 505-243-5300
www.americanclay.com

Photo: Addison Doty

American Clay is a 100% natural earth plaster veneer made from clay, aggregates (including 65–75% post-industrial recycled marble dust), nontoxic mineral pigments, and a boric acid mold inhibitor. Designed for interior use, the product can be applied to many substrates (including painted surfaces, though a primer is required). American Clay Earth Plaster is breathable and is not for areas that come into direct contact with water such as shower stalls (areas subject to splashing can be sealed to resist damage). Available in 12 standard colors; custom colors may be ordered. American Clay Earth Plaster is mixed with water to apply, and can be rewet and reworked indefinitely if left unsealed. Produced in New Mexico exclusively with U.S.-sourced materials. No water or heat is used in production, and virtually no waste is generated, according to the company.

Clay Plaster

Clay Mine Adobe, Inc.
6401 W. Old Ajo Hwy.
Tucson, AZ 85735

Phone: 520-578-2222
www.claymineadobe.com

Clay Mine Adobe offers 95-lb. bags of clay plaster, both cement-stabilized and unstabilized, in a variety of earth tones.

St. Astier Natural Hydraulic Lime Plasters

TransMineral USA, Inc.
201 Purrington Rd.
Petaluma, CA 94952

Phone: 707-769-0661
www.limes.us

St. Astier Natural Hydraulic Lime, or NHL, is a 100% natural product imported from France that has been in production since 1851. Used in construction as plaster, stucco, mortar, and paint, its high level of vapor exchange and mineral composition can help reduce the risk of mold development and dry rot. NHL products are breathable, elastic, low shrinking, zero VOC, self-healing, and recyclable. Transmineral USA also offers Le Decor Selection, a line of high-end, all-natural interior/exterior limestone finishes which require trained installers and crushed limestone aggregate imported from France instead of the domestically available aggregate used for the St. Astier NHL products.

Terramed

Med Imports
1710 N. Leg Ct.
Augusta, GA 30909

Toll-free: 866-363-6334
Phone: 706-364-6334
www.medimports.net

Med Imports is the North American distributor for Terramed, an all-natural interior wall coating made from clay, sand, and cellulose. Terramed is available in 12 colors that are derived from clays from the Mediterranean plate of Europe. The product is shipped dry and mixed with water prior to application.

Tierrafino Clay Plaster

Hopper Handcrafted Specialty Finishes
302 S. 30th St.
Phoenix, AZ 85034

Phone: 602-273-1338
www.hopperfinishes.com

Tierrafino® is a 100% natural clay interior finish made from colored sands and clays mined from European quarries. The product

contains no pigment or chemical additives. Mother of pearl or straw can be mixed in to add interest. Because Tierrafino sets mechanically and not chemically, it may be reworked over and over again and the surface refreshed by wiping down with a wet sponge and rubbing with a soft brush. Tierrafino is available in several colors, which can be changed after installation by applying fresh Tierrafino powder with a wet sponge. The manufacturer claims the finish is suitable for areas of high humidity, though use should be avoided where it can come in contact with streams of water or excessively wet walls such as in cellars.

Paint Strippers

Conventional paint strippers, including those containing methylene chloride, are notoriously hazardous and should be avoided. Less-hazardous alternatives are becoming increasingly available. Look for low-VOC, nontoxic, biodegradable products.

Soy-Gel

Franmar Chemical, Inc.
P.O. Box 97
Normal, IL 61761

Toll-free: 800-538-5069
Phone: 309-452-7526
www.franmar.com

Soy Gel is a soy-based paint remover suitable for stripping lead-based paint. The product contains methylated soybean oil and mild surfactants, N-Methyl-2-Pyrolidone.

Recycled Paints

Some recycled paints are commingled paints from partially used containers, often collected under municipal waste programs. These are sometimes referred to as consolidated or reusable paint and are typically sold as primers because the color is variable. Other recycled paints are collected and reprocessed or remanufactured to achieve higher quality and consistency. The two resulting products are generally very different. The better recycled paint brands have sophisticated testing and quality control.

Amazon Select Recycled Paint

Amazon Environmental, Inc.
P.O. Box 9306
Whittier, CA 90608

Toll-free: 800-566-2396
Phone: 562-789-9191
www.amazonpaint.com

Amazon Select Recycled Paint is available in whipped white, ivory white, concrete gray, tawny beige, and chocolate brown. Custom colors are available upon request. Recover Brand recycled paint is sold exclusively through Dunn-Edwards Paint Co. in California, Colorado, Nevada, Texas, Arizona, and New Mexico. Amazon Select is sold directly through the manufacturer in all markets. The manufacturer has certified the following recycled-content levels (by weight): total recovered material 95% typical, 50% guaranteed; post-consumer material 95% typical, 50% guaranteed.

E-Coat Recycled Latex Paint

Kelly-Moore Paint Co.
987 Commercial St.
San Carlos, CA 94070

Toll-free: 800-874-4436 ext. 157 (corporate offices)
Phone: 916-921-0165
www.kellymoore.com

E-Coat is an interior/exterior line of paint made from recycled latex paint. Typically available in a flat finish, semi-gloss is also available by special order. Six standard colors are available, as well as a wide range of custom colors. The manufacturer has certified the following recycled-content levels (by weight): total recovered material 80% typical, 50% guaranteed; post-consumer material 80% typical, 50% guaranteed.

Local Color Recycled Latex Paint

The Environmental Depot
1011 Airport Pkwy.
S. Burlington, VT 05403-5804

Phone: 802-863-0480
www.cswd.net

Local Color recycled latex paint is made from 100% recycled, filtered latex paint that has been sorted by color and reblended. The cost is less than half the price of new paint, and quality satisfaction is guaranteed. Local Color interior and exterior paints are available for purchase at the Vermont Environmental Depot in a variety of colors including off-white, tan, green, gray, and blue. All paint is eggshell finish.

Recycled Paint

NU-BLEND Paints, Inc.
40 E. McMicken Ave.
Cincinnati, OH 45210

Phone: 513-651-5111
www.nublendpaints.com

NU-BLEND reblends unused latex paint into various colors and finishes for resale in the Cincinnati, Ohio marketplace. The manufacturer has certified the following recycled-content levels (by weight): total recovered material 100% typical, 100% guaranteed; post-consumer material 100% typical, 100% guaranteed.

VRI Remanufactured Latex Paint

Visions Recycling, Inc.
4205 S. Market Ct.
Sacramento, CA 95834

Toll-free: 800-770-7664
Phone: 916-564-9121
www.visionsrecycling.com

Visions Recycling, Inc. (VRI) produces recycled latex paint from post-consumer (contractor overstock and city and county paint collection sites) and secondary recycled sources (mistints and overstock from factory and store-level distributors). Minimum post-consumer/secondary recycled content is 50%. The paint is checked for quality, sorted, and reblended with virgin materials and additives to produce a high-resin paint that the company claims is comparable in quality to major brands of virgin, one-coat latex paints for roughly one-third the cost. The paints are available for interior and exterior applications, and they come in flat, eggshell, and semi-gloss in six stock colors (custom colors are available upon request). VRI is also working on a low-VOC recycled paint and a recycled traffic paint.

Specialty Sealers

Some low-toxicity sealers are formulated specifically to help reduce offgassing from interior finishes and furnishings.

Safecoat Safe Seal and Carpet Seal

American Formulating & Manufacturing (AFM)
3251 Third Ave.
San Diego, CA 92103

Toll-free: 800-239-0321
Phone: 619-239-0321
www.afmsafecoat.com

Safecoat® Safe Seal is a clear sealer designed to limit offgassing from particleboard and other manufactured wood products containing formaldehyde. It lends water repellency and serves as the base coat for adhesives and finishes on porous surfaces, including wood and concrete products. SafeChoice® Carpet Seal is designed to help prevent the offgassing from synthetic carpet backing and adhesives. Applied directly after shampooing carpet, Carpet Seal cures into a clear membrane. According to the company, Carpet Seal is odorless and remains effective for up to a year, depending on traffic and cleaning frequency. It cannot be applied to wool carpet.

SoySeal

Natural Soy, LLC
2 Liberty St.
Watkins, IA 52354

Toll-free: 888-655-0039
Phone: 319-227-7418

SoySeal is a water-based, nontoxic, nonflammable sealer suitable for exposed wood surfaces. It contains no VOCs or other known user hazards and cleans up with water. This product spreads water rather than beading it, which reduces the risk of UV magnification and damage, according to Natural Soy. Coverage is 150-300 ft². This product complies with ASTM C-672 and is also used to seal concrete. It is available in 1-, 5-, 55-, and 250-gallon containers.

SOYsolv Soy Seal

SOYsolv®
6154 N. CR 33
Tiffin, OH 44883

Toll-free: 800-231-4274
Phone: 419-992-4570
www.soysolv.com

SOYsolv Soy Seal, made from soybean oil, is a water-based, nontoxic, nonflammable, zero-VOC formulation for sealing cured concrete and wood. According to the company, testing in the upper Midwest shows sealing performance to last over a year outdoors.

Vapor-Retarding Coatings

These paints provide vapor-diffusion retarders on the inside of exterior walls. They're appropriate in climates where the vapor retarder always belongs on the interior side of perimeter walls—cold climates where air-conditioning is rarely used. (In warm climates and mixed climates, wall systems should be designed to dry to either the interior or exterior.) Vapor-retarding paints can provide a simple, low-cost vapor retarder without modifying the building envelope. Note that even without such paints the wall finish material can provide an air barrier, which is generally more important in controlling moisture migration into walls.

Prep & Prime Interior Primer/Sealers

The Glidden Company
925 Euclid Ave.
Cleveland, OH 44115

Toll-free: 800-834-6077
Phone: 216-344-8000
www.iciduluxpaints.com

Prep & Prime Odor-Less Primer Sealer (LM9116) is a zero-VOC tintable primer and sealer for interior use. Prep & Prime Vapor Barrier Interior Primer/Sealer (1060) is a latex primer-sealer formulated to reduce the permeability of wall surfaces. It is low-VOC (85 g/l) and tintable; it may also be topcoated with latex or alkyd paints of any finish. This product has a perm rating of 0.6 when applied at a coverage rate of 400 ft²/gal to smooth surfaces, which compares favorably with the performance of a 2-mil-thick sheet of medium-density polyethylene.

This Space is Available for Your Notes

This Space is Available for Your Notes

Mechanical Systems/HVAC

Heating, ventilation, and air-conditioning (HVAC) are the "engine" that drives the comfort systems in most structures. They directly consume the largest portion of energy in buildings—which makes them critically important from an environmental standpoint. Additionally, good indoor air quality to a significant extent depends on the ventilation they provide, while a problematic mechanical system can create and distribute indoor pollutants.

The first place to look to minimize the impact of a mechanical system isn't the equipment, however; it's the building's design and construction. Careful, integrated design and optimal levels of insulation can minimize the need for supplemental heating, ventilation, or air-conditioning. In situations where a central mechanical system is still necessary, an efficient building envelope can reduce the size of that system. A high-performance domestic water heater is fully capable of supplying heat to a very well-insulated house in most U.S. climates.

In a well-designed building, distribution requirements are also greatly reduced—offering tremendous potential savings in both first cost and operating costs. Houses with very well-insulated walls and high-performance windows, for example, may no longer require heat distribution at the exterior walls to provide comfort. Short duct runs to the closest point in each room save a great deal of money and space, and reduce the potential for wasteful air leakage from the duct system (which should be sealed with duct mastic, not duct tape, at all joints).

After reducing the loads that a mechanical system must meet, it's important to size the system carefully to meet the remaining loads. An oversized system wastes money and materials initially and then operates wastefully, because heating and cooling equipment is at its most efficient when operating at full capacity.

Mechanical equipment should be as efficient as possible, durable, and installed for ease of regular maintenance. As is common practice with heating and cooling, fresh air should be provided to each occupied space and distributed to avoid pockets of trapped, stale air.

To avoid the risk of backdrafting toxic flue gases such as carbon monoxide into a home, only sealed-combustion equipment should be used in houses.

Many air-conditioning systems still rely on HCFC refrigerants, which destroy the ozone layer if allowed to escape. These are being phased out in favor of non-ozone-depleting alternatives. The system efficiency, potential for refrigerant leakage, and ozone-depletion potential of the refrigerant should all be considered when choosing an air-conditioning system.

Good controls are also important. They should have setback options to adjust temperature and fresh air set points according to occupancy levels and time of day, and be easy to understand and use. "Smart" microprocessor-driven controllers with occupancy-detecting sensors can "learn" the activity of a household over time, activating mechanical equipment.

A mechanical system also requires careful *commissioning* to ensure optimal operation. During commissioning, mechanical equipment is checked for proper operation, distribution systems are balanced, and controls are all checked. All too often, careless mistakes in installation and set-up result in poor system performance. Without a commissioning process, these mistakes might not be caught for years. Commissioning is important in both commercial buildings and homes. In large commercial buildings with complex systems, it has been found useful to videotape the commissioning process for future use in training building managers. Clear, thorough documentation is critical to ensure proper ongoing maintenance and operation of systems of any size.

Biomass for woodstoves, pellet stoves, industrial wood-chip boilers, and other combustion devices is renewable as long as production of that biomass is sustainable—i.e., as long as harvesting doesn't outpace regeneration or stress the ecosystems. Some of these heating systems can generate significant amounts of air pollution, however, so appropriate pollution controls such as catalytic converters or secondary burn chambers should always be incorporated.

Air Conditioning Equipment

The two most important issues with compressor-based cooling systems are energy efficiency and potential ozone depletion from refrigerants. Most unitary equipment now uses R-22, an HCFC, as the refrigerant. This refrigerant is slated for phaseout by 2020. A few units use HFC refrigerants, which do not affect the ozone layer but are greenhouse gases that contribute to global warming if released to the atmosphere. Seasonal energy efficiency ratio (SEER) ratings compare cooling capacity (in Btu) to energy inputs (in watts) and are helpful in evaluating central air-conditioner performance. One ton of cooling capacity represents the ability to remove 12,000 Btu of heat per hour. Also consider the moisture-removal capability of air-conditioning equipment.

Elite Series Air Conditioners

Lennox Industries, Inc.
P.O. Box 799900
Dallas, TX 75379

Toll-free: 800-953-6669
Phone: 972-497-5000
www.lennox.com

The Elite series two-speed model HSX19 uses non-ozone-depleting R410A refrigerant, and at 19.2 SEER, it's one of the highest-rated central air conditioning units available. It carries a 10-year limited compressor warranty, and a 5-year limited warranty on covered components. Though it is non-ozone-depleting, HFC refrigerant R410A is a significant greenhouse gas that, like HCFC, contributes to global warming.

Prestige Ultra Line

Amana Refrigeration, Inc.
1810 Wilson Pkwy.
Fayetteville, TN 37334

Toll-free: 877- 254-4729
Phone: 931-433-6101
www.amana-hac.com

Amana's Prestige Ultra line of central air conditioners offers SEER ratings of 14 with furnace coils and to 16.5 with Amana's BBC blower and coil. Six different models range in size from 2 to 5 tons.

Quantum Plus Air Conditioners

Bryant Heating & Cooling Systems
7310 W. Morris St.
Indianapolis, IN 46231

Toll-free: 800-428-4236
Phone: 317-240-2935
www.bryant.com

Bryant uses the chlorine-free refrigerant Puron® as a replacement for Freon-22 in their Quantum™ range of air conditioners. The Quantum model 598b has a rating of up to 16.5 SEER; the 556A, 15.75 SEER; and the 550A, 14 SEER.

Stealth Series and Stellar Ultra Series

York International Corp. - Unitary Products Group
5005 York Dr.
Norman, OK 73069

Toll-free: 877-874-7378
Phone: 405-364-4040
www.yorkupg.com

The Stealth™ Series offers up to 16.2-SEER residential split systems in sizes ranging from 2 to 5 tons. A unique feature allows the compressor to run on only one of its two pistons during low capacity, which increases part-load efficiency. This line is also designed for especially quiet operation. The Stellar Plus residential split system condenser comes in 1.5-5 nominal ton units rated from 12-13.8 SEER; the higher SEER is possible with variable speed. This is a condensing unit only, designed to run with the variable-speed Enhancer air handler or a Diamond furnace.

WeatherMaker Central Air Conditioners

Carrier Corp.
P.O. Box 4808
Syracuse, NY 13221

Toll-free: 800-227-7437
Phone: 315-432-6000
www.carrier.com

The WeatherMaker® line from Carrier includes the company's most efficient central air conditioners (38TDB models), with SEER ratings up to 18.0. The company's somewhat lower-efficiency Weather-Maker 38TSA and 38TXA central air conditioners have SEER ratings of 14 and 13, respectively. All three units use Carrier's new Puron refrigerant (R-410a), which is a blend of three different HFCs.

XL19i Air Conditioners

Trane Residential Products Division
6200 Troup Hwy.
Tyler, TX 75707

Phone: 903-581-3200
www.trane.com

Trane's 2.5-ton XL19i two-stage air conditioner is a highly efficient unit which, when coupled with an optional air-handler, achieves a SEER rating of up to 19.5. The 3-ton unit, with the optional air-handler, is rated up to SEER 19; the 4- and 5-ton units, similarly enhanced, can deliver 17 and 16.5 SEER, respectively. The XL19i uses R-22 refrigerant. The manufacturer's limited warranty covers compressor, coil, and internal functional parts for 10 years.

Air Filters and Air Cleaning Devices

Air filtration is an important part of HVAC design. Quality products should have high filtration efficiency over a range of particle sizes, be energy-efficient (low pressure drop across filters), and durable. Measures of filtration defined by ASHRAE standards include arrestance efficiency, dust-spot efficiency, and Minimum Efficiency Reporting Value (MERV) ratings. High-efficiency particulate air (HEPA) filters are designed to capture extremely fine particulates but require increased duct pressure, which may necessitate an oversized mechanical system. Some lower-efficiency filters use recycled materials or are washable.

Airguard Air Filters

Airguard, Inc.
P.O. Box 32578
Louisville, KY 40232

Toll-free: 800-999-3458
Phone: 502-969-2304
www.airguard.com

Airguard produces a wide range of air filtration products, including rigid-cell filters with MERV 13 and higher ratings and HEPA filters. The company's Permalast® latex-coated natural-fiber (hog's hair) media and foam media, both with arrestance values of 60–70% (MERV 1-2), can be washed for repeated use but are only suitable for filtering the coarsest particulates. StreamLine™ filters, with arrestance values of 85-95% (MERV 5-6), are produced primarily from post-consumer recycled polyester fiber. Variflow filters, including the Compact Series, which rely on ultrafine fiberglass and wet-laid paper filtration, are available with dust-spot efficiencies of 60-95% (MERV 11-14).

Air Outlets and Inlets

These listings include passive fresh-air make-up inlets that replace air removed by exhaust-only ventilation systems. Floor diffusers are used in commercial applications to deliver conditioned air from access-floor plenums.

Fresh 80 and Reton 80 Passive Air Inlets

Therma-Stor LLC
P.O. Box 8050
Madison, WI 53708

Toll-free: 800-533-7533
Phone: 608-222-5301
www.thermastor.com

Fresh 80 and Reton 80 through-the-wall passive air inlets supply controlled trickle ventilation for tight buildings. A single unit is designed to supply fresh air for up to 270 ft² of floor area. Both are available in a larger "100" version, supplying more fresh air for a given indoor-outdoor pressure difference.

Trickle Ventilators

Titon Inc.
6910 North Main St., Ste. 21A - Unit 26
Granger, IN 46530

Phone: 574-271-9699
www.titon.com

Titon produces a range of trickle ventilators designed to suit a variety of window applications, including retrofits. Tests indicate that IAQ is improved with little negative effect on energy costs. The moving air also helps to reduce condensation mold.

Boilers and Accessories

Boilers heat water in hydronic heating systems; the heat is distributed through baseboard radiators (convectors), panel radiators, or radiant-floor piping. These listings include the highest-efficiency oil- or gas-fired boilers and products, as well as biomass-fired alternatives. (Well-designed biomass-fueled boilers have very high burning efficiencies which reduce particulate emissions to less than half of the levels of the best wood stoves.) Some water heaters—especially electronic-ignition on-demand water heaters—can also be used as boilers for heating, particularly in very-low-energy buildings.

FCX Oil-Fired Condensing Boiler

Monitor Products, Inc.
P.O. Box 3408
Princeton, NJ 08543

Toll-free: 800-524-1102
Phone: 732-329-0900
www.monitorproducts.com

The FCX is a small, oil-fired condensing boiler measuring 33½" H x 23" W x 24½" D with a Btu output of 76,100 and an application efficiency of 95%. The unit (which produces heat and domestic hot water) contains a primary, noncondensing heat exchanger coupled to a stainless steel condensing secondary heat exchanger. The FCX is approved as a sealed combustion device and can be fitted to take combustion air from the outside via a concentric vent.

G115 Sealed-Combustion Oil Boilers

Buderus
50 Wentworth
Londonderry, NH 03053

Phone: 603-898-0505
www.buderus.net

The smallest three models in this German hydronic boiler line are among the only true sealed-combustion, oil-fired residential boilers on the market. They are noted for their quiet operation and 86% combustion efficiency. A sophisticated "Logamatic" optional control module allows boiler water temperature control based on outside temperature (outdoor reset), plus priority control for indirect water heating. Buderus also makes indirect water heater tanks.

Multi-Fuel and Wood Boilers

Tarm USA, Inc.
5 Main St.
P.O. Box 285
Lyme, NH 03768

Toll-free: 800-782-9927
Phone: 603-795-2214
www.woodboilers.com

The HS-Tarm Excel 2000 Boiler is a multi-fuel boiler and domestic water heater that operates at over 80% efficiency on wood and 85% on oil. It has fully automatic controls to maintain the wood fire and the oil or gas backup that will automatically turn on the oil or gas burner when the wood fire dies down. The Excel 2000 burns very cleanly and generates very little ash for clean up.

The HS-Tarm Solo Plus-MKII boiler and domestic hot-water heater uses substantially less wood than conventional boilers and outdoor water stoves and also has a very clean burn. Three sizes are available with outputs from 100,000 to 198,000 Btu/hr.

Multi-Pulse Boilers

The Hydrotherm Corp.
260 N. Elm St.
Westfield, MA 01085

Phone: 413-564-5515
www.hydrotherm.com

The Multi-Pulse sealed-combustion gas boiler is available in three sizes. Seasonal efficiency is 90% (AFUE). Units may be joined in modules and linked to heat exchangers for even greater efficiencies.

MZ Boiler

Monitor Products, Inc.
P.O. Box 3408
Princeton, NJ 08543

Toll-free: 800-524-1102
Phone: 732-329-0900
www.monitorproducts.com

Monitor is the U.S. distributor for the fully condensing gas-fired MZ Boiler. All three models are wall-mounted and perform with up to 97.7% efficiency (minimum of 90%, according to the company). The units offer spark ignition, sealed combustion, and zero clearance, and use only 108 watts of electricity to operate. The MZ25S (the only unit of the three to provide both heat and domestic hot water) and the MZ25C have 94,000 Btu/hr input. The MZ40C has 142,500 Btu/hr input in two 71,000 Btu stages (high/low fire). These hydronic heat sources meet German "Blue Angel" environmental standards.

Opus G1 Gas Hydronic Heat Source

Burnham Corporation
1241 Harrisburg Ave.
P.O. Box 3205
Lancaster, PA 17604-3205

Toll-free: 877-567-4328
Phone: 717-397-4701
www.burnham.com

The Opus G1 Hydronic Heat Source for residential or commercial installations is available in three models (50,000 to 250,000 Btu/hr) with AFUEs ranging from 97% to 99%. The fully condensing unit uses a Direct Contact heat exchanger in which hot combustion gases come in direct contact with the water in the unit. The gases are also showered with water inside a "condensation tower." Made from durable components, the G1 offers flexible venting options, including direct-vent (outside air for combustion). Exhaust venting is via standard or thin-wall PVC pipe (with vent lengths up to 60') requiring 0" clearance to combustible surfaces. Units can be installed alone or in tandem; with radiant heat applications, no barrier pipe or mixing valves are required. Domestic water heating is possible when combined with a storage tank. Opus boilers are also available in an oil-fired version.

Opus O1 Oil-Fired Boiler

Burnham Corporation
1241 Harrisburg Ave.
P.O. Box 3205
Lancaster, PA 17604-3205

Toll-free: 877-567-4328
Phone: 717-397-4701
www.burnham.com

The Opus O1 oil-fired, noncondensing, hydronic boiler (AFUE 88.6-90.1) is available in three sizes with three firing ranges for each size (heating outputs from 76,000 to 267,000 Btu/hr). The boiler, constructed of durable materials and designed to minimize noise, can be used for residential or light commercial applications, or installed in tandem for larger applications. A control center automatically adjusts the system-supply water temperature based on outdoor air temperature (outdoor reset). The unit produces water temperatures between 60 and 240°F without need for additional mixing controls and can return water as low as 55°F. Radiant system components (radiant pipe, manifold, etc.) can be added without extra costs and complications of specialized system components. The Opus line also includes a gas-fired version.

Polaris Heating Systems

American Water Heater Company
500 Princeton Rd.
Johnson City, TN 37601

Toll-free: 800-937-1037
Phone: 423-283-8000
www.americanwaterheater.com

Polaris Heating Systems are high-efficiency, combination water and residential space-heating products. The gas-fired unit has a submerged stainless steel flue that transfers combustion energy to the water with 95+% efficiency. Polaris heaters are available in 34- and 50-gal. sizes with outputs of 100,000 to 199,000 Btu/hr and energy factors of 0.86.

Quantum Series Boilers

ECR International, Inc.
2201 Dwyer Ave.
Utica, NY 13501

Phone: 315-797-1310
www.ecrinternational.com

The Quantum Leap condensing, gas-fired, residential hot water boiler features a cast aluminum heat exchanger and an AFUE of 95%. Via a second heat exchanger, hot flue gases heat condensate which is used to saturate and heat combustion air so that 90+% efficiencies can be obtained at return water temperatures up to 160°F. The system is most efficient (up to 98%), however, with lower temperature water returns such as with radiant systems. The boiler offers sealed combustion and direct venting. PVC exhaust piping requires 0" clearance to combustible construction. The other unit in the series, the Quantum 90 (AFUE 90%), is similar but does not use condensate to heat and saturate combustion air. According to the manufacturer, both units substantially reduce CO and NOx emissions (acid rain and smog components)—to less than 10 ppm for the Quantum Leap and 30 ppm for the Quantum 90.

System 2000

Energy Kinetics
Molasses Hill Rd.
Lebanon, NJ 08833

Toll-free: 800-323-2066
www.energykinetics.com

System 2000 has one of the highest seasonal efficiency of any oil heating system on the market with an AFUE rating of 87%. This integrated system produces heat and hot water.

Duct Mastic

Duct leakage is a major problem with forced-air heating or air-conditioning systems. When ducts are run outside of the conditioned space, heating and cooling efficiencies may be cut in half due to leakage. Tightly sealed ducting is extremely important in ensuring high energy efficiency of forced-air HVAC equipment. Experts strongly recommend duct mastics for sealing ducts—not duct tape.

Duct Mastics

RCD Corporation
2850 Dillard Rd.
Eustis, FL 32727

Toll-free: 800-854-7494
Phone: 352-589-0099
www.rcdmastics.com

RCD Corporation is a leading manufacturer of elastomeric, water-based adhesives, sealants, and duct mastics.

Duct Sealants

Hardcast, Inc.
900 Hensley Ln.
P.O. Box 1239
Wylie, TX 75098

Toll-free: 800-527-7092
Phone: 972-442-6545
www.hardcast.com

Hardcast manufactures a line of VOC-free and water-based duct sealants.

UNI-MASTIC 181 Duct Sealer

McGill Airseal Corporation
2400 Fairwood Ave.
Columbus, OH 43207

Toll-free: 800-624-5535
Phone: 614-443-5520
www.mcgillairseal.com

Uni-Mastic™ 181 duct sealer is a water-based product that is designed to remain flexible over time in applications including sheet-metal, flexible, and fiberglass duct. It is UL181 listed and contains antimicrobial agents that remain effective after curing.

Ducts

Air-supply and return ducts can be a medium for mold growth or (with insulated ducts) a source of fiber-shedding, both of which can pose significant indoor air quality concerns. Products listed here allow easy duct cleaning, or protect against mold growth or fiber-shedding.

ToughGard

CertainTeed Corporation
750 E. Swedesford Rd.
P.O. Box 860
Valley Forge, PA 19482

Toll-free: 800-233-8990
Phone: 610-341-7739
www.certainteed.com

CertainTeed's ToughGard™ fiberglass duct board is a ducting material with integral insulation. At 75°F, the company claims an R-value of 4.3 for 1" board, 6.5 for 1$^1/_2$" board, and 8.7 for 2" board. To prevent fiber shedding, ToughGard has both a nonwoven composite interior facing of textile fiberglass and polypropylene, and a reinforced foil-laminate exterior facing. The material's ship-lap design helps minimize air leakage at joints. This product carries the GREENGUARD certification for low emissions.

Fans

Exhaust fans are an important component of today's tightly-sealed buildings. Unless there's a central ventilation system, kitchen and bathroom spot-ventilators may be the only mechanical ventilation system in a house. To increase the likelihood that fans will be used, they should be quiet. To be included in GreenSpec, bathroom ventilators must have some sone ratings no higher than 1.5. ("Sone" is a measure of loudness; one sone is about as loud as a common residential refrigerator.) Quiet

kitchen range-hood fans are much more difficult to find; often the best option is to use a remote, in-line fan. Ceiling fans are designed to mix air in a room and provide airflow for enhanced comfort—they do not provide fresh air. Attic fans are used for whole-house exhaust and airflow or for heat removal from attics. In certain climates, attic fans can be used very effectively for night-flush cooling, in which household air is replaced with cooler air during the nighttime hours.

F. R. Series Fans

Fantech
1712 Northgate Blvd.
Sarasota, FL 34234

Toll-free: 800-747-1762
www.fantech.net

Fantech's in-line duct fans are often specified where minimizing noise is a high priority. These in-line fans range in size from 122 cfm to 649 cfm, 4" to 10" duct diameter, with energy consumption from 19 W to 241 W. Smaller products are generally used for residential applications; larger for commercial. Fantech's F.R. Series fans carry a 5-year warranty.

Fan-Attic

Steeltile Distributing, Inc.
1900 Dobbin Dr.
San Jose, CA 95133

Phone: 408-254-7900
www.fan-attic.com

The Fan-Attic™, formerly available from Sun Tunnel Skylights, Inc., is a PV-powered roof ventilator fan that can move up to 800 cfm. This product is used instead of (or in addition to) ridge or gable vents. This solar-powered fan works hardest when ventilation is needed most and saves on installation costs because electrical wiring is not necessary.

Gossamer Wind Ceiling Fans

King of Fans, Inc.
1951 N.W. 22nd St.
Ft. Lauderdale, FL 33311

Toll-free: 800-330-3267
Phone: 954-484-7500
www.king-of-fans.com

King of Fans is now manufacturing the energy-efficient Gossamer Wind Ceiling Fans for Home Depot's Hampton Bay label. Tests have shown that the production models are 40–50% more energy-efficient than conventional fans.

Panasonic Exhaust Fans

Panasonic Consumer Electronics
  Building Department
Panazip 4A-6
One Panasonic Way
Secaucus, NJ 07094

Toll-free: 866-292-7292
www.panasonic.com

Panasonic manufactures a full line of very quiet high-efficiency exhaust fans and fan-light combination units. All fan motors are high-efficiency and designed for continuous operation. Panasonic was the first company to introduce a truly quiet bathroom fan, and the company remains an industry leader.

Quiet Vent

Therma-Stor LLC
P.O. Box 8050
Madison, WI 53708

Toll-free: 800-533-7533
Phone: 608-222-5301
www.thermastor.com

Quiet Vent is a multiport, central exhaust ventilation system designed to quietly, effectively, and automatically ventilate airtight homes.

SolarCool Attic Vent

Gibraltar Company
3556 Lake Shore Rd.
Buffalo, NY 14219

Phone: 800-247-8368
www.airvent.com

The SolarCool vent from Air Vent, Inc., is a low-profile, galvanized steel dome with a high-efficiency 24-volt DC motor powered by a small solar panel. The photovoltaic panel is mounted either on an adjustable bracket directly on the vent dome or up to 10 feet away, allowing it to be positioned for optimal solar exposure. No auxiliary electricity is required. It ventilates up to 800 cfm for attics up to 1,200 ft², and comes with a 5-year limited warranty.

Solitaire Ultra Silent

Broan-NuTone LLC
926 W. State St.
P.O. Box 140
Hartford, WI 53027

Toll-free: 800-558-1711
Phone: 262-673-4340
www.broan.com

The Solitaire line includes 11 quiet, energy-efficient bathroom ventilation fans with 90–110 cfm of exhaust power.

Ultra-QuieTTest

NuTone, Inc.
2820 Red Bank Rd.
Cincinnati, OH 45227

Toll-free: 888-336-3948
Phone: 513-527-5100
www.nutone.com

NuTone produces the Ultra-QuieTTest® line of bathroom fans.

Vent-Axia LoWatt

Coast Products, Inc.
954 Elliott Ave. W
Seattle, WA 98119

Toll-free: 800-735-7026
Phone: 206-285-5120
www.coastproducts.com

The Vent-Axia LoWatt through-the-wall exhaust fan has an electric opening shutter with positive closure. Its motor's service life is reported to be 5 times longer than that of conventional motors, and the fan delivers an incredible 10.8 watts/cfm.

Ventilation and Airflow Equipment

Tamarack Technologies, Inc.
11 Patterson's Brook Rd.
P.O. Box 490
West Wareham, MA 02576

Toll-free: 800-222-5932
Phone: 508-295-8103
www.tamtech.com

Tamarack Technologies produces specialized ventilators and ventilation controllers. Among its innovative products are the sophisticated whole-house ventilators (HV 1000 and HV 1600-Gold) and the Preventilator 2, a through-the-wall bath exhaust fan. All three fans have motorized, insulated covers that seal the exhaust opening tightly when the units are not in operation.

Furnaces

Furnaces heat air that is then distributed through ducting and warm-air registers. These listings include the highest-efficiency, sealed-combustion furnaces.

Diamond 90 and Diamond 95 ULTRA

York International Corp.
Unitary Products Group
5005 York Dr.
Norman, OK 73069

Toll-free: 877-874-7378
Phone: 405-364-4040
www.yorkupg.com

The Diamond 90 gas-fired, sealed-combustion furnace has an efficiency of up to 94.3% AFUE. This condensing-type furnace is suitable for commercial and residential installation. The Diamond 90 has a primary and secondary heat exchanger to maximize efficiency. The Diamond 95 Ultra comes with a variable-speed fan.

GUVA Air Command 95 IIQ

Amana Heating and Air Conditioning
1810 Wilson Pkwy.
Fayetteville, TN 37334

Phone: 800-647-2982
www.amana-hac.com

Amana's Air Command 95 IIQ two-stage, variable-speed gas furnace has an efficiency of up to 96% AFUE. Heating capacity ranges from 67,000 to 109,000 Btu/hr. The 95 IIQ is available in a variety of airflow configurations.

Plus 90 High-Efficiency Furnaces

Bryant Heating & Cooling Systems
7310 W. Morris St.
Indianapolis, IN 46231

Toll-free: 800-428-4236
Phone: 317-240-2935
www.bryant.com

Bryant's Plus 90i (also known as the 355MAV) series of gas furnaces has AFUEs ranging from to 95.0 to 96.6%. Heating capacities from its two-stage gas valve range from 25,000/38,000 Btu/hr for the smallest model to 73,000/112,000 for the largest. These furnaces have variable-speed fans and advanced humidity-control technology, and are available in upflow, downflow, or horizontal airflow configurations. The Plus 90 (or 350MAV) line is 95.5% efficient, with multispeed blowers (rather than variable speed) and a single-stage valve. Its output ranges from 38,000 to 139,000 Btu/hr.

UltraMAX III

ECR International, Inc.
2201 Dwyer Ave.
Utica, NY 13501

Phone: 315-797-1310
www.ecrinternational.com

Olsen's UltraMAX III high-efficiency furnaces are available in heating capacities ranging from 47,000 to 95,000 Btu/hr. The GTH 85 and GTH 100 models have efficiencies of up to 95% AFUE. GTH 50 and GTH 70 have efficiencies of up to 94% AFUE.

WeatherMaker Infinity Series

Carrier Corp.
P.O. Box 4808
Syracuse, NY 13221

Toll-free: 800-227-7437
Phone: 315-432-6000
www.carrier.com

Carrier's WeatherMaker series of gas furnaces features a smart microprocessor control center and variable-speed motors that minimize electrical usage during both heating and cooling operation. Sealed combustion protects indoor air quality and reduces noise. Models in this series range in heating capacity from 25,000 to 113,000 Btu per hour and are available in a variety of airflow configurations. The 58MVP, with an efficiency of up to 96.6% AFUE, is Carrier's most efficient gas furnace. It has a variable-speed fan, 4-way multipoise, and advanced humidity-removal capabilities. The 9200 (58MXA) has 4-way multipoise but a single-speed fan. It has an efficiency of up to 95.5 AFUE. The 58MTA has a two-speed fan and efficiency of up to 93% AFUE.

Heat Pumps

Heat pumps are similar to air conditioners—but in addition to removing heat, they can reverse their cycle to pump heat into a building when needed. Heat pumps use electricity as the energy input; the heat source is the outside air, the ground, or a body of water. Air-source heat pumps use the outdoor air as the heat source or heat sink. Air-source heat pump heating efficiency is measured as the Heating Seasonal Performance Factor (HSPF), which is the ratio of thermal energy output (in Btu) to electrical energy input (in watt-hours) over a heating season. Similarly derived, the cooling performance of air-source heat pumps is typically measured as the seasonal energy efficiency rating (SEER). Ground-source heat pumps utilize the earth's more stable temperatures as the heat source and heat sink; performance is typically measured as the coefficient of performance (COP)—the instantaneous ratio of energy input in Btus to energy output in Btus. Since the temperatures are usually more moderate underground, geothermal systems typically cost less to operate than conventional heat pumps. Water-source heat pumps are like ground-source heat pumps but use a body of water as the heat source and sink. Some heat pumps can provide water heating in addition to heating and cooling.

Cold Climate Heat Pump

Nyle Special Products, LLC
P.O. Box 1107
Bangor, ME 04402

Phone: 207-942-2865
www.nyletherm.com

The multiple-stage Cold Climate Heat Pump™ (CCHP) from Nyle Special Products rivals many geothermal heat pumps in performance, achieving an average coefficient of performance (COP) of 2.7. In cooling mode, its seasonal energy efficiency ratio (SEER) is 16, higher than most dedicated unitary air conditioners. The system was designed to take full advantage of the non-ozone-depleting refrigerant R-410a, which can withstand up to 70% higher pressure and has 40% better cooling capacity than R-22 (which is scheduled to be phased out in the U.S. in 2010).

Elite Series Heat Pumps

Lennox Industries, Inc.
P.O. Box 799900
Dallas, TX 75379

Toll-free: 800-953-6669
Phone: 972-497-5000
www.lennox.com

The Elite series two-speed model HPX19 uses non-ozone-depleting R410A refrigerant, and at 18.6 SEER (cooling) and 9.3 HSPF (heating), it's one of the highest-rated heat pumps available. It carries a 10-year limited compressor warranty and a 5-year limited warranty on covered components. Though HFC refrigerant R410A is non-ozone-depleting, it, like HCFC, is a significant greenhouse gas that contributes to global warming.

Ground-Source Heat Pumps

ClimateMaster
7300 S.W. 44th St.
Oklahoma City, OK 73179

Phone: 405-745-6000
www.climatemaster.com

ClimateMaster is one of the largest producers of ground-source heat pumps.

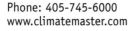

Ground-Source Heat Pumps

ECONAR Energy Systems Corp.
19230 Evans St.
Elk River, MN 55330

Toll-free: 800-432-6627
Phone: 763-241-3110
www.econar.com

The ColdClimate™ GeoSource® 2000 line of ground-source heat pumps are designed for residential (1 to 6 tons) and commercial (8 to 10 tons) applications. These self-contained units have a 25°F design point for regions with higher numbers of heating degree days per year.

Ground-Source Heat Pumps

WaterFurnace International, Inc.
9000 Conservation Way
Fort Wayne, IN 46809

Toll-free: 800-222-5667
Phone: 260-478-5667
www.waterfurnace.com

WaterFurnace International manufactures and distributes E Series, Premier, and Versatec commercial, institutional, and residential lines of ground-source geothermal heat pumps for retrofit or new construction. WaterFurnace produces both water-to-air and water-to-water units with $^3/_4$- to 30-ton capacities. E Series line uses R410-A refrigerant that does not deplete the ozone layer. Wholly owned subsidiary LoopMaster, Inc. is an earth loop contractor.

Quantum Plus 698b Heat Pump

Bryant Heating & Cooling Systems
7310 W. Morris St.
Indianapolis, IN 46231

Toll-free: 800-428-4236
Phone: 317-240-2935
www.bryant.com

Bryant produces the Quantum Plus™ 698b heat pump using non-ozone-depleting Puron™ refrigerant. The heat pump features a quiet fan and pump, two speeds, a SEER rating of 16, HSPF of 8.5, plus a 10-year warranty on the compressor and 5 years on everything else. The 650A heat pump also uses Puron™ refrigerant, has a SEER of 13.0 to 14.5, and the same warranty as the 698b.

Water-Source Heat Pump

FHP Manufacturing
601 N.W. 65th Ct.
Ft. Lauderdale, FL 33309

Phone: 954-776-5471
www.fhp-mfg.com

The EV Series EnviroMiser water-source heat pump is among FHP's most efficient and one of the first ground-source/water-source heat pumps to use the non-ozone-depleting refrigerant R-410a, an HFC mixture.

XL19i Air-Source Heat Pump

Trane Residential Products Division
6200 Troup Hwy.
Tyler, TX 75707

Phone: 903-581-3200
www.trane.com

Trane's 2.5-ton Weatherton® XL19i dual-compressor heat pump is one of the most efficient residential air-source heat pumps on the market, with a SEER (cooling value) of up to 17.9. The 3-, 4-, and 5-ton units have somewhat lower SEER-values. The HSPF (heating value) for this line ranges from 8.3 to 8.9. The manufacturer's limited warranty covers compressor, coil, and internal functional parts for 10 years.

Heat-Recovery and Energy-Recovery Ventilation

Heat-Recovery Ventilators (HRVs) and Energy-Recovery Ventilators (ERVs) are mechanical air-exchange systems that can capture up to 90% of the heat content from stale indoor air being exchanged for fresh outside air. These products work by passing the air streams through a heat-exchange core, generally made with multiple aluminum or plastic plates. HRVs capture heat from the outgoing air during heating season to warm the incoming air; and in cooling season, heat from the incoming air is transferred to the outgoing air to help prevent warming the building while providing fresh air. ERVs also provide humidity conditioning using a desiccant wheel or plates made of a permeable material; these help retain indoor moisture during the heating season and exclude it during the cooling season. The efficiency of the heat exchange is dependent on both the equipment and the climate. Most systems are balanced: the same volume of air is exhausted and taken in.

200S Energy Recovery Ventilators

American Aldes Ventilation Corp.
4537 Northgate Ct.
Sarasota, FL 34234

Toll-free: 800-255-7749
Phone: 941-351-3441
www.americanaldes.com

American Aldes Ventilation 200S Energy Recovery Ventilator (ERV) is designed for climates with long cooling seasons and moderately cold winters, where the temperature remains above 0°F. In the cooling season, the moisture from outdoors is transferred to the exhaust air stream, thus reducing loads on the air conditioning system and enabling more effective humidity control. In the heating season, the ERV tempers the incoming air stream, recapturing needed moisture from the exhaust air stream and directing it to the conditioned space.

Aprilaire Energy Recovery Ventilator

Aprilaire
1015 E. Washington Ave.
P.O. Box 1467
Madison, WI 53701

Toll-free: 800-334-6011
Phone: 608-257-8801
www.aprilaire.com

The Aprilaire Energy Recovery Ventilator (formerly PerfectAire® Fresh Air Exchanger) uses an Energy Max® enthalpic-type air exchanger to recover approximately 77% of the heat in outgoing air and to control moisture, according to the company. Aprilaire also offers a full line of indoor air quality products, such as programmable thermostats, whole-house humidifiers, zoning, and high-efficiency air cleaners.

AVS Solo and AVS Duo

Venmar Ventilation Inc.
550 Lemire Blvd.
Drummondville, PQ J2C 7W9 Canada

Toll-free: 800-567-3855
Phone: 819-477-6226
www.venmar-ventilation.com

Previously known as VanEE, Venmar is the leading manufacturer of advanced ventilation equipment. The company manufactures energy-efficient ventilation equipment including enthalpic wheels, HRVs, and ERVs. Venmar's residential products include the AVS Solo, an HRV, and the AVS Duo, an ERV, meaning that it also reclaims moisture in the air stream. The company offers an extensive line of controls for maintaining comfortable, healthy indoor environments.

Energy Recovery Ventilator

Boss Aire Inc.
685 Bridge St. Center #221
Owatonna, MN 55060

Phone: 507-774-7700
www.bossaire.com

Boss Aire manufactures ERVs for many sizes of residential buildings and for light commercial and industrial buildings.

Guardian Indoor Air Quality Systems

Broan-NuTone LLC
926 W. State St.
P.O. Box 140
Hartford, WI 53027

Toll-free: 800-558-1711
Phone: 262-673-4340
www.broan.com

Broan-NuTone offers the Guardian line of ERVs and HRVs along with appropriate controls for enhancing indoor air quality while maintaining comfort and energy efficiency.

Heat Recovery Ventilators

American Aldes Ventilation Corp.
4537 Northgate Ct.
Sarasota, FL 34234

Toll-free: 800-255-7749
Phone: 941-351-3441
www.americanaldes.com

American Aldes Ventilation makes Heat Recovery Ventilators (HRV) designed to exhaust stale indoor air and supply fresh air for a variety of ventilation requirements. Heat from exhaust air is transferred to the fresh air stream. Models are designed for spaces ranging from 1,100 to 8,000 ft².

Lifebreath Clean Air Furnace

Nutech Brands, Inc.
511 McCormick Blvd.
London, ON N5W 4C8 Canada

Phone: 519-457-1904
www.lifebreath.com

The Lifebreath Clean Air Furnace is an integrated ventilation/heating/cooling appliance that delivers preheated or precooled ventilation air to a house. The system is comprised of a heat-recovery ventilator with an integral, high-efficiency heating coil that uses a conventional domestic water heater (or boiler) as the heat source. For cooling, a plenum-mounted air conditioner can be added. A whole-house air cleaner can also be added. The company claims a combined efficiency of up to 90% and variable heat delivery

of 30,000–75,000 Btu/hr or 50,000–110,000 Btu/hr, depending on the model.

Lifebreath Heat Recovery Ventilators

Nutech Brands, Inc.
511 McCormick Blvd.
London, ON N5W 4C8
Canada

Phone: 519-457-1904
www.lifebreath.com

Lifebreath residential HRVs range in capacity from 95 cfm to 300 cfm. All have a high-efficiency aluminum heat exchanger core. Heat exchange effectiveness ranges from 80 to 90%, according to the company. Commercial models, designed to be integrated into HVAC systems, range in size from 500 to 2,500 cfm. Nutech also makes a 200 cfm Lifebreath for hot, humid climates that exchanges moisture in the core in addition to heat, reducing dehumidification costs.

Perfect Window Fresh Air Ventilator

Honeywell Home & Building Controls
P.O. Box 524
Minneapolis, MN 55440

Toll-free: 800-328-5111
Phone: 612-951-1000
content.honeywell.com/yourhome/

The Honeywell Perfect Window™ line of Fresh Air Ventilator Systems includes HRVs and ERVs.

RenewAire ERVs

RenewAire
2201 Advance Rd.
Madison, WI 53718

Toll-free: 800-627-4499
Phone: 608-221-4499
www.renewaire.com

RenewAire, formerly under the Lossnay name for Mitsubishi Electric, manufactures a full line of commercial and residential ERVs. Among the residential units, the EV 130 is rated at 130 cfm and the EV 200 is rated at 200 cfm with 73 and 76% energy recovery efficiencies, respectively. These units can be installed stand-alone or tied into a furnace.

Ventilation Products

Fantech
1712 Northgate Blvd.
Sarasota, FL 34234

Toll-free: 800-747-1762
Phone: 506-743-9500
www.fantech.net

Fantech manufactures ventilation products with energy recovery cores for residential, commercial, and industrial buildings.

Humidity Control Equipment

Many of the most significant indoor air quality problems in buildings relate to moisture. While preventing rain penetration, plumbing leaks, wicking of moisture from the soil, and unvented moisture sources are the top priorities, it is sometimes also necessary to remove unwanted moisture from indoor air. These listings include high-efficiency dehumidification products.

Sante Fe, Ultra-Aire, and Hi-E Dry Dehumidifiers

Therma-Stor LLC
P.O. Box 8050
Madison, WI 53708

Toll-free: 800-533-7533
Phone: 608-222-5301
www.thermastor.com

Therma-Stor manufactures a range of high-efficiency dehumidifiers for residential and commercial use. Residential products include the Sante Fe and Ultra-Aire APD (air purifying dehumidifier), which provide air filtration in addition to dehumidification. For commercial applications, Therma-Stor offers the Hi-E Dry line of dehumidifiers.

HVAC Instrumentation and Controls

Good HVAC control systems are important for maintaining high levels of comfort as well as energy savings.

Active Ventilation System

SolarAttic, Inc.
15548 95th Cir. NE
Elk River, MN 55330

Phone: 763-441-3440
www.solarattic.com

SolarAttic produces an electronic control for attic ventilation in all seasons. This product is compatible with existing fans or can be a part of a SolarAttic system.

Aprilaire Ventilation Control System

Aprilaire
1015 E. Washington Ave.
P.O. Box 1467
Madison, WI 53701

Toll-free: 800-334-6011
Phone: 608-257-8801
www.aprilaire.com

The Aprilaire Ventilation Control System works in conjunction with an included Aprilaire motorized damper as part of a home's heating/cooling system. The controller monitors interior humidity and outdoor air temperature; user-adjustable controls react to this information, allowing homeowners to manage the quantity and quality of fresh air being brought into the home. Setpoints for high and low outdoor temperature and high indoor humidity override the system to prevent increased heating, cooling, and dehumidification loads; and the system will ventilate only during a heating cycle when outdoor temperatures are below 20°F.

Hunter Set & $ave

Hunter Fan Co.
2500 Frisco Ave.
Memphis, TN 38114

Toll-free: 800-448-6837
Phone: 901-743-1360
www.hunterfan.com

Hunter Fan manufactures a full line of programmable digital and mechanical thermostats.

T8600 Chronotherm IV Thermostats

Honeywell Home & Building Controls
P.O. Box 524
Minneapolis, MN 55440

Toll-free: 800-328-5111
Phone: 612-951-1000
content.honeywell.com/yourhome/

Honeywell produces a wide range of programmable thermostats, including the T8600 Chronotherm® IV line of microprocessor-controlled electronic thermostats for heating and/or cooling. This series allows for programmed temperature setbacks and for gradual temperature recovery. Several T8600 models are available for replacement and new installation applications.

Masonry Fireplaces

Burning wood creates significant pollution. Emissions of particulates, carbon monoxide, VOCs, and methane are significantly greater from wood stoves than from any other common heating fuel. However, when wood is locally available and can be harvested sustainably, it has no net impact on global warming because the carbon emissions from combustion are more than compensated for by growing trees. Thus, if wood is burned in a manner that minimizes pollution, it can be a good fuel choice. The burning efficiencies of masonry heaters and well-designed biomass-fueled boilers help to tip the scale in wood's favor. These products combust wood at very high temperatures, reducing particulate emissions to less than half of the levels of the best wood stoves. The high thermal mass of masonry heaters and biomass-fueled boiler systems can more effectively capture a fire's heat, store it, and release it over time. The downside of a high-mass masonry heater is that the heat of a freshly lit fire may not be felt in the living space until several hours later. In passive solar homes this may make temperature regulation difficult.

Masonry Fireplaces

FireSpaces, Inc.
223 N.W. Ninth Ave.
Portland, OR 97209

Phone: 503-227-0547
www.firespaces.com

FireSpaces is a dealer and manufacturer of masonry fireplaces including Tulikivi and Kakelugn. They also manufacture the masonry Moberg MRC 3042 and the Modern Rumford Masonry Fireplace Kit.

Temp-Cast Enviroheat Masonry Heater Kits

Temp-Cast
3324 Yonge St.
P.O. Box 94059
Toronto, ON M4N 3R1 Canada

Phone: 416-322-6084
www.tempcast.com

Temp-Cast masonry heaters are constructed with Temp-Cast glazed doors, fire grates, clean-out ports, refractory bricks, and separately sourced masonry materials. Units feature corner, 'see through,' and bake-oven models. Temp-Cast provides manuals detailing appropriate chimney construction with each masonry heater kit.

Tulikivi Soapstone Fireplaces, Bakeovens, and Stoves

Tulikivi U.S., Inc.
P.O. Box 7547
Charlottesville, VA 22906-7547

Toll-free: 800-843-3473
www.tulikivi.com

Tulikivi's masonry heaters, available in over 25 different models, are made from soapstone quarried in Finland. Tulikivi masonry heaters produce a hot, clean-burning fire and efficiently transfer the fire's heat to the living space.

Measurement and Control Instrumentation

see *Miscellaneous: Measurement and Control Instrumentation*

Mechanical Insulation

All hot-water pipes should be insulated for optimal performance. Where humidity is a concern, cold-water pipes should also be insulated to prevent condensation and potential moisture problems (mold, mildew, decay). Included here are specialized insulation products for piping and other mechanical equipment. For hydronic heating pipes that experience high temperature (over 150°F), the inexpensive foam-plastic pipe insulation sleeves may not be adequate; high-temperature pipe insulation is required.

UltraTouch Natural Fiber Duct Liner

Bonded Logic, Inc.
411 E. Ray Rd.
Chandler, AZ 85225

Phone: 480-812-9114
www.bondedlogic.com

UltraTouch™ Natural Fiber Duct Liner is an acoustic and thermal insulation for sheet metal ducts made from over 80% cotton fibers. The cotton—reclaimed fibers too short to be used with traditional means of spinning—is combined with a synthetic fiber binder (about 15% of the product) and then "cooked" to fuse the fibers together. The liner is treated with boric acid for microbial and fire resistance, and a black polyester rayon facing material is used as a protective layer to keep particulates from becoming airborne. UltraTouch Duct Liner contains no fiberglass or formaldehyde and has an NRC of .75 (Type A mounting), an R-value of 4.2/in., and a Class A fire rating. Rolls (35" to 60" wide) are available $1/2$" thick x 100' long (3.0 density) and 1" thick by 50' long and 2" thick x 25' long (1.5 density).

Solar Flat Plate Collectors (Air Heating)

see *Renewable Energy: Solar Flat Plate Collectors (Air Heating)*

Space Heaters

In highly energy-efficient homes and small commercial buildings, it is often possible to satisfy all heating demands with space heaters rather than a central, distributed heating system. These listings include high-efficiency, quiet space heaters, along with high-performance panel radiators.

EnergySaver

Rinnai
103 International Dr.
Peach Tree City, GA 30269

Toll-free: 800-621-9419
Phone: 678-829-1700
www.rinnaina.com

The EnergySaver by Rinnai is an 84%-efficient, sealed-combustion space heater. It is 20% more efficient than typical American through-the-wall gas space heaters.

Hydronic Panel Radiators

Buderus
50 Wentworth
Londonderry, NH 03053

Phone: 603-898-0505
www.buderus.net

Buderus Solidoflux-N panel radiators deliver hydronic heat and may interfere with furniture placement less than baseboard radiators. Panel radiators are available in heights of 12", 20", and 24" and depths of $2^1/2$" and 4". They can be fitted with optional individual thermostats and diverter valves to provide individual zoning. Flexible PEX polyethylene piping can be used in place of copper.

Hydronic Panel Radiators

Runtal North America
187 Neck Rd.
P.O. Box 8278
Ward Hill, MA 01835

Toll-free: 800-526-2621
Phone: 978-373-1666
www.runtalnorthamerica.com

Runtal panel and baseboard radiators are designed to operate at lower temperatures than conventional hydronic radiators (convectors). Therefore, a high percentage of the heat will be delivered through radiation rather than convection. The room's mean radiant temperature may be higher, and the thermostat set point (air temperature) can be kept somewhat lower with comparable comfort. Thus, some energy savings can be achieved. Runtal also manufactures the Omnipanel® radiator for bathrooms, which provides additional radiator area. The company's electric Omnipanel may be justified if its use allows whole-house thermostats to be kept lower. Runtal is a Swiss company.

Laser Vented Heaters

Toyotomi U.S.A., Inc.
604 Federal Rd.
Brookfield, CT 06804

Phone: 203-775-1909
www.toyotomiusa.com

The four models in the sealed-combustion Laser kerosene heater line from Toyotomi offer heating efficiencies ranging from 90 to 93% (AFUE rating of 87.7%) while providing outputs from 5,200 to 40,000 Btu/hr. The units have heat-circulation fans and require 120-volt AC power, generating a preheating load of 260–280 watts, and a burning load of 42–76 watts. An external fuel tank is usually required. Units feature electronic ignition (no pilot light), setback thermostat, automatic safety shutoff, and power failure recovery. The cabinet stays cool to the touch.

Oil Miser Space Heaters

Toyotomi U.S.A., Inc.
604 Federal Rd.
Brookfield, CT 06804

Phone: 203-775-1909
www.toyotomiusa.com

The only oil-fired, sealed-combustion space-heating system in North America, Oil Miser model OM-22 from Toyotomi has an AFUE rating of 90%, with output ranging from 8,000 to 22,000 Btu/hr. An external fuel tank is required (No. 1 or No. 2 fuel oil). The unit has a heat-circulation fan and requires 120-volt AC power for a preheating load of 275 watts and a burning load of 46 watts. Units feature setback thermostat, automatic safety shutoff, and power failure recovery. The cabinet stays cool to the touch.

Space Heaters

Monitor Products, Inc.
P.O. Box 3408
Princeton, NJ 08543

Toll-free: 800-524-1102
Phone: 732-329-0900
www.monitorproducts.com

Monitor space heaters are gas-, LPG-, or kerosene-fired, direct-vented, through-the-wall units with 83% efficiencies.

This Space is Available for Your Notes

This Space is Available for Your Notes

Plumbing

Access to fresh water is one of the world's major geopolitical issues, yet in most of the U.S. we still use drinking-quality water as if it were free and unlimited. A substantial portion of this usage happens in buildings where leaky plumbing drips it away and fixtures designed decades ago use exorbitant quantities. In some areas of North America, water is drawn from ground and surface sources at unsustainable rates—in other words, withdrawals from aquifers exceeding annual recharge rates. For much of the year, for example, the Colorado River no longer reaches the Gulf of California. In the U.S., we currently withdraw over 300 billion gallons of fresh water per day from streams, reservoirs, and wells. Even in places where the water supply has traditionally not been a concern, problems are appearing as populations grow or precipitation patterns change (perhaps due to global climate change).

Toilet flushing uses over 4 billion gallons of water per day in the U.S. alone. While older toilets use about 4 gallons per flush, modern toilets conform to the requirements of the Energy Policy Act of 1992 and use no more than 1.6 gallons per flush (gpf). Simply replacing those older toilets with the new ones has been found to reduce a household's overall water use between 10% and 30%. Some toilets use less water—or even none at all. *GreenSpec* includes toilets that provide exceptional flush performance as determined by the Maximum Performance (MaP) testing protocol. Other water-saving designs, devices, and systems are also included when appropriate.

The Energy Policy Act of 1992 also mandates that showerheads and faucets can use no more than 2.5 gallons per minute (gpm); some models use substantially less. Retrofitting these devices in older buildings is usually a very easy and extremely cost-effective investment.

Consumption of potable water can also be reduced by recycling graywater for nonpotable uses, such as irrigation and toilet flushing; however, these systems may be prohibited by local health codes. In most of California it is legal to use graywater for landscape irrigation, provided the system is designed to meet certain conditions.

The drain on limited water supplies can also be reduced by harvesting rainwater. On some of the Virgin Islands, rainwater-storing cisterns provide the primary water supply to most homes. In parts of the U.S., it is not uncommon for collected rainwater to be used for landscape irrigation, toilet flushing, laundry, and other nonpotable uses. For use as potable water, collected rainwater should be filtered and disinfected.

The other end of the plumbing system is wastewater disposal. Many conventional wastewater treatment systems, including both large municipal systems and private on-site septic systems, are inefficient and/or expensive. Alternative technologies are available for systems of all sizes: from composting toilets and recirculating sand filters, to ecological wastewater treatment systems that rely on enhanced biological treatment processes.

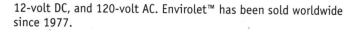
Composting Toilet Systems

Composting toilets convert human waste into nutrient-rich fertilizer for nonfood plants, rather than mixing the waste with potable water and flushing it down the drain—as occurs with conventional toilets. The advantages of composting toilets include dramatic reductions in water use, reduced groundwater pollution or sewage-treatment impacts, and a recycling of nutrients. Some composting chambers can be used with microflush toilets, though most are nonflush. Proper sizing is critical for effective composting; a model with undersized capacity won't function appropriately. If composting toilets are used, graywater treatment and disposal still need to be addressed.

Clivus Multrum Composting Toilets

Clivus Multrum, Inc.
15 Union St.
Lawrence, MA 01840

Toll-free: 800-425-4887
Phone: 978-725-5591
www.clivusmultrum.com

Clivus Multrum popularized the composting toilet in the U.S. and is still one of the most widely recognized manufacturers. The company offers a range of composting toilets for various applications, from small residences to large public facilities. All include a composting chamber below one or more toilet fixtures. In addition to waterless models, Clivus offers a foam flush fixture that uses a soap solution and 3 ounces of water. Electricity is required for ventilation and moistening systems. Design, installation, and maintenance services are available.

Ecotech

Ecotech
50 Beharell St.
Concord, MA 01742

Phone: 978-369-3951
www.ecotechusa.com

EcoTech are "batch" composting toilets that process waste faster and more completely without raking. Available from Gaiam Real Goods.

Envirolet

Sancor Industries Ltd.
140-30 Milner Ave.
Scarborough, ON M1S 3R3 Canada

Toll-free: 800-387-5126
Phone: 416-299-4818
www.envirolet.com

Sancor™ Envirolets are small composting toilets, some self-contained and others with a separate composting chamber below. Available in Waterless and Low Water models in non-electric,

12-volt DC, and 120-volt AC. Envirolet™ has been sold worldwide since 1977.

Equaris Biomatter Resequencing Converter

Equaris Corporation
15711 Upper 34th St. S
P.O. Box 6
Afton, MN 55001

Phone: 651-337-0261
www.equaris.com

Equaris Corporation, formerly AlasCan, Inc., manufactures a composting toilet system that operates as part of a system of integrated technologies to separate toilet and organic kitchen wastes from the wastewater stream at the source. Solid waste is deposited into the Equaris Biomatter Resequencing Converter (BMRC), where 90–95% of the toilet and organic wastes are biologically converted into odorless carbon dioxide and water vapor; the remaining 5–10% can be used safely as a soil amendment. The toilets used with this system require one cup of water or less per flush. Graywater is treated aerobically in the Equaris Greywater Treatment System utilizing a small continuously operating 67-watt linear air compressor to filter and remove most pollutants. This system eliminates septic tanks and reduces leachfields or mounds by 40–90%, according to the manufacturer. The water can then be diverted through the Equaris Water Recycling System to produce potable water using reverse osmosis, ozone and UV treatment, and physical filtration.

ExcelAerator

Bio-Sun Systems, Inc.
R.R. 2, Box 134A
Millerton, PA 16936

Toll-free: 800-847-8840
Phone: 570-537-2200
www.bio-sun.com

Bio-Sun composting toilet systems can serve multiple toilets. The ExcelAerator™ system blows air into the composting chamber and also injects air directly into the waste piles for accelerated decomposition. A vent extraction device is incorporated which simultaneously removes byproduct gases.

Phoenix Composting Toilet

Advanced Composting Systems
195 Meadows Rd.
Whitefish, MT 59937

Toll-free: 888-862-3854
Phone: 406-862-3854
www.compostingtoilet.com

Phoenix Composting Toilet systems are used in residential and public-facility applications such as parks and recreation areas. They have mixing tines for aerating the compost and a system for recycling leachate. The only electrical load is a 12-volt DC, 5-watt exhaust fan.

Sun-Mar Composting Toilet

Sun-Mar Corp.
5370 S. Service Rd.
Burlington, ON L7L 5L1 Canada

Toll-free: 800-461-2461
Phone: 905-332-1314
www.sun-mar.com

Sun-Mar offers over 20 different
models of composting toilets, some
self-contained and others with a
separate composting chamber below.
Composting toilets must be correctly
sized and installed, and appropriately maintained, in order to
function properly.

Domestic Water Heat Exchangers

*In the building industry, "domestic" water includes all potable
water, whether in a residence or any kind of commercial building.
A number of different opportunities exist to use waste heat for
heating water. With refrigeration and air-conditioning equipment, waste heat is typically captured through desuperheating.
Desuperheaters are most common in commercial settings, but
equipment is available for residential use as well. To be cost-
effective, a significant cooling load must support desuperheating
operation—in homes, this means those in southern climates,
and in commercial buildings this applies to businesses such as
supermarkets that have large, year-round cooling and refrigeration loads. Waste heat from fuel-fired boilers can also be
recovered for water heating. The heat content of wastewater
can be recovered as well, using several different heat exchange
technologies; the greater the surface area of contact between
the two fluids, the more efficiently heat recovery can be achieved
(but this must be balanced against the risk of blockage). Wastewater heat recovery systems are available for both commercial
and residential applications.*

GFX Wastewater Heat Reclaimer

Fuel Cell Components & Integrators, Inc.
933 Motor Pkwy.
Hauppauge, NY 11788

Toll-free: 888-871-9679
Phone: 631-234-8700
www.gfxtechnology.com

The GFX (gravity film exchange) drainline heat recovery device
is a section of 3" or 4" copper wastewater drainpipe wrapped by
a coil of $1/2$" copper supply line. Fresh water coming in through
the supply line is warmed by the film of warm water descending
the inner surface of the waste pipe. The GFX is available in various lengths and configurations for residential, institutional, and
industrial uses. When hot water is being drawn, energy savings are
obtained, and the heating capacity of water heaters extended.

Graywater Heat Reclaimer

Earthstar Energy Systems, Inc.
P.O. Box 130
Crozet, VA 22932

Phone: 434-981-5139

Graywater Heat Reclaimer is an insulated 50-gallon tank with
graywater inlet and outlet and a fresh water heat exchange coil.
The manufacturer claims a 40% savings on average annual hot
water energy bills.

HRP - Heat Recovery Option

FHP Manufacturing
601 N.W. 65th Ct.
Ft. Lauderdale, FL 33309

Phone: 954-776-5471
www.fhp-mfg.com

Florida Heat Pump makes a Heat Recovery
Option or desuperheater that uses a heat
exchanger to capture the waste heat from
air conditioning units. The captured heat
is then used for domestic water heating.
System capacities are appropriate for
both residential and commercial applica-
tions. Installation is appropriate where air conditioning loads
are significant.

Domestic Water Heaters

*The most efficient domestic water heaters include electronic-
ignition gas-fired on-demand models, direct-contact commercial
water heaters, heat-pump water heaters, and advanced combination space- and water-heating systems. (All electric resistance
water heaters have the inefficiencies and fuel-source pollution
concerns inherent to electric power generation.) Other factors
to consider include indoor air quality (in terms of combustion
gases) and the ozone-depletion impacts associated with refrigerants for heat pumps and blowing agents for storage tank
insulation. On-demand water heaters have no standby losses
or storage tank insulation concerns, and some models have
sealed combustion and no pilot lights. Gas-fired condensing
storage-tank type water heaters have fuel efficiencies greater
than 90% and use a variety of types of insulation. Heat-pump
water heaters have tremendous efficiencies, but these are still
very uncommon. In combined or integrated systems, efficiencies are boosted by uniting space heating and/or cooling into a
single system that includes water heating. In almost every type
of high-efficiency water heater there are issues of rate-of-use,
climate, and maintenance that require consideration to make
the appropriate selection for optimal results.*

Continuum 2424W and REU 2532FFU

Rinnai
103 International Dr.
Peach Tree City, GA 30269

Toll-free: 800-621-9419
Phone: 678-829-1700
www.rinnaina.com

Continuum 2424W is a forced-combustion, tankless water heater with electronic ignition and the combustion unit installed outside. The heater can deliver 180,000 Btu/hr. Highly sophisticated freeze protection is provided, allowing installation in freezing climates. The REU 2532FFU is a direct-vent version of the Continuum designed for installation inside the building.

Demand Water Heaters

Low Energy Systems
4975 E. 41st Ave.
Denver, CO 80216

Toll-free: 800-873-3507
Phone: 303-781-9437
www.tanklesswaterheaters.com

Low Energy Systems is a specialized distributor of Paloma, Infinion, and Takagi demand gas hot water heaters, the latter of which offers GreenSpec-approved models. They also offer homeowner-friendly maintenance kits. Solar thermal systems and components are also available.

Flash T-K2, T-KD20, and T-KJr.

Takagi Industrial Co. USA, Inc.
3-B Goodyear
Irvine, CA 92618

Toll-free: 888-882-5244
Phone: 949-453-8388
www.takagi-usa.com

Takagi's Flash T-K2, T-KD20, and T-KJr. tankless gas water heaters are suited for residential and commercial applications and have no pilot, so standby losses are negligible. They do use electricity for a power burner and power vent. The T-K2 is a 60 lb. unit with an energy factor of 0.84 for natural gas and 0.85 for propane, self-modulating input ranges from 20,000 to 185,000 Btu, and a max flow rate of 6.9 gpm. The new T-KD20 is a direct vent (uses outside air for combustion) version of the T-K2. The smallest of the line, the Flash T-KJr., measures just 20" x 14" x 6" and weighs 30 pounds. It has an energy factor of 0.83 for natural gas and 0.84 for propane, and self-modulating input ranges from 19,500 to 140,000 Btu, for a maximum flow rate of 5.8 gpm.

Indirect Water Heater Tanks

Buderus
50 Wentworth
Londonderry, NH 03053

Phone: 603-898-0505
www.buderus.net

The TBS-Isocal, ST, L, and LT domestic hot water tanks allow water heating by a gas- or oil-fired boiler. Unlike most domestic indirect water heater tanks, the Buderus uses non-ozone-depleting rigid foam. Because the unit is made in Germany, there are environmental impacts of shipping to consider.

Mobius T-M1 and Flash T-K1S

Takagi Industrial Co. USA, Inc.
3-B Goodyear
Irvine, CA 92618

Toll-free: 888-882-5244
Phone: 949-453-8388
www.takagi-usa.com

The Mobius T-M1 is a tankless, pilotless, computer-controlled gas water heater. It has an energy factor rating of 0.82 for natural gas and 0.84 for propane. The T-M1 has a max flow rate of 9.6 gpm. The unit measures 24" x 18" x 9". The gas valve modulates from 25,000 to 235,000 Btu, accurately metering fuel use. Up to 20 units can be operated by a single control module, and several control modules can be linked together, making the Mobius practical for offices, hotels, hospitals, and other large facilities. The T-K1S pilotless, demand water heater is designed for single-use residential or commercial applications. It has an energy factor of 0.83 for natural gas and 0.84 for propane. Its self-modulating input ranges from 15,000 to 190,000 Btu, for a max flow rate of 7.2 gpm.

Oil Miser Water Heaters

Toyotomi U.S.A., Inc.
604 Federal Rd.
Brookfield, CT 06804

Phone: 203-775-1909
www.toyotomiusa.com

The only oil-fired, sealed-combustion, on-demand water heating systems in North America, Oil Miser Water Heater models OM-148 and BS-36UFF from Toyotomi have efficiency ratings of 88%. Both models provide up to 148,000 Btu/hr—the OM-148 consuming fuel at a rate of 1.05 gal/hr, and the BS-36UFF at 1.1 gal/hr. An external fuel tank is required (No. 1 or No. 2 fuel oil for the OM-148; ASTM No. 1-K Grade Kerosene or No. 1 Fuel Oil for BS-36UFF). The units require 120-volt AC power for ignition loads of 120 watts (no pilot light) and 98 watts while operating. Units may be direct- or chimney-vented and offer overheat protection, ignition safety, and no-water shutoff.

Pro Tankless 635ES

Controlled Energy Corp.
340 Mad River Park
Waitsfield, VT 05673

Toll-free: 800-642-3199
Phone: 802-496-4357
www.controlledenergy.com

The Pro Tankless 635ES water heater supplies two hot water outlets simultaneously at a combined rate of 6 gpm. A sealed-combustion unit that can be vented horizontally or vertically, it can be fueled by either natural gas or propane. It has an electronic ignition, digital temperature control, an energy factor of 0.85, and a 15-year warranty. The Pro Tankless name is trademarked and licensed by Bosch.

Rheem Tankless Gas Water Heaters

Rheem Manufacturing Company
2600 Gunter Park Dr. E
Montgomery, AL 36109

Toll-free: 800-432-8373
www.rheem.com

The Rheem Tankless Water Heater for natural or LP gas features electronic ignition, power venting, low NOx emissions, electric freeze protection, and an exclusive oxygen depletion sensor safety device and overheat limiter. A 0.92 gpm minimum flow rate is required to initiate heating cycle. Suitable for water pressures from 14–150 psi. Input rate ranges from 31,500–118,000 Btu/hr with a 45-degree temperature rise at 4.2 gpm and a 100-degree rise at 1.9 gpm. The unit has an energy factor of 0.81 for both LP and natural gas. It measures $13^3/_4$" x $22^1/_4$" x $5^1/_8$" and weighs 35 lbs.

WatterSaver Heat Pump Water Heater

ECR International, Inc.
2201 Dwyer Ave.
Utica, NY 13501

Phone: 315-797-1310
www.ecrinternational.com

The WatterSaver is an advanced, one-piece, 50-gallon heat pump water heater. Operated in the heat pump mode, the water heater consumes 500 watts and generates approximately 3,500 Btu/hour of cooling. Because heat pump water heaters cool the air, they make the most sense in warm climates dominated by cooling loads. The manufacturer claims an Efficiency Factor of 2.4 and a typical payback (in replacing a conventional electric water heater) of 2.2 to 3.1 years. Relatively low airflow requirements (200 cfm) allow this air-source heat pump to be installed almost anywhere, though it will increase heating loads when located in fully conditioned space. The product uses a non-ozone-depleting refrigerant (R-134a).

Domestic Water Piping

Look for glueless, nonhalogenated products that contain no heavy metals or brominated flame retardants.

Fusiotherm Piping

Aquatherm Piping Systems, LLC
Box 110
Romeo, MI 48065

Phone: 248-830-7037
www.aquatherm-usa.com

Fusiotherm piping from Aquatherm Piping Systems is an exceptionally strong, non-PVC piping for pressurized applications such as potable water distribution and hydronic heating. The polypropylene pieces are heat-joined in the field with an electric fusing tool to create truly monolithic plumbing systems without the use of solvents or glues. Fusiotherm is available in a wide range of diameters from 16 mm to 150 mm (0.63" to 5.9") in three wall-thickness ratios (SDR classifications); over 400 fittings are available. Introduced in the U.S. in 2004, the product has been used in Europe for three decades with great success. (The ICC listing for this product is expected to be complete near the end of September 2004.)

Faucets and Controls

Many conservation efforts—in industrial, commercial, and residential settings—are making significant improvements in water-use efficiency. These advances are also reducing our wastewater treatment burden and expense. Products listed here dispense water efficiently or improve controllability of the water supply.

Bricor Showerheads

Bricor Analytical, Inc.
5210 Champagne Dr.
Colorado Springs, CO 80919-3536

Toll-free: 800-661-4348 then 12
Phone: 719-522-0442
www.bricor.com

Bricor showerheads have a small hole on the side of the throat that generates a vacuum, pulling air into the showerhead. This aerates the water, boosting the pressure. According to the company, this venturi-induction technology increases the shower intensity by $2^1/_2$ times. The company carries 8 models, all of which can be configured by Bricor to deliver 1.5 gpm at either 60 psi or at 30 psi. Other flow rates are possible with custom orders. For multi-level buildings, the company can provide custom manufactured showerheads for each floor to provide consistent flow throughout the building.

EcoPower Sensor-Activated Faucet

Toto USA, Inc.
1155 Southern Rd.
Morrow, GA 30260

Phone: 770-282-8686
www.totousa.com

Toto's EcoPower sensor-activated faucet uses a tiny hydropower generator to keep a manganese dioxide lithium battery charged. Being battery-powered, it does not require hardwiring to the building's electrical system. Battery disposal and the labor of replacing batteries are greatly reduced. Toto estimates the battery will last 10 years with an average of 5 uses/day and as much as 19 years with high usage. The EcoPower faucet uses 0.17 gallons in a standard 10-second cycle and consumes 1.0 gpm when running—both well below the federal standard. EcoPower is available with a Standard or Gooseneck Spout.

ETL Low-Flow Showerheads

Energy Technology Laboratories
2351 Tenaya Dr.
Modesto, CA 95354

Toll-free: 800-344-3242
Phone: 209-529-3546
www.savewater.com

The Oxygenics® line of showerheads, made with DuPont Delrin® 500P acetal resin, employs a venturi air-induction design using a single, centered orifice—rather than a lot of small holes in the face of the showerhead—and stationary fins to break the spray into pulsating droplets. Showerheads in the Oxygenics line are rated to use from 2.0 to 2.5 gpm and are optimized for different water pressures. The products achieve remarkably satisfying shower force and are guaranteed for life never to clog.

Foot- and Knee-Operated Faucet Controls

Kohler Co.
444 Highland Dr.
Kohler, WI 53044

Toll-free: 800-456-4537
Phone: 920-457-4441
www.kohlerco.com

Kohler offers double-pedal, wall- and floor-mounted, foot-operated water faucet controls for commercial and residential applications. Each pedal may be set up to control hot, cold, or tempered water. (For tempered water, conventional hand controls can be used to set temperature balance and flow rate, and the pedal used to turn the flow on and off.) Knee stirrup controls with similar functions are also available, as are single-pedal, temperature-moderated controls for use in showers. Water savings are significant but difficult to quantify.

Foot-Operated Sink Valve

Step-Flow, Inc.
2361 Campus Drive #99
Irvine, CA 92612-1424

Toll-free: 888-783-7356
www.stepflow.com

Step Flow is a retrofit (or OEM) foot-operated valve system, which converts any sink from hand operation to foot operation. This foot-pedal faucet control uses a sheathed flex cable for the pedal-to-valve controller so that no plumbing extends to the foot pedal. "Hands free" usage of sinks results in a sanitary application and conserves water.

Foot-Pedal Faucet Controls

T&S Brass and Bronze Works, Inc.
2 Saddleback Cove
Travelers Rest, SC 29690

Phone: 800-476-4103
www.tsbrass.com

T&S Brass manufactures double- and single-pedal, wall- and floor-mounted, foot-operated water faucet controls. Each pedal may be set up to control hot, cold, or tempered water. (For tempered water, conventional hand controls can be used to set the temperature balance and flow volume, and the pedal used to turn the flow on and off.) Hands-free operation saves water and encourages sanitary sink conditions. Water savings are significant but difficult to quantify.

Metlund Hot Water D'MAND System

ACT, Inc.
Metlund Systems
3176 Pullman St., Ste. 119
Costa Mesa, CA 92626

Toll-free: 800-638-5863
Phone: 714-668-1200
www.gothotwater.com

Metlund Hot Water D'mand System is an electronically controlled valve and pumping system that rapidly distributes hot water from the water heater to fixtures in a home or commercial building. This system can operate either with a return line or by the existing cold-water line. The Metlund System pumps cold tapwater back to the water heater and delivers hot water instead, saving otherwise wasted water and shortening the wait for hot water. Because it circulates the water only on demand, this system avoids the energy penalties of continuously circulating systems. The Metlund System can also be activated by either a low-voltage remote button or a motion sensor.

Omni Products

Chronomite Laboratories, Inc.
1420 W. 240th St.
Harbor City, CA 90710

Toll-free: 800-447-4962
Phone: 310-534-2300
www.chronomite.com

Chronomite Labs/Omni Products makes several faucet flow regulators that reduce water use by over 27%. Omni products use laminar water flow to create the look and feel of a far higher flow rate (these are not faucet aerators; the water looks like a solid stream).

Pedalworks and Footworks

Pedal Valves, Inc.
13625 River Rd.
Luling, LA 70070

Toll-free: 800-431-3668
Phone: 985-785-9997
www.pedalvalve.com

Footworks and Pedalworks are unique, single-pedal faucet controllers. The Footworks product is for commercial applications and bolts into the floor beneath the sink; the residential Pedalworks controller is installed in the base of a kitchen cabinet or bathroom vanity. The conventional hand controls are used to set the temperature balance between hot and cold water, and the foot pedal is used to turn the flow on and off. A lock-on button allows the water to be left running when necessary. Water savings are significant but difficult to quantify. In applications such as hospitals (when water is often left running while surgeons scrub their hands and arms) and commercial kitchens, water savings can be dramatic. The products also help with hygiene and productivity.

Taco Hot Water D'MAND System

Taco, Inc.
1160 Cranston St.
Cranston, RI 02920

Phone: 401-942-8000
www.taco-hvac.com

The Taco D'MAND® System is an electronically activated water-pumping system that quickly delivers hot water to a fixture while returning water that has been sitting in the hot-water pipes back to the hot-water tank. The pump may be activated on demand by pushing a button near the fixture or by remote control. The system switches off when hot water reaches the temperature sensor on the pump at the fixture. Aside from quicker hot water delivery, benefits include energy savings and the elimination of water waste while waiting for hot water. In retrofit applications, the cold-water line serves as the return line; in new construction, a third plumbing line is usually installed.

Tapmaster

Integra Dynamics Inc.
20175 Township Rd. 262
Calgary, AB T3P 1A3 Canada

Toll-free: 800-791-8117
Phone: 403-275-5554
www.integradynamics.com

Tapmaster is a foot- or knee-activated switch that controls the flow to a faucet. The conventional hand controls are used to set the temperature balance between hot and cold water, and the foot switch is used to turn the flow on and off. A lock-on button allows the water to be left running when necessary. Water savings are significant but difficult to quantify, as they depend on user habits. Tapmaster is widely used in dental offices for hygienic reasons.

The Chilipepper Appliance

Chilipepper Systems
4623 Hasting Pl.
Lake Oswego, OR 97035

Toll-free: 800-914-9887
Phone: 209-401-8888
www.chilipepperapp.com

The Chilipepper Appliance is an on-demand water circulation device that speeds the availability of hot water at the tap. This energy- and money-saving appliance is easily mounted at the most remote tap. The 115-volt pump moves cold water out of the hot-water line and back to the water heater via the cold-water line. The Chilipepper is activated by either a wireless remote or a wired controller.

Water-Conserving Fixtures

Niagara Conservation Corp.
45 Horsehill Rd.
Cedar Knolls, NJ 07927

Toll-free: 800-831-8383
Phone: 973-829-0800
www.niagaraconservation.
com

Niagara Conservation Corporation offers water- and energy-conserving products including showerheads, toilets, toilet retrofit kits, faucet aerators, light bulbs, and weatherization products. They also produce a patented tamperproof, flapperless, 1.6-gal. toilet suitable for both 10" and 12" rough-ins.

Graywater Systems

Graywater is defined either as all wastewater other than that from toilets, or as wastewater from baths, showers, lavatories, and clothes washers (not including kitchen sinks and dishwashers). In some states, graywater can be collected and used for below-ground landscape irrigation. Products included here are used in graywater systems.

BioGreen

BioGreen System (Pacific) Ltd.
#4 11443 Kingston St.
Maple Ridge, BC V2X 0Y6 Canada

Phone: 604-460-0203

BioGreen is a biological wastewater treatment system for use in rural and suburban areas and recreational facilities without a central sewage system.

Greywater Treatment Systems

Clivus Multrum, Inc.
15 Union St.
Lawrence, MA 01840

Toll-free: 800-425-4887
Phone: 978-725-5591
www.clivusmultrum.com

Clivus Multrum custom-designs greywater irrigation systems for commercial and residential applications.

Recirculating Wastewater Garden

Ecological Engineering Group, Inc.
50 Beharell St.
Concord, MA 01742

Toll-free: 866-4-ECOENG
Phone: 978-369-9440
www.ecological-engineering.com/

Ecological Engineering Group, Inc. is an engineering design and consulting firm specializing in alternative on-site wastewater treatment systems including graywater systems such as Recirculating Wastewater Garden.

ReWater System

ReWater Systems, Inc.
P.O. Box 210171
Chula Vista, CA 91921

Phone: 619-421-9121
www.rewater.com

The ReWater System is a graywater irrigation system comprised of two primary sections. A self-cleaning filter captures and pressurizes the water, which is then released through a subsurface irrigation system. An electronic controller adds fresh water when required.

Package Sewage Treatment

Biological sewage treatment systems use balanced ecological systems of bacteria, plants, and animals to break down and purify sewage wastes. These systems are usually located in greenhouses and consist of a series of tanks containing complex aquatic ecosystems. Raw sewage is initially broken down by bacteria and algae. Higher plant and animal species further purify the water as it flows through a cascading series of tanks. The discharge water is suitable for reuse, irrigation, or groundwater recharge. The biological diversity inherent in these systems effectively handles periodic fluctuations in the waste stream. The waste-as-food premise that these systems are based on leads to greatly reduced quantities of sludge, compared to conventional sewage treatment systems.

Living Machine Systems

Dharma Living Machines
8018 NDCBU
125 La Posta Rd.
Taos, NM 87571

Phone: 505-751-9481
www.livingmachines.com

A Living Machine® is a biological water reclamation system that accepts sewage wastes as a food source for bacteria, algae, plants, snails, and fish. This system is used both for standard sewage and for specialized waste streams from certain manufacturing processes.

Rainwater Harvesting Systems and Components

Rainwater harvesting is the practice of collecting and using rainwater, most commonly from roofs. Use of collected rainwater can provide building owners with high-quality soft water for irrigation and potable uses, reduce pressure on water-treatment plants, and reduce stormwater runoff and flooding. To use as potable water, filtration and purification are necessary.

Filtering Roofwasher

Water Filtration Company
1205 Gilman St.
Marietta, OH 45750

Toll-free: 800-733-6953
Phone: 740-373-6953
www.waterfiltrationcompany.com

The Filtering Roofwasher is installed between the downspout and cistern to remove dirt and debris from water collected from a roof. Larger debris is collected by screens in "leaf catcher" compartments. The first water to be collected, which washes off dirt and debris that has accumulated on the roof surface between rains, is held in a "quiet chamber" and drains away slowly through a "weep-hole." Use of the Filtering Roofwasher can greatly improve the quality of cistern water and significantly increase the time between cistern cleanings. The unit is constructed of a replaceable filter element, heavy-duty fiberglass, stainless steel, and PVC. The Filtering Roofwasher is often used in conjunction with Water Filtration's Floating Cistern Filter. Additional filtration or sterilization is usually required for potable water applications.

Floating Cistern Filter

Water Filtration Company
1205 Gilman St.
Marietta, OH 45750

Toll-free: 800-733-6953
Phone: 740-373-6953
www.waterfiltrationcompany.com

Water Filtration Company's Floating Cistern Filter is constructed of a replaceable filter element, heavy-duty fiberglass, stainless steel, and PVC. The filter floats near the surface of the cistern to collect and filter the cleanest water in the cistern, thereby reducing final filtration loads. Filter elements need replacement approximately every one to two years. The Floating Cistern Filter, often used in conjunction with Water Filtration's Filtering Roof Washer, is only for filtering dirt and debris and not for sterilization. The company also makes a similar unit for filtering pond water.

Hill Country Rain Systems

Rainwater Collection Over Texas
333 Ella Ln.
Dripping Springs, TX 78620

Phone: 512-858-5395
www.rainco.net

Rainwater Collection provides complete rainwater catchment systems, supplies, consultation, and design work, as well as workshops and water-conserving products.

Plastic Cistern Liners

Thompson Plastics Melita
P.O. Box 456
Melita, MB R0M 1L0 Canada

Toll-free: 866-522-3241
www.thompsoncisternliners.com

Thompson cistern liners are made of polyethylene sheeting seam-welded to fit loosely into a round tank or rectangular cavity used to hold liquid, usually water. These liners are appropriate for rainwater storage.

Rainwater Catchment Systems

Northwest Water Source
P.O. Box 2766
Friday Harbor, WA 98250

Phone: 360-378-8788
www.rainfallcatchment.com

Northwest Water Source offers components and equipment as well as design and consulting for both residential and commercial rainwater catchment and harvesting systems. The company imports European rainfall catchment equipment and stormwater infiltration technology from Germany and Holland. Equipment includes European-made stainless steel demand pumping systems that don't require a pressure tank; UV water purification and filtration; and a variety of water storage tanks including above- and below-ground rotationally molded polyethylene and custom-made in-ground units consisting of a polyethylene "endoskeleton" covered by a welded sheet polypropylene.

Rainwater Catchment Systems

Rain Man Waterworks
P.O. Box 972
Dripping Springs, TX 78620

Phone: 512-858-7020
www.rainharvester.com

Rain Man Waterworks builds and installs turnkey rainwater catchment systems. The company is also a supplier of components used for rainwater catchment systems.

Smart-Valve Rainwater Diverter

FloTrue International Corp
P.O. Box 81596
Austin, TX 78708-1596

Phone: 512-775-8318
www.flotrue.com

Smart-Valve is a kit that transforms an off-the-shelf pipe fitting into a low-cost first-flush diverter valve for roofwater catchment systems. The amount of water diverted is adjustable.

The Garden Watersaver

The Garden Watersaver
8260 Dalemore Rd.
Richmond, BC V7C 2A8 Canada

Phone: 604-274-6630
www.gardenwatersaver.com

During a moderate rainfall, the average roof will shed over 100 gallons of water per hour. The Garden Watersaver is an automatic rainwater collection system that installs on a downspout from the roof's gutter to divert a percentage of this water to a barrel or other container for later use in a garden or other applications.

Vertical Above-Ground Storage Tanks

Holloway Welding & Piping Co.
820 W. Forest Grove Rd.
Allen, TX 75002

Phone: 972-562-5033

Holloway Welding & Piping supplies storage tanks for use with rainwater catchment systems.

Water Cistern and Storage Tanks

Snyder Industries
4700 Fremont St.
Lincoln, NE 68504

Phone: 402-467-5221
www.snydernet.com

Snyder's NuConCept above- and below-ground water storage tanks are rotationally molded with a variety of polyethylene materials, including FDA- and NSF 61-approved high-density (HDLPE) and cross-linked high-density (XLPE) resins. May be used as rainwater catchment cisterns.

Water Storage Tanks

Norwesco, Inc.
4365 Steiner St.
St. Bonifacius, MN 55375-0439

Phone: 800-328-3420
www.norwesco.com

Norwesco's seamless polyethylene storage tanks range from 12 to 15,000 gallons and are manufactured using resins meeting FDA specifications to ensure safe storage of potable water. Applicable tanks are also NSF-approved. Appropriate for rainwater catchment cisterns.

Sanitary Waste and Vent Piping

Most sanitary drain waste and vent (DWV) piping used today is made from PVC or ABS plastic. Both of these have toxic manufacturing intermediaries and require the use of hazardous solvents for welding the joints. PVC can also generate highly toxic dioxins in the case of accidental fire or improper incineration. Cast iron, the traditional DWV pipe material, has high recycled content; it's much heavier, however, and more labor-intensive to work with. Vitrified clay pipe can be used in buildings as drain pipe but is more commonly used for larger-diameter sewage applications (where it competes with concrete and PVC); although heavy and labor-intensive, vitrified clay is the most durable waste and sewage piping material. Finally, there are some polyolefin (polyethylene and polypropylene) plastic pipes that can be used for drainage and venting. If plastic piping products are being chosen, look for recycled content.

Cast-Iron Soil Pipe

AB&I Foundry
7825 San Leandro St.
Oakland, CA 94621

Toll-free: 800-468-4766
Phone: 510-632-3467
www.abifoundry.com

AB&I Foundry is one of three major producers of cast-iron soil pipe.

Cast-Iron Soil Pipe

Tyler Pipe
P.O. Box 2027
Tyler, TX 75710

Toll-free: 800-527-8478
Phone: 903-882-5511
www.tylerpipe.com

Tyler Pipe maintains manufacturing facilities in four locations (Tyler, Texas; Macungie, Pennsylvania; Marshfield, Missouri; and Corona, California) and is one of the three primary U.S. manufacturers of cast-iron drain and soil pipe. The company uses 100% recycled scrap iron—more than 200,000 tons per year. The manufacturer has certified the following recycled-content levels (by weight): total recovered material 100% typical, 100% guaranteed; post-consumer material 100% typical, 100% guaranteed.

Industry Representation

National Clay Pipe Institute
P.O. Box 759
Lake Geneva, WI 53147

Phone: 262-248-9094
www.ncpi.org

The National Clay Pipe Institute represents the manufacturers of vitrified clay waste and sewer pipe. Clay pipe is the environmentally preferable, highly durable, corrosion-resistant alternative to PVC sewer pipe.

The Quiet Pipe

Charlotte Pipe & Foundry Co.
P.O. Box 35430
Charlotte, NC 28235

Toll-free: 800-438-6091
Phone: 704-372-5030
www.charlottepipe.com

The Quiet Pipe is cast-iron DWV pipe made from scrap metal. The manufacturer has certified the following recycled-content levels (by weight): total recovered material 90% typical, 90% guaranteed; postconsumer material 80% typical, 80% guaranteed.

Vitrified Clay Pipe

Building Products Company
P.O. Box 18110
Phoenix, AZ 85005

Phone: 602-269-8314

Building Products Company is a manufacturer of vitrified clay pipe for waste line and sewage piping.

Vitrified Clay Pipe

Gladding, McBean & Co.
P.O. Box 97
Lincoln, CA 95648

Toll-free: 800-776-1133
Phone: 916-645-3341
www.gladdingmcbean.com

Gladding McBean is a manufacturer of vitrified clay pipe for waste line and sewage piping.

Vitrified Clay Pipe

Mission Clay Products
P.O. Box 549
Corona, CA 92878

Toll-free: 800-795-6067
Phone: 909-277-4600
www.missionclay.com

Mission Clay Products is a manufacturer of vitrified clay pipe for waste line and sewage piping. The company has plants located in California, Kansas, and Texas.

Vitrified Clay Pipe

Superior Clay Corp.
P.O. Box 352
Uhrichsville, OH 44683

Toll-free: 800-848-6166
Phone: 740-922-4122
www.superiorclay.com

Superior Clay is a manufacturer of vitrified clay pipe for waste line and sewage piping.

Vitrified Clay Pipe

The Logan Clay Products Co.
P.O. Box 698
Logan, OH 43138-0698

Toll-free: 800-848-2141
Phone: 740-385-2184
www.loganclaypipe.com

The Logan Clay Products Co. is a manufacturer of vitrified clay pipe for waste line and sewage piping.

Septic and Leach Field Systems

Conventional on-site wastewater treatment systems—septic tanks and leach fields—typically deliver the nutrients in the wastewater (nitrogen and phosphorous) directly into the groundwater. Various alternative wastewater treatment systems provide some nutrient removal. Some plastic-matrix products incorporate recycled content.

AdvanTex Wastewater Treatment Systems

Orenco Systems, Inc.
814 Airway Ave.
Sutherlin, OR 97479

Toll-free: 800-348-9843
Phone: 541-459-4449
www.orenco.com

AdvanTex® onsite wastewater treatment systems are particularly appropriate for small lots, poor soils, and environmentally sensitive sites. The standard system accommodates a single-family dwelling; the AX100 model is for multifamily use, resorts, parks, schools, etc. Wastes recirculate five times through a textile filtration media "pod" before discharging into a drain field in small, continuous amounts. Some jurisdictions allow a reduction in drain field area with the system. The pump typically runs 30 to 60 minutes per day, using about 150 kWh per year—about $1 per month in electric costs, based on $.08 per kWh. Installation includes computerized, Internet-based monitoring which allows remote diagnosis and settings adjustment. The textile filter requires periodic replacement. A service contract is required as a condition of the warranty.

In-Drain System

Eljen Corporation
10 N. Main St., Rm. 216
West Hartford, CT 06107

Toll-free: 800-444-1359
Phone: 860-232-0077
www.eljen.com

The Eljen In-Drain System uses recycled-content cuspated plastic sheets in conjunction with Bio-Matt™ fabric, instead of aggregate, to create an effective leach field. The Bio-Matt fabric is suspended between the plastic sheets, adding a second bio-mat to the one at the sand/In-Drain interface. According to the manufacturer, this system is 3 to 10 times more durable than a conventional leach field. The manufacturer has certified the following recycled-content levels (by weight): total recovered material 100% typical, 100% guaranteed.

Puraflo

Bord na Mona Environmental Products U.S., Inc.
P.O. Box 77457
Greensboro, NC 27417

Toll-free: 800-787-2356
www.bnm-us.com

Puraflo® is a biofiltration wastewater system using fibrous peat to treat septic tank effluent. The peat media filters wastewater and provides a substrate for microorganisms that naturally purify wastewater. Puraflo systems may be used for residential and small commercial applications.

Sand Filter Wastewater Treatment

Orenco Systems, Inc.
814 Airway Ave.
Sutherlin, OR 97479

Toll-free: 800-348-9843
Phone: 541-459-4449
www.orenco.com

Orenco Systems is a leading designer and supplier of sand filter wastewater treatment systems. Sand filters are typically positioned between a septic tank and a downsized leach field. Sand filters consist of a contained area of sand that is periodically doused with effluent. The sand filter environment promotes the growth of aerobic bacteria that lower the biochemical oxygen demand (BOD), reduce fecal coliform and pathogens, convert ammonia into nitrate, and reduce total nitrogen by 30 to 50%. Associated leach fields can often be up to 50% smaller, although such downsizing is not accepted by all states.

Solar Aquatics

Ecological Engineering Associates
508 Boston Post Rd.
Weston, MA 02493

Phone: 781-891-5085
www.solaraquatics.com

Ecological Engineering designs and maintains wastewater treatment facilities that accept sewage as a food source for a complex, greenhouse-contained ecosystem including bacteria, algae, plants, snails, and fish.

Sinks

Look for products with recycled content or that can contribute to innovative wastewater treatment practices, such as graywater separation.

Envirosink

Bismart Distributors, Inc.
8584 145 A St.
Surrey, BC V3S 2Z2
Canada

Toll-free: 888-663-4950
Phone: 604-596-5894
www.envirosink.com

The Envirosink® is a secondary kitchen sink that drains to an approved graywater system instead of a sewage or septic system. Collected graywater can then be used for landscape irrigation.

Solar Water Heating Systems and Components

see *Renewable Energy: Solar Water Heating Systems and Components*

Toilets

Since 1992, federal law has mandated that all new toilets use no more than 1.6 gallons per flush (gpf). As toilet flushing is the largest single use of water in most residential and commercial buildings (accounting for up to 40% of residential use), water savings from toilet replacement is very significant. Achieving superb flush performance with 1.6 gpf (or less) has necessitated sophisticated redesign of toilet bowls, flush valves, and tanks; many of the early problems in the wake of the Energy Policy Act of 1992 that led to double-flushing to make up for poor waste removal have been resolved. In addition to improvements to the traditional gravity system, pressure- and vacuum-assisted flushing systems have been developed. The Flushmate® pressure-assist system developed by Sloan employs an air bladder inside the toilet tank that gets compressed by water pressure as the tank fills. This provides a surprisingly forceful and somewhat loud flush. The vacuum-assisted VAC® flushing system from Fluidmaster uses an inverted bottle-shaped vessel inside of the water tank. When the toilet is flushed, a vacuum is created inside the "bottle" as the water empties. That vacuum force is transferred by an air tube to the rear of the trapway to increase the power of the evacuation by pulling, rather than pushing. The Flushmate and the VAC are both licensed to various toilet manufacturers. Dual-flush toilets, available for years overseas and making inroads in the U.S., save additional water by making two flushes available: one for solid wastes and a half-size flush for liquids. To be listed in GreenSpec, 1.6 gpf (6 liters per flush) toilets must evacuate at least 65 grams of solid waste per liter of flush water, as tested under the Maximum Performance (MaP) protocol. (250 total grams is considered to be the lowest reasonable evacuation performance.) For dual-flush toilets, water savings are given additional weight by averaging the flush-water use for both sizes of flush in calculating the grams-per-liter rating.

AquaSaver

The Fuller Group, Inc.
3461 Summerford Ct.
Marietta, GA 30062

Phone: 770-565-8539

AquaSaver is a small, inexpensive, adjustable, water-saving device for gravity-flush, tanked toilets. The product is a plastic manifold that clips over the toilet's overflow pipe. It saves 15–25% of water per flush without impeding the flushing ability of the toilet. It does this by diverting some of the excess refill water that typically overfills the toilet bowl, keeping it in the toilet tank. It saves more water in older, less-efficient toilets. Sales are primarily in bulk to large institutions or water-conservation contractors.

Cadet Pressure-Assist Toilets

American Standard
1 Centennial Way
P.O. Box 6820
Piscataway, NJ 08855

Phone: 800-442-1902
www.americanstandard-us.com

The 1.6-gallon (6 liter) pressure-assisted toilets in the Cadet line from American Standard evacuated a whopping 900 grams of solids with a 5.8 liter flush volume under the MaP (Maximum Performance) testing protocol, giving it a grams-per-liter rating of over 155. These toilets have a 10" x 12" water surface area and a glazed 2" trapway. The Cadet uses Sloan's Flushmate® flushing system.

Champion Flapperless Toilet

American Standard
1 Centennial Way
P.O. Box 6820
Piscataway, NJ 08855

Phone: 800-442-1902
www.americanstandard-us.com

American Standard's Champion toilet with "America's Best™ Flushing System" is flapper-free, gravity-fed, and warranted for 10 years (including tank and trim). The Flush Tower releases 1.6 gallons of water in 0.75 seconds through a 3" flush valve (50% larger than the industry standard) and almost straight down, releasing more water faster for a more powerful flush through its $2^3/_8$" trapway. Champion is available in round front, elongated, and ADA compliant versions. Based on MaP testing, the models had exceptionally high grams-per-liter flushing abilities of 140 (round front) to 144 (ADA).

Cimarron Comfort Height 1.4 GPF Toilet

Kohler Co.
444 Highland Dr.
Kohler, WI 53044

Toll-free: 800-456-4537
Phone: 920-457-4441
www.kohlerco.com

The Kohler Cimarron™ Comfort Height™ is a gravity-flush 1.6 gpf toilet that offers a 1.4 gpf setting option. It has an 11" x 10" water surface, a $3^1/_4$" flush valve, and a $2^1/_8$" glazed trapway with a direct water jet from the tank. This ADA-compliant toilet was designed for residential or commercial applications. Both flush settings underwent MaP (Maximum Performance) protocol testing: the full-flush rating was 108 grams-per-liter, evacuating 700 grams of solid waste with a flush volume of 6.5 liters; the 1.4-gallon setting emerged with 107 grams-per-liter, its 6.1 liter flush volume evacuating 650 grams of solid waste. LEED® Water Efficiency points are available with the 1.4-gallon setting.

Eclipse Mariner II Pressure-Assist Toilets

St. Thomas Creations
1022 Bay Marina Dr.
National City, CA 91950

Phone: 619-336-3980
www.stthomascreations.com

The 1.0-gpf Eclipse Mariner II ™ pressure-assist toilet uses Sloan's Flushmate IV operating system. A supply line with a minimum water pressure of 25 psi is required. Two models were tested using the MaP (Maximum Performance) protocol: both had a 5.9 liter flush volume; the elongated rim model removed 500 grams of solids for a grams-per-liter rating of 85, while the round-front model evacuated 465 grams for a rating of 79.

Ifö Cera Dual-Flush Toilets

DEA Bathroom Machineries
495 Main St.
Murphys, CA 95247

Phone: 209-728-2031
www.deabath.com

Photo: Ifö Sanitas

Ifö toilets have a 50-year track record in Sweden, and theirs were among the first water-conserving toilets to gain acceptance in the American market. Their dual-flush Cera line offers users the choice of a 1.6-gallon full flush, or a 0.8-gallon half-volume flush. Note that Ifö toilets are constructed to European plumbing conventions and require a 4" rough-in rather than 12" or 14", or accommodation for rear-outlet. Retrofitting existing plumbing may not be feasible; refer to rough-in diagrams before ordering. The flush performance of these toilets has not been tested by the MaP (Maximum Performance) protocol; these toilets are included for their water-saving attribute.

Niagara Flapperless Gravity-Flush Toilets

Niagara Conservation Corp.
45 Horsehill Rd.
Cedar Knolls, NJ 07927

Toll-free: 800-831-8383
Phone: 973-829-0800
www.niagaraconservation.com

Niagara Conservation Corporation manufactures a patented tamperproof, flapperless, 1.6-gpf toilet suitable for both 10" and 12" rough-ins. Because this toilet requires no flapper, it avoids the potential problem of increased flush volume that can occur if a generic flapper is used to replace a low-flush toilet's flapper in the course of normal maintenance. The Flapperless evacuated 500 grams of solids with a 5.5 liter flush volume under MaP (Maximum Performance) protocol testing, giving it a grams-per-liter rating of 91.

Pressure-Assist Low-Flush Toilets

Microphor
452 E. Hill Rd.
Willits, CA 95490

Toll-free: 800-358-8280
Phone: 707-459-5563
www.microphor.com

Microphor produces pressure-assisted toilets, including the Microflush® toilets that use 0.5 gpf. Compressed air is used to assist flushing. Noise may be a concern. Microflush is also available in a 12-volt DC version. The flush performance of these toilets has not been tested by the MaP (Maximum Performance) protocol; these toilets are included for their water-saving attribute.

Sfera Dual-Flush Toilets

HCG North America
333 City Blvd. W, Ste. 700
Orange, CA 92868-2984

Phone: 714-919-0622
www.hcgbath.com

HCG offers one- and two-piece, split-handle, dual-flush toilets using 1.6 gal. or 0.8 gal. per flush. These toilets have a bacteria-inhibiting Nano Gloss finish, a 2" siphonic trapway, and a 1-year warranty. The manufacturer has ISO 9002 and ISO 1400 certification. The flush performance of these toilets has not been tested by the MaP (Maximum Performance) protocol; these toilets are included for their water-saving attribute.

Sterling Rockton Dual-Flush Toilet

Kohler Co.
444 Highland Dr.
Kohler, WI 53044

Toll-free: 800-456-4537
Phone: 920-457-4441
www.kohlerco.com

The Rockton™ is a dual-flush, flapperless, gravity-fed toilet from Sterling (a Kohler brand), offering users the choice of a 1.6 gal. or 0.8 gal. flush. The two-button flush actuator is integrated into the tank lid. The flush performance of this toilet has not been tested by the MaP (Maximum Performance) protocol; this toilet is included for its water-saving attribute.

Tasman Dual-Flush Toilet

Caroma USA, Inc.
61 Hazelton Ave.
Toronto, ON M5R 2E3 Canada

Phone: 416-925-5556
www.caromausa.com

Caroma USA, the North American subsidiary of Australian Caroma International Pty Ltd, offers a variety of two-button, dual-flush 1.6/0.8 gpf toilets. All units feature full 4" trapways. The Tasman round-front model emerged from MaP protocol testing with a grams-per-liter removal rating of 134, having evacuated an impressive 775 grams of solids with a full flush of 5.8 liters. When water savings is weighted by averaging the two flush volumes (which comes to 5 liters), the grams-per-liter number jumps to 155—tied for the highest in these listings.

The Controllable Flush

Athena
17175 S.W. TV Hwy.
Aloha, OR 97006

Toll-free: 888-426-7383
Phone: 503-356-1233
www.watersavingdevice.com

The Controllable Flush is a simple, dual-mode flushing device designed to convert most front-flushing standard toilets into low-flush toilets. The Controllable Flush provides the option of the toilet's standard flush or a reduced 1.5-gal. flush, depending on whether the handle is operated in an upward or downward direction. No tools are necessary for installation.

Trocadero Power Lite Dual-Flush Toilet

Kohler Co.
444 Highland Dr.
Kohler, WI 53044

Toll-free: 800-456-4537
Phone: 920-457-4441
www.kohlerco.com

The Kohler Trocadero® Power Lite One-Piece Toilet is a dual-flush (1.1- or 1.6-gal.) toilet that uses a small 0.2 hp submersible pump to force water from the tank to the bowl. This produces a flush the company claims is comparable to a pressure-assist toilet yet is quieter. The pump requires a nearby GFCI outlet. The flush performance of this toilet has not been tested by the MaP (Maximum Performance) protocol; this toilet is included for its water-saving attribute.

Ultra Flush Pressure-Assist Toilet

Gerber Plumbing Fixtures LLC
4600 W. Touhy
Lincolnwood, IL 60712

Phone: 847-675-6570
www.gerberonline.com

The 1.6-gallon pressure-assisted Ultra Flush™ elongated-rim toilet from Gerber evacuated 665 grams of solids with a 6.1 liter flush volume in MaP (Maximum Performance) testing, giving it a grams-per-liter rating of 109. In the same tests, the floor-mounted, rear-discharge model evacuated 575 grams with a 5.3 liter flush to achieve the same grams-per-liter rating of 109. These toilets have a minimum water surface area of 12" x 10", and glazed $2\frac{1}{8}$" trapways. The Ultra Flush line uses Sloan's Flushmate® flushing system, and has a five-year warranty.

Vortens Dual-Flush Toilet

Vortens U.S. Office
1498 Brookpark Dr.
Mansfield, OH 44906

Toll-free: 800-471-5129
www.vortens.com

The Vienna RF W/T412 Dual Flush toilet from Mexican manufacturer Sanitarios Lamosa S.A. de C.V. offers two flush modes: 1.0 gal. or 1.6 gal. This two-piece, two-button toilet has a $2\frac{1}{8}$" trapway and a 5-year warranty. The flush performance of this toilet has not been tested by the MaP (Maximum Performance) protocol; this toilet is included for its water-saving attribute.

Water Supply and Treatment Equipment

Products included here are used to purify water. Such systems can help to ensure high-quality drinking water. Some are also key components of rainwater harvesting systems.

Sol Saver System and Family Sol Saver

Safe Water Systems
2800 Woodlawn Dr., Ste. 265
Honolulu, HI 96822

Phone: 808-539-3937
www.safewatersystems.com

Sol*Saver and Family Sol*Saver can provide inexpensive microbial water purification without electricity, pumps, chemicals, or boiling. The Family Sol*Saver is comprised of a black, double-walled HDPE collector covered by two layers of transparent acrylic glazing. Up to 3.5 gal. of untreated water is poured into the unit and placed in the sun; when pasteurization is complete, an indicator will change color. The Sol*Saver, designed to purify approximately 200 gal. of water a day in sunny climates, utilizes a flat plate collector, a high-efficiency heat exchanger, and a fail-safe thermal control valve. A backup solid-fuel burner and copper heating coil is available for the Sol*Saver for use on cloudy days. Neither unit can be used in freezing temperatures. Also available is the Wood*Saver, which operates only on solid fuels for areas with limited sunlight exposure.

UV Water Disinfection Systems

Sunlight Systems
4-D Pearl Ct.
Allendale, NJ 07401-1611

Phone: 201-934-7772
www.sunlightsystems.com

Sunlight Systems designs, manufactures, and markets ultraviolet (UV) water disinfection systems for residential, commercial, and industrial use and also supplies replacement parts and service. UV purification is suitable for disinfecting water that is microbially contaminated. In certain situations, it may be necessary to pretreat water with another filtration system to remove impurities which can interfere with UV light transmission.

This Space is Available for Your Notes

Electrical

The plastic insulation and jacketing on electric and data wire and cable can contain lead, plasticizers, flame retardants, and chemicals that may be toxic. Polyvinyl chloride (PVC) and fluoropolymers (Teflon®) are commonly used on wire and cable. Toxic compounds may be released in the event of fire or as the wire jacketing deteriorates over time. Wires and cables are available with nonhalogenated insulation and jacketing and with no heavy metals.

Electrical current flow creates electromagnetic fields (EMFs), which—according to some experts—may cause a range of adverse health effects. While many studies have been conducted, these health concerns have yet to be proven to the satisfaction of mainstream scientists. Due to the uncertainty surrounding this issue, it makes sense to take steps to minimize exposure to such fields, as long as these measures aren't expensive (a strategy referred to as "produce avoidance"). Such measures might include locating main electrical service lines away from occupied areas and specifying that wiring be installed in such a way as to minimize EMFs. Electronics may also be sensitive to EMFs, so rooms with computers and other such equipment should be designed with that in mind.

Electrical Power

Fuel cells offer exciting opportunities for clean, efficient, distributed generation of electricity. Very simply, fuel cells generate power by reversing the common high school chemistry experiment in which electric current is used to split water into hydrogen and oxygen. Fuel cells have been used for decades in space. In buildings, fuel cells can be especially useful for back-up power needs. The Four Times Square skyscraper is powered, in part, by two fuel cells providing 400 kW of electricity.

Fuel Cells

Ballard Power Systems
4343 N. Fraser Way
Burnaby, BC V5J 5J9 Canada

Phone: 604-454-0900
www.ballard.com

Ballard Power Systems is recognized as the world leader in developing, manufacturing, and marketing zero-emission proton-exchange membrane (PEM) fuel cells. Ballard is commercializing fuel cell engines for transportation applications and fuel cell systems for portable and stationary products ranging from 1 to 250 kW. The company is also commercializing electric drives for fuel cell- and battery-powered electric vehicles, power conversion products for fuel cells, and other distributed generation products, and is a Tier 1 automotive supplier of friction materials for power train components.

Fuel Cells

IdaTech, LLC
63160 Britta St.
Bend, OR 97701

Phone: 541-383-3390
www.idatech.com

IdaTech, formerly Northwest Power Systems, is developing a small-scale PEM fuel cell for residential, light commercial, backup, and portable applications.

Hazardous Substances Detection and Alarm

see *Miscellaneous: Hazardous Substances Detection and Alarm*

Inverters and Solar Electric Components

see *Renewable Energy: Inverters and Solar Electric Components*

Lighting Controls and Building Automation

Optimizing lighting systems is a complex task involving daylighting and building design issues, careful lamp and fixture selection, and advanced lighting control. The environmental and financial benefits can be significant. Well-designed systems provide high-quality light where and when it's needed, with reduced energy consumption and maintenance costs. Lighting control systems can be as basic as a bathroom light occupancy sensor or as complex as a whole-building, computer-controlled energy management system that handles lighting, HVAC equipment, and sometimes other functions, such as security.

Decora Wall Switch Occupancy Sensors

Leviton Manufacturing Co. Ltd.
59-25 Little Neck Pkwy.
Little Neck, NY 11362

Toll-free: 800-323-8920
Phone: 718-229-4040
www.leviton.com

Decora® Wall Switch Occupancy Sensors are passive infrared sensors that control lighting based upon detected motion. Leviton manufactures wall- and ceiling-mounted, infrared and ultrasonic, commercial and residential occupancy sensors, and lighting control systems.

Isolé Plug Load Control

The Watt Stopper, Inc.
2800 De La Cruz Blvd.
Santa Clara, CA 95050

Toll-free: 800-879-8585
Phone: 408-988-5331
www.wattstopper.com

The Isolé IDP-3050 Plug Load Control from The Watt Stopper consists of an eight-outlet power strip with surge protection and a passive infra-red (PIR) personal occupancy sensor. The occupancy sensor controls six of the eight outlets and is recommended for computer monitors, task lights, printers, personal electric space heaters, and fans. Computers and fax machines should be plugged into uncontrolled outlets.

LightHAWK-MT

Hubbell Building Automation, Inc.
9601 Dessau Rd., Bldg. 1
Austin, TX 78754

Toll-free: 888-698-3242
Phone: 512-450-1100
www.hubbell-automation.com

The LightHAWK-MT™ occupancy sensor combines passive infrared, ultrasonic, and photocell sensors in one unit to optimize lighting control for energy savings. Hubbell Building Automation, Inc., which was formed by the joining of Mytech Corporation and Unenco, produces a full line of occupancy sensors and controls.

Occupancy Sensors and Controls

The Watt Stopper, Inc.
2800 De La Cruz Blvd.
Santa Clara, CA 95050

Toll-free: 800-879-8585
Phone: 408-988-5331
www.wattstopper.com

The Watt Stopper manufactures occupancy sensors and controls for lighting and HVAC equipment in commercial and residential buildings. Products include automatic wall switches, ceiling- and wall-mount sensors, outdoor motion sensors, and sensors for special applications. They include a range of sensing technologies, such as passive infrared, ultrasonic, and dual technology. In addition, The Watt Stopper manufactures lighting control panels, daylighting controls, and plug load controls.

Sensor Switch Occupancy Sensors

Sensor Switch, Inc.
900 Northrop Rd.
Wallingford, CT 06492

Toll-free: 800-727-7483
Phone: 203-265-2842
www.sensorswitch.com

Sensor Switch, Inc. is a leading manufacturer of passive infrared (PIR) and passive dual-technology (PDT) occupancy sensor and photosensor daylighting controls for lighting. Products are available for both commercial and residential applications. PDT combines PIR with sound detection, providing four times the detection reliability, according to the company, and enabling lights to be reactivated by voice if the lights accidentally go out. Sensor Switch also offers a sensor that works on all electrical systems worldwide with a 20-year guaranteed life. Manufactured in the U.S.

Outlet Boxes

Penetrations in exterior walls—such as dryer vents and electrical service entrances—are common sources of air infiltration into buildings. Standard electrical boxes, although they don't penetrate the exterior of the building envelope, can be significant sources of air leakage. Airtight electrical boxes have been designed for use in exterior walls.

Air-Vapor Barrier Box

Low Energy Systems Supply
Co., Inc.
W. 1330 Happy Hollow Rd.
Campbellsport, WI 53010

Phone: 920-533-8690
www.lessco-airtight.com

Low Energy Systems Supply Co. (LESSCO) manufactures special boxes in which electrical receptacle boxes can be mounted. Caulk sealant is used to seal the wire penetrations into the LESSCO box, and contractors tape is used to seal box flanges to the air barrier (polyurethane film).

Photovoltaic Collectors

see *Renewable Energy: Photovoltaic Collectors*

Solar Energy Industry Information

see *Renewable Energy: Solar Energy Industry Information*

Wind Energy Equipment

see *Renewable Energy: Wind Energy Equipment*

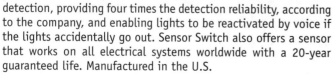

This Space is Available for Your Notes

Lighting

Lighting is a major user of electricity, especially in commercial buildings (which are rarely designed to take advantage of daylight). Besides using electricity, electric lighting also generates heat, contributing to cooling loads that are generally met by using more electricity for air-conditioning. Thus, improving the energy efficiency of lighting has benefits that go beyond the direct electricity savings by the lighting products.

Fluorescent lamps are three to four times more efficient than incandescent lamps. Quality fluorescent lamps today provide far better light quality than the older lamps that often produced a bluish cast. Electronically ballasted fluorescent lighting also doesn't generate the hum and flicker that many people find objectionable in older, magnetically ballasted fluorescent lighting. Both straight-tube fluorescent and compact-fluorescent lamps (CFLs) are widely available. In general, thinner-diameter fluorescent lamps (T-8s and T-5s for example) offer higher efficacy (lumens per watt) than T-10 and T-12 lamps. Other high-efficiency electric light sources suitable for some applications—mostly commercial—include metal halide, high-intensity discharge, and high- and low-pressure sodium lighting. LED (light-emitting diode) light sources are also being introduced. While not yet providing the efficacy of fluorescent lamps, the highly focusable nature of LEDs enable significant energy savings in certain applications. Unlike fluorescent, metal halide, sodium, and other high-intensity discharge (HID) lamps, LEDs do not contain mercury.

Older magnetic ballasts for fluorescent lighting may contain highly toxic PCBs or the less toxic but also problematic DEHP; these should be handled carefully and disposed of properly when changing or servicing fixtures. Fluorescent lamps (as well as all HID lamps) also contain small amounts of the toxic metal mercury. These lamps should never be landfilled or incinerated but instead be recycled by a company that reclaims the mercury. Some new lamps are available with mercury levels far below the industry average, and these should be used whenever possible.

Daylighting strategies must be carefully designed if they're to result in net energy savings. In commercial buildings, savings often don't accrue unless there are automatic controls; but in homes, those controls may not be as necessary to achieve savings. Daylight also introduces heat that can increase cooling loads (though daylight's ratio of heat to light is less than that of all common artificial light sources). Daylight can also cause problems with glare, especially on computer screens. In spite of these potential pitfalls, daylighting is a valuable strategy for saving energy and improving the well-being of occupants—and one of the most important strategies in commercial buildings.

Compact Fluorescent Lamps

Replacing standard incandescent light bulbs with compact-fluorescent lamps (CFLs) can slash electrical consumption in homes and offices where incandescent lighting is widely used. Most CFLs use one-quarter to one-third as much electricity as incandescent bulbs with comparable output. By more efficiently converting electrical energy into light, CFLs generate less heat-which can reduce cooling loads, particularly in commercial buildings. In reducing electrical usage, CFLs also reduce associated carbon dioxide, sulfur dioxide, and nitrous oxide emissions. CFL technology continues to evolve; there are many types to choose from, including straight-tube, folded-tube, and twisted-tube. As CFLs have shrunk in size, they have become suitable for most light fixtures that were designed for incandescent light bulbs. Advances in light quality, lamp durability, and dimming technology have also been significant. Most manufacturers offer 15- and 20-watt models; larger lamps are also available. The average life of CFLs is eight to ten times that of incandescent bulbs.

Compact Fluorescent Lamps

GE Lighting
1975 Noble Rd., Nela Park
Cleveland, OH 44112

Toll-free: 800-435-4448
Phone: 216-266-2121
www.gelighting.com

GE Lighting manufactures a full line of CFLs, with and without integral ballasts. Dimmable integral-ballast CFLs are available.

Compact Fluorescent Lamps

Greenlite Lighting Corporation
    USA
10 Corporate Park, Ste. 100
Irvine, CA 92606-5140

Toll-free: 800-930-2111
Phone: 949-261-5300
www.greenliteusa.com

Greenlite manufactures a wide range of compact fluorescent lamps including Dimmable and 3 Way Spirals. The company's 13-watt "Mini" Spiral is nearly comparable in size to a standard incandescent bulb.

Compact Fluorescent Lamps

Lights of America
611 Reyes Dr.
Walnut, CA 91789

Toll-free: 800-321-8100 ext. 503
Phone: 909-594-7883
www.lightsofamerica.com

Lights of America manufactures twisted-tube, straight-tube, and other electronic-ballasted fluorescent lamps. Durability concerns have been raised with certain LOA products.

Compact Fluorescent Lamps

Link USA International, Inc.
40-22 College Point Blvd.,
    Box 12
Flushing, NY 11354

Toll-free: 877-546-5800
Phone: 312-640-0002
www.linklights.net

Link USA produces several sizes of compact, spiral, and covered CFLs for indoor/outdoor use.

Compact Fluorescent Lamps

Lumatech Corporation
41636 Enterprise Cir. N, Unit C
Temecula, CA 92590

Toll-free: 800-932-0637
Phone: 909-296-3650
www.carpenterlighting.com

Lumatech manufactures a variety of CFLs, including the Reflect-A-Star, Microlamp, and new twist lamps. The twist lamps are available from 11 to 32 watts, the latter producing 1099 lumens (the highest output of any twist lamp).

Compact Fluorescent Lamps

MaxLite SK America, Inc.
19 Chapin Rd., Bldg. B
Pine Brook, NJ 07058

Toll-free: 800-555-5629
Phone: 973-244-7300
www.maxlite.com

MaxLite SK America manufactures CFLs with integral electronic ballasts.

Compact Fluorescent Lamps

Osram Sylvania
100 Endicott St.
Danvers, MA 01923

Toll-free: 800-LIGHT-BULB
Phone: 978-777-1900
www.sylvania.com

Osram Sylvania offers a full line of CFLs, both with and without integral ballasts.

Compact Fluorescent Lamps

Panasonic Consumer Electronics
    Building Department
Panazip 4A-6
One Panasonic Way
Secaucus, NJ 07094

Toll-free: 866-292-7292
www.panasonic.com

Panasonic manufactures CFLs with integral electronic ballasts, including plug-ins and screw-ins.

Compact Fluorescent Lamps

Philips Lighting Company
200 Franklin Square Dr.
P.O. Box 6800
Somerset, NJ 08875

Toll-free: 800-555-0050
Phone: 732-563-3000
www.lighting.philips.com/nam

Philips Lighting Company produces a full line of CFLs, both with and without integral ballasts, including the Philips Marathon™ line of compact fluorescent bulbs. Lamps in the Marathon line are guaranteed for at least 6,000 hours and are the first CFLs to have the look of standard incandescents. These high-efficacy lamps offer a high color rendering index (CRI) and the energy-saving benefits associated with compact fluorescent technology. Philips introduced CFL lamps.

Compact Fluorescent Lamps

Technical Consumer Products, Inc.
300 Lena Dr.
Aurora, OH 44202

Toll-free: 800-324-1496
www.tcpi.com

TCP manufactures a full range of compact fluorescent lamps, such as integral ballast and modular ballast configurations, reflector lamps, spiral- and folded-tube configurations, and candelabra-base lamps.

Compact Fluorescent Lamps

U.S. Way Lighting
410 S. Warren Ave.
Palatine, IL 60074

Phone: 847-255-4021

U.S. Way Lighting offers CFLs in 14 styles and a variety of wattages and color temperatures. High output up to 105 watts (500-watt incandescent equivalent). Lamps achieve 95% illumination at start up with full brightness within 3 seconds.

NanoLux CFLs

Westinghouse Lighting Corporation
12401 McNulty Rd.
Philadelphia, PA 19154

Phone: 215-671-2000
www.westinghouselighting.com

NanoLux™ CFLs incorporate tiny electronic ballasts in the screw base so that the smallest lamp is about half the size of a standard incandescent bulb. Available in 3 designs—half-spot, spot, and globe—in various sizes and colors, the line ranges from 7 watts to 13 watts. All NanoLux lamps have a standard threaded base. The globe lamps are UL-approved for wet locations, and the medium and large globe lamps are rated to -13°F. The spot and half-spot allow CFLs to be used in place of high-design halogen lamps in track, spot, and pendant applications. NanoLux CFLs are sold through electrical distributors for use in such commercial-sector markets as hospitality, entertainment, restaurant, and retail. They are rated for an 8,000 hour life—20% less than for most CFLs.

Twisted-Tube CFLs

Star Lighting Products
11350 Brookpart Rd.
Cleveland, OH 44130

Toll-free: 800-392-3552
Phone: 216-433-7500
www.starlightingproducts.com

Star Lighting Products offers several sizes of compact, twisted-tube CFLs.

Twisted-Tube CFLs

Sunpark Electronic Corp.
1850 W. 205th St.
Torrance, CA 90501

Toll-free: 866-478-6775
Phone: 310-320-7880
www.sunpkco.com

Sunpark Electronic Corp. produces several sizes of compact, twisted-tube CFLs.

Compact Fluorescent Luminaires

Compact fluorescent lamps (CFLs), especially the smaller twisted-tube models, can readily be used in standard lighting fixtures. There are also many lighting fixtures designed specifically for use with CFLs, most of which have integral ballasts and plug-in CFLs. The popular torchiere-style CFL floor lamps have been developed, in part, as a response to the fire hazard of halogen torchiere fixtures. The cooler CFL torchieres are not only safer but also far more energy-efficient.

CFL Fixtures

Technical Consumer
Products, Inc.
300 Lena Dr.
Aurora, OH 44202

Toll-free: 800-324-1496
www.tcpi.com

Technical Consumer Products produces many indoor, outdoor and portable CFL fixtures including table and floor lamps, ceiling fixtures, and outdoor and portable fixtures. Their electronically ballasted CFL torchieres have a 65-watt T6 lamp configuration and 3-way light levels (30/36/65 W) in polished brass, matte black, glossy white, and brushed steel; average lamp life is 10,000 hours, and average ballast life 50,000 hours.

CFL Recessed Downlights

Juno Lighting, Inc.
1300 S. Wolf Rd.
P.O. Box 5065
Des Plaines, IL 60017

Toll-free: 800-367-5866
Phone: 847-827-9880
www.junolighting.com

Juno Lighting manufactures an extensive line of commercial-quality recessed downlights using CFLs. All models have separate ballasts—most electronic—with plug-in twin-tube, quad-tube, or triple-tube CFLs. Fixtures designed for lamp wattages of 13 to 42 are available. Some fixtures have the CFL oriented vertically, others horizontally. Full photometric data are available for all fixtures.

CFL Recessed Downlights

Technical Consumer
Products, Inc.
300 Lena Dr.
Aurora, OH 44202

Toll-free: 800-324-1496
www.tcpi.com

TCP produces complete retro-fit kits to change an existing recessed-can fixture into an energy-efficient CFL system. Kits are available in wattages ranging from 18 to 32 watts, which are equivalent to 75 to 125 incandescent watts. Kits feature reflector, two-piece SpringLamp®, and screw-in adapter for medium base sockets. According to the manufacturer, this product uses 75% less energy than equivalent incandescent products. The replaceable lamp lasts for 10,000 hours, while the ballast lasts 50,000 hours.

CFL Torchieres

Catalina Lighting
18191 N.W. 68th Ave.
Miami, FL 33015

Toll-free: 800-966-7074
Phone: 305-558-4777
www.catalinalighting.com

Catalina Lighting offers energy-efficient, torchiere-style floor lamps that use a single 55-watt fluorescent bulb.

CFL Torchieres

Good Earth Lighting
122 Messner Dr.
Wheeling, IL 60090

Toll-free: 800-291-8838
Phone: 847-808-1133
www.goodearthlighting.com

Good Earth Lighting produces energy-efficient, fluorescent torchiere standing fixtures.

Fluorescent Light Fixtures

Sunpark Electronic Corp.
1850 W. 205th St.
Torrance, CA 90501

Toll-free: 866-478-6775
Phone: 310-320-7880
www.sunpkco.com

Sunpark Electronics produces a wide range of compact-fluorescent and linear-tube fluorescent lamp fixtures, including fluorescent torchieres, ceiling fixtures, recessed downlights, table lamps, floor lamps, outdoor fixtures, and under-counter fixtures. Electronic ballasts are also available.

Frankie Goes Fluorescent, Parallel Universe, Lulu, Flipster and Fibonacci Series

Fire & Water Lighting/David
 Bergman Architect
241 Eldridge St. 3R
New York, NY 10002

Phone: 212-475-3106
www.cyberg.com

Most Fire & Water fluorescent lighting fixtures are green both from a materials standpoint and an energy efficiency standpoint.

Frankie Goes Fluorescent fixtures use either 4-pin CFLs or dimmable, integral-ballast CFLs and are made from Environ™ (a composite of soy flour and recycled paper) and 100% recycled glass (post-consumer content varies). The series includes two wall sconces, a ceiling fixture, and a table lamp; sconces are ADA-compliant.

The Lulu series, available in table, floor, wall and ceiling versions, utilizes the same lamping options and is made of 50% post-consumer recycled plastic.

The Parallel Universe series (floor, table, wall and ceiling) incorporates recycled and sustainable content materials and utilizes pin-based (dedicated) CFLs.

Fibonacci's shades are made of formaldehyde free, 70–100% post-industrial recycled wood, and process chlorine-free (PCF) paper liners. Flipster's shades are made of up to 40% recycled content resin. Both series are lamped with pin-based replaceable ballast CFL's, are ENERGY STAR®-compliant and are available in table, floor, wall and ceiling models.

Exterior Luminaires

Outdoor lighting is common around buildings. Incandescent, metal halide, and high-pressure sodium are the most common outdoor lighting options. Environmental issues include lamp efficacy (lumens per watt), luminaire efficiency, controllability of the light source, potential for PV power, and control of light pollution. To control light pollution, full-cutoff luminaires should be specified.

Full-Cutoff Luminaires

Gardco Lighting
2661 Alvarado St.
San Leandro, CA 94577

Toll-free: 800-227-0758
Phone: 510-357-6900
www.sitelighting.com

Gardco Lighting produces a wide range of full-cutoff luminaires for various lamp types.

Full-Cutoff Luminaires

Kim Lighting
P.O. Box 60080
City of Industry, CA 91716-0080

Phone: 626-968-5666
www.kimlighting.com

Kim Lighting produces a wide range of full-cutoff luminaires for various lamp types.

Full-Cutoff Luminaires

Sterner Lighting Systems, Inc.
P.O. Box 805
351 Lewis Ave. W
Winsted, MN 55395

Toll-free: 800-328-7480
Phone: 320-485-2141
www.sternerlighting.com

Sterner Lighting produces a wide range of full-cutoff luminaires for various lamp types.

LED and Solar- and Wind-Powered Full-Cutoff Luminaires

MoonCell, Inc.
P.O. Box 3068
Stafford, VA 22555-3068

Toll-free: 877-396-3142
www.mooncell.com

The Enviro-Lum™ outdoor luminaire provides off-grid illumination using both solar and wind power. Each luminaire uses 12 LEDs. The self-contained unit has a deep-cycle, lead-acid battery that is trickle-charged by a wind turbine and an integrated PV module. A second PV panel can be added to boost power generation. MoonCell luminaires are "cutoff" fixtures, limiting light pollution. Enviro-Lum is available with a variety of power-management features, including timers, motion sensors, and remote switches. MoonCell has also introduced several grid-connected outdoor light fixtures that rely on LEDs. All of these products reduce energy consumption by 50–70% compared to conventional lighting technologies, according to the company.

Sonne Solar-Powered Outdoor Luminaire

Selux Corporation
5 Lumen Ln.
P.O. Box 1060
Highland, NY 12528

Toll-free: 800-735-8927
Phone: 845-691-7723
www.selux.com

Sonne solar-powered Type III full-cutoff luminaires from Selux come equipped with 80W or 120W solar panels, mounted singly or in pairs on a fully tilting and rotating mount for maximum solar exposure. One or two 12V, 82AH sealed gel batteries power a compact fluorescent lamp rated at 18, 26, 32, or 42 watts, providing initial lumens between 1250 and 3200. A regulator/controller prevents overcharging and backflow; senses and remembers dusk and dawn time; and may be programmed to illuminate during set periods of time relative to sunrise and sunset. A motion detector is optional. Steel parts are hot-dip galvanized; some parts are made with recycled ABS.

Fluorescent Lamps

Fluorescent lamps have long been preferable to incandescent lighting, relative to energy efficiency. New developments with fluorescent technology, including the high-efficacy T-5 lamps, have pushed the energy efficiency envelope further. Recently, attention has also been paid to the mercury content of fluorescents and the consequences of mercury releases into the environment. As with all resource use and pollution issues, reduction is the best way to limit the problem. Even with low-mercury lamps, however, recycling of old lamps remains a high priority.

SILHOUETTE T5 Lamps

Philips Lighting Company
200 Franklin Square Dr.
P.O. Box 6800
Somerset, NJ 08875

Toll-free: 800-555-0050
Phone: 732-563-3000
www.lighting.philips.com/nam

The Silhouette T5 and Silhouette T5 High Output fluorescents are available in a variety of popular wattages (ranging from 14 to 80 watts), with an average rated life of 20,000 hours. They are particularly suitable for offices, retail stores, hotels, schools, and hospitals, especially where small fixtures are required.

Interior Luminaires

Many innovative, energy-efficient luminaires are available, most of which are primarily relevant to commercial buildings. Envi-

ronmental characteristics to consider include fluorescent lamp use, effective reflectors, and application-appropriate design. Fluorescent high-bay fixtures can replace conventional HID lighting in gymnasiums, warehouses, and other high-ceiling spaces, offering both direct energy savings and the benefit of instant-on (so they are more likely to be turned off).

Indirect Fluorescent Fixtures

SPI Lighting Group
10400 N. Enterprise Dr.
Mequon, WI 53092

Phone: 262-242-1420
www.spilighting.com

The Opera line of indirect lighting fixtures includes a selection of stylish pendant fixtures that have integral electronic ballasts and 21-watt 2D or twin-tube lamps (27, 39, 40, 50, or 55 W). The Options line includes wall, sconce, ceiling, and pier-mount fixtures. Designed primarily for commercial buildings.

Lamp and Ballast Recycling

Fluorescent and HID lamps and older magnetic ballasts contain hazardous materials that should be disposed of in an environmentally responsible manner. Fluorescent and HID lamps contain the toxic heavy metal mercury, and pre-1970 ballasts contain polychlorinated biphenyls (PCBs). The quantity of mercury in a fluorescent lamp is small (a few grams), while about an ounce of PCB was typically used in every pre-1970 ballast! Both substances are very persistent in the environment, bioaccumulating in animal tissues. Bioaccumulated mercury levels in fish can be 250,000 times as high as in the surrounding environment. Human health risks associated with these toxins include neurological, reproductive, and liver disorders. Recycling services are equipped to recycle and reprocess fluorescent and HID lamps and ballasts safely without releasing these toxins into the environment. Before sending fluorescent lamps and ballasts to out-of-town recycling facilities, check with your local solid-waste agency; many handle lamps and ballast disposal through toxic waste programs.

Fluorescent and HID Lamp Recycling

AERC.com, Inc.
30677 Huntwood Ave.
Hayward, CA 94544

Toll-free: 800-628-3675
Phone: 510-429-1129
www.aercrecycling.com

AERC.com, Inc. recycles spent fluorescent and High Intensity Discharge lamps. Their technology recovers mercury and other metals from the lamps, then segregates the glass, metal end caps, and phosphor powder for further recycling and reuse.

Fluorescent Lamp and Ballast Recycling

Ecolights Northwest
9411 8th Ave. S
P.O. Box 94291
Seattle, WA 98124-6591

Phone: 206-343-1247
www.ecolights.com

Ecolights Northwest provides storage/shipping containers, transportation, handling documents, and final recycling for fluorescent and HID lamps and fluorescent ballasts. Ecolights Northwest is sister company to Total Reclaim, Inc., which offers CFC reclamation/recycling, as well as electronic and battery recycling programs.

Fluorescent Lamp and Ballast Recycling

Environmental Light Recyclers, Inc.
2737 Bryan Ave.
Fort Worth, TX 76104

Toll-free: 800-755-4117
Phone: 817-924-9300

Environmental Light Recyclers safely processes used fluorescent and HID lamps and ballasts. ELR handles both PCB ballasts and non-PCB, DEHP-containing magnetic ballasts. Certificates of Recycling are provided to ELR's customers as protection against hazardous materials liabilities.

Fluorescent Lamp and Ballast Recycling

Full Circle Recyclers
509 Manida St.
Bronx, NY 10474

Toll-free: 800-775-1516
www.fcrecyclers.com

Full Circle, Inc. is one of the largest recyclers of PCB ballasts and fluorescent lamps in the U.S. Headquartered in New York City, the company operates facilities in at least ten cities to provide disposal/recycling services for the entire country. In addition to handling PCB ballasts and fluorescent lamps, the company recycles non-PCB ballasts, HID lamps, mercury thermostats and switches, batteries, thermometers, etc. With fluorescent lamps, 100% of the material is separated and recycled; with PCB ballasts, 80% is recycled and the rest sent to hazardous-waste incinerators for complete thermal breakdown of the PCBs.

Fluorescent Lamp and Ballast Recycling

HTR-Group
P.O. Box 185
Lake Ozark, MO 65049

Toll-free: 888-537-4874
Phone: 537-302-7575
www.htr-group.com

HTR-Group is a resource-recovery facility for mercury-containing

lamps and for ballasts. The company maintains a fleet of vehicles covering the entire U.S. for material pick up and a 4-acre recycling facility with a processing capacity of 1,500,000 lamps per month. Certificates of Recycle are provided as protection against hazardous materials liabilities. HTR-Group recycles 100% of all lamp parts.

Fluorescent Lamp and Ballast Recycling

Institution Recycling Network
7 S. State St.
Concord, NH 03301

Phone: 603-229-1962
www.ir-network.com

The Institution Recycling Network (IRN) offers fluorescent, HID, as well as other lamp and ballast recycling for member institutions. Services are typically organized in a "milk run" setup, through which pickup is coordinated for several members at a time to minimize handling and transportation costs to each member organization. Single pickups can be arranged as well. IRN is a cooperative recycling company that works with colleges and universities, hospitals, and other institutions to provide single-point recycling for dozens of different materials, including C&D waste and battery recycling. IRN fluorescent and ballast recycling services are typically limited to member organizations in the New England and Hudson Valley Regions.

Fluorescent Lamp and Ballast Recycling

Northeast Lamp Recycling, Inc.
250 Main St.
P.O. Box 680
East Windsor, CT 06088

Phone: 860-292-1992
www.nlrlamp.com

Northeast Lamp Recycling (NCR) is a licensed hazardous waste transporter operating a fluorescent and HID lamp and ballast recycling facility. NCR separates lamp components of glass, metal, mercury, and phosphor powder for recycling and reuse. Certificates of Recycling are issued as protection against hazardous materials liabilities.

Fluorescent Lamp and Ballast Recycling

Onyx Special Services
1275 Mineral Springs Dr.
Port Washington, WI 53074

Toll-free: 800-556-5267
Phone: 262-243-8900
www.onyxes.com

Onyx, through its Electronics Recycling Division, is one of the world's largest recyclers of fluorescent and HID lamps and other items containing toxic and hazardous materials. Packaging and pick-ups are available for some items, including lamps, ballasts, computer and electronic equipment, batteries, and electrical equipment containing PCBs. For prepaid recycling, visit www.onyxpak.com

Lighting Accessories

Electronic ballasts for fluorescent lighting are much more energy-efficient than traditional magnetic ballasts, saving as much as 35%. Electronic ballasts are commonly available in new fixtures and for retrofitting existing fixtures. These products are quiet and do not have the characteristic flicker of magnetic ballasts. Additional energy savings are possible with electronic dimming ballasts. Advanced dimming ballasts can now reduce light levels to below 10% of total output. Besides the energy savings that dimming affords, building occupant comfort is enhanced, especially through lessened eye fatigue from reduced computer screen glare.

Dimming Electronic Ballasts

Lutron Electronics Co., Inc.
7200 Suter Rd.
Coopersburg, PA 18036

Toll-free: 888-588-7661
Phone: 610-282-3800
www.lutron.com

Lutron's extensive line of dimming electronic ballasts includes products for T12, T8, and T5 linear fluorescent lamps and for CFLs. Dimming to 1% available with some products. New products include personal remote dimming controls for workstations.

Electronic Ballasts

Advance Transformer Co.
10275 W. Higgins Rd.
O'Hare International Ctr.
Rosemont, IL 60018

Toll-free: 800-322-2086
Phone: 847-390-5000
www.advancetransformer.com

Advance Transformer manufactures a wide range of leading-edge energy-efficient ballasts, including electronic, electronic-dimming, and electronic HID and CFL ballasts.

Electronic Ballasts

Howard Industries, Inc.
P.O. Box 1590
Laurel, MS 39441-1588

Toll-free: 800-956-3456
Phone: 601-422-0033
www.howard-ballast.com

Howard Industries manufactures a full range of electronic ballasts.

Electronic Ballasts

Universal Lighting Technologies
26 Century Blvd., Ste. 500
Nashville, TN 37214

Toll-free: 800-BALLAST
Phone: 615-316-5100
www.universalballast.com

Universal Lighting Technologies, formerly MagneTek Lighting Products Group, manufactures a comprehensive line of energy-efficient electronic ballasts and controls, including the ULTim8 family of ballasts for T8 applications. The ULTim8 line saves up to 40% compared to T12 energy saving systems, and up to 6% versus standard electronic T8 ballasts, according to the company.

Special Purpose Lighting

These listings include heavy-duty work lights using high-efficiency compact fluorescent lamps, as well as other solutions for special purpose lighting needs.

Limelite

EI Products
1009 W. 6th St., Ste. 208
Austin, TX 78703

Phone: 512-339-6765
www.limelite.com

Limelite® is a lime green electroluminescent exit light with a current draw of 0.2 W.

SideKick Worklytes

Stonco Lighting
2345 Vauxhall Rd.
Union, NJ 07083

Phone: 908-964-7000
www.stoncolighting.com

Stonco Lighting has introduced a line of portable CFL worklights and cord reels under the name SideKick™. These energy-efficient worklights reduce heat buildup and the risk of contact with hot surfaces. SideKick WorkLytes come in a range of styles for a variety of applications. Included in the series is the Ratchet Lyte™, which ratchets into 8 positions and gives 60-watt light output from a 13-watt quad CFL. Also available is the 13-watt fluorescent Lyte Rover Cordless WorkLyte, which converts any extension cord into a portable light source.

Appliances

Appliances are significant ongoing users of energy and potable water. Federal standards for some appliances are helping to ensure that certain new appliances will be far more efficient than models they are replacing, but some manufacturers offer products that significantly exceed federal standards. Many of the most efficient appliances come from Europe, where energy is more expensive than in North America.

There is a revolution under way in the world of clothes washers—it's called "horizontal axis." Horizontal-axis washing machines have long been the standard among commercial-quality washers and in Europe. They use much less water than the typical American top-loader, are gentler on the clothes, use less detergent, wash more effectively, and—because they spin faster—remove more of the moisture from a load of laundry, which reduces the amount of energy needed for drying. For years these models were almost impossible to find in the U.S., but now most major American manufacturers are producing them. Although more expensive than standard top-loaders, the extra cost of a horizontal-axis washer will be covered by detergent savings alone—even before the water savings, energy savings (by using less hot water and reducing drying time), and wear-and-tear on clothing are factored in.

As with other appliances, seek out an efficient dishwasher that meets the convenience and feature requirements—and don't use energy-guzzling features, such as heat drying, when it isn't necessary. Most models have a water-saving cycle that should be used for lightly soiled dishes or partial loads (though it usually makes the most sense to wash only full loads). Note that hand-washing dishes may use more water and energy than a dishwasher, depending on how one does the hand-washing.

Driven by national standards, the energy efficiency of refrigerators has improved greatly over the past few decades. Unfortunately, a common practice when buying a new refrigerator is to keep the older one for storing beer and soda; this practice should be avoided. In general, refrigerators in the 16- to 20-cubic-foot range tend to be most efficient (because these are the most popular sizes, so this is where manufacturers invest the most R&D funding), as are those with freezers on top instead of side-by-side. Avoid extra convenience features like ice-makers unless they'll *really* get used.

For ranges and cooktops, electric elements should be preferred over gas simply to avoid the toxic byproducts of gas combustion in the house. If a gas appliance is used, an effective, exhausting vent-hood (rather than one that simply filters and recirculates the air) should be used whenever the burners are on. As quiet a range-hood fan as possible should be selected to increase the likelihood that it will be used by homeowners. Halogen electric elements provide the instant-on, instant-off performance that many cooks seek in a gas range.

Most gas ovens use a significant amount of electricity because they have a glow-bar that is on continuously in order to reignite the gas flame immediately if it is blown out somehow. In fact, a microwave oven can use less electricity to bake a potato than a gas oven! While microwaves are a more efficient way to cook, there are some concerns about the possible leakage of microwaves if the door seals aren't perfect.

Residential Clothes Washers and Drying Equipment

A significant amount of the energy used for clothes washing is for heating the water, so machines that use less water are usually more energy-efficient. Manufacturers have made tremendous strides in increasing the energy efficiency of clothes washers in recent decades. This has been aided by U.S. Department of Energy (DOE) minimum efficiency standards, the federal ENERGY STAR® program, and efforts of the Consortium for Energy Efficiency (CEE). To be included in GreenSpec, clothes washers must have a minimum "Modified Energy Factor" of 1.42 and a maximum "Water Factor" of 9.5, as defined by CEE. These thresholds are the requirements for Tier 2 of the CEE's list of energy-efficient residential clothes washers and are significantly more stringent than ENERGY STAR standards. The modified energy factor (MEF) combines the "Energy Factor" of the federal appliance standard with "remaining moisture content" (RMC, which is predictive of dryer energy use). The higher the MEF, the more efficient the washer is in the entire laundry cycle, including drying. The water factor (WF) is a measure of the number of gallons of water used per cubic foot of laundry. The majority of the washers listed here are horizontal-axis models, which use less water—thus requiring less water to be heated. Some manufacturers also offer condensing dryers; these do not require exterior venting, and they release all generated heat inside the building (an advantage in the winter but a disadvantage in the summer). The primary problem with washer-dryer models (single units that both wash and dry laundry in a common drum) is that the volume required for drying a load of laundry is larger than the volume required for washing, so when one drum has to serve both needs, the wash volume is reduced. They can also increase water consumption by running cold water through condensation coils.

Asko H-Axis Clothes Washers and Dryers

AM Appliance Group - Asko
P.O. Box 851805
Richardson, TX 75085-1805

Phone: 972-644-8595
www.askousa.com

Asko manufactures seven models that meet the requirements for *GreenSpec*. Models W6221 (Tier 2) and W6021 (Tier 3) have 1.96 ft³ capacity, a WF of 7.48, and an MEF of 1.58 and 1.66, respectively. Models W6441 and W6641 are Tier 3 washers with 1.96 ft³ capacity, a WF of 7.48, and an MEF of 1.74. Qualifying for Tier 4A, Models W6661 and W6761 have a 1.84 MEF, with 1.96 ft³ capacity, and a WF of 7.48. In Tier 4A as well, model WCAM1812 is a washer/condensing-dryer combo with a volume of 2.46 ft³, an MEF of 2.5, and a WF of 7.48. All of these washers have internal water heaters and are front-loading. Asko also manufactures dryers with integral moisture condensers so that outside venting is not required. Asko appliances are manufactured in Sweden.

BSH Axxis Clothes Washers and Dryer

BSH Home Appliances Corp.
5551 McFadden Ave.
Huntington Beach, CA 92649

Toll-free: 800-944-2904
Phone: 714-901-6600
www.boschappliances.com

Bosch Axxis™ horizontal-axis washer models WFL2060UC and WFR2460UC are among the top-rated washers in the country, rating Tier 4A. Both front-loading machines offer internal water heating and have 1.85 ft³ of volume, a WF of 6.547 and 5.73, and an MEF of 1.8 and 2.08, respectively. Bosch also manufactures a condensing dryer.

Ecosmart Clothes Washers

Fisher & Paykel
27 Hubble
Irvine, CA 92618

Toll-free: 800-863-5394
www.fisherpaykel.com

Fisher & Paykel's Ecosmart models GWL10 and GWL11 qualify for Tier 3. Made in Australia, these top-loading, vertical-axis machines have a volume of 3 ft3, with MEF ratings of 2.2 and 1.91 and WF of 8.9 and 8.5, respectively.

Equator Combination Washer-Dryers

Equator Corporation
Equator Plz.
10067 Timber Oak Dr.
Houston, TX 77080

Toll-free: 800-935-1955
Phone: 713-464-3422
www.equatorappliances.com

The Equator Clothes Processor combination washer-dryers qualify for the highest level, Tier 4B. Models EZ3612CEE (ventless condenser dryer) and EZ1612VCEE (vented dryer) both are front-loading, have a 1.92 ft³ capacity, MEF ratings of 1.92 and 2.04, respectively, and a WF of 5 and 4.9. In Tier 4A, front-loading model EZ2512CEE has 1.6 ft³ capacity, an MEF of 1.83, and a WF of 6. Made in Italy.

Eurotech Clothes Washers

AM Appliance Group - Eurotech
P.O. Box 851805
Richardson, TX 75085-1805

Phone: 972-644-8595
www.eurotechappliances.com

The Eurotech EWF172 Extra Large Capacity H-axis front-loading clothes washer offers integral water heating and qualifies for Tier 2 with a volume of 2.5 ft³, an MEF of 1.52, and a WF of 8. Qualifying for Tier 4A, model EWC177 is a front-loading washer combined with a ventless condensing dryer with a volume of 2.46 ft³, an MEF of 2.5, and a WF of 7.48. Eurotech washers are distributed by AM Appliance Group, which also distributes Asko appliances.

Frigidaire, Gibson, and White-Westinghouse H-Axis Clothes Washers

Electrolux Home Products
250 Bobby Jones Expy.
Augusta, GA 30907

Toll-free: 800-451-7007
Phone: 706-651-1751
www.frigidaire.com

Electrolux Home Products offers Frigidaire, Gibson, and White-Westinghouse brands of clothes washers. Frigidaire lists more than a dozen that meet requirements for Tier 2, including models GLTF1040A, FTF630A, FTR630A, and FWT645RH; each with a volume of 2.65 ft³, a WF of 9.43, and an MEF of 1.68. Gibson offers two Tier 2-qualifying models, both with a volume of 2.65 ft³, a WF of 9.44, and an MEF of 1.44. White-Westinghouse offers model WTR1240A, which has a volume of 2.65 ft³, a WF of no more than 9.5, and an MEF of 1.44; this model qualifies for Tier 2.

GE Clothes Washers

GE Appliances
General Electric Answer Center
9500 Williamsburg Office Plz.
Louisville, KY 40222

Toll-free: 800-626-2000
www.geappliances.com

Front-loading GE models WPXH214A and WSXH208A qualify for Tier 2 with a WF of 9.5 and MEFs of 1.47 and 1.59, respectively. Both models have a volume of 2.65 ft³ and are manufactured for GE by Electrolux. Model WPGT9350C, also in Tier 2, is a top-loader providing a large 3.53 ft³ of capacity, 1.45 MEF, and a 6.3 WF. This model is manufactured for GE by LG Electronics.

Kenmore H-Axis Clothes Washers

Sears
3333 Beverly Rd.
Hoffman Estates, IL 60179

Toll-free: 800-549-4505
www.kenmore.com

Kenmore, manufactured for Sears by Electrolux and Whirlpool, offers a number of models that meet the requirements for *GreenSpec*, including several that qualify for Tier 4A and are among the most energy-efficient washers in the country. Models with the highest MEF include 4304, 4305, and 4314.

LG Combination Washer-Dryers

LG Appliances
1000 Sylvan Ave.
Englewood Cliffs, NJ 07632

Toll-free: 800-942-3786
www.lgappliances.com

All models from LG Appliances are front-loading and, except as noted, have a capacity of 3.22 ft³. Models WM1811C and WM1832C qualify for Tier 3, each with an MEF of 1.76 and a WF of 4.3. LG Appliances also has 8 models in the highest level, Tier 4B—several more than any other manufacturer. Models W0532H, WM2032H, WM2011H have a 1.83 MEF and a 4 WF. Models WM2432H and WM2411H have a 1.87 MEF and a 4 WF. Models WM3611H and WM3632H are washer/condensing-dryer combos with an MEF of 1.87 and WF of 4. Models WD-324RHD and WD-327RHD, are also combination washer/condensing-dryers with a volume of 1.96 ft³, a WF of 5, and a 2.1 MEF. These ventless units feature integral water heating and are manufactured in Korea.

Maytag Neptune Washers

Maytag Appliances
403 W. Fourth St. N
P.O. Box 39
Newton, IA 50208

Toll-free: 888-462-9824
Phone: 641-792-7000
www.maytag.com

Maytag models MAH55FLB, MAH5500B, MAH6500A, MAH7500, MLE2000 (stacked washer/vented electric dryer), MLG2000 (stacked washer/vented gas dryer), all are front-loading, have a volume of 2.9 ft³, WF ratings between 8 and 8.5, and qualify for Tier 3 with MEFs of 1.47, 1.47, 1.55, 1.66, 1.69, and 1.69, respectively. Manufactured by Maytag in the U.S.

Miele H-Axis Clothes Washers

Miele, Inc.
9 Independence Way
Princeton, NJ 08540

Toll-free: 800-843-7231
Phone: 609-419-9898
www.mieleusa.com

Miele offers five models that qualify for Tier 3. Models Novotronic W1918 (volume of 1.69 ft³, WF of 8.3), W1926 (volume of 2.01 ft3, WF of 7.6), W1930 (volume of 1.69 ft³, WF of 8.3), and W1966 (volume of 2.01 ft³, WF of 5.1) all have an MEF of 1.64. Model W1968 has a volume of 2.01 ft³, a WF of 5.1, and a slightly better 1.63 MEF. These models all are front-loading, have integral water heating, and are made in Germany.

Splendide Clothes Washers

Splendide
15650 S.E. 102nd Ave.
P.O. Box 427
Clackamas, OR 97015

Toll-free: 800-356-0766 Ext. 6
www.splendide.com

Westland Sales

Splendide offers models WDC6200CEE and WD2100, washer/condensing-dryer combos that qualify for highest level, Tier 4B. Each has a capacity of 1.92 ft³ and a WF of 5.2, with 1.62 and 1.74 MEF, respectively. In Tier 4A are models WDC5200 (a washer/condensing-dryer combo) and WD2000S (a vented washer/dryer combo), each with a 1.55 MEF and 5.9 WF, and capacities of 1.92 and 1.6 ft³, respectively. All models are front-loading.

Staber Clothes Washers

Staber Industries, Inc.
4800 Homer Ohio Ln.
Groveport, OH 43125

Toll-free: 800-848-6200
Phone: 614-836-5995
www.staber.com

Staber is the only top-loading horizontal-axis washer made in the U.S. Staber model HXW2304 qualifies for Tier 2 and has a volume of 2.0 ft³, a WF of 7.11, and an MEF of 1.48. Because of its unique top-loading h-axis tub design, the entire tub volume can be utilized and fit up to 16 full-size bath towels in one load. Staber has a patented stainless-steel tub design with no transmission and a removable front panel for total front access to parts. Staber models HXW2404 and HXW2504 also qualify for Tier 2.

The Dryerbox

In-O-Vate Technologies
6190 Sand Pine Ct.
Jupiter, FL 33458

Toll-free: 888-443-7937
Phone: 561-743-8696
www.dryerbox.com

The Dryerbox™ is a 21"-high aluminized steel box designed to be installed in the wall behind a dryer to eliminate bends in the flex transition hose. According to the manufacturer, this reduces lint build-up and the attendant risk of fire. The company also claims it shortens the necessary drying time to save the typical household $6 per year (based on testing carried out by the company). Because the dryer can then be installed right up against the wall, about 1 ft² of living space is gained, and the elimination of a 90° bend gives the HVAC contractor a 5' credit in duct run length. The company's website contains a wealth of information on dryer venting.

Thor Combination Washer-Dryers

Thor Appliance Company
268 Ave. Montalvo, Ste. 9
San Clemente, CA 92672

Toll-free: 877-877-0540
www.thorappliances.com

Thor offers two front-loading combination washer/condensing dryer units that qualify for *GreenSpec*. Model WD9900, with a volume of 2.0 ft³, an MEF of 1.59, and a WF of 7.4, qualifies for Tier 2. Thor Softline™ Model XQG65-11, with a volume of 2.01 ft³, an MEF of 1.85, and a WF of 5.7, rates Tier 4A and is among the most efficient washers available.

Whirlpool Duet, Duet HT, and Calypso Washers

Whirlpool Corporation
2000 N. Hwy. M-63
Benton Harbor, MI 49022-2692

Toll-free: 800-253-1301
www.whirlpool.com

Whirlpool offers four models that qualify for *GreenSpec*. The Whirlpool® Calypso™ Model GVW9959K (volume 2.99 ft³, MEF 1.53, WF 8.02), is a top-loading vertical-axis machine that has been rated for Tier 2. Horizontal-axis front-loading Whirlpool Duet™ and Duet HT™ (Models GHW9100L and GHW9200L) both have a volume of 3.18 ft³ and qualify for higher-rated Tier 3 (MEF 1.69 and 1.68, and WF 4.28 and 4.36, respectively). The Whirlpool Duet Frontloader GHW9250M is also in Tier 3 (volume 3.18 ft³, MEF 1.68, and WF 4.36). These washers are made in Europe by Whirlpool.

Residential Dishwashers

Most of the energy consumed by dishwashers is used to heat the water; therefore, water-efficient dishwashers are also energy-efficient. As with other home appliances, national energy standards have catalyzed the development of more efficient dishwashers. As a measure of efficiency, the Energy Factor (EF) describes energy performance under carefully defined conditions, and provides a basis of comparison among different models. The national energy standard adopted in 1994 requires all standard size dishwashers to have an energy factor of at least 0.46. The Energy Star program qualifies dishwashers exceeding that standard by at least 25% (EF of 0.58). To be included in GreenSpec, dishwashers must exceed the national minimum energy standard by at least 45% (EF of 0.67 or higher). In mid-2002 a problem was noted with the DOE test procedure used to determine the EF numbers—the test used clean dishes, and for models with soil-sensing features, the rated energy efficiency was overstated. (When dishes are heavily soiled, sensor-equipped models heat the wash water more or use additional water.) The DOE has instituted a revised test procedure, and all EF numbers are being revised accordingly. Be aware that the rated energy performance (as indicated on the yellow EnergyGuide labels or on ENERGY STAR labels) may not be accurate on dishwashers with soil-sensing features manufactured before February 25, 2004.

Asko Dishwashers

AM Appliance Group - Asko
P.O. Box 851805
Richardson, TX 75085-1805

Phone: 972-644-8595
www.askousa.com

Asko manufactures 21 dishwasher models that are among the most energy-efficient available, with energy factors as high as 1.19. Some models include the SensiClean™ Sensor, which may affect actual energy efficiency. Made in Sweden.

Danby Designer Dishwashers

Danby Products Inc.
101 Bentley Ct.
P.O. Box 987
Findlay, OH 45840

Toll-free: 800-26-DANBY
Phone: 419-425-8627
www.danby.com

Canadian company Danby offers built-in model DDW1802W, and portable version DDW1805W. Both have an energy factor of 0.71 and currently do not employ soil-sensing technology. Manufactured in China.

Equator Dishwashers

Equator Corporation
Equator Plz.
10067 Timber Oak Dr.
Houston, TX 77080

Toll-free: 800-935-1955
Phone: 713-464-3422
www.equatorappliances.com

Equator offers 6 full-size dishwashers with energy factors of 0.68, as well as 8 compact models with energy factors of 1.29. Equator dishwashers do not use soil-sensing. Made in Germany.

Eurotech Dishwashers

AM Appliance Group - Eurotech
P.O. Box 851805
Richardson, TX 75085-1805

Phone: 972-644-8595
www.eurotechappliances.com

Eurotech, a division of Texas-based AM Appliance Group, manufactures two *GreenSpec*-qualifying models. EDW154E has an energy factor of 0.72, and EDW174E has an energy factor of 0.74. They do not use soil-sensing technology.

Fisher & Paykel Dishwashers

Fisher & Paykel
27 Hubble
Irvine, CA 92618

Toll-free: 800-863-5394
www.fisherpaykel.com

Fisher & Paykel's DishDrawer® (model DD603-USA) is a double-drawer dishwasher with an energy factor of 0.72. It does not use soil-sensing. Made in New Zealand.

Frigidaire and Gibson Dishwashers

Electrolux Home Products
250 Bobby Jones Expy.
Augusta, GA 30907

Toll-free: 800-451-7007
Phone: 706-651-1751
www.frigidaire.com

Frigidaire offers 7 dishwasher models meeting *GreenSpec* requirements. Models FDB658RA, FDB751SC, FDB780RC, FDBC56BA and GLDB756A have energy factors of 0.67, and models FDR252RB and FDS252RB have an energy factor of 0.68. Some models include a feature called "Smart Soil Sensor," which may affect their actual efficiency. Companion brand Gibson sells two *GreenSpec*-qualifying models (GDB754RC and GDB755RJ) with energy factors of 0.67. These models may include soil-sensing technology, which could affect their actual efficiency. Made in the U.S.A.

GE Dishwashers

GE Appliances - General Electric Answer Center
9500 Williamsburg Office Plz.
Louisville, KY 40222

Toll-free: 800-626-2000
www.geappliances.com

GE offers 35 dishwasher models that have energy factors ranging from 0.68 to 0.83. These models include soil-sensing features that may affect their actual energy efficiency. Made in the U.S.A.

The Monogram series from GE includes 7 dishwasher models with energy factors of 0.72 that do include soil-sensing technology, which could affect their actual efficiency. The Monogram series is made in Germany and Italy.

Kenmore Dishwashers

Sears
3333 Beverly Rd.
Hoffman Estates, IL 60179

Toll-free: 800-549-4505
www.kenmore.com

Sears carries two models of Kenmore dishwashers, models 1424 and 1724, that have an energy factor of 0.68. These models are not soil-sensing. Kenmore dishwashers are made in the U.S.A. by Electrolux.

Miele Dishwashers

Miele, Inc.
9 Independence Way
Princeton, NJ 08540

Toll-free: 800-843-7231
Phone: 609-419-9898
www.mieleusa.com

Miele offers 5 dishwasher models meeting *GreenSpec* criteria. Models G605 and G805 have an energy factor of 0.68; model G811, an energy factor of 0.67; and models G818 and G832 have energy factors of 0.71 and 0.73, respectively. None of the Miele dishwashers include soil-sensing. Made in Germany.

Viking Dishwashers

Viking Range Corporation
111 Front St.
Greenwood, MS 38930

Toll-free: 888-845-464

The Viking Professional Series dishwasher models VUD040 and VUD141 have energy factors of 0.79 and 0.93, respectively. Designer Series model DFUD140 has an energy factor of 0.79; and DFUD141, an energy factor of 0.84. Viking dishwashers do not use soil-sensing. Made in the U.S.

Residential Refrigerators

The energy efficiency of refrigerators has improved dramatically in the last several decades. National standards have helped reduce the energy use of refrigerators to less than one-third that of pre-1973 models. Developments in refrigerator design, including increased insulation, tighter door seals, and more efficient compressors, are continuing that trend. ENERGY STAR-qualified refrigerators exceed the minimum federal efficiency standards for refrigerators by 10% or more. To be included in GreenSpec, top-freezer models (the most efficient configuration) must exceed the federal standards by at least 13%, and side-by-side and bottom-freezer models must exceed it by at least 15%. Also listed here are super-efficient refrigerators that are usually sold for use in houses that generate their own electricity; these generally haven't qualified for ENERGY STAR because the companies are too small to be required to submit to testing.

Conserv

Equator Corporation
Equator Plz.
10067 Timber Oak Dr.
Houston, TX 77080

Toll-free: 800-935-1955
Phone: 713-464-3422
www.equatorappliances.com

Conserv™ is a specialized very-low-energy-usage refrigerator designed for homes with or without connection to the utility grid. A Danish product formerly marketed as Vestfrost™, the manual-defrost Conserv is built with all recyclable parts, CFC-free foam and refrigerant, and separate compressors for the refrigerator and freezer.

GE Refrigerators

GE Appliances
General Electric Answer Center
9500 Williamsburg Office Plz.
Louisville, KY 40222

Toll-free: 800-626-2000
www.geappliances.com

General Electric produces 13 models that exceed federal standards for side-by-side refrigerators by 15%. All of them have a projected energy usage of 613 kWh/year and are roughly 25.5 ft^3.

Kenmore Refrigerators

Sears
3333 Beverly Rd.
Hoffman Estates, IL 60179

Toll-free: 800-549-4505
www.kenmore.com

Sears offers a whopping 58 full-size models under the Kenmore brand name that qualify for *GreenSpec*, including some of the highest ENERGY STAR-rated in the top-freezer and side-by-side configurations. Rated 20% better than the federal standard, top-freezer models 7390, 7393, 6397, 6398, 7397, and 7398 are 18.8 ft^3 models with a projected energy use of 392 kWh/year. Top-freezer models 7320 and 7323 are 21.7 ft^3 models rated 19% better with a projected energy use of 428 kWh/year. Most of these models are manufactured for Sears by Whirlpool.

KitchenAid Refrigerator

KitchenAid
P.O. Box 218
St. Joseph, MI 49085

Toll-free: 800-422-1230
www.kitchenaid.com

KitchenAid offers 27 side-by-side refrigerator models rating 15% higher than the national standard for that configuration. They range in capacity from 20.96 to 29.92 ft^3 with projected energy usage from 540 kWh (for 21.7 ft³ model KSRA22KK) to 659 kWh/year. Eight bottom-freezer models rated at 15% better than the federal standard are also offered, each with a volume of 20.38 ft³ and a projected annual energy usage of 482 kWh.

LG Refrigerators

LG Appliances
1000 Sylvan Ave.
Englewood Cliffs, NJ 07632

Toll-free: 800-942-3786
www.lgappliances.com

Achieving new levels of efficiency for refrigerators with bottom-mounted freezers, LG Electronics has five models to choose from with volumes of 19.7 and 22.4 ft³, using 440 and 475 kWh/year and rating 23% and 15% better, respectively, than federal standards for that configuration. LG also manufactures four side-by-side models that qualify for *GreenSpec*: three 25.5 ft³ models with a projected energy usage of 626 kWhr/year (18% better than the federal standard) and one 23.7 ft³ model with a projected energy usage of 625 kWhr/year (16% better).

Maytag Refrigerators

Maytag Appliances
403 W. Fourth St. N
P.O. Box 39
Newton, IA 50208

Toll-free: 888-462-9824
Phone: 641-792-7000
www.maytag.com

Maytag manufactures two refrigerator models sold under the Magic Chef brand that exceed the new federal standards for refrigerators by 14%. Models CTL1511GEW and CTN1511GEW each have a projected energy usage of 386 kWh/year and a volume of 14.96 ft³.

Sun Frost Refrigerators

Sun Frost
P.O. Box 1101
Arcata, CA 95518

Phone: 707-822-9095
www.sunfrost.com

Sun Frost produces refrigerators and freezers with extremely low energy use—some models exceed federal standards by more than 50%. Capacities range from 10.12 to 16.14 ft³, with annual energy usage tested to be 171 to 254 kWh, depending on the model. Available in 12- and 24-volt DC, and 110- and 220-volt AC models, they are especially suited to homes not connected to the utility grid.

Whirlpool Refrigerators

Whirlpool Corporation
2000 N. Hwy. M-63
Benton Harbor, MI 49022

Toll-free: 800-253-1301
www.whirlpool.com

Whirlpool model ET5WSE is a 14.54 ft³ top-freezer unit that exceeds the federal standard by 16% with a projected annual energy usage of 372 kWh. Eight other top-freezer Whirlpool models with volumes ranging from 18.8 to 21.7 ft³ (projected annual energy usage 491 to 528 kWh) are rated 15% better than the federal standard. Whirlpool also makes 11 side-by-side models that exceed federal standards for that configuration by 15%. They have projected annual energy usages ranging from 572 to 619 kWh and volumes ranging from 21.93 to 25.55 ft³. Whirlpool also makes a number of other *GreenSpec*-approved units that are sold under Kenmore and KitchenAid labels.

This Space is Available for Your Notes

This Space is Available for Your Notes

Furniture & Furnishings

The introduction of furnishings that offgas hazardous chemicals can undo all the care given to using "clean" building materials. Furniture and furnishings incorporate many separate products and all of the issues that go with them. As a result, they can be a significant source of IAQ problems—coming from binders in wood composites such as particleboard, from finishes used on the products, from flame retardants used in foam cushions, and from adhesives used to assemble the products. Those items incorporating fabric, such as upholstered furniture and workstations, can also collect dirt and airborne contaminants, releasing them later.

Most of the plastic laminates used on inexpensive furniture is made from phenolic resins. These compounds are somewhat toxic to work with but relatively stable—and they're easy to keep clean after manufacture.

Hardwoods—especially tropical hardwoods—used in furniture manufacture should be third-party certified according to Forest Stewardship Council (FSC) standards to ensure that they were harvested in an environmentally responsible manner. FSC certification involves third-party evaluation and monitoring of sustainable forestry practices.

Most fabrics used on commercial furniture and workstations are primarily polyester. Wool is a durable and attractive natural alternative, though it is sometimes treated with toxic mothproofing agents. The polyurethane foam padding used in furniture generally contains polybrominated diphenol ethers (PBDEs), which are bioaccumulating relatives of PCBs. These flame retardants are released into the building as the foam padding ages.

Furniture should be as simple as possible, with a minimum of different materials, and it should be assembled with mechanical fasteners rather than adhesives.

Some innovative designers have produced lines of furniture made from various recycled materials and with high recyclability.

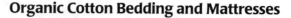

Ag-Fiber Particleboard

see *Interior Finish & Trim: Ag-Fiber Particleboard*

Bedding

Products included here are produced from recycled materials, from organic cotton, or without chlorine bleaches and other hazardous chemicals.

Cotton Mattresses and E-Foam Futons

Futon Man
5280 N.W. Hwy. 99 W
Corvallis, OR 97330

Phone: 541-753-6395
www.fatfuton.com

Natural Life Furnishings manufactures beds, tables, and futon frames of FSC-certified alder (upon request) and futons of E-foam (recycled PET, foamed with CO_2-injected foam) with untreated cotton and wool. Futon mattresses and innerspring cotton mattresses can be made from organic cotton on request.

Coyuchi Organic Cotton Bed Linens

Coyuchi, Inc.
11101 State Rte. 1
P.O. Box 845
Point Reyes Station, CA 94956

Toll-free: 888-418-8847
Phone: 415-663-8077
www.coyuchi.com

Coyuchi offers a full line of organic-cotton bed linens, including comforter covers, blankets, throws, bedskirts, and pillow shams. Percale and checked damask fabrics in both natural and hydrogen peroxide-bleached white are available, as well as printed sateen and 6-oz. flannel.

Natural Fiber Bedding and Mattresses

Crown City Mattress by Vivetique
11134 Rush St.
South El Monte, CA 91733

Toll-free: 800-365-6563

Crown City natural-fiber mattresses are available in three types: standard cotton, organic cotton, and an organic cotton/wool blend. Organic cotton mattresses are made without the use of fire-retardant chemicals and, therefore, require a doctor's prescription showing chemical sensitivity to purchase. The organic cotton/wool blend mattress contains naturally fire-resistant wool. Organic cotton and wool pillows and wool mattress covers and comforters are also available.

Organic Cotton Bedding and Mattresses

Furnature
86 Coolidge Ave.
Watertown, MA 02172

Phone: 617-926-0111
www.furnature.com

Furnature's bedding and mattresses are made with chemical-free organic cotton fabrics. The company provides a kit for chemically sensitive customers that includes samples of all materials used in the furniture so that customers can test for sensitivity. In some cases, substitutions can be made for objectionable materials. Pillows, as well as fabrics made from organic fibers, are also available.

Wellspring Futon Mattresses and Covers

Rising Star...Stellar Home Furnishings
35 N.W. Bond St.
Bend, OR 97701

Toll-free: 800-828-6711
Phone: 541-382-4221

Wellspring Futon Mattresses are made with 100%-recycled PET fiber batt, and cases are made from 100% organic cotton or a 50/50 cotton/polyester blend.

Certified Wood Furniture

The furniture included here is produced using wood certified under standards established by the Forest Stewardship Council (FSC). SmartWood and Scientific Certification Services are the primary FSC-accredited third-party certifying organizations in North America.

Certified Hardwood Furniture

Berkeley Mills
2830 Seventh St.
Berkeley, CA 94710

Phone: 510-549-2854
www.berkeleymills.com

Berkeley Mills is a manufacturer of high-end custom and limited-production furniture available in FSC-certified hardwoods including cherry and maple. Distribution is nationwide though primarily on the West Coast.

Certified Hardwood Furniture

Cotswold Furniture Makers
904 Sawyer Rd.
Whiting, VT 05778

Phone: 802-623-8400
www.cotswoldfurniture.com

Cotswold Furniture Makers offers handcrafted home and office furniture. Pieces are typically made from American black cherry from FSC-certified sources. Other hardwoods—such as oak, maple, and walnut—may be offered, but may not be available FSC-certified, depending upon supply.

Certified Wood Furniture

Beeken Parsons
Shelburne Farms
1611 Harbor Rd.
Shelburne, VT 05482

Phone: 802-985-2913
www.beekenparsons.com

Beeken Parsons offers Vermont Forest Furniture, a line of FSC-certified forest furniture handcrafted out of character wood incorporating knots, grain textures, and colors that reflect the life of the tree and "tell the story of the forest." Character Wood often comes from trees that are relegated to such low-value uses as firewood and paper pulp. Increasing the value of these trees will help to offset the costs of responsible forest stewardship. Beeken Parsons has been designing and building custom furniture for more than 20 years. Its shop is located at historic Shelburne Farms in Shelburne, Vermont.

Certified Wood Furniture

Island Pond Woodworking, Inc.
306 Meadow St.
P.O. Box 236
Island Pond, VT 05846

Phone: 802-723-6613
www.islandpondwoodworkers.com

Founded by displaced workers after a multinational furniture manufacturer shut its doors on a local plant, employee-owned Island Pond Woodworking produces handcrafted residential, business, and institutional furniture from locally harvested FSC-certified lumber.

Certified Wood Furniture

South Cone Trading Company
19038 S. Vermont Ave.
Gardena, CA 90248

Toll-free: 800-466-7282
www.southcone.com

South Cone Trading Company is an FSC-certified furniture manufacturer with factories in Lima, Peru (FSC-certified) and Santa Fe, Argentina (FSC certification in progress). According to the manufacturer, about 30% of their production is certified, but they expect to have 90% certified by the end of 2005. The company offers a variety of home furnishings sold nationwide through approximately 300 independently owned retail stores and also sells to hotels and resorts on a contract basis. South Cone is the founder of PaTS (Partnerships and Technology for Sustainability), a nonprofit organization pursuing sustainable development in the Peruvian rainforest through the implementation of market-driven forms of forest conservation.

Certified Wood Furniture

The Joinery
4804 S.E. Woodstock
Portland, OR 97206

Phone: 503-788-8547
www.thejoinery.com

The Joinery hand-crafts a wide variety of home and office furniture with lines reflecting Mission, Shaker, Asian, and French styles. FSC-certified hardwood, mostly cherry, is used in 75% of their work. Custom orders are commonly filled. The Joinery guarantees its furniture for life.

Certified Wood Furniture

Wiggers Custom Furniture
173 Reach Industrial Park Rd.
Port Perry, ON L9L 1B2 Canada

Phone: 905-985-1128
www.wiggersfurniture.com

Wiggers Custom Furniture crafts high-end furniture made from FSC-certified woods.

Certified Wood Furniture and Futons

Futon Man
5280 N.W. Hwy. 99 W
Corvallis, OR 97330

Phone: 541-753-6395
www.fatfuton.com

Futon Man, formerly Natural Life Furnishings, manufactures beds, tables, and futon frames of FSC-certified alder (upon request) and futons of E-foam (recycled PET, foamed with CO_2-injected foam) with untreated cotton and wool.

Eco-Furniture

Hardwood Artisans
12266 Rockville Pike
Rockville, MD 20852

Toll-free: 800-842-6119
www.hardwoodartisans.com

The Eco-Furniture line includes FSC-certified red oak beds and bookcases. Hardwood Artisans also crafts custom furniture and store fixtures of certified woods.

Low Toxicity Furniture

Karp Woodworks
136 Fountain St.
Ashland, MA 01721

Phone: 508-881-7000

Karp Woodworks specializes in building custom furniture for chemically sensitive people. Low-VOC finishes are used, as well as organic cotton and special batting for upholstered designs.

Modular Furniture

IKEA, North American Service Office
496 W. Germantown Pike
Plymouth Meeting, PA 19462

Phone: 610-834-0180
www.ikea.com

Swedish-based IKEA has taken a number of steps to reduce the environmental impact of its modular, build-it-yourself furniture products. An FSC member, IKEA's long term goal is to have all wood used in its products certified by the Forest Stewardship Council (FSC) or an equivalent program. Currently all high-value tropical wood species must originate from forests certified by the FSC. PVC has been eliminated in all products except the isolating plastic of electric cables, and the company is looking to find an alternative for this as well. Bromine fire-retardants have been eliminated entirely. IKEA uses water-based and UV-cured coatings, powder coatings for metal components, and white and hot-melt glues. A line of air-filled seating products is available as well.

Cork Furniture

Cork is a renewable material; it's the bark from cork oak, Quercus suber, *which grows in the Mediterranean region. Cork oak bark can be harvested about every 10 years.*

Cork Furniture

KorQinc
155 E. 56th St.
New York, NY 10022

Phone: 212-758-2593
www.korqinc.com

KorQ furniture, made from natural cork, is constructed much like wood furniture. The KorQ line includes pull-up chairs, lounge chairs, armchairs, benches, and side tables. The products come in a granulated pattern in natural and flame or scorch colors.

Fiberboard and Particleboard Panels

see *Interior Finish & Trim: Fiberboard and Particleboard Panels*

Fixed Tackboards

Cork is the traditional, natural solution for vertical tackable surfaces, and it remains an excellent green option. Cork is obtained from the outer bark of the cork oak tree (Quercus suber). *After harvesting, the bark regenerates and can be harvested again in about 10 years. The substrate for some tackboards is made from recycled paper and paraffin.*

Bulletin Board

Forbo Linoleum, Inc.
P.O. Box 667
Hazleton, PA 18201

Toll-free: 800-842-7839
Phone: 570-459-0771
www.forbolinoleumNA.com

Bulletin Board is a colored, $1/2$"-thick, granulated linoleum-cork composite product sold in full-size sheets for use as tack panels, or as a decorative finish for furniture, doors, or moveable partitions. Bulletin Board is self-healing, durable, washable, low-glare, and will not warp or crumble. It is available in 13 solid colors.

Dodge Cork

Dodge-Regupol, Inc.
P.O. Box 989
Lancaster, PA 17608

Toll-free: 866-883-7780
Phone: 717-295-3400
www.regupol.com

Dodge cork comes in 36" x 36" sheets and 36"- or 48"-wide rolls.

Natural-Fiber Fabrics

Natural fibers are traditional fabric materials such as cotton, linen, ramie, wool, silk, jute, and hemp. Unlike their polymer-based replacements, natural fibers require little energy to process and are biodegradable—but they may have other environmental impacts. Cotton is typically grown with significant chemical fertilizer and pesticide use, although the availability of organically grown cotton is increasing. Silk and wool, both animal products, are obtained primarily from overseas sources; both are prone to moth attack and microbial growth, so are often treated with chemicals. Hemp and jute, also primarily from overseas sources, are relatively resistant to pests, both as plants and after manufacture into fabrics. Natural dyes are sometimes used with these fabrics, but synthetic dyes are more commonly employed for greater color retention. Natural-fiber fabrics may be used as furniture upholstery, workstation fabrics, draperies, etc.

Cotton Plus

Cotton Plus, Inc.
822 Baldridge St.
O'Donnell, TX 79351

Phone: 806-428-3345
www.cottonplus.com

Cotton Plus fabrics are made from 100% organically grown cotton fiber, woven into chambray, twill, canvas, oxford, and flannel. In addition to natural-color cotton fabrics, some fabrics are dyed using low-impact materials.

Foxfibre Colorganic Fabric

Vreseis Ltd.
P.O. Box 69
Guinda, CA 95637

Phone: 530-796-3007
www.vreseis.com

Vreseis manufactures upholstery fabrics from Foxfibre® Colorganic® organic cotton, which has been selectively bred and grown to produce cotton in shades of green, brown, and natural off-white. The

brown color is naturally flame-retardant, though additional chemicals have to be added to meet most commercial standards.

Office Furniture

Conventional office furniture may offgas formaldehyde and VOCs and is often very resource-intensive to produce. Some products included here are remanufactured or refurbished. Others are produced from materials or in ways that will not compromise indoor air quality or that carry particularly low life-cycle environmental burdens.

Office Furniture

Steelcase, Inc.
901 44th St. SE
Grand Rapids, MI 49501

Toll-free: 888-STEELCASE
Phone: 616-247-2710
www.steelcase.com

Steelcase has adopted a broad range of corporate environmental principles that have contributed to more efficient materials usage and reductions in VOC and other emissions. The company conducts extensive IAQ testing of all products.

Recycled/Remanufactured Office Furniture

Creative Office Systems, Inc. (COS)
2470 Estand Way
Pleasant Hill, CA 94523

Toll-free: 800-400-7787
Phone: 925-686-6355
www.creativeoffice.com

Creative Office Systems specializes in the recycling and remanufacturing of UL-listed Herman Miller and Haworth systems furniture and other products. The manufacturer has certified the following recycled-content levels (by weight): total recovered material 89% typical, 80% guaranteed; post-consumer material 86% typical, 75% guaranteed.

Refurbished and Remanufactured Office Furniture

Mansers Office Interiors
185 Paularino Ave., Ste. A
Costa Mesa, CA 92626

Toll-free: 800-473-3393
Phone: 714-754-1696
www.mansers.com

Mansers Office Interiors refurbishes Haworth and Steelcase system furniture, workstations, desks, chairs, and files. Mansers also refurbishes and/or remanufactures Herman Miller office furniture.

Refurbished Office Furniture

Conklin Office Furniture
45 Lyman St.
Springfield, MA 01103

Toll-free: 800-817-1187
www.conklinoffice.com

Conklin Office Furniture has been offering salvaged office furniture since 1981. Panel systems and furniture are sold "as is" (when available) as well as refurbished. Conklin also offers leasing and rental. The company's main location is in Springfield, Massachusetts with branch offices in New York City and Philadelphia.

Refurbished Office Furniture

Davies Office Refurbishing, Inc.
Retail Outlet
38 Loudonville Rd., Entrance A
Albany, NY 12204

Toll-free: 888-773-3872
Phone: 518-449-2040
www.daviesoffice.com

Davies Office Refurbishing offers "as is" salvaged and refurbished office furniture from all major office furniture manufacturers. The company also offers rentals, a trade-in and banking program, powder coat finishes, and recycled content fabric options.

Refurbished Office Furniture

R.A.C.E.
1000 N.W. First Ave., Ste. 28
Boca Raton, FL 33432

Toll-free: 888-893-7223
Phone: 561-347-7666
www.race-inc.com

R.A.C.E. refurbishes Herman Miller office furniture and partitioning systems.

Refurbished Office Furniture

Sonrisa Furniture
7609 Beverly Blvd.
Los Angeles, CA 90036

Toll-free: 800-668-1020
Phone: 323-935-8438
www.sonrisafurniture.com

Sonrisa sells refurbished vintage American steel furniture, including office and institutional products, ranging from chairs and desks to lamps and lockers. Old paint is removed from the furniture, and a clear sealer is used in the refinishing process.

Remanufactured Office Furniture

RBF Interiors
1225 Western Ave.
Cincinnati, OH 45203

Phone: 513-232-3363
www.rbfinteriors.com

In business since 1984, RBF Interiors remanufactures Steelcase, Herman Miller, and Haworth office furniture. RBF uses powder-coat finishes on most high-wear parts and offers a 100% recycled-content fabric option. The company has retail locations in Cincinnati, Ohio, and St. Louis, Missouri; its manufacturing facility is in St. Louis.

Verde Business Furniture

Verde Interior Products
P.O. Box 1507
Goldenrod (Orlando), FL 32792

Phone: 407-673-7474
www.verdeproducts.com

Verde Interior Products manufactures a line of standard and custom-made business furniture relying on high recycled-content, low- or no-VOC, and biobased materials. The core material for many of the offerings consists of 100% recycled-content SONOBoard3D made by Sonoco, a lightweight, high-strength material with no added binders. Other materials used are recycled-denim acoustical insulation; nontoxic, low-VOC paints and finishes; and Climatex® Lifecycle™ or industrial hemp fabrics. Worktop surfaces can be finished with a choice of linoleum or plastic laminate. Some of the products are adjustable for height and other dimensions and can be reconfigured to suit many different situations. No PVC is used in any of Verde's products.

Reclaimed Wood Furniture

These listings have significant wood content that was reclaimed or salvaged from other uses (barns and buildings slated for demolition, for example). Some salvaged wood sources are certified through the SmartWood Rediscovered Wood Program, but that's not a requirement to be included here.

Furniture and Kitchen Cabinetry from Urban Trees

CitiLog™
6 Bywood Ln.
Ewing, NJ 08628

Phone: 609-538-8680
www.citilogs.com

CitiLog, also known as D. Stubby Warmbold, is SmartWood-certified for the harvesting of trees in urban areas of New Jersey and Pennsylvania. Wood is sent by rail to Amish craftsmen in central Pennsylvania who take extra care to turn the lesser graded wood into higher quality products such as flooring, lumber, custom architectural millwork, furniture, and kitchen cabinets. Where appropriate, wood is now harvested using horses.

Furniture from Urban Trees

Urban Hardwoods
5021 Colorado Ave. S
Seattle, WA 98134

Phone: 206-766-8199
www.urbanhardwoods.com

Photo: Jeff Curtis Studio

Urban Hardwoods salvages urban trees from within a 50-mile radius of the company and mills them into furniture, flooring, and other millwork. Urban Hardwoods continually designs products to make use of manufacturing "fall-down." The remainder of the waste material is given away, sold as firewood, or used to heat their facility. The company utilizes plant-based solvents, when needed, to clean tools and machinery, and ships 99% of their products blanket-wrapped (all blankets are reused). They will also accept products back at the end of their useful life and refurbish them or reuse the material to manufacture new products. The company is seeking certification from SmartWood under the "Rediscovered Wood" category.

Millennium Oak

Ecologic, Inc.
921 Sherwood Dr.
Lake Bluff, IL 60044

Toll-free: 800-899-8004
Phone: 847-234-5855
www.ecoloft.com

Ecologic's Millennium Oak furnishings are made from recycled plantation-grown hardwood with an oak color. The product line includes beds and lofts, desks, dressers, nightstands, and bookcases.

Reclaimed-Wood Furniture

Antique Woods & Colonial Restorations, Inc.
121 Quarry Rd.
Gouverneur, NY 13642

Toll-free: 888-261-4284
www.vintagewoods.com

Antique Woods & Colonial Restorations, Inc. (formerly Vintage Barns, Woods & Restorations) sells reclaimed and remilled wood products including flooring, siding, and whole barn frames.

Reclaimed-Wood Furniture

Vintage Material Supply Co.
4705 E. 5th St.
Austin, TX 78702

Phone: 512-386-6404
www.vintagematerialsupply.com

Vintage Material Supply Co. offers custom furniture—including tables, desks, chairs, and beds—made from wood recovered from such sources as demolished buildings, ranch recovery, urban logging, and river bottoms. Furniture design services are also offered. Species include primarily old-growth longleaf pine, cypress, mesquite, and walnut.

Recycled-Content Furniture

A number of innovative furniture products have been introduced in recent years with high recycled content.

Bicycle Part Tables and Furnishings

Resource Revival, Inc.
2267 N. Interstate Ave.
Portland, OR 97227

Toll-free: 800-866-8823
Phone: 503-282-1449
www.resourcerevival.com

Resource Revival crafts furniture and other home decor items from discarded bicycle and automotive parts and other recycled materials. All items are handmade. The manufacturer has certified the following recycled-content levels (by weight): total recovered material 90% typical, 90% guaranteed; post-consumer material 90% typical, 90% guaranteed.

ECO+Plus

Ecologic, Inc.
921 Sherwood Dr.
Lake Bluff, IL 60044

Toll-free: 800-899-8004
Phone: 847-234-5855
www.ecoloft.com

Ecologic designs and manufactures furniture of recycled HDPE. Founded in 1992 to manufacture better college dormitory furniture, the company has expanded to include products for other markets, including federal and municipal office buildings and fire stations. Eco+Plus is an attractive line of desks, bookcases, lofts, beds and bunks, dressers, nightstands, and wardrobes. Products generally do not require tools for assembly.

MetaMorf Furniture

MetaMorf Design, Inc.
362 Sudden Valley
Bellingham, WA 98229

Phone: 206-818-8960
www.metamorfdesign.com

MetaMorf Furniture is made from post-consumer recycled plastic materials. MetaMorf offers durable, weather-resistant furniture for residences, cafes, resorts, restaurants, public parks, and children's facilities.

Pulp Furniture

Poesis Design
P.O. Box 246
Norfolk, CT 06058

Phone: 860-542-5152
www.poesisdesign.com

The Pulp Armchair (31" x 31" x 26", cube-shaped with upholstered cushions) is made of recycled newspaper blended with water and wax, and is designed with maple or walnut trim. FSC-certified wood may be specified. Pulp end tables, coffee tables, beds, bureaus, and file cabinets are also available.

Recycled-Paper Tabletops

All Paper Recycling, Inc.
502 Fourth Ave. NW, Ste. 7
New Prague, MN 56071

Phone: 952-758-6577
www.shetkastone.com

All Paper Recycling manufactures tables and countertops using a patented process and 100% recycled paper. The material, called Shetkastone, can be recycled over and over again through the same process. This process uses no binders or adhesives, just pre-consumer and post-consumer waste paper, including items such as wax paper and phone books. The material has a Class A fire rating without the addition of chemicals and a 400-pound screw test. The company will provide samples and additional information for a $35 fee.

Recycling Equipment

see *Miscellaneous: Recycling Equipment*

Storage Shelving

Look for shelving products with recycled content, low-VOC coatings, and other green features.

Dura-Shelf, Dunnage Rack, Benchmaster, and Modular-Kart

Structural Plastics Corp.
3401 Chief Dr.
Holly, MI 48442

Toll-free: 800-523-6899
Phone: 810-953-9400
www.spcindustrial.com

Structural Plastics specializes in recycled HDPE plastic products for commercial and industrial shelving and storage. Dura-Shelf™, Dunnage Rack™, and Benchmaster® are bulk-storage and display-shelving systems. Modular-Kart™ is a similar product with wheels in the form of a multilevel mobile cart. The manufacturer has certified the following recycled-content levels (by weight): total recovered material 82% typical, 82% guaranteed.

Synthetic Fiber Fabrics

Although most synthetic fabrics are made from virgin polymers, polyester products are available from 100% post-consumer recycled PET (from plastic soda bottles). Polyester fabrics are often specified in commercial settings for panel and workstation applications because of their inherent fire-resistant qualities and relatively low cost.

Many Happy Returns and Please Be Seated

Deepa Textiles
333 Bryant St., Ste. 160
San Francisco, CA 94107

Toll-free: 800-333-3789
Phone: 415-621-4171
www.deepa.com

Many Happy Returns is a line of polyester panel fabric made from 100% post-industrial recycled polyester from photographic film manufacturing. The film is fiberized using a closed-loop process called Terratex®. The yarn is solution-died, which reduces environmental impact while offering optimum durability and cleanability. Many Happy Returns is available in three patterns: Ciao, Au Revoir, and Hasta La Vista, and in over 300 colorways. Custom color combinations are also available.

As part of the Please Be Seated Collection, Deepa also now produces piece-dyed A San Francisco Treat panel fabric made from 100% recycled polyester (63% post-industrial and 37% post-consumer content), and solution-dyed Pour It On upholstery fabric made from 100% post-industrial recycled polyester. Both of these fabrics are also produced using the Terratex process.

The Venture Collection

ICF Group
607 Norwich Ave.
Taftville, CT 06380

Toll-free: 800-237-1625
www.unikavaev.com

The Venture Collection from Unika Vaev, a division of ICF Group, is upholstery fabric made from 100% recycled post-industrial polyester. New techniques allow recycled polyester fabrics to be made with a softer texture and feel. The fabric is also recyclable and contains no UV or flame inhibitors.

Tub and Shower Doors

Look for recycled content and other environmental attributes.

UltraGlas

UltraGlas, Inc.
9200 Gazette Ave.
Chatsworth, CA 91311

Toll-free: 800-777-2332
Phone: 818-772-7744
www.ultraglas.com

Photo: US Horizons, Inc.

UltraGlas is sculpted/embossed, molded architectural glass with 15–30% recycled-glass (cullet) content. A variety of decorative patterns are available with varying levels of transparency. If so specified, UltraGlas can be made from 100% recycled glass.

Window Shades and Quilts

see *Windows: Window Shades and Quilts*

This Space is Available for Your Notes

Renewable Energy

Renewable energy sources offer environmentally attractive alternatives to fossil fuels and nuclear power. Although no energy system can claim to be 100% pollution free, renewables are orders of magnitude better than our conventional energy systems. The U.S. Department of Energy estimates that the annual influx of accessible renewable resources in the U.S. is more than 200 times the total amount of energy used. Technologies for converting these energy sources into electricity or usable heat are improving in efficiency and dropping in price.

The simplest way to utilize renewable energy in buildings is with climate-responsive design—passive solar heating in winter, summertime cooling with natural ventilation, and daylighting.

The field of building-integrated photovoltaics (BIPV) is expanding dramatically, with enormous arrays of PV panels on large, institutional buildings and smaller arrays integrated into individual homes. These typically come in the form of panels that can be wall- or roof-mounted, though PV panels that serve a dual role as glazing and power production are now also available. Solar-domestic hot water systems have quick paybacks in climates where sophisticated freeze-control systems aren't needed. In colder climates the paybacks are longer, but such systems can still be a very worthwhile investment.

Large-scale hydroelectric facilities are associated with some significant environmental problems—most notably the displacement of humans and other species, and the interruption of fish migration. Carefully sited small-scale hydropower may be a good option, however. Related tidal and wave power systems are also becoming feasible.

Large-scale wind power is becoming cost-competitive with fossil fuel-fired power plants. Utility-sized wind turbines can produce more than 750 kilowatts of power; small, home-based wind machines range in output from 250 watts to 10 kilowatts. The Union of Concerned Scientists estimates that wind power could supply one-fifth of U.S. electricity demand.

One issue affecting many renewable energy sources is that their power production varies with the time of day and season. In some cases, the peak production actually matches peak demand—for example, photovoltaic systems on commercial buildings generate the most electricity on hot days, when cooling loads are highest. In other cases, different forms of energy storage are needed to match the energy demand with energy production.

Inverters and Solar Electric Components

Inverters convert the direct-current (DC) power produced by the renewable energy system into alternating-current (AC) power needed for most conventional appliances or for feeding site-generated electricity into the power grid. Other power-conditioning equipment and controllers are also included here.

Inverters

Xantrex Technology
5916 195th St. NE
Arlington, WA 98223

Toll-free: 888-800-1010
Phone: 360-435-8826
www.xantrex.com

Xantrex Technology, formerly Trace Engineering, manufactures energy-efficient DC-to-AC inverters for residential, commercial, mobile, remote, and emergency applications. These are the most widely used inverters for PV and wind power systems. Inverters specially designed for feeding power into the electric grid are available.

Smart Power Inverters

Beacon Power Corporation
234 Ballardvale St.
Wilmington, MA 01887

Toll-free: 888-938-9112
Phone: 978-694-9124
www.beaconpower.com

Beacon Power Corporation introduced the Smart Power line of inverters in 2003, with inverter technology acquired from Advanced Energy, Inc. (previously of Wilton, New Hampshire). The first product, a 5 kW M5 model, is designed for grid-connected applications with battery back-up. The company claims 90% efficiency at full output and 93% efficiency at 50% output.

Solar Controllers

Heliotrope PV
3698 Franklin Blvd.
Eugene, OR 97403

Phone: 541-284-2426
www.heliotrope-pv.com

Heliotrope PV manufacturers electronic charge controllers for PV systems. Though marketed to recreational vehicle users, they are appropriate for any small PV system.

Sunny Boy Inverters

SMA America, Inc.
12438 Loma Rica Dr., Unit C
Grass Valley, CA 95945

Phone: 530-273-4895
www.sma-america.com

SMA America offers 2,500-, 1,800-, and 700-watt inverters designed for residential-scale photovoltaic applications. These German-made inverters carry a 5-year warranty and are being specified by some of the leading PV system designers today. The company also offers a larger, 125 kW inverter, as well as PV control and monitoring equipment.

Masonry Fireplaces

see *Mechanical Systems/HVAC: Masonry Fireplaces*

Photovoltaic Collectors

Photovoltaics (PV) enable the direct conversion of sunlight into electricity. Some PV modules are integrated into building components, such as roofing and wall glazings—these are often referred to as building-integrated photovoltaics (BIPV).

PV Controllers

Solar Converters Inc.
C1-199 Victoria Rd. S
Guelph, ON N1E 6T9 Canada

Phone: 519-824-5272
www.solarconverters.com

Solar Converters Inc. is a designer and manufacturer of highly efficient power control products for the renewable energy field. Included among the products the company has developed are Linear Current Boosters, Battery Equalizers, Power Tracker™ charge controllers with Maximum Power Point Tracking (MPPT), Cathodic Protection Controllers, Generator Starters, Battery Desulphators, Constant Voltage Pump Drivers, Voltage Controlled Switches, Solar Lighting Controllers, DC-DC Converters, and more.

PV Modules

BP Solar
989 Corporate Blvd.
Linthicum, MD 21703

Phone: 410-981-0240
www.bpsolar.com

BP Solar is one of the world's largest solar electric companies, with manufacturing plants in the U.S., Spain, Australia, and India.

They manufacture, design, market, and install a wide range of crystalline silicon solar electric products. The highest percentage of BP Solar's sales are to homeowners, builders, and businesses, and they are the largest supplier to the rural infrastructure market, where solar is the core power source for off-grid communities. In 1999, BP-Amoco acquired Solarex and folded it into BP's PV Division to form BP Solar.

PV Modules

Evergreen Solar, Inc.
259 Cedar Hill St.
Marlboro, MA 01752

Phone: 508-357-2221
www.evergreensolar.com

Evergreen Solar is a manufacturer of PV modules and the innovator of the String Ribbon™ method of producing solar cells. This technique uses approximately half the amount of silicon as the industry norm. The company manufactures panels suitable for both grid-tied and off-grid installations and offers a 20-year warranty on all its products. Evergreen products are available through various distributors.

PV Modules

First Solar, LLC
4050 E. Cotton Center Blvd., Ste. 6-68
Phoenix, AZ 85040

Phone: 602-414-9300
www.firstsolar.com

First Solar develops and manufactures Cadmium Telluride (CdTe) thin-film photovoltaic modules. First Solar has invested heavily in developing advanced, high-volume manufacturing processes that are considered essential to achieving the low cost required to make solar electricity economically viable across a broad range of applications.

PV Modules

Sharp Electronics Corp. - Solar Systems Division
5901 Bolsa Ave.
Huntington Beach, CA 92647

Toll-free: 800-BE-SHARP
Phone: 630-378-3357
www.sharpusa.com

Sharp Electronics Corporation, a worldwide leader in solar electric technology, offers single-crystal and polycrystalline PV panels. Available modules range from 70 to 185 watts for grid-tied or stand-alone systems. Sharp modules carry a 25-year warranty. Product introductions planned for the future include green, golden brown, and light blue PV cells; triangular modules; AC modules; and thin-film, virtually transparent modules.

PV Modules

Shell Solar
4650 Adohr Ln.
Camarillo, CA 93011

Phone: 800-272-6765
www.shell.com/solar/

Shell Solar is one of the world's largest manufacturers of PV modules, producing single-crystal, multi-crystal, and CIS thin-film modules. Shell also offers EarthSafe™ PV kits for residential and commercial installations. These solar electric rooftop kits include mounting hardware, inverter, and 25-year warranty panels. Shell Solar was previously Siemens Solar (and before that Arco Solar) before Shell acquired Siemens in April 2002.

PV Systems

Kyocera Solar, Inc.
7812 E. Acoma Dr.
Scottsdale, AZ 85260

Toll-free: 800-544-6466
Phone: 480-948-8003
www.kyocerasolar.com

Kyocera is one of the world's largest manufacturers of polycrystal PV modules.

Renewable Energy Systems

RWE Schott Solar, Inc.
U.S. Sales & Marketing
4051 Alvis Ct., Ste. 1
Rocklin, CA 95677

Toll-free: 888-457-6527
Phone: 916-625-9033
www.rweschottsolar.us

RWE Schott Solar, Inc. (formerly Applied Power and then Schott Applied Power) is a leading manufacturer and distributor of solar power components and systems, such as the SunRoof RS packaged residential system and the world's largest solar power module, the ASE 300. The company maintains a large inventory of renewable energy equipment for distribution, serving markets such as grid-connected residential and commercial systems, and grid-independent agricultural, industrial, and governmental applications. RWE Schott combined forces in 2002 with solar wafer, cell, and module manufacturer ASE Americas, Inc., which had acquired silicon-ribbon PV manufacturing technology from Mobil Solar in 1994. RWE Schott Solar is a joint venture of the RWE Group, a global multi-utility concern with core businesses in electricity, gas, water, waste management, and recycling.

Solar Turtle

Solar Turtle, Inc.
4901 S. Cactus Wren
P.O. Box 425
Tucson, AZ 85746

Phone: 520-883-3356

The Solar Turtle is a photovoltaic power supply and water purification system mostly used for remote cabins and RVs. These systems include 120-watt panels, deep-cycle batteries, an inverter, and General Ecology's SeaGull IV water purification systems. The system can output up to 720 W DC or 2,500 W AC. Most Solar Turtle units include custom features to match customer needs.

Sunslates

Atlantis Energy Systems, Inc.
9275 Beatty Dr., Ste. B
Sacramento, CA 95826

Phone: 916-438-2930
www.atlantisenergy.org

Atlantis Energy Systems produces Sunslates™, which serve as both a roofing product and a solar-electric power source. Sunslates are fiber-cement shingles into which PV cells have been laminated. Each shingle has a plug-in wiring connection.

SunUPS and SunLine

AstroPower
Solar Park
461 Wyoming Rd.
Newark, DE 19716

Toll-free: 800-800-8727
Phone: 302-366-0400
www.astropower.com

AstroPower is a leading PV manufacturer, producing primarily single-crystal silicon PV modules. SunUPS® is a packaged system for backup electrical power. SunLine™ is a packaged system designed for grid-connected applications. Astropower is also developing an advanced, lower-cost, thin-crystal PV module.

UNI-SOLAR PV Shingles and Standing Seam Panels

United Solar Ovonic LLC
3800 Lapeer Rd.
Auburn Hills, MI 48326

Toll-free: 800-843-3892
Phone: 248-475-0100
www.uni-solar.com

Uni-Solar Ovonic LLC PV Shingles and Standing Seam Roofing Panels are installed much like conventional roofing products. They generate electricity while protecting the structure from weather. PV Shingles, measuring 86.4" x 12" with 7 tabs, are interspersed among conventional 3-tab shingles. Standing Seam Panels are available for laminating onto conventional roofing or as a PV-integrated, standing-seam product. Lead wires from each shingle or panel enter the structure through drilled holes in the roof decking. Uni-Solar roofing products use triple-junction amorphous silicon technology.

Solar Energy Industry Information

Industry Representation

Solar Energy Industries Association
1616 H St. NW, 8th Floor
Washington, DC 20006

Phone: 202-628-7745
www.seia.org

The Solar Energy Industries Association (SEIA) is the national trade association of solar energy manufacturers, dealers, distributors, contractors, and installers. SEIA's primary mission is to expand the use of solar technologies in the global marketplace. Membership exceeds 500 companies providing solar thermal and solar electric products and services.

Solar Flat Plate Collectors (Air Heating)

These listings include flat-plate solar collectors and solar collector systems used for ventilation-air preheating and space heating.

Air-Heating Solar Collector

Sunsiaray Solar Manufacturing, Inc.
4414 N. Washburn Rd.
Davison, MI 48423

Phone: 810-653-3502

Sunsiaray Solar Manufacturing produces air-heating solar collectors.

Solar Water Heating Systems and Components

These listings include specialized components and materials for solar thermal systems used for water heating. A wide range of technologies are employed for solar water heating, including integral-collector storage (ICS) systems, evacuated-tube collector systems, and flat-plate collector systems. Flat-plate collectors can be configured for drain-down, drain-back, or closed-loop solar water heating systems (the latter requiring propylene glycol antifreeze in all but the warmest climates). Higher-temperature solar

thermal systems typically use parabolic reflectors to concentrate the solar energy and heat-transfer fluids other than water.

CopperSun

Sun Systems, Inc.
2030 W. Pinnacle Peak Rd.
Phoenix, AZ 85027

Toll-free: 800-777-6657
Phone: 623-869-7652
www.sunsystemsinc.com

Sun Systems manufactures the Copper Sun™ integral collector storage (ICS) solar water heater. The unit is designed for integration into a roof, with flush mounting and a flashing kit for roofing right up to the textured-glass cover plate. Systems are available with either a 40- or 50-gallon capacity. The company is primarily pursuing the new-home builder market in the Sun Belt, as the CopperSun system is not appropriate for heavy-freeze climates.

Evacuated Tube Solar Collectors

Thermo Technologies
5560 Sterrett Pl., Ste. 115
Columbia, MD 21044

Phone: 410-997-0778
www.thermomax.com

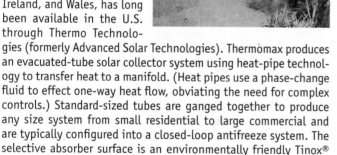

Thermomax, a European company with manufacturing facilities in Italy, Northern Ireland, and Wales, has long been available in the U.S. through Thermo Technologies (formerly Advanced Solar Technologies). Thermomax produces an evacuated-tube solar collector system using heat-pipe technology to transfer heat to a manifold. (Heat pipes use a phase-change fluid to effect one-way heat flow, obviating the need for complex controls.) Standard-sized tubes are ganged together to produce any size system from small residential to large commercial and are typically configured into a closed-loop antifreeze system. The selective absorber surface is an environmentally friendly Tinox® titanium nitride oxide coating from Germany.

Fireball 20-01

ACR Solar International Corporation
5840 Gibbons Dr., Ste. G
Carmichael, CA 95608

Phone: 916-481-7200
www.solarroofs.com

The Fireball 20-01 is a solar water-heating system.

Gobi Solar Collectors and Helio-Pak Solar Water Heater

Heliodyne, Inc.
4910 Seaport Ave.
Richmond, CA 94804

Phone: 510-237-9614
www.heliodyne.com

Heliodyne is a manufacturer of flat-plate solar collectors and heat-transfer systems for residential and commercial water heating—considered the top-of-the-line by catalog retailer Real Goods.

ProgressivTube Passive Water Heating Systems

Thermal Conversion Technology
101 Copeland St.
Jacksonville, FL 32204

Phone: 904-358-3720
www.tctsolar.com

Thermal Conversion Technology produces the ProgressivTube® line of integral collector-storage (ICS) systems with 4"-diameter copper pipes in a glass-glazed collector. The collectors are typically for solar preheating of water and are used extensively in Caribbean and Hawaiian hotels. Founded in 1974, the company has sold thousands of the current ProgressiTube® line since its introduction in 1982.

Solahart Solar Water Heating Systems

Solahart / Rheem USA, Inc.
101 Bell Rd.
Montgomery, AL 37117

Phone: 334-213-3804
www.solahart.com

Solahart's BCXII series is a closed-circuit thermosiphoning solar water-heating system utilizing a heat-transfer fluid that circulates around a jacketed water tank. The BCXII series comes with a 12-year warranty in a range of tank sizes and panel configurations. Other models, also available in various sizes, have specific design criteria—including the J series for areas with medium to good solar radiation, poor water quality, or frost conditions; the K series for low to medium solar radiation, poor water quality, or frost or snow conditions; and the L series for frost-free areas with medium to high solar radiation and relatively clean water supplies. The J, K, and L series have a five-year warranty. Solahart, a division of Rheem Australia Pty Ltd, also offers large commercial solar water-heating systems.

Solar Collectors

R&R Services Solar Supply
922 Austin Ln., Bldg. D
Honolulu, HI 96817

Phone: 808-842-0011

R&R Services Solar Supply is a manufacturer of copper-tube/absorber flat-plate collectors. The company packages solar water-heating systems for sale throughout Hawaii.

Solar Collectors

Radco Products, Inc.
2877 Industrial Pkwy.
Santa Maria, CA 93455

Toll-free: 800-927-2326
Phone: 805-928-1881

Radco Products manufactures flat-plate solar collectors and complete drainback solar water-heating systems. The company also produces a line of unglazed solar pool-heating systems.

Solar Collectors

Sealed Air Corp. - Solar Pool Heating
3433 Arden Rd.
Hayward, CA 94545

Toll-free: 800-451-6620
Phone: 510-887-8090
www.sealedair.com

Sealed Air Corporation is primarily in the packaging business but also produces a line of flat-plate solar collectors for pool heating.

Solar Pool Heating Systems

Aquatherm Industries, Inc.
1940 Rutgers University Blvd.
Lakewood, NJ 08701

Toll-free: 800-535-6307
Phone: 732-905-9002
www.warmwater.com

Aquatherm produces unglazed polypropylene collectors designed for pool heating. These are used with existing conventional filtration systems to circulate pool water through the collectors then back into the pool. Most systems utilize an automatic temperature control. The swimming pool serves as the heat-storage reservoir.

Solar Pool Heating Systems

Fafco, Inc.
435 Otterson Dr.
Chico, CA 95928-8207

Toll-free: 800-994-7652
Phone: 530-332-2100
www.fafco.com

Fafco is the oldest manufacturer of solar water-heating equipment in the U.S.—since 1969. The company manufactures a line of pool-heating systems.

Solar Pool-Heating Systems

Heliocol Solar Pool Heating
13620 49th Street N
Altamonte Springs, FL 33762

Phone: 727 572 7922
www.heliocol.com

Heliocol manufactures unglazed polypropylene, solar pool-heating systems.

Solar Systems

Thermo Dynamics Ltd.
101 Frazee Ave.
Dartmouth, NS B3B-1Z4 Canada

Phone: 902-468-1001
www.thermo-dynamics.com

Thermo Dynamics manufactures a full range of solar water-heating systems with liquid flat-plate, glazed collectors with fused copper tubing and aluminum absorbers. The company also produces the Solar Pump™—a PV-powered pump—and a thermosiphoning heat exchanger.

Solar Thermal Equipment

Alternate Energy Technologies
1057 N. Ellis Rd., Unit 4
Jacksonville, FL 32254

Toll-free: 800-874-2190
Phone: 904-781-8305
www.aetsolar.com

Alternate Energy Technologies is a manufacturer of copper-tube, flat-plate collectors with a nontoxic collector coating.

Solar Water Heating Systems

SunEarth, Inc.
8425 Almeria Ave.
Fontana, CA 92335

Phone: 909-434-3100
www.sunearthinc.com

SunEarth, Inc., a manufacturer of solar water-heating equipment since 1978, produces flat-plate solar collectors and ICS solar water-heating systems.

Solar Water Storage Tanks

Morley Manufacturing
P.O. Box 1540
Cedar Ridge, CA 95924

Phone: 530-477-6527

Morley manufactures storage tanks used for solar water-heating systems.

Solar Water Storage Tanks

Vaughn Manufacturing Corporation
26 Old Elm St.
P.O. Box 5431
Salisbury, MA 01952

Toll-free: 800-282-8446
Phone: 978-462-6683
www.vaughncorp.com

Vaughn Manufacturing produces stone-lined storage tanks specifically for solar water heating systems. Vaughn tanks have removable copper-finned heat exchangers enabling periodic cleaning of the coil to maintain maximum performance. The tanks—which are lined with centrifugally applied Hydrostone for corrosion protection—come in 65-, 80-, and 120-gallon capacities, and can also be made to custom dimensions.

SunTube Collector

Sun Utility Network, Inc.
4952 Coringa Dr.
Los Angeles, CA 90042

Phone: 232-478-0667
www.sunutility.com

Sun Utility Network is the U.S. distributor of NEG's SunTube evacuated-tube solar water-heating systems. SunTube panels can be used for residential and commercial water heating, space heating and cooling, water pasteurization, and desalination applications.

Winston Series CPC Collector

Solargenix Energy, LLC
2101-115 Westinghouse Blvd.
Raleigh, NC 27604

Phone: 919-871-0423
www.solargenix.com

Photo: Fred Stewart

The Winston Series CPC Collector from Solargenix Energy is a residential and commercial solar water-heating system. The basic system is comprised of 12 small compound parabolic collectors (CPC) which focus light onto absorber tubes through which heat-transfer fluid is piped. One to three collectors are commonly used for residential solar water-heating systems, depending on the size of the hot water storage tank. A roof-integrated thermosiphoning configuration is possible with new construction. The collectors carry a 10-year warranty. The system's heat exchanger, SOLPAC, is also available as a separate item. Coupled with one or more solar collectors, it prepackages the components needed to convert existing electric or gas water heaters into solar water-heating systems.

Wind Energy Equipment

Most large wind-power systems are installed in centralized wind farms, with the power being fed into electric utility grids. Smaller wind turbines are available that are more appropriate for individual homes or commercial buildings.

AIR and Whisper Series Wind Turbines

Southwest Windpower
2131 N. First St.
Flagstaff, AZ 86004

Phone: 928-779-9463
www.windenergy.com

Southwest Windpower manufactures 400-, 900-, 1,000- and 3,000-watt wind turbines for on- and off-grid residential and industrial power generation. The 400-watt unit can also be used to power telecommunication stations, and the 1,000-watt unit can be used to pump water.

AWP 3.6 Wind Turbine

Abundant Renewable Energy
22700 N.E. Mountain Top Rd.
Newberg, OR 97132

Phone: 503-538-8298
www.abundantre.com

African Windpower wind turbines are distributed in North America by Abundant Renewable Energy. The manufacturer is located in South Africa. African Windpower's generator model AWP 3.6 is rated at 1,000 watts. It is available in 24v, 48v and high-volt batteryless grid connect.

BWC Excel Wind Turbines

Bergey Windpower Co., Inc.
2001 Priestley Ave.
Norman, OK 73069

Phone: 405-364-4212
www.bergey.com

Bergey Windpower manufactures three models of wind generators for residential and small-scale commercial applications. The BWC XL.1 is rated at 1,000 watts, the BWC Excel-R is rated at 7,500 watts, and the BWC Excel-S is rated at 10,000 watts.

Jacobs 31-20 Wind Turbine

Wind Turbine Industries Corp.
16801 Industrial Cir. SE
Prior Lake, MN 55372

Phone: 952-447-6064
www.windturbine.net

Wind Turbine Industries' Jacobs 31-20 generator is rated at 20,000 watts. Other Jacobs turbines (also known as "Jakes" and made in the 1930s) are no longer manufactured but, due to their exceptional durability, are still widely available as used and rebuilt machines.

Wind Turbines

Proven Engineering Products, Ltd.
Wardhead Park
Stewarton, Ayrshire KA3 5LH Scotland, UK

Phone: +44 (0)1560 485 570
www.provenenergy.com

Proven Engineering Products, Ltd. manufactures four turbine models, rated at 600, 2,500, 6,000 and 15,000 watts. Proven Engineering has two American distributors: Lake Michigan Wind and Sun can be reached by phone at 920-743-0456 and is online at www.windandsun.com; Solar Wind Works can be reached by phone at 530-582-4503 and is online at www.solarwindworks.com.

This Space is Available for Your Notes

Distributors & Retailers

Green building products are increasingly available from mainstream distributors and building suppliers, but only a few U.S. cities are fortunate enough to have specialized green building suppliers that stock a significant range of products. In most places, green building products that aren't available through mainstream suppliers will need to be purchased directly from the manufacturer, by mail order, or from regional distributors specializing in those products. Specialized distributors and retailers of green building products are addressed here.

Distributors: Certified Wood

Distributors of FSC-certified wood products are subject to the same rigor of inspections as manufacturers and land managers. "Chain-of-custody certification" is the term used to describe the documentation of certified-wood product sourcing, processing, handling, and distribution. Accurate paperwork and careful separation of certified and noncertified wood must be maintained for compliance with FSC standards.

Certified Flooring Distributor

Hoboken Floors
181 Campanelli Pkwy.
Stoughton, MA 02072

Toll-free: 800-255-1600
Phone: 781-341-2881
www.hobokenfloors.com

Hoboken Floors is a large distributor of flooring products that can provide unfinished and prefinished wood flooring from three different FSC-certified Canadian sources. They also distribute multi-ply, laminated flooring products made from certified ash, hackberry, maple, and oak.

Certified Hardwood Lumber

Pittsford Lumber and Woodshop
50 State St.
Pittsford, NY 14534

Phone: 585-586-1877
www.northfieldcommon.com/pittsford%20lumber.htm

Pittsford Lumber and Woodshop stocks FSC-certified tropical hardwoods for cabinet and furniture construction. They also carry Tried & True nontoxic oil finishes.

Certified Hardwood Lumber

YWI
P.O. Box 211
Cornish Flat, NH 03746

Phone: 603-675-6206

YWI specializes in bird's-eye and curly maple, as well as other figured woods, for fine furniture and musical instrument markets. The company also has available clear, wide, flat, and quartered white pine for the preservation/restoration markets.

Certified Wood Distributor

Craftmark Reclaimed Wood, Inc.
P.O. Box 237
McMinnville, OR 97128

Phone: 503-472-6929
www.craftmarkinc.com

Craftmark Reclaimed Wood, Inc. is a distributor of flooring, decking, paneling, wainscoting, timbers, and specialty wood products such as architectural moldings produced from a wide variety of FSC-certified species. Custom-milling is a specialty. The company is also a manufacturer of wood products from reclaimed timber.

Certified Wood Distributor

EcoTimber
1611 4th St.
San Rafael, CA 94901

Toll-free: 888-801-0855
Phone: 415-258-8454
www.ecotimber.com

EcoTimber® offers a wide range of domestic and tropical wood flooring from ecologically sound sources. EcoTimber branded items include reclaimed and FSC-certified woods, as well as a full line of bamboo flooring products. Prefinished and floating floors are available.

Certified Wood Distributor

Edensaw Woods
211 Seton Rd.
Port Townsend, WA 98368

Toll-free: 800-745-3336
Phone: 360-385-7878
www.edensaw.com

Edensaw Woods' selection of FSC-certified wood includes alder, ash, cherry, Honduras mahogany, maple, poplar, and red and white oak. Edensaw also has a location in Seattle, Washington.

Certified Wood Distributor

Endura Wood Products, Ltd.
1303 S.E. 6th Ave.
Portland, OR 97214

Phone: 503-233-7090
www.endurawood.com

Endura offers FSC-certified hardwood and softwood flooring, lumber, and decking in a wide variety of exotic and domestic species. Endurawood butcher blocks and countertops are produced from certified woods such as rock maple. Endura also sells reclaimed wood products as well as straw particleboard and agfiber composite sheet goods.

Certified Wood Distributor

J. E. Higgins Lumber Company, Purchasing Division
6999 S. Front Rd.
Livermore, CA 94550

Toll-free: 800-241-1883
Phone: 925-245-4300
www.higlum.com

J. E. Higgins Lumber sells FSC-certified hardwood, plywood, and flooring.

Certified Wood Distributor

Northland Forest Products
P.O. Box 369
Kingston, NH 03848

Phone: 603-642-3665
www.northlandforest.com

Northland Forest Products carries FSC-certified kiln-dried Northern and Appalachian hardwood lumber for flooring and architectural millwork, as well as fixed widths, special widths, and figured woods. Species include cherry, maple, ash, yellow birch, red oak, mahogany, eastern white pine, and others, depending on availability.

Certified Wood Distributor

Plywood and Lumber Sales, Inc.
Earth Source Forest Products
1618 28th St.
Oakland, CA 94608

Toll-free: 866-549-9663
Phone: 510-208-7257
www.earthsourcewood.com

EarthSource Forest Products, a division of Plywood and Lumber Sales, Inc., sells FSC-certified hardwood plywood and lumber of the following species: maple, cherry, red oak, white oak, ash, Honduras mahogany, walnut, machiche, amapola, and many more. EarthSource also sells salvaged and rediscovered lumber such as fir, redwood, and hickory.

Certified Wood Distributor

Windfall Lumber and Milling
210 Thurston St.
Olympia, WA 98501

Phone: 360-352-2250
www.windfalllumber.com

Windfall Lumber and Milling is a distributor of FSC-certified hardwoods, flooring, and structural lumber. Windfall also manufactures specialty wood products such as flooring and moldings.

Distributors/Retailers: Energy Conservation

The companies listed here specialize in energy conservation products, including lighting, weatherization materials, and specialized energy-conserving products.

Energy-Conserving Products

Gaiam Real Goods
360 Interlocken Blvd., Ste. 300
Broomfield, CO 80021-3440

Toll-free: 800-919-2400
Phone: 303-222-3500
www.realgoods.com

Gaiam Real Goods sells a broad range of energy-conserving, alternative energy, and environmental-living products through its catalogs and retail stores. Real Goods catalogs are available by mail upon request or can be accessed on their Web site. Real Goods and Jade Mountain merged in 2001 to become the largest provider of renewable energy systems (solar, wind, and hydro) in the world. These companies have been involved with solarizing more than 50,000 homes since 1978.

Energy-Efficient Lighting

Fred Davis Corp.
93 West St.
Medfield, MA 02052

Toll-free: 800-497-2970
Phone: 508-359-3610

Fred Davis Corporation is a national wholesaler of energy-efficient lighting. The company offers thousands of products including: compact, low-mercury, and T8/T5 fluorescent lamps; electronic ballasts; energy-efficient fixtures; and LED exit signs.

Lighting, Ventilation, and Weatherization

Energy Federation Incorporated
40 Washington St.
Westborough, MA 01581

Toll-free: 800-876-0660 Ext. 1
Phone: 508-870-2277
www.efi.org

Energy Federation Incorporated (EFI) is a retailer and wholesaler of energy-efficient lighting, ventilation, and weatherization products.

Radon Control Equipment

Infiltec Radon Control Supply
108 S. Delphine Ave.
P.O. Box 1125
Waynesboro, VA 22980

Toll-free: 888-349-7236
Phone: 540-943-2776
www.infiltec.com

Infiltec Radon Control distributes and installs radon-control equipment.

Ventilation and Energy-Conserving Products

Shelter Supply, Inc.
151 E. Cliff Rd., Ste. 30
Burnsville, MN 55337

Toll-free: 800-762-8399
Phone: 952-516-3400
www.sheltersupply.com

Shelter Supply offers products for better indoor air quality and greater energy efficiency. Shelter Supply specializes in residential building ventilation products.

Weatherization and Energy-Conservation Products

Positive Energy
P.O. Box 7568
Boulder, CO 80306-7568

Toll-free: 800-488-4340
www.positive-energy.com

Positive Energy publishes a catalog of hard-to-find energy-conservation products. The selection includes products for ventilation, weatherization, heating control, lighting, safety, and water conservation and purification.

Weatherization and Energy-Conservation Products

AM Conservation Group, Inc.
430 Sand Shore Rd., Ste. 7
Hackettstown, NJ 07840

Toll-free: 800-466-3289
Phone: 908-852-6464
www.amconservationgroup.com

AM Conservation Group, Inc. introduces, manufactures, markets, and distributes a wide array of products for weatherization, as well as water and energy conservation.

Certain green building materials can be found in most lumber-yards and home centers; a few building supply centers in the U.S. specialize in green products. Among the broad selection of products offered by these companies are low-toxic paints and finishes, cabinets, flooring products, formaldehyde-free panels, and FSC-certified lumber. (FSC certification involves third-party evaluation and monitoring of sustainable forestry practices.) In most cases, online or print catalogs are available with listings of the products offered. In addition to sourcing products, these companies have knowledgeable sales experts. A few have buildings that serve as demonstrations of high-performance green building.

Green Building Materials

BigHorn Materials
1221 Blue River Pkwy.
Silverthorne, CO 80498

Phone: 970-513-1575
www.bighornace.com

In business for 18 years and offering green building products for four years, BigHorn Materials supplies general building materials and hardware, sustainable forest products, CFLs, and set-back thermostats. The company caters mainly to contractors but serves the general public as well.

Green Building Materials

Building For Health Materials Center
102 Main St.
P.O. Box 113
Carbondale, CO 81623

Toll-free: 800-292-4838
Phone: 970-963-0437
www.buildingforhealth.com

The Building For Health Materials Center is a centrally located, nationwide supplier of healthy, environmentally conscious building products for consumers and contractors. The company states that each product is evaluated in relationship to environmental impact and human health effects. Catalogs are available upon request.

Green Building Materials

Eco-Products
3655 Frontier Ave.
Boulder, CO 80301

Phone: 303-449-1876
www.ecoproducts.com

Eco-Products primarily supplies exterior and interior finish materials, composite decking, and household items and equipment. The company currently serves Colorado and neighboring states but is expanding to serve the national market.

Green Building Materials

Eco-wise Building Supplies
110 W. Elizabeth St.
Austin, TX 78704

Phone: 512-326-4474
www.ecowise.com

Eco-wise Building Supplies carries a wide variety of green building materials, including such items as rainwater catchment systems, cotton insulation, recycled-glass tiles, reclaimed woods, plant-based finishes, milk paint, recycled-content carpeting, bamboo flooring, and ENERGY STAR® appliances.

Green Building Materials

Environmental Building Supplies
819 S.E. Taylor St.
Portland, OR 97214

Phone: 503-222-3881
www.ecohaus.com

Environmental Building Supplies sells environmental building materials and interior finishes to trade professionals and to both residential and commercial end-users. Products include flooring and floorcoverings, FSC-certified and salvaged wood, finishes, cabinetry, tiles, and furniture. The company distributes to retailers as well as offers products to the public from their showroom location in Portland, Oregon. Environmental Building Supplies also has a second retail location in Bend, Oregon.

Green Building Materials

Environmental Construction Outfitters of NY
901 E. 134th St.
Bronx, NY 10454

Toll-free: 800-238-5008
Phone: 718-292-0626
www.environproducts.com

Environmental Construction Outfitters of NY offers a full line of environmental and hypoallergenic building products. They cater to the needs of the chemically sensitive. Home inspections and consultations on greening homes and workplaces are available.

Green Building Materials

Environmental Home Center
1724 Fourth Ave. S
Seattle, WA 98134

Toll-free: 800-281-9785
Phone: 206-682-7332
www.environmentalhomecenter.com

Environmental Home Center sells a wide variety of environmental building products to trade professionals, dealers, and commercial

and residential customers across the country through their showroom and call center in Seattle, as well as through the company's website. Wholesale pricing is available to trade professionals.

Green Building Materials

Green Building Supply
508 N. 2nd St.
Fairfield, IA 52556

Toll-free: 888-405-0222
Phone: 641-469-5558
www.greenbuildingsupply.com

Green Building Supply offers hundreds of name-brand, sustainable, and energy-efficient construction products for residential and commercial projects, including nontoxic paints, stains, sealers, cleaners, furniture and cabinetry; air and water purification equipment; water-efficient toilets and non-water-using urinals; linoleum, cork and bamboo flooring; wool carpeting; cotton insulation. Contact the company for a catalog.

Green Building Materials

Hayward Corporation
P.O. Box 16009
Monterey, CA 93942

Phone: 831-643-1900
www.haywardlumber.com

Hayward Corporation, formerly Hayward Lumber, with six building supply centers in California, is reported to have the largest stock of certified lumber in the country. They also carry an expanding stock of other green building materials, including high-performance windows, ACQ- and borate-treated lumber, cotton insulation, and wood alternatives. In 2000, the company began producing its own line of FSC-certified roof trusses, now manufactured in a solar-powered facility soon to be LEED®-certified.

Green Building Materials

Livingreen, Inc.
218 Helena Ave.
Santa Barbara, CA 93101

Phone: 805-966-1319
www.livingreen.com

Livingreen offers environmentally sustainable building and finishing materials, accessories, and retail products highlighting natural and recycled alternatives to standard building materials. The company's showroom provides product samples for both homeowners and trade professionals. As a resource center, Livingreen maintains a green book store and provides consultation

Kitchen design by Scott Lenox; material and photo by Livingreen

and information on design, energy and water conservation, and product searches for home, work, and marine environments.

Green Building Materials

Planetary Solutions
2030 17th St.
Boulder, CO 80302

Phone: 303-442-6228
www.planetearth.com

Planetary Solutions caters to contractors, the design professions, and the general public in the Rocky Mountain region with a range of environmentally sound products including cork flooring, linoleum, 100% natural wool and recycled PET plastic carpet, reclaimed and FSC-certified wood flooring, bamboo flooring, recycled-glass tile, and natural paints and finishes.

Green Building Materials

Truitt & White
642 Hearst Ave.
Berkeley, CA 94710

Toll-free: 877-600-1470
Phone: 510-841-0511
www.truittandwhite.com

An institution since 1946 in Berkeley, CA, builder's supply store Truitt and White has committed to developing and promoting green products and practices. Environmentally preferable products, such as FSC-certified wood, low-VOC paints and caulks, and energy-efficient items, are clearly labeled throughout the store, making them easy to find. Truitt and White is a founding member and sponsor of educational nonprofit Bay Area Build It Green.

Natural Fiber Bedding and Floorcoverings

Natural Home Products.com
P.O. Box 1677
Sebastopol, CA 95473

Phone: 707-824-0914
www.naturalhomeproducts.com

Natural Home Products.com carries an extensive line of commercial and residential natural floor coverings including New Zealand wool carpet, linoleum, cork, sisal, and seagrass. The company sells organic paints and wood finishes, as well as organic-cotton sheets and wool bedding.

Distributors/Retailers: Renewable Energy Equipment

Most of these companies supply a wide range of renewable energy equipment, including photovoltaic systems, solar water-heating equipment, batteries, and inverters. A few also supply wind-energy and micro-hydro equipment.

PV Systems

Mr.Solar.com
P.O. Box 1506
Cockeysville, MD 21032

Phone: 410-308-1599
www.mrsolar.com

Mr.Solar.com designs and sells PV systems using BP, Siemens, Kyocera, Trace, and Solarex components for residential and commercial use.

Renewable Energy Equipment

Backwoods Solar Electric Systems
1395 Rolling Thunder Rdg.
Sandpoint, ID 83864

Phone: 208-263-4290
www.backwoodssolar.com

A company of six solar-electric technicians, most of whom live in solar-electric homes themselves, Backwoods Solar Electric Systems has been in business in the same off-the-grid mountain home location since 1978. The company is catalog-based (web and print) and is dedicated to serving remotely located homeowners/builders.

Renewable Energy Equipment

Creative Energy Technologies
10 Main St.
P.O. Box 149
Summit, NY 12175

Phone: 518-287-1428
www.cetsolar.com

Founded in 1998, Creative Energy Technologies (CET) offers a wide range of renewable and energy-efficient equipment through its online catalog. The company operates a pilot franchise store, the CET Solar Store (in Cavendish, Vermont), from which they also offer workshops and an energy audit weatherization service. According to CET, they test all the products they offer to verify the claims of the manufacturers and will provide free technical support for the life of a purchased product.

Renewable Energy Equipment

Electron Connection
P.O. Box 203
Hornbrook, CA 96044

Toll-free: 800-945-7587
www.electronconnection.com

In business and producing its own power since 1976 (with its owner utilizing renewable energy since 1970), Electron Connection designs, sells, installs, and maintains renewable energy systems. The company does not publish a paper catalog but provides information about some products on its website. Manufacturers' literature is also provided on products determined to be suitable for a specific customer's needs. Electron Connection is fully licensed, bonded, and insured to install and service renewable energy systems in California and Oregon. The company also maintains a worldwide network of Electron Connection dealer/installers.

Renewable Energy Equipment

Energy Outfitters, Ltd.
543 N.E. "E" Street
Grants Pass, OR 97526

Toll-free: 800-467-6527
Phone: 541-476-4200
www.energyoutfitters.com

In business since 1991, Energy Outfitters is a renewable energy distributor supplying products either as components or assembled systems, and offering technical design services for a wide range of renewable energy products and systems including PV, wind, and micro-hydro. The company also distributes Sharp photovoltaic modules.

Renewable Energy Equipment

Gaiam Real Goods
360 Interlocken Blvd.,
  Ste. 300
Broomfield, CO 80021

Toll-free: 800-919-2400
Phone: 303-222-3500
www.realgoods.com

Photo: Rob Ashmore, Real Goods

Real Goods and Jade Mountain merged in 2001 to become the largest provider of renewable energy systems (solar, wind, and hydro) in the world. These companies have been involved with solarizing more than 50,000 homes since 1978. The combined company provides products and technical assistance for customers wanting to improve energy efficiency in their homes and businesses, and for those wanting to become totally independent from the power company. Their Design and Consulting division deals with commercial and eco-tourism projects from initial feasibility and design to product procurement and turnkey installation. Free catalog available upon request.

Renewable Energy Equipment

New England Solar Electric, Inc.
401 Huntington Rd.
P.O. Box 435
Worthington, MA 01098

Toll-free: 800-914-4131
www.newenglandsolar.com

New England Solar Electric, formerly Fowler Solar Electric, offers renewable energy equipment and systems from a 104-page catalog and product guide. The company also publishes "the Solar Electric Independent Home book."

Renewable Energy Equipment

Northern Arizona Wind & Sun, Inc.
2725 E. Lakin Dr.
Flagstaff, AZ 86004

Toll-free: 800-383-0195
Phone: 928-526-8017
www.solar-electric.com

In business selling and installing solar electric systems since 1979, Northern Arizona Wind & Sun offers renewable energy equipment through its catalog, an online store, and a retail location in Flagstaff. The company also offers a Solar Design Guide.

Renewable Energy Equipment

RWE Schott Solar, Inc.
U.S. Sales & Marketing
4051 Alvis Ct., Ste. 1
Rocklin, CA 95677

Toll-free: 888-457-6527
Phone: 916-625-9033
www.rweschottsolar.us

RWE Schott Solar Inc. (RSS; formerly Schott Applied Power) is a leading manufacturer and distributor of solar power components and systems. RSS produces the world's largest available solar power module available, the ASE 300. A pioneer in the design and development of complete solar power solutions, RSS serves a highly diverse market including grid-connected residential and commercial systems, and grid-independent agricultural, governmental and utility applications. RWE Scott Solar Inc. is a joint venture of the RWE Group, a global multi-utility concern with core businesses in electricity, gas, water, waste management, and recycling.

Renewable Energy Equipment

SBT Designs
25840 IH-10 W
San Antonio, TX 78257

Toll-free: 800-895-9808
Phone: 210-698-7109
www.sbtdesigns.com

SBT Designs' Alternative Energy Catalog includes design guides, product descriptions, and prices on solar modules, wind generators, and a variety of renewable energy products.

Renewable Energy Equipment

Solar Works, Inc.
64 Main St.
Montpelier, VT 05602

Phone: 802-223-7804
www.solar-works.com

Solar Works, Inc. has been installing and selling renewable energy systems and energy-efficient equipment since 1980. The company headquarters are in Montpelier, Vermont, and sales offices are located in CA, CT, ME, MA, NH, NY, and RI. Solar Works also maintains a network of subcontractors and sales "partners" across the U.S. The company provides a full range of turnkey solar electric and solar thermal systems for residential, commercial, and institutional clients, and services that include systems design, engineering, installation, system commissioning, and servicing. Solar Works also develops and manages utility, state government, and community-supported renewable energy programs; plays an active role in helping to shape state and local energy policies; and offers renewable energy training programs.

Renewable Energy Equipment

Southwest Photovoltaic Systems, Inc.
212 E. Main
Tomball, TX 77375

Toll-free: 800-899-7978
Phone: 281-351-0031
www.southwestpv.com

In business since 1986, Southwest PV Systems designs and supplies PV, wind, and hybrid-power systems. The company offers training seminars on-site and maintains a large in-stock distribution warehouse.

Renewable Energy Equipment

Sunnyside Solar
1014 Green River Rd.
Guilford, VT 05301

Phone: 802-257-1482
www.sunnysidesolar.com

Sunnyside Solar, Inc., founded in 1979, is a small, family-owned firm specializing in photovoltaic electric systems. The company provides design, engineering, sales, installation, service, and education in the field of off- and on-grid residential and commercial photovoltaic installations. Sunnyside Solar has also recently reintroduced solar domestic hot water systems into its product line, with design, installation, sales, and service.

Used Building Materials

Clearly, reusing building materials can be environmentally advantageous. The companies listed here commonly have varying selections of doors, windows, cabinets, brick, stone, wood flooring, and plumbing fixtures. Also check the Yellow Pages under "salvage" for local suppliers. Avoid the use of old, inefficient windows in exterior envelopes, or plumbing fixtures that don't meet current water conservation standards. In these cases, new products will save more than the environmental costs of their manufacture. Testing for lead paint is recommended for items such as salvaged doors and millwork. Raw, unsealed wood can be a source of lead dust in a building even if lead paint has been removed. If lead paint residue is found or suspected, the wood should be sealed after paint is stripped.

Green Building Resource Guide

Salvaged Building Materials Exchange
www.greenguide.com/exchange/

The salvaged building materials exchange section of this website is set up for sellers and buyers to connect by way of free listings.

Industry Representation

Used Building Materials Association
1702 Walnut St.
Boulder, CO 80302

Phone: 303-440-0703
www.ubma.org

The Used Building Materials Association is the nonprofit North American organization representing firms that deconstruct buildings, retail used building materials, or both. Its website gives current contact information for all members nationwide.

Materials Exchange

Vermont Business Materials Exchange
P.O. Box 430
Newfane, VT 05345

Toll-free: 800-895-1930
www.vbmex.net

Vermont Business Materials Exchange (VBMeX) is a free service that connects businesses or institutions that have surplus commercial materials with other businesses or individuals who can put the materials to good use. VBMeX maintains a database of available and wanted materials, and publicizes the listings in the form of "classified ads" through their website, specialized listserves, and *Vermont Business Magazine*. The database normally contains about 150 active listings of materials offered free or at low cost, updated daily. Offerings include surplus wood and plastic materials, construction salvage, and containers, among other items.

Salvaged and Sustainably Harvested Wood Finder

Woodfinder
P.O. Box 493
Springtown, PA 18081

Toll-free: 877-933-4637
www.woodfinder.com

Woodfinder can be used to locate both salvaged and sustainably harvested wood.

Salvaged Architectural Antiques

North Shore Architectural Antiques
521 Seventh St.
Two Harbors, MN 55616

Phone: 218-834-0018
www.north-shore-architectural-antiques.com

North Shore Architectural Antiques salvages antique residential and commercial building materials. The company operates a retail showroom and will deliver regionally and ship anywhere.

The IRN Surplus Network

Institution Recycling Network
7 S. State St.
Concord, NH 03301

Phone: 603-229-1962
www.ir-network.com

The Surplus Network, a service of The Institution Recycling Network (IRN), provides surplus furniture, office equipment and furnishings, classroom furnishings, dormitory/bedroom furniture, and other surplus salvaged products from their over 100 members. The Network operates in an online auction format. Most items are available for pickup at the Surplus Network's warehouse in Chelsea, Massachusetts. Some items are sold directly from IRN member campuses, and delivery can also be arranged in most cases.

Used Building Materials

1st Saturday Construction Salvage
R.R. 3, Box 405
Spencer, IN 47460

Phone: 812-876-6347

1st Saturday deconstructs small buildings and carries everything from lumber to doors to stained glass.

Used Building Materials

American Salvage
7001 N.W. 27th Ave.
Miami, FL 33147

Phone: 305-836-4444
www.americansalvage.com

A source for general home furnishing items, American Salvage carries a wide variety of finished building components such as paneled doors and specialty windows.

Used Building Materials

Austin Habitat for Humanity Re-Store
310 Comal, Ste. 101
Austin, TX 78702

Phone: 512-478-2165
www.re-store.com

The Austin Re-Store carries a broad range of salvaged building materials in part supplied by deconstruction activities of the local Habitat for Humanity affiliate.

Used Building Materials

Building Materials Resource Center
100 Terrace St.
Boston, MA 02120

Phone: 617-442-8917
www.bostonbmrc.org

The Building Materials Resource Center (BMRC) is a nonprofit organization that accepts donations of good quality used and surplus building materials and offers them for a modest fee to the general public. A 50% discount is offered to low- to moderate-income homeowners (proof of income is required) and nonprofit organizations. BMRC maintains a 6,000 ft² retail location and also offers workshops, in-home consults, a lending library, and other homeowner-assistance services. Donations to the BMRC are tax-deductible on the estimated fair market value of the item.

Used Building Materials

Caldwell Building Wreckers
195 Bayshore Blvd.
San Francisco, CA 94124

Phone: 415-550-6777
www.caldwell-bldg-salvage.com

Caldwell Building Wreckers salvages a wide variety of building products including lumber, beams, doors, windows, bricks, and cobblestones.

Used Building Materials

Center for ReSource
Conservation
1702 Walnut St.
Boulder, CO 80302

Phone: 303-441-3278
www.conservation
center.org

ReSource is a program of the
Center for ReSource Conservation to salvage and resell
building materials from con-
struction and demolition projects. Available materials include
lumber, door, window, and cabinet packages as well as architectural
artifacts including timbers, hardwood flooring, and other items of
significance. ReSource also now offers a complete line of millwork
and flooring from reclaimed timbers.

Used Building Materials

Centre Mills Antique Floors
P.O. Box 16
Aspers, PA 17304

Phone: 717-334-0249
www.centremillsantiquefloors.com

Centre Mills Antique Floors salvages and remills a variety of
hand-hewn wood products made from such species as chestnut,
oak, white pine, and hemlock. Centre Mills also has 7 acres of
architectural artifacts, including bricks, mantles, wavy glass, old
doors, and used slates.

Used Building Materials

Odom Reusable Building Materials
5555 Brentwood Ave.
Grawn, MI 49637

Phone: 231-276-6330

Odom salvages and deconstructs commercial and residential buildings and sells lumber, cabinets, doors, windows, and a variety of
fixtures to the public at a retail warehouse.

Used Building Materials

Rejuvenation
1100 S.E. Grand Ave.
Portland, OR 97214

Phone: 503-238-1900
www.rejuvenation.com

Encompassing over 5,000 ft², the Salvage Department of the Rejuvenation store in Portland, OR offers a wide variety of salvaged
architectural products. The company's Restoration Department
refurbishes, repairs, and sells antique lighting fixtures. Rejuvenation is also a manufacturer of period lighting fixtures, including
a line equipped with energy-efficient CFLs and small electronic

ballasts. The company has taken a number of steps to reduce its
environmental impact.

Used Building Materials

Rejuve Seattle
2910 1st Ave. S,
Seattle, WA 98134

Phone: 206-382-1901
www.rejuvenation.com

Rejuve Seattle, a branch of Rejuvation in Portland, OR, offers a wide
variety of salvaged architectural products at its 6,000 ft² facility.
The company's Restoration Department refurbishes, repairs, and
sells antique lighting fixtures. Rejuvenation is also a manufacturer
of period lighting fixtures, including a line equipped with energy-
efficient CFLs and small electronic ballasts. The company has taken
a number of steps to reduce its environmental impact.

Used Building Materials

Renovators ReSource
6040 Almon St.
Halifax, NS B3K 1T8 Canada

Toll-free: 877-230-7700
Phone: 902-429-3889
www.renovators-resource.com

Renovators ReSource stocks a wide variety of quality used building materials, including entire dismantled buildings, and carries
a line of furniture and household items elegantly designed from
used building materials.

Used Building Materials

Reuse Development Organization
2523 Gwynns Falls Pkwy.
Baltimore, MD 21216

Phone: 410-669-7245
www.redo.org

Reuse Development Organization is a national nonprofit organization providing technical assistance in reuse, deconstruction, and
building materials salvaging. It's a great information resource for
all types of secondhand consumer products as well as building
materials, office equipment, and furniture.

Used Building Materials

Second Use Building Materials
7953 Second Ave. S
Seattle, WA 98108

Phone: 206-763-6929
www.seconduse.com

Second Use Building Materials operates a retail yard of salvaged
building materials in Seattle, WA.

GREEN BUILDING PRODUCTS

Used Building Materials

Sound Builders Resource
210 Thurston Ave.
Olympia, WA 98501

Phone: 360-753-1575
www.sbroly.org

Sound Builders Resource recently took over the Olympia, Washington branch of Second Use Building Materials, Inc. Sound Builders is a nonprofit organization donating all profits from the sale of a wide variety of used building supplies to Habitat for Humanity. The company offers pick-up and delivery, and operates a building materials retrieval operation at the local waste recovery center that diverts usable building materials from the landfill before they reach the scales.

Used Building Materials

The Brass Knob and The Back Doors Warehouse
2311 18th St. NW
Washington, DC 20009

Phone: 202-332-3370
www.thebrassknob.com

The Brass Knob and The Back Doors Warehouse offer salvaged building supplies, carrying everything from salvaged antique hardware to chandeliers, stained glass, and radiators. The two locations are within walking distance of each other, with The Back Doors Warehouse carrying larger items in greater volume.

Used Building Materials

The Rebuilding Center of Our United Villages
3625 N. Mississippi Ave.
Portland, OR 97227

Phone: 503-331-1877
www.rebuildingcenter.org

The Rebuilding Center accepts and carries lumber, doors, windows, cabinets, sinks, tubs, toilets, carpets, and more. The Rebuilding Center also offers deconstruction services for commercial and residential structures.

Used Building Materials

The ReUse Center
2216 E. Lake St.
Minneapolis, MN 55407

Phone: 612-724-2608
www.greeninstitute.org

Run by the Green Institute, The ReUse Center supplies its retail operations through a partner deconstruction business and as a donation-based resale business.

Used Building Materials

Urban Ore, Inc.
900 Murray St.
Berkeley, CA 94710

Phone: 510-841-7283
www.urbanore.citysearch.com

One of the oldest used building materials retail operations in the country, Urban Ore carries large quantities of a wide variety of exterior and interior building materials.

Used Building Materials

Used Building Materials Exchange
RecycleNet Corporation
P.O. Box 24017
Guelph, ON N1E 6V8 Canada

Phone: 519-767-2913
build.recycle.net/exchange/index.html

Used Building Materials Exchange (UBM) is a free worldwide information exchange for those companies and individuals who buy/sell/trade used building materials.

Used Building Materials

Whole House Building Supply
1955 Pulgas Ave.
E. Palo Alto, CA 94303

Phone: 650-856-0634
www.driftwoodsalvage.com

Whole House Building Supply offers a complete range of used building materials, including salvaged clear and virgin growth redwood, and a great website picturing quality materials as well as beautiful uses of salvaged building materials.

This Space is Available for Your Notes

Miscellaneous

- Hazardous Materials Testing and Remediation

- Hazardous Substances Detection and Alarm

- Insect Control

- Lamp and Ballast Recycling
  see Lighting: Lamp and Ballast Recycing

- Measurement and Control Instrumentation

- Recycling Equipment

- Wood Products Certification and Information

Hazardous Materials Testing and Remediation

Asbestos and lead are among the most common hazardous materials encountered in older buildings. Use of asbestos as an insulating and fireproofing material, and lead as a primary ingredient in paint, ended in the 1970s as awareness of these dangers grew. Lead and asbestos remediation in buildings should generally be done by professionals, through either removal or encapsulation. Some of the following products aid in managing lead and asbestos with minimal additional environmental and health risks. Radon—a naturally occurring, odorless gas that is considered by the EPA to be the second most common cause of lung cancer (after cigarettes)—can seep into buildings from the ground. Proper detection, abatement, monitoring, and building ventilation provide effective radon control. Rechargeable nickel-cadmium (Ni-Cad) batteries have become ubiquitous on building sites. Despite their durability, they do wear out; the health and environmental risks posed by the heavy-metal content of Ni-Cad batteries makes their recycling a very high priority, so facilities for recycling them are included here. Fluorescent lighting products—fluorescent lamps as well as older ballasts—should also be disposed of only through specialized recycling facilities, some of which are listed here. All fluorescent lamps (as well as mercury-vapor and other high-intensity-discharge—HID—lamps) contain elemental mercury, which is a very serious environmental contaminant. Fluorescent lighting ballasts made prior to 1979 contain significant quantities of PCB (polychlorinated biphenyls)—each ballast containing 0.6 to 1 ounce—which is highly toxic and bioaccumulates in natural systems. Before sending fluorescent lamps and ballasts to out-of-town recycling facilities, check with your local solid-waste agency; many handle lamps and ballast disposal through toxic waste collection programs.

A-B-C and L-B-C

Fiberlock Technologies, Inc.
150 Dascomb Rd.
Andover, MA 01810

Toll-free: 800-342-3755
Phone: 978-623-9987
www.fiberlock.com

A-B-C® (Asbestos Binding Compound) is a high-solids asbestos encapsulant. This product can be used for effective in-place management of asbestos hazards.

L-B-C® (Lead Barrier Compound) is an elastomeric-thermoplastic water-based copolymer paint for lead encapsulation. L-B-C is available for indoor and outdoor applications in 1-, 5-, and 55-gallon containers.

Air Check Radon Test

Air Check, Inc.
1936 Butler Bridge Rd.
Fletcher, NC 28732-9365

Phone: 828-684-0893
www.radon.com

Air Check offers a series of radon test kits, each designed for different exposure times. The company provides fully certified analysis of mailed-in air samples for as little as $10 per test. Air Check performs same-day tests upon receipt of samples and provides a complete written report describing the results and their implications for indoor air quality.

LeadCheck

HybriVet Systems, Inc.
P.O. Box 1210
Framingham, MA 01701

Toll-free: 800-262-5323
Phone: 508-651-7881
www.leadcheck.com

HybriVet Systems offers several tests for lead in paint, soil, and water, as well as tests for other heavy metal pollutants. LeadCheck® swabs are a quick means of detecting lead in paint and other materials.

LeadLock and AsbestoSafe

Global Encasement, Inc.
132 32nd St.
Union City, NJ 07087

Toll-free: 800-266-3982
Phone: 201-902-9770
www.encasement.com

Photos: inc3

AsbestoSafe® and LeadLock™ are water-based, low-VOC, protective acrylic coatings for long-term, in-place management of asbestos and lead-based paint. Both products provide waterproofing yet allow water vapor to pass through the protective coating, and both are highly impact- and seismic-resistant. One impressive characteristic of Global Encasement's PrepLESS Primer is that it can eliminate and/or minimize surface preparation prior to application of TopCoats.

Ni-Cad Battery Recycling

Inmetco
One Inmetco Drive.
Ellwood City, PA 16117

Phone: 724-758-2800
www.inmetco.com

Inmetco maintains a nationwide battery recycling program for nickel-cadmium, nickel-metal-hydride, zinc, alkaline, lithium-ion, and nickel-iron batteries.

Safe Encasement Systems

SAFE Encasement Systems
7860 Dana Point Ct.
Las Vegas, NV 89117

Toll-free: 888-277-8834
Phone: 702-360-6111
www.safeencasement.com

Safe Encasement Systems manufactures a two-step encasement process for in-place abatement of lead-based paint and asbestos-fibers. SE-110 Penetrating Stabilizer, also available with corrosion inhibitors or mold-resisting additive, is a clear primer suitable for penetrating and sealing friable fibrous insulation materials and damaged paint surfaces. SE-110 can be used for interior and exterior applications on a variety of surfaces. When dry, SE-110 is followed by the application of SE-120 Protective Skin, a high-solids, 100% acrylic coating available with or without a mold-resisting additive. Both the Stabilizer and Protective Skin are water-based, nontoxic, nonflammable, zero-VOC formulations that clean up with soap and water. Safe Encasement Systems products can be warranted for 5-20 years.

The Professional Radon Gas Test Kit

Pro-Lab, Inc.
3300 Corporate Ave., Bldg. 112
P.O. Box 26773
Weston, FL 33331

Phone: 954-384-4446
www.prolabinc.com

Each EPA-recognized Pro-Lab test kit comes with a pair of radon detectors. The detectors use liquid scintillation technology with silica-gel desiccants, so they require only 96 hours of exposure before they are sealed and sent back to the lab for analysis. Results will be returned within one week; express 2-day analysis is also available. Pro-Lab also offers kits to detect pesticides, molds, carbon monoxide, asbestos, and bacteria in water, paints, dust, and on surfaces.

Hazardous Substances Detection and Alarm

Alerting building occupants about toxins or contaminants is important in many situations. With some toxins, an immediate warning is needed; with others, long-term exposure is the concern.

Air Ion Counter

AlphaLab, Inc.
1280 S. 300 W
Salt Lake City, UT 84101

Toll-free: 800-769-3754
Phone: 801-487-9492
www.trifield.com

AlphaLab's handheld, battery-operated Air Ion Counter detects natural and artificial ions, including radon gas.

Photo: Bill Lee

Atwood CO Alarm

Atwood Mobile Products
4750 Hiawatha Dr.
Rockford, IL 61103

Phone: 815-877-5700
www.atwoodmobile.com

Atwood Mobile Products' CO alarm is certified by the Canadian Standards Association, which includes specifications for both alarm longevity and time-of-manufacture testing. Atwood uses a patented electrochemical technology to alert building occupants to the presence of carbon monoxide. According to the company, the sensor is more accurate, more energy efficient, and less sensitive to humidity than competing models. A digital display updates CO levels every 30 seconds and indicates battery and sensor conditions. The unit requires 3 AAA batteries. A picture-frame leg allows installation in various locations. The Canadian Standards Association certifies Atwood CO alarms for use in RVs.

CO Detector

Senco Sensors
700 W. Pender St., Ste. 1408
Vancouver, BC V6C 1G8 Canada

Toll-free: 800-858-0158
Phone: 604-687-6011
www.sencosensors.com

Senco Sensors manufactures a range of three electrochemical carbon monoxide (CO) detectors.

IAQ Test Kit

Aerotech Laboratories, Inc.
1501 W. Knudsen Dr.
Phoenix, AZ 85027

Toll-free: 800-651-4802
Phone: 623-780-4800
www.aerotechlabs.com

Aerotech provides a wide array of sampling devices for measuring IAQ, including Zefon Air-O-Cell Cassettes for gathering mold and bioaerosol samples. Samples are returned to Aerotech for analysis. Aerotech also supplies and rents equipment for gathering specimens.

IAQ Test Kits

Air Quality Sciences, Inc.
1337 Capital Cir.
Marietta, GA 30067

Toll-free: 800-789-0419
Phone: 770-933-0638
www.aqs.com

Air Quality Sciences produces a variety of IAQ test kits to screen for molds and other allergens, as well as VOCs and formaldehyde. These self-administered kits are simple to use and fairly economical. Results are analyzed by AQS, including comparisons to existing standards, and delivered in an easy-to-read report.

Low Level CO "Health" Monitor

CO-Experts, Div. of G. E. Kerr Companies, Inc.
19299 Katrina Ln.
Eldridge, MO 65463-9102

Phone: 888-443-5377
www.coexperts.com

The Low Level (LL) CO Monitor displays carbon monoxide (CO) levels as low as 5 ppm with an audible and visual warning at 10 ppm. A more intense warning sounds at 25 ppm. Unlike most CO detectors, these monitors (in addition to sensing higher levels) are designed to alert occupants to low levels of CO that may be harmful, but not necessarily fatal, so that corrective measures may be taken. Most CO detectors sound an alarm only after much higher levels are sustained for a protracted period of time. The CO-Experts LL Monitors update their readings every 10 seconds and are accurate to 1 ppm, according to the manufacturer. The units include hush button features, with override if CO levels rise to next level. Diagnostic failure warnings and data recall features are also included. The unit comes with a 1-year warranty—an extended warranty is available for a small fee per year for a maximum of 5 years. An annual 1 ppm recalibration/warranty renewal service is also available for an additional charge.

Nighthawk CO Detector

Kidde Safety
1394 S. Third St.
Mebane, NC 27302

Toll-free: 800-654-9677
www.kidde.com

The Nighthawk CO detector uses electrochemical technology to alert building occupants to the presence of carbon monoxide (CO). The Canadian Standards Association certifies Kidde's Nighthawk CO dectectors for use in homes.

Insect Control

Termite control in buildings has traditionally been accomplished with pesticides—in the past with chlordane and heptachlor, more recently with chlorpyrifos. With all of these pesticides no longer in use because of health and environmental concerns, there's tremendous interest in alternatives. Products listed here include totally nontoxic termite barrier systems as well as less toxic, or more precisely targeted, chemical treatments. Termite barriers and full-control bait systems are generally quite expensive.

Basaltic Termite Barrier

Ameron Hawaii
2344 Pahounui Dr.
P.O. Box 29968
Honolulu, HI 96820

Phone: 808-832-9200
www.ameronhawaii.com

Basaltic Termite Barrier is a regionally available product made from basaltic aggregates (a coarse sand) on the Hawaiian Islands. These aggregates, when graded to a specific size, shape, and weight, form an effective, nontoxic barrier to standard subterranean and Formosan termite entry. The aggregates are too large and heavy for termites to move and the spaces between too small to move through.

Exterra

Ensystex, Inc.
P.O. Box 2587
Fayetteville, NC 28302

Toll-free: 888-398-3772
www.exterminate.com

The Exterra® Termite Interception and Baiting System is similar to the Sentricon System, using a chitin synthesis-inhibitor called diflubenzuron. A unique feature of Exterra's bait station, the Labyrinth, is the ability to install pesticide in the bait core without disturbing termites feeding on the bait box perimeter.

Sentricon Termite Colony Elimination System

Dow AgroSciences, LLC
9330 Zionsville Rd.
Indianapolis, IN 46268

Toll-free: 800-352-6776
www.sentricon.com

The Sentricon® Termite Colony Elimination System eliminates termites with a highly targeted hexaflumuron-based bait. This bait is approved under the EPA's Reduced Risk Pesticide Initiative and is considered to be highly targeted because worker termites carry it back to the colony to feed others. The chemical affects chitin formation in termites. In a management-intensive approach that limits environmental impact, the hexaflumuron pesticide is employed only when regularly inspected bait stations reveal termite activity. The Sentricon System is offered as part of an ongoing service contract.

Termi-Mesh System

Termi-Mesh USA
9519 Interstate 35 N
Austin, TX 78753

Phone: 512-997-0066
www.termi-mesh.com

The Termi-Mesh™ System is a termite barrier from Australia made from a tight-weave stainless steel mesh. Proper installation of Termi-Mesh may avoid the repeated application of pesticides. Currently this system is available only in a few Southern states.

Underseal XT Waterproofing Membranes

Polyguard Products, Inc.
3801 S. Business 45
P.O. Box 755
Ennis, TX 75120

Toll-free: 800-541-4994
Phone: 972-875-8421
www.polyguardproducts.com

The Underseal XT line (formerly Borderguard) resists termites, radon, pesticide migration, soil fungi, puncture, and tearing while providing waterproofing and stress relief for concrete slabs and walls. XT 750 is a peel-and-stick sheet membrane applied to the outside of finished flat concrete walls. XT 751 has a nonwoven textile top layer that bonds with the concrete when monolithic walls are poured. XT 850 is similar to XT 751, but designed for subslab use; XT 851 is a split-slab version. Underseal XT has been shown by testing at Texas A&M to deter Formosan and eastern subterranean termites. The adhesive is asphalt-based. Other ingredients include polymers, resins, and fillers.

Lamp and Ballast Recycling

see *Lighting: Lamp and Ballast Recycling*

Measurement and Control Instrumentation

Blower doors and duct pressurization systems are invaluable diagnostic tools for air-sealing buildings and ducts and for measuring the airtightness of buildings. Other instruments listed here can provide information on electricity usage.

Brand Digital Power Meter

Brand Electronics
421 Hilton Rd.
Whitefield, ME 04353

Toll-free: 888-433-6600
Phone: 207-549-3401
www.brandelectronics.com

The Brand Digital Power Meter monitors energy usage of 120-volt AC plug loads (up to 1,850 watts). It calculates instantaneous watts, accumulated kWh, and monthly cost. The higher-end models also display peak demand, power factor, and volt-amps, and are capable of datalogging and transferring data to a PC (Win 95/98/XP). Other models are available for multichannel metering, including 240-volt and DC channels. All models measure accurate (+/-2%) wattage—including power factor—by sampling volts and amps at 4 kHz.

KILL A WATT

P3 International Corporation
132 Nassau St.
New York, NY 10038-2400

Phone: 212-346-7979
www.p3international.com

The Kill A Watt™ energy monitor records appliance electrical consumption by kilowatt-hour within 0.2% accuracy and shows it in a large LCD display by the hour, day, week, month, or up to a year. Also displays volts, amps, watts, hertz, and volt-amps. It is more affordable than most energy-monitoring products on the market.

Watt's up?

Electronic Educational
   Devices, Inc.
2345 S. Lincoln St.
Denver, CO 80210

Toll-free: 877-928-8701
Phone: 303-282-6410
www.doubleed.com

Watt's up? electricity monitors
show users the electricity usage of
any 120-volt AC load. The monitor
displays 16 values including watts,
current volts, duty cycle, and dollars and cents based upon a specified electricity rate. The Pro version records this data, and with
a PC interface, provides graphs of the collected data over time.
Watt's up? is an educational tool that is also useful for people
planning their off-the-grid energy needs.

Recycling Equipment

*Enabling homeowners and commercial building occupants to
be good environmental stewards is important. Systems that
make it easy to recycle wastes should be provided in houses,
apartment buildings, offices, and institutions. Some of the
products described here are themselves made from recycled
waste materials.*

Curbside or Work-Area Recycling Bins

Microphor
452 E. Hill Rd.
Willits, CA 95490

Toll-free: 800-358-8280
Phone: 707-459-5563
www.microphor.com

Microphor recycling bins, made from plastic, are designed for
curbside or office-paper recycling. These stackable bins have large
handles and measure 12^1/$_4$" x 12^1/$_2$" x 20^1/$_2$". Standard colors are
white, navy blue, blue, red, green, and yellow.

Feeny Recycling Center with Lids and Rotary Recycling Center

Knape & Vogt Manufacturing Company
2700 Oak Industrial Dr. NE
Grand Rapids, MI 49505

Phone: 616-459-3311
www.knapeandvogt.com

Knape & Vogt offers two products for residential recyclable collection. The Feeny Recycling Center with Lids is intended for base
cabinet applications; it has 3 bins and rolls out. The Feeny Rotary
Recycling Center has 3 bins and works like a lazy susan.

Recycling Equipment

Recy-CAL Supply Co.
42597 De Portola Rd.
Temecula, CA 92592

Toll-free: 800-927-3873
Phone: 909-302-7585
www.recy-cal.com

Recy-CAL Supply is a distributor
of recycling containers, waste receptacles, and mobile collection
containers. Many styles and sizes of
products from more than 30 manufacturers are available to fit various
needs, budgets, and decors.

Recycling Receptacles

Busch Systems
   International Inc.
130 Saunders Rd., Unit 7
Barrie, ON L4N 9A8
   Canada

Toll-free: 800-565-9931
Phone: 705-722-0806
www.buschsystems.com

Busch Systems International
provides recycling container
solutions to industries, municipal governments, and educational
systems. They produce dozens of styles of curbside, deskside, and
centralized recycling containers, as well as carts and compos-
ters. Most products contain a minimum of 25% post-consumer
recycled material. They also offer novelties to promote recycling
and composting.

Wood Products Certification and Information

*Forest certification in North America is conducted primarily by
two third-party certifying organizations: SmartWood and Scientific Certification Systems (SCS). SmartWood and SCS certify
forest lands and chain-of-custody forest products based on Forest
Stewardship Council (FSC) standards.*

Forest Stewardship Council

Forest Stewardship Council - US
1155 30th St. NW, Ste. 300
Washington, DC 20007

Toll-free: 877-372-5646
Phone: 202-342-0413
www.fscus.org

The Forest Stewardship Council (FSC) is a nonprofit international organization committed to the conservation, restoration, and protection of the world's working forests through standards setting and accreditation. Founded in 1993, FSC is comprised of more than 600 members from 70 countries, including major environmental groups like Greenpeace and World Wildlife Fund, social organizations representing indigenous peoples and forest workers, and progressive forest-management and wood-products companies. The FSC checkmark-and-tree logo indicates that wood and wood products bearing the logo came from a well-managed forest. The FSC is the only forest certification standards program recognized in evaluating wood products for GreenSpec.

Third-Party Certifier of Wood Products

Scientific Certification Systems
2000 Powell St., Ste. 1350
Emeryville, CA 94608

Toll-free: 800-832-1415
Phone: 510-452-8000
www.scs1.com

Scientific Certification Systems (SCS) is an independent certification organization that offers a range of services. SCS certifies manufacturers' claims of building product attributes such as recycled and recovered content and absence of added formaldehyde. The company also conducts life-cycle impact assessments and the certification of environmentally preferable products such as paints, carpets, technologies, services, and electricity. In addition, SCS is accredited by the FSC to certify well-managed forests and conduct chain-of-custody certification for forest products based on FSC standards.

Third-Party Certifier of Wood Products

SmartWood
Goodwin-Baker Bldg.
65 Millet St., Ste. 201
Richmond, VT 05477

Phone: 802-434-5491
www.smartwood.org

SmartWood is the sustainable forestry program of the Rainforest Alliance, an international conservation organization that works to protect ecosystems and the people and wildlife that depend on them by transforming land use practices, business practices, and consumer behavior. Established in 1989, SmartWood was the first certification program in the world and is accredited by the Forest Stewardship Council. SmartWood's headquarters is located in Richmond, Vermont.

This Space is Available for Your Notes

This Space is Available for Your Notes

Index of Products & Manufacturers

#930 Epoxy Caulking Compound 184
#965 Flooring and Tread Adhesive 144
1st Saturday Construction Salvage 281
200S Energy Recovery Ventilators 212
234 Natural Metal Primer.................... 189
2nd Site Systems 19
3-D Panel Construction System 50
3-D Panel Construction Systems............ 50
380 Natural All-Purpose Floor Adhesive 144
389 Natural Wallpaper Adhesive 182
4-Way Floor Deck, N.C.F.R., and Firestall
    Roof Deck 72
9400W Impregnant........................... 191
9400 Impregnant 188
A-B-C and L-B-C............................. 286
A. B. Chance 40
A. E. Sampson & Son, Inc. 97, 140
AB&I Foundry 228
Abundant Renewable Energy 272
Accent Windows, Inc. 105
ACCOA Aerated Concrete Corporation
    of America 45
Accurate Dorwin Company 100
ACFoam 128
Acousti-Cork 145
ACQ Preserve Treated Wood................. 58
ACR Solar International Corporation 269
Acsys Inc. 64
Acsys Panel System 64
ACT, Inc. Metlund Systems.................. 224
Active Ventilation System................... 214
Adobe Block.................................... 44
Adobe Factory 44
ADO Products 127
Advanced Composting Systems............ 220
Advanced Fiber Technology, Inc........... 113
Advance Foam Plastics, Inc. -
    California Division 55, 65, 119
Advance Foam Plastics, Inc. -
    Colorado Division 55, 65, 119
Advance Foam Plastics, Inc. -
    Nevada Division 55, 65, 119
Advance Foam Plastics, Inc. -
    Utah Division 55, 65, 120
Advance Guard.................................. 58
Advance Transformer Co. 246
AdvanTech OSB................................. 72
AdvanTex Wastewater Treatment
    Systems 230

Aeolian Enterprises, Inc. 18, 29
AERC.com, Inc.................................. 244
Aerotech Laboratories, Inc.................. 288
AERT, Inc. (Advanced Environmental
    Recycling Technologies, Inc.) 31
Affordable Building Systems LLC... 160, 180
AFG Industries, Inc............................ 102
AFM Corporation 65, 120
Aged Woods / Yesteryear Floorworks
    Company.................... 150, 174, 177
Agriboard 64
Agriboard Industries, L.C...................... 64
Air-Care Odorless Paints 192
Air-Heating Solar Collector 268
Air-Vapor Barrier Box........................ 237
Airguard, Inc................................... 205
Airguard Air Filters 205
AIR and Whisper Series Wind Turbines .. 271
Air Check, Inc................................... 286
Air Check Radon Test 286
Air Ion Counter............................... 287
Air Krete, Inc. 125
Air Krete Foam Insulation................... 125
Air Quality Sciences, Inc. 288
Alamo Foam, Inc............................... 118
Albany Woodworks, Inc. 149, 174
Algoma Hardwoods, Inc....................... 97
All-Weather Insulation 113
All-Weather Insulation Co............. 4, 113
Allard Lumber Company......................46
Alliance to Save Energy...................... 100
Allied Foam Products, Inc..............65, 120
Allied Mat & Matting, Inc.................... 147
Alluvium Construction........................ 91
All Paper Recycling, Inc. 165, 262
Aloha Plastics Recycling......... 6, 9, 20, 30
Alpen Glass 102
AlphaLab, Inc.................................. 287
Alpine Grade Douglas Fir Flooring 158
Alternate Energy Technologies 270
Alterna by Doorcraft 97
Amana Heating and Air Conditioning.... 210
Amana Refrigeration, Inc.................... 204
Amazing Recycled Products, Inc....6, 10, 19,
    27, 200
Amazon Forms One, Inc....................... 52
Amazon Grid-Wall ICFs 52
Amazon Select Recycled Paint............. 200
AMERGREEN Roof Garden System 86

American Aldes Ventilation Corp... 212, 213
American Clay Enterprises, LLC 198
American Clay Natural Earth Plaster 198
American ConForm Industries, Inc. 56
American Ecoboard, Inc. 5, 27, 37
American Formulating & Manufacturing
    (AFM)..................................36, 158, 188,
    189, 190, 195, 196, 200
American PolySteel, LLC 54
American Pride Vegetable-Oil-Modified
    Latex Paint.................................. 192
American Recreational Products....9, 19, 20
American Recycled Plastic, Inc. ...6, 10, 24,
    29
American Roof Manufacturing, LLC........ 88
American Rubbertech.......................... 11
American Salvage.............................. 281
American Sprayed Fibers, Inc. 130
American Standard 231
American Water Heater Company 207
American Wick Drain Corporation 86
AmeriSlate...................................... 88
Ameron Hawaii 288
Amorim Flooring North America, Inc. ... 144
Amorim Industrial Solutions 145
Amtico International Inc. 155
AM Appliance Group - Asko.......... 248, 251
AM Appliance Group - Eurotech 248, 251
AM Conservation Group, Inc................. 276
Andersen Windows 107
Anderson-Tully 163
Antique Drapery Rod Co., Inc. 108, 194
Antique Speciality Flooring................. 150
Antique Woods & Colonial
    Restorations, Inc......... 59, 79, 150, 261
ANTIWASH/GEOJUTE and GEOCOIR
    DeKoWe 2
Applegate Insulation Manufacturing 4, 113
Applegate Loosefill and Applegate
    Stabilized Cellulose Insulation.......... 113
Applegate Mulch 4
Appleseed Wool Corp. 138
Aprilaire 212, 214
Aprilaire Energy Recovery Ventilator..... 212
Aprilaire Ventilation Control System 214
Aquafin, Inc. 35
Aquafin-IC Crystalline Waterproofing 35
AquaSaver...................................... 231
Aquatherm Industries, Inc. 270

Aquatherm Piping Systems, LLC 223
Aqua ZAR 197
Arbor Guard and Universal Barriers 15
Architectural Accents 178
Architectural Timber and Millwork. 150, 174
Archovations, Inc. 78, 118
Arch Treatment Technologies, Inc. 58
Arctic Insulation, Inc. 113
Ark-Seal 125
Armstrong World Industries, Inc. .. 146, 160
Artisan Sound Control, LLC 160
ART (American Rubber Technologies,
     Inc.) 14
Arxx Building Products 52
Arxx High Performance Wall System 52
Ashford Formula 188
Asko Dishwashers 251
Asko H-Axis Clothes Washers and Dryers 248
Asphalt Release 37
Astec Coatings 85
Astro-Foil 128
Astro-Mulch 4
AstroPowerSolar Park 268
Athena 233
Atlantis Energy Systems, Inc. 268
Atlas Roofing Corp. 128
Attic Insulation and Wall Cavity Spray .. 113
Attic Vents Chutes 126
Atwood CO Alarm 287
Atwood Mobile Products 287
Aurora Glass 178
Austin Habitat for Humanity Re-Store .. 281
Authentic Roof 2000 88
Autoclaved Aerated Concrete 45
AVS Solo and AVS Duo 212
AWP 3.6 Wind Turbine 272
Aztec Recycled Plastic Lumber 27
AZ Energy Saver 113
A Reclaimed Lumber Co.... 63, 79, 154, 177
A W I Mulch 4
B. W. Creative Wood Industries Ltd. 164
Babb International Inc. 45
Backwoods Solar Electric Systems 278
Baleblock System 52
Ballard Power Systems 236
Bamboo Depot 136
Bamboo Flooring 135
Bamboo Flooring Intl. Corp. (BFI) 137
Bamboo Hardwoods, Inc. 136
Bamboo Hardwoods Flooring 136
Bamboo Paneling and Veneer 162
BamPlank Bamboo Flooring 136
Bamtex Bamboo Flooring 136
Bamtex Bamboo Paneling 162
Barco Products Co. 6, 11, 22
Barnwood and Hand-Hewn Beams 59
BarrierPanel, TechShield Radiant
     Barrier, and BarrierFloor OSB 72
Basaltic Termite Barrier 288
BASF Corporation 119

BASWAphon Acoustic Insulation 160
Battic Door Attic Stair Covers 112
Beacon Power Corporation 266
BEANedoo Mastic Remover 198
Bedford Technology, LLC 10, 29, 90
Bedrock Industries 179
Beeken Parsons 257
Belton Industries, Inc. 2
Benches, Picnic Tables, and
     Landscape Ties 20
Benches, Picnic Tables, and Planters 20
Benches, Picnic Tables, and Recycling
     Receptacles 20
Benches, Picnic Tables, and Trash
     Receptacles 20
Benches, Picnic Tables, Waste
     Receptacles, and Planters 20
Benches, Tables, Chairs, Waste
     Receptacles, and Planters 21
Benches and Picnic Tables 19
Benches and Recycling and Waste
     Receptacles 20
Benches and Table Sets 20
Benjamin Moore & Co. 195
Benjamin Obdyke Inc. 79, 89
Benolec, Ltd. 4, 113
Benotherm 113
Benovert 4
Bentonite Waterproofing Systems 35
Bergey Windpower Co., Inc. 272
Berkeley Mills 256
Best Duracryl Exterior Paint 189
Best Paint, Inc. 189, 193
Best Paints 193
Better Than Wood 27
Better Than Wood - Benches and Picnic
     Tables 21
Better Than Wood Car Stops 9
Better Wall System 181
Bicycle Part Tables and Furnishings 261
Bigfoot System Footing Forms 39
BigHorn Materials 276
Big Creek Lumber Company 47
Big Sky Insulations, Inc. 55, 66, 120
Big Timberworks, Inc. 60, 79, 150, 174, 177
Bio-Based Systems 125
Bio-Floor Collection 156
Bio-Form 37
Bio-Sun Systems, Inc. 220
BioBase 501 125
BioFence 2
BioGreen 226
BioGreen System (Pacific) Ltd. 226
BioShield Cork Adhesive #16 144
BioShield Exterior Stains 191
BioShield Exterior Transparent Finishes. 191
BioShield Interior Paint 193
BioShield Interior Stains 196
BioShield Interior Transparent Finishes. 197
Bismart Distributors, Inc. 230

Bitterroot Restoration, Inc. 7
BJM Industries, Inc. 24, 28
Black's Farmwood 60, 79, 150
Blazestone 179
Bonded, Insul Therm, and Tasco 113
Bonded Insulation Co., Inc. 113
Bonded Logic, Inc. 117, 129, 216
Bord na Mona Environmental Products
     U.S., Inc. 230
Boss Aire Inc. 213
Bostik Findley 158
BP Solar 266
Branch River Foam Plastics, Inc...... 66, 120
Brand Digital Power Meter 289
Brand Electronics 289
Brick Nuggets 2
Bricor Analytical, Inc. 223
Bricor Showerheads 223
Brighten Up and SolaMaster Tubular
     Skylights 103
Broan-NuTone LLC 209, 213
Broda Coatings Ltd. 192
Broda Pro-Tek-Tor 192
Bryant Heating & Cooling Systems 204,
     210, 211
BSH Axxis Clothes Washers and Dryer ... 248
BSH Home Appliances Corp. 248
BTW Industries 9, 21, 27
Buderus 206, 216, 222
Building For Health Materials Center 276
Building Logics, Inc. 86
Building Materials Resource Center 281
Building Products Company 229
Bulletin Board 258
Burnham Corporation 206
Busch Systems International Inc. 290
ButtHanger and EZ-Backer 170
BWC Excel Wind Turbines 272
Cabinet King, Inc. 166
Cadet Pressure-Assist Toilets 231
Caldwell Building Wreckers 60, 281
California Bamboo Flooring Co. 135
Can-Cell Industries, Inc. 114
Capitol Ornamental Concrete
     Specialties, Inc. 12
Caraustar Concrete Column Forms 39
Caraustar ICPG Corp. 39
Cardinal IG 102
Carefree Xteriors Composite 31
Carefree Xteriors HDPE 27
Carefree Xteriors Structural Pilings 36
Carlisle Restoration Lumber 150, 176
Caroma USA, Inc. 233
Carousel Carpet Mills 157
Carpet Padding 138
Carrier Corp. 204, 210
Car Stops 9
Car Stops and Speed Bumps 9
Cascades Re-Plast, Inc. 20, 28
Cascadia Forest Goods, LLC... 26, 46, 140, 163

GREEN BUILDING PRODUCTS

Cast-Iron Soil Pipe 228
Catalina Lighting 242
CavClear EPS Insulation System 118
CavClear Masonry Mat 78
CavClear Weep Vents 78
CDS Cast Stone Panels 81
CDS Manufacturing, Inc. 81
Cecco Trading, Inc. 26, 46
Cedar Breather 89
Cedar Grove Compost 3
Cedar Grove Composting, Inc. 3
Celestial Construction, Inc. 52
Cell-Pak, Inc. 113
Cell-Pak Advantage 113
Cellofoam and Fan-Fold 118
Cellofoam North America, Inc. 118, 127
Cellulose Insulation 113
Cemplank, Inc. 77
Cemplank and Cempanel 77
Cempo Form 52
Cempo Forms, Inc. 52
Center for ReSource Conservation 282
Central Fiber Corp. 114
Central Maui Landfill / Maui Eko-Systems . 3
Centre Mills Antique Floors 60, 79,
    150, 174, 282
Century Products 16
CertainTeed Building Insulation 123
CertainTeed Corporation 77, 123,
    124, 130, 208
Certified Butcher Block Countertops 165
Certified Cherry Flooring 140
Certified Decking 26
Certified Engineered Wood 49
Certified Flooring Distributor 274
Certified Hardwood and Softwood
    Lumber 45
Certified Hardwood and Softwood
    Lumber and Timbers 46
Certified Hardwood Flooring 140
Certified Hardwood Furniture 256
Certified Hardwood Lumber 46, 274
Certified Hardwood Lumber and Timbers 46
Certified Ipe Outdoor Furniture 21
Certified Iron Woods Decking 26
Certified Iron Woods Lumber 46
Certified Lumber 46
Certified Lumber and Timbers 47
Certified Millwork 47, 163
Certified Outdoor Furniture 21
Certified Parquet Flooring 140
Certified Particleboard 167
Certified Pine Plywood 73
Certified PR Shingles 93
Certified Redwood Lumber 47
Certified Spruce-Pine-Fir (SFP) Lumber ... 47
Certified Stair Parts 164
Certified Stave Core Doors 97
Certified Teak Outdoor Furniture 21
Certified Tropical Hardwood 47

Certified Tropical Hardwood Decking 26
Certified Veneer-Faced Trim 168
Certified Wainscot 164
Certified Wood Distributor 274
Certified Wood Doors 97
Certified Wood Flooring 140
Certified Wood Furniture 257
Certified Wood Furniture and Futons 258
Certified Wood Moldings 164
Certified Wood Products 47
Certified Wood Windows 108
CETCO 91
CETCO - Building Materials Group 35
CFL Fixtures 242
CFL Recessed Downlights 242
CFL Torchieres 242
CF 128 185
Champion Flapperless Toilet 231
Champion Insulation, Inc. 117
Charlotte Pipe & Foundry Co. 229
Chem-Safe Products Company 193
Chemical Specialties, Inc. 58
Chestnut Specialists, Inc. 59, 79, 151
Chicago Adhesive Products Co. 145
Children's Playstructures, Inc. 18
Chilipepper Systems 225
ChoiceDek 31
Chronomite Laboratories, Inc. 225
Cimarron Comfort Height 1.4 GPF
    Toilet 232
CitiLog™ 63, 148, 173, 260
Classic American Heart Pine Millwork ... 173
Classic Products, Inc. 88
Claylite and ClayMax 84
Clayville Insulation 114
Clay Mine Adobe, Inc. 44, 199
Clay Plaster 199
Clay Roofing Tiles 84
Clean and Xcell 114
ClimateMaster 211
Climate Pro Blowing Wool 123
Climatizer Hydroseeding Mulch 4
Climatizer Insulation, Ltd. 4, 114
Climatizer Plus and Enviro-Batt 114
Clivus Multrum, Inc. 220, 226
Clivus Multrum Composting Toilets 220
CO-Experts, Division of G. E. Kerr
    Companies, Inc. 288
Coast Products, Inc. 209
Cobra Ridge Vents 90
Cocoon Loose-Fill and Cocoon2
    Stabilized Insulation 114
Cohalan Company, Inc. 190
Cold Climate Heat Pump 211
Colin Campbell & Sons, Ltd. 157
CollinsWood Certified Wood Products 47
Collins Companies 26, 47, 163
Collins Products, LLC 76, 167
Colonial Craft 164
Comfort-Zone 114

ComfortTherm 123
Comfort E2, Comfort Ti, and Solar Glass 102
Comfort Line 101
Commercial and Residential Carpet 156
Compact Fluorescent Lamps 240
Concrete Porous Pavers 12
Conklin's Authentic Antique Barnwood ... 59,
    151
Conklin Office Furniture 260
Conserv 252
Conservancy Series - Benches, Picnic
    Tables, and Recycling Receptacles 21
Conspec® 38
Construction Film 130
Continental Turf Systems, Inc. 14
Continuum 2424W and REU 2532FFU 222
Contours Steel Doors 96
Contour Products, Inc. -
    Kansas City Division 120
Contour Products, Inc. -
    Newton Division 66, 120
Contractor Products International, Ltd. ... 112
Controlled Energy Corp. 223
Convenience Products 185
Coon Manufacturing, Inc. 172
CopperSun 269
Cork Floating Floor and Parquet Tile 143
Cork Furniture 258
Cork Underlayment 145
Cork Wall Covering 165
Coronado Paint Company 192
Cosella Dörken Products Inc. 36
Cotswold Furniture Makers 257
Cotton Mattresses and E-Foam Futons .. 256
Cotton Plus 259
Cotton Plus, Inc. 259
Counter Production 166
Coyuchi, Inc. 256
Coyuchi Organic Cotton Bed Linens 256
Cozy Curtains 107
CO Detector 287
CP and DWP Root Barrier Panels 16
Craftmark Reclaimed Wood, Inc. 60, 151,
    174, 274
Creative Energy Technologies 278
Creative Office Systems, Inc. (COS) 259
Cresset Chemical Company 38
Crete-Lease 20-VOC 38
Crossroads Recycled Lumber 60, 151, 176
Crossville Porcelain Stone 139
Crowe Building Products Ltd. 88
Crown City Mattress by Vivetique 256
CSSI 155, 156
Cunningham Bricks 76
Cunningham Brick Co., Inc. 2, 76
Curbside or Work-Area Recycling Bins ... 290
Curecrete Distribution, Inc. 188
Cure and Seal 34
CushionWalk Pavers 155
Custom Tile Roofing, Inc. 85

D-5 Premium and D-40 Duraflex
Thin-Set Mortar....................... 158
D. Litchfield & Co. Ltd. 60
Danby Designer Dishwashers 251
Danby Products Inc. 251
Davies Office Refurbishing, Inc............ 260
Davis Colors 142
Daylighting Technologies, Inc. 104
DC1 Drywall Clip 170
DEA Bathroom Machineries 232
Debris Series Ceramic Tile 139
Debris Series Paver Tile 147
Decorative Metalwork 96
Decora Wall Switch Occupancy Sensors .. 236
Deepa Textiles 262
DeepRoot Partners, LP 15
Degussa Building Systems / MBT
Protection and Repair 35
Degussa Building Systems / Radiance... 195
Delta-MS 36
Demand Water Heaters 222
Demilec USA, Inc. 126
Designer Series SmartSash 109
DesignWall, NovaCork, and Burlap Panels 172
Design Materials, Inc. 156, 179
Devoe Paint: Wonder Pure................. 193
Devoe Paint 196
Dharma Living Machines.................... 226
Diamond 90 and Diamond 95 ULTRA 210
Diamond Bond Cushion 138
Diamond Pier....................................40
Dimming Electronic Ballasts................ 246
Dinoflex Manufacturing, Ltd............... 155
Direct to Metal Coating 189
DiversiFoam Products................. 123, 127
DLW Linoleum 146
Dock and Piling Cap 37
Dodge-Regupol, Inc................... 143, 259
Dodge Cork 259
Dodge Cork Tile 143
Door-Tite, Inc..................................96
Door-Tite Strike Plate 96
Doty & Sons Concrete Products, Inc. 20
Dow AgroSciences, LLC...................... 289
Dow BioProducts..................... 146, 161
Dow Chemical Co., Styrofoam Brand
Products 128
Draincore² 12
Drainstone and Turfstone 12
Drapery Rods................................ 108
Drew Foam, Inc. 118
Dry Pac Wall System 115
Duct Mastics 207
Duct Sealants 207
Duluth Timber Co. 62, 80, 151, 174
DuMor, Inc. 23
Duogard II 38
DuPont Commercial Flooring 138
Dura-Shelf, Dunnage Rack,
Benchmaster, and Modular-Kart 262

Durable Slate Co. 91
DuraBord Plastic Lumber 27
DuraBuild 56
Durapalm Palm Flooring 148
DuraWeave 181
Durisol Building Systems Inc................52
Durisol Wallforms 52
DUROVENT and proVent 127
Duxton Windows & Doors 101
Dwight Lewis Lumber / Lewis Lumber
Products 46, 140, 163
DynoSeal Waterproofing Sealer 36
E-Coat Recycled Latex Paint............... 200
E-Crete 45
E.Z. Oriental, Inc. 136
EagleOne Golf Products 20
Early New England Restorations 151
Earthcare Series 22
Earthshade................................... 107
Earthshade Natural Fiber Window
Treatments 107
Earthstar Energy Systems, Inc. 221
Earthstone International 170, 182
EarthTech 193
EarthTech Paints and Finishes 193
Earth Weave Carpet Mills, Inc...... 138, 156
Easiboard/Easiwall Panels 180
Easy Dock 19
Echeguren Slate 92
Eclipse Mariner II Pressure-Assist
Toilets 232
Eclipse Plastic, Inc. 41
ECO+Plus 261
ECO-Block, LLC 53
ECO-Block ICFs 53
Eco-Cycle and Eco-Cycle Stone 139
Eco-Furniture 258
Eco-House, Inc. 190
Eco-House Mineral Silicate Paint 190
Eco-Products 276
Eco-Roof Systems 86
Eco-shake 88
Eco-Tile 139
Eco-wise Building Supplies 277
Ecoboard Landscape Timbers.................. 5
Ecoboard Marine Pilings 37
Ecoboard Plastic Lumber 27
EcoGrid Porous Pavers 12
Ecolights Northwest 245
Ecologic, Inc. 22, 261
Ecological Engineering Associates........ 230
Ecological Engineering Group, Inc. 226
Ecological Interior/Exterior Paint 190
EcoLog Homes 50
ECONAR Energy Systems Corp. 211
EcoPower Sensor-Activated Faucet 224
Ecosmart Clothes Washers.................. 248
EcoSoft Carpet Cushion 138
EcoStar 89, 157
Ecotech 220

EcoTimber............................... 274
Eco Design/BioShield Paint Company ... 144,
191, 193, 196, 197
Eco Outdoor Series 22
Eco Panels 171
ECR International, Inc. 207, 210, 223
Edensaw Woods 274
Edison Coatings, Inc. 190
Eggers Industries 97
EI Products 246
Electrolux Home Products 249, 251
Electronic Ballasts.......................... 246
Electronic Educational Devices, Inc. 290
Electron Connection 278
Elite Series Air Conditioners 204
Elite Series Heat Pumps 211
Eljen Corporation 230
Emack Slate Company, Inc. 92
Emaco T415 and Emaco T430 35
EMCO Building Products Corporation 73
Endurance II 138
Endura Wood Products, Ltd. ...60, 140, 154,
165, 177, 274
Enercept, Inc. 64
Enercept Super Insulated Building
System 64
Energy-Conserving Products 275
Energy-Efficient Lighting................... 275
EnergySaver 216
Energy Brace and Thermo Ply 73
Energy Control 115
Energy Control, Inc. 115
Energy Federation Incorporated 275
Energy Kinetics 207
Energy Outfitters, Ltd. 279
Energy Recovery Ventilator 213
Energy Sentry Solutions 112
Energy Technology Laboratories........... 224
EnerMax Radiant Barrier Sheathing 73
Engineered Plastic Systems...6, 22, 28, 171
Ensystex, Inc................................ 288
Enviro-Pro, Sound Wall, and Spray-On ... 115
Enviro-Safe Paint 193
Enviroform and Aquastrip 38
EnviroKote Interior Low Odor Paint 193
Envirolet 220
Environmentally Safe Products, Inc. 129
Environmental Building Products, Inc.....29
Environmental Building Supplies 277
Environmental Construction Outfitters
of NY 277
Environmental Home Center......... 197, 277
Environmental Light Recyclers, Inc. 245
Environmental Recycling, Inc.............. 29
Environmental Research Corps............... 2
EnvironOxide Pigments 142
Environ Biocomposite, Dakota Burl,
and Biofiber Wheat 172
Envirosafe Manufacturing Corporation ...34,
188

Enviroshake 88
Envirosink 230
Envirotec Floor Covering Adhesives 144
EnVision 181
EPS and Polyurethane SIPs 64
EPS Foam............................ 118
EPS Foam Insulation Components 119
EPS Plastic Landscape Timbers 6
EPS Plastic Lumber..................... 28
EPS Plastic Plywood 171
EP Henry Corporation.................. 13
EP Henry ECO Pavers 13
Equaris Biomatter Resequencing
    Converter 220
Equaris Corporation 220
Equator Combination Washer-Dryers 248
Equator Corporation 248, 251, 252
Equator Dishwashers 251
Erie Energy Products, Inc.......... 4, 116
Ernst Conservation Seeds................ 7
Erosion Control Blankets 2
Erosion Control Products 2
ETL Low-Flow Showerheads 224
Eurolux Waterborne Acrylics 193
Euroslate 89
Eurotech Clothes Washers 248
Eurotech Dishwashers 251
Evacuated Tube Solar Collectors 269
Evergreen Solar, Inc. 267
EverKote 300........................ 190
ExcelAerator........................ 220
Executive Door Company 98
Expanko Cork Co. 143
Expanko Cork Tiles 143
Exterra 288
Extreme Panels/Insulspan™ 67
EZ-Shim 63
F&S Manufacturing, Inc............... 39
F-2, FSKF, and Type 4, 5, & 6 128
F. R. Series Fans.................... 208
Fab-Form Industries Ltd.............. 39
Fafco, Inc......................... 270
Falcon Products, Inc................ 23
Fan-Attic 208
Fantech 208, 214
Fastfoot, Fastbag, and Fast-Tube
    Fabric Forms..................... 39
Faswall Wallforms.................. 53
FCX Oil-Fired Condensing Boiler 205
Feeny Recycling Center with Lids
    and Rotary Recycling Center 290
Fencing 18
FHP Manufacturing 212, 221
Fiber-Cement Siding 77
Fiber-lite, Pk Class 1, Wal-Mat, SATAC,
    and In-Cide PC 115
Fiberboard - Regular and High Density ...73
Fiberglass Insulation 123
Fiberiffic 2000 125
Fiberlock Technologies, Inc............ 286

Fiberock Aqua-Tough Underlayment...... 145
Fiberock Gypsum Fiber Panels............ 169
Fibertec Window & Door Mfg. Ltd........ 101
Fiber Mulch 4
Fiber Turf 4
Fibre-Wool Cellulose 115
Fibrex 4
Filtering Roofwasher................ 227
Fine Paints of Europe 193
Fireball 20-01 269
Fireclay Tile 139, 147
FireFree Plus PMFC 85
Fireplace DraftStopper 112
FireSpaces, Inc. 215
Firestone Building Products Company 93
Fire & Water Lighting/David Bergman
    Architect 243
First Solar, LLC 267
FischerSIPs, Inc..................... 67
Fisher & Paykel 248, 251
Fisher & Paykel Dishwashers 251
Fiskars, Inc. - Fiskars Garden Tools......... 2
Fiskars Soaker Hose and Sprinkler Hose ... 2
Flash T-K2, T-KD20, and T-KJr. 222
Flat-Fast, Inc. 170
Flexi-Wall Systems.................. 180
Flexible Packaging Company 121
Flexstake, Inc....................... 9
FlexStake Highway Safety Products 9
Floating Cistern Filter 227
Flooring from Urban Trees 148
Flooring from Urban Trees 148
Florida Playground and Steel Co. 21
FloTrue International Corp............ 227
Fluorescent and HID Lamp Recycling 244
Fluorescent Lamp and Ballast Recycling 245
Fluorescent Light Fixtures.............. 242
Foam-Tech, Division of Building
    Envelope Solutions, Inc............ 126
Foam Laminates of Vermont............. 67
Foot-Operated Sink Valve 224
Foot-Pedal Faucet Controls 224
Foot- and Knee-Operated Faucet
    Controls 224
Forbo Linoleum, Inc. 147, 258
Forefront Designs................... 166
Forest Stewardship Council 290
Forest Stewardship Council - US 290
Forest World Group 21, 26
ForeverDock 19
Formaldehyde-Free Insulation Batts 124
FORMSHIELD WB 38
Fountains and Bird Feeders............ 22
Foxfibre Colorganic Fabric............ 259
Frankie Goes Fluorescent, Parallel Universe,
    Lulu, Flipster and Fibonacci Series...... 243
Franklin International................ 186
Franmar Chemical, Inc. 37, 198, 199
Frazee Paint 193
Fred Davis Corp.................... 275

Fresh 80 and Reton 80 Passive Air
    Inlets 205
Frigidaire, Gibson, and White-Westinghouse
    H-Axis Clothes Washers 249
Frigidaire and Gibson Dishwashers 251
FSC-Certified TruWood Siding 76
FSC-Certified Wood Paneling 164
FSC Pau Lope........................ 27
Fuel Cells........................ 236
Fuel Cell Components & Integrators,
    Inc. 221
Fuhr International LLC ..189, 191, 196, 198
Full-Cutoff Luminaires............... 243
Full Circle Recyclers 245
Furnature......................... 256
Furniture and Kitchen Cabinetry from
    Urban Trees 260
Furniture from Urban Trees 261
Fusiotherm Piping 223
Futon Man 256, 258
G-P Gypsum Board.................. 169
G-P Gypsum Corporation............. 169
G115 Sealed-Combustion Oil Boilers.... 206,
    217
GAF Materials Corp. 77, 90
GAF Siding 77
Gaiam Real Goods 275, 279
Gardco Lighting 243
Gavin Historical Bricks 13, 76, 137
GCP 1000 192
GEM, Inc.......................... 89
Gempak........................... 130
General Panel Corporation 67
Genesis Coatings, Inc. 192
Geocel Corporation.............. 185, 186
Gerber Plumbing Fixtures LLC............ 233
GE Appliances................ 249, 251, 252
GE Clothes Washers 249
GE Dishwashers................... 251
GE Lighting 240
GE Refrigerators 252
GFX Wastewater Heat Reclaimer......... 221
Gibraltar Company................. 209
Gilkey Window Company, Inc........... 106
Gladding, McBean & Co.........84, 229
Global Encasement, Inc............. 286
Globus Cork....................... 143
Globus Cork Flooring............... 143
GNR Technologies, Inc. 10
Gobi Solar Collectors and Helio-Pak
    Solar Water Heater 269
Gold Bond Gypsum Wallboard 169
Gold Label Premium Enviro Paints........ 193
Goodwin Heart Pine Company 80, 154,
    177, 178
Good Earth Lighting 242
Good News - Reused 115
Good News - Reused, House Blanket,
    Weather Blanket, and Comfort Control 115
Good Shepherd Wool Insulation.......... 128

Gorell Enterprises, Inc. 106
Gossamer Wind Ceiling Fans 208
Granulated Rubber 13
Graywater Heat Reclaimer 221
Greenblock 53
Greenblock Worldwide Corp. 53
GreenCore Plyform 39
Greenheart Durawoods, Inc. 27
Greenland Corporation 38
Greenline 166
Greenlite Lighting Corporation USA 240
Greenplus Form Release Agent ES 38
greenscreen 18
greenscreen Trellising System 18
GreenWood Bamboo Flooring 136
GreenWood Products Company 136
Green Building Materials 276
Green Building Resource Guide 280
Green Building Supply 277
Green Leaf Series 166
Green Mountain Woodworks 151, 158
Green River Lumber 140
Green Roof Plants 86
Green Roof Plants - Emory Knoll Farms 86
Greywater Treatment Systems 226
Ground-Source Heat Pumps 211
Guardian Indoor Air Quality Systems 213
GUVA Air Command 95 IIQ 210
Haliburton Forest: EcoLog Concepts 50
Hamilton Manufacturing, Inc. 116
Hanlite Bamboo Flooring 136
Hanlite Enterprises Corp. 136
Hanover Architectural Products 12
Hardcast, Inc. 207
Hardiplank, Hardipanel, and Hardie Shingleside 77
Hardwood Artisans 258
Harmony Coating System 194
Harwood Products 26, 47
Havillah Shake Company 63, 151
Hayward Corporation 69, 277
Hayward Truss 69
HCG North America 232
HealthySeal 125
HealthySeal Spray-in-Place Foam Insulation 125
Healthy Milk Paint 194
Heartland EPS, Inc. - Headquarters 66, 121
Heartland EPS, Inc. - Illinois Division 121
Heartland EPS, Inc. - Iowa Division 121
Heartwood Industries 62, 152
Heart Pine Lumber and Millworks 149
Heat Mirror Glass 102
Heat Recovery Ventilators 213
Heat Smart 109
Heliocol Solar Pool Heating 270
Heliodyne, Inc. 269
Heliotrope PV 266
Henry GreenLine Flooring Adhesives 145
High-Performance Fiberglass Windows 100

High-Performance Non-PVC Thermoplastic Windows 100
High-Performance Vinyl Replacement Windows 105
High-Performance Wood Windows 109
Hilltop Slate Inc. 92
Hill Country Rain Systems 227
Hilti, Inc. 185
Hoboken Floors 274
Holloway Welding & Piping Co. 228
Homasote 440 SoundBarrier and ComfortBase 146
Homasote Company 37, 72, 146, 172
Homex 300 37
Home Slicker 79
Honeywell Home & Building Controls 213, 214
Hoover Color Corporation 142
Hopper Handcrafted Specialty Finishes 199
Horse- and Biodiesel-Harvested Hardwood and Softwood Lumber 48
Howard Industries, Inc. 246
HRP - Heat Recovery Option 221
HTR-Group 245
Hubbell Building Automation, Inc. 237
Huebert Brothers Products, LLC 73
Humane Manufacturing LLC 90
Hunter Douglas Window Covering 107
Hunter Fan Co. 214
Hunter Set & $ave 214
HUVCO, Proactive Energy Solutions 103
HUVCO Skylights 103
HybriVet Systems, Inc. 286
Hydro-Spray 4
Hydro-Spray Mulch 4
Hydronic Panel Radiators 216
IAQ Test Kit 288
IceStone, Inc. 165
IceStone Countertops 165
ICF Block System 53
ICF Group 263
ICF Industries, Inc. 53
ICI Paints 194
Icynene, Inc. 126
Icynene Insulation System 126
IdaTech, LLC 236
Ifö Cera Dual-Flush Toilets 232
Igloo Cellulose, Inc. 115
Igloo Cellulose Insulation 115
IKEA, North American Service Office 258
illbruck Sealant Systems, inc. 131, 186
Impact-Curb 9
Impact-Post 28
IMSI Block 48
In-Drain System 230
In-O-Vate Technologies 250
Indirect Fluorescent Fixtures 244
Indirect Water Heater Tanks 222
Industries Maibec, Inc. 93
Infiltec Radon Control Supply 276

Inline Fiberglass Ltd. 101
Inmetco 286
Inno-Therm Fiber Insulation 117
InnoTherm 117
Innovations in Wallcoverings, Inc. 181
Innovative Energy 128
Innovative Formulations Corporation 190
Innvironments Collection 181
Instant Foundation System 40
InStar Straw-Panel Acoustical Ceiling System 160
Institution Recycling Network 245, 281
Insul-Beam 49
Insul-Deck® 53
Insul-Deck ICFs for Floors, Roofs, and Walls 53
Insul-Tray 127
Insulated Building Systems, Inc. 67, 121
Insulated Concrete Forms 53
Insulating Coatings Corp. (ICC) 85
Insulation Solutions, Inc. 127
Insulfoam (Division of Premier Industries, Inc.) 55, 118
InsulSafe 4 124
Insulspan 65
Insulspan SIPs 65
IntegraSpec ICF 54
Integra Dynamics Inc. 225
Integrity Windows and Doors 101
Inteq Corp. 10, 11, 18, 20, 29, 87, 89
Interface Flooring Systems, Inc. 139
Interface FLOR with Ingeo PLA Fiber 139
Interior and Exterior Doors 97
International Black Jewel 135
International Cellulose Corporation 116
Intrinsic Perennial Gardens, Inc. 86
Inverters 266
Invisible Structures, Inc. 3, 12
Ion Exchange 7
Iowa Plastics, Inc. 172
Island Pond Woodworking, Inc. 257
Isolé Plug Load Control 236
Isolite, Thermalite, and Isopro 115
J. E. Higgins Lumber Company, Purchasing Division 275
J. Hoffman Lumber Co. 61, 80, 152, 175
J. L. Powell & Co., Inc. 149, 175, 178
J. M. Huber Wood Products 72
J. S. Benson Woodworking & Design, LLC 108
Jackel Enterprises 174
Jackson Industries LLC 135
Jacobs 31-20 Wind Turbine 272
Jager Building Systems 51
Jarwin Bamboo Flooring 136
Jeld-Wen, Inc. 96, 97
Jeld-Wen Windows & Doors, Willmar Collection 109
JH Lumber & Wood Products 48
Johnsonite 144, 184

Johns Manville Corporation.....90, 123, 124
Juno Lighting, Inc. 242
K&M Bamboo Products, Inc. 137
K-X Faswall Corp. 53
Kane Hardwood, A Collins Company...... 141
Karp Woodworks...................................... 258
Kay Park Recreation Corp. 9, 20
Keeva ICFs 54
Keeva International, Inc. 54
Keim Mineral Silicate Paint 190
Kelly-Moore Enviro-Cote 194
Kelly-Moore Paint Co. 194, 200
Kenmore Dishwashers 251
Kenmore H-Axis Clothes Washers 249
Kenmore Refrigerators 252
Kensington Windows, Inc. 106
Key Solutions Marketing 128
Kidde Safety... 288
KILL A WATT 289
Kim Lighting 243
King of Fans, Inc. 208
KitchenAid... 252
KitchenAid Refrigerator 252
Knape & Vogt Manufacturing Company ... 290
Kohler Co............................. 224, 232, 233
KoirMat and KoirLog 3
KorQinc 143, 147, 165, 258
Kurfees Fresh Air 194
Kyocera Solar, Inc. 267
K Shield Reflective Barrier 128
L.I.F.T. Foundation Systems 41
Lafarge North America (Chicago and
    Hamilton Slag) 41
LaFayette Home Nursery, Inc............... 7
Landscape Structures Inc...................... 19
Landscape Timbers 6
Land Ark Wood Finishes 197
Laser Vented Heaters 216
Lashway Lumber, Inc. 45
Lawn Edging, Lattice, and Privacy
    Fencing 5
Lawn Edging and Tree Rings.................. 5
LeadCheck 286
LeadLock and AsbestoSafe 286
Leahy-Wolf Company 37
LED and Solar- and Wind-Powered
    Full-Cutoff Luminaires 243
Lees Carpets, Division of Burlington
    Industries 156, 157
Legacy Antique Woods 61, 80, 152, 175
Leggett & Platt, Inc. -
    Fairmont Division 138
Leisure Deck 28
Lennox Industries, Inc. 204, 211
Les Produits Forestiers Becesco 163
Leviton Manufacturing Co. Ltd. 236
LG Appliances.......................... 249, 253
LG Combination Washer-Dryers 249
LG Refrigerators 253

Lifebreath Clean Air Furnace 213
Lifebreath Heat Recovery Ventilators.... 213
LifeMaster 2000............................. 194
LifeTime 58
LightHAWK-MT 237
Lighting, Ventilation, and
    Weatherization.................................... 275
Lights of America 240
Limelite.. 246
Link USA International, Inc. 240
Linosom Linoleum 146
Liquid Nails Brand Super Caulk and
    Painter's Caulk 184
Litchfield Industries 10, 22
Lite-Form and Fold-Form 54
Lite-Form International.......................... 54
Livingreen, Inc. 277
Living Machine Systems 226
Local Color Recycled Latex Paint.......... 200
LodeStone Companies 76
LodeStone Fly-Ash Based Veneer Block ...76
Loewen Windows.................................... 109
Longleaf Lumber 61, 80, 152, 175
Louisiana Pacific Corp. - WeatherBest
    Premium Decking................................ 32
Low-E Insulation 129
LowFlow 3
Low Energy Systems 222
Low Energy Systems Supply Co., Inc..... 237
Low Level CO "Health" Monitor.......... 288
Low Toxicity Furniture 258
Lo E2 102
LP 72
LP SmartSide 77
LP SmartSide Siding and Exterior Trim
    Products 77
Ludlow Coated Products 73
Ludowici Roof Tile, Inc. 84
Lumatech Corporation.......................... 240
Lutron Electronics Co., Inc. 246
M-D Building Products 130
Maaco Adhesives.................................... 184
Maine Woods Company, ...46, 140
Majestic Slate Tiles 89
Mansers Office Interiors 259
Many Happy Returns and Please Be
    Seated 262
Marine Lumber.. 28
Marmoleum and Artoleum.................... 147
Marshfield DoorSystems™ 97
Marvin Windows and Doors 109
Masonry Fireplaces 215
Mason City Recycling 114
Master Mark Div., Avon Plastics, Inc... 5, 32
Materials Exchange................................ 280
Materiaux Blanchet, Inc. 47
MaxiPlank and MaxiPanel...................... 78
MaxiTile, Inc. 78
MaxLite SK America, Inc...................... 240
Maxwell Pacific............................61, 152

Mayse Woodworking Co. 149, 173, 178
Maytag Appliances 249, 253
Maytag Neptune Washers.................... 249
Maytag Refrigerators 253
Maze Nails 51
MCA Clay Tile 84
McDowell Lumber Company, Inc.....46, 141, 164
McGill Airseal Corporation 208
Meadoboard Straw Panels 172
Meadowood Industries, Inc. 172
Medex and Medite II................................ 167
Medite MDF Molding 168
Med Imports 199
MemBrain Smart Vapor Retarder 130
Menominee Tribal Enterprises.........47, 163
Met-Tile 87
Metacrylics 85
Metafloor 156
MetalCoat Acrylic Metal Primer 189
MetalWorks Steel Shingles.................... 87
MetaMorf Design, Inc. 262
MetaMorf Furniture................................ 262
Metlund Hot Water D'MAND System 224
Michael Evenson Natural Resources 61
Microphor 232, 290
Midwest Hardwood Corporation 47
Midwest Trading - Horticultural
    Supplies, Inc. 91
Miele, Inc. 249, 252
Miele Dishwashers.................................. 252
Miele H-Axis Clothes Washers 249
Milgard Manufacturing, Inc................. 101
Milk Paint 194
Millennium Lumber 28
Millennium Oak 261
Millwork from Urban Trees 173
Mineral Fiber and Glass Based Drop-in
    Ceiling Tile.. 160
Mineral Resource Technologies, LLC......... 34
Mintec Corporation 136, 162
Miraflex.. 124
Mission Clay Products 229
MiTek Industries....................................... 51
Mobius T-M1 and Flash T-K1S 222
Modern Insulation.................................. 115
Modern Outdoor...................................... 21
Modular Furniture 258
Mohawk Industries, Inc....................... 156
Moment.. 181
Mondo America Inc................................ 155
Mondo Commercial Flooring 155
Monitor Products, Inc. 205, 206, 217
Mono-Therm 116
Monoglass, Inc. 124
Monoglass Spray-On Insulation 124
MoonCell, Inc. 243
Morley Manufacturing 271
Mortar Net 78
Mortar Net USA, Ltd. 78

MOSO International NA, Ltd. 135, 162
Mountain Fiber Insulation 115
Mountain Lumber 61, 152, 175, 178
Mr.Solar.com 278
MRT / Atlanta Distribution Center 50
MRT Blended Hydraulic Cement............34
MRT E-Z Joint.................................50
Mt. Baker Plywood 163
Mule Creek Adobe............................44
Multi-Fuel and Wood Boilers 206
Multi-Pulse Boilers 206
MultiLayer and Solid-Plank Antique
    Wood Flooring 149
Murco LE-1000 and GF-1000 194
Murco M100 Joint Compound 170
Murco Wall Products 170, 194
MZ Boiler....................................... 206
NanoLux CFLs 241
National Clay Pipe Institute................. 229
National Fenestration Rating Council.... 100
National Fiber 4, 116
National Gypsum Company.................. 169
National Shelter Products, Inc. 173
Native American Seed 8
Native Plant Supplier 7
Native Seed and Plant Supplier.............. 7
Natural Cork, Inc. 143, 145, 165
Natural Cork Wall Tile 165
Natural Design Collection and Natural Tex-
    tures Collection............................ 156
Natural Fiber Bedding and
    Floorcoverings 278
Natural Fiber Bedding and Mattresses... 256
Natural Fiber Floor Coverings 157
Natural Home Products.com 278
Natural Paints 194
Natural Soy, LLC............. 34, 38, 201
Natural Wood Flooring, Inc. 149
Nature's Carpet 157
NatureStain.................................... 191
NatureStain Co. 191
NatureWood 58
Nedia Enterprises, Inc...................... 3
Neil Kelly Cabinets 166
Neil Kelly Naturals Collection 166
Newcastle Fabrics Corp..................... 182
New England Classic 162
New England Classic Raised Panel
    System 162
New England Solar Electric, Inc. 279
New Mexico Earth Adobes 44
New TJI Joists 49
Nexwood 31
Nexwood Industries, Ltd. 31
Ni-Cad Battery Recycling.................. 286
Niagara Conservation Corp. 225, 232
Niagara Flapperless Gravity-Flush
    Toilets 232
Nichiha Fiber-Cement Rainscreen Siding 78
Nichiha USA, Inc..............................78

Nicolock 13
Nighthawk CO Detector 288
Nisus Corporation.............................58
No-Flame Sisal Wallcovering 179
No-Nail and Stud Claw 170
No-VOC Paints 195
Northeast Lamp Recycling, Inc. 245
Northern Arizona Wind & Sun, Inc. 279
Northern Cross Industries 108
Northland Forest Products 275
Northwest Water Source 227
North American Insulation Manufacturers
    Association 124
North Shore Architectural Antiques 281
North West Rubber Mats, Ltd........... 15, 90
Norwesco, Inc. 228
Nova Cork 143
Nova Distinctive Floors 143, 146, 147
Nova Linoleum 147
Nova Underlayment 146
Nova Walkway Pads 157
No Mow 14
NU-BLEND Paints, Inc. 200
Nu-Wool Co., Inc. 5, 116
Nu-Wool Engineered Cellulose
    Insulation 116
Nu-Wool HydroGreen 5
Nutech Brands, Inc. 213
NuTone, Inc. 209
Nu Look Concrete & Masonry Cleaner.....34
Nyle Special Products, LLC 211
Occupancy Sensors and Controls 237
Oceanside Glasstile Co. 179
Oceanside Glass Tiles 179
ODL, Inc. 103
ODL Tubular Skylight 103
Odom Reusable Building Materials 282
Office Furniture 259
Oil Miser Space Heaters 217
Oil Miser Water Heaters 222
Oldcastle Architectural Products Group ... 12
Old Fashioned Milk Paint Co. 194
Old Pueblo Adobe Company 44
Omni Block 49
Omni Block, Inc. 49
Omni Products 225
Ondura 84
Onyx Special Services 245
Open-Web Trusses 51
OPTIMA 124
Opus G1 Gas Hydronic Heat Source....... 206
Opus 01 Oil-Fired Boiler 206
Orenco Systems, Inc. 230
Organic Cotton Bedding and Mattresses 256
Origins 171
OSI Sealants 184
OSI Sealants, Inc. 184
Osmose Wood Preserving, Inc..............58
OSMO Hardwax Oil 197
Osram Sylvania 241

Ottawa Fibre, Inc. 123
Owens Corning.......................... 124, 125
P3 International Corporation 289
Pacemaker Plastics Co., Inc. 53, 68
Pacific Allied Products, Ltd. 66, 121
Palmer Industries, Inc.................. 188, 191
Panasonic Consumer Electronics ... 209, 241
Panasonic Exhaust Fans 209
Panel Source International 161, 168
Par/PAC™53 Cove Side Rd. 115
Paramount Windows, Inc.................... 109
Park-It and Easy Rider 10
Parker International Ltd. / USA 188
Parking Stops 10
Parking Stops, Speed Bumps, and
    Bollards 10
Parking Stops and Bollards 10
Parking Stops and Speed Bumps 10
Parquet By Dian 140
Paul's Insulation 4, 113
Pecora Corporation 184
Pecora Sealants 184
Pedalworks and Footworks 225
Pedal Valves, Inc........................... 225
Pella Corporation 109
Penetrating Waterstop 188
Pentstar, Corp............................... 54
Pentstar Concrete Form Masonry Units....54
Perennial Park Outdoor Furniture 22
Perfect Window Fresh Air Ventilator 213
Perform and Perform Guard EPS 119
Perform Wall, LLC........................... 54
Perform Wall Panels 54
Perma-Deck 28
Perma-Deck Plastic Lumber 29
Perma-Turf Playground Safety Surface.... 14
Perma-Vent 127
PermaVent Attic Baffle 127
Perma "R" Products 118, 127
Phenix Biocomposites, LLC 172
Phenoseal................................... 184
Phenoseal and Sealant 184
Phil-Insul Corp............................. 54
Philips Lighting Company.......... 241, 244
Phoenix Composting Toilet 220
Phoenix Recycled-Plastic Landscape
    Timbers 6
Phoenix Recycled Plastics..........6, 19, 22,
    31, 171
Phoenix Recycled Plastic Panels 171
Phoenix Recycled Plastic Site
    Furnishings 22
Phoenix Recycled Products, Inc. 5, 16
Picnic Tables, Benches, Planters,
    and Waste Receptacles 22
Picnic Tables and Benches 22
Pierce Enterprises, Inc. 180
Pilkington Energy Advantage 102
Pilkington NA............................. 102
Pilot Rock Site Furnishings................23

PINK Fiberglas Building Insulation 125
Pinocchio's 59
Pin Foundations, Inc. 40, 41
Pioneer Millworks 62, 152, 175, 178
Pittsford Lumber and Woodshop 274
Plain Herringbone-Weave Cocoa Matting 147
Planetary Solutions 278
Planters.. 23
Plaster in a Roll and Faster Plaster
    Underliner 180
Plasti-Fab Ltd. 122
Plastic Cistern Liners 227
Plastic Fences 18
Plastic Lumber................................... 29
Plastic Panels 172
Plastic Pilings, Inc. 28
Plastic Recycling of Iowa Falls, Inc. .. 9, 22,
    30
PlastiSpan Insulation 122
Playfield Equipment............................ 18
Playground Equipment 19
PlayGuard 155
Plaza Hardwood, Inc. 141
Plus 90 High-Efficiency Furnaces 210
Plyboo America, Inc. 137
Plyboo Bamboo Flooring 136
Plyboo Bamboo Paneling, Plywood,
    and Veneer 162
Plymouth Foam Incorporated 119, 126
Plywood and Lumber Sales, Inc. 275
PL and DublBac Series Carpet Cushion .. 138
Poesis Design 262
Polar-Ply Radiant-Barrier..................... 73
Polaris Heating Systems 207
Polar 10 and Polar Guard Rigid EPS 122
Polar Industries 122
Poly-Foam, Inc. 66, 122
Poly-Wood 23
Poly-Wood Inc. 23
Polyguard Products, Inc. 3, 289
PolySteel Forms 54
Polywood, Inc. 23, 30
Polywood Plastic Lumber.................... 30
Polywood Site Furnishings.................. 23
Portable Traffic Delineators.................. 15
PORTERCorp 68
Posi-Strut... 51
Positive Energy 276
Power-Stop 11
PowerSand Sanding Blocks 182
PPG Architectural Finishes 195
Prairie Nursery, Inc......................... 8, 14
Prairie Restorations, Inc...................... 8
Premier Building Systems - Division of
    Premier Industries, Inc................. 49, 68
Premier ICFs..................................... 55
Premium Compost, Clay Buster, and
    Lawn Topdressing 3
Prep & Prime Interior Primer/Sealers ... 201
Pressure-Assist Low-Flush Toilets 232

Prest-on Company 170
Prest-on Corner Clips 170
Prestige Ultra Line 204
Prestowall...................................... 180
Presto Products Company 15
PrimeBoard 161
PrimeBoard, Inc. 161
Pristine Eco-Spec 195
Pro-Lab, Inc. 287
Profile Products, LLC............................ 4
ProgressivTube Passive Water
    Heating Systems 269
Progress Aluminum Roofing 87
Progress Paint Manufacturing Co., Inc. 194
Progress Plastic Roofing Shingles.......... 89
Promat - H 5
ProntoKorQ 143
Prontolino 147
Proven Engineering Products, Ltd. 272
Pro Tankless 635ES 223
Pulp Furniture 262
Puraflo 230
PUREKOR Composite Panels................. 161
Pure Performance 195
Pure Tung Oil 197
PurFil IG 185
PV Controllers 266
PV Modules 266
PV Systems 267, 278
Pyroblock Fire-Retardant Particleboard,
    MDF, and Plywood 168
QUAD-LOCK Building Systems Ltd........... 55
QUAD-LOCK ICFs................................ 55
Quad Lock Building Products................. 36
Quantum Plus 698b Heat Pump 211
Quantum Plus Air Conditioners 204
Quantum Series Boilers 207
Quarry Tile Company........................ 139
Quartzitec...................................... 158
QuartzStone 158
Quick Shield VOC-Free Sealant 185
Quiet Vent 209
QuikSand Sanding Blocks 170
R&R Services Solar Supply 270
R-Control ICF System 55
R-Control Panels 65
R-Control SIP Panels........................... 67
R-U Seal 112
R.A.C.E. 260
R. J. Thomas Manufacturing Co., Inc. 23
R. W. Rhine Inc. 61
Radcon Formula #7 188
Radco Products, Inc. 270
Radiance Paints 195
Radon Control Equipment 276
Rainhandler and Doorbrella 15
Rainwater Catchment Systems 227
Rainwater Collection Over Texas 227
Rain Man Waterworks 227
Rain Run 15

Randall Custom Lumber, Ltd.... 26, 47, 141,
    164
Rauhsaser...................................... 181
RayLite, BackerBoard, and StyroStud.... 123
RBF Interiors 260
RCD Corporation.............................. 207
Re-Bench 23
Re-Con Building Products, Inc. 85
Re-New Wood, Inc. 88
Re-Source Building Products 30
Re-Tech Wood Products 61, 152, 175
Rebar Supports 41
Recirculating Wastewater Garden 226
Reclaimed-Wood Flooring 154
Reclaimed-Wood Furniture 261
Reclaimed-Wood Millwork 177
Reclaimed-Wood Siding....................... 79
Reclaimed-Wood Stair Parts 177
Reclaimed-Wood Timbers..................... 63
Reclaimed and Urban-Harvested
    Millwork 174
Reclaimed Flooring........................... 149
Reclaimed Hand-Hewn Beams 59
Reclaimed Heart Pine Flooring 149
Reclaimed Lumber............................. 59
Reclaimed Lumber and Timbers 59
Reclaimed Lumber Trestlewood Division ... 62
Reclaimed Millwork 174
Reclaimed Paneling 176
Reclaimed Paneling and Trim 177
Reclaimed Roofs, Inc. 92
Reclaimed Timbers 62
Reclaimed Timbers and Millwork........... 62
Reclaimed Tropical Hardwood Flooring.. 149
Reclaimed Wood Flooring 150
Reclaimed Wood Products.................... 62
Reclaimed Wood Timbers..................... 63
Recy-CAL Supply Co. 290
Recycled-Content Wood Doors.............. 98
Recycled-Glass "Terrazzo" Tile 158
Recycled-Glass Tiles 179
Recycled-Paper Countertops............... 165
Recycled-Paper Tabletops................... 262
Recycled-Rubber Roofing Underlayment ..91
Recycled/Remanufactured Office
    Furniture 259
Recycled Metal Shingles......................87
Recycled Paint 200
Recycled Paper Formworks/Brick Ledger
    Void Forms 40
Recycled Plastics, Inc. 171
Recycled Plastics Marketing, Inc...... 20, 27
Recycled Plastic Lumber...................... 30
Recycled Plastic Man, Inc. 10, 30, 37
Recycled Plastic Site Amenities 23
Recycled Technology, Inc. 11
RecycleTech Products 19
Recycle Design Site Furnishings 23
Recycling Equipment 290
Recycling Receptacles....................... 290

Reddi-Deck Floor and Roof-Deck ICFs 56
Reddi Form, Inc. 56
Redi-Therm Insulation, Inc. 114
Reeski, Inc. 24
Reflectix 129
Reflectix, Inc. 129
Refurbished and Remanufactured
    Office Furniture 259
Refurbished Office Furniture 260
Regal Industries, Inc. 116
Regal Wall Net and Insulweb 116
Rejuvenation................................. 282
Rejuve Seattle 282
Reliance Carpet Cushion Division 138
Remanufactured Office Furniture......... 260
Renaissance Roofing, Inc. 92
Renewable Energy Equipment............. 278
Renewable Energy Systems 267
RenewAire 213
RenewAire ERVs 213
Renewal by Andersen Windows 107
Renovators ReSource 282
Republic Paints.............................. 195
Residential Steel Framing Systems 48
Resincore-I Particleboard 167
Resin Technology Division of Henry Co. 126
Resource Conservation Technology,
    Inc. 130, 185
Resource Revival, Inc. 96, 261
Resource Woodworks, Inc. 62, 153, 177
Restrictor Speed Humps 11
Reuse Development Organization......... 282
Reward Wall Systems 56
Reward Wall Systems, Inc. 56
ReWater System 226
ReWater Systems, Inc. 226
Rheem Manufacturing Company 223
Rheem Tankless Gas Water Heaters 223
Rhino Deck 32
Rinnai 216, 222
Rio Abajo Adobe 44
Rising Star...Stellar Home Furnishings .. 256
River-Reclaimed Wood Flooring 154
River-Reclaimed Wood Millwork 177
River-Reclaimed Wood Siding 80
River-Reclaimed Wood Stair Parts 178
Rodda Low-VOC Exterior Paint 190
Rodda Paint 190, 195
Rodda Zero-VOC Interior Paint........... 195
Rodman Industries 167
RoLanka International, Inc. 2
Rolath 90
ROMEX World Trade Company, LLC -
    sales agent for ROM 39, 46, 73
Roof-Guard Pads 90
Roofmeadow 86
Roofscapes, Inc. 86
Rooftop Planting Media......................91
Roof Walkway Pads and Paving Risers 90
Roof Windows And Skylights 105

Roof Windows and Skylights with
    Heat Mirror 105
Roos International Ltd. Inc................. 181
Roto Frank of AmericaResearch Park..... 105
RTC Polyurethane Insulation 126
Rub-R-Wall Foundation Waterproofing.....36
RubberStuff 14
Rubber Granulators, Inc. 13
Rubber Polymer Corp. 36
Rug-Hold - Division of Leggett and
    Platt, Inc. 138
Rug-Hold 100% Natural..................... 138
Rumber Lumber 30
Rumber Materials Inc. 30
Runtal North America 216
Rustic Shingle 88
RWE Schott Solar, Inc. 267, 279
S&L Designs 108
S&S Seeds, Inc. 8
S. J. Morse Company 168
S365, S366, S367 Wall Bracing..............69
Safe-Set Adhesives.......................... 145
Safecoat 3 in 1 Adhesive................... 158
Safecoat Enamels............................ 195
Safecoat Exterior Satin Enamel........... 190
Safecoat Safe Seal and Carpet Seal 200
Safecoat Zero-VOC Flat, Eggshell, and
    Semi-gloss 196
SAFE Block 56
SAFE Encasement Systems 287
Safe Solutions, LLC.............. 59, 80, 153
Safe Water Systems 234
Sailshade/Cloth Construction 107
Salvaged-Brick Flooring.................... 137
Salvaged and Sustainably Harvested
    Wood Finder 281
Salvaged Architectural Antiques 281
Salvaged Brick and Cobblestone Pavers...13
Salvaged Building Brick 76
Salvaged Building Materials Exchange .. 280
Salvaged Clay and Concrete Tile Roofing....85
Salvaged Native Plants....................... 8
Salvaged Slate and Clay Tile Roofing 91
Salvaged Slate Roofing 92
Sancor Industries Ltd....................... 220
Sandhill Industries 179
Sandhill Plastics 172
Sandhill Plastics Sheeting 172
Sand Filter Wastewater Treatment 230
Sante Fe, Ultra-Aire, and Hi-E Dry
    Dehumidifiers 214
Savetime Corporation 15
SBT Designs 279
SCHÜCO Homecraft, LP..................... 106
Scientific Certification Systems........... 291
Scientific Developments, Inc. 11, 15
Sealants 185
Sealection 500 126
Sealed Air Corp. - Air Cellular
    Insulation 129

Sealed Air Corp. - Solar Pool Heating ... 270
Sealoflex, Inc. 85
Sealoflex Waterproofing System 85
SealTight Green Line........................ 35
Sears 249, 251, 252
SeaTimber.................................... 31
Seaward International, Inc. 31
Second Use Building Materials 282
SelecStops and SelecBumps 11
SelecTech, Inc. 7, 11, 23
SelecTimber 7
Selux Corporation........................... 244
Senco Sensors 287
Sensor Switch, Inc. 237
Sensor Switch Occupancy Sensors 237
Sentricon Termite Colony Elimination
    System 289
SF-RIMA 13
Sfera Dual-Flush Toilets 232
Shades & Blinds 107
Sharp Electronics Corp. - Solar Systems
    Division 267
Shaw Contract Group 138
Sheetrock Brand Gypsum Panels 169
Shell Solar 267
Shelter Enterprises, Inc. 68, 119
Shelter Supply, Inc. 276
SideKick Worklytes 246
SierraPine Ltd...........................167, 168
Silacote Mineral Silicate Paint............. 191
Silacote Textured Coating 189
Silacote USA LLC 189, 191
SILHOUETTE T5 Lamps 244
Silkroad Bamboo Flooring.................. 137
Simpson Drywall Stop (DS) 171
Simpson Strong-Tie Connectors.......69, 171
Sinan 160 Series Natural Stain 196
Sinan Co............. 144, 182, 189, 194, 196
Sisal Rugs Direct............................ 157
Site Furnishings.............................. 24
SI Geosolutions 2
Ski and Snowboard Furniture............... 24
Sky-Tech Industries, Inc. 104
Slate Roofing Shingles......................92
Slopetame^2 3
Smart-Valve Rainwater Diverter 227
SmartBlock 56
SmartWood 291
Smart Power Inverters 266
SMA America, Inc............................ 266
Smith & Fong Company 136, 148, 162
Smith and Hawken 21
Snyder Industries 228
Softpave 156
Solahart / Rheem USA, Inc. 269
Solahart Solar Water Heating Systems .. 269
SolarAttic, Inc. 214
SolarCool Attic Vent 209
Solargenix Energy, LLC 271
Solar Aquatics 230

Solar Bright Corporation.................. 103
Solar Bright Tubular Skylights 103
Solar Collectors 270
Solar Controllers 266
Solar Converters Inc. 266
Solar Energy Industries Association...... 268
Solar Pool-Heating Systems 270
Solar Systems 270
Solar Thermal Equipment.................. 270
Solar Turtle 268
Solar Turtle, Inc. 268
Solar Water Heating Systems............... 271
Solar Water Storage Tanks 271
Solar Works, Inc. 280
Solatube International, Inc. 103
Solitaire Ultra Silent 209
Sol Saver System and Family Sol Saver ... 234
Sonne Solar-Powered Outdoor Luminaire 244
Sonoco Products Co. 40
SONOTUBES 40
Sonrisa Furniture 260
Sound Builders Resource 283
Southern Diversified Products, LLC 192
Southwall Technologies.................... 102
SouthWest Management 48
Southwest Photovoltaic Systems, Inc. .. 280
Southwest Windpower....................... 271
South Cone Trading Company 257
Soy-Gel 199
SoySeal 201
SOYsolv® 38, 201
SOYsolv Concrete Form Release Agent..... 38
SOYsolv Soy Seal.......................... 201
Soy Form Release and Natural Form Oil... 38
SpaceJoist 51
Space Heaters 217
Spectra-tone Paint Company 193
Speed Bumps 11
Speed Grip 186
SPI Lighting Group........................ 244
Splendide 250
Splendide Clothes Washers................. 250
St. Astier Natural Hydraulic Lime Mortar...51
St. Astier Natural Hydraulic Lime
     Plasters 199
St. Thomas Creations 232
Staber Clothes Washers 250
Staber Industries, Inc. 250
Stanark Foam / R-CONTROL...... 56, 66, 122
Standard ICFs............................. 56
Standard Structures, Inc. 49
Stanek Vinyl Windows Corp. 106
Star Lighting Products 241
Stealth Series and Stellar Ultra Series... 204
Steelcase, Inc............................ 259
Steeltile Distributing, Inc. 208
Step-Flow, Inc. 224
Sterling Rockton Dual-Flush Toilet 233
Sterner Lighting Systems, Inc. 243
Stevens EP 93

Stevens Roofing Systems 93
Stonco Lighting 246
StoneyCrete 13
Stoney Creek Materials, LLC 13
Stratica 155
Street Smart Traffic Control Units........... 15
Structural Insulated Panels.................. 67
Structural Insulated Panel Association....64
Structural Plastics Corp. 262
Stud Claw USA 170
Styrofoam High Performance
     Underlayment 128
StyroVent.................................... 127
Sun-Dome Tubular Skylights.................. 104
Sun-Mar Composting Toilet 221
Sun-Mar Corp. 221
Sun-Tek Manufacturing....................... 104
Sun-Tek Tube................................. 104
SunEarth, Inc. 271
Sunlight Systems 234
Sunnyside Solar 280
Sunny Boy Inverters 266
SunOptics Skylights 103
Sunpark Electronic Corp. 241, 242
SunPipe Tubular Skylights 104
SunScope Tubular Skylights 104
Sunsiaray Solar Manufacturing, Inc. 268
Sunslates.................................... 268
SunTube Collector 271
SunUPS and SunLine........................... 268
Sun Brand Bamboo Flooring 137
Sun Frost 253
Sun Frost Refrigerators...................... 253
Sun Pipe Co., Inc. 104
Sun Systems, Inc. 269
Sun Tunnel Tubular Skylights 104
Sun Utility Network, Inc. 271
SuperFlexx Paver Tiles 156
Superglass Quad with Heat Mirror 102
SUPERGREEN FOAM 126
Superior Clay Corp........................... 229
Superior Radiant Insulation 73, 128
Superior Walls 57
Superior Walls of America, Ltd............... 57
Superior Wood Systems 49
SureVoid Products, Inc. 40
Sustainable Forest Systems LP........ 26, 47
Sutherland Welles, Ltd. 197
Sutherland Welles Low-Toxic Wood
     Finishes 197
SWII Headers 49
Sylvan Brandt................................ 153
Syndecrete................................... 166
Syndesis..................................... 166
Synthetic Fiber Carpet Cushion 138
System 2000 207
T&S Brass and Bronze Works, Inc. 224
T8600 Chronotherm IV Thermostats 214
Taco, Inc. 225
Taco Hot Water D'MAND System 225

Takagi Industrial Co. USA, Inc. 222
Tallant Industries, Inc.....................84
Tamarack Technologies, Inc. 209
Tamko Roofing Products, Inc. 87
Tamms Industries...........................38
Tandus Group / C&A Floorcoverings.......11
Tapeter Decorative Wall Solutions, LLC.. 181
Tapmaster................................. 225
Tarkett Commercial....................... 146
Tarm USA, Inc. 206
Tascon, Inc. 5, 115
Tasman Dual-Flush Toilet.................. 233
Taylor Creek Restoration Nurseries 8
Team Industries, Inc..................67, 122
Technical Consumer Products, Inc... 241, 242
Tech Block................................57
Tech Block International, LLC..............57
Tembec, Inc., Huntsville Division 141
Temp-Cast................................ 215
Temp-Cast Enviroheat Masonry
     Heater Kits 215
Temple-Inland Forest Products 169
Temple-Inland Gypsum..................... 169
TempShield Material 129
Teragren Bamboo Flooring, Flooring
     Accessories & Stair Parts 137
Teragren Bamboo Panels and Veneer..... 162
Teragren LLC 137, 162
Termi-Mesh System 289
Termi-Mesh USA 289
TerraMai 59, 149, 153, 175
Terramed 199
Terra Classic and Terra Traffic 179
Terra Green Ceramics..................... 179
Texas Contec, Inc. 45
Texturglas............................... 181
TF System Vertical ICFs 57
Therm-O-Comfort Co. 5, 117
Therma-Stor LLC 205, 209, 214
ThermaFiber Insulation Products 129
ThermaFiber LLC 129
Thermal-Pruf, Dendamix, and
     Sound-Pruf 130
Thermal Conversion Technology........... 269
Thermal Foams, Inc. 57, 68, 123
Thermal Foams/Syracuse, Inc. 122
Thermal Foams EPS........................ 123
Thermal Foams TF ICF 57
Thermal Foam SIPs........................ 68
Thermal Industries, Inc. 106
Thermal Line Windows, Inc. 100
Thermapan Structural Insulated Panels ...68
Therma Foam, Inc......................67, 122
Thermo-Cell Industries, Ltd.............. 117
Thermo-Cel and Cel-Pak.................. 116
Thermo-Kool of Alaska 4, 116
Thermo-Mulch 5
Thermo-Vu Sunlite® Industries, Inc...... 105
ThermoCon Manufacturing /
     Applegate Inc......................... 113

Thermoguard Co. 4, 115
Thermolok and Thermospray 116
Thermotech Windows, Ltd. 102
Thermo Dynamics Ltd. 270
Thermo Technologies 269
Therm Shield 116
The Battic Door Attic Stair Cover 112
The Bead & Batten Door 97
The Brass Knob and The Back Doors
    Warehouse 283
The Chilipepper Appliance 225
The Controllable Flush 233
The Dryerbox 250
The Efficient Windows Collaborative ... 100
The Energy Guardian 112
The Environmental Depot 200
The Footing Tube 40
The Forever Deck 31
The Fuller Group, Inc. 231
The G. R. Plume Co. 176
The Garden Watersaver 228
The Glidden Company 193, 201
The Hydrotherm Corp. 206
The Insulator 129
The IRN Surplus Network 281
The Joinery 257
The Logan Clay Products Co. 229
The Millennium Group, Inc. 171
The Nailer 171
The Plastic Lumber Co. 6, 10, 21, 28, 30
The Professional Radon Gas Test Kit ... 287
The Quiet Pipe 229
The Real Milk Paint Co. 196, 197
The Rebuilding Center of Our United
    Villages 283
The ReUse Center 283
The Reveg Edge/Ecoseeds 7
The Roof Tile and Slate Company 92
The Sherwin-Williams Company
    Stores Group 194
The South Seas Collection 182
The Venture Collection 263
The W. W. Henry Company 145
The Watt Stopper, Inc. 236, 237
The Woods Company, Inc. 153
Third-Party Certifier of Wood Products .. 291
Thompson Plastics Melita 227
Thor Appliance Company 250
Thor Combination Washer-Dryers 250
Tierrafino Clay Plaster 199
TileSearch, Inc. 92
Tim-Bor and Bora-Care 58
TimberStrand LSL Studs, Headers,
    and Rim Boards 50
Timeless Timber 63
Timeless Timber, Inc. 63
TIREC Corporation 14
Tire Turf 14
Titebond Solvent Free Construction
    Adhesive 186

Titon Inc. 205
Toc-Light 117
Todol Products 185
Tomorrow's Timber Bamboo Flooring 137
Torrens Sculpture Designs 22
Toto USA, Inc. 224
Touch'n Foam 185
ToughGard 208
Toyotomi U.S.A., Inc. 216, 217, 222
Traffic & Parking Control Co., Inc.
    (Tapco) 9
Traffic Calming Products 11
Traffic Cones and Safety Delineators ... 11
Trane Residential Products Division ... 204,
    212
TransMineral USA, Inc. 51, 199
Tree Rings 16
Tremco, Inc. 185
Tremflex 834 and Tremco Spectrem 1 ... 185
Trestlewood 63, 80, 153, 176
Trestlewood Timbers 63
Trex 32
Trex Company, Inc. 32
Tri-Chord Steel Systems 48
Tri-Chord Steel Systems, Inc. 48
Tri-State Insulation Co. 115
Tri-Steel Homes 48
Tricel Corp. 173
Tricel Honeycomb 173
Trickle Ventilators 205
Tried & True Wood Finishes 198
TrimJoist 51
Tri State Foam Products, Inc. 119
Trocadero Power Lite Dual-Flush Toilet .. 233
Trojan Masonry Sealer 188
Tru-Lite Skylights, Inc. 104
Tru-Lite Tubular Skylights 104
True Lite Slag Concrete Aggregate 41
Truitt & White 278
Trus Joist-Weyerhaeuser 49, 50, 51
TTD, Inc. 21
Tubular Skylight 104
Tubular Skylight, Inc. 104
Tuff-Strand Certified OSB 73
Tulikivi Soapstone Fireplaces,
    Bakeovens, and Stoves 215
Tulikivi U.S., Inc. 215
Turtle Plastics 148
Turtle Tiles 148
TWB and RCWB Wall Bracing 69
Twisted-Tube CFLs 241
Tyler Pipe 228
U.S. Architectural Products 167
U.S. GreenFiber, LLC 114
U.S. Plastic Lumber, Ltd. 23, 27, 31, 36
U.S. Rubber Recycling, Inc. 156
U.S. Way Lighting 241
Ultra-QuieTTest 209
UltraGard PVC WBP-100 Heavy Duty
    Walkway Pad 90

UltraGlas 263
UltraGlas, Inc. 263
UltraMAX III 210
UltraPly TPO 93
UltraTouch Natural Fiber Duct Liner ... 216
UltraTouch Natural Fiber Insulation ... 117
Ultra Flush Pressure-Assist Toilet ... 233
UnderFleece 138
Underseal XT Waterproofing Membranes 289
UNI-Group U.S.A. 13
UNI-MASTIC 181 Duct Sealer 208
UNI-SOLAR PV Shingles and Standing
    Seam Panels 268
Unicor 173
United Gilsonite Laboratories
    (UGL) 192, 197
United Solar Ovonic LLC 268
Universal Foam Sealant 186
Universal Lighting Technologies 246
UNI Eco-Stone 13
Urban Hardwoods 148, 173, 261
Urban Ore, Inc. 283
Used Building Materials 281
Used Building Materials Association ... 280
Used Building Materials Exchange 283
USG Corporation 145, 160, 169
USP Structural Connectors 69, 170
US Tile Company 84
UV Water Disinfection Systems 234
Valhalla Wood Preservatives, Ltd. 58
Vaughn Manufacturing Corporation 271
Velux 104, 105
Venmar Ventilation Inc. 212
Vent-Axia LoWatt 209
Ventilation and Airflow Equipment 209
Ventilation and Energy-Conserving
    Products 276
Ventilation Products 214
Verde Business Furniture 260
Verde Interior Products 260
Vermont Business Materials Exchange ... 280
Vermont Structural Slate Co., Inc. 92
Versaroc Cement-Bonded Particleboard ... 167
Vertical Above-Ground Storage Tanks ... 228
Vetrazzo 166
Victor Stanley, Inc. 19
Viking Dishwashers 252
Viking Range Corporation 252
Vintage Log and Lumber, Inc. 62, 176
Vintage Lumber Co. 153
Vintage Material Supply Co. ... 62, 154, 176,
    178, 261
Vintage Timberworks 62, 149, 176
Virginia Slate Company 93
Visio 157
Visions Recycling, Inc. 200
Vitrified Clay Pipe 229
Vortens Dual-Flush Toilet 233
Vortens U.S. Office 233
Vreseis Ltd. 259

VRI Remanufactured Latex Paint......... 200
VT Industries, Inc. 97
W. F. Taylor Company 144
W. R. Meadows, Inc. 35, 38
Walkote Mix II, Loose Fill, and
  Craftkote............................. 117
Warm Windows 107
Water-Conserving Fixtures 225
Water-Source Heat Pump 212
WaterFurnace International, Inc. 211
Water Cistern and Storage Tanks 228
Water Filtration Company 227
Water Storage Tanks 228
Watt's up?................................. 290
WatterSaver Heat Pump Water Heater ... 223
Wausau Tile, Inc. 158
Weather-Bos Finishes..................... 192
Weather-Bos International.......... 188, 192
Weather-Bos Sealers 188
WeatherBest Decking 32
Weatherization and Energy-Conservation
  Products 276
WeatherMaker Central Air Conditioners . 204
WeatherMaker Infinity Series............. 210
Weathershield............................. 117
Weatherstripping and Gaskets 130
Weatherstripping and Joint Sealants 131
Weather Blanket, House Blanket, Comfort
  Control, and Good News - Reused...... 117
Weather Shield Manufacturing, Inc....... 109
Wellington Polymer Technology Inc........88
Wellmade USA, Inc. 135
Wellspring Futon Mattresses
  and Covers 256
Welsh Mountain Slate Inc. 89
Welsh Simulated Slate Shingles 89
Western Fibers, Inc........................ 117
Westinghouse Lighting Corporation...... 241
Weyerhaeuser 167
Weyerhaeuser Particleboard and MDF.... 167
WE Cork.................................. 144
WE Cork Flooring.......................... 144
WFI SingleStrip - The American
  Quartered Collection 142
What Its Worth, Inc........62, 154, 176, 178
Wheel Stops, Speed Bumps, and Bollards ... 11
Whirlpool Corporation................ 250, 253
Whirlpool Duet, Duet HT, and
  Calypso Washers.......................... 250
Whirlpool Refrigerators 253
Whitethorn Construction 141
White Premium Organics, Inc. 91
Whole House Building Supply............ 283
Wicanders Natural Cork 144
Wiggers Custom Furniture.................. 257
Willowell Nursery 8
Windfall Lumber and Milling... 141, 164, 275
Window Coverings 107
Window Quilt 108
Window Treatment Hardware 108

Wind Turbines 272
Wind Turbine Industries Corp. 272
Winston Series CPC Collector............. 271
Winter Panel Corporation 64
Wisconsin Thermo-Form, Inc. 57
Wolmanized Natural Select Wood 58
Wonder-Pure No-VOC/Odor................. 196
Woodfinder 281
WoodStalk 161
WoodStalk Underlayment................... 146
Wood Ceilings............................ 164
Wood Flooring International   (WFI).... 142
Wood Materials from Urban Trees.......... 63
Wool and Cotton Carpet 157
Wool Insulation 128
X-Technology, Acoustone, and
  Auratone Panels and Tiles.............. 160
Xantrex Technology 266
XL19i Air-Source Heat Pump 212
XL19i Air Conditioners 204
XPotential Products Inc............... 6, 9, 28
Xypex Chemical Corporation 36
Xypex Concentrate...........................36
Yemm & Hart Ltd. 171
York International Corp. 204, 210
YWI 274
Zappone Manufacturing......................87
Zar Exterior Polyurethane 192
ZVOC Exterior Waterbased Stain.......... 191
ZVOC High Solids Clear Coat, Wax Seal &
  Finish, and Sanding Sealer.............. 198
ZVOC White Primer and Topcoat.......... 196

ABOUT THE EDITORS

Alex Wilson is president of BuildingGreen, Inc. and serves as executive editor of *Environmental Building News*, a monthly newsletter on environmentally responsible building design and construction, and as coeditor of the *GreenSpec®* product directory. He consults and lectures widely on sustainable design and serves as Secretary of the board of directors of the U.S. Green Building Council. Prior to starting his own company in 1985 (now Building-Green), he was executive director of the Northeast Sustainable Energy Association for five years; and in the late '70s, he taught workshops on passive solar design and construction in New Mexico. Alex has written about energy-efficient and environmentally responsible design and construction for more than 25 years and is author, coauthor or editor of several books and manuals, including *Greening Federal Facilities* (U.S. Dept. of Energy), *The Consumer Guide to Home Energy Savings* (ACEEE, 8th edition, 2003) and the Rocky Mountain Institute's comprehensive textbook *Green Development: Integrating Ecology and Real Estate* (John Wiley & Sons, 1998). He has also written hundreds of articles for other publications, including *Fine Homebuilding, Architectural Record, The Construction Specifier, Landscape Architecture,* and *Popular Science.* Alex is a trustee of the Vermont Chapter of The Nature Conservancy.

Mark Piepkorn is associate editor of *Environmental Building News* and the lead products researcher for *GreenSpec®*, both publications of BuildingGreen, Inc. His knowledge of conventional and alternative construction methods, materials and building science—in applications as diverse as underground structures, vernacular timber construction, and earthen techniques, as well as the rehabilitation and remodeling of conventional structures—lends an interesting and important perspective to the understanding of the roles of manufactured products and materials in our built and conditioned environments. Active in the natural building movement, Mark has also been the editor of *The Last Straw*, an international newsletter about straw-bale construction and natural building.

NEW SOCIETY PUBLISHERS

ENVIRONMENTAL BENEFITS STATEMENT

New Society Publishers has chosen to produce this book on recycled paper made with **100% post-consumer waste**, processed chlorine free, and old-growth free.

For every 5,000 books printed, New Society saves the following resources:[1]

95	Trees
8,620	Pounds of Solid Waste
9,484	Gallons of Water
12,371	Kilowatt Hours of Electricity
15,670	Pounds of Greenhouse Gases
67	Pounds of HAPs, VOCs, and AOX Combined
24	Cubic Yards of Landfill Space

[1]Environmental benefits are calculated based on research done by the Environmental Defense Fund and other members of the Paper Task Force who study the environmental impacts of the paper industry. Contact the EDF for more information on this environmental benefits statement, a copy of their report, and the latest updates on their data.